11.18.08

only textual (book-ish)
and personal experience as
a Malaysian Chinese in the U.S.
(How long will be a visiting professor...)

Hong Kong - Metropark (Kowloon) 12-5-08

Heup-Young Kim in K. Barth's Sanctification and Wong Yang Ming's
金 氏 恆 王 compares the similarity, but keeps them separate
self-cultivation

without any attempt to "christianize Confucianism or Confucianize
Christianity."

R.K. Yeo - sees what is weak or strong in one tradition and
supplements the weaker with the stronger. His is a "selective
inheritance" that is possible for a bicultural person. The question
is - Is this possible for a collective, a community, the "body of
christ" in Chinese churches? (That goes for any theological position
being accepted collectively; theologians can only try.)   (Diane
Theology is prior to "objective" study of religion   Obenchain)
Yeo's assumption. Both Confucian + Christian ideal is a trajectory
towards the neighbor, the outsider, and for Christianity even the
enemy. Confucianism is an incarnated life without an
incarnator. Its self-cultivation (though human effort alone)
is (as Kim notes) a sanctification process without
any personal sanctifier. Confucian life in short is
part of the natural process of 天, however
abstract and impersonal!

③

To care — 孝 — a trajectory of caring
is larger + love circles
is self-cultivation

愛和平
講孔節
能吃苦

importance of ritual

to Koi Tse at table

Chinese trial of
all the parents. trusts
the children
which is 孝 (constant filiality)

how parents sacrifice for the children

Fixing
Dec 5th
(Ho 等 returned)

Guangzhou

Can Virtue be taught? (It needs to be caught in an environment)
rituals at the 120th celebration (建校)
ritualistic — environment is the collective

priority, a day will be most inspiring person

The meaning of being
Human (仁)

Dr. K. K. Wong's memorial

It means practicing gods chin "I rededicate" points to
standard very moment
Testimonies — science from elegance
remembrance the limit
Ever reinventing a
rededication.

Sermon —
very Buddhistic
from a Christ's mode

Norman — honoring the event
Transitive to
Above going thru
Osmosis

(this second book for a year)
Reflecting death.

Humility / imperfection —
imovement, how blue achieves
transcends.

I love music in this Echos!

Another journey to Hong Kong within a Half Century — Metropark Hotel 4 a.m.
{ 1. Lo
2. 3Ec $\frac{1}{2}$
3. 學
4. Walker

No. 7 中學 — Guangzhou Saturday Dec 7th, 2008

2008

If I were asked to speak (as at UK Povi To former at the Tsinan private school Middle School campus,

寶血中學

I would elaborate on the 大學

(Taken from the Book of Rites 禮記, as well as 中庸)

MUSING with

CONFUCIUS and PAUL

70 years later

大學 has nothing to do with the modern use of the term university which was based on the medieval European term of universities of primarily the meeting of theologian + medical people (Maimonides)

1988 —

大學 is for a big people —

a nation, a small, but going + going adult.

20 years later 桂林街 精神 of Chien Mu

education is primarily for virtue or morality.

明明德 — great

知正 德

Mou Tsung-san on Confucianism

Manifest for Renewal of Chinese Culture.

1958 {

for response — ability (hopefully Spontaneous)

良知 of Wang Yang Ming

habits of the best

"truth is in order to goodness — (wisdom)

止 於 致 善 — stopping at the highest excellence (Noah E. Fehl)

(虞) 先天下之憂而憂

MUSING with
CONFUCIUS and PAUL

Toward a Chinese Christian Theology

K. K. YEO

CASCADE *Books* · Eugene, Oregon

MUSING WITH CONFUCIUS AND PAUL
Toward A Chinese Christian Theology

Cascade Books
A Division of Wipf and Stock Publishers
199 W. 8th Ave., Suite 3
Eugene, OR 97401

www.wipfandstock.com

ISBN 13: 978-1-55635-488-5

楊克勤

Cataloging-in-Publication data:

Yeo, Khiok-Khng.　(Malaysian Chinese)

　　Musing with Confucius and Paul : toward a Chinese Christian theology / K. K. Yeo.

　　xxviii + 480 p. ; 23 cm.

　　Includes bibliographical references (p. 433–51) and index.

　　ISBN 13: 978-1-55635-488-5 (alk. paper)

　　1. Confucius. 2. Paul, the Apostle, Saint. 3. Bible. N.T. Galatians—Criticism, interpretation, etc. 4. Christianity and culture. 5. Bible—Hermeneutics—Cross-cultural studies. I. Title.

BS476 Y36 2008

Manufactured in the U.S.A.

Guest Hotel
Xiamen U., Dec. 8, 2008
3:20 p.m.

Opening ceremony of <u>Pai To's</u> new campus.

Spring ~~2009~~ 2010)

Dedicated to
Timothy, Joseph, and Phoebe
and their generation of Chinese Christians
whose world *tian* has graced with moral goodness
and *Theos* has created with cruciform love

Last December 6, 2008 (Saturday)
at the Precious Blood Middle School campus
special activity = the mentally disabled.
"social harmony"

quoted the 天 [字]

many of you will want to go to a <u>university</u>.
"what do you want to be when you grow up?"

Astronomer (Scientist)
Banker
Computer expert
Doctor
Engineer
Farmer – noble profession that feeds
humanity

天 [字] has nothing to do = what to do when you
grow up; ... something emphasis on "grading exam"
nothing to do = going to HKU or HK
... university or ... institute
of "higher learning"

(See p.4 for rest of the address
Submit MSS to Ms Tseng for
emendation.)

Contents

[handwritten notes: 11.18.08 · facile equating one tradition 2 another? · too christian-centric? privileging christianity? to the point of christianizing Confucianism (fulfillment?)]

Foreword

In the past, under the influence of Lin Yutang, I took it for granted that, were we to compare Christianity with Confucianism, it was more suitable to compare Jesus with Confucius, and St. Paul with Mencius. As Lin Yutang said in *The Wisdom of China*, "Jesus was followed by St. Paul, Socrates by Plato, Confucius by Mencius, and Laozi by Zhuangzi. In all four cases, the first was the real teacher and either wrote no books or wrote very little, and the second began to develop the doctrine and wrote long and profound discourses." For me this insight of Lin Yutang was true to a great extent. That's why I was surprised to see the manuscripts of K. K. Yeo's book titled *Musing with Confucius and Paul*. I asked myself: Why not deal with Jesus, the founder of Christian tradition, and Confucius, the founder of Confucian tradition?

Now, the deeper I delve into K. K. Yeo's manuscript, the more I understand the meaning of this work, which is not only an essay on comparative theology, but indeed an excellent attempt to formulate a Chinese Christian theology based on his reading of Confucius' *Analects*, one of the founding texts of Chinese Culture, and Paul's Galatians, arguably one of the earliest among Paul's letters to be introduced by the Nestorians into China, as evidenced by the very rare Dunhuang Syriac manuscripts. Not only has K. K. Yeo corrected the commonly accepted mechanical comparison of Lin Yutang, he has indeed launched a dynamic comparison and mutual enrichment of Confucianism and Christianity. It's most interesting for me that K. K. Yeo puts this Chinese Christian theology in the context of today's world in the process of globalization full of conflict, violence, and suffering caused by the self-assertion and self-enclosure of different genders, ethnic groups, economic interests, political powers, and religious faiths. Chinese Christian theology finds its sources in the profound Confucian *ren* (humanness) and Christian *agape*. This theological project concerns itself with the contrasting virtue and violence, freedom and bondage, and the eternal problem of who we are in a world of violence and difference, hoping for a peaceful coexistence despite so many in difference. This book has well blended conceptual analysis and logical argumentation with the use of narratives, both historical and personal, to illustrate a vision of comparative theology and Chinese Christian theology. Indeed, this is one of the most fascinating books produced in recent years on Chinese Christian theology that intrigues us with a profound understanding of Christianity and Confucianism, focusing in particular on Confucius and Paul.

To my understanding, Paul's tireless traveling after his miraculous conversion to Christ, from Damascus to Arabia, to Jerusalem, to Antioch, to Syria, to Cyprus, to Asia Minor, to North Galatia, to Macedonia, to Corinth, to Troas, to Miletus, to Rome . . . etc., for the purpose of evangelization and bringing Christ to the gentile peoples, constitutes indeed an unceasing process of strangification and relentless effort of generosity to the Multiple Other. His travel for the good of Multiple Other goes beyond the Jewish Law that keeps itself to circumcision and other nomistic services. Paul refers to the faith in Christ, the perfect union of God and Man, as the only criterion for the gentile peoples to become Christians. He always goes beyond boundaries, not only geographical but also ideological. I use the term "strangification" to denote the act by which one goes beyond the boundary of oneself to Multiple Other, beyond one's familiarity to strangeness, to foreigners and strangers. Also, I use the term "Multiple Other" to replace the concept of "the Other" used by Levinas, Derrida, and Deleuze. We humans are born into Multiple Other, which is more concrete than and ontologically prior to the Other. In Multiple Other, there could be the Other as well as the Thou and the They.

Historically speaking, Paul was at the beginning of Christianity's historically dynamic expansion to the gentile peoples. The process in which Christianity has extended from Judea to Rome and Greece, to Asia Minor, to Europe, to Africa, to East Asia and America, and finally to every corner of the world, could be seen as an unceasing process of strangification and act of generosity. This dynamism is essential to the history of Christianity that has entered into diverse civilizations and cultures in the world, to become one of their constitutive factors and, again, to push them, each in its own way, to go out side of itself and to go beyond.

This is to say that Christianity is a religion of generosity and strangification par excellence. Creation of the world could be seen as God's generosity, God's originally generous act of producing creatures out of his infinitely powerful and immensely abundant creativity. The emergence of various forms of existence in the universe and their successive evolution are therefore understood as produced by this original act of generosity and successive act of transformation. In the first version of Genesis, to what He has created, God says, "it was good." The ontology of goodness is therefore the outcome of divine generosity. After creation, God lives in the universe by the laws of nature that regulate not only all creatures' movement and life but also bring them to go beyond themselves, to better perfection, to the emergence of higher forms of being. Human being, created in the image of God, should also go beyond him/herself for better perfection, even if in the meantime, because of his/her free will, he/she is also able to choose to stay in his/her self-enclosure in the imagined subjectivity, without caring about his/her relation with others, and be bound miserably to the selfish-enclosure, that is what is meant by original sin. The incarnation of Christ is an act of generosity and love, that God becomes human and takes the form of human body, even sacrifices his own life for the benefit of human beings and the whole world. Redemption should be understood in the sense of being saved from one's finite self-enclosure to be open again to Multiple Other, horizontally to other people and Nature, and vertically to God. Christ, core to the faith of all forms of Christianity, is the paradigm of strangification and generosity, so that all human beings and all beings in the universe should go outside of their finite self-enclosure and go always beyond, so as to return eventually to their infinite perfection.

Generosity to strangers and effort of strangification are most important for today when we're facing the challenge of globalization, basically understood as a process of deterritorialization or border-crossing, to the extent of involving all humankind on the globe as a whole. This spirit of crossing borders, of going beyond oneself to Multiple Other, best exemplified by Paul's act of evangelization for the gentile peoples, is indeed very inspiring for Confucianism, the essence of Chinese culture, which has focused mostly on the ethics of reciprocity. As I see it, the message that Christianity has brought to the Confucian China, a message still urg-

ing us today, is this generosity to Multiple Other by way of strangification; in a way that makes Chinese people more balanced in the dynamic
contrast of immanence and transcendence, love and justice, construction
of life-meaningfulness, and further strangification.

If we look for something in Confucianism that could contribute
to this process of globalization, it must be the Confucian way of life as
an ethical extension based on *ren* (humanness), *cheng* (sincerity), and
shu (altruistic empathy). Given that much discussion has been made
by scholars on *ren* (humanness) and *cheng* (sincerity), I would like to
feature here *shu* and its relation with *ren*. Although in the *Analects*, not
much was said about *shu*, it was told by Confucius to be the expression
to act upon till the end of one's life. When Zigong asked, "Is there one
expression that can be acted upon till the end of one's days?" The master
replied, "There is *shu* 恕: do not impose on others what you yourself do
not want." Here *shu* was understood in the spirit of negative golden rule.
The same negative golden rule was repeated by Confucius when answering Zhonggong's question about *ren*. We can see therefore a very close
relationship between *ren* and *shu*, given the fact that they have the same
definition. On the other hand, a positive golden rule was given as answer
to the question about the concept of *ren*, also to Zigong: "A man of humanity, wishing to establish his own character, also establishes others;
wishing to be prominent himself, also helps others."

In Confucianism, the tension between self and Multiple Other is
to be solved in reference to golden rules, both negative and positive,
based ultimately on the principle of reciprocity. In the Confucian world,
where all human behaviors have to be regulated by *li*, even the act of
going outside oneself to the other and the original generosity it implied
have to be regulated by reciprocity. That's why the *Liji* (*Book of Rituals*)
says, "What the rules of propriety values is that of reciprocity. If I give
a gift and nothing comes in return, that is contrary to propriety; if the
thing comes to me and I give nothing in return, that also is contrary to
propriety." Confucius understands generosity also in term of reciprocity. He says, when answering to Zizhang's question about *ren*, "One who
can practice five things wherever he may be is a man of humanity. . . .
Earnestness, liberality, truthfulness, diligence, and generosity." As we can
see among these five virtues, *kuan* (liberality) and *hui* (generosity) are
related to the virtue of being generous, although all five are related to
reciprocal virtues. Confucius explains, "If one is liberal, one will win the

heart of all; . . . if one is generous, one will be able to enjoy the service of others." Note that reciprocity here is shown in people's responses to one's liberality and generosity.

For sure, reciprocity at the basis of the golden rule is still fundamental to ethics. But, as I see it, there should be first of all an original generosity to go outside of oneself to the Multiple Other before there could be any reciprocity. Original generosity and strangification are therefore the condition *sine qua non* of all reciprocal relationships. Before the establishment of any reciprocity, emphasized for example in Marcel Mauss' *Essai sur le don* as the principle of sociability, there must be previously a generous act of going outside of oneself to the Multiple Other, so that there can be established accordingly a relation of reciprocity. In both classical world and modern times, golden rules are much emphasized, and reciprocity seen as the basic principle of sociability. Now in the postmodern world and in the world of globalization, we need a new principle more than that of reciprocity. This must be the original generosity of strangification.

Unselfish love and generosity to the other are indeed the true spirit of Christianity, always urging Christians and all human beings to take a generous initiative before any reciprocity. This is something that Confucianism and Daoism didn't do in the past. The *Liji* might have synthesized the Confucian mind, all in emphasizing the reciprocity of *li*, in saying, "I have heard [in accordance with *li*] that scholars come to learn; I have not heard of [the master] go to teach." Though the emphasis here was put on the value of truth and dignity of master, unfortunately the original generosity was quite often forgotten. This explains why Confucianism, essential to Chinese civilization, never made the effort in the past, like Christianity did from St. Paul on, to strangify itself to the West and to the whole world. Therefore, Confucian reciprocity is not yet complete. What it needs is this dynamism of strangification launched by an original generosity as revealed by Christianity and from God Himself.

In this sense, we are all grateful to K. K. Yeo for bringing Paul and Confucius together in this book in an effort to construct a Chinese Christian theology. This precious effort to make Christianity understandable to the Chinese and Confucianism to the Christians is itself an outcome of mutual strangification and intellectual generosity, as witnessed not only by his theological discourse, but also by his narrative accounts of his own life story, and those of Confucius and Paul, rendering thereby a sense of concreteness to the theological discourse itself. For all these, I would invite all readers to savor this text about Chinese Christian theology supported by narratives related to Confucius, Paul, and the author himself.

repetitive

Professor Vincent Shen
Lee Chair in Chinese Thought and Culture
University of Toronto

strangification
(an awful term)
11-17-08

Preface

TERROR, VIOLENCE, AND THE NEED
OF A THEOLOGY OF PEACE
(theological)

I live in two worlds: one is a Chinese world shaped by Confucian ethics, and the other a Christian world informed by Pauline theology. Despite the stark differences between the two worlds, both Confucius and Paul advocate peace and wholeness. Confucius believes that cultivation of virtues will bring about harmony; Paul believes that a faithful reception of God's grace through the work of Christ will bring about salvation. This sacred wisdom of shalom and freedom is constantly challenged by terror and mistrust throughout history.

It seems that more people seek to resolve conflict with militarism, mistrust with fear. Two books, *Jesus in Beijing* and *China Inc.*, raise the specter of the increasing power of China, thus implying that China is now—or is increasingly becoming—a threat to the West.[1] In an article entitled, "How We Would Fight China," Robert D. Kaplan writes: "The Middle East is just a blip. The American military contest with China in the Pacific will define the twenty-first century. And China will be a more formidable adversary than Russia ever was."[2] When we encounter those whose worldview, cultural framework, or way of life differs from our own, we oftentimes allow our fear to guide us toward a fight or flight. Confucius and Paul believe that genuine encounter and mutual accep-

---

1. Aikman, *Jesus in Beijing*, passim; Fishman, *China Inc.*, passim.
2. Kaplan, "How We Would Fight China," 49.

[handwritten marginalia: multiple Other]

tance can overcome fear. The lack of knowledge of the true identity of the others causes one to stereotype, that is, to objectify them. To romanticize or to demonize China is unhelpful, for these approaches will surely lead to violence between China and the West.

I am an overseas Chinese living in the West, and I am aware of the escalating violence in the world and the increasing fear in the psyche of Western nations. Nations are determined to kill one another; suicide bombers are so desperate they seek "honor" by sacrificing their own lives in order to take the lives of others. If "the axis of evil" uses tactics of terror, "we civilized nations" use military might and threaten preemptive measures. If there is any similarity between "they" and "we," it is in the appeal to God for blessings, and both are ready to use evil against the other—resulting in the dehumanization of both. The spiral of evil does not end, no matter how fervent the rhetoric of "jihad" or "God bless America" may be.

The present context reminds me of similar fear and violence described in the two ancient texts. The *Analects* and the Epistle to the Galatians are canonical texts of Confucianism and Christianity respectively.[3] Each text has been studied by followers of each religious tradition faithfully over the last two millennia. The *Analects* is a compilation of Confucius' (551–479 BCE) and his disciples' teachings on their social and political ethics to the rulers and kings of their day. It contains twenty chapters of mostly the Master's (Confucius) sayings and also the interpretation of his major disciples. It was believed that the compiling, editing, and interpretation of the *Analects* began soon after the death of Confucius. The main thesis in the *Analects* is that, human beings are endowed with benevolence, and that the cultivation of virtues is the way for people to live in a world of difference and violence. While the *Analects* is a compendium of wisdom literature, the Epistle is a letter written by the Apostle Paul to Christians in Galatia. It was written by Paul (ca. 6–64 CE) in the early 50's and is found in the New Testament. Paul defends his understanding of the gospel of Christ, which invites Gentiles to become the people of God without the requirements of the Jewish law. Paul also argues that the power of the Spirit and the way of love should be the guiding force

---

3. On Confucianism see Yao, ed., *RoutledgeCurzon Encyclopedia of Confucianism*, 1:2–11; on Confucianism and Christianity, see ibid., 106–9.

of Christian ethics in order to form a cohesive community of Jewish and Gentile Christians.[4]

The *Analects* of Confucius and Paul's letter to the Galatians may be ancient texts, but the problems they dealt with re-appear in our world today. "The Analects Problem" concerns forming community by means of violence or virtue. The problem has not left us. We have witnessed the propensity of modern nation states to use military force to resolve conflict or simply to cause terror. "The Galatian Problem" is about becoming the people of God by means of religious observance or in freedom. The historical problem was an inner-Jewish or inner-Christian dispute as to whether the relationship of humankind with the divine was established through law-obedience or whether it was a gift freely given and freely accepted (or declined). Some forms of Islam are ready to die, even by suicide, to preserve the law (such as the law of *shariʿah* in the belief that the divine-human relationship is observed by submission to specific demands and regulations. There are some American leaders who are convinced that they have been divinely called to establish among the Near Eastern legalists democratic rule in which the divine-human relation is a matter of individual free-choice, and that no religious law can be imposed by one culture on another. Although, of course, like "the circumcision party" before him, the American leadership is ready to impose "freedom of choice" (now with quite a different meaning).

The "Analects Problem" and the "Galatian Problem" reappear not just in the Middle East and North America, in China and the West where violence and virtue, bondage and freedom are in conflict. This volume wrestles, alongside Confucius and Paul, with the old problem of who we

---

4. For more on the *Analects* and Galatians, see Chapter One. To speak of Jesus, his followers, and those believers in the first-century context as "Jews or Jewish" and "Christians" may be imprecise and misleading. In this book I use these traditional terms, but I am basically in agreement with John Elliott's view, which is reflected in the title of his article: "Jesus the Israelite was Neither a 'Jew' nor a 'Christian': On Correcting Misleading Nomenclature." According to Elliott, in the first century, *Ioudaios* did not refer to a "Jew" in the sense of religious affiliation, but a Judean in terms of ethnicity. *Ioudaios* is a term used often by non-Israelite to refer "those connected to Judea by blood relations, Torah allegiance, patriotism, and loyalty to Judea, the holy city of Jerusalem and the Temple" (ibid., 146). The first followers of Jesus "were identified by fellow Israelites also as 'Galileans,' 'Nazarenes,' or members of 'the Way,' but never as 'Judeans'" (ibid.). See also Mason, "Jews, Judaeans, Judaizing, Judaism: Problems of Categorization in Ancient History"; Amy-Jill Levine, *The Misunderstood Jew*, passim.

are in a world of violence, fear, and difference—and the hope that diverse groups can coexist peacefully in this "global village" of ours.

The hermeneutical task of finding wisdom in scriptures and in the Chinese classics in order to construct a Chinese Christian theology of peace and salvation has been a personal quest. My family, both in Malaysia and in China, had suffered because of war. Memories were too painful for my parents to speak about their lives during the Japanese occupation of Malaysia. Relatives in China told us of the suffering they had endured during the Cultural Revolution. I lived through the 5/13 Incident (May 13, 1969) in Malaysia, and have been horrified by the casualties of race riots.[5] In the comfort of my living room in the seminary apartment, I witnessed the June 4th (1989) conflict at the Gate of the Heavenly Peace (Tiananmen Square), and am still chilled by the thought that even such "human sacrifice" may not be enough to guarantee freedom. I was equally shocked by the 9/11 (2001) event when thousands were evaporated in flame and smoke, and I too felt the worldwide panic and uncertainty that followed.

As a teenager and even as a young man, I held the naive assumption that Coke and McDonalds would one day unite Israelis and Palestinians, Americans and Russians, North and South Koreans. I also dreamed that one day Honda, Sony, and IBM would help China and Taiwan to coexist peacefully. Yet, the more alike our material possessions have become, the more divergent our ideologies and beliefs seem to be. The smaller the global village becomes, the greater the distance and the greater the difficulty there is in crossing the thoughts and feelings of others. What can link human hearts? What can unite the human spirit? Can capitalism or democracy or science bring us closer?

As a Malaysian Chinese living in America, my reading of the Bible is filtered through my American context. I seek to make sense of current events in dialogue with the scriptures. For my family and for many of my American friends, the tragic events of 9/11 are a reminder that none of us is invulnerable. We live in a land of freedom, power, and affluence, and the 9/11 event proved that our freedom can be taken away, our power weakened, our prosperity ruined, our security threatened, and life itself destroyed. To think that we are invincible and can therefore respond with our own alienating measures may eventually be to dig our own graves.

---

5. See Pan, *Sons of the Yellow Emperor*, 253.

Great empires in the past have spent huge amounts of their national resources on preserving their national security. Is spending eighty-seven
billion dollars fighting terrorism justifiable? Is the "Homeland Security"
project a repetition of the Great Wall the Chinese Empire devised to keep
out the barbarians and terrorists? The project of the Great Wall was a
failure. It merely served to keep the Chinese from reaching out to the
world rather than keeping the invaders out. It burdened China with such
heavy economic (taxation) and human (3,500,000 people worked on it
and a million of them died) costs that this "imperial project" became
a death blow to the Qin dynasty (255–206 BCE)—one of the shortest
dynasties in China.

In this volume, I am not ready to address the issue of America and its
role in the world of nations, though this is one cultural context that constantly drives me to read sacred texts, paying attention to the questions of
political ethics and the coexistence of humankind. I may return to study
the American national security issue from the perspective of a Chinese
American in the future. For now, I have the more immediate concern
of addressing the issue of Chinese coexistence in a politically, ideologi-
cally, religiously, linguistically, and ethnically diverse world, such as the
situation between China, Taiwan, Hong Kong, and overseas Chinese. My
hermeneutical interest is also driven by the problem of clans and dialects
and divisiveness that mark many Chinese societies throughout the world.
My basic inquiry is twofold in its intertextual reading of the *Analects*
and the Galatians: first, regarding the cultural etiology (beginning) of
Chinese Christian theology and, second, regarding a hybrid identity of a
Chinese Christian. The first enquiry asks: "What makes Chinese Chinese,
Christian Christian?" "How has Confucius shaped China, up to its present?" "How has Paul shaped the Protestant West?" And "What scriptures
can provide resources for a Chinese Christian theology?" The second
enquiry asks: "What will Chinese Christian theology look like?" "What
will the moral and theological identity of Chinese Christians be?" "How
will such identity and theology be helpful to China and the universal
Church?"

not PRC?

PREVIEW OF THE BOOK: MUSING WITH CONFUCIUS AND PAUL FOR A CHINESE CHRISTIAN THEOLOGY

The Overture and Epilogue chapters contain the hermeneutical interests I use to frame the six chapters (or movements) of the book. "Overture" and "epilogue" are musical metaphors that provide aesthetic harmony and open-endedness to the expression of themes. The framing chapters are narrative in style, dealing with the moral and theological identities of the Chinese. My story and my people's story are intertwined with the Confucianist and Pauline traditions. As a cultural critic, I identify with Confucius and Paul as I observe how they were cultural critics in their own day (Overture chapter). The Epilogue seeks to delineate the cultural, political, and theological identity of Chinese in Hong Kong, Taiwan, and elsewhere overseas. Nothing definitive is claimed in the framing chapters—they are suggestive pointers for my own people, to work out ways to live in the "beautiful harmony" of coexistence, of diversity in unity, of individual freedom in mutual service.

The book as a whole uses cross-cultural hermeneutics, moving between the historical meaning and the "applied" meaning of the texts. Readers will discover that just as the historical reading sets a certain limit to the way I do my hermeneutical reading, my hermeneutical lenses also condition me to read the classical texts from a certain perspective. The Overture chapter discusses the intertextual approach I use in crossing back and forth between the *Analects* and the Galatians. Both texts are well read in both the West and the East, but seldom are they read together. My close reading of both texts intertextually here may be the first attempt to bring these two texts into dialogue. Since I am more interested in practice rather than in theory, I have demonstrated throughout the book how Confucius and Paul are helpful for Chinese Christians to construct a theological understanding of virtue, violence, politics, anthropology, coexistence, and so forth. Thus, the framing chapters serve to construct a Chinese Christian theology.

Between the framing chapters of Overture and Epilogue are six chapters that focus on the major themes that emerge from the intertextual readings between the *Analects* and Galatians. The six chapters, which constitute the core of the book and the dynamic of a Chinese Christian theology, are grounded more in the literary and exegetical interpretation of texts. These chapters are my interpretation of the classical texts; I admit that other plausible readings exist, ones that may in fact be better than mine when the cross-cultural contexts of the interpreters shift or change.[6] Chapter One is an introduction to the texts and the critical issues of the two books—*Analects* and Galatians. They constitute the textual basis of a Chinese Christian theology, thus the scope of my study; as indicated they are very different from one another. I conclude, however, that their intertextual or common thread lies in the theological ethics they share with each other—concern for the common good within a community of difference. Chapter Two confronts the obvious question of incommensurability between the *Analects* and Galatians, between "Chinese" and "Christian" in a Chinese Christian theology, differences I want to maintain. Despite the different presuppositions underlying Confucian ethics and Pauline theology, I find in my intertextual readings that shifting their lenses slightly is mutually enriching. Confucius' relative weakness in theology (notably Christology) can find its counterpoint in Paul, and Paul's relative weakness in ethics can find its amplification in Confucius. Chapters Three through Six demonstrate various counterpoints between Confucius and Paul in my constructive Chinese Christian theology. These chapters investigate their straightforward and critical dialogues on law and *li* (propriety), music and harmony, ritual and style, on what it means to be human and to be *renren* (benevolent or humane persons), to be holy (pious) and to be *shengren* (a holy person), to be *zhongshu* (loyal-empathetic) and *jing* (respectful), and to have *xin* (trustworthiness) and *pistis* (faith).

I find delineating the differences between Confucius and Paul necessary to the understanding of Chinese Christian identity and theology. I also find the combined wisdom of Confucius' and Paul's theological ethics still to be useful to our modern world. For example, I try to show in Chapter Five that Confucius and Paul were aware of the cultural ills of bondage, patriarchy, and violence. Though they did not know our modern terminologies of sexism, racism, slavery, and so forth, their less than "(post-)modern" theological ethics remains a persuasive paradigm for me and for many Chinese Christians.

The book is a manifesto or *apologia* for Chinese Christians. It seeks to articulate how it is possible to maintain a Chinese identity and a

---

6. On the criteria for discerning the plausibility and legitimacy of interpretations, see Yeo, "Culture and Intersubjectivity."

Christian identity *concomitantly* without capitulating to some western or other cultural model of Christian identity. To be a Chinese Christian is to adopt a distinctive, unique identity that owes much to both traditions but is *sui generis*. Providing great resources for the construction of a Chinese Christian theology, Confucius and Paul converge across a surprisingly broad front. Yet, the Christ of the Cross completes or extends what is merely implicit or absent in Confucius; and Confucius amplifies various elements of Christian faith (e.g., community, virtues) that are underplayed in individual, western Christianity.

This book is not written specifically for scholars in Pauline or Confucian studies, but more generally for college-educated readers. These readers may find theological ethics; or cultural studies of Confucius and Paul; or intertextual (cross-cultural) hermeneutics on ethnic, political, and theological identities subjects interesting to study. Because of my background in the ethical reading of the Confucianist texts and on the exegetical study of the Pauline epistles, my presentation of both texts may be partial. I have worked to provide as much balance as possible on thematic material from the Confucianist and Pauline texts. Much more scholarly material has been published on Pauline texts than on Confucianist texts. However, an exhaustive review of scholarship for both texts (*Analects* and *Galatians*) is not my point; my intention is not to be consumed by exegetical details. Rather, I wish to work from a sufficient knowledge of both texts and move confidently toward a creative intertextual reading.

THE HENRY LUCE FAMILY
AND THEIR CHRISTIAN PASSION

In praise of ?! Henry Luce?

Without a critical theological understanding of culture and politics, some missionaries regarded the Chinese as benighted heathen practicing the infidel Confucianism.[7] Some "belittled Chinese politics and institutions and even insisted that Confucius was expiating his sins in hell."[8] Patricia Neils writes,

---

7. Even before becoming a Luce Fellow, I identified with the Luce legacy of cherishing the intertwining relationship between theology, politics, and the Chinese culture. Ralph G. Martin, biographer of the Luces, once wrote, "God and country and China: this was the passionate core of the Luce heritage." Martin, *Henry and Clare*, 16.

8. Swanberg, *Luce and His Empire*, 19.

The negative stereotyped images of China at that time were often reinforced, if not created, by the missionaries themselves in their sermons and speeches and in their prolific writings for magazines, journals, and textbooks. Generally the missionaries were not well acquainted with Chinese accomplishments in science, art, philosophy, and literature and purveyed instead debasing images of opium dens, female infanticide, long fingernails, bound feet, pigtails, ancestor worship, superstitions, floods, and famine, and of the cunning, inscrutable, heathen Chinese. They wrote and told about all these conditions and thus may have been America's most powerful China image-makers in the era before photo-journalism and television.[9]

By contrast, Henry Winters Luce (1868–1941) and his wife Elizabeth Middleton Bloodgood Root (1869–1948) were unusually astute missionaries to China. Pastor Charles E. Robinson, who married them before their departure of China, urged them to "[s]trive to learn the Chinese way of looking at things."[10] When they set foot in Shantung province, the birthplace of Confucius, Luce preferred to call himself a "missionary in reverse"—rather than "bestowing the American way of life upon a heathen backward nation. Luce felt that it was at least equally important for him to educate Americans to the philosophies, traditions, and achievements of the Chinese. 'He must become a missionary from China to his own native land.'"[11]

Henry Winters Luce was passionate for Chinese culture. "The Chinese gave him the name Lu Suiyi, 'one who seeks righteousness.'"[12] The word righteousness in Chinese has a rich Confucian meaning, connoting the virtue of sacrificial love based on heavenly (*tian*) endowed human bonding. Luce was convinced that China could integrate its culture with Christian theology.

Many missionaries were shortsighted, wanting the immediate result of individual conversion. Luce, however, had the telescopic vision of educating the Chinese for Christian leadership. He helped finance and enlarge a number of Christian universities in China, for example,

9. Neils, *China Images in the Life and Times of Henry Luce*, 19.
10. Martin, *Henry and Clare*, 17.
11. Neils, *China Images in the Life and Times of Henry Luce*, 23.
12. Martin, *Henry and Clare*, 19.

the Cheeloo (Shantung) University at Tsinan, the capital of Shantung Province, and Yanjing University in Beijing.

Henry Winters moved to Tengchow in September 1897. The following year (April 3), Henry Robinson Luce was born, and the Chinese gave him the name, "small boy Luce," Lu Shaoyi. It was the father's open-minded and ecumenical attitude that "would later become one of the finer qualities in the character of his son and would be manifested in *Time* and *Life* magazines' treatment of world religions."[13] The younger Luce grew up to be an editor and publisher whose initial goal was to educate readers of the East and the West to better understand one another. Against the background of negative, inaccurate, stereotypical, patronizing, and prejudicial images of the Chinese in the nineteenth century, Henry Luce's publishing empire sought to change peoples' understanding of one another. And through the Luce Foundation, God's creative and redemptive work continues to touch the lives of many. In this age of hatred and violence, the empathic missionary spirit of the Luce family is to be admired and emulated. I am grateful to be named one of the Henry Luce III Fellows in 2003-2004—Luce III passed away in September 2005. Many missionaries to China risked their lives so that the new identity of the Chinese Christian might be conceived. Of these I am graced to be one. Many missionaries to China "have died, yet they continue to speak" (Heb 11:4). This "Luce Project" is a testimony to the creativity of life as intended by the Creator God, for God is the God of Life, and Death is not the end of our human story.

ACKNOWLEDGEMENTS

I cannot begin to list all the names of friends and scholars who have helped me in this project. I am particularly grateful to Garrett-Evangelical Theological Seminary for granting me a sabbatical year, to the Henry Luce Foundation—especially to Henry Luce III and President Michael F. Gilligan—and to the Association of Theological Schools—especially Daniel O. Aeshire, Christopher I. Wilkins, and William R. Myers—for the Luce Fellowship and the stimulating conferences with the Fellows: Ana María Díaz-Stevens, Paul D. Hanson, Blake Leyerle, Walter Lowe, Rebekah L. Miles, and Randall C. Zachman. I want to express my heartfelt

13. Neils, *China Images in the Life and Times of Henry Luce*, 42.

gratitude to the following sojourners, supporters, critics, and editors who have made my research and writing sustainable, and even delightful at times. They are Dr. Vincent Shen (for his preface), Dr. Donald Alexander, Dr. Charles H. Cosgrove, Dr. David Rhoads, Dr. Daniel Patte, Dr. Brook Zipporyn, Dr. Ron Anderson, Dr. Steve Long, Dr. Brent Water, Ms. Claire Matheny, Prof. David and Mrs. Grace Smart, Mr. Wu Yong, Rev. Hii Kong-hock, and Ms. Tsen Fui-tshin. I appreciate their care and critique, support and suggestions, prayer and queries. Dr. Richard Soulen has meticulously worked on the manuscript and helped me craft the work with care. I am grateful to him for being a conversation partner on Paul and Confucius, and being a mentor on writing. A weekly meeting of studies and prayers with my following friends at First Presbyterian Church Evanston has sustained my work: Dr. Terry Halliday, Dr. Don Wagner, Dr. Christopher Miller, Rev. Dave Handley, and Dr. Ken Vaux. I am indebted to my family—Lau Kung-siu, Timothy, Joseph, and Phoebe Yeo—whose forbearance and love on a daily basis have infused this work. I dedicate this book to the generations of Chinese Christians of my children, who are marked by God's cruciform love and *tian's* moral goodness.

March 25, 2004 (Feast of Annunciation)
Revised May 11, 2007 (at the Philosophy Department, Peking
University)

Abbreviations

GENERAL

BCE	Before the Common Era
CE	Common Era
NT	New Testament
OT	Old Testament

BIBLE VERSIONS AND TRANSLATIONS

ASV	American Standard Version
AV	Authorized Version [King James Version]
LXX	Septuagint [Old Testament in Greek]
MT	Masoretic Text [Old Testament in Hebrew]
NIV	New International Version
NRSV	New Revised Standard Version
RSV	Revised Standard Version

HEBREW BIBLE/OLD TESTAMENT

Gen	Genesis
Exod	Exodus
Lev	Leviticus
Num	Numbers

Deut	Deuteronomy
Judg	Judges
1–2 Kgs	1–2 Kings
1–2 Chr	1–2 Chronicles
Job	Job
Ps (pl. Pss)	Psalm/Psalms
Prov	Proverbs
Isa	Isaiah
Jer	Jeremiah
Ezek	Ezekiel
Dan	Daniel
Hos	Hosea
Joel	Joel
Amos	Amos
Mic	Micah
Hab	Habbakuk
Zech	Zechariah
Mal	Malachi

NEW TESTAMENT

Matt	Matthew
Mark	Mark
Luke	Luke
John	John
Acts	Acts
Rom	Romans
1–2 Cor	1–2 Corinthians
Gal	Galatians
Eph	Ephesians
Phil	Philippians
Col	Colossians
1–2 Thess	1–2 Thessalonians
1–2 Tim	1–2 Timothy
Titus	Titus
Phlm	Philemon
Heb	Hebrews

Jas	James
1–2 Pet	1–2 Peter
1–3 John	1–3 John
Rev	Revelation

OTHER ANCIENT TEXTS

1–2 Macc	1–2 Maccabees [Apocryphal book]
Cra.	Plato, *Cratylus*
Jub.	*Jubilees* [Pseudepigraphal book]
m. Aboth	Mishnah *Aboth* [Rabbinic text]
m. Sab.	Misnah *Sabbath* [Rabbinic text]
Sir	Sirach/Ecclesiasticus [Apocryphal book]
War	Josephus, *Judean War*

JOURNALS AND REFERENCE WORKS

BAGD	*A Greek-English Lexicon of the New Testament and Other Early Christian Literature*
CBQ	*Catholic Biblical Quarterly*
ChF	*Ching Feng*
JBL	*Journal of Biblical Literature*
JCP	*Journal of Chinese Philosophy*
NTS	*New Testament Studies*
PEW	*Philosophy East and West*
TDNT	*Theological Dictionary of the New Testament*

OVERTURE: Identifying with the Life-World of Confucius and Paul

CULTURAL AND THEOLOGICAL IDENTITIES   *inner dialogue "*

Through a study of Confucius and Paul, this project is autobiographical in its search for the cultural and religious identities of being a Chinese Christian—Chinese Christian as "a self-identical essence and . . . a construction constantly being remade."[1] More generally this project is about the "logic" and "dynamics" of Chinese Christian identity. The aspiration to construct and affirm one's identity—personal or corporate—is what Daniel Boyarin means by the "politics of identity,"[2] a meaning-creating process for one's life.

Religion and culture, though inseparable, are two of the most important aspects of the meaning-making process in my search of self-identity. With this hermeneutical interest in mind, I use the word religion in concert with Clifford Geertz's definition: "a system of symbols which acts to establish powerful, pervasive and long-lasting moods and motivations in [human beings] by formulating conceptions of a general order of existence and clothing these conceptions with such an aura of factuality that the moods and motivations seem uniquely realistic."[3] My religious

---

1. Boyarin, *A Radical Jew*, 3, where Boyarin describes Paul's identity as a Jew.
2. Ibid.
3. Geertz, "Religion as a Cultural System," 4.

1

identity is, therefore, the relations I have with God and with others that engender meaning in life. It entails the quest for faith and the pursuit of truth as my ultimate concerns. Religious identity grants me a system of signification for interpreting the world into a meaningful order. Notably, my religious identity is shaped by the Christ event, Christ makes sense for me a meaningful world through God's creation and redemption.

In defining culture, I find the working definitions of Richard Peterson and Peter Berger helpful. Peterson sorts out the different ways people use the word culture, which include material substance, norms of behaviors, values or significant virtues, beliefs or worldview, expressive symbols or representations.[4] Berger argues that human beings are compelled by nature to impose meaningful order upon reality.[5] The objective meaning one brings to reality through the process of transposition is what Berger terms "interpenetration," through which the meaning-system and life-world interact.[6] When Berger defines culture as "the totality of man's products,"[7] he includes both the material culture as such and human reflection on reality in general. Culture exists "only as people are conscious of it."[8] In other words, culture and meaning are intertwined in the meaning of life-world. I will expand and differentiate the nuances between "religion" and "culture" in later chapters.

Finding religious and cultural identity is more than a historical task of recovering who I was, who my family and various affiliated communities were. It is also a meaning-creating process. Janet Gunn aptly points out the fact that autobiography is not "the private act of a self writing" but "the cultural act of a self reading."[9] This act of writing is an identity-forming process whereby one reads one's story in light of the cultural and religious resources that already have shaped one's identity. The authenticating moment of one's identity happens in the self-reading process, for in discovering one's identity, one also creates a new identity.

---

4. See Peterson, "Revitalizing the Culture Concept." I have added "material substance," which might overlap with his "expressive symbols." See also Tanner, *Theories of Culture*, passim.

5. Berger, *Sacred Canopy*, 22. See also Tanner, *Theories of Culture*, 33.

6. Berger and Kellner, *Sociology Reinterpreted*, 42.

7. Berger, *Sacred Canopy*, 6.

8. Berger and Luckmann, *The Social Construction of Reality*, 78.

9. Gunn, *Autobiography*, 8. Rebecca Chopp speaks similarly of "the poetics of testimony" in theology; see her "Theology and the Poetics of Testimony."

Finding identity is more than the political activity of fighting for power and acceptance, of claiming one's rights, or seeking justice in a pluralistic world. It is also a process of contributing to the common good of society. In other words, rather than letting this work become a self-absorbing and narcissistic task, I would want my own politics of identity to fulfill, in part, my civic duty to serve others whose lives also shape mine. My ethical responsibility to serve others is predicated upon the truth about love. Ethics is not some legal dictate or burdensome regulation one is forced to observe. Ethics is a communal exchange and edification that moves everyone to share in the open spirit of love and trust, and in the ambiguous context of vulnerability.

Below is my story, moving as it does toward that of Confucius and Paul. This is my religious and cultural identity in which I find the larger identity of the encounter between Confucius' China and Paul's Protestant West.

A DIASPORIC CHINESE: A HYBRID CHINESE CHRISTIAN IDENTITY

Malaysian Chinese

I am an overseas Chinese, born and raised in Malaysia, a multi-cultural and religious country that has shaped my diasporic Chinese identity. In the early 1920s, my grandparents and parents came to Borneo Island in search of better living conditions while escaping the civil war in southern China (Santou). In the late 1930s and early 1940s, the Japanese army occupied Malaysia, and my parents witnessed the brutality of one race against another in the expansionism of a political and economic East Asia empire. I learned from a young age that ethnic identity and ideology can be lethal, that when asserted with radicalism, history itself bears witness to the horrific events that follow, such as the Holocaust (in which the Nazis starved or executed an estimated six million Jews, along with millions of Poles, Roman Catholic religious, gypsies, and homosexuals) and World War II massacres (Japanese against Chinese, in which in Nanjing alone an estimated 300,000 people were killed in two weeks).

Living in diaspora was the conscious yet desperate choice of my grandparents and parents. While in Malaysia, we lived in a Chinese neighborhood, celebrated Chinese festivals, and ate Chinese food as ways to maintain our Chinese identity. However, to be Chinese can take on a wide range of practices and ways of life, such as being Buddhist, Daoist, Confucianist, polytheist, atheist—or a modern intellectual who believes in science and democracy and capitalism, or some hybrid of those listed above. Because culture, like any religion and ideology, changes across space and time, my family's cultural identity also changed. But I would locate it in the Confucianist ethical tradition and in the modern intellectual quest characteristic of many Chinese sub-identities.[10] For my family, "Chinese-ness" means to follow the social ethics of Confucius' teaching. We believe the Confucian ethic of becoming human. To be human is to affirm the creativity of Heaven in one's self and in others and to be social and ethical beings who establish themselves and others. Rather than to secure a good job, what my parents and other elders often instructed us was to learn to be a good person—to learn to be human (*xue zuoren*). "To do things" (successful in one's occupation, *zuoshi*) is paired with "to be human" (*zuoren zuoshi*). The description of a good and successful person as "virtuous and talented" (*decai jianbei*) is a Confucian ideal I heard early in life.

Ethnic consciousness and its accompanying symbolism became our means of survival. This was especially true in diaspora, in Malaysia and worse still in Indonesia, where at times the institutionalized mechanism to de-Sinicize mainland immigrants challenged Chinese to know who they were. *Paihua* was a form of racist policy supported by local governments to ostracize Chinese, prohibiting or controlling Chinese newspapers, Chinese schools, and/or Chinese names. Because of political dynamics, local governments at times considered Chinese-ness a threat to national security. In the 1960s, when I was in grade school, I heard the news that Chinese Communists in Malaysia (probably working with those in China) were terrorists, who vowed to takeover Malaysia. During that period of national insecurity, being Chinese was to live in a zone of suspicion.

I became aware of the value of co-existence among the various groups in Malaysia, as different races tried to celebrate diversity and to

---

10. Lionel Jensen observes that "Confucianism has long been considered the definitive ethos of the Chinese—their civil religion, their official cult, their intellectual tradition. Indeed, the term 'Confucianism' . . . has become indistinguishable from what it signifies—China." See Jensen, *Manufacturing Confucianism*, 4.

respect uniqueness. I knew that my Chinese ethnicity mattered to my family. Being a Chinese in Malaysia meant that no matter which socio-economic class one belonged to, one often gained the respect and the jealousy of other ethnic groups. Generally speaking, Chinese are industrious and family-oriented, they pay attention to education and morality, and they are successful business persons. But in a socially diverse society where the rich and the poor, the haves and the have-nots, are sharply contrasted, anti-Chinese sentiment is common. This is true in Malaysia.

When I was five, I knew that, whereas options were available for me to attend primary school in Chinese, English, or Malay, my parents chose to send me and all my siblings to Chinese schools—schools sponsored by Chinese associations and subsidized by the government. My parents wanted us to be educated as Chinese, to learn Chinese morality, Chinese ways of thinking, and the Chinese language. As a student in grade school, I thought the English language was easier to learn than the Chinese language, but I appreciated the aesthetic and the representation of Chinese characters, and I especially appreciated Chinese calligraphy. One of my Chinese teachers liked to emphasize that to write Chinese words was to form one's character and to shape one's personality, because the writer has to be patient and observant, and has to seek to express his will and emotion through the practice of thousands of brush-strokes, and the control of ink and pressure on the brush.

I still remember vividly how our school masters gave us moral instruction in the morning assembly every week. Each semester's report card contained our academic score, but also a progress report on our moral aptitude and physical fitness. The grade school curriculum emphasized how to be a good person and how to do the right thing. There was an incident during my grade school years when I visited a public library. A group of Malay adolescents attacked me on my way home. I was not hurt physically, but psychologically I was hurt, and I wanted to take revenge, as the legends of the knights had taught me. I wished I were Bruce Lee, who could get even. Despite my hurt, I kept on reminding myself that to fight with "wild dogs and pigs" is to do an evil thing to myself. I learned then to keep a distance from the "enemy" and to extend my helping hands only to my neighbors—those in need.

When I attended the English secondary (middle and high schools) schools, I noticed that the Confucianist categories of goodness and rightness were absent from the curriculum. There were two reasons my parents wanted to send us to English school. First, they thought that having six years of Chinese/Confucianist education was an adequate foundation and, though in an English school, we still could continue to learn Chinese and Malay. Second, they thought that an English education would guarantee us better employment opportunities than a Chinese or Malay education could offer. An English education would serve us better if we were thinking of going overseas for further education. I enjoyed the cross-cultural education of my secondary school, where a racially mixed student body challenged me to be sensitive to the co-existence of all people.

Chinese Christian

It was in secondary school that Christian theology began to impact the way I thought about cultural and religious identities. Malaysia was a British colony until the late 1950s. Christian missionaries established high-quality English secondary schools in Malaysia with standard examinations offered by Cambridge University (at the Ordinary and the Advance Levels). I went to an Anglican high school and had the option to take Bible as a course elective. I did not do that, but it was there in the secondary school that my Confucianist ethos encountered Christian theology. I was brought up in an atheistic family, with a strong belief in the power of the person over nature, of reason over feeling. For me at the time religion was superstition, created for those who did not have a strong self-image. I did not associate myself with any Chinese gods. But I appreciated the beautiful greenery, the deep blue sea, mysterious nature, and the gorgeous flora and fauna around my hometown. These things often caused me to wonder whether a Creator-God existed. It was at the Anglican high school in Kuching that I began a search for the meaning of existence and my life.

My quest for truth started with looking into Eastern philosophy. An informal study left me with the following impressions: Confucius advocated my keeping away from gods and ghosts, and to be a superior and humane person; Laozi (Lao Tze) taught me that one's finite mind could not understand the infinite *Dao*, and that all I could do was to strive to be a part of nature ("self-being/becoming" in Chinese); Buddha asked me to be compassionate, to deny myself, and to do good until I became enlightened as he was. Later, I began to explore western philosophy, literature, arts, and science.

Then, a Christian friend of mine shared Christ with me at school. For a few months, we discussed and argued about the person and work of Christ, about salvation by faith, about the existence and incarnation of God, and about the meaning of life. I began to have a basic understanding of Christ's incarnation. One night I read Rev 1:8 in the New Testament. The Spirit must somehow have helped me to understand that Jesus is indeed God, for he is the First and the Last, before and after the existence of time and space. That truth struck me, for the Creator is the Almighty God who broke into the realm of space and time to save sinners from the power of sin and death and to grant them their full humanity. The conversion experience from being simply a Chinese (cultural identity) to a Chinese Christian (theologico-cultural identity) was sealed for me, not through intellectual clarification, but through the reality of the community of love. I wanted to become a Christian because I saw the Confucianist ideal of community love realized in the Christian Fellowship at my high school. There was nothing so evident and irrefutable than the love of God that radiated through the body of Christ in that school. I knew Christ was alive and had the power to grant fullness of life. I thought then that to be a *Christian Confucianist* was not to destroy my cultural tradition but to fulfill it. Over the years, the Cross has become the most meaningful of symbols and the event that has enabled me to construct my Chinese Christian identity.

Becoming a Christian was a high point in my life. It was more than a transformation of a moral being, from doing evil to doing good and having the resources (grace) to love God and neighbor. It was also a pilgrimage to becoming a *Chinese Christian*, or better still a *Christian Chinese*—a journey of rendering rich meaning to my cross-cultural identity as both a Chinese *and* a Christian. At that time, when discussing with my Christian friends questions regarding a "cultural God," and the possibility of becoming an authentic Chinese and a genuine Christian, I was not aware of what lay in store. Sometimes I mocked my Christian friends who were racially Chinese yet did not know the Chinese language, any of the Chinese classics, or Confucianist ethics. I found it problematic that the Chinese Bible did not read like Chinese prose. I wrestled with the many biblical narratives that were not universal in scope but highly contextualized in their Palestinian and Mediterranean worlds. I wondered, if the Bible is the word of God for everyone, why that divine revelation sounds so limited to particular groups only. My favorite biblical books were the wisdom literatures of the Old Testament. I did not like the historical books, for they did not contain the history of other peoples. To me Pentateuchal (first five books of the Old Testament) theology was "racist" in many respects, except for the first two chapters of Genesis, where I appreciated the poetry and openness of the creation account. Even then, the story I heard about Adam and Eve from my Christian friends sounded like the ancestors of westerners—they could not possibly include the Chinese as their descendants, since we have the famous *Pangu kaitian* account of the origin of the Chinese.[11]

As for the New Testament, I respected the Gospels as personal stories of our Savior and his earliest disciples. I found it difficult to reject them as a Chinese believer. But I liked Luke and John better than Matthew and Mark—later I discovered as a young Christian that I shared views regarding the Bible similar to those of the heretic Marcion. It was Paul's writings that opened my eyes. It was he who taught me how to be resourceful as a Chinese Christian. Paul's skill in interpreting Jewish stories and Jesus' life and works interested me. Paul's erratic mood and edginess captured my attention. He was counter-cultural and that was an asset to me. I used my Confucianist lenses to read Paul; for example, I found his understanding of a life of holiness freed from the bondage of sins (e.g., Romans 5–7) fascinating. I dismissed his understanding of eschatology (end of the world and coming of Christ) as a cultural bias—partly because I was suspicious of the preaching in local churches that only taught the dispensationalist reading of Christ's second coming. Despite all these questions I had as a new believer, I had a passionate interest in beginning a careful reading of Confucius' Four Books and in studying the Pauline epistles alongside them. But no one in my church or my school showed any interest in my intertextual reading.

After high school, I worked for a few years at the Internal Revenue Department. That job never satisfied my interest in philosophy and lit-

---

11. See Chiu, *The Tao of Chinese Religion*, 122–36. *Panku* was born from the *Huntun*, the Cosmic Egg. The myth also describes the primordial chaos, as in the Genesis account, but the Chinese myth does not attribute the creating process to the god(s). In Chinese tradition especially of the Confucianist, this creation myth does not play any role in their ethical thought. Heaven (*tian*) is central in Confucianism, see my discussion later in this chapter (pp. 13–25) and also Chapter Two (pp. 114–27).

erature. I decided to come to America to pursue a theological degree and to work on cross-cultural interpretation of the New Testament, sensing the calling to be a Christian theologian. At first I applied for a psychology and counseling major, thinking it would be needed for ministry in Malaysia; but more importantly, I wanted to study theological anthropology—humanity as created by and in relation to the Creator God. I wanted to go to America because I thought America was a Christian nation, where everyone lived in freedom there.

My undergraduate study at St. Paul Bible College, in the small town of Waconia, Minnesota, gave me—together with my wife—three years of deep reflection. We arrived two days after the Fourth of July (1984) celebration. We loved America, being a land of freedom and great resources, especially in academic pursuits. We were shocked, however, to witness racism in the land of freedom. We began to have a more realistic view of America. We disliked the fact that the history of the Native Americans and the slavery of the African Americans resurfaced in the perpetuation of institutional racism. We tried to forget our first encounter with the Immigration officer at the Los Angeles Airport, who questioned my wife and me with a condescending tone. But when that unwelcome attitude repeated itself thirteen years later when we applied for our Permanent Resident Card at the U.S. Immigration and Naturalization Service in Chicago, we knew every generation had to take freedom's quest into its own hands. At college, I was told of racism against Asian, Black, Hispanic/Latinos, and Native Americans in the United States of America. I was told that in the summer of 1982, Vincent Chin's

> brains were beaten out with a baseball bat by Ronald Ebens, a forty-three-year-old laid-off Chrysler foreman in East Detroit.... Ebens has taken Vincent Chin for a Japanese, one of those people whose car exports had put so many Americans out of work, . . . When the court handed down its sentence it outraged the Chinese community: for killing Vincent Chin, Ebens and his stepson were merely placed on three years' probation and fined $3,780 each.[12]

I rationalized to myself then: America was an open society, and such incidents were part of the parcel of freedom.

My wife and I were far away from our family in Malaysia, and three years of homesickness deepened my conviction that we could not be

---

12. Pan, *Sons of the Yellow Emperor*, 293.

Americanized, we must remain Chinese Christians. We experienced "culture shock" (positively and negatively), not only in our immersion into American ways of life, but also by American Chinese (e.g., the invention of fortune cookies). However, I met a wonderful mentor and friend, Donald Alexander. He had been my wife's professor during his seven years of missionary teaching in Hong Kong. His doctoral work in Confucian texts intrigued me. He constantly encouraged me to do an intertextual reading between Chinese culture and the Bible. After three years of undergraduate study majoring in Bible and theology, I came to Garrett-Evangelical Theological Seminary to do a Master of Divinity degree.

I met Robert Jewett at Evanston and decided to stay on to pursue a Doctor of Philosophy program at Northwestern University, majoring in a cross-disciplinary study of the New Testament (at the seminary) and Greco-Roman rhetorics (in the Classics and Communications Departments of the University). Robert Jewett did his doctorate at the University of Tübingen, and perhaps because of his diasporic experience there, he was led to read Paul as an Apostle to America.[13] His works on the Captain America Complex and his cultural readings of Paul are samples of cross-cultural hermeneutics I learned from. My doctoral dissertation dealt with Chinese cross-cultural hermeneutics, and as a test study, I extended the rhetorical move of Paul in 1 Corinthians 8 and 10 to address the challenge of ancestor worship in many Chinese Christian homes.[14] It is evident that my aspiration over the last twenty years has been to construct a cross-cultural hermeneutic.

I am convinced that "cross-cultural hermeneutics" is practiced by the New Testament writers, the Church Fathers, and many theologians in the West. Hellenization impacts the translation of the Hebrew Scriptures. Greek philosophical thoughts are readily expressed through the New Testament and patristic writings. Augustine, Aquinas, and Calvin used Greek philosophies so well that the process of their indigenization (intertextual reading between Christian doctrines and Greek philosophy) was never regarded as "cross-cultural" but simply Christian. My envy of theologians in the West turns into a challenge I must face; that is, how can I read Paul and Confucius intertextually? How can I read the New Testament through which Chinese cultural ideals are critiqued and

13. See Jewett, *Paul the Apostle to America*, passim.

14. See my dissertation in its revised form, Yeo, *Rhetorical Interaction in 1 Corinthians 8 and 10*.

fulfilled? I am convinced that this kind of biblical hermeneutic in turn makes the biblical text "sacred," that is, to have the power to speak across space and time.

Migrant/Diasporic Chinese

After my doctoral work, I went to Hong Kong to teach for almost four years; that itself was also a cross-cultural experience. Because of dialect problems (I spoke Chaozhou and Fujian dialects and very little Cantonese), I lectured in Mandarin and engaged in conversation with students and colleagues in simple Cantonese. I noticed, however, that for those who could not speak Cantonese life in Hong Kong could be a painful experience. Many times I felt unwelcome simply because I was a Malaysian speaking Mandarin. Some of my close friends explained my feelings of alienation as a normal reaction to an "island emotion," that is, being slow to open up to outsiders for the sake of survival in a limited space. However that may be, in my cross-cultural work I began to understand the complexity of even Chinese identity: Is it one or many?

I do not see a uniform, fixed Chinese identity. It is commonly known that the internal conflicts among various Chinese clans or families or political groups can be as bad as any interracial conflict, if not worse. Chinese movies and martial arts novels of the "knights" variety do reflect the harsh reality and self-destructive nature of being obsessed with the issue of Chinese identity. I once immersed myself in this hypnotizing fiction of revenge, all in the name of righteousness and justice. Where does salvation lie in such self-destruction? Is there any way out for any racial group trying to resolve its cultural or ethnic (sub-)identity without destroying others?

I think the answer lies in a transcendent cross-cultural hermeneutic. It is true that we can only read from one vantage point. But to stand too long at one point and to think that what one sees is complete and absolute is the idolizing process we need to avoid. Idolizing one's own identity rarely leads to tolerance, even less to the appreciation of the viewpoint of others. In my second English book, *What Has Jerusalem to Do with Beijing?*[15] my goal was to work toward bridging the gap between Scripture

---

15. Yeo, *What Has Jerusalem to Do with Beijing?* My work, *Chairman Mao Meets the Apostle Paul*, is an extension of the previous work, with the narrower focus of reading the

(with Jerusalem as the metaphor) and Chinese culture (with Beijing as the metaphor). I approached Chinese culture in terms of the concrete specificities of *yin-yang* thinking, Confucianist ethics, Daoist spirituality, the June Fourth massacre (in 1989), etc. Then I brought in biblical ethics, eschatology, theology, and the concept of salvation to dialogue with these aspects of Chinese culture. The end-result of that work was that in the cross-cultural reading process I began to recognize the blind spots in my own culture and that of the biblical texts, and I came to appreciate more fully than ever how other cultures can illuminate one's own.

In the last twenty years I have learned now to assimilate into another culture, especially the West. But assimilation often brings ambiguous feelings. The writer Ien Ang speaks of his own experience as a Chinese migrant born in Indonesia but living in a number of western countries, including Australia:

> But assimilation, as Zygmunt Bauman has forcefully shown, can never be successful. The modern project of assimilation, which literally means 'making alike', is inherently contradictory, because the very acquired—rather than inherited or ascribed—character of cultural traits gained in the process of assimilation turns the assimilating subject into a less than real, and thus somehow inferior Westerner. Even the most westernized non-Western subject can never become truly authentically Western. The traces of Asianness cannot be erased completely from the westernized Asian: we will always be 'almost the same but not quite', because we are 'not white' (Bhabha).[16]

Assimilation in the sense of "a melting pot" does not happen. As immigrants to America, we were not assimilated into its Anglo-Saxon core. "A more accurate image . . . would be a 'stew' or 'salad bowl', a mosaic of different groups co-existing in a multiracial, multicultural or pluralistic society, the tomatoes remaining tomatoes, distinguishable from the lettuce and the chicory."[17]

My diasporic journey in an increasingly globalized, postcolonial, and multicultural world, has led me to discover the hybridity of my cross-cultural identity and has caused me to turn now and again to Confucius and Paul, the icons of my identity. Their stories reflect the hybrid charac-

---

Thessalonian correspondence in the context of the Cultural Revolution in China.

16. Ang, *On Not Speaking Chinese*, 9.

17. Pan, *Sons of the Yellow Emperor*, 289.

ter of their own equally multicultural worlds. For me, Confucius and Paul are two major pieces in the mosaic of my religious/theological and cultural identity. For this reason I will give the biographies of Confucius and Paul in the following two sections before proceeding to the section on the "Intertextuality of Confucius and Paul." Readers familiar with these two figures may skip the biographies, my focus of which is the political and academic teaching of Confucius and the cross-cultural theology of Paul.

CONFUCIUS: THE ETHICS OF MORAL EDUCATION AND BECOMING A SAGE-RULER[18]

Family Background

The English word Confucius (551–479 BCE) is a Jesuit's latinization of the Chinese word Kong Fuzi, meaning Master Kong. In the Chinese speaking world, he is most often referred to as simply Kongzi.[19] Confucius was born in the state of Lu during the Spring and Autumn period (717–472 BCE).[20] It was a period of disorder and violence because of constant

18. See the following sources: *Zuo Zhuan* [*The Commentary of Zuo*], *Gongyang Zhuan* [*The Commentary of Gongyang*] and *Guliang Zhuan* [*The Commentary of Guliang*]—all three are commentaries on the *Spring and Autumn Annals*, *Shiji* [*Records of the Historiographer*], *Kongzi Jiayu* [*Master Kong's Family Sayings*] in *Baizi Quanshu* [*Complete Works of All Teachers*]; Huang, *The Analects of Confucius*, 191–200; Lau, trans., *The Analects*, 209–40; Yang, *Lunyu Yizhu*, 3–8; Van Norden edited, *Confucius and the Analects*, Introduction; Brooks and Brooks, *The Original Analects*, 163–94. On *Zuo Zhuan*, I use the Chinese text made available online by Peking University (http://chinese.pku.edu.cn/david/zuozhuan.html). On the Chinese text of *Shiji*, I use the ten-volume work published by Xinhua Bookstore (Beijing) in 1972; for the selected English translation, I consult the seven-volume work edited by William H. Nienhauser Jr., *The Grand Scribe's Records* (Bloomington: Indiana University Press, 1994–).

Formerly, the standard source for a biography of Confucius was the Han historiographer, Sima Qian's (145–86 BCE) work, *Shiji, Kongzi Shijia* [*Records of the Historiographer, The Hereditary House of Master Kong*]. Since the publication of *Zhusi Kaoxinlu* [*A Study on the Authenticity of Confucian Literature*] by Cui Shu (1740–1816) in the Qing dynasty, most scholars think that Sima Qian's work may contain myths and legends of Confucius.

19. Confucius' family name is Kong, and his personal name is Qiu, and his "style name" (in Chinese called Zi, i.e., the name employed by those not familiar with him) is Zhongni, given when he was an adult (ca. 533 BCE).

20. Confucius was born in the county of Zou (near modern Qufu), in the state of Lu, at the time when Lu Xiang Gong was the Duke of Lu for twenty-one years. Confucius was born on September 26, 551 BCE, toward the end of the Zhou dynasty, commonly known

warfare. Out of this context emerged the political ethics of Confucius. Unfortunate events occurred in Confucius' family, out of which came his ethical concerns. Confucius' forbearers, who were originally from the Song state, belonged to the upper class. Kong Fujia, Confucius' sixth-generation ancestor, served as minister of military affairs to Duke Shang of Song but was murdered, and the family fled to Lu to escape further persecution. Though his forebearers were nobles, upon moving to Lu they lived in obscurity until Confucius' father, Kong He (personal name: Shuliang), served as the magistrate of Zou county. At sixty years of age, Kong He married a young girl named Yan Zhengzai, who was much younger than he, and they gave birth to a son and called him Qiu or Zhongni—Confucius.

Kong He died soon after Confucius was three years old. It is suggested that this experience of losing his father at a young age influenced him to abide by the "Way of one's father" and be a "filial son" (*Analects* 1:11; 4:20). His mother was a knowledgeable woman, for as a single parent she raised Confucius to become a government official and a great teacher. She died when Confucius was seventeen years old. Little wonder then that Confucius often mentioned fathers and mothers in his discussion of filial piety (*Analects* 1:7; 2:6; 4:18, 19, 21; 11:5; 17:21). Despite the hierarchical distinction between parents and children, Confucius did emphasize the responsibility of children to guide their parents to do the right thing: "In serving your father and mother you ought to dissuade them from doing wrong in the gentlest way. If you see your advice being ignored, you should not become disobedient but should remain reverent. You should not complain even if you are distressed" (*Analects* 4:18).[21]

In his pre-teen years, Confucius had to work to support his mother and himself. In his youth, he held lowly offices while deeply engaged in self-education. *Analects* 9:6 tells us that he had learned many menial things because of his poor background.

---

as the Spring and Autumn period.

21. Lau, trans., *Analects*, 33. I will note the source of the English translation of the *Analects* used, or mention if it is my own translation. The citation of the *Analects* in Chinese scholarship simply gives the title of the book or chapter without the numbering of the verse. However, the citation of the *Analects* in non-Chinese scholarship often gives the precise numbering of passages from the *Analects*. The problem is that the numbering of passages from the *Analects* is not always the same in different editions. For the English citation of the *Analects* in this paper, I will follow the numbering of Lau or Ames and Rosemont, indicating them as e.g., "1:3" and noting which source I use.

Below, his biography is divided into two areas: political career and academic achievement—the former a failure, the latter a success—though both aspects of his life were greatly influential in the development of Chinese culture.

Political Career

Since the age of fifteen, Confucius had already committed himself to study and learning music and rituals especially of the Zhou dynasty, with the ambition of bringing peace and prosperity to the society. His heroes were the sage kings of the ancient past, especially of the Zhou dynasty. And he wanted to learn about rituals and music because, he thought, they had created a culture (*wen*) that had made the Zhou rulers sages and their society humane and harmonious. There were no schools for Confucius to attend, so he consulted professionals.[22] He excelled in learning, and was popularly sought after by noble houses.[23] By the time he was thirty years old, the Master said of himself, "I was established" (*Analects* 2:4), meaning that he had already established a good career in government. He was scrupulous in ritual propriety as practiced by the government.

The political career of Confucius occupied a long period of his adult life. He traveled from one state to the next in search of a ruler who would practice his idea of benevolent government. Unfortunately, he not only encountered hardships in his travels, but also he was never sincerely offered a position by a ruler, except a short period in the state of Lu. Below are chronological snapshots of the challenges and disappointments in his political career.

---

22. In 525 BCE he consulted the Viscount of Tan, prince of a vassal state of Lu, on how to name government offices (see *Zuo Zhuan* 48.3b–9a). He consulted Lao Dan, court librarian of the Zhou royal house, on rituals. He consulted Zhou minister Changhong on music; he learned music also from the grand master of music at the state of Qi (see Huang, *Analects*, 193).

23. On their state visit to Lu (in 522 BCE), the Duke Jing of Qi (or Jing Gong) and his Prime Minister Yan Ying consulted Confucius on rituals and statecraft. In 518 BCE, Meng Xizi wanted his two sons, Meng Yizi and Nangong Jingshu, to learn rituals from Confucius. See *Zuo Zhuan* 49:21b.

In the State of Qi

In 517 BCE when Confucius was thirty-four years of age, he fled to the state of Qi to avoid the political upheaval in the state of Lu.[24] At Qi he had a conversation with Duke Jing (*Analects* 12:11, 16:12), hoping that the Duke would offer him a position. Confucius aspired to realize his political ideal in Qi, and hoped Qi would be transformed into Lu and Lu transformed to attain the Way of benevolent government (*Analects* 6:24).[25] Unfortunately, the Duke did not extend an offer to Confucius because the Bei and Zhen ruling families at Qi were competing for power.[26] Duke Jing, however, often consulted Confucius on statecraft and rituals.[27]

Return to the State of Lu

When the political situation in Qi worsened, Confucius returned to Lu. The situation in Lu was no better than that in Qi. A Ji family steward, Gongshan Furao, rebelled against Ji Huanzi, one of the ruling families in the state of Lu.[28] Gongshan Furao asked Confucius to join him. Confucius was not too keen on the idea, but he did consider the offer. His disciple Zilu was annoyed with Confucius' consideration, "We may have nowhere to go, but why must we go to Gongshan?" Confucius replied, "The man who summons me must have a purpose. If anyone's purpose is to use me, perhaps I can create another Zhou in the east?" (*Analects* 17:5). Confucius

24. That year Duke Zhao of Lu attempted to seize power from the three ruling families (Jisun, Shusun, and Mengsun). However, he was defeated and had to flee to the Qi state northeast of Lu.

25. See Qian, *Lunyu Xinjie*, 216 (*Analects* 6:22); Zhu ed., *Sishu*, 153; Yang, *Lunyu Yizhu*, 136.

26. The Duke said about Confucius, "I am unable to accord him such exalted treatment as the Ji family receives [in Lu]. . . . I am afraid I will not be able to put his talents to use" (*Analects* 18:3). See Lau, trans., *Analects*, 183; Yang, *Lunyu Yizhu*, 410.

27. Earlier on Yang Hu, a house steward of Ji Huanzi, usurped the power by holding Ji Huanzi under house arrest. When Yang Hu rebelled, he was defeated and was forced to flee to Qi and later moved to Jin. *Analects* 12:11 accounts the discussion between Confucius and Duke Jing. Confucius responded to the issue of the ruling families, "Let the ruler be a ruler, the subject a subject, the father a father, the son a son." The Duke then said, "Splendid! Truly, if the ruler be not a ruler, the subject not a subject, the father not a father, the son not a son, then even if there be grain, would I get to eat it?" (Lau, trans., *Analects*, 113; *Analects* 12:11.)

28. Huang, *Analects*, 194.

was clearly not serious in assuming the position, but his dream of restoring the ideal society of Zhou was obvious. In the meantime, Confucius kept busy with his teaching.

Another opportunity came when Yang Huo, a government official in the state of Lu,[29] asked Confucius to serve with him, but Confucius declined (*Analects* 17:1).[30] Finally in 501 BCE, when Confucius was fifty years old, Duke Ding of Lu (Ding Gong) appointed Confucius to be the magistrate of Zhongdu (a county of Lu). Confucius was promoted to the position of deputy minister of public works the next year, then to the "minister of justice" (*sikou*). He was appointed by Ji Huanzi, the chief minister of Lu.[31] Confucius' achievement in the government includes setting up a diplomatic meeting between Duke Ding of Lu and Duke Jing of Qi in 500 BCE at Jiaku to promote friendship between the two states. Confucius served as master of ceremonies at that conference.[32] During the meeting, Duke Jing's men attempted to abduct Duke Ding at a dance performance. Confucius saw the deception and stopped the performance, thus rescuing Duke Ding. Confucius renounced the shameful act of Duke Jing. Duke Jing apologized and returned to Lu the lands of Wenyang, Guiyin, and Huan, which they had seized earlier.[33] Confucius' political career was at its height at this time.

29. Yang Hu is not the same person as Yang Huo. See Lau's discussion (*Analects*, 215–16) on the identity of Yang Huo and Yang Hu. Lau thinks that Yang Huo in the *Mencius* 3b.7 passage is Yang Hu. I see these two as different persons. Lau is correct in identifying Yang Hu and Yang Huo as two different persons in the *Analects*. Huang (*Analects*, 194) and Yang (*Lunyu Yizhu*, 388) see these two persons as one, and most commentators think so: Qian, *Lunyu Xinjie*, 614; Ames and Rosemont, *The Analects of Confucius*, 202.

30. Yang Huo then asked that a pig be given to Confucius as a gift. Confucius then purposely went to Yang Huo's residence to acknowledge the gift when Yang was not at home—to do according to the *li* (ritual) of receiving gifts, and yet to reject his invitation. But on road, they met each other. Yang asked Confucius, "To pocket one's gem and allow one's state to go awry—can this be called humane [*ren*]? I'd say: 'It cannot.' To love to engage in state affairs but to have repeatedly missed the opportunity—can this be called wisdom? I'd say: "It cannot.' The days and moons are flitting away; the years do not wait on us" (Huang, *Analects*, 165; *Analects* 17:1). Confucius was shamed by Yang Huo's word and was persuaded to take office. Yet, we have no evidence that Confucius did serve Yang.

31. Cf. *Mencius* 6b.6 (see Legge, trans., *The Four Books*, 215).

32. *Zuo Zhuan* 56.2a–4a.

33. Huang, *Analects*, 194.

For a number of years when Confucius served as the minister of justice, Lu was governed well and became powerful. Qi, the neighboring state, became insecure. Li Chu, the minister of Duke Jing of Qi, proposed that extravagant gifts be given to Duke Ding of Lu and Ji Huanzi to distract them. Confucius resigned the position of "minister of justice" when the Duke and Ji Huanzi accepted eighty singers and dancers and thirty truckloads of precious material from Qi. For three days the Duke and Ji Huanzi failed to administer their duty (*Analects* 18:4).[34] Confucius' counsels were ignored by Ji Huanzi, and at one particular sacrificial ceremony, Ji Huanzi did not follow the rite in distributing the meat to the government officials. Confucius left the ritual hastily with his cap still on and felt angry toward Ji Huanzi.

Confucius left his home state, Lu, once more. For the next fourteen years or so, he traveled around a number of states with a group of his disciples. They searched for a wise prince who would accept his concept of a benevolent government and allow them to implement their sage-king politics.

In the State of Wei

Duke Ling of Wei welcomed Confucius but was not interested in his political theories, for the duke was preoccupied with military might and women (cf. *Analects* 6:16, 28; 13:3; 15:1). Confucius said that Duke Ling had lost the Way of benevolent government.[35] Nanzi, the wife of Duke Ling, showed interest in consulting Confucius. Nanzi was known for her licentiousness, though she was politically powerful. Confucius was reluctant to see her,[36] but she was a cunning woman who was planning to use Confucius to boost her career and power, and in return wanted to offer

34. See Yang, *Lunyu Yizhu*, 410 on the Chinese *kui* (歸, meaning "return") is *kui* (饋, meaning "give").

35. When asked why Qi had then not declined, Confucius replied, "He had Zhongshu Yu to receive envoys and guests, Priest Tuo to administer ancestral temple, Wangsun Jia to command the military" (*Analects* 14:19). According to Zhu Xi (in his edited, *Sishu*, 265), though these ministers were not virtuous, they were still capable of helping the Duke.

36. Confucius went to speak to Nanzi, and that agitated Zilu. Zilu did not want his Master to associate with such a woman. In any case, *Analects* 6:28 records the reply of Confucius to Zilu: "If I have done anything wrong [with her], may heaven despise me, may heaven despise me!" (*Analects* 6:28).

Confucius a high position. Confucius found it difficult to deal with her and tried to avoid her.[37]

Despite the fact that Confucius did not have an official position in Wei, Wei would become his second home.[38] Confucius left Wei the day after Duke Ling consulted him regarding military formation. Confucius replied that he had never studied how to command troops, but he had studied the use of sacrificial vessels (*Analects* 15:1). In a benevolent government, according to Confucius' political thinking, violence was never a means either to achieve peace or to overcome conflict. Confucius was disgusted with the military resolution of Duke Ling.

In the States of Chen, Cai, and Chu

When Confucius and his disciples passed through the state of Song to go to Chen state, they were almost assassinated.[39] Eventually, they arrived safely at the state of Chen. Duke Min of Chen gave Confucius a position in his government.

Three years later, Wu attacked Chen, and Confucius and his followers fled to Cai. Before arriving in Cai, they went seven days without food, and some of his disciples fell sick, many becoming so weak that they could not stand. Facing this adversity, Zilu resentfully questioned Confucius: "Do even exemplary persons face such adversity?" Confucius replied, "Exemplary persons remain steadfast in adversity, while petty persons

37. Perhaps in that context, Confucius said "women and petty men are difficult to keep: if you go near them they become insolent, and if you keep a distance with them, they are resentful." Though most commentators interpret women and petty men here as referring to concubines/maid servants and men servants/eunuchs respectively. See Qian, *Lunyu Xinjie*, 645–46; see Chapter Five of this book (pp. 320, 325–32) on Confucius' view on gender and social ethics.

38. In Wei Confucius acquainted with Qu Boyu, a good minister, and a number of Confucius' disciples managed to be officials there. See *Analects* 14:25, 15:7.

39. Confucius and his disciples were almost killed by Huan Tui (Huan Sima in *Mencius* 5a.8). Huan Tui was the minister of military affairs. *Analects* 9:5 records this experience, yet we see Confucius' conviction that heaven had protected him in order to continue the culture/civilization (*wen*) of King Wen: "King Wen has already died, but does his cultural heritage still exist with us? If heaven were to let that legacy die, then we latecomers would not have that culture. But if heaven is not going to destroy this culture, then what can people of Kuang do to me?" (*Analects* 9:5) *Analects* 7:22 also echoes the providential act of heaven toward Confucius, as he said, "Heaven has bestowed upon me virtue, what can Huan Tui do to me?"

become reckless in adversity" (*Analects* 15:2). Finally, King Zhao of Chu sent an army to escort Confucius and his disciples to the state of Chu. The King considered making Confucius a lord and offered him a position in the court, but the Prime Minister Zixi blocked the plan. During his brief stay at Chu, Confucius was content that he met a good prince—Prince of She, who asked Confucius how to govern (*Analects* 13:16). But soon Confucius began to feel homesick for the state of Lu (*Analects* 5:22).

Return to the States of Wei and Lu

On his way to Lu, Confucius and his disciples visited the state of Wei (in 489 BCE). Confucius and his disciples were hosted by Duke Ling while in the state of Wei. The family feud for power among the duke's family made it impossible for Confucius to promote his political ethics.[40] Confucius returned to Lu in 484 BCE when he was sixty-seven years old. In 493 BCE Ji Kangzi had succeeded his father's position and became the chief minister of Lu. Ji Kangzi did not show interest in Confucius; instead he offered Confucius' disciple, Ran Qiu (a.k.a. Ran You), a position in the court.[41] Upon the recommendation of Ran Qiu (in 484 BCE), Confucius eventually was given some kind of ceremonial or advisory position (*Analects* 14:21), rather than a position where he had executive power.[42]

40. In 496 BCE, Kuaitui, the son of Duke Ling attempted to kill Nanzi, wife of the Duke. Kuai Kui was too ashamed of what Nanzi had tried to do. The attempt failed, Kuai Kui fled to the state of Jin. Three years later, Duke Ling died (493 BCE), and his exiled son, Kuai Kui, was not able to rule, so the grandson Zhe became the Duke. Duke Zhe was thinking of appointing Confucius to a position, but it never happened. In the mean time, Kuai Kui never gave up the revolt. With the help of the Jin army, he set up his base in the city of Qi, and waited for the opportunity to topple his son Zhe. Kuai Kui was to wait for thirteen years to regain power (480 BCE). Confucius was not pleased with their family struggle for political power. See *Analects* 7:15; Lau, trans., *Analects*, 223–24.

41. In 484 BCE, Ran Qiu led an attack on behalf of Ji Kangzi and defeated the invading forces of Qi.

42. In the same year, Ji Kangzi consulted Confucius through Ran Qiu on the matter of taxation. *Analects* 11:17 may be referring to this case, see Lau, trans., *Analects*, 225. *Analects* 11:17 tells us that the wealth of the Ji family surpassed that of Duke Zhou. Yet Ran Qiu collected more tax and increase the wealth of Ji's family. Confucius was furious and asked his students to "beat the drum and attack him publicly" (*Analects* 11:17)." Whether Confucius was too stubborn in insisting on reviving the ancient Zhou or whether Ran Qiu was simply politically shrewd in wanting to help Ji Kangzi whom Confucius would not help is open to question. In any case, we see here the irreconcilable conflict between a teacher and his his student.

Confucius advised Duke Ai of Lu[43] to defend the state of Qi and to punish Chen Chengzi when Chen Chengzi assassinated Duke Jian, the ruler of Qi. Duke Ai rejected Confucius' advice.[44] Confucius was now of the age when he did not intend to take any office, and he was given a low-ranking position. He spent the rest of his life engaging in academic works of editing, writing, and teaching.

Last Years

During his last years, Confucius' life was difficult. He was lonely and heartbroken. Those close to him passed away, one after another.[45] The Master himself died in 479 BCE at the age of seventy-two.[46] The apotheosis of Confucius began soon after his death. Mencius wrote, "Ever since man came into this world, there has never been another Confucius" (*Mencius* 2a.2).[47]

43. Duke Ai of Lu had come to power in the state of Lu in 194 BCE.

44. Duke Ai asked Confucius to report to the three lords of the ruling families. The ruling families also rejected Confucius' counsel (*Analects* 14:21; see also *Zuo Zhuan* 59.19a–b).

45. A year before he returned to Lu (485 BCE), his wife died, without his presence. Before he arrived home at the state of Lu, his step-brother (see *Analects* 5:2, 11:6) also passed away. The immediate family members who welcomed him back home were his son and his grandson. His only son, Li (Boyu) died in 482 BCE (16:13), two years after his return to Lu. His grandson, Kong Ji was the only one who lived with him. The next year (481 BCE), his favorite disciple, Yan Hui died unexpectedly at the age of forty. The year after (480 BCE), his faithful disciple Zilu died in a civil fight in Wei. Zilu resisted the invasion of Kuai Kui but failed.

46. See *Zuo Zhuan*, 60.2a. He was buried by River Si, north of Qufu, the capital of Lu. His disciples mourned the Master for three years, according to Confucius' teaching on mourning. At the end of the mourning, they all parted in grief, except Zigong who built a little shed by the grave and mourned for another three years.

47. See Lau, trans., *Mencius*, 79; Brooks and Brooks, *The Original Analects*, 215. Master Kong has over seventy-seven generations of descendants. His grandson Zisi (491–431 BCE) may have been one of the editors of *Zhongyong, the Doctrine of Mean*, and also a teacher to Mengzi. The seventy-seventh generation progenitor is Kong Decheng (1920–), the ex-minister of examinations in Taiwan.

Academic Career

Most scholars consider Confucius' political career a failure, if one is to gauge the result in terms of how rulers then received his political ideas. The legacy of Confucius is best known in his teaching and writing.

In 538 BCE, at the age of fifteen, Confucius studied rituals and music, in addition to four additional arts (*liuyi*)—shooting, riding, writing, and arithmetic. Compared to other states, the state of Lu prided itself in its cultural heritage, which it traced to Zhou sage-rulers such as King Wu, King Wen, and the Duke of Zhou (Zhou Gong). The rituals and music of the early Zhou, commonly known as Zhou-*li*, were mainly the work of the Duke of Zhou. The son of the Duke of Zhou, Po Qin, served the Lu as Duke. He was able to use music and ritual to govern Lu and thus made Lu one of the most powerful states of its time. When Confucius was eight years old (544 BCE), a prince of Wu state by the name of Ji Zha visited Lu and was amazed to see how Lu preserved and fully made use of Zhou music and rituals. When Confucius was eleven years old, Jin state's ruler Han Xianzi visited Lu and remarked that Zhou-*li* was found only in Lu. From these two incidents, we can tell why Confucius was attracted to Zhou ritual and music in his studies. Unfortunately, even before Confucius was born, the music and ritual of Zhou were deteriorating in Lu and even more in other states. *Libeng yuehuai* means "ritual propriety has fallen, music has been ruined"—this saying characterized the morale of those days. This was another reason Confucius was so desperate to revive Zhou-*li* (the ritual of the Zhou dynasty) in his political ideology and teaching. He was determined to make Lu into a "state of ritual and music" (*liyue zhi bang*).

By the age of thirty, after fifteen years of serious study, Confucius was established in his family and professional life.[48] He was well versed in the classics and had proven himself to be a great teacher. He started a private school, the first in China. His teaching career in the state of Lu was severely interrupted when he fled to the state of Qi to avoid the political upheavals between Duke Zhou of Lu and the three noble ruling families.

Confucius' forbearers were from the knight class, but misfortune had cast his family into the lowest aristocratic stratum of the time.

---

48. At nineteen (534 BCE), he married a daughter of Jianguan, family of the Song state. The following year they had a son, named Li, and later a daughter named Kong Yao. The daughter later married his disciple Gongye Chang (cf. *Analects* 5:1).

Because of family misfortune, Confucius believed that education was the means to restore himself to the knight class of *junzi*—"son of the lord," the noble class. An autobiographical statement in the *Analects* (9:6) tells us, "I was lowly when young, therefore I have many skills and have done many jobs." His own childhood experience taught him the importance of giving educational opportunity to everyone (*Analects* 7:7). He taught others to move up the social ladder by means of learning (scholarship) and self-cultivation (virtue). It was a revolutionary idea, because being an aristocrat was an ascribed, not achieved, status. Confucius transformed the status of the aristocracy into an achievable one, open to all as long as they became educated and morally superior beings. Of his disciples, many of the well-known ones, such as Yan Hui, Zilu, Zhonggong, and Zengshen, came from lowly backgrounds (see *Analects* 6:11; 7:7; 9:27; 15:39).

Another reason why Confucius educated the common people may have something to do with the contemporary culture in which education was the way to become a government official. Those from the upper classes could afford to hire teachers for their children, almost guaranteeing them a future in the royal court. But now Confucius made this path available to all by offering them an opportunity for education.

Part of his legacy in education is the works edited after his retirement from a frustrating political career. To rediscover his curriculum one must look at the six classics—*Shijing (Book of Odes), Shangshu (Book of History), Liji (Record of Rituals), Yuejing (Classic of Music), Yijing (Classic of Changes), Chunqiu (Spring-Autumn Annuals)*—which many believe were his basic texts. However, in *Analects* 7:25 we are told that Confucius taught four subjects: culture, conduct, loyalty, and trust.[49]

Confucius edited *Chunqiu (Spring-Autumn Annuals)*, which is one of the oldest historical books in China; it preserved a total of 242 years of Zhou dynastic history called the Spring-Autumn period, from 722 BCE to 481 BCE. It contains Confucius' political ideas. While these ideas were not received by the rulers of his day, they are nevertheless the ideals of a thoughtful and practical ethicist. The book has its main historical thrust in Lu, the ideal state closest to the Western Zhou—in Confucius' opinion. The book accounts the rise and fall, the glory and the shame, of twelve dukes in Lu. In retrieving history, Confucius also looked back at the Xia,

49. See Chapter One (pp. 61–64) on *wen* and culture and refinement (cultured).

Shang, and Zhou dynasties.[50] The book relies on the premise that, rituals and music bring about peace and order, whereas a lack of ritual and music ensure a reign of violence.

Another book Confucius edited was *Yijing*, the *Classic of Changes*. It is an ancient book of divination, but it is full of philosophical reflections on cosmological phenomena, the decrees of heaven, the natural laws, human behavior, and relationships. Had Confucius studied the *Yijing* several years earlier, when he was fifty, he would not have committed gross errors (as he did in the years of his exile in his mid-fifties, even to the point of putting his disciples in danger while traveling in the lands of Chen and Chai; *Analects* 7:17). Even though the *Yijing* contains numerous oracles and divinations that were either used at the time or later for various superstitious purposes, Confucius' editing and teaching of *Yijing* seemed to "demythologize" the ancient wisdom. In *Analects* 13:22 Confucius quoted a text from *Yijing*, "If one does not show constancy in one's virtue, one will, perhaps, suffer shame." But to that quotation, Confucius offered an interpretation: "The import of the saying is simply that in such a case there is no point in consulting the oracle."[51]

In the area of historical works, Confucius also critically edited *Shangshu*, which contains the history of four dynasties: Yu, Xia, Shang, Zhou. Confucius' purpose in editing this book is to praise the Duke of Zhou for his establishment of Zhou rituals, music, and statutes. In Confucius' mind a state could be governed by *li* (ritual propriety) and music (*yue*). He often dreamed of the Duke Zhou, perhaps, imagining himself as the next Duke Zhou, who would restore the glorious days of Western Zhou by means of a benevolent or humane (*ren*)[52] government.

50. Modern scholarship tends not to believe that Confucius wrote *Chunqiu*, but as early as the fourth century BCE, Mencius already attributed *Chunqiu* to Confucius (*Mencius* 3b.9), saying that Confucius' own legacy would be judged by the work of *Chunqiu*.

51. Lau, trans., *Analects*, 129.

52. Confucius did not have a definitive answer to various questions about *ren*; his answer depended very much on the person asking question about it and the situation in which it was asked. That's why it allows us to have quite a flexible translation of the term, sometimes as humanness/humanity, sometimes humaneness/benevolent, and other times compassion, love. I will have a more elaborate discussion of *ren* in Chapter Four (pp. 261–76). My rendition of the term *ren* in this book will be flexible, assuming the overlapping nuances of the term, and its meaning as dependent on the context used. The same can also be said of the following terms used in the *Analects*: *li* (rite, ritual, propriety, ritual propriety), *junzi* (gentleman, exemplary person, best moral self, best humanity),

In his old age, he lamented that he no longer dreamed of the Duke of Zhou (*Analects* 7:4).

Besides historical books, he also edited other genres such as poems, music, and liturgy—thus the three major books of *Shi, Yue, Li*. These works have more to do with the expression of emotion than with the elucidation of the intellect. The work of *Li* contains the liturgies of various ceremonies the Zhou people used; the liturgies helped the participants to express their emotions through ceremonial exercises and music. Confucius also edited *Yue*, that is, the *Classic of Music*.

There would be other great ethicists, politicians, scholars, editors, interpreters, and teachers after Confucius, but there has been none like him in Chinese history who combined all these talents in one. The life and work of Confucius has been so influential that Chinese culture would not be what it is, apart from Confucius. I find locating my cultural identity in this tradition meaningful.

PAUL: APOSTLE OF THE CROSS-CULTURAL GOSPEL

Childhood and the Hellenistic Jewish World

Paul was a Hellenized diaspora Jew (Phil 3:5–6; Gal 1:11–24) living in a multi-cultural world. His *praenomen* or given name was, in Hebrew, *Sha'ul* (Acts 7:58; 8:1, 3; 9:1, 4, 17; 22:7; 26:14). His *cognomen* or family name in Latin, was *Paullus*, or in Greek *Paulos*. Paul was born and raised in the city of Tarsus (Acts 9:11, 30; 11:25; 21:39 ["no mean city"]; 22:3) about 6 CE, during the reign of the Emperor Augustus. Paul was a Roman citizen by birth (Acts 22:27–28).[53]

As a boy Paul experienced the multiculturalism of Tarsus. Being the capital of Cilicia, Tarsus was the political, commercial, intellectual, and cultural center of the region. His basic education was at home and in synagogue. Studying in Tarsus and Jerusalem, Paul learned Hebrew and Aramaic besides Greek, his native language, and some Latin (Acts 21:40, 22:2, 26:14). When he cited Scripture it was the Greek Septuagint, not

---

zhong (loyalty, dutifulness), *shu* (empathy, self-forgetting), *xin* (trust, faith, trustworthiness, fidelity), *jing* (respect, reverence, honor).

53. Though his own letters do not highlight his Roman citizenship; in fact, the punishment he received of thirty-nine lashes (2 Cor 11:25) was contrary to Roman law, which withheld the penalty for Roman citizens.

the Hebrew Bible, that he turned to. Hellenistic education generally did not train one in critical reasoning, as in our day, for it focused on the transmission of classical culture through the works of Homer, Euripides, Menander, and Demosthenes. Paul's own letters indicate that he was trained in the Greco-Roman rhetorical tradition, which was an essential aspect of ancient oral and literary cultures. He was "thoroughly at home in the Greek idiom of his time."[54]

Paul's letters tell us of his Jewish heritage and these we can find a similarity with Confucius. Confucius and Paul belonged to high social classes. But whereas Confucius aspired to live as the son of a noble (*junzi*), Paul found pride in being an Israelite, a descendant of Abraham, a member of the tribe of Benjamin (Rom 11:1). To assert his Jewish heritage he declares proudly that he was "circumcised on the eighth day" (Phil 3:5) according to the Torah. In the eyes of the Roman world, circumcision was a permanent mutilation; so he was "marked" as a Jew. Paul was proud of his hybrid identity, primarily of his ancestry: born "of the people of Israel, of the tribe of Benjamin" (Phil 3:6). When Paul was challenged by his Jewish Christian opponents regarding his apostleship and the truth of his gospel, he defended himself by recounting how steeped he was in the Jewish religion and how zealous he was for the traditions of his fathers (Gal 1:13–14).[55]

Despite living in diaspora amid a mix of Greco-Roman and Jewish cultures, Paul was familiar with the ancient tongue of his people (Hebrew/Aramaic), with the old traditions (Abraham and Torah), and with the Holy City of Jerusalem. Having received his basic education in Tarsus, Paul went to Jerusalem in 15 CE, at about the age of twenty, for more advanced study (Acts 22:3) in his own religious traditions of the law (*torah*). Paul was a Pharisee with respect to the law (Phil 3:5).[56] There is a parallel

54. Kennedy, *New Testament Interpretation through Rhetorical Criticism*, 10. But 2 Cor 10:10 records the accusation that his spoken words were unimpressive and unmoving.

55. Likewise, when so called super-apostles arrived in Corinth and questioned his credentials as an apostle of Christ, Paul replied passionately, "Are they Hebrews? So am I! Are they Israelites? So am I! Are they descendants of Abraham? So am I!" (2 Cor 11:2).

56. If Luke is correct, Paul studied at the feet of Gamaliel I the Elder, one of the leaders of the Pharisaic movement (Acts 22:3, 23:6). Interestingly enough Paul himself never mentions Gamaliel, even when he is defending his zeal for, and blamelessness under, the law (Gal 1:14; Phil 3:6). There were two wings of the Pharisee party: Hillel (a lenient, humane group, less opposed to Rome, that survived the Jewish-Roman war to become the predecessors of modern Judaism) and Shammai (a strict and radical group, which

here between Confucius and Paul in terms of their commitment to and retrieval of the glorious traditions of the past—the *Zhou-li* and the Torah. The Pharisees were the most devout of all Jewish groups in their study of the law. In addition to the written Torah, there were also oral laws (Mark 7:3–13; Matt 15:2–6; cf. Gal 1:14) to which observance was due.

It was as a zealous Pharisee that Paul persecuted the church of God violently (Gal 1:13; 1 Cor 15:9; Phil 3:6; Acts 8:3; 9:1–2; 22:3–9; 26:9–11). He looked upon the followers of Jesus as proclaiming a message contrary to Pharisaic interpretations of the law. As a Christian he spoke of the crucified Messiah as a scandal to Jews, or Jews could not accept the notion that one cursed by the law could be the Messiah of Jews and Gentiles. From the time he witnessed the stoning of Stephen (Acts 7:58; cf. 6:11–14; 8:1), Paul looked upon the followers of Christ as those who blasphemed against Mosaic traditions and the sanctity of the Temple.

Jewish Christian

Conversion[57] at Damascus, Arabia, Jerusalem

Paul's zeal and devotion to his ancestral Jewish faith, specifically to the law is stated in his letter to the churches in Galatia (1:13–14). He describes here as well his conversion from being a Jew to being a Jewish Christian. It is a turning from a monocultural law-abider to a cross-cultural missionary of Christ. Paul saw the Messiah in a new perspective as one who had changed the relationships of Jews and Gentiles and altered their identities as the people of God. God was active both in the first stage of Paul's life, as a Jew, and now in his life as a Christian (cf. Gal 1:3, 6, 15; 2:9, 21; 5:4; 6:18). Throughout the process of his life he was set apart before he was born (Gal 1:15) for service (see Exod 13:1; 19:12, 23; Rom 1:1; Acts 13:2) and finally called to "preach Christ among the nations."

---

was sympathetic to zealots and was discredited by the Jewish-Roman War).

57. "Conversion" is used here not in the anachronistic sense of changing religious faith from Judaism to Christianity; in Paul's day, these two religious faiths were not yet differentiated into two systems. "Conversion" is used here in the sense of a radical change in Paul's view of the Torah tradition and how Christ as the Messiah fit into the picture of God's salvation for Jews and Gentiles. The experience was so radical the term "conversion" is appropriate.

Gaventa's position is that Paul's Damascus experience is a transformation, rather than a conversion or alternation. See Gaventa, *From Darkness to Light*, 40.

God called him through grace (1:15)[58] and "was pleased" (*eudokēsen*) to reveal his Son to him (1:16). Paul did not trace his call back to his Jewish training and education as a youth. Rather, he traced his call to the God who was the author of grace and the God of the prophets—because although his Jewish tradition was sacred to him, his call to service was apocalyptic, that is, it came as God's intruding and claiming act upon him. The gospel that came to Paul did not originate in the form of tradition; it was "revealed" (*apocalypsai*) to Paul in the death and resurrection of the Messiah.[59]

After his conversion sometime around 36 CE, Paul did not go directly to Jerusalem, "but I went away into Arabia; and again I returned to Damascus" (Gal 1:17). The first thing Paul did was to go to Arabia (Gal 1:17). This may refer to the Nabatean kingdom of Aretas,[60] perhaps going there to make converts.[61] Paul was forced to return to Damascus after getting into trouble with Nabataeans in Arabia.[62]

Only three years after his conversion did he go to Jerusalem (Gal 1:18), perhaps in 39 CE; and for fifteen days he met only Peter and James, the brother of the Lord (Gal 1:18–19); and he adds, "I went up [to Jerusalem] by revelation" (Gal 2:20). Paul did not seek validation from authoritative sources. He makes it plain that the direct encounter with the risen Christ was sufficient for him (Gal 1:1). Paul's three-year stay at Damascus came to an end when the Nabataeans seized control of that city in 39 CE, and this time he fled to Jerusalem, never to return to Damascus.[63]

---

58. See also Gal 1:6; 5:8, 13; 1 Cor 15:10.

59. The apocalyptic invasion of God into Paul's life may sound mysterious. The phrase "*en emoi*" (to me or in me) in Gal 1:16 seems to describe a subjective experience (cf. also 2 Cor 4:6; 12:1–10 which describe a more esoteric and subjective visionary experiences), but Luke's accounts in Acts (9, 22, 26) appears to be more objective (at least eye witnesses were reacting to the Christophany also). See Martyn, *Galatians*, 158 on his argument for the translation "to me."

60. 2 Cor 11:32 relates how the governor of Damascus under orders from King Aretas IV [9BCE–40CE] attempted to seize Paul; Gal 4:35 uses Arabia in the more general sense of wilderness. See Murphy-O'Connor, "Paul in Arabia," 732–37.

61. Murphy-O'Connor, *Paul, A Critical Life*, 82.

62. "In Damascus the governor under Aretas the king guarded the city of the Damascenes in order to take me: and through a window was I let down in a basket by the wall, and escaped his hands" (2 Cor 11:32–33, ASV; cf. Acts 20: 3, 9 and 23:30).

63. Murphy-O'Connor, *Paul, A Critical Life*, 5–7.

Antioch and Tarsus

According to Acts 11:25–26, Barnabas went to Tarsus and brought Paul to Antioch to preach the gospel there. Paul then went to the districts of Syria and Cilicia. Antioch was the capital of Syria and Tarsus, the capital of Cilicia. Paul was not known by the church in Judea despite his brief visit (Gal 1:21–22). The Judean churches accepted his apostleship, though perhaps provisionally: "They only heard it said, 'He who once persecuted us is now preaching the faith he once tried to destroy.' And they glorified God because of me" (Gal 1:23–24).

(First) Missionary Journey (46–49 CE)[64]

Paul's life is highlighted by the missionary activity of traveling from one city to another. Scholars, following the book of Acts, traditionally divide Paul's missionary activity into three somewhat arbitrary journeys as a simple way to chart them on a map of the eastern Mediterranean. These journeys are not mentioned in Paul's letters as such. Acts 13:3—14:28 portrays Paul's missionary journey from Antioch in Syria to Cyprus, accompanied by Barnabas and John Mark. They continued on to the cities of Perga, Pisidian Antioch, Iconium, Lystra, and Derbe. John Mark departed at Derbe, and Paul and Barnabas returned to Antioch in Syria (49 CE). Paul took the gospel to Gentile communities after facing opposition in the synagogues.

It is not to be assumed that Paul was the first Christian preacher among the Gentiles. There were others before Paul who made Christian converts among the Gentiles (Acts 10:44–48, 11:20–21).[65] Paul was the first apostle to the Gentiles who adamantly declared that becoming God's people did not require circumcision and other nomistic services. In Paul's mind faith in Christ was sufficient. Paul believed that, as people of God,

---

64. See Brown, *Introduction*, 428–36 for information on the missionary journeys of Paul, followed here.

65. Judaism itself permitted Gentiles to give gifts to the Temple or to the worship of Yahweh. Herod's Temple in Jerusalem had a courtyard for Gentiles. Other Gentiles attended synagogues, some kept many of the 613 commandments. Thus Gentiles did participate in Jewish religious life, ranging from "God-fearers" to full-fledged proselytes, but in all cases of conversion to Judaism, circumcision was required. Akenson, *Saint Saul*, 147–48.

Gentiles need not adhere to the Jewish law, including circumcision. This was a controversial issue that finally required a meeting in Jerusalem to clarify for both Jewish and Gentile Christians what was necessary in order to be a Christian.

Jerusalem and His Apostleship (49 CE)

"Fourteen years later" (after Paul's conversion in 36 CE, that is, in 51 CE) Paul went to Jerusalem (Gal 2:1). Paul's purpose in going up to Jerusalem was to explain clearly to the Jerusalem apostles the nature of his gospel, since there was confusion regarding the acceptance of Gentiles into full membership in the people of God through Christ. Paul traveled with a Levite by the name of Barnabas and took along (*symparalabon*) a Greek by the name of Titus. Paul "laid before them [the apostles] the gospel," which he had preached among the Gentiles. Paul's concern in "laying the gospel before them" was not to gain their approval but lest he be preaching ("running" Gal 2:2) in vain.[66] Paul's fear concerned not peer acceptance but the perversion of the truth of the gospel, the gospel that he had directly received from Christ. Instead of a public meeting, Paul spoke privately to those apostles who were most influential—to Cephas, James, and John, the so-called "pillar apostle" (Gal 2:9).

The result of the conference was a division of labor. Paul was to preach to the Gentiles, the Jerusalem apostles to the Jews (Gal 2:7–8). Jerusalem was significant symbolically for Paul's missionary activities, because of the conference imposed Jewish legal restrictions, except circumcision, on Gentile believers (Acts 15).[67] Gentile Christians were also

66. The running metaphor is used elsewhere (1 Cor 9:24–27; Gal 5:7; Phil 2:16), describing the persistent stamina of a Christian life. Here it is employed to connote the persistent conviction and preaching of the gospel of Christ to the Gentiles that would bring enduring freedom (thus salvation) to the Gentiles.

67. Gal 2:1 states that both Paul and Barnabas attended the Jerusalem conference, representing the Gentile mission (2:9; see also 1 Cor 9:6). According to Acts 18, Paul stayed in Corinth for 18 months (18:11), then sailed for Syria, landed at Caesarea, and went up to Jerusalem (18:22), finally returning to Antioch (18:18–22) again (probably 51 CE). Fourteen years had passed since his last visit to Jerusalem (Gal 2:1). But this time, his visit to Jerusalem has to do with clarifying the truth of the gospel for Gentile Christians, since there were false brothers "secretly brought in to spy upon" the freedom of Antioch Christians (Gal 2:4–5). It is very likely that Acts 15 is Luke's version of the Jerusalem conference.

asked "to abstain from the pollutions of idols and from unchastity and from what is strangled and from blood" (Acts 15:20, RSV).

(Second and Third) Missionary Journey (50–57 CE)

Sometime after the Jerusalem Conference, Paul and Barnabas went back to Antioch, and both Acts 15:30 and Gal 2:11, 13 seem to agree on this account. According to Gal 2:12–14 a major dispute occurred between Peter and Paul. Up to this point there had been no contention between Paul and the Jerusalem apostles. According to Paul, the problem arose when "false brethren were secretly brought in to spy on the freedom we have in Jesus Christ so that they might bring us to bondage" (Gal 2:4).[68]

The Jerusalem apostles recognized the grace and the apostolate bestowed on Paul (Gal 2:9; cf. Acts 15). However, the pillar apostles (Peter and James) did not back up the decision of the Jerusalem conference. Peter who had been eating with the Gentiles backed down when James' men and the circumcision party arrived at Antioch (Gal 2:12). Other Jewish Christians and Barnabas were influenced by the action of Peter and withdrew fellowship from the Gentile Christians. Paul failed to win his case of the gospel without law in Antioch.

As Paul traveled extensively along the coastal regions of the Mediterranean world after the Jerusalem and Antioch incidents, he was convinced that the identity of Gentile Christians was constituted by the freedom they had in Christ. During the so-called "second missionary journey" (50–52 CE; see Acts 15:40—18:22), Paul revisited the places in Southern Anatolia he had evangelized earlier. Then he headed north bringing the gospel for the first time to Galatia and Phrygia, and crossed over to Macedonia (Europe) from Troas. He founded churches in Philippi, Thessalonica, Beroea, Athens, and Corinth. He wrote from Corinth to the Thessalonian congregations that he evangelized in 50–51 CE. He admonished them to trust in God and love each other in the hope of Christ's coming despite their suffering and affliction. He stayed at Corinth for eighteen months, longer than with any other congregation thus far in his ministry. Despite the gifts and graces they had, they were

---

68. If Acts 15:1, 24 are reliable, the evidence seems to tell of Jewish Christians coming to Antioch from Jerusalem arguing for the necessity of Gentile Christians being circumcised in order to become a part of the people of God.

the most challenging of all his congregations, as is evident in 1 and 2 Corinthians. Paul left Corinth to go to Ephesus with Aquila and Priscilla, Jews from Rome and now Christian converts (see Acts 18). From Ephesus, he sailed to Jerusalem.

Paul's "third missionary journey" (53–58 CE; Acts 18:23—21:15) began again in Syrian Antioch. He made one more round through Galatia and Phrygia to Ephesus, where he remained for three years (54–57 CE; Acts 20:31).[69] Paul left Ephesus for Troas in 57 CE, heading north along the Asiatic shore of the Aegean, and then crossing over to Europe at Macedonia. Here he met Titus. Titus had been sent earlier to Corinth to bring the Corinthian congregation back to Paul, and Titus brought good news of reconciliation. Hearing the good news, Paul wrote 2 Corinthians in response. Finally, Paul went to Achaia and to Corinth and spent three winter months (57/58 CE) collecting an offering for the poor of Jerusalem (Rom 15:24-26) as well as writing his letter to the Romans, and planning an evangelizing mission to Spain based on the support of the churches in Rome.

According to Acts 20:2–17 (58 CE), Paul traveled from Corinth to Jerusalem via Macedonia. He spent Passover at Philippi, then sailed to Troas, then to Miletus where he gave a farewell speech to the Ephesian elders (20:17-38). Acts 21:15—28:31 recounts the last years of Paul: his arrest in Jerusalem, his two-year imprisonment in Caesarea, being sent to Rome followed by two-years of imprisonment there. Paul probably died in 64 CE in Rome during Nero's persecution of Christians.

Legacy: Death and Apotheosis

Neither Confucius nor Paul died as a sage or a saint. Their last years were full of desolation and unfulfilled dreams. While he was living, Confucius' *rendao* (the way of humanity) was not accepted by any ruler of his day, and Paul's apostleship and his gospel were doubted and rejected by many who heard him. A few hundred years later, the Han emperors conferred on Confucius the status of a sage and built temples throughout the em-

---

69. It is generally thought that he was imprisoned in Ephesus, although Acts did not record such imprisonment (cf., however 1 Cor 15:32, 16:8-9, 2 Cor 1:8, 11:23-26), and that he wrote letters to the Philippians and to Philemon while in the Ephesus jail. Most scholars also think that Paul wrote Galatians and the Corinthian correspondence at Ephesus.

pire to honor him. Paul's apostleship gained such great admiration that he was regarded as "the Apostle" and sainthood was conferred on him by the year 258. Statues were built throughout the world to honor Saint Paul. Devotees of both Confucius and Paul collected their works, edited them, circulated them, canonized them, and their students wrote books and commentaries to interpret their masters' work. There is resurrection after death; death does not conclude one's life. Death may begin the apotheosis process for great people; soon they become demigods. While they were living, the lives of Confucius and Paul were marked by faithfulness to the ideals by which they lived—be they ethical, political, or theological.

INTERTEXTUALITY OF CONFUCIUS AND PAUL: TOWARD A MORAL AND THEOLOGICAL IDENTITY OF CHINESE CHRISTIAN

Confucius and Paul are "bigger than life" figures. Their so-called "historical facts" are also inevitably *interpretive* data that color and shape the facts. It is impossible to separate interpretation from history. Events are filtered by perception. My intent here is not to be an archaeological detective, explaining what is legend and what is history (important as that is); my intent is to discuss Confucius and Paul as pivotal figures in the cultural development of China and the Protestant West, which become the matrix of the moral and theological identity of Chinese Christians.

Intersubjectivity and Intertextual Reading

Since my work is based heavily on the interpretation of two texts, Confucius' *Analects* and Paul's letter to the Galatians, it will be helpful to say something about the kind of intertextual reading I will employ. Julia Kristeva coined the term *intertextuality* to indicate that a "text"—whether it is a person, an interpretation, a reading, an object—exists not in a closed system of its own but in interrelation with other "texts"—that preceded it or co-exist with it through quotations, references, allusions, and other influences of various kinds.[70] This *intersubjective* influence conveyed through the medium of a "text" is clearly seen in the "various cultural

70. Kristeva, "Word, Dialogue and Novel," 34.

discourses"[71] because "the text is a tissue of quotations drawn from innumerable centers of culture."[72] Both axes of intertextuality—via the writer (who is the first reader) and his/her readers (who are co-producers of textual meaning)—allow us to dialog with the texts in the production of meaning.

This reproductive and productive process of reading allows the text/ writer and reader/interpretation to be intersubjective. A text not only carries meaning but allows, and even requires, the reader to create meaning in the act of reading. Similarly, readers not only interpret texts, they are being *read* by texts, that is, their own stories are made meaningful by the texts themselves. Because understanding and reading are processes that are reproductive and productive, a writer cannot control the meaning of a text, or limit its meanings to his or her own original intention. It is my conviction that the authority of interpretation does not reside in the text itself or in the first writer alone, but is to be found in the interactive process of the text, involving both the writer and the reader, which I have previously called "rhetorical interaction."[73] From the example of Paul's letter to the Galatians, Paul does a "rhetorical interaction" with the Scriptures as he engages with two, historically separated events, viz. Abraham and Christ. Paul shows what the Scriptures actually say: "The Scripture preproclaimed (*proeuaggelizomai*) the gospel to Abraham that 'all the Gentiles will be blessed in you'" (Gal 3:8b). Paul argues that the gospel that comes through Abraham to all Gentiles (nations) is a gospel "beforehand," which means "preaching the gospel by anticipation" (it does not mean, "preaching a preliminary gospel")[74] Paul can say the Scripture proclaims the gospel in advance (*proeuaggelizomai*; found only here in the New Testament) because of his Christological interpretation.[75] This

---

71. Culler, *On Deconstruction*, 32.

72. Barthes, *Image, Music, Text*, 146.

73. Yeo, *Rhetorical Interaction in 1 Corinthians 8 and 10*, 15–49.

74. Hanson, *Studies in Paul's Technique and Theology*, 64.

75. Gal 3:9 draws out the implications of the scriptural proof in verse 8: "So then, those who are of faith are blessed with Abraham who had faith" (RSV). The relationship between the old people of God and the new people of God could be understood in terms of Abraham and Christ. Paul understands the original promise as made to include all humankind and he sees its fulfillment in the mission to the Gentiles. The promise to Abraham is a pre-announcement of the gospel that God would set right the Gentiles by their faith. From this it follows ("as" in Gal 3:9) that those persons who have trusted God are blessed as Abraham was blessed.

point is significant to our work here because it allows the indigenization of the gospel of Christ into the cultural language of Confucianism even though historically the Christ event happened centuries after Confucius. My purpose is not to argue that a certain "proto Gospel of Christ" existed in the *Analects*, this kind of historical argument is unnecessary. I prefer to use Paul's Christ-hermeneutics in reading history backward from Christ (c. first century CE) to Abraham (1800 BCE) to Confucius (c. 550 BCE) and claim this is simply a valid hermeneutical move.

Overarching Concepts in Confucius' and Paul's Worldviews[76]

The intertextual perspective will help us see the commonality and commensurability between Confucius and Paul. It is their profound differences that distinguish the cultural-specific of Confucian China from the cultural context of the Protestant West. These differences "are both real and fundamental. They can be either an obstacle or a resource, depending on how we engage them."[77] Confucius and Paul did not live at the beginning points of China and Western histories respectively; their thoughts, however, are the defining points for their respective cultures.[78] The premise of this section is that it is helpful to investigate the etiology of the cultural differences between Confucius and Paul in order to understand Chinese Christian identity, and to grasp different destinies of China and the Christian West. It can be said without undue exaggeration that the difference between Confucius and Paul is the difference between China and the West. No texts in Western history have had more of an impact than the Gospels and the letters of Paul in the New Testament; no texts in Chinese history are more foundational than the teachings of Confucius

---

76. I have drawn insights from Bodde, "Harmony and Conflict in Chinese Philosophy," 19–80. Other helpful sources are Northrop, *The Meeting of East and West*, 312–46, 386–89; Tang, *Zhonghua Renwen Yu Dangjin Shijie*, passim; Capra, *The Tao of Physics*, 101–12.

77. Hall and Ames, *The Democracy of the Dead*, 6.

78. Thompson, *The Chinese Way in Religion*, 1: "'Beginnings' are always intriguing, and because the psychology of cultures, like that of individuals, seems inescapably bound up with the molding experiences of infancy and childhood, we must seek the meaning of mature institutions at least partly in those beginnings."

and the traditions that developed around them. In passing one may note that Karl Marx does not define Chinese culture and tradition.[79]

Confucius and Paul are very close at certain points while differing radically from each other in terms of the larger frames of reference of their thought. On the one hand, these basic differences of the origin or cause of determinative concepts of Confucius and Paul shape in a complementary way the contours of my identity as a Chinese Christian, just as they make up the principles of my hermeneutical investigation. On the other hand, there are basic differences that are simply irreconcilable, and holding on to them in radical tension is an ever-present challenge. The incommensurability between Confucius and Paul does not mean that one is right and the other wrong. Rather it means that on different issues both are incomplete and that one is needed for the fulfillment of the other. In this section I simply provide an outline of their worldviews with indications of chapter references where I will pick up the themes and elaborate much more extensively later in the book.

Naturalistic Cosmos and Created Universe (cf. Chapter Two)

The Judeo-Christian tradition, of which Paul is part, holds to the cosmogonic (origin and history of the universe) belief that the universe is "initially created, and since then externally controlled, by a Divine Power who 'legislates' the phenomena of the nonhuman natural world."[80] Speculation and theological deliberation abound in the religious and philosophical literature of the West, and it is the Bible which has functioned as both source and springboard for it. Even the great Hellenistic traditions of Plato and Aristotle most often served in the subordinate role of hermeneutes to scripture. However, in ancient China, though the concept of deities and *Di* (Supreme Deity)[81] was present, popular religions of

79. Marxism occupies less than sixty out of the five thousand years of China history, and the Marxist thesis is becoming weaker in China since the introduction of modernization programs some of which were the works of Deng Xiaoping (1902–1997).

80. Bodde, "Harmony and Conflict in Chinese Philosophy," 20.

81. Chinese people in the Shang dynasty (1783–1045 BCE) believed in the Supreme Deity called *di* (Lord) or *shangdi* (the Lord from Above [Heaven]). Other deities were known as well, such as God of Wind, God of Cloud, God of Sun, God of Moon. See Thompson, *The Chinese Way in Religion*, 4–5. There was a period in which Zhou people used both *di* and *tian*, before its transition to merely using the concept of *tian*. But Confucianism never develops the worship of *di*; its focus is on *tian* (Heaven). See

"ghosts and gods" (*gui* and *shen*) were seldom considered proper belief. Confucian tradition regarded speculation of gods as superstition;[82] that is why many Confucianists object to calling Confucianism a religion. *Tian* (Heaven) was originally a tribal god of the Zhou people. In Confucian thought, however, Heaven is the cosmic power of creativity that rules over the natural and the human world; Heaven "is both the creator and the field of creatures."[83] Heaven is the Creator but does not have a creative and redemptive narrative. The transcendent nature of Heaven is benevolence or humaneness *(ren)* of the moral order and its immanent nature is expressed in human nature as virtues. Heaven is the ethical matrix of the cosmos; Heaven is the ultimate symbol of Order/Principle (*li*, 理). Heaven is as "natural" as the natural world is, but less personal than the human world. One of the Chinese words for the universe is "nature." The word "nature" in Chinese literally means "self-so" (*ziran*), referring to the world *as it is*; the world exists by itself according to the principle of changes and creativity therein.

The implications stemming from this basic assumption regarding the naturalistic cosmos for Confucius and the created universe for Paul are tremendous in terms of their respective views of history, society, anthropology, ethics, law, freedom, and destiny. In the cosmogonic story of the Christian West, history begins with God, specifically the creation of the universe as God's victory over chaos and non-existence (formless void). It is a divine story of the God of love and power who is intimately involved in his creation as well as his human creatures. In Confucian China, history begins with the order of things, the order that does not overcome chaos. The understanding of the universe as "self-so" assumes chaos can co-exist with order since chaos is thought to be a part of the order. For Confucian China, history begins with self-understanding (who they are as human beings), the unifying culture of the civilized/Chinese people (*huaxia*), or what Hall and Ames called "the 'myth' of Han identity."[84] The fundamental meaning structure of the West is mythology or

---

Chapter Two (pp. 114–31) on the discussion of *Tian*.

82. Yang, *Lunyu Yizhu*, 10–11.

83. Ames and Rosemont, *Analects*, 47.

84. Hall and Ames, *The Democracy of the Dead*, 23–24. "*Huaxia*" literally means the illustrative Xia—Xia being the first legendary dynasty of the Han Chinese. The myth tells of the founder of Xia dynasty, the sage-king Yu, tamed the floods of the Yellow River, and thus making it possible for the early Han to live in that part of world. See the Epilogue

theology (divine narrative); that of Confucian China, however, is cultural history and genealogy (lineage through the family). Revelation for the West comes from the world of gods; for China revelation comes from the natural world.

Cyclical History (Golden Age) and the *Telos* of Eschatology (cf. Chapter Two)

Because of the worldview that the cosmos simply existed without a first cause, Confucius viewed history as moving in perpetual oscillations of change or in eternal cycles.[85] Influenced by the *yin-yang* understanding of time, Confucius had a cyclical view of history.[86] Confucius was familiar with a *yin-yang* worldview based on climatic or natural phenomena. In the traditional *yin-yang* symbol, the shaded area, *yin*, and the sunlit slope, *yang*, represent the movement of the earth and the moon. The Chinese world "*as it is*" is a harmonious one, comprises of *yin* and *yang*.

Since the collapse of the kingdoms and ideals of the ancient-sage-kings, Confucianists have hoped for a reemergence of the Golden Age. The Golden Age for Confucius spanned past dynasties (of Xia [2205–1783 BCE] and Shang [1783–1045 BCE]), especially the idealized Western Zhou dynasty (1122–770 BCE), when sagacious kings and virtuous rulers such as King Wen, King Wu, and the Duke of Zhou brought about peace and order. The Golden Age is considered to be the period when the cultural achievement of the Chinese was at its height. For the Chinese, history does not come to an end; it will go on forever as will the world. "In the Chinese language, 'the world' is *shijie*, literally 'the succeeding generational boundaries' which conjoin one's own generation to those who have come before, and to the generation that will follow this one."[87]

---

of this book for my discussion of the Han Chinese and its relationship to other Chinese ethnic groups.

85. Bodde, "Harmony and Conflict," 21 mentions Zhuangzi's view of "a process of endless return within a closed circle rather than of forward movement along a straight line. Thus we read in his twenty-seventh chapter: "All things are species which, through variant forms, pass on into another. Their beginnings and endings are like those in a ring—incapable of being definitely located. This is called the Equilibrium of Heaven."

86. Bodde, "Harmony and Conflict," 21 mentions Appendix III of *Classic of Changes* (*Yijing*): "The alternation of the *yin* and *yang* is what is called *Dao.*"

87. Hall and Ames, *The Democracy of the Dead*, 34.

Confucius' understanding of history is different from the linear framework of Paul's historical thought. Paul's understanding of history focuses on Christ, especially the death, resurrection, and the future but imminent return of Christ. For Paul, God has acted in Christ, and will act again soon in earthly transformation. Human beings are responsible for preparing themselves to participate in this New Creation that has begun *proleptically* in Jesus Christ as evidenced by his resurrection from the dead.[88] It is a New Creation believers share in symbolically in baptism and are to manifest ethically in their lives, but its full realization is still yet to be.

Good and Evil, Chaos and Sin: The Nature of the Universe and Human Being (cf. Chapters One, Three, Five)

The naturalistic view of a self-contained cosmos in the Chinese worldview assumes that "the universe is actually a natural harmony, and therefore imbued with a principle of goodness."[89] It also assumes that human nature (*xing*) is part of that cosmic harmony and its moral order; human nature is the vital link between the human world and the cosmic world.[90] Self-cultivation is to refine and to realize one's basic human nature that is essentially good and beautiful. Confucius believes that ritual propriety and music—as natural instruments of goodness and beauty respectively—can cultivate one to be virtuous, to become a human being par excellence (*shengren, junzi*), to become a benevolent or humane person (*renren*).

Confucianists understand that evil and goodness are not opposing forces. Evil is a moral deficiency; it is not seeing the cosmic pattern (*li*) of goodness. Such a deficiency can be overcome by education. Confucian thought posits that "evil," as Christian theology understands it, is not a real force. The Confucian worldview does not seek to eradicate "evil." Undesirable events, such as natural disasters, social turmoil, and vissici-

88. It is the kingdom of God present in Jesus Christ (the "already"), but to be realized fully only in the future (the "not yet"). It is the kingdom of God proleptically present, indicating what the kingdom will be.

89. Bodde, "Harmony and Conflict in Chinese Philosophy," 39; Mou, *Xinti Yu Xingti*, 1:217–24; idem, *Zhongguo Zhexue De Tezhi*, 25: "The moral order is the cosmic order."

90. The Chinese word *xing* for human nature has to do with "life," perhaps similar to the Greek understanding of *physis* and the Latin *natura*. The root of *physis* is *phuō*, and that of *natura* is *nascor*; both root words are about birth or growth.

tudes of life, are not attributed to evil forces, but instead, are interpreted in light of the cosmic order and challenge persons to reach their highest moral potentials.

Paul understands evil as opposing the good, as the privation of good. While Paul does not say human nature itself is evil, he believes the power of sin holds human nature captive and therefore human beings are impotent to exercise their will to do good. Paul would have repudiated Confucius' idea that one could follow the path of rituals (*li*) to become a sage. Paul takes the destructive and chaotic power of sin seriously. In Protestant theology, "Adam's Fall" is the representation of human depravity, of the broken image of God in mankind, and of the captivating power of sin in the fallen world. Confucius would find it difficult to understand "sin" in Christian theology. In the Chinese Bible sin is translated as "crime" (*zui*), something one "does" becomes something one "is." Most Chinese, especially Confucianists, would understand the phrase, "we are all sinners" (cf. Rom 3:9) as "we are all felons and misdemeanors"! To the Confucianists, sin refers to social conflicts, wrongdoings, and insincerity toward Heaven; but sin does not refer to one's existential estrangement with *Tian*.[91] The "fall" Confucius knows of is the ritual impropriety, the moral collapse, the decadent music, that is, the fallen culture that drifts away from the cosmic order of life.

Ethics and Theology; Virtue and Faith (cf. Chapters One, Four, Six)

Confucian and Pauline anthropologies are distinctly different from each other. The correlation of Confucian mind/heart and morality is foundational to the Confucian ethics. Alexander explains:

> The Chinese mind . . . refuses to become rationalistic and also refuses to separate form from context. . . . The Chinese would rather trust common sense, and they believe that analogies and symbolism tell us more bout real life than abstract logical reasoning. Hence, reasoning is directed toward moral or humane conduct rather than in abstract, logical conclusions divorced from daily life. Whether personal, social, political or religious, the focus of reflective thought is principally directed toward moral concerns

91. In the *Analects*, the word *zui* ("sin") occurs only once, and it means offending the will of Heaven (3:13: "If one offends against *tian*, he has nowhere to pray").

and ethical conduct, with the ultimate goal of creating a moral-humane community.[92]

The difference between Confucius' ethics and Paul's theology is the difference between virtue in self-cultivation and faith in God's grace. Unlike Paul's starting point, so thoroughly rooted in Judaism, that God is holy, the starting point of Confucius is that human community is sacred, because human nature is the best expression of the moral order of *Tian*. In response to the problem of wrongdoing and evil, Confucius asks the question, "How is one to be human?" Paul asks, "How is one to be holy?" Put simply, Paul's thought is theological, Confucius' ethical. Confucius gives the ethical answers of being benevolent (*ren*), respectful (*jing*), trustworthy (*xin*), and empathetic (*ming*), that is, of being virtuous. In Paul's theology the problem with the world is sin, a broken relationship with the Creator, God. That relationship is restored by faith, which itself is a gift of divine grace. Paul's answer echoes that of the Gospel: "to be holy/perfect as your heavenly Father is" (Matt 5:48) is to know the acceptance (blessedness) of a forgiving God.

Faith (*xin*) in Heaven is not explicit in Confucius' teaching—except that the idea of "mandate of Heaven" (*tianming*) assumes faith in Heaven because its "*ming* [mandate] refers to the whole range of circumstances that are both external to the Confucian practice and beyond the control of human beings. It is therefore not only pointless, but also morally wrong, to struggle against it."[93] However, he prominently expresses faith in people throughout his ethical teaching of *ren* (compassion) and *li* (rites). Confucius understands the cosmic order (*tianli*) as a moral law. For Paul, faith in Christ is the only possible way to overcome sin and its evil consequences. Paul asks Christians to believe that God, the Creator of the Universe, has acted in Jesus Christ, revealing his nature and will as forgiving love. He who has faith in Christ is asked to die to the "old self" and rise a New Creation, symbolized in the ritual of baptism; and he is called to be Christ-like in everything he does, ethically and spiritually.

92. Alexander, "The Face of Holiness," 9.
93. Slingerland, trans., *Confucius Analects*, 238.

Law and Spirit: Ethics (Doing) and Christology (Being in Christ)
(cf. Chapters Four, Five, Six)

Paul calls individuals to live according to the Spirit and to bear the fruit of the Spirit. It is a call to the transformation of one's *being*, not to submission to externally imposed laws in acts observable by all. Once an individual knows that, although he is a sinner separated from God, he has been forgiven in Christ Jesus and restored to a loving relationship with God. In gratitude to God's love and forgiveness, he can now be merciful toward his neighbor.

Confucius attempts to shift the emphasis from doing to being as well. The fallenness of his age means the forms of rituals, music, and offices are still there, but "obsession with externalities (5:27, 14:24)"[94] selfishness, manipulation, and chaos abound in his society (*Analects* 3:11, 8:20, 19:19). In his teaching of ritual propriety (*li*), of aesthetic delight (*yue*), and of *wuwei* (effortless action) ethics, Confucius does not think, for example, that bowing itself means anything unless one's attitude is right. He calls "filial pietists" those who simply take care of parents out of a sense of duty and equates them with animal-keepers "feeding their cattle" (*Analects* 2:7). Confucius admonishes them to respect their parents out of a feeling of gratitude, respect, and empathy. "Persons are not perceived as agents independent of their actions, but are rather ongoing *events* defined functionally by constitutive roles and relationships."[95] His *wuwei* ethics teaches neither passivity nor no-action but "the *manner* in which something is done [in] spontaneous, unselfconscious, and perfectly efficacious [ways.]"[96] Just as Heaven governs the cosmos naturally and effortlessly (*Analects* 17:19), rulers, being Heaven's proxy on earth, should not rule with force. They must rule by *wuwei*, without resolve to force, but by *de*, the virtuous power endowed by Heaven (*Analects* 15:5).[97]

Confucius' teachings do not contain many imperatives. However, because his teachings deal mainly with ethics that has a strong disposition in advocating action and cultivation, Confucianists and Confucianism have inevitably mistakenly focused on the doing (ritual propriety) rather

94. Slingerland, trans., *Confucius Analects*, xxiii.
95. Hall and Ames, *The Democracy of the Dead*, 193.
96. Slingerland, trans., *Confucius Analects*, xix.
97. Ibid., xix.

than on the being (*renren*, sage, *junzi, etc.*) aspects of Confucius' teaching. With such distortion, one may equate Confucianism to Chinese Pharisaism—apart from whether or not there is a strong concept of Heaven or God. In the New Testament, Pharisees believed that the observance of religious laws signified an obedience to God's will. Likewise, Confucianism, if taken from a similar perspective, places undue authority on doing rather than *being,* on duty rather than intention. From the perception of the Pharisees, these laws were true, and leaders were zealous about keeping them. The conversion of Paul from Pharisaism to a believer in Christ is a radical change from doing to being. For Paul, to love God is to embody love of God's creation, including God's children, thus to *be* loving.

In Paul's thought, human beings are creatures with a *telos*, just as a seed has its *telos* in fruition. The *telos* of *being* the people of God is *to be* people of love. Paul saw the task of being human as *becoming* what one *is* by God's design. In the age of the Messiah, the Spirit of God poured down on all nations, creating a new people of God inclusive of Jews and Gentiles apart from any ethical or religious laws. By God's salvific design, the *telos* of humanity is found in the loving community which the church, as the people of God, is called to be.

Inequality and Equality: Social Harmony and Individual Freedom (cf. Chapter Five, Epilogue)

Confucius assumes that society is made up of smaller units of different groups, which, because of inherent differences (*bie*) between them, inevitably produce inequalities, hierarchies, and conflicts. The Confucian understanding of harmony is not based on an egalitarian vision, but on "hierarchical differences."[98] Hall and Ames write, "Ancestor reverence as the defining sensibility, family as the primary human unit, co-humanity (*ren*) and filiality (*xiao*) as primary human values, ritualized roles, relationships, and practices (*li*) as a communal discourse, are all strategies for achieving and sustaining communal community."[99] Confucius says, "Let the ruler be ruler, the minister minister, let the father be father, and

98. Bodde, "Harmony and Conflict in Chinese Philosophy," 54.
99. Hall and Ames, *The Democracy of the Dead*, 193.

the son son" (*Analects* 12:11),[100] each fulfilling his role in its proper place within the society for the common good. Unfortunately, those lower on the social ladder are often victimized by the elite in many Chinese societies; those with less power are asked to sacrifice for the sake of the common good; social harmony is privileged and the freedom of the individual suppressed.

There are distortions in churches of Pauline traditions as well, and there are Christians whose lives depart from or betray Pauline theology. According to Paul, however, the believer lives within eschatological history, a time that is already and not-yet. It is a history that has begun with the death and resurrection of Jesus, which, through faith, creates for believers a freedom and an equality within the community of faith that will only be fully realized in the future with the coming of God's kingdom. Paul would disagree with Confucius that true social harmony in this world is possible, given the enslaving power of sin. Borrowing from Stoic philosophy, Paul sees the worshiping community, not society as a whole, functioning in harmony as a body with many members, forming together the body of Christ, the church, in service to each other and to the larger community.[101] For Paul, freedom is the result of dying with Christ, dying to the desires and fears of the old man, and of rising with Christ into the new life of the Spirit, bearing the fruit of the Spirit: faith, hope, and love.

Identifying with Confucius and Paul

"Diasporizing Identity"

The first thing I identify with in Confucius and Paul is that both were born away from their ancestral homes—Confucius in the state of Lu (originally from Song), Paul in Tarsus (rather than Judea), and myself in Sarawak, Malaysia (rather than China). Mobility, whether in ancient or modern times, does form one's interest in a cross-cultural reading of the world and it causes one to pay attention to the dynamics of community living. Living in a foreign land requires finding ways to affirm one's identity within a complex web of relationships—"diasporizing identity."[102]

---

100. Translation of Bodde, "Harmony and Conflict in Chinese Philosophy," 47.

101. See Engberg-Pedesen, *Paul and the Stoics*, 131–71.

102. Boyarin, *A Radical Jew*, 242–46.

As the psalmist put it: "How shall we sing the LORD's song in a foreign land?" (137:4, RSV). While I was brought up in multi-cultural Malaysia, I yearned to know more about my ethnic roots. In hindsight, it was while pursuing theological degrees in the United States that I became preoccupied with the task of cross-cultural reading of the Bible. The experience of knowing the world of differences nudges one into pursuing an identity that helps stabilize one's sense of direction. The same experience forces one to be conscious of the delicate interaction of persons within a community, so that one can find belonging in the midst of multiplicity.

Confucius and Paul value the personal style of mutual-interaction; both, as *cultural critics* of their times, emphasized the "crossing over" of boundaries. While Paul is concerned with Jews and Gentiles, Confucius is concerned with interaction between sets of positions such as parents and children, lords and common people, husbands and wives. Both see the perfect life as a seamless web, though Paul explains in theological terms how Jews and Gentiles are God's people, and Confucius advocates *junzi* (the exemplary person or the best moral self) as the person of virtue, excellence, and benevolence.

Learning Traditions

Secondly, both Confucius and Paul influence me to appreciate learning as an essential part of my growing identity. Both Confucius and Paul are steeped in the scholarly traditions of their own cultures. Confucius' devotion to study and Paul's pharisaic zeal for the Torah have inspired me in the pursuit of learning. The tradition of study is one of the characteristics of being a Pharisee, as Murphy-O'Connor writes,

> The mild Hillel is reported as saying, 'he who does not learn [the Law] is worthy of death', whereas the strict Shammai merely counselled, 'make your [study of the] Law a fixed habit', and Gamaliel I proffered the practical advice, 'provide yourself with a teacher and remove yourself from doubt' (*m. Aboth* 1:13–16).[103]

Again,

> Do not separate from the community. Do not trust yourself until the day of your death. Do not judge your fellow until you stand

---

103. Murphy-O'Connor, *Paul, A Critical Life*, 59.

in his place. Do not say of a thing which cannot be understood that it will be understood in the end. And do not say, 'When I have leisure I will study!' Perhaps you will never have leisure (*m. Aboth* 2:5).[104]

Both Confucius and Paul belonged to the tradition that values the keen observation of the rules of life. Zeal for the "tradition of the fathers" (Gal 1:14) caused Paul and Confucius to value classical writings and to creatively appropriate them for their generation. In Galatians Paul does not feel regretful or deficient regarding the traditions of the fathers; he is proud of his learning in the Pharisaic tradition.

The Confucian tradition is commonly called the *Rudao* meaning the way of the teacher or counsellor.[105] In the old days before Confucius, *ru*'s responsibility is to educate children of the nobility with the curriculum of the six arts at the elementary level, and then the six classics in the advanced level.[106] Confucius strengthened and transformed the way of *ru*. The *Analects* is full of texts that describe Confucius' attitude toward learning (*Analects* 1:6, 8); consider, for example, his description of the stages in his development: "At fifteen, I bent my mind on learning; at thirty, I was established; at forty, I was free from delusion; at fifty, I knew the decree of Heaven; at sixty, my ears became subtly perceptive; at seventy, I was able to follow my heart's desire without over stepping the rules of propriety" (*Analects* 2:4).[107] He was determined to study at age fifteen, and by thirty already well accomplished in the areas of ritual and the cultivation of virtue (see *Analects* 8:8, 16:13, 20:3). He spent another ten years learning to be free of delusion (see *Analects* 9:29, 14:28). And by

---

104. Taken from Murphy-O'Connor, *Paul, A Critical Life*, 60.

105. *Rujia* means school, tradition, sect or family of teachers (literati); *rujiao* refers to Confucianism as an ethical and/or religious institution; *rushu* refers to the books; *ruxue* is the study of Confucianism or "learning of the literati"; *rudao* is the way or principle of the Confucianist school. See the usage of this word *ru* in *Analects* 6:13. Confucius was teaching his disciple Zixia to be a virtuous *ru* and not a morally deficient *ru*. See Slingerland, trans., *Confucius Analects*, 57; Yao, *An Introduction to Confucianism*, 26–30.

106. See Liu Xin's (?–23 CE) discussion of *ru* as ranging from ministers of education in government office (*situ zhi guan*) to teaching of six arts (*liuyi*—rituals, music, shooting, riding, writing, and arithmetic) and six classics (*Shijing* [*the Classic of Odes*], *Shangshu* [*the Book of History*], *Liji* [*Record of Rituals*], *Yuejing* [*the Classic of Music*], *Yijing* [*the Classic of Changes*], *Chunqiu* [*Spring-Autumn Annuals*]). According to *Shiji*, only 72 of the 3000 disciples of Confucius are skillful of the six arts.

107. Huang, *Analects*, 53.

fifty he knew his own mandate of Heaven.[108] At sixty he was able to differentiate the subtlety of what he heard. At seventy, his mind and heart, his will and desire were in unity; he was pleased that he constantly walked the path of propriety (*Analects* 7:17–18). This commitment to learning is found in another autobiographical statement: "I set my heart on the Way, base myself on virtue, lean upon benevolence for support and take my recreation in the arts" (*Analects* 7:6).[109]

Messianic Mission and Concern for the World

Thirdly, both men felt a "messianic mission" toward the worlds they cared about. Confucius' understanding of himself as the bearer of the Heaven-sent mandate to preserve the refined culture, that is, to bring about the ideal of the Golden Age; and this "messianic" pathos resonates with Paul's calling to be an apostle of Christ. Xu Fuguan, a Neo-Confucianist, interprets the "messianic pathos" of Confucius as the "consciousness of concern about the vicissitudes and turmoil" of the age (*youhuan yishi*).[110] Confucius identified himself with the Duke of Zhou (Zhou Gong), the brother of the founder of the dynasty, King Wu ("Warrior King"). The *Analects* often mentions the Duke of Zhou, and some scholars have suspected that perhaps Confucius longed to be such a personality and restore in his home state, Lu, the Golden Age of Zhou.[111]

The self-perception of a messianic role is the legacy of Confucianism; thus every Confucianist seems to have the conviction and the aspiration of serving his country after completing a moral education. That legacy also makes Confucian moral philosophy political in function. After all, the semantic domain of the Confucius' title, *zi*, is political. The title *zi* was first used to refer to royal princes and kinsmen, then to wise counselors

---

108. As recorded in this *Analects* Confucius has used the term "mandate of heaven" not simply as divine right to rule. It has a new emphasis on the moral order of Heaven for everyone to become fully human. Even for the divine rights of rulers, its meaning is different from that of the West. Thompson (*The Chinese Way in Religion*, 8) points out that "The Chinese sovereign held his commission on sufferance; Heaven gave it to reward virtue, and when virtue vanished, Heaven would revoke it and confer it upon a deserving house."

109. Lau, trans., *Analects*, 57.

110. Xu, *Zhongguo Renxinglun Shi*, passim. See Chapter Six (pp. 356–57).

111. Bauer, *China and the Search for Happiness*, 22–23.

of feudal lords, and finally to philosopher-teachers. The significant point of Confucius' yearning for the restoration of peace and order in the world is seen in his understanding of the heavenly mandate, i.e., the calling he felt from Heaven to save fallen society. Throughout Chinese history, few people had as clear a calling as Confucius.

Some suspected that Confucius had the ambition to become king, but that hope was unfulfilled. Confucius' despair is recorded in *Analects* 9:9: "The Phoenix does not come, the River does not emerge forth the map, and my life is done."[112] The phoenix is a mythical creature belonging to the heavenly realm that is to send forth a sign announcing the arrival of the sage-king Shun. It was believed that when the legendary sage-king Fu Xi was enthroned, a dragon would come up from the Yellow River, so Fu Xi drew a map of his empire called the River Map. The River Map was a gift given to Zhou King at the time of his enthronement. It mapped out the boundaries of his kingdom for the sake of a peaceful reign.[113]

Paul's mission as an apostle, the Messiah's (Christ's) representative, is also notable (Gal 1:11–12). Now whether Paul's opponents in Galatians or the apostles in Jerusalem were questioning Paul's apostleship or the validity of his gospel is difficult to ascertain. Perhaps both. If we read Paul's words in Galatians as a counter-argument to the opponents' teaching, then the autobiographical material in Galatians 1 looks like an *apologia* (a defense). Paul's vocation as an *apostle* was certainly not without controversy, not least of which was his claim to that title. Paul's conversion experience on the Damascus road (according to Acts 9:3 and 22:3) was difficult for his contemporaries to comprehend. Not only his gospel, but also his apostleship was doubted and challenged. J. C. Beker has painted a convincing picture of why Paul defends primarily his gospel and secondarily his apostleship in his letter to the Galatians:

> To be sure, the opponents do not intend to apostatize from the gospel, they only want to perfect what Paul has commenced (Gal 3: 3). . . . [But] if they can undermine Paul's apostolate, they can undermine his gospel as well. The issue is sensitive and explosive, because Paul also posits apostolate and gospel as interlocking re-

---

112. Translation mine.

113. Ching, *Mysticism and Kingship in China*, 211; Slingerland, trans., *Confucius Analects*, 89.

alities. Paul, however, intends to subordinate his apostolate to the gospel.[114]

Paul's call on the Damascus Road is more than a call to become a Christian; it is a call to become the Apostle to the Gentiles. If the first speaks of Paul's conversion in the sense that he now sees the Crucified Messiah as the divine paradigm addressing cross-cultural and cross-religious problems, the second speaks of Paul's call in the sense that he now sees *himself* as one commissioned to be a cross-cultural apostle. Paul argues that "the *permanent* origin . . . [of the gospel] is *and remains* God himself, not any ecclesiastical group wherever located."[115]

Paul's "conversion experience" of encountering the risen Christ suggests that the gospel is revealed through Christ (thus a subjective genitive; see Acts 9, 22, and 26). It is helpful to link the revelation that comes from Jesus Christ with the gospel whose content is the Christ of God, i.e., God's Son. Taken within the context of the Galatian controversy, the gospel of Jesus Christ is foundational to the preaching of the apostle Paul, and that gospel is directed to the Gentiles. The gospel is not simply a Torah-free gospel, the gospel for Gentiles is defined so centrally in Jesus Christ that even the Torah has to be reinterpreted by Christ. Christological theology thus becomes the core hermeneutical enterprise of Paul. Paul and his opponents in Galatia are arguing about the basis of the truth of the gospel: Does it rest on tradition or come out of the future, by revelation (is it apocalyptic)? Does the truth of the gospel found in the Torah or in the crucified Messiah? Before his conversion, Paul is sure that God is on the side of the tradition/Torah only, not on the side of the crucified Messiah/apocalyptic. What about post-conversion Paul: Does he think God is on the side of the crucified Messiah and not on the Torah? The answer phrased by J. Louis Martyn is: "Yes! (Gal 3:13) and No! (4:21b; 5:14; 6:2)."[116]

Though Confucius and Paul give different messianic visions of serving people placed in their care, both of them are committed to their calling. To be a Chinese Christian is to consider what the ethical and theological insights of Confucius and Paul, and to imitate them.[117]

---

114. Beker, *Paul the Apostle*, 42.

115. Martyn, *Galatians*, 151.

116. Ibid., 163.

117. See the work of the New Confucianists who seek to combine the wisdom of

HYBRIDITY OF A CHINESE CHRISTIAN IDENTITY AND THEOLOGY

Confucius' political ethics and Paul's cross-cultural gospel resonate with me because they help describe the strangeness of the other and the newness of journeying into the other. This way of life is one that is vulnerable and risky but also necessary and rewarding, particularly in a world where co-existence is the first challenge of being human. Confucius and Paul knew well the world of differences and the necessity for human beings to live together.

The hybridity of my Chinese Christian identity has gone through various mutations because of my multiple migrations, the effects of globalizations, and my own critical reflection. I can identify with Malaysia (where I was brought up), America (where I studied and worked and now live), Hong Kong (where I also worked), and both Taiwan and China (where I have visited my relatives and lectured). Yet, I never feel completely at home in any one of these places. Such diasporic consciousness is one of constant ambiguity. As a *huaqiao* (Chinese sojourner), I am also a *mestizo*—constantly living in the crossroads. The *mestizo* is the hybrid citizen par excellence of the borderlands. Rita Felski has spoken of this hybridity and the "doxa of difference" well:

> Metaphors of hybridity and the like not only recognize differences within the subject, fracturing and complicating holistic notions of identity, but also address connections between subjects by recognizing affiliations, cross-pollinations, echoes and repetitions, thereby unseating difference from a position of absolute privilege. Instead of endorsing a drift towards ever greater atomization of identity, such metaphors allow us to conceive of multiple, interconnecting axes of affiliation and differentiation.[118]

I want to hold onto the hybridity of living at the crossroads, not because the diasporic consciousness is comfortable, but because I believe the "unsettling" consciousness of hybridity is, in the words of Ien Ang, "a

---

Confucius and Western culture for sake of contributing toward global issues including politics, economics, ethics, and religions: Carson Zhang Junmai, Xu Fuguan, Mou Zongsan, and Tang Junyi, "Wei Zhongguo Wenhua Jinggao Shijie Renshi Xuanyan" ["A Manifesto on the Reappraisal of Chinese Culture"]. Originally published in January, 1968 issue of *Minzhu Pinglun*.

118. Felski, "The Doxa of Difference," 12.

source of cultural permeability and vulnerability which, in [my] view, is a necessary condition for living together-in-difference."[119] Ing continues, "In short, hybridity is not only about fusion and synthesis, but also about friction and tension, about ambivalence and incommensurability, about the contestations and interrogations that go hand in hand with the heterogeneity, diversity and multiplicity we have to deal with as we live together-in-difference."[120] This idea of hybridity is a Chinese Christian reality to be described, and thus an ideal to which a Chinese Christian can pursue, and hopefully attain. The following chapters of this book attempt to illustrate and clarify the hybridized relationship between a Chinese and a Christian identity, and the implication of their relationship to a Chinese Christian theology. The engagement between a Chinese and a Christian identity is neither a static nor a fixed equation. To use H. Richard Niebuhr's classical categories of "Christ and culture," I attempt to show that the logic of hybridity for a Chinese Christian identity and theology is not always that of "Christ against culture," but sometimes that of "Christ above culture," of "Christ and culture in paradox," and of "Christ the transformer of culture."[121] An intertextual reading allows me to pay attention to the relationship between the specific of cultural ideals, or ills, and the concreteness of Christian theology, thus avoiding the mistake of seeing only one normative relationship between Christ and culture. For example, in many areas (such as God and *tian*, ethic based on the Spirit and ethic based on self-cultivation) they are incompatible (Chapter Two). Yet, Paul's understanding of cruciform love fulfills the Confucius' ideal of *ren* (benevolence); Confucian ethics on propriety (*li*) and music (*yue*) supplements Pauline theology that does not spell out their significance (Chapter Three). The relationship between human nature and grace (for Paul) and the relationship between human nature and goodness (Confucius) are antithetical (Chapter Four), yet, Confucius and Paul would agree that only love of neighbors can hold their theses in a healthy tension (paradoxical). Despite the different assumptions Confucius and Paul have regarding human nature, both speak of freedom, though one's freedom is moral and the other's spiritual, and both discourses mutually transform each other's freedom (Chapter Five). Another example of

119. Ang, *On Not Speaking Chinese*, 199.

120. Ibid., 200.

121. Niebuhr, *Christ and Culture*, passim.

mutually transformation reading between Confucius and Paul is their understandings of *xin* (trust) and *pistis* (faith) (Chapter Six). The hybridity of Chinese Christian theology will be illustrated and clarified in the main chapters (One to Six) enclosed by the framing chapters that deal with the hybrid identity of a Chinese Christian.

To live in hybridity is the life of the Cross (see Chapter Two). A Christian life is to live in "a gradual spectrum of mixed-up differences,"[122] celebrating cultural diversity and respecting uniqueness.[123] Through the act of self-reading, I narrate a Chinese Christian identity; Confucian and Pauline ideals are essential aspects of many Chinese Christian identity. Autobiography is never just a personal narrative, it is also a collective and cultural act. My story will have its commensurability with other Chinese Christians. By examining Confucius and Paul I am studying the logic and dynamics of Chinese Christian identity more generally, as these are shaped by two important sources of Confucius and Paul.

122. Geertz, *Works and Lives*, 148.

123. Ongoing historical and cultural changes are powerful factors in creating our experience of indeterminacy, ambiguity, and pluralism. My diasporic consciousness has come to accept religious and cultural pluralism while not necessarily embracing the vision of religious syncretism. Religious relativism shares the risks of polytheism—multiple salvation narratives claiming equally validity (out of political correctness or theological justification) may mean that none is unique. Knowing that danger, I find it difficult to articulate the difference between pluralism and relativism, because they are twins—however easily they may be defined with words, they are difficult to recognize in reality. My intertextual approach does work hard at coping with the challenge and complexity of religious pluralism in the world today. Although I do not end with a theology of religious relativism that does not mean I envision another Christian century. On the issue of religious pluralism, I follow Lesslie Newbigin's hermeneutics but add the intertextual layer of reading. See Newbigin, *The Gospel in a Pluralist Society*, passim; Obenchain, "The Study of Religion and the Coming Global Generation," 3:59–109.

1

The Textual Worlds of the *Analects* and the Letter to the Galatians

INTERTEXTUAL READING OF CLASSICS

Laozi once said to Confucius: "Those of whom you speak have all already rotted away, both the men and their bones. Only their words are here."[1] So it is that those who seek to glean wisdom from historical figures encounter the challenge that "only their words are here." Yet, behind the words is a life, and our effort here is to read the texts of Confucius and Paul in order to reconstruct something of their lives. Inevitably, we read ourselves into their texts, since interpreters read from their social locations, bringing with them presuppositions that are both limiting and creative. A faithful reading is not simply a historical recovery of what the text meant, but a creative engagement with the text that continues to speak to the later generation of readers.

Intersubjective Reading, Exegesis, and Eisegesis

Ward Gasque is a historical critic who desires an objective interpretation of Paul, and his lament at perspectival and subjective reading is quite true

---

1. This translation is found in Nienhauser, ed., *The Grand Scribe's Records,* Vol. VII: *The Memoirs of Pre-Han China by Ssu-ma Ch'ien,* 7:21–22; see *Shiji* 63:1.

and apt when he writes, "So often the Paul who emerges from a scholar's study is a Paul created in the scholar's own image, one limited by the scholar's own theological or ideological perspective, the issues of his own day."[2] I am honored when I can read Galatians and *Analects* as a Chinese Christian, creating a Confucius and a Paul in my image. Gasque's perspective is lopsided, since every reading process is intersubjective, and is therefore a constant shifting of images between the writer and the reader. It cannot be otherwise. I want to qualify what Gasque has said: Even the purportedly "objective" reading based on historical-critical methods is not without its own assumptions, for the presuppositions of exegetes are conditioned by their language and culture. Exegesis based on grammatical analysis is often deemed to render the most objective reading of the biblical text. Biblical scholars assume that the Greek grammar and syntax can reveal the objective meaning of the text. However, interpreters of the Bible using the same grammatical reading may offer diverse meanings of the same text. For we understand grammar and history not according to objective and abstract principles, but in relation to our subjective, partial, and changing assumptions about language and history. Thus even grammatical reading is not without subjective input. Words become archaic, their referents unknown. Some texts contain words found nowhere else, and require an educated guess as to their meaning. In times past, much has been made of the precise explication of a text (exegesis), with warnings against reading into the text what is not there (eisegesis).

The classic distinction between "exegesis" (reading objective, historical meaning out from the text) and "eisegesis" (reading subjective meaning into the text) may not be helpful once we move to a cross-cultural interpretation that seeks to honor perspectival readings. At best the "exegesis/eisegesis" concern might be a construct that assumes a scholar can transcend his culture and detach himself from his own time and place, yet be able to become immersed in the past and know it with certainty. At worst, the "exegesis/eisgesis" differentiation is a scholarly fear of living in partial knowledge, the insecurity of shared ownership of any text, or the alienation of self from the network of texts with which we all work. I am here assuming that a purely objective reading of Confucius and Paul that transcends culture is unrealizable. The language of Confucius (fifth century BCE Chinese) and Paul (first century CE Greek) is not always

2. Gasque, "Images of Paul," 8.

clear, and our knowledge of their worlds is limited. But these assumptions do not lead us to despair; we need to be all the more diligent in seeking understanding. They are, after all, "classics."

The Meanings of "Classics"

The letter of Paul to the Galatians is indisputably one of the most influential canonical texts of the Christian tradition. The *Analects* is also well regarded as one of the classics. The Chinese word "classics" (*jing*) carries the connotation of "weaving"—implying the intertextual responsibility of text, author, and reader in the discovery, transmission, and practice of wisdom, whether by way of an oral/auditory or written medium. The ancient Chinese language, the language of the *Analects*, is not so much comprised of descriptive statements of what the world is, but performative and prescriptive utterances for guiding people into action and moving them toward the world as it should be.[3] The classics are texts containing communal wisdom, have stood the test of time, and continue to empower the community to live in wholeness. In our modern (Western) world, "the classics" refer to enduring normative texts that have a revelatory, transcendental, and objective nature. The classics contain the eternal principles of the cosmic order; they are works whose ideals and precepts transcended the historical circumstances of their origins and formed the basis of the social, political, economic, and religious institutions that followed.

The classics in the modern Western sense are concerned with truth, ancient Chinese classics with practical wisdom, a wisdom that is generative of life abundant. There is no lexical equivalent for truth in classical Chinese. In the West (especially in modernity), truth is equated with "objective reality." Modern epistemology tells us that we discover "objectivity" through the discovery of "the Eternal One," that "it is by virtue of analogy with this 'objective One' that we are able to disengage from our contexts, thereby resolving them into 'objects' independent of ourselves."[4] The suggestion here is not a dichotomous understanding between classical Chinese and modern Western languages—as though one were pre-

3. See Hansen, *Daoist Theory of Chinese Thought*, 33–52, on *dao* as linguistic communication for leading people on the way (*dao*).

4. Ames and Rosemont, *Analects*, 31.

scriptive, the other descriptive, and one about event, the other substance. I am suggesting that for me as a modern Chinese, trained in the Western mode of discourse, the *Analects* may not be discounted simply because it does not proclaim truth in the same way Paul believes he is doing in Galatians. By bringing the *Analects* into an intertextual relationship with Galatians, I am not trying to resolve the issue of which is more authoritative. Intertextuality answers that question by acknowledging the *mutually reinforcing authority* of both texts. The *Analects* and Galatians are received texts that continue to speak to their respective global communities by virtue of their founding, canonical, and commentarial functions.

Because the languages of the *Analects* and Galatians (classical Chinese and Koine Greek respectively) are alien to our modern Western experience, I have deemed it even more necessary for us to examine with care individual words, concepts, and phrases. This close interpretive process will prove helpful to us as we cross over from our cultures to that of antiquity. Furthermore, such a procedure will help us avoid letting our own cultural assumptions flatten out the otherness of the foreign culture. Most importantly, looking at the texts this way will help us personalize, perhaps even internalize, the wisdom of the classics, thus rejuvenating new life into the texts.

I will summarize the basic rhetorical argument of the *Analects* and Galatians below with the purpose of constructing the theological ethics of the two texts.

THE *ANALECTS*: TEXT, LANGUAGE, AND CONTENT

The Classic Text and Its Composition

The *Analects* (*Lunyu* in Chinese), a term coined by a Scottish Congregationalist missionary to China called James Legge (1815–1897), means "categorized conversation" or "collection of sayings."[5] The *Analects* is one of four Confucian classics, which, together with the Five Classics, were integrated into a Confucian canon in the Former Han era (201 BCE—25 CE). The Four Books were the core texts of Confucianism—the *Analects* (*Lunyu*), *Mencius* (*Mengzi*), the *Doctrine of the Mean* (*Zhongyong*), and

5. See an excellent discussion on the Chinese title of the work and its textual history: Cheng, *Lunyu Jishi*; Yang, *Lunyu Yizhu*, 3–8; and Slingerland trans., *Confucius Analects*, xiii–xxv.

the *Great Learning (Daxue)*.[6] They became unified texts only in the Sung dynasty (960–1279 CE). They are considered classical (*jing*) texts (*wen*) because they have long been regarded as containing a comprehensive understanding of the moral, philosophical, and political worlds of human endeavor. The *Analects* has special place because it collects the teachings of China's greatest master, Confucius. Later commentators have found in the *Analects* the essence of the Sage's teaching and the master key to the classics as a whole.[7]

The composition of the *Analects* began soon after Confucius' death (in 479 BCE) by his disciples and successors for the next two centuries (probably before 220 BCE). By the time of the Han dynasty (206 BCE–200 CE), there were three versions of the *Analects* (according to *Hanshu, History of the Han Dynasty*), and the received text (the *Lunyu*, which we have today) is made up of these three versions, edited first by He Yan (190–249 CE). The *Analects* is a record of the Master's teaching as preserved by his earliest disciples with material added by different Confucian sects, sometimes of the same mind, sometimes of a competing spirit. Each composer or editor had his own intention in the editing process.[8] The present form of the *Analects* (containing 15,935 words altogether) is comprised of twenty books (or sections, sometimes referred to as chapters). Each book is divided into divisions (or paragraphs, and sometimes referred to as chapters, about five hundred in all) of individual

6. See Legge and Yang, trans., *The Four Books*.

7. According to the prominent Qing historian of the classics, Chen Li (1810–1882), "the essentials of classical studies are all in the *Analects*" (Henderson, *Scripture, Canon, and Commentary*, 18). Liu Fenglu remarked that "the *Analects* sums up the great meanings of the Six Classics (Henderson, *Scripture, Canon, and Commentary*, 19). The *Analects* was considered a classic by Jesuit missionaries in China and Japan during the sixteenth through eighteenth centuries. Protestant missionaries in the nineteenth century were also attracted to it; James Legge translated the classics into English. Among the best English translations of the *Analects* are those by James Legge, Arthur Waley, D. C. Lau, Roger T. Ames and Henry Rosemont Jr., Chichung Huang, and Edward Slingerland. The four Chinese commentaries on the *Analects* I use are: He and Xing, *Lunyu Zhushu*; Yang, *Lunyu Yizhu*; Qian, *Lunyu Xinjie*; Chen, *Lunyu Duxun Jiegu*; and Zhu ed., *Sishu*. An excellent online resource on Confucianism is: http://www.confucius2000.com/.

8. On the technical study of the redaction of the *Analects*, see Norden ed., *Confucius and the Analects*, 14–18; Waley, *The Analects of Confucius*, 21–26. Following Waley, Norden sees Books 3–9 as the earliest portion, with explicit topics, yet Book 10 is irrelevant and Book 1–2 without explicit topics. Brooks and Brooks, *The Original Analects*, propose the accretion theory. They see only Book 4 is the original and dated 479 BCE, right after the death of Confucius, and the last book (20) was dated 249 BCE.

dialogues or sayings. Most of the sayings are concerned with political ethics and with the cultivation of virtue.[9]

9. The result of the redaction process is the work we have today that has titles to every book (or section). Below are the titles of the books and their component sections with a brief summary of their content in parenthesis:

Book 1–2: The sayings of Confucius and his disciples
    Book 1: Xue Er—On Learning (On studying, life, language, truth, etc.)
    Book 2: Weizheng—On Governing (On government, poetry, Confucius' own life of study, *junzi* [exemplary person], etc.)
Book 3–9: Core Books (Probably the earliest material with topical discussions)
    Book 3: Bayi—Eight Rows of Dancers (On ritual and music)
    Book 4: Liren—To Live Benevolently/Humanely (Aphorism on *ren*)
    Book 5: Gongye Chang—Gongye Chang (A major disciple of Confucius, contains sayings on judgment about others)
    Book 6: Yong Ye—Yong Ye (a major disciple of Confucius, also known as Ran Yong or Ran Bo-niu, a discussion on judgment and official responsibility)
    Book 7: Shu Er—To Transmit (Biographical material on Confucius)
    Book 8: Tai Bo—Tai Bo (The eldest son of the Zhou dynasty's first king; contains Master Zeng's analects [chap. 3–7] and a discussion on the sage kings [chap. 18–21])
    Book 9: Zihan—Master Seldom (The title is based on the first two words of the book, "The Master seldom . . . " The book contains biographical material of Confucius.)
Book 10–11: Topical Discourses
    Book 10: Xiang Dang—Native Place (On Confucius's behavior in his native region and maxims concerning ritual.)
    Book 11: Xian Jin—Those Who First Entered (On rituals, music, and government)
Book 12–20: Dialogues between the Disciples and the Master
    Book 12: Yan Yuan—The disciples ask about *ren* (humaneness), *junzi* (the exemplary person), clear-sightedness (*min*), government (*zheng*), etc.
    Book 13: Zilu—The disciples ask about government, *ren* [benevolence], *junzi* [exemplary person], etc.
    Book 14: Xian Wen—Xian, a disciple of Confucius, also known as Yuan Si. He asks about shame, and other disciples ask about being human, government, *junzi* [the exemplary person], etc.
    Book 15: Wei Ling Gong—Duke Ling of the state of Wei, who asks about Confucius. Confucius' responses on virtue, *junzi* [exemplary person], his own teaching, *dao* [the way], etc.
    Book 16: Ji Shi—Ji Kangzi, one of the ruling families in the state of Lu, asks about warfare, and Confucius' discourses on *dao* [the way], friendship, *junzi* [the excellent person], etc.
    Book 17: Yang Huo—Yang Huo, a government official who asks to see Confucius, but Confucius refuses. Confucius' discourse on human nature, *ren* [humaneness], ritual, etc.

To translate the title *Analects* as "The Sayings of Confucius" is incorrect. There is not one author, there are multiple voices with the Master's as the dominant one. Eight of the sixteen chapters in Book 1 are not even the teachings of Confucius; Book 2 begins with the voice of Master You; Books 12–20 contain sayings of the disciples; and Books 14 and 18 even contain anti-Confucian stories. Of all the four canonical texts—the *Analects, Mencius, the Doctrine of the Mean,* and the *Great Learning*—the *Analects* is the one that contains sayings closest to the spirit of the Master's teachings.

Language of the Analects: Wenyan

The *Analects* was written in the classical Chinese language called *wenyanwen*, the imperial language of ancient China in which most classics of history, philosophy, and literature were written. Classical Chinese is different from *baihuawen* ("the plain language" or modern Chinese), the vernacular written language widely used throughout the Chinese speaking world today.[10] *Wenyan* (classical Chinese) texts, such as the *Analects*, are more poetic, ambiguous, and polyvalent than *baihua* (modern Chinese) texts.[11]

Book 18: Weizi—Accounts of the viscount of Wei who left the tyrant ruler, Duke Jing of Qi, etc. This book contains few of Confucius' sayings.

Book 19: Zizhang—Sayings of Zizhang, Zixia, Ziyou, Master Zeng, Zigong. This book does not contain sayings of Confucius.

Book 20: Yao Yue—Yao Said (On government and the mandate of heaven.)

10. The 1919 May Fourth Movement brought about the *baihuawen,* the vernacular written language widely used throughout the Chinese speaking world. It is more or less a transcription of how one speaks. The *wenyanwen* and *baihuawen* have different styles, grammars, and vocabularies. Generally speaking, *wenyanwen* is more grand and formal; it has stricter rules or patterns of expression, especially in poetic compositions. *Baihuawen* literally means "plain-saying." It has a simpler style, looser sentence structure, and therefore needs more words to express the same idea than *wenyanwen.* Because of the history, wisdom, and beauty of *wenyanwen,* most writers today use *baihua* but then draw on the rich tradition of *wenyan* in the form of "short sayings," called *chengyu* (proverbial sayings or anecdotes).

11. Ames and Rosement have published substantial studies on the philosophical and linguistic background of *wenyan* (classical Chinese). They argue that *wenyan* is probably not the exact language the people of antiquity spoke because of the high number of homonyms in the language, "with anywhere from two to seven different characters pronounced identically. Today the situation is worse. In a common five-thousand-word dictionary, for example, even when the tones are taken into account, forty semantically

It is important to note also that the Chinese language, whether *wenyan* or *baihua*, does not have moods, voices, tenses, articles, declensions, prepositions, or distinguishing features regarding parts of speech. Sometimes a word in a sentence can function as a noun, a verb, or another part of speech. This dynamic aspect of the Chinese language adds another layer of challenge to the modern mind that expects precision. These elliptical features of classical Chinese pose difficulty for interpreters of the *Analects*. F. S. C. Northrop understands this dynamic aspect of the Chinese language as the "intuitive, aesthetic, undifferentiated experience" of ancient Chinese epistemology:

> Western type of knowledge tends to be formally and doctrinally expressed in logically developed, scientific and philosophical treatises. . . . The Easterners, on the other hand, uses bits of linguistic symbolism, largely denotative, and often purely ideographic in character, to point toward a component in the nature of things which only immediate experience and continued contemplation can convey. This shows itself especially in the symbols of the Chinese language, where each solitary, immediately experienced local particular tends to have its own symbol, this symbol also often having a directly observed form like that of the immediately seen item of direct experience which it denotes. . . . Since the symbols tend to be related merely as the items in the concrete, individual aesthetic experience are associated, the rules of grammar are less definite.[12]

The language of the *Analects* is poetic. The nature of language is such that it invites "immediately introspected imagination of the reader, with a minimum of symbols, the maximum amount of rich, subtly related, immediately felt aesthetic content."[13] All the practical moral precepts are presented in the *Analects* as if they are immediately available to the readers, and the readers are expected to draw upon their experience in reading the *Analects*. For Confucius, the ethical is grounded in the aesthetic.

---

dissimilar [pictographs or characters] are pronounced identically /yi/; the sounds /shi/ and /ji/ each have thirty-two lexical entries; /zhi/ has thirty-one; and so on, with almost no phoneme having only one semantic correlate." Ames and Rosemont, *Analects*, 38. See the "Introduction" and "Appendix II" in their book—very helpful material to proper understanding of Chinese language. Another valuable source on Chinese language is Northrop, *The Meeting of East and West*, 312–46.

12. Northrop, *The Meeting of East and West*, 315–16, 319.

13. Ibid., 319.

Ethics is not to arrive at a doctrinal, logical formulation of behaviors. Ethics is leading people to participate in the beauty of the great order of life, as the cosmic *dao* (way or pattern) or universal principle (*tianli*) has it eternally, and as individuals fulfill the harmony (aesthetic delight) of the *dao* (the Way) in their moral life.

The Power of the Analects:[14] *From* Yan *(Word) to* Wen *(Culture)*

We have noted in the previous chapter that Confucius came in the tradition of teachers called *ru* who advocated a culture of studies and self-cultivation in place of physical force and domination, Confucius strengthened the teachings to become the so-called the school of Confucianism (*Rujia*). In the *Analects* we see Confucius' emphasis in the power of the word as his means to redefine the role of teachers (*ru*). In the *Analects* the rhetoric of *yan*, word or speech, is especially important. The word *yan* is used 116 times throughout, and is often linked to virtue (*Analects* 12:10). Confucius contends that "[a] person of virtue is sure to speak eloquently, but a person who speaks eloquently is not necessarily virtuous" (*Analects* 14:4). Confucianism holds the view that moral character is revealed in one's speech (*Analects* 20:3). Lu writes, "The conceptualization of *yan* is Confucius's invention and creation, and his *Analects* is the first treatise on Chinese speech and communication."[15]

Confucius approves of using speech to persuade, to learn, and to cultivate oneself, but he does not approve of using speech for immoral gain. "It is rare, indeed, for a man with cunning words and an ingratiating face to be benevolent" (*Analects* 15:27).[16] Confucius "distastes clever talkers who overturn states and noble families" (17:18).[17] The exemplary person is described as "being slow in speech" (4:24) and "eager to show respect to his audience" (5:16). The rhetorical *topoi* to avoid include "feats of strength, disorder, and spiritual beings" (7:20).

To be eloquent without ethical integrity does not persuade; to be virtuous is to be persuasive. As Robert Oliver has noted, "In constructing

14. On rhetoric of Confucianism, see Lu, *Rhetoric in Ancient China*, 154–94; Qian, *Lunyu Xinjie*, 1–3.

15. Lu, *Rhetoric in Ancient China*, 163.

16. Lau, trans., *Analects*, 155.

17. Ibid., 177.

a moral perspective of *yan*, Confucius proposed the following categories of speech: *deyan* (virtuous speech), *xinyan* (trustworthy speech), *weiyan* (upright speech), *shenyan* (cautious speech), and *yayan* (correct speech)."[18] All these locutions are related to the rhetor's ethos. According to Oliver, Confucius gives seven distinct reasons for persuasive discourse:

> . . . 'to communicate ideas clearly' (*Analects* 15:39); to 'captivate the will of those whose loyalty must be won' (9:24); to maintain social functions, for as he said: 'Human relations not rectified, speech would grate; speech grating, activities would not carry on' (13:3); to reform the conduct of a prince or friend, for 'how can one help . . . rectifying, through persuasion, the one to whom he is loyal?' (14:7); to win personal advancement, since experience shows that 'Unless gifted with the artful tongue of Ceremony Master T'o and the handsomeness of Prince Ts'ao of Sung, one can hardly get on these days' (6:15); to gain a truer understanding of other people, since 'he who does not know the value (force) of words will never come to understand his fellow men' (20:3); and to represent clearly and accurately the true nature of the speaker, for 'There are three facets of a gentleman. Looked at from a distance he seems stern; at close range he is pleasant; as we listen to his words, they are clear cut' (19:9).[19]

Confucius is the master of language, his metaphorical speech invites his disciples then and his readers now to join him in creating an orderly moral world. That invitational style includes using contrasts and open-ended definitions (this sounds like an oxymoron, but it has a pedagogical purpose). For instance, it would be difficult for us to determine the precise definition of the following terms: *ren, zhong, shu, li, xiao, junzi*. For Confucius, effective teaching requires the creative definition of concepts, leaving them open for disciples to explore their derivative and connotative paths, and thereby to internalize them. Jay G. Williams gives the examples of how Chapters (Books) I and II of the *Analects* are invitational in their discussion of the gentleman's study and practice of *ren*.

> Initially, the connection between Chapter I and Chapter II seems unclear, though one has an inkling that the filial and the fraternal are old friends revisited. II.2, however, introduces the *junzi* once more. The true aristocrat, *Lunyu's* ideal, is said to bend his atten-

---

18. Lu, *Rhetoric in Ancient China*, 164. *Yayan* can be translated as "elegant speech."
19. Oliver, *Communication and Culture*, 136.

tion to the root which, in the case of *ren* (human heartedness), are filial piety and fraternal submission. . . . Chapter III supplements II, providing an indication of where not to look for *ren*. *Ren*, it announces, is seldom associated with fine words and insinuating appearance. This is typical of the *Lunyu*: no definition, but a series of pointers. . . . Ideas are introduced but the definition of them is left up to the reader.[20]

Thus, the text of the *Analects* preserves the dynamic definitions of Confucius opening up the possibility for the reader to reconceptualize how to be fully human in a multitude of diverse situations.

Consistent with the Master's pedagogy, the editors of the *Analects* seek to draw forth the reader's participation as he engages the text. Jay G. Williams suggests that 1:1 sets the tone for the whole book:

Chapter I is not meant to be read like an Aristotelian treatise, as a series of arguments terminating in a conclusion. Its rhetoric is that of the intellectual puzzle which calls upon the reader to supply, through imaginative insight, the missing links. The reader is invited, not to follow the argument, but to construct it.[21]

The life disciplined in study is an enjoyment derived from a journey of discovery, rediscovery, imagination, and internalization. This path of discovery is made possible through *yan* (word or rhetoric).

Another significant word in the *Analects* interrelated with *yan* is *wen*, which can mean "knowledge," "learning" (*Analects* 1:6), "culture" (3:14, 9:5), "fond of learning" (5:15), "embellishment" (6:18, 19:8), "classics" (7:25), "knowledge" (9:11), "knowledge of classics" (9:27), or "refinement" (8:24), as seen in Lau's translation. *Wen* often means "pattern" as well (1:6). *Analects* 5:13 talks about the *wenzhang* of Confucius. What is the *wenzhang* of Confucius? The history of interpretation gives different meanings:

It could refer to Confucius' personal displays of culture. In *Analects* 5:15, Zigong asks why an official named Kong was given the posthumous name *the cultured one* (*wenzi*). But equally plausible is the idea that *wen* refers to the cultural forms of the Zhou dynasty. One finds support for this reading in *Analects* 9:5, where

---

20. Williams, "On Reading A Confucian Classic," 109–10; Slingerland, trans., *Confucius Analects*, 1–16.

21. Williams, "On Reading A Confucian Classic," 108–9.

Confucius thought that Heaven was delegating to him the task of rebuilding the culture of Zhou.[22]

These two interpretations can be seen as mutually compatible: "Confucius was the repository of knowledge about this culture and he displayed it in his personal conduct. . . ."[23] Today we might use the words "civilized" and "cultured" to describe the meanings of *wen* in the *Analects*, while using the word "culture" anthropologically to refer to stylized ways of living. I will pick up this discussion in the section below on "culture and cultured."

The Analects *and the Scholarly Tradition of Learning to Becoming Human*

The Confucian culture is the context in which the Chinese human character has been shaped. Confucius believed that human beings are born with similar natures, but they drift apart through repeated practices caused by educational and environmental influences (*Analects* 17:2). Confucius founded the *rujia*, "the scholarly tradition" or the "Learning School,"[24] and emphasizes studying as the way to becoming fully human (cf. *Analects* 15:9). Confucius advocates wide learning in *wen* (culture), in order to become an exemplary person (*junzi*) who disciplines himself with *li* (ritual propriety). Such a person will not likely go astray (*Analects* 6:27).

The scholarly tradition of Confucianism believes that teachers are life-long learners who keep reviewing and preserving the old and acquiring the new (*Analects* 2:11). To be a great teacher, one takes the historical and prophetic task of knowing the classics well and transmitting them to the contemporary audience. *Analects* 7:1 says: "I transmitted and did not

22. For more interpretative discussion on these verses, see Yang, *Lunyu Yizhu*, 104, 194; Qian, *Lunyu Xinjie*, 165, 307; Chen, *Confucian Analects*, 72, 154; Slingerland, trans., *Confucius Analects*, 87–88.

23. Ivanhoe, "Whose Confucius? Which *Analects*?" 131, n. 9: "Other plausible interpretations exist, as well. For example, Liu Xie (465–522) in the second chapter of his *Wenxin diaolong* says that Confucius' *wenzhang* is his "style of composition" (*wenci*). Huang Kan (488–545) in his commentary on the *Analects* identifies *wenzhang* as the six classical works (*liuji*)."

24. On *ru*, *rujia* and its legacy, see Eno, *The Confucian Creation of Heaven*, 190–97; Jensen, *Manufacturing Confucianism*, Part 2.

describe." It means that he passed on the knowledge of the classics but did not create new rituals and music, he trusted and loved antiquity. *Analects* 7:1 means that knowledge has its foundation in past wisdom.

The great Master, Confucius himself, was an exemplary learner. He was omnivorous and described himself as a person who was fond of learning. Confucius learned from the way of the sage-kings, King Wen and King Wu, but also from the common people. He was not ashamed to ask inferiors for information,[25] he never denied anyone who came to him for learning (*Analects* 7:7).[26] Learning, he believed, was not limited to the classroom or to formal education, learning can happen in any social setting. Confucius said that when there were three persons together, he could find a teacher among them, he could learn from the good points of others; the bad points he could also learn from them and he could correct the same weak points in himself (*Analects* 7:22).[27]

The *Analects* is full of discourses on learning. Studying involves not just thinking but, foremostly, observation and listening (*Analects* 2:18).[28] Learning must be supplemented with critical reflection to be fruitful; critical reasoning must be supplemented with study to be coherent. Learning without reflection is futile; reflection without learning is perplexing (Analects 2:15). Confucius expected his students to take initiative in studying, to think hard, for "no vexation, no enlightenment; no anxiety, no illumination" (*Analects* 7:8).[29] He also expected his students to draw inferences and not just do rote memory (*Analects* 7:8).

25. When asked why the minister of Wei Kong Wenzi was called "wen" (meaning "refined") Confucius replied to his disciple Zigong that, because he was intelligent and fond of studying, he was not ashamed to ask his inferiors and learn from them, and this was the meaning of *wen* (*Analects* 5:15). See Yang, *Lunyu Yizhu*, 104.

26. In his studies, Confucius started from the basic and gradually worked his way to the upper levels. If he was understood by anyone, perhaps it was heaven, so he did not complain against heaven, he did not blame any person (14:35). See Qian, *Lunyu Xinjie*, 234.

27. See Chen, *Lunyu Duxun Jiegu*, 122.

28. "When Zizhang asked how to seek an official's salary, the Master said: 'Hear much, leave out what is doubtful, discreetly speak about the rest, and you shall make few mistakes. See much, leave out what is hazardous, discreetly practice the rest, and you shall have fewer regrets. If you make fewer mistakes in speech and have fewer regrets in action, an official's salary lies therein" (Huang, *Analects*, 55–56; *Analects* 2:18). See Yang, *Lunyu Yizhu*, 39.

29. Huang, *Analects*, 88.

Thinking too hard, to the extent of fasting and sleepless nights may yield nothing. Confucius believed that speculative knowledge may not be helpful, while learning moral and self-cultivation would make one wise. Study should be well rounded, for all disciplines lead one to be a person of excellence for the sake self-cultivation. And because virtue formation is a life-long process, so is learning; as the first sentence of the *Analects* reads: "What a joy it is to learn and to constantly *practice* or *cultivate* it."[30]

Confucius did not claim to be a sage or a benevolent person; but he said he was committed to learning the way of benevolence and to teaching others to do the same, that much could be said of himself (*Analects* 7:34). Is the goal of learning to establish oneself (and others) or just to boast about one's knowledge? Confucius lamented that in the old days, scholars learned for themselves whereas now scholars learn to brag about themselves (*Analects* 14:24). Confucius taught that benevolence is the goal of learning, and in this pursuit of benevolence, one need not yield precedence even to one's teacher (*Analects* 15:36).

Indeed, learning is for the sake of the Way: "The Master said: 'Those who, after three years of learning, have never contemplated an official's salary, are not easy to find.' The Master said: 'Firmly believe in it, diligently learn it, and adhere to the good Way until death. A perilous state, do not enter; a rebellious state, do not inhabit. When the empire possesses the Way, reveal yourself; when it loses the Way, conceal yourself. When the state possesses the Way and you are poor and lowly, it is a shame; when the state loses the Way and you are rich and noble, it is also a shame'" (*Analects* 8:12–13).[31] Again, "The Master said: 'What the gentleman seeks is the Way and not food. If he farms, hunger lies therein; if he learns, an official's salary lies therein. What the gentleman worries about is the Way and not poverty" (*Analects* 15:32).[32]

The scholarly tradition of Confucianism is designed for the sake of leading people to the Way (*dao*), the cosmic pattern of all things. Those who are born with *dao* (the way of humanity) are rare but superior. Most people know the *dao* through learning. Many may learn when forced, but

---

30. See Chen, *Lunyu Duxun Jiegu*, 1; Yang, *Lunyu Yizhu*, 3–4.

31. Huang, *Analects*, 98.

32. Ibid., 157.

it is the last group that is undesirable, for they do not even learn when forced (*Analects* 16:9).

The Dao *of "Human Becoming" and the Confucian Project of an Aesthetic Culture*

The *Analects*, a collection of anecdotal sayings of Confucius and his disciples, is challenging to summarize. I shall examine the key concepts, terms, and sayings *in their contexts* later in this book. Here I wish to note the language and metaphysical worlds of the *Analects*, and consequently, to examine the major thrust of its teaching and the thesis.

The work of Ames and Rosemont is an insightful resource for non-Chinese readers of the *Analects* who seek to understand the linguistic and philosophic world of the *Analects*. Ames and Rosemont point out that the Chinese world emphasizes the function of "correlation" and not the function of essence or substance. They describe the Confucian worldview as "intrinsic and constitutive," that is,

> The Chinese made sense of personal identity "by fitting it into the cyclical rhythms of natural and social process." . . . The early Chinese thinkers never seem to have perceived any substances that remained the *same* through time; rather in our interpretation they saw "things" relationally, and related differently, at different periods of time. *Dao*, the totality of all things *(wanwu)*, is a process that requires the language of both "change *(bian)*" and "persistence *(tong)*" to capture its dynamic disposition. This processional nature of experience is captured in *Analects* 9:17: "The Master was standing on the riverbank, and observed, "Isn't life's passing just like this, never ceasing day or night!"[33]

Unlike the Greek metaphysical and Judeo-Christian theology that possess a worldview

> where an independent and superordinate principle determines order and value in the world while remaining aloof from it, . . . ancient Chinese thinkers did not view language basically as a way of describing the world, or of communicating one's beliefs about it, but rather as a means of guiding actions in the world.[34]

33. Ames and Rosemont, *Analects*, 24–26.
34. Ibid., 30–31.

As such the text of the *Analects* is a *dao* in the sense that it is a "guiding discourse." The Chinese word *dao* means "to lead through [on foot]" "foremostly" ("head").[35] The Confucian teachings in the *Analects* are guiding discourses (*dao*) of "human *becoming*"—in the dynamic and relational process of change and persistence.

The *Analects* does not speculate the genesis of the world, it "*does* something to the world and recommends *how it should be*."[36] Because there is no creation myth in the Chinese worldview, Confucius and his disciples believe that *tian* (Heaven) is the creative order and the field of creatures. "There is no apparent distinction between the order itself, and what orders it. . . . *Tian* is not just 'things'; it is a living culture—crafted, transmitted, and now resident in a human community."[37] The "ten thousand things" (*wanwu*) and the human world are immanent of creativity and life; they are "at once continuous one with another, and at the same time, unique."[38] A moral subjectivity, which is also the subjectivity of *tian*, distinguishes the human creature from other creatures.[39] The way of becoming human is to realize the way of *tian*, as one cultivates virtues in correlation with others.

As we turn to the letter to the Galatians, we will notice sharp contrasts between Galatians and the *Analects*. The thesis of the *Analects* concerns the cultivation of one's subjectivity, that is, one's moral mind or one's heart.[40] The *Analects* does not pursue the question of the Objective One, who is believed to provide a transcendental answer to the question "what causes the world to be here?" and consequently to provide the basis for the meaning of life. In the *Analects*, the world does not appear deceptive, and accordingly the *Analects* is not preoccupied with the *why* of the world.[41] Instead, the *Analects* as a teacher (*ru*) is concerned with "*how to get on* in the world"—"the way (*dao*) is made in the walking of it."[42] Thus, the language and the teaching are training grounds for readers and learners to walk on the path of becoming human as they are being culti-

35. Ibid., 45.

36. Ibid.; emphases mine.

37. Ibid., 47.

38. Ibid., 30.

39. Mou, *Xinti Yu Xingti*, 1:22–23.

40. Mou, *Zhongguo Zhexue De Tezhi*, 16–27.

41. Ames and Rosemont, *Analects*, 32.

42. Ibid., 33.

vated in the stylized rituals and beautiful music of the sages in the past. Slingerland correctly notes that "Confucius seems to have been the first to use the term *dao* ('the Way') in its full metaphysical sense. Referring literally to a physical path or road, *dao* also refers to a 'way' of doing things, and in the *Analects* refers to *the* Way—the unique moral path that should be walked by any true human being, endorsed by Heaven and revealed to the early sage-kings."[43]

The teaching of Confucius, as it advocates for the path of becoming human, provides a moral response to a fallen society "whose rulers have lost the Way and the common people have therefore becomes confused" (*Analects* 19:19). The Way is lost because people of Confucius' day are obsessed with mechanically fulfilling the outward forms of the rites and pursuing self-cultivation with ulterior motives.[44] According to Confucius, fallen culture is the inevitable product of such a corrupt society. Thus, to restore the way of becoming human is to restore the Way of Heaven (*tian*)—and that, for Confucius, means to build an aesthetic culture (*wen*) of Virtue (*de*) for its own sake. Confucius is convinced that the aesthetic culture was once manifested in the Western Zhou, and in his own time, he wants to make his home state of Lu to be a "second Zhou in the East" (*Analects* 17:5).

Heaven neither endows nor endorses a manipulative, artificial, and glib set of rules; Heaven gives "natural, spontaneous, unselfconscious harmony"[45] as Virtue (*de*) to all people. Heaven governs the natural world "effortlessly" (*wuwei*), without even speaking, yet all living things grow (*Analects* 17:18).[46] Confucius believes that the political and the social world should function in the same effortless manner as the natural world—without resort to force. The stylized ritual and the harmonious music are not about the external forms, they are the fields of an aesthetic culture in which one immerses and consequently, one's being is cultivated into a mature moral self (*junzi*).

We will return to this discussion below as we deal with Confucian ethics in relation to Pauline theology. Let us turn now to the letter to the Galatians written by Paul.

43. Slingerland, trans., *Confucius Analects*, xxiii–xxii.

44. Ibid., xxiii–xxiv.

45. Ibid., xxiii–xxi.

46. *Analects* 17:18: "The Master said: 'What does Heaven say? Yet the four seasons revolved and a hundred things grow. What does Heaven say?'" (Huang, *Analects*, 170).

THE LETTER TO THE GALATIANS: TEXT, SETTING, AND PAUL'S RESPONSE TO THE CRISIS IN GALATIA

In Pauline scholarship today there are three broad plausible readings of Paul's letter to the Galatians, with a fourth as a creative synthesis of one or more of the other three: (1) the older Lutheran view that Galatians is about faith versus works as the means of salvation, that the sinner is justified in the presence of a holy and righteous God by faith alone, which itself is a gift of God's grace;[47] (2) the view that Galatians is about covenant membership, that is, about the status and identity of Jews and Gentiles as God's people and whether the symbol of that identity is the law or Christ;[48] (3) the view that Galatians is about living an ethical life within the controversy concerning the role of the law and the Spirit.[49] My reading attempts to combine the last two without rejecting the first view completely. My view interprets the eschatological events of baptism into Christ and the ushering in of God's Spirit not only as defining more inclusively the people of God, but also of creating a new people of God as "moral charismatics" in which the Spirit of God enables the people of God to be morally pure and victorious in overcoming the reign of sin.[50]

The Crisis and the Congregation in Galatia[51]

∾ The Background of Galatians

Paul's letter to the Galatians was written to a group of Gentile Christians who were Celts (known as Keltoi to the Greeks) or the Gallic people (known as Galli to the Romans). The Celtic tribes dwelt in villages in

---

47. Represented by Bultmann, *Theology of the New Testament* 1:25–90; Ridderbos, *The Epistle of Paul to the Churches of Galatia*; Hübner, *Law in Paul's Thought*, 4–21.

48. See Sanders, *Paul, the Law, and the Jewish People*, 75, 173, 176; Dunn, "The New Perspective on Paul," 95–122.

49. See Cosgrove, *The Cross and the Spirit*, 31–86, 173–94. See also Betz, *Galatians*, passim on especially the paraenesis of Galatians (pp. 5–9, 28–33); Lull, *The Spirit in Galatia*, 7–10, 30–39, 42–53; Hays, *The Faith of Jesus Christ*, passim.

50. Cosgrove, *The Cross and the Spirit*, 86.

51. There are three explicit places in Galatians that discuss the birth and life of the Galatian congregations (3:1–4; 4:13–14; 5:7a). See Martyn, *Galatians*, 13. For a historical understanding of "Galatia and Galatians" see Betz, *Galatians*, 1–3.

northern Galatia (central Turkey).[52] Their main occupations were fighting and farming. They resisted the hellenization that had surrounded the Galatian cities. They had a strong sense of identity with their traditional culture, its values of honor and shame, which were clearly seen in competitive contests, games, benefactions, and feasts. They believed in cosmic elements, such as water, light, sky, sun, for they believed that these elements were endowed with divine powers.[53] Celts were afraid of manifestations of cosmic power, such as lightning and thunderstorms, because they reminded them of the end of the world. They worshipped the forces of nature out of fear.[54] Paul's letter to the Galatians contains the rhetorical *topoi* of Celtic culture: the androgynous Attis may lie behind the expression "not 'male and female'" (3:28);[55] Paul's stigmata (6:17) and his identity with Christ "in me" (2:20) resonate well with the Galli belief in possession by respective deities;[56] Jerusalem as "our mother" (4:26) and "works of the flesh" are not responses to moral laxity, but to Celtic ritual practices of paganism;[57] "those who by nature are not gods" (Gal 4:8) is a reference to the Celtic religion,[58] and "days, months, seasons, and years" (Gal 4:10) refers to the Celtic religious calendar rather than the Jewish.[59]

✤ Paul's Rhetoric and the Crisis in Galatia

From the *pathos* of Paul's rhetoric, it is not difficult to tell that he was in distress, full of anguish and pain. Paul is at times harsh, forceful, and interrogative in his argumentation. His rebuking tone is obvious in Gal 1:6–9, in which the Galatians are warned of abandoning the gospel. He calls them "foolish" (3:1). He uses a double curse formula against those who dare preach another gospel (1:8–9). He equates the pangs of child-

---

52. Cf. Lightfoot, *Galatians*, 13–17; Guthrie, *Galatians*, 72; Cole, *Galatians*, 16; Rankin, *Celts and the Classical World*, 190.

53. Rankin, *Celts and the Classical World*, 60.

54. Ibid., 260.

55. S. M. Elliott, "Rhetorical Strategy," 629.

56. Ibid., 625.

57. Ibid.

58. Schweizer, "Slaves of the Elements," 455–68.

59. T. W. Martin, "Pagan and Judeo-Christian Time-Keeping Schemes," 105–19.

birth with his own anguish (4:12–20) as he had compassionately awaited their formation in Christ. But now he is heart-broken. The Galatian Christians have given in to those who demand circumcision and have perhaps returned to paganism. He wishes that those who pervert the gospel (1:7) would "castrate themselves" (5:12).

↦ The Occasion of the Letter and the Opponents[60]

The occasion of Paul's letter to the churches of Galatia was a dispute over the place of the law in Christian identity, faith, and practice. The opponents of Paul were conservative Jewish Christian missionaries from Jerusalem,[61] inspired by zealous Pharisaism (cf. Acts 15:1). They challenged Paul's authority, and they required (Gal 6:12) the Gentile Christians of Galatia to be circumcised (5:2, 6:12–13) and to observe the "works of the law" (3:2, 5:4).[62] Their argument was that by doing so Gentile Christians would be fully accepted as true people of God belonging to the line of Abraham, and that they would be able to enjoy the benefits of the "full gospel" (Gal 2:12). They had intruded the Galatian church with a "different gospel" (1:7) in order to "perfect" Paul's partial gospel. These intruders were

60. For an excellent history of interpretation see Martyn, *Galatians*, 27–42, also Boyarin, *A Radical Jew*, 41–52 gives an excellent review of the traditional readings of Paul and the five current views. My reading of Galatians is influenced by the works of Sanders and Dunn with regard to the "identity symbol" of the people of God, and Cosgrove, Hays, and Martyn have informed my thinking on the Spirit, the faithfulness of Christ, and eschatology respectively.

In describing the Galatians and Paul's opponents (the Judaizers), I tend to take Paul's words at face value in the sense that I assume he is engaging in a dialogue with either the Galatians or the opponents. Barclay, "Mirror-Reading a Polemical Letter: Galatians as a Test Case," 73–93 suggests caution on mirror-reading. Here I assume that my knowledge of Paul and his conversation partners is implied in Paul's words. One cannot know the integrated theology of the opponents. In my reconstruction, I may have been able to identify some individual elements, but by and large Paul's words project his view of the opponents' position as well as his own teaching among the Galatians. Thus to delineate precisely what the opponents' teachings were is a methodological conundrum. See also, Cosgrove, *The Cross and the Spirit*, 16–38.

61. After Paul's last visit to Galatian churches (Acts 18:23), the itinerant Jewish Christian missionaries arrived (cf. Gal 1:7, 4:17, 5:10, 6:12). Watson, *Paul, Judaism and the Gentiles* (p. 60) identifies the opponents as men from James (Gal 2:2) who defeated Paul at Antioch and now came to Galatia to compete with Paul.

62. Cf. Jewett, "The Agitators," 200, who says that 6:12 *houtoi anagkazousin hymas peritemnesthai* "refers to the 'necessity' of circumcision."

probably related to the Judaizers from Jerusalem. According to Gal 2:4, those who opposed Paul were brethren who had been secretly brought in from Jerusalem to spy on the freedom Paul and the Galatian Christians had in Christ Jesus.

✣ The Motives of the "Disturbers"

Paul describes of his opponents as "some (*tines*) disturbers" (*tarassontes*; 1:7, 5:10; *parechetō* 6:17) who "pervert (*metastrepsai*) the gospel of Christ" (1:7). Paul wants to know who (*tis* in 3:1) had bewitched the Galatians and hindered them from obeying the truth (5:7). He suspects that the intention of the opponents "to exclude" (4:17) the Galatians is a false tactic of enticement. He writes that the opponents want to make "a good showing in the flesh," trying to compel the Galatians to be circumcised so that they might not be persecuted for the cross of Christ (6:12).

Why did these opponents attempt to pressure the Gentile Christians into accepting circumcision? Paul offers a few reasons. To begin with (Gal 6:12a), as noted, they want to make a "good showing in the flesh" (RSV). The Greek word, here, *euprosōpēsai* ("good showing"), appear only once in the New Testament. It means to have good manners as perceived by others.[63] The term suggests that disturbers are the Judaizers who were more concerned with the symbol of Jewish identity (i.e., circumcision and observance of the law) than with the reality to which the symbol points (i.e., the covenanted love of God). Relatedly, they want "to escape the persecution of the cross" (6:12b).

While circumcision was a religious act, its symbolic meaning for the Judaizers in mid-first century CE had more to do with Jewish identity in a politically unstable world. The persecution and violence they encountered had caused many Jews (Christian or non-Christian alike) to see circumcision as the solidarity sign of Jewish ethnicity.[64] The Judaizers were themselves Jewish Christians from Judea and their campaign to circumcise Gentile Christians was a response to Jewish zealots, hoping that if the Gentile Christians of Galatia subscribed to their circumcision campaign, they themselves would not be persecuted by the Jewish zealots.[65]

---

63. Cf. Lohse, "Sun-Meta," 779; Lightfoot, *Galatians*, 222.

64. Murphy-O'Connor, *Paul, A Critical Life*, 141.

65. Jewett, "The Agitators," 205.

The Judaizers may have been subject to persecution by non-Christian Jews because of their belief in Jesus as the Messiah, and for this reason sought to convince Gentile Christians to abide by the old traditions and thus to belong to the "true people" of God. Non-Christian Jews would not object to Jewish Christian affiliation with the Cross. The reason for preaching a "gospel of circumcision"[66] is that these Jewish believers thought they could convince their Jewish compatriots, that their preaching (i.e., that Jesus was the Messiah) was in line with Jewish identity. In other words, Paul's opponents meant to tell conservative Jews that they were not betraying Jewish nationality, culture, or religion just because they believed in the Messiah. If the Gentiles succumbed to the opponents' plan, then the opponents would escape persecution from their compatriots.[67]

The Judaizers' strategy of (a) "completing" the Pauline mission (Gal 3:3: the offer of "finishing up/making complete" [epiteleisthe]), and (b) "perfecting" the Abrahamic covenant (Gal 3:6–18) is a matter of theological articulation. It looks good, but it is false.

The opponents also slander Paul: Paul, they say, got his gospel from Jerusalem (Gal 1:11; 1:18—2:1); he used to preach circumcision (Gal 5:11) and the law (Gal 1:14); he had softened the requirements of the gospel to win pagan converts (Gal 1:10). Paul defends his preaching of Christ as valid: "But if I, brethren, still preach circumcision, why am I still being persecuted? If so [preaching circumcision], the scandal of the cross is abolished" (5:11).

Paul pronounces a judgment on the opponents: "The one who disturbs *you* (plural) will bear the judgment, whoever he is" (Gal 5:10b). "The one who disturbs" (1:7) will receive rejection and punishment from God (1:8–9). And Paul expresses this judgment sarcastically: "Would that those disturbing you might castrate themselves!" (5:12) The word castrate (*apokoptein*) shares the root word (*kop-*) with "cut off" (*egkoptein*) in 5:7. That is, those who preach the gospel of circumcision to the Galatians are now asked to cut the member off completely (note a similar tone in Phil 3:2). To mutilate oneself is to cut oneself off from God's community,

---

66. Gal 2:7 is the only time this expression "the gospel of circumcision" occurs in the New Testament. It refers to the gospel to the uncircumcised, rather than referring to the gospel whose content is circumcision.

67. Martin explains Paul's opponents as those circumcised Jewish Christians whose political motive was to escape persecution, so they wanted to convince Gentile Christians to abide with the law's demands. See R. P. Martin, *New Testament Foundations*, 2:55.

since both Paul and his opponents would have known Deut 23:1: "No one whose testicles are crushed or whose penis is cut off shall be admitted to the assembly of the Lord."

✥ The Incident in Antioch and Peter's Behavior

Paul's letter to the Galatians was also triggered by an incident in Antioch involving Peter whose behavior parallels the motives of the Judaizers. Peter had been eating with Gentiles (Gal 2:12), thus ignoring the legal division between "clean and unclean," that is, between Jews and Gentiles as prescribed in the old covenant (cf. Acts 10:14, 28).[68] Observing the fundamental distinction between clean and unclean food was a matter of principle for Jews (1 Macc 1:62–63) because of the requirement of the covenant. With whom one shared meals was an identity marker of the Jewish religion. "Separate yourselves from the nations, and eat not with them (Jub. 22.16)."[69] Early Judaism, not least of which were the Pharisees, strictly observed dietary laws for the sake of self-identity as the people of God. For a Jewish Christian to lay aside dietary law would be the same as "Peter living like a Gentile"[70] (Gal 2:14). For Gentiles to practice dietary laws would be the same as being proselytes.

The problem of the fellowship meal was not a major one in Jerusalem; it was a serious one, however, in Gentile lands such as Antioch in Syria. In Antioch, the eating customs of Jews and Gentiles, social or religious, did not have clear demarcations.[71] The Jewish- and Gentile-Christian communities in Antioch did not have huge public spaces like basilicas or synagogues to go to; instead, they attended "house churches," or cell groups, with the fellowship meal as a way of networking with the larger

---

68. Gentile meals are considered "unclean" (Ezek 4:13) because: (1) the food has been offered to idols (Exod 34:15); (2) the food comes from an unclean animal (Lev 11:1–20); or (3) the food is not properly prepared (Exod 23:19). See Matera, *Galatians*, 85. On details of Paul's use of Second Temple Judaism's intra-Jewish polemical language in Galatians, see Dunn, "Echoes of Intra-Jewish Polemic," 459–77.

69. Murphy-O'Connor, *Paul, A Critical Life*, 150.

70. The word "living" in Greek is present tense and suggests the basic principle of Peter's life, i.e., living like a Gentile. Cf. Lightfoot, *Galatians*, 114.

71. See a helpful discussion of Jewish and Gentile relations in first century Antioch by Bockmuehl, *Jewish Law in Gentile Churches*, 49–83; Fredriksen, "Judaism, the Circumcision of Gentiles, and Apocalyptic Hope," 235–60; Nanos, "What Was at Stake in Peter's 'Eating with Gentiles' at Antioch?" 282–318.

group of Christians. In the ancient Near East a meal was a social event that expressed friendship and built community. For early Christians the Eucharist was often celebrated in the context of such a social meal.

In a mixed community such as Antioch Jews would bring their own food when dining with Gentiles, if they knew kosher food was not being served. Table fellowship among Christians in Antioch was going on well until "certain people came from James" (2:12).[72] Peter "began gradually withdrawing (*hypestellen*) and separating (*aphōrizen*) himself" from the Gentile Christians (2:12).

For first century Jews and ancient Chinese alike ritual and propriety were not simply social conventions and therefore insignificant. In fact, they were *identity symbols* that express the core being of a people. Thus, "works of the law," such as circumcision, the observance of days, and dietary laws, for Jewish Christians were a matter of decency and honor. Paul took identity symbols not as a sociological variant, but as matters of *theological anthropology*—who we are in relation to what is sacred. To destroy the identity of a person is to destroy that person created in the image of God. For this reason, Paul was harsh on Peter and the Jewish Christians. Paul sympathized with the Gentile Christians and his understanding of their faith in Christ.[73] Given the food regulations placed on the Jews, the pressure of sharing a fellowship meal was on the Jews, not on the Gentiles. Jews like Peter, James, and Barnabas had no problem in Jerusalem, where Jews were in a majority. When Peter came to Antioch, "he was accustomed to eating with Gentiles" (the use of the imperfect [*synēsthein*] suggests Peter has been doing that for quite sometime) (2:12).[74] James' delegation, representing the Jerusalem Church, pressured

---

72. These "certain people from James" are *not* identical with the "false brethren" (2:4) because Peter and James did not agree with the false brethren (Contra Watson, *Paul*, 58, who holds that this group from James are the opponents). "Certain people from James" may be investigating delegates sent by James *or* people who wished to show their allegiance to James but not sent by James. The former is probably true because, according to Paul's interpretation, Peter "feared those from the circumcision (*tous ek peritomēs*)" (2:12). On the circumcision party as a group of Christian Jews in the Jerusalem Church, see Martyn, *Galatians*, 236–40.

73. See Bockmuehl, *Jewish Law in Gentile Churches*, 82, where he writes of "James's intervention, Peter's accommodation and Paul's rigid refusal" regarding the halakhic law for Gentile believers in Antioch.

74. According to Acts, Peter was at least once criticized by Jewish Christians because he shared a fellowship meal with Gentiles (Corneilus' household), see Acts 11:3.

Peter to observe strict Jewish dietary laws whereas Peter himself, after coming to Antioch, was accustomed to living like a Gentile (i.e., not observing dietary laws). James' party checked on Peter's behavior in order to maintain Jewish identity and unity.

The problem Peter faced did not stop with him. Paul observed that "even the rest of the Jews joined in hypocrisy with Cephas, so that even Barnabas was led away by their hypocrisy" (Gal 2:13). Before the Antioch incident, Peter and the Jerusalem apostles had understood and accepted Paul's gospel to the Gentiles. It was a gospel without "nomistic services"—a term used by J. Tyson, which is his translation of Lohmeyer's phrase, "Dienst des Gesetzes."[75] But now these same apostles had been persuaded to return to the old boundaries between Jewish and Gentile Christians. With the return to strict dietary laws, Gentile Christians had to live like Jews (*Ioudaïzein*)[76] or face the consequences, viz., expulsion or persecution.

Paul's Theological Response to the Crisis

✤ Paul Rebuked Peter for Hypocrisy

That Paul opposed Peter to his face shows that he was outraged. In Gal 2:14, Paul singles Peter out and rebukes him in front of everyone, saying, "if you being a Jew live as a Gentile and not as a Jew, how can you force the Gentiles to live as Jews?" Paul's verdict regarding Peter is that he stood condemned (*kataginōskein*, 2:11). Paul charged that "the rest of the Jewish Christians (at Antioch) joined in the hypocrisy (*synypekrithēsan*, also translated "insincerity")" with Peter (2:13). In Paul's mind it was hypocrisy because it constituted betrayal of their agreement at the Jerusalem Council. It is possible that some had either changed their minds about that agreement or that some did not accept the agreement in the first place. The agreement was ambiguous in matters concerning the fellowship meal. In Acts 15 the agreement focuses on the manner in which Gentile Christians were accepted as full members of the people of God, but the agreement does not spell out how or whether Jewish and Gentile

75. Tyson, "Works of Law in Galatians," 425.

76. *Ioudaïzein* (Gal 2:14) occurs only here in the New Testament. It means to accept partially or totally Judaistic customs (Gutbrod, "*Ioudaios*," *TDNT* 3:383).

Christians should eat together, and that was the problematic issue for Peter and Barnabas at Antioch. When Paul is compelled to visit the Jerusalem apostles (2:1–10) he mentions the issue of circumcision. Circumcision is a precisely defined matter. A fellowship meal, however, is a matter of social interaction between Jewish and Gentile Christians. Furthermore, the Jerusalem Conference advised Gentile Christians not to eat food offered to idols and food with blood, but it does not tell Jewish Christians what to do in a Gentile setting when kosher food is not served.

Hypocrisy is a social problem in the context of the coexistence of Jewish and Gentile Christians. But in this instance hypocrisy is interpreted by Paul *theologically*. Peter and the Judaizers "were not straightforward with the *truth* of the gospel" (2:14).[77] The theological implication of withdrawing fellowship from Gentile Christians is no less than the rejection of the gospel of Christ. Indeed, for Paul culture and theology are inseparable; Peter's social behavior is a theological act. As a Jewish Christian Peter had lived like a Gentile Christian (*ethnikos*) when he shared in Gentile (Christian) fellowship meals (Gal 2:12). In his empathetic acceptance of the Gentile lifestyle Peter has already accepted Gentiles as full members in the people of God. Now Peter pressures (*anagkazeis*) Gentile Christians to live as though they were Jewish (Gal 2:14); that is, to strip off their Gentile identities and to take up Jewish customs—even when Peter himself is not observing them strictly. Under the gospel of Christ Peter has the right to live without the law; but he cannot force Gentile Christians to take up the yoke of the law when he himself has set them aside.

✧ Works of the Law and Faith in Christ

Paul's letter to the Galatians contains both his *ad hoc* response to his opponents as well as his more foundational theological reasoning. Without attempting to delineate the two, I here prefer to read Galatians in terms of its theological understanding of Christ as the inclusive and sufficient identity symbol for both Jewish and Gentile Christians as God's people. That symbol guarantees freedom for all. Paul believes that if "works of the law," such as circumcision, dietary restrictions, and Sabbath observance,

---

77. So Matera, *Galatians*, 90.

are added to Christ in a theological-cultural formulae, bondage happens to the Gentiles as a result of Jewish religious coercion.

Paul's understanding of culture is theological. His genius is in not differentiating faith from culture, theology from religion. As we have already seen, in both the meaning-creating worldview and in the identity symbol of a people, faith, theology, and culture are intertwined. Paul's genius lies in his sensitivity to cultural and religious behaviors that marginalize others and bring them into bondage. In the case of Galatia, Paul views "works of the law" as *nomistic services,* ones that define Jewish identity *culturally and religiously* before the coming of Christ. But this covenantal nomism characterizes Jewish cultural *and* religious identity and is exclusive of Gentiles,[78] therefore when imposed upon Gentile believers the "works of the law" also define them to be Jewish culturally and religiously. Today we call such cultural and religious imposition "imperialism."

Paul's opponents are not able to differentiate the cultural and religious dimensions of nomistic services. But Paul is able to discern the "works of the law" in light of the Christ event (especially the Cross), based on whether a behavior contributes toward the freedom or salvation of a community. The truth of the gospel as Paul sees it is able to avoid cultural imperialism. He knows theologically that in the age of the Messiah the "works of the law" cannot serve as the identity symbol for Jewish and Gentile Christians—only Christ can. By contrast, the problem with Peter's hypocritical behavior lies in the theological ambiguity of trying to syncretize the "works of the law" with "faith in Jesus Christ" as the symbol for both Jewish- and Gentile-Christian identity.

From Paul's point of view the basic theological issue between his opponents and himself is "Christ or the law," not "faith or works." The basic issue is how to conceive of Gentile Christians as the people of God, as children of Abraham and part of the commonwealth of Israel and yet be *Gentiles.* Can Gentiles be the beneficiaries of God's salvation in this eschatological age according to Jewish prophecy (as e.g., according to Isa 2:2–4, 49:6, 56:6–7, 60:4–7; Zech 2:11, 8:20–3)?

The opponents are not preaching a gospel *without Christ.* They only want Gentile Christians to fulfill nomistic services, such as sabbath observance and circumcision. In other words, Christ-plus-law-observance would truly make Gentile Christians full members of the people of God.

---

78. On "covenantal nomism," see Das, *Paul, the Law, and the Covenant,* 70–94.

Neither Paul nor the opponents are talking about *individual* salvation, but about group identity and what is required to be a full member of God's people. The polemic is neither about whether righteousness is obtained through law observance or through faith in Christ, nor about the cultural superiority of Jew or Gentile. Rather, the polemic resolves around which identity symbol best defines the people of God.

TOWARD A CHINESE CHRISTIAN UNDERSTANDING OF THEOLOGICAL ETHICS

Theology and Culture

I have used the word "religion" loosely in the Overture chapter to refer to distinct traditions of belief in God (or the gods) as a meaning-creating process. As a Confucianist, I am hesitant to speak of Confucianism as a religion (though many Chinese do worship Confucius and his disciples as gods in Confucian Temples), because for me and many Chinese it is more a way of life in pursuit of virtue and in the formation of community. I recognize that the broad understanding of religion would categorize all passionate devotions, whether to God, or the gods, to nation, or science, or culture, or money as religion. In this sense all "isms," whether paganism, secularism, capitalism, or nationalism, can be as "religious" as Christianity or Buddhism. No one advocates the view that all these "religions" are benign or equally holy and good, that they are just like brands of food found in supermarkets. While our (post)modern tendency is to think of religion with a consumer's mentality (choosing what is most profitable or preferable, or considering all to be equally valid), most would agree that child sacrifice or female circumcision is evil. Satanic cults and Trinitarian beliefs are not the same. Every religious belief, ethical practice, or aspect of cultural life mirrors a certain theology. Behind each is an understanding of who God is, and how God relates to human beings. My contention is that every ethic, culture, or religion—which of course overlap and interact with each other—contains a theology by which it is shaped and directed. Theology is queen of the sciences (as Karl Barth once said) because theology gives birth to and qualifies all the disciplines. Thus, when I use the phrase "theological ethics" or "theological culture," I am assuming (1) that there is no ethics without theology, and (2) that a certain kind of theological belief will inevitably produce a certain kind of ethic or culture; e.g., a Confucianist understanding of *tian* (Heaven[79]) leads to a particular ethic of virtue (*de*)—virtue as good habits acquired through constant practice and virtue as power residing in a person endowed from Heaven for harmonious living with others and Heaven.[80] Similarly, the controversy surrounding Paul's letter to the Galatians permits a discussion of this understanding of "theological culture."

↩ Theological Culture

From the standpoint of Paul's opponents, Gentile Christians ought to embrace the Jewish law in addition to embracing Christ as the Messiah in order for them to legitimately become full members of the people of God, possessing in their flesh the symbol of their identity in the commonwealth of Israel. For Paul, such theology is not only insensitive to Gentile culture, it also betrays the work of Christ who has come to liberate all people.

This difference in understanding the truth of the gospel hinges on how culture and theology are to interact with one another. As much as theology is a part of culture, culture is also a part of theology. That is, theological reflection is undertaken and theological beliefs lived out within a dynamic historical process, while cultural processes and social practices reflect the consequent relationship with God. Theology and culture are inseparable. To the opponents, the gospel was a matter of sharing the conviction that a particular "religious" symbol (circumcision) appertains to belonging to the true people of God. To Paul, the opponents' theology is imperialistic (our term) because one would be unable to tell when the required religious observances had become theologically and culturally oppressive to the Gentiles. The law, as defined in Galatians, involves circumcision, sabbath keeping, the observance of food laws and festivals. These are the *nomistic services* that define a Jew from a non-Jew. These nomistic services function both as *religious and as ethnic* identity symbols. When such symbols are required of Gentile Christians, Paul implies, they are as enslaving. How so?

79. See Chapter Two on *tian* (pp. 114–27).

80. Slingerland, trans., *Confucius Analects*, 242 mentions the original Latin *virtus* means power residing in a person, such as the usage preserved in modern English "by *virtue* of his intelligence."

Circumcision and fellowship meals are not simply physical acts, they are also religious and social identity symbols, as Daniel Boyarin rightly argues.[81] Troy Martin also asserts that, "practicing circumcision also means maintaining distinctions between the circumcised and the uncircumcised (Gen 17:14), especially by refusing to engage in table fellowship."[82] Martin translates Gal 6:13a as "those who practice the *distinctions* of circumcision."[83] However, this symbol of distinction and honor to Jews meant castration or "strong sexual arousal" to the Galli of the Phrygio-Celtic people—the Gentiles of Galatia.[84]

"Theological culture" means that a culture reflects its understanding of God since theology and culture are intertwined. Paul's hermeneutic of theological culture is that he judges the validity of personal and communitarian identity in terms of Christ and his works. The notion of theological culture is significant in the case of Galatians because Paul deliberately holds in tension Christ's work of salvation *and* the ethnic identity of the Gentiles. Both freedom/salvation and ethnic identity are rooted culturally *and* theologically. The salvation of God is always contextual and incarnational, thus salvation has its cultural embodiment. Racial identity is often seen as merely cultural, in the sense of having its physical characteristics only. This view is partial. For a society cultural identity also has affinity with the pursuit of truth, allegiance to ideals, and the creation of an ethical system of goodness, beauty, and harmony.

For the Jewish Christians, the "opponents" in Galatia, the problem is that the law constitutes a "sacred culture." What one might say of the Galatian opponents today is that they are ethnocentric and monocultural. Standing within their own culture and looking out, they cannot tell in what areas the law may be theologically *and* culturally destructive to Gentile identity. On the other hand, though, Paul's cross-cultural sensitivity does not enable him to differentiate what is religious from what is cultural, as an apostle to the Gentiles (Gal 1:16), he proposes a cross-cultural hermeneutic that is not hegemonic, because it is centered in Christ.

---

81. Boyarin, *A Radical Jew*, 67.

82. T. W. Martin, "Apostasy to Paganism," 452.

83. Ibid.; emphasis mine.

84. S. M. Elliott, "The Rhetorical Strategy," 506–38.

In fact, his cross-cultural interpretation of the Bible is informed and enlightened by the Risen Christ who confronted him on the Damascus road. We have already seen that Paul's conversion experience (Gal 1:13–17) was life transforming in the sense that it made him conscious of his own past insensitivity as a zealous Pharisee. He had persecuted the Christian church because they had refused to follow the law. The Damascus experience caused him to believe that the Messiah had been crucified as part of the divine plan to include the Gentiles within God's people.

How then does Paul deal with the problem of cultural and religious imperialism? The answer lies in the crucifixion of Christ. Such a christology has a number of theological implications for the identity of Jews and Gentiles. First, Christ was condemned to die as a law-breaker because he did not blindly obey the law. Paul's previous experience as a zealous Pharisee might be attributed to an idolatrous devotion to the law in which love for others took a back seat. The Galatian controversy is on the one hand about upholding the law as an absolute and sacred system and, on the other, about caring for the freedom/salvation of the Gentiles.

Secondly, Paul believes that the crucifixion of Christ has revealed to humanity its fear and insecurity. People put trust in their culture rather than in God for their security and their peace. They boast in themselves and hold tight to their cultural absolutes. Christ crucified is the inclusive symbol devoid of any hegemonic connotations, because the paradigm of Christ is one that deconstructs his own culture. It portrays the shortcomings of any culture, no matter how sacred. Even though circumcision and dietary laws were sacred and valid for the Jews, they were not so (in Paul's understanding) for the Gentiles. Because the Messiah has come, the question of whether nomistic services are valid for the Gentiles had to be ascertained in light of the Christ event itself. Paul believes that Christ is the only and sufficient symbol for the inclusion of the Gentiles into the people of God.

Thirdly, the crucifixion paradigm suggests that no culture can be transformed and renewed without self-critique. The work of critique for the sake of transformation can be challenged by outsiders, but the process has to be carried out by insiders themselves. Paul articulates a theology on behalf of the Gentiles in Galatia, but he also helps his own people engage in critical reflection on their cultural assumptions. Paul explains how the crucified Christ can serve as the identity symbol for

Jewish Christians as well, noting that the crucified Christ fulfilled the requirements of the law.

Does Paul make the law obsolete by his argument that Christ is an inclusive symbol? His reasoning is presented in terms of salvation history. The law's function to protect Jews from assimilation into Gentile culture and to lead them to the Messiah is temporary. Its role is fulfilled once the Messiah has come. In the messianic age, Jesus Christ is the new identity symbol for both Jews and Gentiles, viz., Jesus unites both groups in the new covenant as the people of God while he accepts Jews as Jews and Gentiles and Gentiles. This does not mean that Jews stop being Jews. The law continues to serve as a valid symbol for Jews ethnically (bearing the theological identity as the chosen people of God). To the Gentiles, the *ethnic* function of the law had never been a valid one (which is why they were called Gentiles in the first place, they were outside the covenant), whereas the law's ethical function had to be reinterpreted in Christ, in whom there is now a New Covenant, so that the law of Christ becomes the new law (Gal 6:2). In Galatians Paul argues that the lineage of Gentile Christians goes back not to Adam or to Noah, but to Abraham. It is an argument rooted in the Jewish thought world. Hence, at the end of his letter, he uses the term "the Israel of God" (Gal 6:16) for Galatian Christians—presumably including both Jewish and Gentile Christians.

The ethical function of the law for the Jews had always been operative, and in the age of the Messiah this function needed to be reinterpreted in light of Christ. Thus, Paul does not make the law obsolete for Jewish Christians. Paul reinterprets the law through Christ so that the law would not be imperialistic to Gentiles; it could offer ethical guidance for both Jewish and Gentile Christians.

✎ The Ethics of Holding to Cultural Assumptions

The cross-cultural lens through which Paul critically views his own sacred cultural tradition, transforming it through Christ for the benefit of the Gentiles, is a critical tool applicable to my own reading of the Confucianist culture in which I was raised. The task of appropriating traditional texts, such as the *Analects* and Galatians, in our contemporary era poses a challenging question: How can a cross-cultural and global interpretation of such texts not be trapped by ethnocentrism? I am aware that how I reappropriate these texts for the establishment and clarification of my own identity does not mean it is the only way of being a Chinese Christian. I understand that many Chinese Christians will find John, or James, or Buddhist, or Daoist—or other cultural and religious—texts more prominent for and meaningful in their lives.

Apart from the question of whether to utilize a multiplicity of texts in the formation of one's identity, we need to bear in mind the ethics of our choice. Culture and theology are not value-free entities in a *lazze faire* world. That Paul's opponents preach circumcision and Paul rejects it is indicative of the fact that not all theologies are acceptable. Similarly, for Confucius to promote Zhou-*li* (the ritual propriety of Zhou's culture) and for others to disagree with him is indicative of the fact not all cultural assumptions are equally valid to everyone. To some, the *Analects'* understanding of *wen* (culture) may sound elitist, exclusivistic, if not ethnocentric. But one needs to give a reasoned account of its alleged elitism. Simply because the *Analects* is Chinese does not make it valid or invalid. The criteria of inclusivity and plurality cannot alone determine the correctness of a point of view; otherwise, polytheism becomes a valid religion, and racism becomes a valid way of social interaction. While the *Analects* contains discourses on human flourishing, it does not have a totalizing theory of a global culture. Also, while it presents an ethic of virtue and attempts to argue for it persuasively, it does not seek to conquer other, non-Chinese nations by its supposedly superior Zhou-*li* (propriety of the Zhou dynasty). The rhetoric of the *Analects* seeks to invite readers to participate in the pursuit of virtue, and it uses the rhetoric of consent rather than of domination.

Paul consistently uses the criterion of Christ's salvation for all humanity to define the gospel truth, and Confucius consistently uses the ideal of the virtuous life to define the *telos* (purpose and goal) of ethics. Any thought or action adverse to such a criterion or ideal is rejected. As a Chinese Christian, my work in cross-cultural hermeneutics supports inclusivity and plurality *only in ways* that fit the criteria of Christ's work of salvation and Confucius' ideal of ethics of virtue. Thus, I do not believe that hatred saves a person, I do not accept that violence or war can form virtue in a community.

❧ Culture and Cultured

I have used "culture" and "cultured" in this work to mean "ways of life" and "human flourishings" respectively. My usage hinges on the classical debate regarding the understanding of the word "culture"[85]—in Chinese, *wenhua*. There are generally two broad perspectives of how people look at culture: the first is the humanities school, and the second is the social sciences especially entailing an anthropological perspective.[86]

The humanities school has literary and philosophical roots that trace back to the Greco-Roman understanding of culture as that which "cultivates" virtue, perfection, and excellence in all human endeavors. Confucius' understanding of *wen* as culture shares this perspective. Culture enables the human mind and spirit to rise above the mundane societal norms and expectations to what is excellent, true, and beautiful. In other words, a culture has its *telos* (purpose) in forming a *cultured* people. The means by which human excellence is cultivated is education. The older German usage of *Kultur*, referring principally to high culture, falls within this view; so also does Confucius' understanding of *wen*—and as well as his understanding of *li* (ritual propriety) and *yue* (aesthetic delight).[87]

Matthew Arnold (1822–1888) argued that civilization is different from culture. He was critical of Victorian England's worship of industrialization, machinery, materialism, and progress. Civilization so pursued and so idolized only ends in dehumanization, mindlessness, and the capitalistic reduction of human values. In the name of modernization and progress society may end up in philistinism in which technological advancement not only does not guarantee cultural refinement; it may create in fact, the opposite: Technological advancement, he argued inadvertently, brings about a barbaric and depraved human spirit. Arnold believed that only culture could restore "sweetness and light" (beauty and wisdom) to society and civilization.[88]

---

85. On definitions of culture, see Kroeber and Kluckhohn, *Culture*, passim. The authors gathered no less than 160 definitions of culture used in the social sciences. See also Tanner, *Theories of Culture*, 3–37.

86. Tanner, *Theories of Culture*, 3–15.

87. See Chapter Three (pp. 189–230).

88. Arnold, *Culture and Anarchy*, 48–49.

The humanistic understanding of culture, such as the view advocated by Arnold, gives it a positive perspective and equates it with human flourishing. By contrast, civilization (though capable of providing a society with material advancement) tends to restrain, disharmonize, distort, and jeopardize human flourishing. The humanistic perspective seeks to preserve and *refine* culture through education, artistic events, and cultural archives.

The humanities view of culture can inspire people to aspire to be their best. This view helps us see the possibility of human yearning for goodness, truth, and beauty. This view seeks to preserve virtue and inspire people for excellence. That is why "high" culture is differentiated from popular, mass, or "low" culture. The humanistic perspective, once linked to ultimate concern, to moral excellence, or to the meaning of human existence, works well with theology. The humanistic understanding of culture corresponds to my reading of the Confucian texts on the ethics of virtue.

While the humanities view of culture maybe elitist and too restrictive, nevertheless it has its own criteria for making value judgments, which the sociological view does not. The social sciences or anthropological school is nevertheless also important. It defines culture as the "complex whole" that makes up a society.[89] In the words of Edward B. Tylor: "Culture or Civilization, taken in its wide ethnographic sense, is that complex whole which includes knowledge, belief, art, morals, law, custom, and any other capabilities and habits acquired by man as a member of society."[90] Sociological definitions pack the whole complex social phenomena into its definition of culture, and that each discipline within the school studies culture ethnographically on the field. But it has its own weaknesses. Tanner points out that rarely does a culture exhibit its complex whole.[91] This view of culture tends to explain complexity away too easily, reducing theological aspects into sociological ones.

The strength of the sociological understanding is that culture is not always the prestigious preserve of intellectual elites, it is also the ways common peoples live their daily lives.[92] Each society has its own culture:

89. See for example the usage of culture by Tylor, *Primitive Culture*, 1:1.

90. Ibid.

91. Tanner's helpful critique of modern understandings of culture in her *Theories of Culture*, 38.

92. Culture is not only something to be found in professional writing, the science

its own patterns of belief; its own ethical practices, values and ways of life; its own institutions; etc.—all of which are formed and reformed in the changing dynamic of the historical process.[93]

This broad understanding of culture by the social sciences may avoid the ethnocentrism inherent in the humanities-based viewpoint. Yet, lumping all human experience, activities, and thinking under the rubric "culture," as in some sociological views, is simply too broad a definition and makes this view of culture less useful as an analytical device. The sociologist's assumption that each culture has its own legitimating way of life should not be distorted. Yet how would one explain the burning of wives with their deceased husbands without critiquing it as evil? How would one explain child sacrifice without pointing out the fallacy of the religious assumption on which it is based? Or, to use a more contemporary example, how does one justify the devaluation of women within the spectrum of human rights? Wherever these practices were considered acceptable, it took a prophet to point them out as evil. A prophet is a person who sees things beyond the cultural limits and is able to preach something new. His is a word against cultural blindness and expectation, so that change takes place. In other words, a cross-cultural critique is necessary for any culture to transform its limits and is inherent evils. Though Confucius and Paul are pre-modern persons, they understood the beauty of a world of differences, and they also believed in inspiring their audience to be their best and to confront sin and evil where they found it.

Theological Ethics—Ethics and Theology

The intertextual reading of the *Analects* and Galatians reveals the first connection between theology and culture. The second connection is between ethics and theology.

The shared concern of the *Analects* and Galatians lies in their concern for the formation of a community rule that leads to freedom, integrity, and harmony. As a Chinese Christian, I find that Confucius' ethical

---

lab, art museum, concert hall, and archival library; it also includes those creative human activities found in popular magazines, on refrigerator doors, in churches and subway stations. It includes folklore, story telling, and talks at social gatherings.

93. See Tanner, *Theories of Culture*, 38–58.

teaching can be enriched by Paul's understanding of God's Spirit—as that which gives birth to and enables the ethical life. But I also find the ethical reading of Paul's letter to the Galatians to be helpful, because Galatians is often read as theology without ethics. Here, I see the intertwined relationship between theology and ethics in both texts; this relationship is what I call "theological ethics." I use the Confucian notion of *de* (morality or virtue) in reading Paul's understanding of God's Spirit; I use Paul's understanding of the Spirit as the initiator of ethics when reading Confucian *de*. In Gal 3:1–5 God's Spirit is not just a moral force. It is God who works miracles among the Galatians because they have heard the gospel and believed.[94]

Both Confucius and Paul believe that the good life is governed not by violence but by virtue. Both understand the power dynamic behind all human relationships, be they rulers or common citizens, Jews or Gentiles. The notion of ruling with virtue is paradoxical. The virtue of the ruler is seen to be such a persuasive force that subjects are expected to be obedient. Subjects obey not because of physical force, but because of the superior virtue of the leader. In the case of the Galatian controversy, the question arises: Could Jewish Christians have expected Gentile Christians to submit to Jewish propriety because the former understood the law to be the means of virtue formation in their own lives and in the lives of the Gentiles? We can translate this question into a general enquiry: Is one not free to do good to others in order to gain goodness for oneself? In Confucian social ethics, self-denial on behalf of others is a means of gaining virtue for oneself. It is also the means by which society arrives at peace, even though the motive involved is ultimately self-serving, that is, for the sake of self-cultivation. However, Confucius' notion of *de* (virtue) explains the effect of morality on both the actor and the recipient of *de*.

✧ *De* and Moral Force

The semantic domain of *de* in the *Analects* is often politics. *Analects* 2:1 reads: "Those who rule with *de* (virtue) are like the North Star that is seated in its place yet surrounded by a multitude of stars."[95] In the realm

94. See Cosgrove, *The Cross and the Spirit*, 39–50.
95. My translation of the *Analects* 2:1. See Qian, *Lunyu Xinjie*, 29–30; Chen, *Lunyu*

of politics *de* refers to the magnetic force of the virtuous ruler, who guides the nation through the power of his moral excellence without exerting physical force. To speak of a good emperor is to speak of the emperor's *de* inspiring the people to serve the country. In his work on ancient Chinese philosophy, A. C. Graham aptly translates *de* as "potency."[96] Arthur Waley, in his study of *Daodejing*, translates the phrase as "The Way and Its Power." He defines *de* as moral force or moral persuasion, a kind of psychic power over or influence upon others.[97] Norden also has a similar understanding of *de*:

> *De* was from very early on (perhaps originally) a sort of charisma or power a king has over others, which causes them to willingly follow him, without the need for physical coercion. This charisma was associated with good character; hence, it can be thought of as almost a 'moral force' which radiates out from a good ruler, ensuring obedience.[98]

By extension we can say *de* is a moral act that has religious or spiritual force. The classic example of *de* in Chinese political ethics is found in the story of King Zhou (Di Xin) of Shang dynasty, King Wu of Zhou dynasty, and later in the Duke of Zhou dynasty. When the infamous King Zhou, the last ruler of the Shang dynasty, was defeated by King Wu in 1040 BCE, it was said that King Zhou did not live a virtuous life therefore lost the Virtue (*de*), the power from the Lord on High to rule the people. The Lord on High gave the mandate to rule to the Zhou dynasty.

From the time of the Shang dynasty (1783–1122 BCE), there had been a tradition that rulers and diviners were to offer sacrifices to Heaven (*tian*) and to the spirits of their ancestors so that peace and prosperity might be ensured for all "under heaven" (*tianxia*).[99] There were cases when a king offered himself as a sacrifice to the spirit world in order to heal the illness of others, but because of the king's act of compassion

---

Duxun Jiegu, 12; Yang, *Lunyu Yizhu*, 23.

96. Graham, *Disputers of the Tao*, 13–15.

97. Waley, *The Way and Its Power*, 24.

98. Norden, ed., *Confucius and the Analects*, 21.

99. The word *tianxia* occurs in the *Analects* 23 times. In the early usage, the term *tianxia* probably does not refer to the world, but to the inhabitants of the civilized world (*huaxia*), the barbarians (*yidi*), and the animals.

his virtue increased and his own life spared.[100] *Shangshu* (the *Book of History*) tells the story of King Wu and his younger brother Dan, known as the Duke of Zhou, regarding his demonstration of *de*, the compassionate virtue that moves *tian* (Heaven) to bring about the blessing of all. King Wu was taken ill in the second year of the conquest of the Shang dynasty. Dan performed divination and offered his life to the spirits in return for the King's recovering from illness. In his analysis of this story David Nivison concludes that it was not the burnt offerings themselves (his divination), but the fragrance of the kings' *de* that was pleasing to the spirits. As he writes, *de* "appears to be a quality or psychic energy in the king that the spirits can perceive and are pleased to see in him; and it appears to be something he gets, or something that becomes more evident in him when he denies or risks himself, does something for another—for another human being. . . ."[101] Nivison continues,

> The idea is repeated over and over in Zhou bronze inscriptions and in early literature: the king must 'reverently care for his 'virtue'—*jingde*. . . . The king must seek to occupy a role defined as a *de*-manifesting role. As one adviser to a king in a *Shangshu* chapter tells him, 'as king you must rest your position in the primacy of your 'virtue.' And yet the king is to do this in all religious humility, with no pride in being 'virtuous.'[102]

Nivison cites the bronze vessel made by a nobleman, He, who listened to King Zheng's address to his officials at the newly founded capital city Luoyang of the Zhou dynasty:

> Even though you are only junior princes, surely we can expect that you will emulate [your] princely [fathers] in the noble status they earned in Heaven's regard, attending dutifully to Heaven's bidding and caring reverently for the sacrifices! Help [me] the king to uphold [my] virtue, so that Heaven will make me compliant when I am not earnest.[103]

This aspect of royal virtue is the spiritual force that moved Heaven (*tian*) to bless him, that engendered self-denial on the part of the king in the first place, and caused all to emulate him in his compassion. This aspect

---

100. See Nivison, *The Ways of Confucianism*, 23.

101. Ibid., 24.

102. Ibid., 26.

103. Ibid., 27; Nivison's translation.

of royal virtue (*de*) is a popular idea in ancient China. "A king with 'virtue' listens to advice; wise counselors are attracted to his service. A king without 'virtue' spurns advice."[104] A virtuous king is "self-denying—in this case ego-denying—and so is self-restrained."[105] A king without *de* is "self-assertive, arrogant, and guilty of other forms of unrestraint, including violence, lust, and cruelty."[106]

The *Analects* asserts that the power of persuasion lies not in military forces but in *de*. Nivison cites the example of Duke Huan of Qi and his minister Guanzhong in their confrontation with Chu. The Chu envoy told Guan Zhong: "If your lordship . . . by your virtue (*de*) seeks the tranquility of the states, who will dare not to submit to you? But if you depend on your strength, our state of Chu has the mountains of Fancheng for a wall and the Han River for a moat. Great as your multitudes are, you could not use them."[107] The *Analects* recounts how Confucius counseled Ji Kangzi not to employ capital punishment, for "If you desire what is good, the people will at once be good. The *de* of the superior [Ji Kangzi] is wind. The *de* of the people is grass. Let the wind be over the grass and it must bend" (*Analects* 12:19).[108]

✧ The Paradox of Virtue

In ancient China, a king was expected to embody the spiritual power of *de*. He performed sacrificial duties, the spirits were grateful and persuaded by his moral influence; the spirits in turn granted the king greater virtue. In effect, the king got his virtue/*de* from the spirits. What if a king knew the *dao de*—the way of virtue—so that he offered sacrifices in order to manipulate the spirits? There is no guarantee that the spirits would respond favorably, or even whether the spirits would respond at all when sacrifices were offered. When one made sacrifice in order to use the spirits in selfish or wrong ways, *de* was already absent from that person. "The

---

104. Ibid., 29.

105. Ibid.

106. Ibid.

107. Ibid., 25.

108. Qian, *Lunyu Xinjie*, 439 states that the virtue of the leaders is responsible for the actions of those below.

favorable response of the spirit is approval of the *de* I already have, and my religious performances are acts of maintenance."[109]

How does one practice *de* without desire for selfish gain, power, repute, or substance? Nivison gives three solutions to this "paradox of virtue." The first is practicing *de* in secret, such as the Duke of Zhou offering his life in secret to the spirits, and the myth states that this secret was known only after his death. Similarly, Tai Bo being the oldest son of the dynasty founder (Tai Wang), Dan Fu, willingly gave up his right of succession to his younger brother's son—the later Wen Wang. Confucius praised Tai Bo for attaining the highest degree of *de*, and then for absenting himself so that no one could praise him.[110] The second way of practicing this paradox of virtue is in doing good to the extreme so that no one could match or repay it with another virtuous act. The story of Houying is a good example. After first ignoring the invitations and gifts of Prince Wuji of Wei, Hou Ying finally accepted a gift with such impoliteness as to cause the prince maximum embarrassment. By doing this, Hou Ying sacrificed his own *de* and enhanced that of the Prince. However, once his act was understood, Hou Ying had lifted his own *de* and become *shangke*, the distinguished guest.[111] The third way is to practice *de* without thinking of gaining *de* at all.[112]

✤ *De* as Mutual Indebtedness

In the time of Confucius the word *de* did not refer just to the quality of a good ruler, but also to *any* good person to whom Heaven had given protection and courage in fulfilling Heaven's will. For example, when Confucius was traveling through Song state with his disciples, he was almost killed by Huan Tui, the brother of his own disciple Sima Niu. Fortunately, Huan Tui was not successful in his attempt to kill Confucius. Confucius' response to Huan Tui's threat was: "Heaven granted me *de* (moral force), what can Huan Tui do to me?" (*Analects* 7:23).[113] Whether for Confucius *tian* (Heaven) is personal or impersonal, it is implied

---

109. Nivison, *The Ways of Confucianism*, 26.

110. See *Analects* 8:1.

111. See *Shiji* 1:77.

112. Nivison, *The Ways of Confucianism*, 35.

113. My translation. See Yang, *Lunyu Yizhu*, 160 on the identity of Huan Tui.

in this verse that *tian* bestows upon him gifts such as moral force and protects him from harm. *Analects* 9:5 also tells of another threatening incident when Confucius encountered the men of Kuang city. Besieged, Confucius said that though Wen Wang (King Wen of Zhou, father of King Wu) was dead, Confucius' participation in the culture (*wen*) of Wen Wang had not ended, that Heaven had given Confucius the task of being involved in and contributing to this culture through Zhou's *li* (propriety) (cf. *Analects* 19:22).[114]

Another way of explaining *de* is in terms of its relationship to government and *wuwei* ("natural" or "effortless" action), which is a prominent theme in the *Analects*.

✏ *Zheng* (To Govern) and *Wuwei* (Natural or Effortless Manner)

Because Confucius thinks of government as a form of ruling by means of virtue *(de)* rather than by force, he believes that "a ruler achieves order [by means of] '*wuwei*.'" Confucius uses the example of Shun (2257–2205 BCE)—a sage ruler before the Xia dynasty (2205–1783 BCE)— as the exemplary ruler of "*wuwei*." Confucius asks a rhetorical question: "What is there to do but to assume a deferent posture and to sit on the throne facing south?" (*Analects* 15:5)[115] In other words, simply *let it be,* allowing one's virtue to affect its natural course of getting things done. Though the words *wuwei* literally mean "doing nothing" or "non-action," they mean "not asserting," "effortless action,"[116] or "refraining from activity contrary to nature."[117] Daoism has an elaborate explanation of *wuwei*. In the *Analects* (Books 2 and 10, 14:13, 8:18–19, 12:19, 13:6, 15:5, and 17:19) *wuwei* refers to action that "is spontaneous, unselfconscious, and perfectly efficacious."[118] Slingerland writes, "The state of *wuwei* represents a perfect harmony between one's inner dispositions and external move-

---

114. See Chen, *Lunyu Duxun Jiegu*, 154; Yang, *Lunyu Yizhu*, 194–95 on the meaning of *wei* as threat.

115. My translation.

116. Slingerland, trans., *Confucius Analects*, 176, 243.

117. Joseph Needham translated *wuwei* as "refraining from activity contrary to nature" (*Science and Civilisation in China*, 2:68) as he used Zhuangzi to justify his definition on p. 69: "Non-action does not mean doing nothing and keeping silent. Let everything be allowed to do what it naturally does, so that its nature will be satisfied."

118. Slingerland, trans., *Confucius Analects*, 243.

ments—effortless and free of strain—as well as a state of harmony between the individual and Heaven, which means that a person in he state of *wuwei* also possesses virtue [*de*]. In the political realm, *wuwei* refers to ruling by means of Virtue [*de*]."[119] Confucius' ideal of government is a ruler who has so united his power with virtue that all the people under heaven (*tianxia*) willingly pay him respect. The use of physical force is indicative of bad government, the unpersuasiveness of the ruler's virtue, hence the need to impose that which lacks virtue. *Analects* 2:1 uses the metaphor of the North Star to speak of governing properly by means of *de* (virtue). The people are then like the multitude of stars paying tribute to the ruler.[120] Another example: When Confucius wanted to go live among the nine clans of barbarians, he was asked how he would deal with their crudeness. Confucius replied, "When an exemplary person (*junzi*, one's best–self or the virtuous person) lives among them, will there still be crudeness?" (*Analects* 9:14).[121]

⋄ *Zheng* (To Govern) and *Zheng* (To Correct)

We have mentioned already Confucius' conviction that: "The moral force of a leader is like the wind that bend the grass as it blows" (*Analects* 12:19). To govern is to lead, and to lead is to shape a virtuous humanity, beginning with oneself. To lead or to rule takes more than power and more than skill in the art of administration. *Analects* 3:19 mentions the rites that rulers, such as Duke Jing, must follow in ruling and leading the people, and dutifulness that ministers, such as the Three Families of Lu, must have in serving the Duke. Here Confucius is speaking to Duke Ding, who is "the kind of ruler who 'held the blade of the sword and offered the handle to his enemies,' therefore Confucius wants him to protect himself by means of ritual. The Three Families were the type of ministers of whom one might say, 'the tail is wagging the dog,' and therefore Confucius wishes to instruct them in the ways of dutifulness."[122]

119. Ibid. Qian, *Lunyu Xinjie*, 551 interprets *wuwei* as a ruler does nothing because of his wisdom in appointing the right persons to do the job needed done.

120. My translation. See Qian, *Lunyu Xinjie*, 29–30.

121. My translation.

122. Slingerland, trans., *Confucius Analects*, 25 on the context of *Analects* 3:19. The Three Families are Jisun, Mengsun, and Shusun, whose wealth and power exceed that of the Duke of Lu. See Chapter Six (pp. 364–66) on proper relationship between a ruler and

According to Confucius, to govern is to correct oneself (*Analects* 12:17, see also 12:18, 13:13). In Chinese the words "govern" (*zheng* 政) and "correct" (*zheng* 正) can be used interchangeably. The scholar Wejen Chang writes,

> From his [Confucius's] various remarks on government we get the impression that to be correct [*zheng*] a ruler must have certain attitudes and take certain responsibilities. First of all, he should 'rectify the names'—establish a set of standards [*Analects* 13:3]. Then he should conduct himself with dignity [2:20]. He should be filial to his parents and kind to his children [13:3]. He should be respectful to the worthy and tolerant to the masses [2:20]. He should reward the good and be sympathetic toward the less able [2:20]. He should observe the rites and be righteous and trustworthy [19:3]. . . . He should never cruelly impose penalties without attempting first to reform the people, never expect results without first giving warning, never be slow in giving orders but quick in demanding the meeting of a deadline, and never be miserly in rewarding the people [20:2]. He should realize that while it is not easy to be a subject, it is more difficult to be a ruler, and he should never take satisfaction as ruler from the mere fact that his words are never disobeyed [13:15].[123]

We have seen thus far that Confucius' political ethics sees the goal of government in cultivating and benefiting the people. His political ethics advocates that kings rule by their virtue. It is an ethic grounded upon the mandate of Heaven (*tian*) that rulers honor Heaven by their rule. What then is the significance of the *de* of the common people? As a moral force *de* carries the reciprocal meaning of mutual indebtedness and mutual appreciation. Confucius not only democratized his political ethics, he also redefined *de* as the fundamental psychic configuration of being human. Nivison's study of *de* helps explain this concept well,

> The feeling of a debt of gratitude for a kindness or gift or service is something we all know. It is part of being human. But in some societies it is greatly magnified, in countless ways, by socialization and social pressure, until it comes to seem to be an ambient psychological force. Chinese society is like this [ideally]. . . . When you do something for me or give me something, a compul-

---

his ministers according to Confucius' thought.

123. Chang, "Confucian Theory of Norms and Human Rights," 123.

sion I feel so strongly that I come to think of it not as a psychic configuration in myself, but as a psychic power emanating from you, causing me to orient myself toward you. That power is your *de*—your 'virtue' or 'moral force.'[124]

We shall expand this idea of the mutual indebtedness of *de* in Confucius' understanding of *ren, zhong,* and *shu* later. For the moment, let us use the Confucian understanding of *de* to interpret the Galatian polemic.

⊕ Judaizing Gentiles, Jerusalem Leaders, Paul's Mission and *De*

Reading Galatians by way of Confucius can be enlightening. Though Paul is not talking about the political ethics of kings, his discussion of the role of the Spirit of God in the lives of believers is about the *rule* of God. We will discuss at length in the next chapter how Paul is aware of the political ideology of the Roman Empire, and that his proclamation of the gospel is in subtle ways a critique of Rome's domination and violence. Since Paul is concerned with presenting an alternative vision of the true community, one ushered in by God's Spirit, then his discussion of the Spirit does imply an ethical choice: Be aligned either with the force that is spiritual or the force that is physical.

The tactic employed by Paul's opponents in Galatia of forcing Gentile Christians to submit to the requirements of Jewish law is analogous to Rome's political strategy of military domination. To pressure others into conformity is akin to domination by force. Paul contends that the true but surreptitious (*kataskopēsai,* "to spy") motive of the false brethren was to bring Gentile Christians into "bondage" (*katadoulōsousin*), thus robbing them of their freedom in Christ (Gal 2:4). "The truth of the gospel" has to do with freedom (see *eleutheria* in 3:28; 4:22, 23, 26, 30, 31; 5:1, 13) in Jesus Christ. The opponents' insincere motives, bewitching tactics, and surreptitious demeanor, as well as their hypocritical behavior reveal their own insecurity—the uncertainty of their own identities. In short, by dominating others, they also entrap themselves in bondage—not being able to live freely, having to live in falsehood and insincerity.

In his letter to the Galatians Paul adamantly opposes to those who require circumcision, because (1) their piety is false ("they do not themselves observes the law," 6:13), and (2) it is "enslaving," i.e., it forces Gentile

124. Nivison, *The Ways of Confucianism,* 25.

believers to become what they are not—becoming Jews through circumcision, food laws, observance of special days. In the language of Confucius, the opponents and false brethren are not practicing *de* (virtue).

Even when there is a problem between certain false brethren and Paul, the Jerusalem apostles affirm the mission of Paul and Barnabas (Gal 2:6–10)—that is, they exhibit *de*. In the understanding of *de*, compassion is basic to political virtue, the goal of which is harmony (*Analects* 13:23). In describing his Jerusalem support, Paul points out that (1) "those considered to be reputable" (*ton dokountōn einai ti* in Gal 2:6; note Gal 2:2 has "*tois dokousin*," presumably referring to the same group) "did not *impose* anything upon" him, that is, there is agreement between Paul and the apostles of repute; (2) the Jerusalem apostles had recognized Paul's gospel and God's grace in his calling (Gal 2:7–9a); (3) these reputable apostles had given Paul and Barnabas the right hand of fellowship even after they understood the *different* callings of Paul and Peter; (4) the apostles have mutually agreed on a division of labor among themselves (Gal 2:9c), that Peter should preach to the Jews and Paul to the Gentiles; (5) the Jerusalem apostles had requested that Paul as representative of Gentile Christianity, remember to support the Jerusalem poor (Gal 2:10). This reciprocal respect and support is indicative of the mutual indebtedness of all human relationships, which is the essence of *de* in Confucius' understanding.

Paul does not need his gospel or his call to be authenticated by the Jerusalem apostles. Nevertheless, Paul feels compelled to go up to Jerusalem so that his missionary preaching might not be in vain (Gal 2:2). So Paul is also exhibiting *de* (virtue) by not making a unilateral decision to get his way. Gal 2:6–10 lists the three requests the apostle agrees to, suggesting that *de* is fundamental to Paul's relationship to the Jerusalem apostles.

First, God is impartial in his love even though his call of different apostles pertains to differing ethnic groups. God is One and people are many. God's impartiality eventually works its way out to reach all humanity. God's impartiality (see Rom 2:11) means that his grace is given to all who are called to, or who are entrusted with (*pepisteumai*; see 1 Thess 2:4) purposive life. So Paul is entrusted with "the gospel of uncircumcision" and Peter "the gospel to the circumcised" (Gal 2:7). Theology necessitates ethics; it encompasses ethics. God's impartiality requires the recognition that no one is complete without another. As the poet John Donne says, "No man is an island entire unto itself."

Second, even if their mission seems to be directed toward two different groups, the apostles still have *koinōnia* (communion) with one another. The phrase "right hand of *koinōnia*" (1:9; see also Phil 1:5) is equivalent to the modern handshake by which collegiality, friendship, or mutual esteem is conveyed. This unity (fellowship) in diversity (ministry) between Paul and the other apostles points to the Oneness of God. "The one who worked" through Peter (God) also worked through Paul (Gal 2:8). There is only *theological* ethics. Hence the (ethical) life of the believing community must mirror God's reality in their midst. Human relationships are theologically based, *de* is grounded in *dao* and *tian*.

Third, the Jerusalem apostles understood and accepted Paul's mission to the Gentiles, but they asked that Paul and Barnabas remembered the poor. The poor were those who utterly depended on God because they were deprived of human support, such was the case with some Jerusalem Christians. This plea was not something imposed on Paul; it was something Paul was eager to do (Gal 2:10). Indeed, Paul was seriously committed to taking a monetary offering to Jerusalem (Rom 15:25–33; 2 Cor 8–9; 16:1–4). Paul's determination to help the Jerusalem poor was more than a humanitarian concern. Rather, the offering again suggests the Oneness of God, i.e., God is the Lord of Jews and Gentiles. From an ecclesiological perspective, the offering also meant that the two bodies, Jewish and Gentile Christians, were united in the gospel of Christ. This cross-ethnic *koinonia* further implied the legitimacy of the gospel of Christ for the two peoples. The mutual support between Jewish and Gentile churches confirmed the legitimacy of the gospel preaching by both the Jerusalem apostles and by Paul. As Confucius noted whenever virtue or moral force (*de*) is demonstrated to benefit the less-powerful, the whole body is built up.

The remark in Gal 2:6 ("what they were then makes no difference to me") suggests by its polemical tone that something has changed. The polemical tone expressed here surely refers to the inconsistency of the Jerusalem apostles regarding fellowship with Gentile Christians. These apostles had withdrawn from such fellowship when they themselves were pressured by Judaizers. Unfortunately, unity between Jew and Gentile, between Paul and the Jerusalem apostles was never fully achieved. As Paul J. Achtemeier writes:

It is clear from Paul's report of his dispute with Peter, and ultimately with Barnabas and 'the rest of the Jews,' that he did not
fare well in that encounter. The dispute was not resolved in his
favor . . . . Following that dispute, Paul lost Antioch as his power
base and, as Acts itself indicates, had to move further and further
west to find room for his missionary activity. Yet even there he
was hounded by opponents, ... The one chance that remained to
Paul to restore the unity between himself and Jerusalem was the
agreed-upon collection for the poor (Gal 2:10). . . . Yet even here,
as Paul had feared (Rom 15:30–31), he met with no success. . . .
[H]is offering was not accepted and he was in fact not delivered
from 'the unbelievers in Judea' (Rom 15:31). . . . Thus that elusive
unity for which Peter yearned and which Paul sought to achieve,
which James attempted to preserve and which Luke labored to
portray in his account of the primitive church—that unity in fact
was not achieved.[125]

⊷ God's Spirit, the Cross, and *De*

In Galatians, Paul's first use of "Spirit" is at 3:2. Paul is convinced that the
activity of God's Spirit in the Christ event has resulted in the creation of
the new people of God at the end of time. This new people of God is born
by the Spirit who comes not through the law but through the preaching
of Christ crucified. This point is made with great emphasis in Gal 3:1–5:
The Galatians came to faith by hearing the gospel, not by doing work;
their "coming to faith" had been the "work of the Spirit." There are many
biblical references that point to the gift of God's Spirit to the Gentiles at
the end time for the purpose of their salvation. This Jewish perspective
appears with the prophets of the Old Testament. It expresses a universalist theology in which Gentiles are included in the salvation plan of God
(see Acts 2:17–21; Joel 3:3–15; Isa 2:2; 10:45). Paul's understanding of the
Gentiles' reception of God's Spirit is based on the Jewish prophetic and
eschatological tradition that the Messiah will come to save the Gentiles at
the end of time, and that the sign of the end will be the gift of the Spirit.
The account of the Jerusalem Council in Acts 15 provides corroborating
evidence to this view. Here Peter informs his Jewish colleagues about the
conversion of the Gentiles to Christian faith: "God who knows the heart

125. Achtemeier, "An Elusive Unity," 24–26.

bore witness to them [the Gentiles], giving them the Holy Spirit just as he did to us; and he made no distinction between us and them, but cleansed their hearts by faith [in Christ]. Now therefore why do you make trial of God by putting a yoke upon the neck of the disciples which neither our fathers nor we have been able to hear? But we believe that we shall be saved through the grace of the Lord Jesus, just as they will" (Acts 15:8–11).

In Gal 3:2, 5, Paul asks his misguided audience two rhetorical questions containing the same antithesis: works of the law or hearing with faith. The six rhetorical questions in Gal 3:1–5 expresses Paul's utter frustration and disappointment with his readers who, he believes, are abandoning the reality of God's Spirit in their midst—the very reality they had once so powerfully experienced. The six questions underscore the absurdity of the opponents' unethical tactics (they have acted without *de*) and the way the Galatian Christians have fallen under their spell. Paul's public preaching demonstrates his willingness to proclaim the truth of the gospel. To respond to the gospel of Christ is neither a matter of "personal choice," nor a matter of falling under a "spell," it is a conviction arising from the public portrayal of God's love in Christ crucified.

Paul is also convinced that the persuasiveness of the gospel of Christ is grounded in the public portrayal of God's work in Christ, especially in the death of his Son, the Messiah (3:1). From a Confucian Christian's perspective this is the divine paradigm of *de*, Christ the embodiment of *de*—the image of God in humanity, the self-sacrificing virtue, the moral force of compassion, the essential element in human relationships.

As it is interpreted by Paul, the Cross of Christ fulfills the Confucian ideal of *de*, since the moral force or power of virtue derived from and endowed by *tian* (Heaven). And the death and resurrection of Christ, as well as the giving of God's Spirit at the end of time, suggests that God makes plain the nature of divine/human bonding by means of Christ's work, centering on the Cross.

A CHINESE CHRISTIAN ETHIC OF VIRTUE

Theological Ethics and Moral Choices

Even though Confucius' *tian* (Heaven) and Paul's *Theos* (God) are not exactly the same (see next chapter), I have argued that *ethics* in both the Confucian and Pauline traditions is always *theological.* In socio-religious matters like the Antioch incident Paul refers to (Gal 2:11–14), I use the term "moral choice" to refer to the decisions the Judaizers made, and the ways they lived their lives. The Antioch incident shows the problem inherent in the opponents' coercive tactics (6:12–13) and of Peter's vacillation regarding fellowship with Gentile Christians (Gal 2:12). Both actions represent concern for Jewish identity. The issue was how to include Gentiles in the people of God. They had to make moral choices, and they revolved around rules of food and fellowship in a community of difference.

As Paul struggled with what had occurred in Antioch he may have reflected on his own conversion experience. That experience also involved a "moral choice." It involved Paul's view of the law and whether he would persecute or accept followers of Christ.

Paul's experience is a microcosm of what Christ means to the law and to Jewish identity (and therefore Gentile identity as well). It is significant that in Galatians Paul argues for Christ as the identity symbol not just for Gentile Christians, but also Jewish Christians. Paul does not argue for "works of the law"—their function is exclusivity. Paul believes that the Messiah has come; he brings a new world order, one in which God calls upon all people to become children of Abraham through the one seed of Abraham—Jesus Christ. The temporary role of the law is superseded by Christ and the Spirit (cf. Gal 3:14). Paul also believes in newness of life, when one does not just get rid of the law, but reinterprets it in light of the crucified Messiah. The spirit of the law now takes on new life in the Spirit-filled community of the people of God.

The Antioch incident also enables Paul to see that a gospel limited to one group (whether Jews or Gentiles) would be a distortion of the true gospel. One sees this in the agreement arrived at by the Jerusalem Council (Acts 15: 20, 29). What is expected of the Gentile Christians is made clear; but what is asked of Jewish Christians? Nothing is mentioned. The Antioch incident had shown that when Jewish and Gentile believers entered into table fellowship, the diversity of their symbols of identity was bound to clash.

I want to propose that despite the fact that many of the ethical and theological problems raised in the *Analects* and in Galatians involve moral choices, the two books are not about "crisis ethics" or "decision-making ethics." They are about *theological ethics*. They are about the social dimension of being human, that is, about interconnectedness and the necessity of living for the sake of the common good.[126] Life forces us to make moral choices, but there is a subtle difference between making decisions at the crossroads and living virtuously as a way of life.

The kind of western ethical education I received was often preoccupied with moral choices, with making decisions at the crossroads. Whether, for example, to have an abortion, or to endorse capital punishment, or to approve certain sexual lifestyles, or to use military force preemptively. These were some of the dominant issues I was asked to resolve in my Theological Ethics course in seminary. These are the issues that still dominate moral discourse at my place of work. Because so many attendant factors are left unaddressed, the legal consequence of the various choices often becomes the heat of the debate. Ethical discussions, when pursued in this way, are often hijacked by lawyers or obfuscated by simplistic answers rather than thought through in a comprehensive way by moral philosophers whose conceptual framework ought to lead us to look at ethics more broadly and deeply. A moral philosopher of Confucian ethics, Teemu Ruskoka, recognizes how Confucian ethics can help enrich modern Western moral philosophy:

> While Western moral philosophy more often than not tends to dissociate itself from the prosaic business of finding a morally viable *modus vivendi* and concerns itself with lofty ends and universalizable maxims instead, Confucius advocates a way of *living* and thereby implicitly recognizes that the choices between the means in our every-day lives are of profound moral significance. The means are, in the most concrete sense, the end as well.[127]

I use the Confucian concept of virtue, which I call "the ethics of virtue," to underline ethics *as* virtue and to highlight moral identity, as well as its accompanying "community of character,"[128] as the goal of virtue cultivation. I use this understanding of an ethics of virtue in reading Galatians 5–6 while paying attention to the theme, *freedom as the common good in a pluralistic community.*

126. See Aristotle's *Nicomachean Ethics* (A commentary by Joachim) Book 10, 9. Numerous articles have been published in recent years on comparing Confucius with Aristotle. For a good secondary source on Aristotle's ethics, see Macintyre, *After Virtue,* passim.

127. Ruskola, "Moral Choice in the *Analects,*" 294.

128. See Hauerwas, *A Community of Character,* passim; Kotva, *The Christian Case for Virtue Ethics,* 16–47.

The Ethics of Virtue and Doing Good for Goodness Sake

Readers who are familiar with Aristotle's ethics of virtue will note parallels in Confucian ethics: Aristotle's concern for the *polis* (community),
his identification of *eudaimonia* (blessedness or happiness) as the good in
being human, and his belief that virtue forms the basis of social harmony
and justice are similar to Confucian ethics.

Lee H. Yearley argues that in Confucian ethics, virtuous behavior
is not only acquisitive but also expressive of ethical action.[129] In other
words, virtuous behavior acquires the ethical good for the sake of the
good itself, knowing that such action will contribute to the good, and
that doing good is a means of acquiring it. Virtuous behavior expresses
the good knowing that it is the good thing to do. Ultimately, what matters
is the good that is expressed, rather than the benefit or profit of doing a
good deed—since the result is often not evident. Even without receiving
some return for their good works, good persons still pursue good works;
for them virtue (*de*) is the way (*dao*) of life. Yearley writes,

> A person appropriates or chooses a way of life (and, thus, a set of
> personal qualities) that, for her or him, defines the good life and
> thereby constitutes flourishing. . . . [O]ften one [i.e., human flour-
> ishing] whose form changes as circumstances change. . . . [So the
> need to reaffirm] will always rest on the good that is expressed,
> not on the benefits that will or could be produced.[130]

Such is the kind of ethics of virtue Confucius was teaching. A wise person will choose the way of benevolence/humaneness (*ren*): "The Master
said, 'Of neighborhoods benevolence is the most beautiful. How can a
man be considered wise who, when he has the choice, does not settle in
benevolence?'" (*Analects* 4:1)[131] The benevolent person will keep doing
good in easy and difficult situations. "The Master said, 'One who is not
benevolent cannot remain long in straitened circumstances, nor can he
remain long in easy circumstances.' 'The benevolent man is attracted to
benevolence because he feels at home in it. The wise man is attracted

---

129. Yearley, "An Existentialist Reading of Book 4 of the *Analects*," 258.

130. Ibid.

131. Lau, trans., *Analects*, 29. See also Qian, *Lunyu Xinjie*, 111–12; Chen, *Lunyu
Duxun Jiegu*, 46; Yang, *Lunyu Yizhu*, 75.

to benevolence because he finds it to his advantage'" (*Analects* 4:2).[132] A benevolent person is at home with virtue, he does good for the sake of the good. The benevolent person has the moral will to like or dislike others. But ultimately, it is in setting her heart on benevolence that grants her freedom. *Analects* 4:3: "The Master said, 'It is the benevolent man alone who is capable of liking or disliking other men.'"[133] *Analects* 4:4: "The Master said, 'If a man were to set his heart on benevolence, he would be free from evil.'"[134] Yearley's reflection on *Analects* 4 is worth our attention here. He writes,

> [E]xpressive virtue differs fundamentally from acquisitive virtue and that distinction helps us understand the characteristics of different kinds of people. The lowest levels of people (small people or lesser people) will have virtually no understanding of expressive virtue and will only pursue profit (4:16), . . . Higher levels of people, categorized as the wise, will pursue virtue, but because they recognize it is to their advantage to do so (4:2, and perhaps 4:14). What distinguishes the virtuous, however, is that they seek virtue as an end in itself, a goal that needs no further justification (4:2, 5, 14, 16). Moreover, they understand that, in fact, virtue may not produce some benefits, such as position and good food (4:9, 14), but that finally those benefits do not provide them with fully adequate goals and may even need to be surrendered.[135]

Joel J. Kupperman has argued that despite the emphasis on "a person's special relationships and connectedness with others" in current feminist ethics and recent ethics of virtue, what Confucian ethics can contribute toward filling the *lacuna* of western ethical theories is the "systematic account of how people could self-consciously attempt to integrate personal style, connectedness with others, and virtues into a way of life that would both be worth living on a minute-by-minute basis and also be civically useful."[136]

132. Lau, trans., *Analects*, 29. See Chen, *Lunyu Duxun Jiegu*, 46–47; Yang, *Lunyu Yizhu*, 76.

133. Lau, trans., *Analects*, 29. See Chen, *Lunyu Duxun Jiegu*, 47; Yang, *Lunyu Yizhu*, 76.

134. Lau, trans., *Analects*, 29. See Chen, *Lunyu Duxun Jiegu*, 47; Yang, *Lunyu Yizhu*, 77.

135. Yearley, "An Existentialist Reading of Book 4 of the *Analects*," 259. Cf. Slingerland, trans., *Confucius Analects*, 29–38.

136. Kupperman, "Naturalness Revisited," 40.

The ethics of virtue is what Fingarette calls *dao*, "A Way without a Crossroads," in his *Confucius—Secular as Sacred*.[137] There is only one right set of values, choosing is not the issue, rather "discovering which is the true Path [*Dao*]" is the task. "We need only make the tacit assumption that there is a Way, a self-consistent, self-authenticating way of universal scope."[138]

Just as Confucius was true to the *tiandao* (Way of Heaven), so was Paul to the gospel of God in Christ. We are now dealing with the different understanding of the ultimate concern between Confucius and Paul, viz., *Theos* (God) and *tian* (Heaven)—a topic we will begin in the next chapter. Despite the different starting points, the theological ethics of Confucius and Paul share the same commitment of fidelity to the ultimate concern. Confucius regards virtue as gift of Heaven, and therefore being human is to accrue virtues in a natural way through cultivation. Paul does not see union between nature and nurture possible in Christian life, he regards virtue as fruit of the Spirit. We will discuss this topic in chapters Five and Six. I want to conclude this chapter on the intertextuality of the *Analects* and Galatians by reading Galatians 5–6 using the Confucian virtue ethics.

The Ethics of Virtue, Coexistence of All, and the Common Good

Paul's description of freedom and the Christian person, found in Galatians 5–6, has provided a platform for modern Western ethical reflection, which has tended to postulate the notion that human beings are caught in a conflict between the human spirit and human flesh. Depending on the path they followed, human beings are destined to produce the fruits of the spirit or the fruits of the flesh. As a young believer, I was taught that Galatians 5–6 is about the inner struggle of the Christians, because the soul (and the divine component of the self) is trapped in the body of flesh (earthly and carnal existence). I was terrified to learn that becoming a Christian meant having to choose between spirit (both the human spirit and God's Spirit) and the flesh. The conflict between "desire" and "will" was thus heightened and intensified. I acknowledge the long theological controversy in Western Christianity regarding the freedom or the

137. Fingarette, *Confucius—The Secular as Sacred*, 18–36.
138. Ibid., 24.

bondage of human will, dating at least to Pelagius (free) and Augustine (bound), Erasmus (free) and Luther (bound). I was taught that Christians do not live in a spiritually or morally free zone, that in every moment of their lives they are forced to make a decision either for God's Spirit or for human flesh. This, I now believe, is a Gnostic reading of life, and I want to discuss in the following two main problems with such a reading.

First, Paul's theological anthropology does not view the human flesh as sinful or evil—an anthropology that Confucius can concur.[139] He does accept the impotence of moral judgment in human beings absent God's Spirit, and he accepts the reality of the binding force of the "evil age" (Gal 1:4) as well as the controlling power of Sin.[140] A brief survey of the word *sarx* (flesh) in Galatians indicates that it is an anthropological term with the following possible meanings: (a) human existence in the neutral sense ("all flesh" [1:16], "flesh and blood" [2:16], "live in the flesh" [2:20]); (b) human existence under the dominion of the cosmic elements, or under the dominion of sin which is in opposition to, or a consequence of the absence of, the Spirit (3:3, 6:13; 4:23; 5:13, 16, 17, 19, 23; 6:8); (c) symbolic reference to circumcision ("the flesh" in 4:13–14 [2x], "in flesh" in 6:12). In these three meanings, there is no indication at all that Paul holds to the view that human flesh in and of itself is sinful or evil.

Secondly, although in Galatians Paul never discusses the existence of an ethical "free zone," throughout these chapters his juxtaposition of flesh and Spirit may suggest to later readers that human beings are morally free persons. However, this suggestion is erroneous, for we are *not* created merely to be free, that is, we are not created to be independent selves and we are not independently capable of making decisions without the influence of others. That is why as a young Christian, I was frustrated to the point of giving up, because the harder I tried to make a decision for my spirit (in which I assumed God's Spirit dwells), the more miserable I became. My Confucianist propensity was to be diligent in living a virtu-

---

139. See Chapter Four (pp. 254–61).

140. Sin is used with a capital S to refer to the realm and power of sin and sin's capacity to make people to be less than human. Thus, all human beings are: sinners (Romans 3; all human beings are equal in their religious [idolatry] and moral [immoral] predicament), in the realm of death (Romans 5; all are children of Adam), in bondage to Sin (Romans 6), and all reveal their bondage by their own evil acts (Rom 1:18–32, 6:23; cf. 5:12–13). They are above all victims, "sold under sin" (7:14). Sin is perceived as a personified ruling power or tyrannical lord-ruler (*basileuei* in Rom 5:21 and 6:12; *kyrieusei* in 6:14) which makes all human beings "captives," enslaving them (*douleuei* in 6:6; *douloi* in 6:17, 20).

ous life for God (Heaven). Yet, the anxiety of always trying to do my best seemed to hinder God's Spirit at work in me. This is where Paul's theology of God's Spirit of grace at work in believers offers constant critique to Confucian ethics of virtue. I was so relieved to discover that God's Spirit dwells not just in my spirit, but also in my body, my flesh, for I do not *have* flesh and soul, body or spirit, *I am* a bodily soul, I am a soul-filled body. I discovered that Paul was concerned not just with our own freedom, but also with the freedom of others, and the freedom of a pluralistic community.

While most commentators identity the last two chapters of Galatians as parenetic,[141] or exhortational material,[142] many have difficulty seeing how the last two chapters (5:13—6:10 particularly) fit into the whole argument of the letter (especially with 1:11—4:31). There are even scholars who see the last two chapters as interpolations by a later redactor.[143] Following Barclay and Esler,[144] I read the last two chapters of Galatians as a continuing clarification of the truth of the gospel begun as early as 1:11.[145]

The argument between Paul's gospel of faith and the opponent's gospel of works revolves around whether Christ or the law—or the rituals of Zhou dynasty for Confucius—grants a life freed from evil and bondage. Paul's opponents could easily have convinced the Galatians that the law and all its works granted life, since all the precepts were prescribed in detail. After Paul describes the temporary function of the law in salvation history—as well as the sufficiency of Christ in granting a life of righteousness and freedom (Galatians 2-4)—he still has to prove how life in Christ can guide the *ethical life* of Jewish and Gentile believers. Moreover, after Paul has shown that the Gentiles are included in the covenant of Abraham

141. Dibelius, *From Tradition to Gospel*, 238.

142. Betz, *Galatians*, 282–83.

143. On interpolation theory, see Barclay, *Obeying the Truth*, 9–23 for a quick summary.

144. Esler, "Group Boundaries and Intergroup Conflict in Galatians," 215.

145. Scholars such as Lull (*The Spirit in Galatia*, 113–30), Brinsmead (*Galatians— Dialogical Response to Opponents*, 163–85), and Howard (*Paul: Crisis in Galatia*, 11–19) have seen the last two chapters of Galatians as integral parts of the whole argument in Galatians, but they read Paul's response as against the law theology of the opponents. It is true that Paul's response is at times reactive to the opponents' theology, but Paul's argumentation in Galatians are not limited to that. Barclay's research is helpful in this regard (*Obeying the Truth*, 216–20).

and have become heirs of God through the endowment of the Spirit, he still has to prove that the Spirit guides the communal life of God's people in an ethically vital way without the help of the law. Thus Gal 5:13—6:10 is a continuation of Paul's preceding proof. Here he explains how God's Spirit guides God's people to live *in unity and in freedom*. If this *moral* dimension of the gospel were either absent or inadequate, Paul's theological argument in Gal 1:11—4:31 would be unrelated to the real world. But the argument in 5:13—6:10 is practical and exhortational, it is also theological and Christ centered, and it fits within the framework of salvation history. Paul contends that freedom in Christ is the purpose of our redemption from the present evil age. In other words, whether Christ or the law should best symbolize the identity of the people of God is ultimately to be determined by the virtuous life of the community. Virtue without freedom is not virtue; it is compulsion. And freedom without the fruit of the Spirit is not freedom, but licentiousness. Christ's work of salvation is to bestow upon the community God's Spirit, so that the community bears the fruit of the Spirit. And the fruit of the Spirit is manifested by "love, joy, peace, patience, kindness, goodness, faithfulness, gentleness, self-control"—behaviors exhibited in the life of a virtuous community (Gal 5:22–23).

A Chinese Christian interpretation of the *Analects* and Galatians concludes that God's Spirit is the initiator of virtue (*de*), and that Christ's work shows human beings the divine paradigm for being a community. Christ's community lives out the virtuous life by imitating Christ and yielding to the Spirit. The Spirit grants freedom and out of that freedom comes the fruit of the Spirit. This is a Chinese Christian reading of the *theological ethics* of Confucius and Paul.

2

Theological Ethics in a World of Violence

I understand that Confucius and Paul have grave differences. Confucius' desire to recover the Golden Age of the Zhou dynasty is different from Paul's eschatological proclamation of salvation in Christ. Confucius' ethics is incommensurable with Paul's theology. Confucius' interest in the political world is radically different from Paul's interest in the new age of Christ. Confucius' Heaven (*tian*) is not the same as Paul's God (*Theos*). All these differences can be traced to the etiological understandings of the universe. Paul believes that God is both Creator and Redeemer of the world. To Confucianist Chinese the universe is a "self-contained and self-operating organism."[1] The universe and all therein was not created. Joseph Needham rightly states that the Confucian worldview believes in "the harmonious cooperation of all . . . [as] all parts in a hierarchy of wholes forming a cosmic pattern, and what they obeyed were the internal dictates of their own natures."[2] The "Laws of Nature" in thinking of the Christian West indicate the wisdom of a Supreme Creator. This line of thinking remains an alien concept in Confucius' China.

In the past the discussion of the differences between Confucian and Christian worldviews bred contempt, even hostility. In his essay,

---

1. Bodde, "Harmony and Conflict," 20.

2. Needham, "Human Laws and Laws of Nature," 230, cited in Bodde, "Harmony and Conflict," 20.

"What Does Heaven Say?" Robert B. Louden recounts how Christian Wolff, professor of theology at the University of Halle, was dismissed and condemned by the king of Prussia because of his 1721 lecture declaring Confucius to be a "prophet or teacher, given to us by God."[3] Today we are beginning to recognize that difference is a blessing, not a curse. Differences can attract and not just repel. Thus, I want to work with the differences between Confucian ethics and Pauline theology and see how their alleged incommensurability can enrich each other.

COMMENSURABILITY: *TIANMING* IN CONFUCIUS AND GOD'S WILL IN PAUL

Religion, Zongjiao, Jia, *and Piety*

In Western Christianity it is quite common to distinguish theology from ethics, faith from works, doctrine from practice. In Chinese cosmology, however, these sets of seemingly bipolar concepts are intentionally held in tension so that the fluidity between them is maintained.

In the earliest forms of Confucianism, Daoism, and *yin-yang* world-views were ways of life practiced as "schools of thought" (often influencing each other), and were only later institutionalized, becoming "religions." At their inception these schools of thought were lived-out realities; their emphasis was always on the practical and ethical dimensions of *being human*—although intellectual rigor was not rejected. A life of study and a life of ethical and religious freedom, it was thought, went hand in hand. The pursuit of learning is for the sake of living in freedom.

After becoming a Christian, I continued to use this ethical understanding of "religion" in living my Christian faith. For me, to know God is the beginning of a free and happy life. "Knowing" God involves the intellectual comprehension of and a relationship with God. Of course, it is not the human capacity to "know" God that counts, rather knowledge of God is predicated on divine revelation. It is *God's knowing us* and God's self-revelation to us that make it possible for us to know God. Noting this

---

3. Louden, "'What Does Heaven Say?'" 73–93. For the original text, see Wolff, *Oratio,* 18–19 (in Latin and German). The sentence "What does Heaven say?" has its source in the *Analects* 17:18: "The Master said: 'What does Heaven say? Yet the four seasons revolved and a hundred things grow. What does Heaven say?'" (see Huang, *Analects,* 170).

distinction Paul qualifies his observation that the Galatians "have come to know God, *or rather to be known by God*" (Gal 4:9).

In his language about God, Paul is explicit. Confucius is implicit. The latter's emphasis upon knowing the intention of *tian* (Heaven) is for the sake of ethics. Most Chinese schools of thought have the same ethical posture, and have often been misunderstood as purely humanistic. But these schools of thought rest on cosmological assumptions and religious presuppositions. The Chinese have a functional view of "religion," and they perceive truth as practical wisdom. In Chinese cosmology theology and ethics are fused together.

In Chinese the word "religion (*Zongjiao*)" is a later development of the traditional concept of "school/family (*jia*)."[4] *Zong* means ancestral tradition, *jiao* means teaching or education; when the word *jiao* is used alone, as in *Rujiao*, it is difficult to decipher whether it refers to Confucianism as a religion or as an educational system based on ancestral teaching; most frequently the latter meaning is intended. The pictograph *jiao* portrays a teacher holding a staff giving instruction, thus stressing the authority of the instructor. *Zongjiao* denotes ancestral teaching. Tradition and history conjoin to prove the ancestral teaching's credibility and usefulness.

Jia literally means family, and it is an older term than *zongjiao*. *Jia* denotes a group of instructions or a school of teaching that has authority over one's life. *Jia* stresses the familial structure and tradition of Chinese communities. The *family* is considered the basic unit or social grouping. It is so basic that larger social groups are modeled after it; a country is called *kuojia*—national family.

The word "Confucianism" is a Western neologism, created by the Jesuit missionary who treated the teaching of Confucius and his followers as a religion. In Chinese, *rujia* or Confucian school or family of teaching, and *rujiao* or Confucian Learning or Confucian Religion are standard terms. Neo-Confucians in the Post-Sung period (Yuan [1280–1368], Ming [1368–1662] and Qing [1662–1911] dynasties) called this school *rujia daoxue*—the Study of the Way. In the modern period, the Confucian scholars Tu Weiming, Liu Shu-hsien, and Cheng Chungying have argued for the *religious* dimension of the Confucian tradition, and they

---

4. The English word "religion" may be traced to the Latin word *religare*, which refers to the bond between God and human beings. See Chiu, *Tao of Chinese Religion*, 2. On the debate about the religiosity of Confucianism, see Chen, "On the Rhetoric of Defining Confucianism as a 'Religion.'"

use the word Confucianism in that sense.[5] According to Mou Zongsan, Confucianism is a "moral religion" (*daode zongjiao*) or "moral spirituality" (*daode jingshen*) in that it sees ritual and music as sacred ways of self-cultivation and realizing *ren* (humaneness) as knowing Heaven (*zhitian*).[6] Mou argues for the moral quality of *ren* (benevolence) as the basic human nature and the basis of communal life.[7] *Ren* is moral awareness or the "character of humanity as a creative agent and not a mere physiological type or class of being. . . . This effort, this persistence in the face of the powers of privatized materialization is how Mou defines Confucian spirituality."[8] My reading of the Confucian texts and thoughts is similar to the interpretations of these scholars, some of them have strong conviction to use Christian theological frameworks to reread Confucian thoughts.[9]

Because of Confucius' preoccupation with political ethics, many categorized him as a humanist with no awareness of religiosity; this is inaccurate. Worse still, Confucius is said to be "antireligious," as allegedly evident in those "antireligious texts" of the *Analects* (5:13, 6:22, 7:21,

---

5. See Berthrong, *All Under Heaven*, 189–207. In the modern period, scholars such as Tang Junyi (T'ang Chün-I), Qian Mu, Chen Shihchuan, Hsü Fu-kuan and Mou Zongsan, as well as their students Liu Shuhsien, Cheng Chungying, Julia Ching, Tu Weiming, Antonio Cua, Yü Ying-shih, and Ts'ai Jen-hou have also used the word "Confucianism" (or *rujiao* in Chinese) to speak of the religiosity of *rujia*.

6. Mou, *Xinti Yu Xingti*, 1:22–23. In another book, *Shengming De Xuewen*, 88–89, 119, Mou refers to Confucianism also as a "humanistic religion" (*renwen jiao*) and its distinctiveness is the subjectivity of the heart. See also Mou, *Zhongguo Zhexue De Tezhi*, 16–27.

7. Mou, *Xinti Yu Xingti*, 1:14, 17.

8. Berthrong, *All Under Heaven*, 117. On the religiosity and transcendence of Confucianism, see Mou's articulation, as explained by Berthrong, *All Under Heaven*, 103–31. See Mou, *Xianxiang Yu Wuzishen*, passim, and his *Xinti Yu Xingti*, 1:144.

9. There are three generations of scholars of New Confucianism in the twentieth century. The first-generation scholars are Ma Yifou, Xiong Shili, Zhang Junmai, Liang Suming, and Fung Yulan who do not think Confucian thoughts are concerned with religious matters. I disagree with them. I side with the second- and third-generation scholars. The second-generation scholars (Qian Mu, Fang Dongmei, He Lin), especially Xu Fuguan, Tang Junyi and Mou Zongsan employ the theological and philosophical perspectives found in Western metaphysics to explore the religious dimension of Confucianism. They believe that Confucianism is an "ethical religion" or a "humanistic religion." The third-generation scholars of New Confucianism include Cai Renhou, Cheng Chungying, Liu Shuhsien, Tu Weiming. They see their works as ushering in a third epoch of Confucianism. These scholars seek interreligious dialogues between Confucianism and other world religions, and advocate Confucianism to learn from Christian theology. See Liu Shuhsien, *Rujia Sixiang Yu Xiandaihua*, 310.

11:12).[10] I used to think the text, "The Master does not talk about extraordinary things, feats of strength, disorder, and gods" (*Analects* 7:21).[11] meant that Confucius rejected religion and did not want to discuss religion. I now think Confucius was merely *cautious* about gods, fasting, war, and sickness (7:13)[12] for fear of fostering superstition and being religious without ethical integrity. As James Legge suggests, Confucius is "unreligious rather than irreligious."[13] Louden argues that Confucius does not speak on matters of death and advocates keeping a distance from gods and ghosts (6:22, 7:21), not because Confucius does not believe in these things, but because of his practical ethics, as opposed to speculative philosophy: "Speculative chatter would only detract people's attention away from the more fundamental moral task of deciding how to live and act."[14] *Analects* 11:12 does record Confucius' saying that, "If you don't know how to serve people, how can you serve the spirits? . . . . If you don't understand what life is, how will you understand death?" but such sayings are not antireligious as some suggest. Confucius' priority is to express religiosity in terms of its socio-political reality. Wisdom dictates that people keep an appropriate distance from spirits and earnestly attend to ethical responsibilities toward others (*Analects* 6:20). The tradition of his day required staying in good terms with the "stove spirits," but Confucius says that one who sins against *tian* (Heaven) will have no gods to pray to (*Analects* 3:13). Confucius had his own religious life. When he was ill and his disciples prayed to "*tian* and earth" on his behalf, Confucius responded that he had been praying for a long time (*Analects* 7:34). He also participated in sacrifice rituals (2:5; 3:17), which were also a part of religious practices.

Confucius lived in an age when superstition dominated people's lives. His rational tendencies critiqued these archaic supernatural beliefs, but he also retained "those ritual practices as an aesthetic, moral, political, and spiritual foundation."[15] Hence, much of the religious tradition of the past held true for Confucius, such as ritual and sacrifice.

10. See Liu, "On Confucius' Attitude Toward Gods, Sacrifice, and Heaven," 16–27.

11. Superstitions and bizarre spiritual forces and exploits and disorders are not the scope of Confucius' discussion. See Qian, *Lunyu Xinjie*, 250.

12. See Chen, *Lunyu Duxun Jiegu*, 114.

13. Legge, trans., *Confucian Analects*, 99.

14. Louden, "'What Does Heaven Say?,'" 80.

15. Rosemont, Jr., "On Confucian Civility," 192.

Tian, Tianming: *Heaven and the Mandate of Heaven*

Concerning Confucius' religious worldview, H. G. Creel writes, "If we look for a firm and frankly stated conviction on the part of Confucius as to things religious, we shall find it most clearly in connection with *tian*, Heaven."[16] It will be shown that Confucian ethics emphasizes *tianming* (mandate of heaven) rather than *tian* (heaven).[17] In the Chinese language *tian* has multiple meanings, similar, perhaps, to the word "god" or "heaven" in English. Chinese script has no analogy to the usage of capital letters in English to indicate a proper noun. Thus, it is difficult to tell if *tian* refers to the cosmic heaven or to Heaven as God.

First, *tian* can refer to the sky, without necessarily telling the audience what the speaker means by that word, or whether he or she believes in the personhood or creative power of "sky." It is common to hear in conversations "*wo de tian*" ("my heaven" or "my god"), expressing disbelief or ridicule, as is the case in English language. This meaning of *tian* is used twice only in the *Analects* (7:19, 8:19).[18]

Secondly, *tian* communicates its will through the four seasons and through things coming into being (*Analects* 17:19). Ames and Rosemont suggest that *tian* occasionally refers to all things: "*Tian* is both *what* our world is and *how* it is. The 'ten thousand things (*wanwu*),' an expression for 'everything,' are not the creatures of a *tian* which is independent of what is ordered; rather, they are constitutive of it. *Tian* is both the creator and the field of creatures. There is no apparent distinction between the order itself, and what orders it."[19] *Tian* "is wholly immanent, having no

---

16. Creel, *Confucius*, 116, also his *Chinese Thought*, 35–36. Schwartz has the same view, *The World of Thought in Ancient China*, 122.

17. Qian, *Gongzi Yu Lunyu*, 194.

18. Yang, *Lunyu Yizhu*, 12; Slingerland, trans., *Confucius Analects*, xvii: "Early graphic forms of *tian* seem to picture a massive, striding, anthropomorphic figure, who is from the earliest times associated with the sky. Hence 'Heaven' is a fairly good rendering of *tian*, as long as the reader keeps in mind that 'Heaven' refers to an anthropomorphic figure—someone who can be communicated with, angered, or pleased—rather than a physical place."

19. Ames and Rosemont, *Analects*, 47. The assumption of *tian* as the creator and the field of creatures is the self-contained universe. Jiang Wenye mentions that in the *Classic of Changes*, *tian* is defined as the beginning of all things, including the earth. Jiang, *Confucius On Music*, 38. Mou, *Xinti Yu Xingti*, 1:21–23 discusses the quasi-personal *tian* and *tian* as the "metaphysical reality."

existence independent of the calculus of phenomena that constitute it."[20] This would still put *tian* in an "unreligious" but not necessarily "antireligious" category.

Though the word *tian* as used in the *Analects* does not provide a precise and elaborate sense of what it means (Fingarette),[21] Eno and Louden argue that its use in the *Analects* is fairly consistent and clear.[22]

Thirdly, as to the question "Does *tian* speak?" (*Analects* 17:19), Confucius thinks *tian* does not need to use speech to be creative; *tian* by being natural is awesome and therefore respected by all the sages (16:8); *tian* has intentions (9:5, 3:24); *tian* possesses understanding (14:35, 9:12); as, more importantly, for Confucius *tian* is the source of moral power, of rightness and principle, as seen from the following texts—but *tian* is not a personal Being *and* it does not have a redemptive narrative with the world:

> (1) *Analects* 7:23 tells of Confucius, besieged in Song, when Huan Tui, the Minister of Military Affairs wanted to kill him. Confucius said, "*Tian* has bestowed virtue upon me, what can Huan Tui do to me?" (*Analects* 7:23).

> (2) *Analects* 9:5 records either the same incident or a similar one. In both Confucius states his conviction that *tian* has protected him to preserve the culture (*wen*) of King Wen (1099–1050 BCE): "King Wen has died, but his cultural heritage still exists with us. If *tian* were to let that legacy die, then we latecomers would not have that culture. But if *tian* is not going to destroy this culture, then what can the people of Kuang do to me?"[23]

---

20. Hall and Ames, *Thinking through Confucius*, 207.

21. See also *Analects* 3:24. Fingarette, *Confucius—The Secular as Sacred*, 62; similarly Hall and Ames, *Thinking Through Confucius*, 208. See also Qian, *Lunyu Xinjie*, 107–8; Chen, *Lunyu Duxun Jiegu*, 154.

22. Eno, *The Confucian Creation of Heaven*, 84, though on p. 96 he qualifies this remark by saying that the *Tian* (Heaven) Confucius believed in might not be the one found in the *Analects*. Louden argues that "the *tian* passages do form a consistent whole, one from which we can reliably infer both that Confucius was a strong religious believer in a controversial sense, and that his moral orientation was itself dependent upon his religious outlook" (Louden, "'What Does Heaven Say?'," 77). This is basically what my published position in *What Has Jerusalem to Do with Beijing*, 122.

23. These references are taken from Louden, "'What Does Heaven Say?'," 78.

(3) *Analects* 8:19 speaks of the greatness of *tian* and how sage king Yao modeled his life upon *tian*.[24]

(4) In *Analects* 9:6, a government official queries Zigong about Confucius, whether he possessed many talents and is a sage. Zigong replies that *tian* has lavished upon his Master sagehood and many talents (9:6).

(5) There is an incident in the County of Yifeng in state of Wei when a frontier warden wanted to speak to Confucius. The warden, an anonymous person, was a gifted person but had been assigned the humble position of keeping watch at an outpost of the state. He told the disciples of Confucius not to lament the lowly position of Confucius in the state of Lu, because the empire had long ago lost its Way. *Tian* would use the Master as a wooden bell (3:24). Huang, a commentator of the *Analects*, explains that the bell was actually "a bronze [bell] with a wooden tongue, used to . . . assemble the multitudes when the emperor had a decree to proclaim or saw a need to edify the people; a metaphor signifying a great teacher of the people."[25]

(6) Confucius admits to Zigong that many do not understand him, but if there is anyone, it will be *tian* (14:35).[26] Either *tian* is a personal being or there is a certain kind of personal relationship between *tian* and Confucius that consists of understanding and respect. The same text speaks of Confucius never blaming *tian* but of respecting *tian* (*jingtian*).[27] *Analects* 2:4 speaks of Confucius knowing the mandate of *tian* (*zhitianming*).

(7) *Analects* 11:9 says that *tian* abandoned Confucius in the death of his beloved disciple Yuan Hui. Yuan Hui's death means that there will be no successor to Confucius to continue his Way of humane government. The idea that *tian* blesses and curses is found in Confucius' thinking. When Zilu is angered by Confucius' visit to the licentious wife of Duke Ling of Wei (Nanzi), Confucius

---

24. Just as *tian* rules "without the need for words" (*Analects* 17:19), King Yao's virtue rules without force (cf. *Mencius* 7a.13; see Legge and Yang, trans., *The Four Books*, 400–1). Slingerland, trans., *Confucius Analects*, 84.

25. Huang, *Analects*, 66.

26. See Qian, *Lunyu Xinjie*, 526.

27. See also *Analects* 16:8 on *junzi* respecting *tian*.

says to Zilu that if he has done anything wrong, let *tian* abandon or curse him (6:28).

(8) When one offends *tian*, there is no one else one can pray to (3:13).[28] The word "offends" in Chinese is "sin," used in the Chinese Bible. But "sin" in the *Analects* does not refer a broken relationship with Heaven; rather, it speaks of moral violation of Heaven's mandate.

(9) *Analects* 9:12 speaks of the impossibility of deceiving *tian*.

We can assume that there was a belief in ancient China before and during the period of Confucius regarding a transcendental Being called *Tiandi*.[29] The worship of *Tiandi* in the Xia, Shang and Zhou dynasties was expressed in the religious aspects of ritual, music, politics, and ethics. Notably, ethics and politics are not simply humanistic in ancient China. In fact, *Ru*, as in Confucianist Schol (*Rujia*), are religious teachers, not simply moralists. An excavation at Anyang in 1899 unearthed more than 100,000 pieces of oracle bones of ox scapula and tortoise shells that refer to divination practices in the Shang dynasty (1783–1045 BCE). The diviner—in most cases the Shang king himself—consulted the spirits of the ancestors of Shang for answers and intercessions regarding the political decisions (such as warfare and ceremony), natural events (such as flood or irrigation), and social life (such as marriage or health) of the people. There is evidence that Chinese people at that time believed in the Supreme Deity called *di* (the Lord) or *shangdi* ("the Lord on High"). "The ur-ancestor known as the 'Lord on High' seems originally to have been a nonhuman god who gradually came to be viewed as the first human ancestor of the Shang people, and therefore—by virtue of seniority—the most powerful of the ancestor spirits."[30] Emperors in later Chinese history adopted the title of *huangdi* (King the Lord), believing that their positions as kings on earth mirrored that of the Supreme Deity in Heaven (*tian*), and that they had the divine right to rule. Kings communicated with *di* through shamans (*wu*), skillful craft-men (*shu*), and scholars (*shi*);[31] *ru* (Confucianist) was one of these groups of religious professionals. *Di* or

28. See Chen, *Lunyu Duxun Jiegu*, 35–36.
29. He, "Zhongguo wenhua de gen yu hua," 53.
30. Slingerland, trans., *Confucius Analects*, xvi.
31. Thompson, *The Chinese Way in Religion*, 36–38.

shangdi was believed to be the Benefactor and Judge of the human world. Since the Shang dynasty, *di* or *shangdi* was thought to be the ur-ancestor of the Shang people. It was thought that the spirits of the ancestors could intercede for the descendents in the presence of *shangdi*. In Confucius' day, "worship and war were the two most important affairs of the state, and worship of the ancestors was set even above war as a determinant factor of the fate of a nation. Ghosts were diligently worshiped and reverentially feared."[32]

The Zhou people had their own tribal god called *tian* (Heaven), and *tian* eventually replaced the Shang high god "Lord on High" (*shangdi*). "Heaven possessed all of the powers of the Lord on High and in addition had the ability to charge a human representative on earth with the 'Mandate' (*ming*) to rule."[33] Heaven (*tian*) became the Supreme Deity in Zhou dynasty. Confucius did not reject the religious traditions of Shang and Zhou altogether. He never developed the worship of *di*; his foci are on *tian*, the Creator and Being of moral order (thus rituals and virtues), and on the ethics of family (thus ancestor worship). This shift of Confucius makes from deities to *tian* (Heaven), and from fear to intellect (*zhi*) and sincerity (*cheng*) does not mean that he rejected the belief of Deity and became an atheist.

He Guanghu is convinced that ancient Chinese worldview is theistic, because of some evidences regarding the understanding of *tiandi*, *huang-tian* as the supreme being, the ultimate order and source, creator and sustainer of the universe, final judge and rewarder, and revealer.[34] However, the work, personality, and revelation of *tiandi* in ancient Chinese texts are either illusive or minimum. Thus, *tian* is often understood as lacking strong personality and story with the people. Ames and Rosemont are correct in explaining that:

> The God of the Bible, often referred to as metonymically "Heaven," *created* the world, but *tian* in classical Chinese *is* the world. *Tian* is both *what* our world is and *how* it is. The "ten thousand things (*wanwu*)," an expression for "everything," are not the creatures of a *tian* which is independent of what is ordered; rather, they are

32. Ibid., 5.

33. Slingerland, trans., *Confucius Analects*, xviii.

34. He, "Zhongguo wenhua de gen yu hua," 35. He Guanghu is convinced that Christian theology has much to offer to Confucianism regarding the personhood of *Tian*.

constitutive of it. *Tian* is both the creator and the field of creatures. There is no apparent distinction between the order itself,
and what orders it. . . . *Tian* does not speak, but communicates
effectively although not always clearly through oracles, through
perturbations in the climate, and through alterations in the natural conditions of the human world.[35]

Though Heaven can communicate, it does not speak; Heaven has
will and does care for the creation, but it acts naturally without direct involvement with humanity. Heaven will reward or punish, but its actions
are mysterious. For Confucius "inner virtue is not always rewarded with
external goods, which means that, the true servant of Heaven should focus
solely upon his virtue and leave its recompense to fate [*ming*] (4:9, 4:14,
4:16, 11:18, 12:4–5, 14:36; 15:32."[36] For many people *tianming* (mandates
of Heaven) as their *fate* (*ming*) can be a nihilist or fatalistic idea, because
they understand their fate as predetermined by Heaven. Mandates of
Heaven (*tianming*) are heavenly rules and moral principles that one must
simply accept. Not to accept Heaven's mandates is to disrupt the natural
order of things. One is able to accept the mandates and to respect *tian*
because *tian* is the source of benevolence, and *tian* is omniscient and
thus cannot be fooled (*Analects* 9:12). In Christian theology, one speaks
of the sovereign will of God as predestination but not predeterminism
(Rom 8:28–30), of God's will as salvation and sanctification but neither
damnation nor ethical despair (1 Thessalonians 4), and of God as Love (1
John 4:8; Rom 5:8).[37]

Despite *tian's* naturalistic being and movements, Confucius transforms the meaning of *tian* and its mandate into a moral principle of
goodness and beauty. Confucius also transforms the mandate of Heaven
from a political idea to a moral privilege of all people. In the *Analects*,
tian is mentioned directly seventeen times, of which ten are spoken by
Confucius and seven by others. Interestingly enough, in these ten uses
of *tian*, Confucius employs the familiar term "I" in relation to *tian*. An
analysis of this usage by Sung-Hae Kim reveals that what Confucius is
doing here is to transfer the "mandate of Heaven" (*tianming*) from being
the highly political prerogative of the ruling family to one universally

35. Ames and Rosemont, *Analects*, 47–48.
36. Slingerland, trans., *Confucius Analects*, xxiii.
37. See Yeo, "The Rhetoric of Election."

appropriable. That is, Confucius seeks to democratize the elitist and political mandate of *tian* so that everyone can cultivate selfhood and attain
the virtuous life.[38] Confucius envisioned everyone empowered by the
mandate of *tian*, which had been modeled by the sages of past dynasties.
Confucius emphasizes that the sage rulers are to be virtuous, providing
an example for others to follow, and thereby bring about the renovation
of society.[39] Unfortunately, his legacy was often ignored, and the opposite
existed among the ruler-cult of later dynasties, which was then maintained as the status quo.

From this examination of *tian* and *tianming* in the *Analects*, I can
now agree with Louden that Confucius is "religious but not theistic."
Louden explains: "I do not see any evidence that Confucius' *tian* is anything like the 'personal God' of the Western religions. . . . Confucius'
tian is clearly not [simply] a naturalistic concept but a religious one . . .
though it is not very much thought of anthropomorphically.'"[40] I agree
with Louden in maintaining that "dualism between naturalism and religion," or between theology and ethics, is not a helpful way of reading
Confucianism. Louden writes,

> Why couldn't *tian* for Confucius be both a naturalistic and re-
> ligious concept? *Tian* is not transcendent in the sense of being
> above or outside of nature, *in the way* that Western religions con-
> strue God. Rather, *tian* is part of the cosmos itself and thus natu-
> ralistic. But *tian* also serves as the ground of moral norms, and
> the wise feel a sense of awe in contemplating it. In this latter sense,
> *tian* is both transcendent and religious.[41]

---

38. Kim, "Silent Heaven," 195–96.

39. See *Great Learning* 1:1 (Legge and Yang, trans., *The Four Books*, 2–3). *The Doctrine of Mean* likewise states that if a sage-ruler knows how to cultivate his own character, he will know how to govern other people (20:11; see Legge and Yang, trans., *The Four Books*, 46–47). In the West, at least in Greek antiquity, a philosopher-king was the ideal ruler.

40. Louden, "'What Does Heaven Say?'" 79. Similarly, Tang Junyi argues that Confucianism is both transcendent and immanent at the same time, both sacred and secular:
"In Confucianism the individual . . . is expected to practice the utmost sincerity, like
spiritual beings, and to become aware that his own mind is nothing other than the mind
of Heaven; that man is a Heavenly man, and that there is no god outside him." Tang Junyi
speaks of the religious spirit of Confucianism, "Wo duiyu zhexue yu zongjiao jueze,"
8:186–87, 204–5.

41. Louden, "'What Does Heaven Say?'" 91, n. 33.

It is in light of this understanding of *tian* that Confucian tradition (especially that of Mencius) often speaks of *tianren heyi*, meaning either politically the divine right of rulers over their subjects as the mandate of heaven or ethically the fulfillment of the mandate of heaven as in one's cultivation of virtues.

Confucius' understanding of *tian* is not that of a Pauline understanding of God. Paul's understanding of "God's will" (Gal 1:4) is distinctly Christo-centric in that Christ's self-surrender is seen as delivering humanity from its bondage to the present age. Paul has no understanding of ethics as the cultivation of its virtues without the help of God's Spirit; Paul's theology of God and human beings is expressed clearly in narrative and history. But in both Confucius and Paul, the Transcendent, be that God (*Theos*) or Heaven (*tian*), has communicated his mandate or will, which has something to do with saving humanity or cultivating humanity *toward becoming human*. To respect and revere *tian* in one's path toward becoming fully human is, in Paul's language, to grant "glory to God" (Gal 1:5) whose will is to grant us freedom—that is, to be who we are as creatures made in the image of God or *Heaven*.

Dao, Tian Dao, Ren Dao, *and* Dao De

Another key concept in Confucius' religious or theological ethics can be seen in his usage of "dao" (the *Analects, passim*). *Analects* 4:8 reads, "Knowing *dao* in the morning, one can die in the evening."[42] Yearley explains this verse, "To hear about the *dao* in the morning leads one to be able to face death in the evening with an attitude that can be described in related but different ways: contentment [Waley], or acceptance [Ivanhoe], or a lack of regret [Legge], or a not minding of it [Brookses], or a knowing that it is all right to die [Dawson], or perhaps more problematic, a knowing that you have not lived in vain [Lau]."[43] The significant point here is that one ought to know *dao* before one's death, and that the purpose of being human is to live in a harmonious relationship with *dao*. But what is this *dao* Confucius is talking about?

42. See Chen, *Lunyu Duxun Jiegu*, 50.

43. Yearley, "An Existentialist Reading of Book 4 of the *Analects*," 263, and 271–72, n. 39.

Dao is the way, or the vision, of life to be practiced. It is referred to as *"Tiandao"* (the Way of Heaven) in *Analects* 5:13 or *"Rendao"* (the Way of Humanity) in *Analects* 15:29.

(1) *Tiandao* occurs in the *Analects* only in 5:13, and it is one of two texts (the other is 17:2) where *xing* (human nature) appears.[44] *Analects* 5:13 speaks of the way of *tian* as the divine paradigm for culture (*wen*). Building a cultural ethos is not merely a secular, humanistic task, it is foremostly obedience to or the implementation of the will or way of *tian*.[45] A Confucian culture has spiritual force. Here Wilson's reading of the *Analects* regarding *tiandao* and human nature is illuminating:

> What makes the particular way of life Confucius advocates op-timally humane is its expressing perfectly the place of human beings within the context of society, societies within the context of the larger world, and the larger world within the context of what Fingarette calls the 'Cosmic *Dao*.' That is to say, the consum-mation of humaneness is not merely 'fitting in' or being a fully socialized, graceful, and avid participator in society. At least for Confucius, it is virtue, and virtue has everything to do with what one takes to be the nature of human beings and their proper place within their physical and/or metaphysical environment.[46]

Similarly, Mou Zongsan interprets the intrinsic connection between the outer transcendence of heaven (*tian*) and the inner transcendence of hu-man nature (*xing*) as the Confucian ideal.[47] That is, the unity of heaven and human (*tianren heyi*) and the unity of heaven and human in vir-tue (*tianren hede*) are fulfillments of the mandate of Heaven (*tianming*) through moral cultivation of *ren* (humaneness).[48]

44. On various readings of the commentary tradition, see Ivanhoe, "Whose Confucius? Which *Analects*?" 119–33.

45. The word *wenzhang* (culture) is used in this verse, where Zigong says that Confucius' culture can be possessed and understood, but his teaching regarding human nature and *tiandao* cannot be possessed and understood. See Chen, *Lunyu Duxun Jiegu*, 70–71.

46. Wilson, "Conformity, Individuality, and the Nature of Virtue," 99.

47. Mou, *Zhongguo Zhexue De Tezhi*, 52. See He, "Zhongguo wenhua de gen yu hua," 83–93 critiquing the interpretation of "inner transcendence" as contradiction.

48. The terminology "edifying philosophy" is that of Rorty, see his *Philosophy and the Mirror of Nature*, 370: "Edifying philosophers want to keep space open for the sense of wonder which poets can sometimes cause—wonder that there is something new under the sun, something which is not an accurate representation of what was already

(2) *Rendao* in *Analects* 15:29 can be translated as "'a way of becoming consummately and authoritatively human.' As 15.29 tells us: 'It is the person who is able to broaden the way, and not the way that broadens the person.'"[49] In other words, "The Way thus is transcendent, in the sense that it continues to exist even when it is not being actively manifested in the world, but it requires human beings to be fully realized."[50]

Mou Zongsan uses a metaphysical framework of understanding Confucianism as a religion and sees its two essential aspects, viz., practice and principle. He sees practice and principle as equivalent to *rendao* and *tiandao*. He writes,

> From the standpoint of practice, . . . what it [Confucianism] has done is to transform religious ceremonies into the Rites and Music which serve as rules of conduct for daily living. But, in principle, it has a highly religious character. Indeed, it has a most perfect religious spirit. Its religious consciousness and religious spirit are entirely imbued with moral discernment and practical morality [*rendao*]. This is because its emphasis is on how a person should embody and manifest the Way of Heaven [*Tiandao*].[51]

Both *tiandao* and *rendao* explicate the interrelationship of *dao* and *de* in the Chinese worldview, called *daode* ("the Way and the Morality"). It is evident especially, though not exclusively, in *Daojia* (Daoism) but also in *Rujia* (Confucianism).[52] *Dao* is not speculative truth. While *dao* in Chinese refers to one's relationship with the cosmos, *de* denotes the actualization of the self in wholeness within the social and ethical realms.[53] Those who seek to cultivate filial piety seek the union of the *dao* and *de* in the actualization of selfhood in harmony with the cosmos. *Xiaojing* (*Classic of Filial Piety*, Chap. 7) says that "Filial Piety is the first principle

---

there, something which (at least for the moment) cannot be explained and can barely be described."

49. Ames and Rosemont, *The Analects of Confucius*, 45–46.

50. Slingerland, trans., *Confucius Analects*, 186.

51. Mou, "Confucianism as Religion," 39.

52. The encounter between Confucius and Laozi in Sima Qian's *Records of History* (63) reveals the earliest critique by Daoist natural philosophy of Confucianist personal ethics (though this is most likely an apocryphal story), see Lau, trans., *Analects*, 230.

53. See Northrop, *The Meeting of East and West*, plates XIII and XIV; he uses the terms "The Oneness of Knower and Object in the Aesthetic Continuum" and "The Undifferentiated Aesthetic Continuum" to describe the Chinese ways of understanding reality.

of heaven, the ultimate standard of earth, the norm of conduct for the people."[54] Because of the unity between *dao* and *de*, Confucianists seek to follow the pattern of heaven and earth, and hope that they will be led by the rightness of the heavens and the benefits of the earth so that all under heaven might be in harmony.

The word *Dao* in Daoist thought, equivalent to *Tian* in Confucian thought, connotes the universal way or cosmic moral principle. Just like *Tian*, *Dao* is eternal in its existence and creative in its power. *Dao* is self-generative; it is the metamorphosis of a self-contained universe.[55] "*Dao* is a wholly spontaneous principle, without any trace of personality."[56] The word *dao* corresponds to *logos* (word, reason, thing, etc.) in Greek.[57] In both classical cultures (Chinese and Greek) *dao*, *tianli* (cosmic order) and *logos* were used to designate the creative principle, or wisdom, that generates that way of life which is harmonious and fulsome.

The worldview of a naturalistic cosmos does not imply that Confucian thought lacks a theory of transcendence. Transcendence is an aesthetic or ethical category in Confucian thought, referring, for example, to the awe one senses in encountering another person, the charisma of a stylized behavior called etiquette (*li*), or the delightful beauty of music (*yue*). Confucius did not conceive of a personal divine *Tian* or *Dao* who is sovereign and transcendent, and intimately engaged in the world. *Dao* (the Way) is not a total mystery, it embodies a cosmology that acknowledges the transcendent aspects of *tian* (Heaven) within a self-generative universe. Transcendence in classical Confucian thought is not understood as having a relationship with a Supreme Being outside the universe. Rather, it is understood as transcendence of moral power within one's heart to relate to others. In fact, *dao*, understood in Chinese culture as the Way, often means the concrete expression of the Transcendent; the realization of moral order reflects cosmic order (*tianli*). Thus, the dialectical relationship between *dao* (Way) and *de* (morality) in classical Confucianism encompasses the union between theology and ethics, which in turn is

---

54. Translation of Chiu, *Tao of Chinese Religion*, 348.

55. See, for example, Laozi's understanding in *Daodejing* (42): "Tao produced Oneness. Oneness produced Duality. Duality evolved into trinity, and trinity evolved into the myriad things" (translation of Bodde, "Harmony and Conflict," 23).

56. Bodde, "Harmony and Conflict," 23.

57. For more, see Zhang, *The Tao and the Logos*, passim.

based on the union between *tian* (Heaven) and *ren* (humanity), that is, *tianren heyi* (union between heaven and humanity).

Dao is the ungraspable quality of ultimate reality conceived as self-eternal and self-creative. The Chinese understanding of *dao* as the Way that originates in the ultimately timeless and unknown is different from Paul's interpretation that God has been made known in Christ. When Paul wrote his letter to the Galatians he believed he lived at the end of time. Such a belief is called, collectively, eschatology. He also believed that the end of time had been inaugurated by the crucifixion and resurrection of Jesus Christ, an event that came totally unexpectedly in history, as out of the future, by revelation—that is, apocalyptically. These conceptual elements together are called apocalyptic eschatology and together they provide the background for understanding Paul's Christology and soteriology (salvation) as well as his understanding of freedom and the ethical life. When Paul speaks of "the present evil *aeon*" (age; Gal 1:4b), he is not making the Gnostic distinction between an evil material creation and a good world of the Spirit. Such a distinction dismisses history. Rather, Paul's eschatological dualism distinguishes between the present *aeon* (Gal 1:4; Rom 12:2; 1 Cor 1:2; 2:6; 2:8; 3:18; 2 Cor 4:4) and "the new creation" (Gal 6:15). The distinction points to the reality of newness and hope and salvation in Christ—despite the fact that the present age is still dominated by the power of sin, evil, and death. The distinction between the two aeons elevates history. Eschatological dualism does away with the cosmological dualism of Gnostics (and others) and presents the possibility of redemption and wholeness in Christ now.

Paul's apocalyptic eschatology is grounded in Christ. Christ reveals (*apocalypse*) the mystery and the pattern of the cosmos, and Christ defines the end, the *telos*, the goal and purpose of the cosmos. The issue here is not about disclosing God's acts of salvation that were hidden in the past. Rather, the issue is the breaking-in of God into the cosmos and the present age in a way that is redeeming to all. The word *apocalyptein* is customarily translated as to unveil or to reveal, but both prove to be less satisfactory. Martyn is correct in asserting that, "apocalypse is the *invasive* act that was carried out by God when he sent Christ and Christ's Spirit into the world and into human hearts (3:23; 4:4, 6)."[58] This is to say that, Paul's gospel is about more than the revelation of something that

58. Martyn, *Galatians*, 144.

had been hidden for ages and is now revealed. The gospel is about God's breaking into the present age by sending his Son and Spirit. In Paul's words, "when the fullness of time came, God sent his Son . . . the Spirit of his son into our hearts" (Gal 3:23, 24, 25; 4:4, 6). Before God's breaking into the present evil *aeon* (age), human beings were in bondage; after the revelation of Christ human beings can live in freedom. This is God's will for salvation (Gal 1:5) realized in history (4:4) and is not the result of a natural process: "when the fullness of time came, God sent his Son." "The fullness of time" (*To plerōma tou chronou*) refers to a "predetermined time," impregnated with *God's will for salvation*. Gal 4:3 speaks of "the time appointed by the father" (4:3), which is parallel to "the fullness of time" in Gal 4:4. These terms denote the time when humanity gains its legal right to become heirs of God's promises and blessings through Christ. The new age is the age of maturity and freedom with regard to attaining God's salvation through Christ's faithfulness.

Framed within the eschatological motif of current Jewish expectation, Paul's theology of resurrection points to the new openness of the human condition and the clarity of the future. As an aspect of Paul's theology the concept of resurrection is a challenge to Confucius' ahistorical understanding of *dao*. Confucianist cosmology does acknowledge the open-endedness of the Way (*dao*). The goal (*telos*) of Confucius' moral world is harmony between Heaven (*tian*) and humanity/humaneness (*ren*). According to Confucius, it is the ethical life that actualizes the creativity and goodness of Heaven (*tian*). Confucius sees being human as loving others (*renren*), and that loving others fulfills the mandate of Heaven (*tianming*).

From the perspective of *dao* (Way), freedom exists only within the order of things. Whether as an individual or as a community, freedom results from following the right course, being in tune with how things are, as ordered by *dao* (the cosmic Way).[59] Paul's ethic of freedom is rooted

---

59. More research could be done regarding a comparative study of Confucius' ethic and Western moral traditions. One tradition sees moral obligation ("oughtness") inferred from ontological "is-ness" by means of *phronesis* (practical wisdom). Thus to be a moral being, or to live a good life for Aristotle does not need require a moral god, although the *summa bonum*, one may argue, is his understanding of ultimate reality. Another tradition sees morality as the duty to obey and love God, the Creator. This is a Christian view, such as Paul would understand. But in Rom 1:18–32 Paul seems to derive morality from the general revelation of God in creation. Paul assumes that God is a moral being, and therefore those who suppress the truth will end up with immoral consequences, incurring the

in God's act of forgiving love in Jesus Christ, which liberates, through faith, those enslaved by the power of sin and death. While Confucius explains the moral life as the way of *dao*, Paul places hope for the human predicament of sin, evil, and death in the imminent coming of the kingdom of God. It is the resurrection of Jesus that points humanity toward God's future. It is humanity's destiny to be saved because the *telos* (goal) of history, proleptically revealed in Jesus' resurrection from the dead, is salvation, not destruction.

Despite the differences between Confucius and Paul, they are not irreconcilable, as an intertextual reading shows. Confucius' moral world can be illuminated by the theology of Paul. We hope to show in the following discussion that several concepts central to the thought of Confucius and Paul are mutually complementary. They are: *dao, tian*, word, ethic, theology.

1. In Confucius' cosmology the understanding of *dao* (as Transcendence) is akin to the Jewish concept of *dabar* (word). As M. Fishbane has written, from the Jewish perspective

> the humanly communicable language inscribed in Scripture is but a reflex of the divine infinity. It is but the outer garment, so to speak, of the eternal feminine within God that draws us erotically—platonically, and with religious ardor—into the consummate depths of God.[60]

This is to say that although Scripture is encoded with the infinite divine *logos*, the loci and existence of meaning do not evolve until speech breaks the silence of the text. In the interaction and communion of the divine text (Scripture) and the human "text" (narrative) comes the possibility of meaning for human existence. Both the Chinese and the Pauline traditions have some similarity with the Hebraic notion of *dabar* as dynamic and auditory.[61]

The apostle Paul would agree with this understanding of *dao* and *dabar*; he speaks of the eschatological reality revealed in the risen Christ and in the eschatological reign of God. The reign of God is eschatological,

---

wrath of God. Confucius' ethic (of *dao* and *li*) aligns more with the first tradition, though in his understanding of *tian* and *ren*, it moves closer to the Christian tradition.

60. Fishbane, *The Garments of Torah*, 125.

61. Etymologically speaking, *dabar* means "to say," "to arrange," connoting the eternal order of being, in the words of Plato, "how a being is" (*Cra.* 385b). *Dabar* is a deed, a continuous happening, and is an oral/aural phenomenon.

so is the truth of God; neither is yet fully realized or consummated. Thus, to understand the truth of God and to participate in the reign of God, our knowledge and our involvement are always partial, for in the next "eschatological moment" more will be revealed.[62]

2. Paul's discussion of divine self revelation and of the divine-human relation, found in Rom 1:18–32, is comparable to the Confucian understanding of *dao* (Way) and *tian* (Heaven), as well as to the dialectical relationship between the transcendent and immanent *tian* (Heaven) and thus between *dao* (Way) and *de* (ethics). In Romans 1 Paul explains that his gospel of Jesus Christ contains the power of God for salvation based not on works but on faith. Paul argues that despite the revelation of God's (invisible) nature and the moral obligation of humanity arising from it, all people sin against him and fall short of his glory. According to Confucius, *tian* (Heaven) is both transcendent and immanent: Creative *dao* (Way) is transcendent, an elusive aspect of *tian*; immanent *tian* is the all-pervading life-force that expresses itself in virtue.[63] For Confucius transcendence is best known in its immanence; it is virtue that reveals one's relationship with *tian*. The mandate of *tian* is to be moral selves, the free expression of oneness with *tian*.[64] While the cultural contexts and the issues addressed are different in Confucius and Paul, their arguments are similar. They include (1) the ethical quality of the eternal power and divine nature of God; (2) the ethical demand implicit in the self-revelation of God's righteousness; (3) the universality and clarity of God's self-revelation in creation (for which reason humanity is "without excuse" [Rom 1: 20]); (4) the criterion by which God judges humanity is its response to the universal self-revelation of God. Let me elaborate.

In the opening chapter of Paul's letter to the Romans (1:18–32) Paul argues that every human being is accountable to God on the basis of their knowledge of God. The nature of the truth about God, he contends, is available to all (1:19 and 32). It is not innate in human beings but is rather something revealed to them (as is *dao* in Confucianist understanding). Everyone knows the invisible qualities of God, viz., his "eternal power"

---

62. Critiquing the Corinthian Gnostics' claim of full knowledge, Paul says, "Now we see in a mirror dimly; but then face to face. Now I know in part; then I shall understanding fully, even as I have been fully understood" (1 Cor 13:12; RSV).

63. Mou, *Zhongguo Zhexue De Tezhi*, 30–31, writes of *tian* as both immanent and transcendent Reality.

64. Chen, "Confucian Onto-Hermeneutics," 35.

and "divine nature." "Eternal power" refers to the awesomeness of creation, its power, and mystery. "Divine nature" refers to God's transcendence over all principalities and powers, even over creation itself. God's power and nature are clearly manifested by creation itself, which God alone sustains. This revelation alone is sure enough for people to worship God as the Creator-God.

Another manifestation of God's is power and deity resides in humankind's awareness of moral endowment and obligation. Confucius sees this sense of moral endowment and obligation as responsible for the formation of virtue (*de*) in persons, even when (if not especially when) they face crises and trials. Virtue begins to show its strength most clearly in exemplary persons during times of trial and testing. The Master said, "Only when the year turns bitter cold will one know pines and cypresses are the last to wither" (*Analects* 9:28).[65] For Paul the sense of moral obligation comes from "God's righteous decree" (Rom 1:32). "God's righteous decree" is righteousness itself, decreed by God. There are certain elementary ethical precepts all human beings know. The desire to do good rather than evil is evident in all cultures, despite cultural nuances of the definition of what is good and what is evil. For this reason, says Paul, all "are without excuse" (Rom 1:20). The knowledge of moral obligation is itself clear and sufficient cause for everyone to be held accountable to God. Paul goes on to say that, tragically, humankind at large has not responded in accordance with the knowledge they have of God or of themselves: they "suppress the truth" (Rom 1:18); "knowing God, they do not acknowledge God as God" (1:21); they "do not give thanks to God" (1:21); they "exchange the glory of the immortal God for images" (1:23); they "exchange the truth of God for a lie" (1:25); they "do not consider it worthwhile to retain the knowledge they know" (1:28); and they "not only continue to do these very things but also approve of those who practice them" (1:32). Is this not the same as one finds in the "*Dao de*" or the "Transcendent and Immanent *Tian*" of Confucian thought?

3. The difference between Pauline and Confucian thinking is that Paul concludes in dismay that all are guilty and fall short of God's glory and live in the bondage of sin. "None is righteous, no, not one" (Rom 3:10). From there, Paul posits the means of salvation in Christ's work on the Cross, an act of divine grace, to be accepted by faith. The divine

---

65. My translation. See Chen, *Lunyu Duxun Jiegu*, 166.

alternative to God's wrath is the Christ-event, which manifests the righteousness and the forgiving love of God.

In the Confucian understanding of *dao*, creation and redemption are processes within nature. As such, human beings can be a part of that process, becoming moral beings by way of self-cultivation and by being in harmony with the cosmic pattern. By contrast, for Paul the eschatological nature of cosmic and divine truth—even truth about ourselves—requires faith in union with Christ. "Faith" is not a rigid subscription to religious ideology or dogma. Faith is not a spiritual opium that saves believers from vulnerability. Faith is not immunity from pain and suffering. Rather, to have faith is to live in trust and hope and love. In these ways the *incarnated Christ was faithful.*

Conclusion

Cross-cultural hermeneutics has enabled us to see the many ways the Chinese and Christian traditions overlap. The two traditions, represented by Confucius and Paul, touch on the three fundamental issues of transcendence of God (*Theos*) and Heaven (*tian*), the immanence of God in love and suffering, and the new community initiated by God for the good of all.

Admittedly, Confucius' understanding of *tian* (Heaven) is limited (to as sky, moral creativity, or impersonal fate [*Analects* 9:12; 14:35; 17:19]) and *tian* is never conceived of as being incarnate in a human being, nor are human beings ever thought of as becoming *tian*/divine. But Confucius does understand *tian* as both a transcendent and an immanent cosmic principle. Herein lies the thread of connection.

One might also say that Confucius' redefinition of *tianming* (the mandate of Heaven)—from being an imperial claim of divine right to rule by virtue—if taken seriously today, could give hope for the future of China's political system. The next section will discuss how the Christian understanding of the Cross can help in the redefinition of the old understanding of *tianming*; conversely, it looks at how the Confucian suspicion of religion can help Christians be cautious about religious uses of violence.

THE POLITICAL ETHICS OF CONFUCIUS AND PAUL

Religious Violence Despite Piety

Confucius' cautious attitude toward ghosts and spirits may be explained in terms of his fear of superstition (because it hinders the pursuit of virtue) and of religion (because it often results in violence). To phrase Confucius' rationale for this cautious attitude simply: religious zeal is easily misdirected, its faith easily distorted, resulting in violence toward or disinterest in others. With this rationale in mind, let us look at Paul's confession in his letter to the Galatians. First, a brief sketch of Paul's absolute devotion to the Torah and its unfortunate consequence in his zealous suppression of the Christian church is in order. Autobiographical material is found in Gal 1:13–15 (cf. Phil 3:6; 1 Cor 15:9; Acts 8:3). As a zealous Pharisee prior to his conversion Paul persecuted the church of Jesus Christ. Where did this zealotry come from? Is there a political reason for it? He tells us that he was advanced in *Ioudaïsmos*, that is, not Judaism in general, but a movement within Judaism committed to traditional, Judean ways of life—as opposed to *Hellenismos* (Hellenized Jewry), which had adopted Greek ways. Palestinian Jews being in closer proximity to their past, had greater accessibility to the temple in Jerusalem and to its rituals and sacrifices, practices that were not only essential to their religious lives but crucial to their identity. Diaspora Jews as well used rituals and practices as ways of preserving their identity, and that was evidently the case with the Pharisaic Paul and, later, with his Galatian opponents. As Murphy-O'Connor has written,

> The touchstone of Jewish observance has always been the sabbath, and there can be little doubt that the complexity of Pharisaic legislation which culminated in the 39 types of work forbidden on the sabbath had already begun in the time of Jesus (*m. Sab.* 7:2). Thus it is not surprising that the Gospels record a number of controversies in which Pharisees challenge Jesus on what is permissible on the sabbath (Mark 2:23–28; 3:1–6; Luke 6:6–11; 14:1–6; John 9:1–40). . . . By his [Jesus'] action and response precisely on God's day, the sabbath, he was criticizing current Jewish halakha in order to emphasize that God's love expressed in healing power

was available at each and every moment, and not merely when permitted by the law.[66]

What is being noted here is that Jesus' teaching and the Jesus movement were a threat to zealous Pharisees because Jesus had dared to *reinterpret* the old Jewish law, the keystone of their identity as Jews. Jesus is guilty of subverting the authority of the holy laws. It is suggested that the *Ioudaïsmos* of which Paul boasted sought independence from Rome and resisted the cultural assimilation characteristic of many Jews. At the same time Paul and his company were neither overtly anti-Roman nor militant for fear of provoking Roman. In the context of this historical reconstruction, the Jesus movement is seen as getting too radical for the Pharisaic group. In their "role as the professional cultivators and guardians of the traditional Judean-Israelite way of life, they attempted to hold Judean society together according to 'the laws of the Judeans' (Josephus's term), while also serving, as the mediators of the Roman imperial order, under their high priestly patrons who served as client rulers for Rome."[67]

In addition to their political reasoning, I suspect a religious motivation as well. As a loyal Pharisaic Jew, Paul was concerned with how Gentiles might come into full citizenship of the people of God. His early answer was by adopting the law of Israel. In Jewish tradition, Gentiles are sinners. Lloyd Gaston has shown that some of Paul's rabbinic contemporaries expressed the view that both Jews and Gentiles could have a relationship with God, especially in the end-time, but only through Torah-observance.[68] E. P. Sanders has rightly observed that "in the entire body of Palestinian Jewish literature between *Ben Sirah* and the redaction of the Mishnah, with only the exception of *4 Ezra*, membership in the covenant is considered salvation."[69] According to this Pharisaic belief, both Jews and Gentiles can achieve and maintain their status in the household of God only by observing the Torah. Paul's zeal for the Torah in persecuting the church should be seen in this light.

The word *nomos* (law or Torah), as it is used in Galatians, refers to a cultural and religious code. Stephen Westerholm has appropriately described the Torah as "a collection which spells out Israel's covenantal obli-

66. Murphy-O'Connor, *Paul, A Critical Life*, 76.

67. Horsley, "Introduction," 207.

68. Gaston, *Paul and the Torah*, 28.

69. E. P. Sanders, "The Covenant as a Soteriological Category," 15.

gations."[70] These covenantal obligations have their basis in Deuteronomy (4:8; 30:10; 32:46). In both its symbolic and practical function law is an essential part of every group's life. It is fundamental to its sense of identity (religious, national, or cultural). Law is sacred tradition; it is what society considers upright. For Paul Torah is a cultural and religious code that identified him as a Jew, and more particularly as a Pharisee (cf. Acts 23:6; 26:5; 22:3; 5:34). Paul's attitude did not stand for Jews in general but represented his distorted practice when he was a Pharisee persecuting the Christian church. The law became a form of cultural arrogance, rather than the way of righteousness.[71]

Today, we speak of religious imperialism or proselytism. Those words seem to describe what the Pharisaic Paul was about. The result can be frightening: Loving God can lead to murder. Paul's righteousness within his circle of conviction and his persecution of people outside that conviction is ironical. In Gal 1:13–17, Paul recalls his former life (*pote*) when he "advanced in Judaism" (*proekopton en tō Ioudaïsmō*) beyond his peers.[72] At that time he possessed extreme zeal for the traditions of his ancestors—the law. Paul's zeal expressed in extreme form his commitment and adoration. When Paul was not careful, his zeal lead him to use violence in "persecuting [Christians] to the extreme" (Gal 1:13).[73] Paul's zeal, therefore, contradicted the sacred intention of his advancement. As far as the zealous practice of the law was concerned, in his former life of Judaism Paul was blameless—he was righteous under the law (cf. Phil 3:6). But maintaining that righteousness and zeal across cultural and religious differences often results in persecution (Gal 1:23; 4:29; 5:11; 6:12; Acts 9:4; 22:7; 26:14), in this case of God's church (see 1 Cor 15:9 and Phil 3:6).

---

70. Westerholm, *Israel's Law and the Church's Faith*, 330–31.

71. See Yeo, "Culture and Intersubjectivity," 81–100. There I use Romans 7 to reconstruct Paul's pharisaic experience of wanting to love the law and its result in persecuting the church.

72. A term coined in the Hellenistic period to refer to the religion of the Jews (cf. 2 Macc 2:21; 8;1). In the New Testament, it occurs only in Gal 1:13, 14, cf. 2:14. See Martyn, *Galatians*, 163–64.

73. The phrase *kath' hyperbolēn* (violently) expresses the act of Paul's persecution, it therefore connects Paul's zeal for his ancestral religion ("the traditions handed down from my forefathers" [Gal 1:15]) and the ironic outcome of that zeal—violence towards others outside the tradition.

Let us take a moment to look at this phenomenon so troubling to our age. It is a persistent problem in all religions that their adherents kill in the name of the God they worship. Devotees of any religion are committed to their faith and its traditions and seek to observe all its laws and rituals. A person who advances in his faith by following the principles of his religion (charity and justice) would not persecute others. Yet, we often see persons of high personal morality can at the same time also be violent persecutors of others because they demand of others what they require of themselves. The problem is not only inner-cultural, it is cross-cultural, inter-religious as well.

Paul's own zealous obedience to the Jewish faith and its traditions resulted in his demanding the same of others. The fact that he "persecuted God's church violently" and tried "to annihilate it"[74] is indicative of his cultural and religious imperialism, even though his motives arose out his zeal for his own faith.

That Jews should devote themselves totally to the law or that Christians should believe in a crucified Messiah is of itself of little concern to others. But when a zealous Jew wants a Christian to be a faithful Jew, subscribing totally to the traditions of the Torah, or when a Christian proclaims the crucified Messiah as the end of the law, then fear and hatred are aroused. According to Torah tradition, zeal for God's commandments lies at the heart of Israel's loyalty to Yahweh. Israel's well being (cf. Sir 48:1–2 and 1 Macc 2:23–26) and redemption depend on it (cf. Num 25:6–13). Any violation of the Torah, as in believing in a crucified Messiah or engaging in a critique of the law (cf. Acts 7 and 8), is a threat to the well being of Israel. It is significant that in these few autobiographical sentences Paul contrasts his former loyalty to the law with his later life transformed by God's grace through the revelation of the crucified Messiah.

As a Pharisee, Paul accepted only observant Jews as the true congregation of Israel (*qahal* Yahweh), whether they were Jews or proselytes. He rejected the notion that the "people of the Way" (the *ekklēsia* or church of God) was an extension of "the congregation of Israel" (Deut 23:2–3). After his call, Paul came to believe that the followers of the crucified Messiah, the church, were also members of "the household *of God*." As a

---

74. The two verbs "persecuted" (*ediōkon*) and "destroyed" (*eporthoun*) are in the imperfect tense, the first indicates a continuous action in the past, and the second indicates a volitional action. Cf. Phil 3:6; 1 Cor 15:9.

Pharisee he was appalled that a Jewish sect would confess a crucified man as the Messiah *of God*, because the law explicitly condemned anyone who dies on a tree, i.e., was crucified (Deut 21:23; Gal 3:13). As a Pharisee he knew that such a confession constituted blasphemy. But that understanding was prior to the revelation of the risen Lord.

Paul's autobiographical account in Gal 1:13–14 is not simply a rhetorical device, it is also an essential point of his argument—showing that the "Galatian problem" between Jews and Gentiles is what Paul had wrestled with in his conversion experience. His encounter with Christ on the road to Damascus (according to the book of Acts) brought about a "conversion experience"—not of religion but of piety. In Confucian language, Paul moves toward being more fully human. Paul recognized the potential of religion becoming evil, of the impotence of the law in breaking the power of sin, of the burden of the law in its exclusion of Gentiles as people of God, and of the danger of segregating the heirs of God from one another. Paul realized that his faithfulness to the law had betrayed him to the power of sin by his persecution of Christ's followers. In those moments when he thought he was expressing love of God, he was in fact hurting others in ways even non-religious people cannot do—by invoking the name of God! The conundrum of any religion is that its zealots use holy swords, to kill the infidel, and to crucify their neighbors.

Paul's autobiographical reflection leads him to use the crucified Messiah as the interpretive principle for defending his gospel. As a Pharisee, he had rejected the notion of the crucified Messiah as absurd and scandalous. After all, how could the violence and evil of a cross triumph over God's Anointed? What kind of Messiah is he who dies to save?

Violence against the Son of God is presented to Paul in his first encounter with the risen Christ on the Damascus Road, the backdrop to which is his own violence against the church. There are at least two points arising from this encounter that are pertinent to our discussion here. First, violence and God's Son as the Messiah are intricately intertwined. It is not foolishness, not weakness, not profanity to say that God's Son, as Messiah, is crucified. Rather, the Crucified Messiah symbolizes God's wisdom, God's power, and God's holiness. The Cross of crucifixion is the divine paradigm for addressing the problems of cultural superiority and distorted religious zeal. Violence and persecution result when of a cultural or religious group views its own wisdom or power or sanctity above all others. In contemporary terminology, this is called ethnocentrism or cultural imperialism. Paul's conversion begins with his realization that the Messiah did not worship the law, did not hold on to his power as Messiah, did not retaliate. On the contrary, the Messiah gave himself up, died as a law-breaker, and accepted the suffering of the cross. It is little wonder that the crucified Christ, not the resurrected Christ, becomes the sufficient and inclusive symbol for both Jewish and Gentile Christians in Galatia.

The second point rests on the union between Christ and this church. They are not the same, but they are related to the point that when Paul persecutes the church, he persecutes Christ. This connection focuses the discussion on the elect people of God. What constitutes the people of God? Is it the law, or the Christ, that constitutes the identity symbol of the people of God?

Is Paul's Christology anti-law, thus anti-Jewish? In Gal 5:14 the whole Jewish law is said to be "fulfilled in one word" (*en eni logō*), i.e., one commandment—Lev 19:18 "You shall not take vengeance or bear a grudge against any of your people, but you shall love your neighbor as yourself: I am the Lord" (NRSV). Paul wants to keep the whole Jewish law alive by reinterpreting it with the emphasis on loving others as the fulfillment of the law. The word "fulfill" means " to render it effective," or "to realize its purpose." In other words, Paul is committed to seeing that the Jewish law be restored to its rightful place and used in its rightful service. How so?

Paul emphasizes how *loving one's neighbor* is to *love one's God* and comprises the essence of fulfilling the Jewish law. The textual source (Lev 19:18) is Jewish, but the content of the law is not singularly Jewish or Christian; it is human. The law asks believers to love their fellow beings. Confucianists also understand loving people as a mandate from Heaven. In Galatians, Paul singles out Lev 19:18 ("You shall love your neighbor as yourself") and does not mention the *Shema* from Deut 6:4–6 ("Hear, O Israel: The LORD is our God, the LORD alone. You shall love the Lord your God with all your heart, and with all your soul, and with all your might" [NRSV]). This is not simply an omission. It is intentional. Loving God in confessional acts of worship is easy and widely practical. But it is more difficult to love one's neighbors either as an expression of love for God or as a duty toward the neighbor. The absence of the *Shema* from Galatians does not imply Paul downplays religious duty; Paul's concern is with hypocrisy and self-delusion. Here Confucius' critique of hypocrisy is helpful: "Before we know how to serve people, how do we know how to serve spirits?" (*Analects* 11:12).[75]

The ethics of love is the only answer to the world of violence. In the Pauline context, love is less the completion than the persistent performance of the law. The constant obligation to love arises not because the law is defective or cannot be perfectly obeyed, but because the people of God live out of the experience of grace—and the fruit of grace is love.

Violence and the Galatian Community

While Confucius holds a moral understanding of *tian*, evil, and bondage, Paul's theological understanding of curse, bondage, and the gospel of freedom is also not without ethical significance. To put it differently, Paul turns the ethical dilemma faced by the churches in Galatia into a theological issue. It regards the violence done them, the bondage imposed on them, and the message that will curse them should they subscribe to it.

Galatians 1:7 mentions "*those* who disturb" the Galatians, who are both "mentally and spiritually agitated."[76] Gal 5:10 uses the same word "disturb" (*tarassein*) to describe the result of forcing the Galatians to be circumcised.[77] While the Jerusalem apostles are named (James, Cephas, and John [Gal 2:9]), the opponents ("some" in Gal 1:7, and "false brothers" in Gal 2:4) are not named, although their tactic is intimidation ("who frighten you," Gal 1:7; so also in 5:10, 12; cf. 4:17, 6:12). Paul interprets supplementing the gospel of Christ with works of law as "agitating." Such an act perverts the gospel and contradicts the gospel he preached. Instead of opening his letter with the traditional thanksgiving so characteristic of his other letters (see Rom 1:8–15; 1 Cor 1:4–9; 2 Cor 1:3–11; Phil 1:3–11; 1 Thess 1:2–10; Phlm 4–6), Paul here (1:8–9) opens with a double curse ("Let such a one be cursed"). It is aimed at anyone (including angels from heaven), who preach contrary to what Paul had received by revelation and was now preaching.[78] Agitation of this nature is a "perversion"

75. See Chen, *Lunyu Duxun Jiegu*, 200.

76. "*Tarassō*," BAGD, 805.

77. Matera, *Galatians*, 46 points out that Acts 15:1–24 uses the same verb to describe the agitation in the Antioch Church caused by certain individuals who had come from Judea.

78. The word "preach" (*euaggelizein*) appears six times (out of seven) in Chapter One (1:8 [2x], 9, 11, 16, 23; 4:13), indicating its importance in Paul's mission to Galatia.

(*metastrepsai*) of the gospel of Christ (Gal 1:7). Paul denies that "there is another gospel" (Gal 1:7).

The consequence of preaching a gospel different from Paul's gospel is expressed in double imperatives: "Let him be accursed" (Gal 1:8, 9). The word "*anathema*" connotes punishment by divine wrath or intense refutation by divine will (Gal 1:8, 9; see also Rom 9:3; 1 Cor 5:3–5; 12:3; 16:22).[79] No human being has the power to bless or curse anyone, the most one can do, as Paul does here, is to deliver that person to God, to be subject to God's will and judgment.[80]

From Paul's point of view, his gospel is the norm against which other gospels are to be measured for their truth or falsehood. Paul believes his gospel is "both God's apocalyptic deed and the apostle's tradition, doubtless the former before the latter, but also the former *in* the latter."[81] The word "received" (*parelabete*) has a technical meaning and refers to a body of tradition (1 Cor 11:23; 15:1, 3; Phil 4:9; 1 Thess 2:13; 4:1). Paul did not simply create his gospel out of whole cloth, he received the gospel from the risen Lord and passed it to the Galatians as something he had received—as tradition.[82] His reception of the gospel could be described as the *apokalypsis* (revelation) of God, so that any turning away from that gospel would be a rejection of God's call (1:6) and a fall from grace (1:6, 5:4). The word "tradition" does not mean human creation. As Paul had experienced it the apocalyptic intrusiveness of the Christ event was not a human creation. Similarly, the Torah, though received as a revelatory act from God through Moses, was in Paul's day guarded as sacred tradition and not as a human creation. Nevertheless, in Paul's mind the Christ event was something totally new. It was the redemptive act of God, which had broken into history. The old aeon had passed and a new age had begun. It meant deliverance from bondage, wholeness from chaos, freedom from domination, whether principalities and powers—both cosmic and temporal or social (e.g., male or female, free or slave).

79. Behm, "*Anathema*," 354.

80. The human responsibility towards those who preach a counterfeit gospel is to deliver them to the divine realm (to God or to Satan), as is the case also in 1 Cor 5:3-5, which means excommunication from the body of Christ. Later in 4:30 Paul does indeed asks the Galatian believers to "cast them out."

81. Martyn, *Galatians*, 116.

82. Ibid., 150.

The issue of contention between Paul and his opponents was "the truth of the gospel" (2:5, 14), which is stated in Gal 5:1: "For freedom Christ has set us free." The "agitators" (whether Judean Christians [Acts 15:1] or Pharisees [Acts 15:5]) were pressuring Gentile Christians to be circumcised. In Paul's mind, to submit to this requirement meant to live in bondage. "False brethren" (as Paul describes them) were brought in to spy on the freedom Gentile Christians now had under Paul's gospel (Gal 2:4–5). In response to the false brethren, Paul urges the Galatians not to give in to any gospel requiring them to take up works of the law. The truth of the gospel of Christ grants freedom; it does not burden believers with bondage. Paul does not want Jewish Christians to force Gentile Christian to live like Jews. To do so would violate the truth of the gospel (Gal 2:14). Any burden added to one's identity constituted a violation of freedom. Pressuring Gentiles to be Jewish because they followed the Messiah must be construed as violence against them.

To be bound to an external and physical requirement as a mark of spiritual identity constituted, as far as Paul was concerned, a violation of the freedom given in Christ. The issue at hand was a matter of behavior and identity, not simply that Jewish Christians were "troubling" Gentile Christians.[83] When Paul was still in Galatia, Gentile Christians had a clear understanding of their identity. They accepted Paul's gospel and imitated Paul's way of life in the Spirit. Still, they were marginalized by their own people, having abandoned their pagan heritage. After Paul left Galatia, these Christians were unsure of the ethical guidelines by which they were to live, and the message of those who would impose the Jewish law upon them sounded convincing. It clarified their new identity. Jesus had been a Jew. And the Jewish law did provide clear ethical codes and guidelines for religious behavior.[84] Paul is sympathetic to them for adopting the ethical values of the Jewish law, but he is adamantly opposed to their adopting circumcision, the observance of days, and food laws. Why?

Paul was worried that the very ones he had called into discipleship were now reverting to old ways: "But then, not knowing God, you were enslaved to things that by nature are not gods; but now, knowing God, rather being known by God, how is that you are turning again to weak

---

83. Philip Esler's work points to communal identity as the central problem, and notes especially the scandal mixed table-fellowship caused in the mind of some Jewish members. Esler, "Group Boundaries," 230.

84. Barclay, *Obeying the Truth*, 52–74.

and beggarly elements whose slaves you want to be once more" (Gal 4:8–10, RSV). As pagans, the Gentiles "did not know God"[85] (4:8b), they "were enslaved to things that by nature are not gods" (4:8c). They "did not know God" because they worshipped things that were not gods at all, yet by them they were enslaved.

How can these Christians, after knowing and be known by God, "turn again to beggarly elements which [they] wish to serve (as slaves) again?" (Gal 4:9) The bewitching tactics of the opponents as well as the foolishness of the credulous (Gal 3:1), account for their return to paganism. At least from Paul's point of view that is what they are doing. The works of the law, such as circumcision, constituted the identity symbols of Judaism. That they were demanded and accepted is viewed by Paul as political expediency on the one hand and superficiality on the other. The opponents compelled Gentile Christians to be circumcised, so that they themselves would avoid persecution (Gal 6:12–13, "even they themselves do not keep the law") at the hands of Jewish zealots.[86] The Gentiles accepted circumcision, not in order to keep the law as an ethical guideline, but as an act of reversion to paganism.[87] For both the opponents and the Gentile Christians, works of the law were practiced not to cultivate virtue or create a spiritual relationship with God, they were used to bind others into a particular identity—violently. This is how Paul interpreted the actions of his opponents.

From Paul's perspective, to give in to circumcision or to revert to paganism meant remaining in bondage. If the Gentiles "bought into" the works of the law, thinking that putting on Jewish identity would help them, they were in fact rejecting who they were created to be as Gentiles. If they returned to paganism, they were again submitting themselves to psychological enslavement under the so-called elemental spirits of the cosmos. Either way was to violate themselves and to submit to bondage. Either way constituted spiritual capitulation.

---

85. That they "did not know God" is a Jewish way of saying that Gentiles who are without the law cannot know the one true God of Israel, see Jer 10:25; 1 Thess 4:5. Matera, *Galatians*, 152.

86. Jewett, "The Agitators," 198–212.

87. Martin, "Apostasy to Paganism," 443. For more, see "Galatian Crisis and Congregation" in Chapter One (pp. 70–80).

Hegemonic System (Ba) and Roman Ideology

Paul knew the danger of religious and political violence. Political violence was also pervasive in the world of Confucius, where the institution of force called *ba* (a hegemonic system or Lord Protector[88]) was
unprecedented.

⤷ The Institution of the Hegemonic System

The political context of Confucius' ethical teaching was the institution of
the hegemonic system during the final years of Zhou dynasty. Dynasties
rose and fell. The Zhou dynasty was no different. By 771 BCE, the Zhou
Emperor had lost his power and a coalition of Chinese feudal lords, with
a barbarian leader, usurped the empire, and killed the emperor. One heir
to the throne survived and succeeded in moving the capital to regions
in the east, continuing to rule only as a figurehead. The Zhou dynasty
is divided historically into Western Zhou (1041–771 BCE) and Eastern
Zhou (771–221 BCE). The last Eastern Zhou king stepped down in 256
BCE, and a new dynasty did not begin until 221 BCE. The transitional
period (256–221 BCE) is called the Qin dynasty (255–206 BCE), under
the leadership of Qin Shihuangdi, who ruled with an iron fist. The Eastern
Zhou period, from 771 to 221 BCE, constituted a long 550 years of interstate warfare. Two subperiods in the reign of the Eastern Zhou were
called the Spring and Autumn period (*Chunqiu*, 771–403 BCE), and the
Warring States period (*Chanquo*, 403–221 BCE), denoting the changing
and violent character of those days. This was the socio-political context
when Confucius appeared; he lived during the later part of the Spring
and Autumn period. *Zuo Zhuan* gives a vivid portrayal of the brutality
of this period.[89]

   During that time, the institution of the hegemonic or overlord system (*ba*) created a *reign of force* as the norm of governance. Because the
weakened Eastern Zhou kings could neither protect themselves from
external powers nor dispute the internal power of their lords, powerful
overlords emerged both to challenge and to offer help. Duke Zhuang of
the state of Zheng (ruled 743–701 BCE) was the first overlord to estab-

---

88. Slingerland, trans., *Confucius Analects*, 239.
89. See Watson, *The Tso Chuan*, passim.

lish the hegemonic system (*ba*). The system enabled a superpower to help weaker states maintain peace; it preserved the old feudal system, and protected Chinese states from barbarian invasions—meaning from various non-Chinese tribes, such as the Man, the Rong, and the Yi. After Duke Zhuang's death, Dukes Huan of Qi (ruled 685–643 BCE) and Wen of Jin (ruled 636–628 BCE) maximized the power of the overlords in controlling other dukes. As the Eastern Zhou was losing its power, the overlords of other states, such as Zheng, Qi, Jin, Wu, and Yue were gaining in power. These overlords saw themselves not only as protectors but, gradually as the conquerors of weaker states. Military capability accelerated in Qi, Jin, Qin, and Chu, until finally, in 579 BCE, the overlords of these states met to discuss disarmament. Peace lasted a short while, then the overlord kings of Wu and Yue entered into military conflict. King Goujian of Yue (ruled 496–465) defeated King Fuchai of Wu and became the last overlord. Without overlords to maintain peace, military conflict worsened and the time of the Warring States began.

A hegemon is a "legitimate" feudal lord who convinces others to accept his leadership. Of course, this submission of other lords was achieved by manipulation and domination. In eras of anarchy, the institution of *ba* did bring brief moments of order. But "the *ba* became a symbol of rule by force as opposed to rule by virtue."[90] As time passed and the situation worsened, not even a hegemon could maintain order, issuing in the era of the Warring States. This context is significant for our understanding of Confucius' life and works. First, the continuous interstate violence drove Confucius to reflect upon the causes of political turmoil. Secondly, the deterioration of ritual and music reminded him nostalgically of the Golden Age of Western Zhou. Thirdly, the state of flux within the social order did bring about a greater mobility of the classes and greater intellectual life. Confucius was among those not from the noble class who had the opportunity to participate in political life. Fourthly, in the maelstrom of social change Confucius was able to set up one of the first educational systems open to all classes of society. In fact, later in the times of the Warring States this period was called the era of the "100 Schools" (*baijia*), due to the number of philosophical schools that blossomed.[91]

90. Norden, ed., *Confucius and the Analects*, 6.

91. Brooks and Brooks, *The Original Analects*, 257–62 on the "Hundred Schools" and Confucianist tradition.

Nevertheless, though turmoil may be a catalyst to creativity, the hegemon never received praise from Confucius.[92]

✎ Roman Ideology and the Political Theology of Paul[93]

Confucius' political thought vis-à-vis his historical context provides a useful hermeneutic for viewing Paul's theology in light of the Roman political reality of his day. We have seen the political context of Confucius' day in the prologue chapter, but seen less obviously that of Paul's context. Galatians is not simply a theological treatise; it contains a theology grounded in the socio-political realities of the Greco-Roman world. I want to suggest among other things, that Galatians is an anti-imperial document. To readers who want to distinguish those issues in Galatians that are explicit from those that are merely tacit, it may seem that I blur the boundaries between exegesis and hermeneutics. But there are a number of terms in Galatians loaded with both *theological and political* nuances.

Paul is well aware of the Roman ideology of conquest and fear. Principalities and powers are expressed as "elements of the cosmos" (4:3) and as evidence of an "evil age" (1:4). "Principalities and powers" are "fallen" powers whose purposes have been demonized, whether they are religious institutions, government departments, financial systems, or political ideologies. In the words of the modern critic William Stringfellow, "Every principality in its fallenness exists in remarkable confusion as to its own origins, identity, and office. The fallen principalities falsely—and futilely—claim autonomy from God and dominion over human beings and the rest of creation, thus disrupting and usurping the godly vocation or blaspheming, while repudiating their own vocation."[94] In such a confusion of identities, many became aggressors out of fear.

The empire's strategy of power consolidation was carried out in the name of the unity of the empire. In reality it was out of insecurity. Though Rome offered to the provinces certain degree of political and economic

---

92. An able prime minister, Guan Zhong, assisted a hegemon called Duke Huan of Qi (Qi Huan Gong; *Analects* 3:22) and received a negative assessment from Confucius. Cf. *Analects* 14:9, 16–17.

93. See Deissmann, *Light from the Ancient East*, 338–78; Horsley, ed., *Paul and Empire*, passim; Nanos, "The Inter- and Intra-Jewish Political Context of Paul's Letter to the Galatians," 396–407.

94. Stringfellow, *An Ethic for Christians*, 80.

autonomy, Rome's glory dictated all its interests. There was no genuine celebration of diversity allowed, only compliance and submission. The problem with power is that its exercise creates rather than overcomes fear. Fear leads to rebellion, and rebellion drives power into becoming absolute, and absolute power destroys without discrimination. The inclination of power toward centralization divides, and power that seeks to be absolute results only in terror, violence, and chaos.

Was Paul aware of how the Roman ideology of conquest, dominion, and unification was at work in the communities of Galatia, even in terms of the co-existence of Jewish and Gentile Christians? I once thought Paul was not at all political, that he was so preoccupied with eschatology that he had no time for politics. But the hermeneutical lens Confucius provides has helped me see differently. Paul had no intention of toppling the Roman Empire, but he believed that the gospel of Jesus Christ pertained to the whole world, Rome included. Paul was not explicitly preaching a gospel that would replace the emperors, but the theological content of his gospel is anti-imperialistic.[95]

Paul's theology had to deal with the political reality of his day, as is evident in Galatians. First, the "assemblies" (*ekklēsia*) of his missionary work are themselves a subtle critique of the political power and groupings of the Roman Empire. Paul is not politically conservative in the sense that he is disinterested in the affairs of the empire or that he simply accommodates to or seeks to maintain the status quo. The political task of Paul's gospel is radical. His reinterpretation of the people of God as an "ekklēsia" (Gal 1:1) including Jews and Gentiles and his reordering of the world according to the Christ event are radical views. One might assume that Pauline Christianity would employ common cultic or socio-religious terms (such as *thiasos, eranos, collegia*) to identify itself, but such terms as well as the language of Greco-Roman worship are absent in Pauline writings.[96] There are external similarities between Pauline Christianity

95. See Yeo, *Chairman Mao Meets the Apostle Paul* (passim on 1 and 2 Thessalonians) where eschatology is seen as a harsh critique of Roman political ideology and the imperial cult; see also Yeo, "A Political Reading of Paul's Eschatology in 1 and 2 Thessalonians," 77–88, and the collection of essays in Horsley, ed., *Paul and Empire*, that explicitly deal with 1 Corinthians, Romans, the Thessalonian correspondence, and Philippians on how Paul's gospel critiques the Roman Empire. See also Hii, "Contesting the Ideology of the Empire," passim.

96. Beker, *Paul the Apostle*, 319. Some scholars have speculated that Pauline communities were modeled on philosophical and religious groups, such as the Pythagoreans,

and the mystery religions with regard to baptism, but there are significant differences as well. Paul consistently refers to his communities as *ekklēsia* (plural *ekklēsiai*), a religious term found in the Septuagint (LXX, the Greek Old Testament) having political overtones. The Greek term *ekklēsia* translates the Hebrew term "synagogue" (or plural *synagogai*), meaning assembly/assemblies of the believers. But in the Eastern Roman Empire where Greek was spoken, *ekklēsia* means "assembly" of citizens, that is, people of the *polis* (or "city," cf. politics).[97] In the diaspora, Roman authorities granted Jewish synagogues *politeuma*—self-government. The *ekklēsiai* (assemblies) of Pauline Christianity are not cultic communities; they are in effect political assemblies with theologically informed activities that constantly critique the political assumption of the day. In contrast to the official city assembly of the Roman provinces (see Gal 1:2; 1 Thess 1:1, 2:14, 1 Cor 16:1, etc.), the churches existed in the principal cities of the empire to carry out God's rule in the land.[98] Horsley writes,

> Paul's *ekklēsiai* are thus local communities of an alternative society to the Roman imperial order. The alternative society, moreover, is rooted in the history of Israel, in opposition to the *Pax Romana*.... [W]hen Paul speaks of 'the *ekklēsia* of God,' the underlying foundation is the *qehal yhwh*, the 'assembly of the Lord,' the assembly of historical Israel.... In God's guidance of human affairs, history, which had been running through Israel and not through Rome, has finally come to fulfillment. The promises to Abraham that all peoples would receive blessings through his seed have now been fulfilled in the crucifixion of Jesus Christ and his seed have now been fulfilled in the crucifixion of Jesus Christ and his exaltation in heaven as the eschatological Lord (over and displacing Caesar, the imperial lord and savior). . . . The movement, especially in Paul's mission area, was thus 'international,' with 'assemblies' in the various provinces.[99]

In other words, Paul's gospel mission, through the *ekklēsia*, is to build an alternative *polis* to that of Rome. The *ekklēsia* for Paul is not the displacement of or a replacement for Israel but its fulfillment, for the *ekklēsiai* are "the Israel of God" (Gal 6:16).

Epicureans, Stoics and Cynics; but see Meeks, *First Urban Christians*, 81–84.

97. Horsley, "Introduction," 208.

98. Georgi, *Theocracy*, 57.

99. Horsley, "Introduction," 209.

Secondly, in Galatians (and other letters), Paul uses terms and concepts that are politically explosive, such as presence (*apanthesis*), lord (*kyrios*), gospel (*euanggelion*), faith/loyalty (*pistis*), savior/salvation (*sōtēr*), righteousness/justice (*dikaiosynē*), peace (*eirēnē*), son of God/rightful heir to the throne (*hyios theou*). *Apantesis* and *kyrios* have royal nuances; the term *apantesis* (e.g., 1 Thess 4:17) denotes a citizens' expectation of a ruler's arrival; thus it too is a political term. *Kyrios*, a common term in all of Paul's writings, also refers to a political lord, a Roman emperor, in addition to its theological reference to Jesus Christ.[100] "Lord" denotes a royal figure, politically the emperor[101] and religiously a god.[102] *Euaggelion* means the good news of the royal person and all the benefactions of that person. A savior (*sōtēr*) brings about world peace and grants benefaction. In the installation of Roman officials, the Roman proconsul suggested September 23, the birthday of Augustus, to be the beginning of the new age (*saeculum*).[103] The salvation brought by Rome is to be worldwide, as is Paul's claim regarding salvation in Jesus Christ. The Augustan expectation of a new age with a divine ruler reigning in Rome constituted a messianic ideology that Roman Empire was the ideal age. Could it be that "the present evil age" (Gal 1:4) refers to Roman rule? The Empire's form of messianism may be compared to Paul's message of Christ. The former based on the divine endorsement of power, the latter on the greater power of love.

Pistis is faithfulness, fidelity, trust, reliability. It has a political dimension as well as religious. Georgi explains: "The Caesar represented the *fides* of Rome in the sense of loyalty, faithfulness to treaty obligations, uprightness, truthfulness, honesty, confidence, and conviction—all, as it were, a Roman monopoly. The ancient cult of the goddess Fides was revived under Augustus. It is significant too, in the period of the principate, that the word appears frequently on coins."[104] Paul uses the same word but argues that *pistis* (fidelity) requires two parties to trust each other enough to co-exist fully as human beings despite their own vulnerability

100. For inscriptions of *kyrios* (lord) referring to Emperor Nero, see Deissmann, *Light from the Ancient East*, 351.

101. Foerster, "*Kyrios*," 1054–58, observes that the imagery was used more and more in the first and second centuries.

102. Radl, *Ankunft des Herrn*, 173–81.

103. Georgi, "God Turned Upside Down," 149.

104. Ibid.

toward each other. *Pistis* requires trust as examplified by the faithfulness of Christ; trust is reciprocal, as God has trusted his children to be his people.

The *Pax Christi* is often understood in the context of the *Pax Romana*. Georgi writes:

> The *Pax Romana* is based on the theory of an eternal Rome, whose foremost representatives are divine and immortal, as well as on the power of the Roman army and Roman money. The result—not only in the view of the rulers—was deliverance from foreign domination and internecine warfare, self-determination, and the freedom to form coalitions with others in a world civilization and world economy that people thought they could enjoy freely but that in fact enslaved them to the principle of achievement and the constraint of possessions.[105]

Georgi continues,

> The *Pax Christi* is based on acceptance of human existence with all its limitations and mutual interdependence. *Pax Christi* means the freedom and the surrender of all privileges by everyone. This renunciation of privilege . . . is the true authority which moves and shapes the world.[106]

The term *parousia* does not appear in pre-Christian apocalyptic literature; its technical usage (in a royal-political sense) points to the arrival of a king or emperor. The term *parousia*, as used in the New Testament, is taken from the semantic domain of the high political or social event. It refers to the return of Christ or the arrival of a significant person such as a dignitary, or the presence of a great person.[107] *Parousia* is related to *epiphania*, which refers to the manifestation of a god or a royal person. Both the religious and the political nuances constitute the semantic domain of the word *parousia* when the church used it to speak of the return of Christ.

Paul's alternative vision, in contrast to imperial ideology, is strongly hinted but not made explicit. "For Paul, Jesus is what the *princeps* claimed

105. Ibid., 154.

106. Ibid.

107. *Parousia* is a festive occasion in which all rejoice in the presence of the royal and authoritative one. The fanfare accompanying such arrivals includes acclamation, joyous celebration, the wearing of bright clothing and crowns. See Oepke, *"Parousia,"* 860.

to be: representative of humanity, reconciler and ruler of the world."[108] For Paul, Jesus is "the *princeps*," the representative of true humanity, humanity living in freedom and righteousness, the ruler and reconciler of the world. His rule and dominion is one of grace. This is the theology Paul expresses in Galatians. When the Judaizers came to Galatia to impose upon Gentile Christians the ideology of the law as an external demand independent of faith, they caused the Gentiles to "fall from grace" (Gal 5:4). Proselytism of this kind is akin to the Roman ideology of conquest. It is so much easier to give in to the demand of others, to be like them for the sake of "unity" and acceptance. And submission to the other's cultural ideal would be the easier path to co-existence, since homogeneity would guarantee peace—as it seemed.

In Paul's theology crucifixion, both as concept and as fact, carried within it sharp political critique. Paul understands the crucified Lord as God's response to power. It can be contrasted to the grasping concentration of power in imperial palaces. Crucifixion was a device of terror used by the Romans on any who would resist the imperial concept of peace and order. Paul writes, "It was before your eyes that Christ was publicly exhibited as crucified!" (Gal 3:1). Paul narrates this terror not for social control but as the ethical and spiritual means for humanity's freedom. In contrast, the "peace of Rome" used terror as a form of social control.

Crucifixion was widely used by Rome to punish sedition and any who were charged with heinous crimes, especially among the lower class (*humiliores*) who were typically slaves.[109] A place for public crucifixion exists on the Campus Esquilinus in Rome, similar to Golgotha in Jerusalem.[110] Crucifixion, the ultimate symbol of terror, was used by Rome to facilitate conquest and maintain peace and order. As Elliott writes, quoting Josephus:

> Crucifixion served as 'a means of waging war and securing peace, of wearing down rebellious cities under siege, of breaking the will of conquered peoples and of bringing mutinous troops or unruly provinces under control.' First among these 'unruly provinces,' of course, was Judea, where the Romans crucified tens of thousands of Jews. . . . During the siege of Jerusalem, the Roman general

108. Georgi, *Theocracy*, 99.

109. Following the slave rebellion of 71 BCE, Rome crucified 6000 followers of the leader Spartacus.

110. N. Elliott, "The Anti-Imperial Message of the Cross," 168.

Titus crucified as many as five hundred refugees from the city per day, until 'there was not enough room for the crosses' outside the city walls (*War* 5.11.1–2). . . .

In the Roman practice [of crucifixion], 'whipping, torture, the burning out of the eyes, and maiming often preceded the actual hanging.' [citing *War* 5.44.9] . . . The Romans practiced crucifixion above all on 'groups whose development had to be suppressed by all possible means to safeguard law and order in the state.'[111]

Elliott continues,

The 'peace' that Rome secured through terror was maintained through terror, through slavery, fed by conquest and scrupulously maintained through constant intimidation, abuse, and violence; through the ritualized terror of gladiatorial games, where the human refuse of empire—captives of war, condemned criminals, slaves bought for the arena—were killed in stylized rehearsals of conquest, . . . ; and on the ideological plane, through imperial cult and ceremonial, the rhetoric of the courts, and an educational system that rehearsed the 'naturalness' of Rome's global hegemony. It was within this civilization of terror that crucifixion played its indispensable role.[112]

In such a context, the political aspects of Paul's gospel cannot be neglected. Though elusive, deceptive, and difficult to resolve, religious and political violence is real.

If the inference to be drawn here is that Paul was "non-violent," it would be inaccurate. We saw in the last chapter the passionate rhetoric of Paul expressing his anguish, pain, and anger. His language is by any measure "violent." He rebukes the Galatians and his Jewish opponents (Gal 1:6–9) for departing from the true gospel, the one he had preached. He pronounces a double anathema on those who preach another gospel. He tells those who preach circumcision (1:7) to "castrate themselves" (5:12). Paul's manner is not mild, his theology not banal. He highlights crucifixion and focus on the cross, perhaps with the hope that that violence would end all violence. His theology of the cross is the powerful symbol of a self-giving love. As Christ suffered the violence humanity inflicted on him, so now Paul endures the pain his congregation caused him by their adoption of the law.

111. Ibid., 168–69.
112. Ibid., 170–71.

Crucifixion and the Evil Age

‹❖ The "Violence" of the Cross and the Self-Sacrifice of Christ

Unlike the Evangelists, Paul nowhere in his letters recounts the story of Jesus, even the story of the crucifixion. He does not track down the villains responsible for Christ's death.[113] He remains in awe of Christ's shameful and horrific death and steadfastly believes that it holds the power of salvation for all. Who crucified the king of glory? he asks (1 Cor 2:6-8). The ruler and wisdom of this age, he answers (1 Cor 2:6, 8). In contrast to the wisdom of this age, Paul writes that it is the "foolishness of the Cross" (1 Cor 1:23) that exhibits God's power and wisdom and salvation. The deutero-Pauline tradition interpreted the reign of Christ as one in conflict with the principalities, powers, and rulers of this present evil age and with the spiritual hosts of wickedness in the heavenly places (Eph 6:12). In Galatians, Paul presents Christ's crucifixion as the means by which humanity is redeemed from bondage to the elemental spirits of the universe (Gal 4:3, 9; cf. Col 2: 8, 20). Paul is convinced that God in Christ had disarmed the principalities and powers of the "present evil aeon" (Gal 1:4), and that Christ had dethroned them all and had been enthroned as Savior/King of the world.

The phrase in Gal 1:6b, "God who raised him from the dead," which is surely an early creedal affirmation, is the only place in Galatians where Christ's resurrection is mentioned explicitly. The dominant Christology of Galatians is crucifixion (Gal 1:4, 2:17-21, 3:1, 13, 26-27, 4:4, 5:11, 6:12-14, 17). Even in Gal 1:1b, the emphasis is on the "God who raised" Jesus, indicating the passivity of Jesus with regard to resurrection—Jesus did not raise himself from the dead, it is God's doing. The contrast between Paul's gospel and that of the opponents' is hinted at in this verse: Both Paul and his opponents believe in God, but Paul affirms that this God is known most vividly and decisively through his act in Jesus, the Crucified Messiah, whom God raised from the dead.

---

113. 1 Cor 2:8 says "the rulers (*archontes*) of this age" crucified "the Lord of glory." But *archontes* is ambiguous and may be intentional to refer to any rule, authority, or power that is "intractably hostile to God and as such doomed to be destroyed by the Messiah at 'the end'"; see the discussion of N. Elliott, "The Anti-Imperial Message of the Cross," 176).

Christ's volitional act of "giving himself over" (*paradidōmi*) to death is for the sake of freeing humankind from the "present evil aeon" (Gal 1:4). The word *paradidomi* is used in the Synoptics (e.g., Mark 9:31; 10:33; 14:21, 41) and by Paul (e.g., Rom 4:25; 8:32; 1 Cor 11:23) to refer to Jesus' being handed over to the authorities (Gal 2:20; 1 Cor 15:3; Eph 5:2, 25; 1 Tim 2:6; Titus 2:14).[114] The effective redemptive work of Christ to deliver humanity from the present evil age is the overarching framework of salvation. In his death Christ "gave himself" to identify with "our sins" so that we might be set free from bondage to the present evil age. Human sin is understood in terms of living in bondage to the present evil age. This transcendent view of sin implies that religion is the mechanisms for the alleviation of social, political, religious, and cultural oppression. Christ's death is to be interpreted in the historical context (cultural, religious, socio-political) of his self-surrender on the cross. Christ suffers even though he is innocent.

In the context of cultural and religious imperialism, Christ's self-surrender models for the community the subordination of privilege and identity, not forcing others to subscribe to one's own zealous convictions, especially if that results in the binding of others. The words, "the Son of God who loved me and gave himself for me" (Gal 2:20) describes Paul's understanding of the loving nature of Christ's sacrificial act. The sentence, "Christ redeemed us from the curse of the law by becoming a curse for us" (3:13) spells out the purpose of the sacrificial act: delivering humanity from condemnation. Christ's self-surrender thus results in the freeing all from the bondage of the present evil age (Gal 1:4).

The human condition as a universal problem is known in both East and West. In the ancient Chinese world, there was a long tradition of elaborate systems of sacrifice and divination. Sacrifices offered to Heaven (*tian*) and to the spirits of the ancestors were to ensure the peace and prosperity of the country and those who made them. The Chinese believed that sickness, catastrophes, and daily problems resulted from the dissatisfaction of the spirits or the disharmony of the cosmic system. Life lived under the law signified to the Jew the notion that doing the requirement of the law (*nomistic services*) served to protect them from human tragedy through the blessing of the covenant. "Thus even we, when we were minors, were enslaved under the elements of the cosmos. But when

114. Martyn, *Galatians*, 43.

the fullness of time came God sent his Son, born of a woman, born under the law, in order that he might redeem those under the law, that we might receive adoption" (Gal 4:3–5). In history God works out mankind's salvation through the law and Christ so that both Jews and Gentiles might be redeemed. The "we" in Gal 4:3 refers to both Jews and Gentiles in their minority, that is, before the age of the Messiah. During the age of the law, both Jews and Gentiles are said to be enslaved under "the elements of the cosmos" (*ta stoicheia tou kosmou*). In the Gentile world, the "elements of the cosmos" described those unseen and evil powers that reigned over the age enslaving all humanity (Gal 4:3). The *stoicheia tou kosmou* is a phrase that variously referred to (1) the physical elements of the universe (air, fire, water, earth); (2) the heavenly bodies, such as the stars; (3) the elemental spirits, demons unseen in the world; and (4) the rudimentary principles of religious knowledge.[115] In light of Gal 1:4, where Christ's salvation is said to deliver and redeem all from the present evil *aeon*, the *stoicheia tou kosmou* refer to the evil principles in the universe that dominate human lives.[116] In Paul's understanding, "Jews *and* Gentiles" (all humanity) are all held captive by these principles. (bad 氣)

↔ Jewish Law and Cosmic Elements

From Paul's point of view, and certainly not only Paul's, the law was given to the Jews as a way of preserving them from sin and from what is here described as bondage to demonic principles. Under the law they are but minors incapable of inheriting God's promises and blessings as fully mature and free persons. The law therefore is not able to bring release to the Gentiles who are also held captive to evil principles. The role of the law in guarding humanity from sin is but temporary. In the age of the law, humanity is only a minor, it does not have the legal right to possess and enjoy its inheritance. As an heir (*klēronomos*) under a guardian or trustee, its life is no different from that of a slave. In Paul's day a guardian was normally a friend or relative of a child's father, who took charge of the

115. On the meaning of *stoicheia* see Bundrick, "*Ta Stoicheia Tou Kosmou* (Gal 4:3)," 353–64; Schweizer, "Salves of the Elements," 455–68. Ancient Chinese had similar worldview also, called the "Five Elements" (*wuxing*), viz., metal, wood, water, fire, and earth. See Thompson, *The Chinese Way in Religion*, 42–43; see also Chapter Three (pp. 215–30) in this book on Confucius' understanding of music.

116. Betz, *Galatians*, 204

education and well being of the minor until such time as he became mature. The trustee might be a slave supervising the estate.[117] Customarily, in his will the father would set a date (*prothesmia*) when the minor would come of age, capable of being responsible for the estate and its well being. Until that date, the minor remained under the supervision of the guardian. This is what Paul has in mind in Gal 4:1–2: "What I am saying is that as long as the heir (*klēronomos*) is a minor (*nēpios*), he is no better than a slave even though he is the owner (*kyrios*) of everything, but is under guardians (*epitropoi*) and trustees (*oikonomoi*) until the time appointed by the father." Paul uses this example of a minor growing into legal adulthood to explain how humanity grows from the age of the law to the age of Christ. The legal example has its theological analogy. God the Father has appointed a time when guardianship and trusteeship is no longer required. The present, ushered in by Christ, is the age of the Messiah. In this new age, humanity lives in the power of the Spirit. That is the offer of the gospel.

The way to escape the human predicament, whether as Jew or Gentile, is to be identified with Christ. Christ's self-sacrificial act has overcome the constraining power of the evil age and ushered in the new age of freedom. The brief greeting in Galatians (1:3) is cut short by a Christological statement. Paul is not happy and he wants to say at the outset that the problem in Galatia is a Christological one. The blessing formula in Gal 1:3 ("grace and peace to you"), though popular in Hellenistic letters, has its Jewish roots in Num 6:24–26: "The Lord bless you and keep you; the Lord . . . be gracious to you; the Lord . . . give you peace." It is significant that Paul would extend this ancient Jewish blessing to the Christians in Galatia. It is the blessing of "God our Father and the Lord Jesus Christ" (see the similar formulas in Rom 1:7; 1 Cor 1:3; 2 Cor 1:2; Phlm 3), and it now includes both Jewish and Gentile believers. This is the Kingdom of Christ that dethrones all principalities and power.

---

117. Matera, *Galatians*, 154.

A CHINESE CHRISTIAN UNDERSTANDING OF HISTORY: ESCHATOLOGICAL AND GOLDEN AGE

The Apocalyptic Theology of Paul

Whether talking about personal or national salvation, ethical or political, the framework and processes of salvation for Confucius and Paul are radically different from each other. For Paul, the idea of redeeming humanity "from the present evil aeon" (1:4) is an apocalyptic one that presupposes two ages, one old and one new (cf. 1 Cor 7:26). It rests upon the common Jewish expectation of a transcendent reign of God beyond national history that included cosmic salvation (cf. Rom 1:20, 25; 8:20–22).[118] The old age is corrupted and filled with evil, sin, imperfection, and alienation. The new age, dawning in the coming of Jesus Christ, is the new reign of God's love and justice over sin and evil. The eschatological redemption of Jews and Gentiles in the present age addresses the universal problem of evil powers, the bondage of Sin, and the elemental spirits of the cosmos.

We have already mentioned the fact that Paul's "cosmological apocalyptic eschatology" is not based on anthropological or cosmic dualism. Paul's dualism is eschatological, and it distinguishes between "the present *aeon*" (Gal 1:4; Rom 12:2; 1 Cor 1:2; 2:6; 2:8; 3:18; 2 Cor 4:4) and "the new creation" (Gal 6:15). It points to the realities of newness, hope, and the salvation of God in Christ. Martyn's description of Paul's apocalyptic theology is worth quoting:

> In *cosmological apocalyptic eschatology*, evil, anti-God powers have managed to commence their own rule over the world, leading human beings into idolatry and thus into slavery, producing a wrong situation that was not intended by God and that will not be long tolerated by him. For in his own time God will inaugurate a victorious and liberating apocalyptic war against these evil powers, delivering his elect from their grasp and thus making right that which has gone wrong because of the powers' malignant machinations. In *forensic apocalyptic eschatology*, things have gone wrong because human beings have willfully rejected God, thereby bringing about death and the corruption and perversion of the world. Given this self-caused plight, God has graciously provided the cursing and blessing law as the remedy, thus plac-

118. See Yeo, "Messianic Predestination."

ing before human beings the Two Ways, the Way of death *and* the Way of life. Human beings are individually accountable before the bar of the Judge. But by one's own decision, one can repent of one's sins, receive nomistic forgiveness, and be assured of eternal life. For at the last judgment the deserved sentence of death will be reversed for those who choose the path of law observance, whereas that sentence will be permanently confirmed for those who do not. A crucial issue is that of determining which of these two "tracks" is dominant in a given source. . . . [W]hereas forensic apocalyptic eschatology is characteristic of the Teachers' theology, Paul's Galatian letter is fundamentally marked by cosmological apocalyptic eschatology.[119]

Paul's cosmological apocalyptic eschatology is christologically grounded since it pertains to cosmic salvation. The idea central to Galatians is that Paul has been called by God at the end of time to receive God's revelation (*apokalypsis*) concerning Jesus Christ: "God's [apocalyptic] revelation of Jesus Christ" (1:12); "when it pleased him [apocalyptically] to reveal his Son to me" (1:15–16); "I went . . . as a result of *apokalypsis*" (2:2); "we were confined . . . imprisoned during the period that lasted until, as God intended, faith was revealed (*apokalypthenai*)" (3:23). It is Paul's mission to proclaim this apocalyptic gospel, which is the *apocalypse* (revelation) of Jesus Christ (Gal 3:23).

Much of Paul's gospel is about God's breaking into the present *aeon* (age) by sending his Son and Spirit (Gal 3:23, 24, 25; 4:4, 6). Before this in-breaking of God's Son and Spirit, human beings were in bondage; and after Christ's revelation, human beings enter into a new age of freedom. However, the present evil *aeon* is not simply followed by, nor does it exist in isolation to, the new creation (Gal 6:15). If it did, we would be confronted by a dualism similar to that of Gnosticism. Rather, the dualism of which Paul speaks is a dynamic one. The pairs of opposites in Galatians need to be read in dynamic relation: "For the Flesh is actively inclined against the Spirit, and the Spirit against the Flesh. Indeed these two powers constitute a pair of opposites at war with one another . . ." (5:17). Martyn's explanation of the conflict between flesh and spirit in Gal 5:17 is helpful:

God's invasion of the present evil age involves warfare. . . . [T]his warfare has been commenced not by the evil powers of the pres-

119. Martyn, *Galatians*, 97–98, n. 51.

ent age, but rather by the redemptive powers of the new creation. The battle is thus characterized by a belligerent and liberating line of movement *from* the new creation *into* the present evil age, God's forces being the ones on the march . . . For Paul . . . liberating redemption does not at all grow out of the present scene. Redemption is a matter of God's invasive movement into that scene. It is this redemptive battle between two groups of forces that is reflected in Paul's numerous references to pairs of opposites.[120]

Since the advent of Christ and the Spirit, Paul sees the Cross as the central event on which redemption takes place: "who gave up his very life for our sins, so that he might snatch us out of the grasp of the present evil age . . . Christ redeemed us from the law's curse, becoming a curse in our behalf" (Gal 1:4; 3:13). For Paul the Christ event bears witness to the need of cosmic liberation from the present evil *aeon*. Accordingly, his view of history is Christological. In his providence God has worked through Israel (the age of tutorage). Now, in the new age, the age of Christ, God has worked through the Christ event to include all people in the way of salvation. Paul sees his role as God's ambassador, proclaiming the good news of salvation to all people, for history is now eschatologically fulfilled in Christ (Gal 1:15—2:10).

Paul's eschatology could be hegemonic. It has often been used in the past by religious groups to oppress others. The key to avoiding any hegemonic distortion is found in the Cross' inherent critique of power. The Cross is both the subversion and reversal of power. The apocalypse of Christ is about God interrupting history in Christ's death and resurrection; that event allows everyone to discern the meaning and intended goal of history. God's involvement in history through Jesus, the firstborn of creation, is the *mythos* by which we can decipher meaning out of chaos, redemption out of violence. No matter how great the magnitude of violence and destruction may be in the final conflict of human history, the Crucified God does not accept any ideology's "will to power": not the violence of the *Pax Romana*, the murderous jealousy of Cain (Genesis 4), or the Lion of Judah (Revelation). The Crucified God, incarnate as the Lamb of God, does not accept tragedy as the ultimate meaning of creation. The blood of Abel cried to heaven from the ground. The resurrection confirms the innocence of Abel ("son of Man [Adam]") and

120. Ibid., 100.

Christ ("Son of Man"). The Cross is a "violent" event—sin and sinners have violated and wounded God, and God on the Cross did not retaliate with force, yet the Cross does not condone violence.[121]

In Pauline Christology the significant point is not incarnation; it is the crucifixion, resurrection and parousia of Christ. The end of the crucified Christ was his true beginning. As a Christian theologian, Jürgen Moltmann explains, "Christian eschatology follows this christological pattern in all its personal, historical and cosmic dimensions: *in the end is the beginning.*"[122] Hope emerges amid all historical ambiguities because God's future transcends history and clarifies all events with salvation. God is the actor in history who personally works out salvation in the midst of the people.

Turning to Confucius we can ask: Does Confucian thought have both the *finis* (termination) of violence and the *telos* (purposive goal) of salvation? I believe the broad brush strokes of salvation would resolve violence in both Paul's and Confucius' thoughts, and in this sense they are similar. But these thoughts are expressed differently. In one there is an eschatological hope for the future and, in the other, a yearning to recover a past Golden Age.

Traditions of the Past

Confucius sees the recovery of Zhou cultural ideals as the hope and salvation of China, whose "*li* (propriety) is fallen and its music broken" (*lipeng yuehuai*). He acknowledged that while history at that moment was degenerating, he was still hopeful, not because of what lay ahead but because of the virtuous path (the *dao*) the ancient sages had shown to be true.[123] Tradition in the Confucianist sense is not rigid history or a persistent pattern of conduct handed down from previous generations; nor is tradi-

121. For perpetrators asking victims to die like Christ did is to reinforce hegemony and abusing Paul's christology. Paul's christology teaches the oppressor to surrender power and it teaches the oppressed to gain freedom.

122. Moltmann, *The Way of Jesus Christ*, x.

123. The Way (*dao*) is "the unique moral path" that any true human being should walk, it is "endorsed by Heaven and revealed to the early sage-kings." And the Way (*dao*) is still "preserved in the state of Lu by a few high-minded, uncompromising *ru* (6:13, 19:22). The 'Way of Kings Wen and Wu has not yet fallen to the ground' (19:22)" (Slingerland, trans., *Confucius Analects*, xxii).

tion the heavy hand of historicity inevitably becoming a burden to new generations. In Confucius' teaching, tradition consists of authenticated norms of conduct accepted and realized by wise sages and rulers.[124]

Chinese royal history is often said to begin with the three dynasties (*sandai*)—Xia, Shang, and Zhou; these were the "good old days" of Chinese political history. Chinese historians often reminisce about these times, especially about the three legendary rulers (Yao, Shun, and Yu), as well as the historical rulers of the Zhou dynasty (King Wen, 1099–1050 BCE and King Wu, 1073–1068 BCE), Zhou regent (Duke of Zhou or Zhou Gong), and Zhou military leader (Tai Gong or Duke of Tai). The traditional dating for Xia is 2205–1767 BCE, for Shang 1766–1123 BCE, for Early (or Western) Zhou 1050–770 BCE, for Late (or Eastern) Zhou 770–221 BCE. Confucius (551–479 BCE), as noted above, lived in the Late Zhou period, and he romanticized the previous sage rulers and regents, especially the early Zhou. Whether the accounts of Yao, Shun, and Yu are the exaggerated writing of historians or the rationalization of myths arising in the Shang period is still a scholarly debate.[125] But these rulers are presented as sages who practiced, not the mandate of Heaven by physical descent, but by electing leaders based on their gifts of governing and virtue. These stories of mythology and history contain small details of a primitive Chinese republic where shared power was practiced. Gifted leaders willingly yielded their thrones humbly (*chan-rang*) to more qualified persons, and they offered to assist and to serve the people. Fighting for power (violence) was not a virtue. Virtue dictated the ways of government. This we see in the first three dynasties of China: Xia Dynasty (2205–1783 BCE), Shang Dynasty (1783–1122/1045 BCE), Zhou Dynasty (1122/1045–255 BCE).

Yao and Shun

Confucius' admiration for Yao centered on his virtue of modeling the Heaven-way (*tian dao*), the wise practice of a sage ruler. Though Confucianism emphasizes family, there is an ideological critique of marriage and blood relations when they became the preoccupation of royal families. I want to look in greater detail at these "bigger than life" sage-

124. See Fingarette, "The Music of Humanity," 335.
125. See Thorp, "Erlitou and the Search for the Xia," 1–38.

rulers whom Confucius admired (*Analects* 8:18–21, 14:5).[126] I believe there is a healthy tension in the political ethics of Confucius in this regard: He admonishes his devotees to cherish and to be responsible for one's family, but at the same time, he warns against idolizing blood relations.

According to Sima Qian (145–86 BCE) in the *Records of History* (*Shiji*),[127] Emperor Yao (previously named Fangxun) was a benevolent and wise ruler, noble and virtuous. Emperor Yao was able to rule for generations, with hundreds of families, and numerous states living in harmony with each other. Under his reign, all who traded or labored on the land were prosperous. One day when he asked who could obey the will of Heaven and be his successor, Fangqi replied, "Your son Danzhu is open and bright." Yao replied, "He is a pompous and mean person, of what use can he be?" Huandou is efficient and diligent, he will serve well." Yao replied, "He knows how to speak eloquently, but his intention is evil, and he is contemptuous of Heaven (*tian*), so he cannot be used." Then Yao was worried about the flood that was causing the people problems. He asked the Four Chiefs of the Sacred Mountains who could solve the problem. They proposed that Gun was the right person. Yao said, "Gun neglected orders in the past and has disgraced his family's name." The assembly before Yao replied, "Try him out before making him the successor." Yao then asked Gun to solve the problem of flooding. But for nine years, Gun could not complete the task. Yao called for the assembly again and said, "For seventy years I have reigned now, who could be my successor?" They suggested to Yao a bachelor by the name of Shun from a place called Yu.

Shun's father, Qiaoniu, was blind and not a disciplined person; Shun's step-mother was unrighteous; Shun's young (step-)brother, Xiang was presumptuous. His family wanted to kill Shun, yet Shun was able to run away when threatened and then he returned to serve his family. Shun's virtue and filial love transformed their lives, and they were able to live in harmony and righteousness. Yao agreed to use Shun. Yao also asked Shun to marry his two daughters, and Yao appreciated Shun's virtuous way of relating to his wives. People loved to listen to Shun's teaching on the five human relationships.[128] Shun did extraordinary well in his

126. See Qian, *Lunyu Xinjie*, 293–99; Chen, *Lunyu Duxun Jiegu*, 147–50.

127. I am paraphrasing Sima Qian's *Shiji* [*Records of History*].

128. These five teachings are explained later in *Shiji* (1:35) as the righteousness of a father, the compassion of a mother, the friendship of an older brother, the respect of a

post. Delegates respected Shun when he received them and bid them farewell. After Shun's three years of service, Yao recommended Shun to be the "Son of Heaven" (*tianzi*), to rule "all under heaven" (*tianxia*, i.e., the empire), not because Shun was his son, but because Shun was a sage, a virtuous person. Here Si-ma Qian in his historical account emphasizes Yao's unselfishness: by not letting his son be his successor, he displeased one person but benefited the whole empire.

Confucius admired Yao's modeling of the heaven-way (*tiandao*) of finding a successor from among the people, rather than blindly following the patrilineal tradition of passing power from father to son. Yao did not simply follow what his ancestors had done before him. Confucius said, "How lofty Shun and Yu were in holding themselves aloof from the Empire when they were in possession of it." The Master said, "Great indeed was Yao as a ruler! How lofty! It is Heaven that is great and it was Yao who modeled himself upon it. He was so boundless that the common people were not able to put a name to his virtues. Lofty was he in his successes and brilliant was he in his civilized accomplishments" (*Analects* 8:18–20).[129]

Shun, it is said, declined to ascend to the imperial throne because he was a commoner and lacked meritorious deeds, but Yao abdicated the throne on the first day of the first month of the new year, and Shun became his successor. When questions arose as to whether Yao had given the empire to Shun, Mencius replied to Wanzhang's doubt, A Son of Heaven cannot give an empire to another person, only heaven can give the empire to Shun.

◆ Shun and Yu

According to Confucius, Yao was a sage, so was Shun. In fulfilling the heavenly mandate (*tianming*), Shun observed the heavenly bodies, and offered sacrifices to God—to the Supreme Deity, to the Six Honored Ones, to the mountains and streams, and to all the deities. After these acts of devotion he began touring various states in the country, inspecting and administering his office as the ruler, and working closely with the governors of each state.

---

younger brother, and the filial piety of a son.

129. Lau, trans., *Analects*, 73–75.

According to *Shiji* (1:44), at the age of thirty Yao chose Shun, and at the age of fifty Shun assumed the duties of the Son of Heaven; at the age of sixty-one, when Yao passed away, Shun acceded to the throne. Yao died after Shun had been emperor for twenty-eight years. People mourned his death as if their own parents had died. For three years no music was played in order to commemorate the death of Yao solemnly. After twenty-eight years, Shun still thought he should yield the throne to Yao's son, Tanchu, and he himself retreated to the Southern River, becoming a commoner, doing some farming and making potter. But neither the court counsels nor the imperial choirs would follow Tanchu. After this test, Shun knew for sure the will of Heaven (*tianming*), so he returned to the capital and acceded to the throne as Emperor Shun, the Son of Heaven.

Shun's reign was characterized by his gift of delegation and by his benevolent and virtuous government. He trusted people and was able to use the talents of Yu, Gao Yao, Xie, Hou Ji, Bo Yi, Kui, Long, Chui, Yi, and Pengzu, whom he made ministers of various departments. Shun admonished the people, "Teach the young people to be upright but warm, liberal but stern, firm but not tyrannical, simple but not presumptuous. Poetry is to express their ideas. Songs are to extend their words. Melody is to follow the way of chanting. Tones are to harmonize the melody. Make the eight sounds capable of being in harmony and do not let them lose their relationship to each other. The spirits and human beings will be harmonized by means of music" (*Shiji* 1:42).[130]

When Shun became the emperor, he still served his father faithfully. Shun appointed his younger brother Xiang to be one of the feudal lords. Shun's son, Shang Jun, proved to be unworthy of the throne, so Shun recommended his minister Yu to Heaven as his successor. When Shun passed away seventeen years later, Yu yielded the position to Shun's son Shang Jun, but the governors and feudal lords all came to Yu, asking him to accede to the position of Son of Heaven, even though Yu was not in the blood line of Shun.

While serving the Emperor Shun, Yu's only intention was to help make the land prosperous by controlling the floods. Yu also admonished the emperor to be a sage, a virtuous ruler, and to serve the mandates of the Supreme Deity with sincerity. Yu's accomplishments made Emperor Shun proud, manifesting his virtue. Yu set the standard for doing things

130. Nienhauser, *The Grand Scribe's Records*, 1:15.

well, in music, and in offering sacrifice. Emperor Shun recommended Yu to the heavens to be his successor. After seventeen years, Shun died, and Yu yielded the throne to Shun's son, Shang Jun, but the lords and all the people wanted Yu.

When Yu became the Emperor, he chose Gao Yao to be his deputy successor. Unfortunately, Gao Yao died, leaving his descendants to serve for a while. Eventually Yu chose Yi to assist him and passed the government on to him following his own death. Yi yielded the throne to Yu's son, Qi, because he had not served with Yu long enough for people to know him and most people preferred Qi. The succession of power from Yu to Qi, though a reign of familial descent, was thus the result of the democratic decision of the people.

Again, we see here the political ethics Confucius admired. The temptation was to pass the throne to one's son, but caring for the welfare of the people had to take priority over one's own interest in his heirs. *Analects* 14:42 recounts the conversation between Zilu and his Master regarding "an exemplary person" (*junzi*)—a virtuous person. The Master said, "He cultivates himself and thereby achieves reverence." Zilu replied, "Is that all?" Confucius said, "He cultivates himself and thereby brings peace and security to his fellow men." "Is that all?" Zilu asked. "He cultivates himself and thereby brings peace and security to the people. Even Yao and Shun would have found the task of bringing peace and security to the people taxing" (*Analects* 14:42).[131] Yao said, "Oh, Shun, the succession, ordained by Heaven, has fallen on you. Hold yourself truly to the middle way. If the Empire should be reduced to dire straits, the honors bestowed on you by Heaven will be terminated for ever." Shun, commanding Yu in like manner, said, "I, Lu, the little one, dare to offer a black bull and to make this declaration before the great Lord. I dare not pardon those who have transgressed. I shall present your servants as they are so that the choice rests with you alone. If I transgress, let not the ten thousand states suffer because of me; but if the ten thousand states transgress, the guilt is mine alone" (*Analects* 20:1).[132]

---

131. Lau, trans., *Analects*, 147.

132. Ibid., 201.

✣ Da Yu (Yu the Great)

Yu came from a royal family. His father was Gun and his grandfather was the Emperor Zhuanxu, his great-grandfather was Zhangyi, and his great-great-grandfather was the Huangdi—the famous Yellow Emperor, the first Chinese ruler. As described in *Shiji* Huangdi is a quasi mythical figure: "[A]t birth, he was perspicacious, as an infant, he was able to speak, as a boy, he was quick, as a youth, he was industrious, as an adult, he was intelligent" (*Shiji* 1:1).[133] Gun and Yu were both from the Huangdi family. Shun banished Kun to die at Mount Yu, because Kun was not successful in solving the problem of flooding, but Shun used Kun's son Yu to continue his father's responsibility for flood control. "Yu was a man both diligent and indefatigable. His character was impartial, his personality was endearing, his words were trustworthy, his voice was the law, his behavior the standard. He demonstrated these qualities in the proper manner. And so earnestly, so reverently, these qualities became the net's head-rope, the yarn's guiding-thread [for his people]" (2:51).[134] Yu was able to lead the lords and all the people to embark on controlling the flood for thirteen years. Yu ruled over nine states, regulated all the lands, opened up nine water ways, made roads through the nine mountains, and there was abundance and bliss throughout the land.

Yu, Poyi, and Gao Yao often deliberated before Emperor Shun. One day, Gao Yao counseled that if a ruler's "character is trustworthy, then his plans will be brilliant and his assistants congenial." Yu asked how that could be. Gao Yao replied, "One should focus on self-cultivation, think for the long term, and bring nine relations to harmony. Then what is done will have enduring effects" (*Shiji* 2:77). Gao Yao added that the art of governing lies in "knowing people and bringing peace to the people." The greatness of Yu, Confucius thought, lay in his perception of the intelligent and capable ruler, i.e., a ruler who would be gracious to his people and have no insecurity. Gao Yao continued to elaborate for Yu the nine virtues of being a sage ruler, "When one sets to work, one should be liberal but strict, gentle but firm, frank but reverent, orderly but alert, compliant

---

133. Nienhauser, *The Grand Scribe's Records*, 1:21. *Shiji* 1:1.

134. Nienhauser, *The Grand Scribe's Records*, 2:51.

but courageous, forthright but warm, easy going but unyielding, resolute but sincere, forceful but righteous" (*Shiji* 2:77).[135]

King Wen, King Wu, and the Duke of Zhou

As noted above, Confucius regarded the Western Zhou royal dynasty to be the utopian political period in China's history, as *Analects* 3:14 states: "How glorious is Zhou's culture, I will follow Zhou." He often looked back to King Wen (literally means "The Cultured King"), his son King Wu (literally means "The Warrior King"), King Chen (literally means "The Perfected King"), and the Duke of Zhou. The state of Lu was Confucius' birth place, and it was the state founded for the descendants of the Duke of Zhou, so Confucius' identification with the Duke of Zhou might have something to do with geography. In Confucius' time Lu was ruled by three families, the Ji, the Meng, and the Shu, of which the *Ji* was the most powerful. These families sometimes usurped the power of the Duke of Lu and performed rites only the Duke could do according to propriety (e.g., having eight rows of dancers in their own courtyards; see *Analects* 3:1; using of the Yong ode in the ritual of the removal of sacrificial vessels, *Analects* 3:2; and offering sacrifice on Mount Tai, *Analects* 3:6). Confucius contended that such abuses of *li* (ritual propriety) were simply intolerable (*Analects* 3:1).[136]

King Wen was a ruler who cherished culture (*wen*), refinement, literature, thus he was the exemplary ruler in Confucius' eyes. King Wen was a scholar and a king in his own right as he was able to combine the eight trigrams of the *Yijing* (the *Classic of Changes*) to form sixty-four hexagrams. Before becoming king, he was a loyal vassal to the last Shang despot. Wen often remonstrated with this ruler, but the evil ruler never changed his ways. When Wen died, his son Wu successfully rebelled against the evil ruler. We have two examples here, one using virtue, the other using force to deal with an evil ruler.

According to *Shiji* many of Wen's ancestors in the Zhou dynasty were benevolent rulers, and King Wen modeled his rule after them. "He was resolute in his kindness, reverent to the old, and compassionate to

135. Ibid., 1:33. *Shiji* 2:77.
136. Norden, ed., *Confucius and the Analects*, 9.

the young" (*Shiji* 4:116).[137] King Wen ruled for fifty years, he settled many disputes between feudal lords and cultivated their rule, but King Wen did not have the title king (though it was posthumously given to him by his son).

When King Wen passed away, his heir Fa became the King, better known as King Wu or Wu Wang—meaning King of Warriors, honoring his struggle against tyrannical lords. *Shiji* (4:124) recounts how King Wu led a 4000-chariot army against the Shang state. When King Zhou (紂王) of the Shang dynasty heard that King Wu had declared war, King Zhou raised an army of 700,000 against him. But King Zhou's soldiers refused to fight; they rebelled against him and turned to King Wu instead. In disgrace Zhou went back to the capital and burned himself to death. The people of Shang rejoiced at King Wu's arrival. The next day sacrifices were offered and a prayer was said, "Zhou, the last descendant of the Yin [Shang dynasty], forsook his ancestors' luminous virtue, defied the deities, did not offer sacrifices, and in his dullness was cruel to the families of the hundred cognomens of the city of Shang. Let these [things] be obvious and known to the Supreme Deity."[138] King Wu knelt twice and bowed his head and declared that he had been given the mandate of Heaven to change the Yin [i.e., the Shang] Dynasty to the Zhou Dynasty. (In Chinese Zhou dynasty [周] is a different word from King Zhou [紂].)

King Wu successfully conquered Shang and set up the Western Zhou based on his understanding of a benevolent government should be. King Wu also emulated the virtues of his ancestors. In commemorating the sage kings of the past, King Wu honored the descendants of Shen Nong by giving them the land of Jiao, Huang Di's with Zhu, Emperor Yao's with Ji; Emperor Shun's with Chen, the great Yu's with Qi. King Wu conferred the title King (Wang) on his father Wen (thus Wen Wang or King Wen), who became the founder of the Western Zhou dynasty. Also, in rewarding the good deeds of his ministers and assistants after the battle, King Wu also honored his younger brother, Dan (Duke of Zhou, or Zhou Gong) presenting him with the city Chufu in the state of Lu, which later became the hometown of Confucius.

King Wu returned to Zhou still thinking of the welfare and future of Shang, so much so that he was not able to sleep at night. In a conversa-

---

137. Nienhauser, *The Grand Scribe's Records*, 1:57; *Shiji* 4:116.
138. Nienhauser, *The Grand Scribe's Records*, 1:62; *Shiji* 4:127.

tion with Dan, his younger brother, King Wu said that heaven did not accept Yin's offerings because of the evil the late ruler had committed. King Wu also vowed to reward and comfort the people, to demonstrate his goodness to all, and to make the land prosperous in a manner akin to a "heavenly residence" (*tian shi*) (*Shiji* 4:131).

The concept of revolution in the political history of China begins as early as the Shang and Zhou dynasties. A mandate from Heaven to replace another reigning power became the grounds for the justification of war. "Revolution" in Chinese literally means "replace-mandate" (*geming*). It should be born in mind that there was no such thing as preemptive war or a theory of just war. King Wu's example of using both force and virtue shows that in Chinese history revolution was justified by the ability of a ruler to persuade the common people on the necessity of war based on his exemplary virtue. That is, only acceptance by the common people could confirm whether a war or a revolution was justified.

Soon, King Wu fell ill, causing all the dukes to be concerned. The Duke of Zhou purified himself and performed an exorcism, offering himself to die in place of the King. Though King Wu initially recovered from the illness, he died soon after. King Chen (1067–1031 BCE) became the next ruler. But Chen was still young. The Duke of Zhou, being the younger brother of King Wu, could have been the next heir. Instead, he served as the most trusted and able regent to King Chen for seven years while Chen was still a minor. The Duke spent the first three years pacifying a rebellion of certain feudal lords, who were suspicious of his motives. The Duke's unselfishness, wisdom, and ethical life gained the respect of Confucius and his followers. Confucius had neither the mandate nor the aspiration to be a ruler. But the concept of an "uncrowned king" (*suwang*), as applied to Confucius, began the long held tradition that one could rule even without crown or throne, yet in the manner of the Duke of Zhou.[139] Confucius knew that to rule was better than to reign, and only a benevolent government with proper rituals and music could guarantee a secure reign. Hoping to find a regent in one of the various states to succeed, Confucius was disappointed when he failed to find a single receptive host. No ruler of great virtue stepped forward.

139. The Han literary critic, Wang Chong (27–97 CE), in *Lunheng* (*Balanced Discourses*) is probably the first one who used the term *suwang* ("uncrowned king") to refer to Confucius. For a comprehensive study of the term "uncrowned king," see Mengce, *Kongzi Weiwang Erwang Lun*.

We have surveyed the tradition Confucius looked to, in particular to those who ruled with virtue, with or without title or crown. It is often said that the political ethics of Confucius ruled China for better or worse, for more than two thousand years. The notion of an uncrowned king may give wings to the belief that kingship need not be lineal and that anyone could become king. Education and wisdom are not the possession of the elitist few. The question for many Confucianists remains: Is the Confucian ideal of the philosopher-king the philosophical legitimation of an old-style kingship, or is it truly the replacement of the old understanding of kingship with a new one?

Confucius' vision of national salvation is a noble one, though his anthropological and moral ideals were grounded, and thus legitimized within a patriarchal society. His intent was to use the sage-ruler paradigm of the past to critique the blind spot of patrilinealism in the ruler cult.

Paul, Confucius, and the Understanding of Time[140]

Confucius' vision of recovering the political ethics of the sage rulers is an ethical one. However, Paul's eschatology is Christ-centered, and encompasses the salvation of every aspect of God's created order, with a future orientation. One difference between Confucius' effort to recover the Golden Age and Paul's eschatology is to be found in their different understanding of time.

Confucius' understanding of history is influenced by the *yin-yang* worldview of time as oscillation between *yin* and *yang* in a cycle. Bodde explains that Tung Chungshu (179–104 BCE), a later Confucianist in the Han dynasty (206 BCE–25 CE), articulated the natural phenomena of *yin-yang* worldview:

> The *yin* and *yang* annually meet each other in the north at the winter solstice, when the *yin* is dominant and the *yang* subordinate, and again in the south at the summer solstice, when the reverse is true. They are annually opposite each other at the spring equinox . . . and again at the autumn equinox, when their positions are reversed; on both occasions they are exactly equal in strength. All this [cosmological movement] . . . constitutes 'the

---

140. For more, see Yeo, "Messianic Predestination in Romans 8 and Classical Confucianism," 266–67, 281–83.

course of Heaven,' when [the cycle] has been completed, [it] begins again."¹⁴¹

History is part of the naturalistic oscillation of *yin* and *yang*, growth and
decay, beginning and ending. History undergoes alternating phases of
order and disorder, peace and war, production and destruction, life and
death, existence and non-existence.

The Chinese concept of time is cyclical, or more precisely, a spiral of
two interlocking sets: "heavenly stems" (*tiangan*) and "earthly branches"
(*dizhi*). Julia Ching explains it well:

> The ancients appear to have believed in the cyclical recurrence of
> sage-kings and good governments within a temporal framework
> that we may call spiral. At the very end of the Book of Mencius we
> have the following passage about the time periods that lapsed be-
> tween sage-kings of old: 'Over five hundred years lapsed between
> [the time of] Yao and Shun and [that of King] Tang . . . . Over five
> hundred years [also] lapsed between [the time of] Tang and that
> of [King] Wen . . . . Over five hundred years lapsed between [the
> time of] Wen and that of Confucius . . . . And over one hundred
> years have lapsed since the time of Confucius. We are so near in
> time to the sage, and so close in place to his home. And yet, is
> there no one [who is now a sage]? Is there no one [who is now a
> sage]?"¹⁴²

Analects 2:23 reads, "The Yin (Shang) dynasty perpetuated the civilization of the Xia; its modifications and accretions can be known. The
Zhou perpetuated the civilization of the Yin, and its modifications and
accretions can be known. Whatever others may succeed the Zhou, their
character, even a hundred generations hence, can be known."¹⁴³ There is
no clearer understanding of the cyclical character of history.

Confucianists have a dynamic understanding of time, unlike the
modern, especially modern western view that time is but a linear progres-
sion of past, present, and future—the past is taken to mean the passing of
the present, the future a prolongation of the present, and the present the
only possession one has. The Chinese seldom talk about absolute time

---

141. Bodde, "Harmony and Conflict," 23.

142. Ching, *Mysticism and Kingship in China*, 210. The English translation of *Mencius*
is Ching's.

143. Bodde, "Harmony and Conflict," 28. *Analects* 2:23.

but about time associated with events—dynamic time. Thomé H. Fang explains this view of time:

> The essence of time consists in change; the order of time proceeds with concatenation; the efficacy of time abides by durance. The rhythmic process of epochal change is wheeling round into infinitude and perpetually dovetailing the old and the new so as to issue into interpenetration which is continuant duration in creative advance. This is the way in which time generates itself by its systematic entry into a pervasive unity which constitutes the rational order of creative creativity. The dynamic sequence of time, ridding itself of the perished past and coming by the new into present existence, really gains something over a loss. So, the change in time is but a step to approaching eternity, which is perennial durance, whereby, before the bygone is needed, the forefront of the succeeding has come into presence. And, therefore there is here a linkage of being projecting itself into the prospect of eternity.[144]

In this process of production and reproduction, time never comes to an end.

Confucianists view history as moving in cycles; Paul sees history as moving linearly to an omega point. The traditional Confucian worldview believes in the constant flux of the universe following a "predictable pattern consisting either of eternal oscillation between two poles or of cyclical movement within a closed circuit. [So] . . . all movement serves in the end only to bring the process back to its starting point."[145]

In Paul's view, historical events are dated backward to the beginning of Creation, whereas the end of history is defined by Christ, an event having already occurred. Dunn writes,

> Paul's view of history . . . is not cyclical, but more of a purpose, formed from the beginning, achieved *through* the process of history, moving toward an intended higher end, not simply returning to the beginning. As Paul has been at some pains to argue, God does not write of the intervening history as a total failure and useless; rather this purpose embraces it, works *through* it, through the travail of a creation subjected to futility, *through* the groaning of believers still beset by sin and under the sway of death, work-

---

144. Fang, "The World and the Individual," 240.
145. Bodde, *Essays on Chinese Civilization*, 239.

ing to achieve not simply a return to pristine purity, but the fuller glory which Adam never attained, including life *from death*.[146]

Paul's view of history is an eschatological vision, and God through Christ and the Holy Spirit is the palpable actor. In short, Paul's worldview is radically oriented toward the future while rooted in a past event, the death and resurrection of Christ, which intrudes into the present. Paul's view arises from a decidedly historical consciousness: act now, time is short. Consumed by the *telos* of history, this consciousness is going somewhere, like a boat through time, and one can either be in the boat or in the water. Unlike Paul, the Confucianist sees no *telos*, no goal to the flow of history.[147]

For Paul, the will of God and the meaning of history are clarified in Christ, and in the Christian West, history is dated according to the story of Christ. "In China, on the contrary, history has no such fixed starting point. Events are dated either according to their occurrence within a recurring sixty-year cycle or according to their position within the reigns of successive rulers."[148] In Chinese history, events are dated cyclically every sixty years, or from the rise of new emperors. The dominant motive in Chinese historiography is to look for a Golden Age in the past. Since history is thought to be characterized by a cycle of generation and degeneration, the cycle is seen as the conscious cultivation of the self in harmony with society and with the cosmos so as to bring back the Golden Age.

As a Christian imbued with Confucian tradition, I find Confucius' and Paul's views of time helpful in achieving a balanced understanding of history and event. A linear view of time (Pauline) is too static; a cyclical view (Confucianist) too closed. A synthesis of both views can be achieved if we understand the biblical concept of past, present, and future as referring not to tenses but to modes of existence and aspects of action.[149] The narrative of God's activity in historical time, which is so central to the Bible, is what predestined Christology is all about. The present is our

146. Dunn, *Romans 1–8*, 484.

147. Bodde, "Harmony and Conflict," 23.

148. Ibid., 28, cites *Mencius* 3b.9: "Since the appearance of the world of men, a long time has indeed elapsed, consisting of alternating order and disorder." See also *Mencius* 2b.13. Legge and Yang, trans., *The Four Books*, 378–79, 344–45.

149. On the differentiation of future, advent, and *novum*, see Moltmann, *The Way of Jesus Christ*, 22–28.

spontaneous and continuous experience of the Holy despite our current historical ambiguity and despair. The past refers to realized acts of God in history. The future is the coming (advent or parousia) of the radically new creation of God assured by the past to be realized in the present. The manifest destiny of history through Christ is God's new creation toward wholeness. Begbie writes,

> Time is divinely *created*—there is no other time. . . . [C]reated time is to be related to the time of Jesus Christ, and Christ's temporality is inseparable from his history as Jesus of Nazareth. Here is a limited, restricted life among us, bound by birth and death. Nevertheless, in his resurrection he is inaugurated as the 'Lord of time' so as not to be bound by our succession of beginning, duration, and end; his time begins but exists before its beginning, has duration but in such a way that his present includes his past and future, and ends but in such a way that the time after its end is that of his renewed presence.[150]

This dynamic understanding of God's working in history is not simply linear or cyclical but is a spiral process. The redemptive event happens at the opportune and meaningful (*kairotic*) time.

Paul's understanding of the goal (the end) of history coming eschatologically out of the future supplements Confucianist readings of history as the retrieval of a past Golden Age. The openness of the future surpasses in potential the past, the New Jerusalem transcends the Garden of Eden, but eschatology does not delete paleontology (such as Confucius's Golden Age called *Datong*)—just as the future does not discount the past. The Chinese-Christian worldview has now been stretched to include past, present, and future in the full spectrum of dynamic time. Despite the recurring (or spiral) movement of dynamic time, its forward and upward thrust is toward the creation of a people of God based on the incarnation of faith and grace. Christian virtue, derived from the virtue of Christ Jesus, is faithfulness and love and hope for the salvation of humanity and the whole cosmos.[151]

---

150. Begbie, *Theology, Music and Time*, 93.

151. For more, see Yeo, "Messianic Predestination in Romans 8 and Classical Confucianism," 281–83.

TOWARD A CHINESE CHRISTIAN POLITICAL ETHIC

There are a number of intersections between Confucius's and Paul's political ethics that we have discussed thus far, and I want to summarize them briefly here.

First, Confucius' critique of dynastic patrilinealism and his emphasis on the sage-ruler was the first such critique in Chinese history. With the centralization of power in patriarchy and the sheer self-interest that is innate to being human, it is to be expected that later Confucianism would distort Confucius' teaching. His ethics were ritualized. Love was subsumed under *li* (holy ceremonies). The history of the dynasties is one full of the corruption of power by the elite, of the domination of the masses, and of imperial claims to be the sons of Heaven without the demonstration of virtue of any kind. Confucius' political ethics sought to overcome these cultural blind spots.

Similarly, Paul's theological critique of political violence, the abuse of power, and the deluded claims of Rome had its long tradition in the Jewish prophets and their anti-imperial language and symbols. In the next few chapters we shall discuss the idolatrous claim of power based on familial or ethnic lineage. By anticipation one may inquire, for example, whether the Galatian Judaizers validated their gospel by laying claim to a distorted form of Mosaic particularism (proselytism and discrimination)? Is not the imposition of the Torah gospel upon Gentile Christians similar to Roman imperialism? Why would Paul argue that the Gentiles had become "heirs according to the [Abrahamic] promise . . . [and received] adoption as [God's] children" through Christ (Gal 3:6—4:7)? How would Christ, as a seed (*sperma*) of Abraham, help resolve the problem of ethnocentrism in the Galatian case? How would Christ help form an inclusive community of God's people—not only for the Christians in Galatia, but also for Chinese Christians today?

The Imperial City in Beijing and the cross of Constantine the Great (274–337) can be seen as symbols of distortion of Confucian ethic and Christian theology respectively. Take the Imperial City as an example: it is a symbol of a Confucianist culture, with the alignment of its gates and buildings to the heavenly position, and then the layout of its interior architecture reflects cosmic order. Confucius' concepts of harmony and hierarchy, ritual propriety and music are overwhelmingly present. However, the City was officially called the Forbidden City, signifying its

sacredness and distance from the "common people" (*pingmin*). The ruling elites assumed that they had the mandate of heaven to reign, and
often used force. Confucian ethics of *ren* (benevolence or humaneness)
and *de* (virtue) is difficult to realize, except if one understands the Cross
of Jesus outside Jerusalem as epitomizing the core of Confucian ethics.
The Cross is a symbol of a Christian narrative of God intervening in his
creation to redeem his people. God's reign of love and justice on earth
through his Son and the church (body of Christ) is the means of God's
salvation for all. The Cross of Jesus is the symbol of God's self-giving love.
Those who respond by faith and gratitude to God's love will in turn love
their neighbors for the sake of God's design and Heaven's intention.

The second intersecting point between Confucius' and Paul's political ethics has to do with divine right and the responsibility of rulers.
Rule by divine right is found in all dynasties—Chinese, Greco-Roman,
or Jewish. The mandate of Heaven, in whatever form, has been claimed
by rulers throughout the ages. A difficult question might be: Whereas
Confucius acknowledged that rulers are ordained to rule, would Paul say
God had given emperors the right to rule the world? Paul does not answer that question explicitly, and Galatians is not as helpful as his letter to
the Romans in this regard. Romans 13:1–7 seems to indicate that governments exist by divine right. Their power is derived from God, therefore
governmental authority is subordinate to God. Its purpose is to serve the
people. Paul's understanding of the authority of government is unique
in ancient Mesopotamian, Confucianist, or Greco-Roman thought because it does not assume the mythological or inherent sacredness of such
power. It enables one to question whether such power serves the purposes of God.[152] Understandably, my reading of Romans 13 is influenced
by my Confucian presuppositions, for I interpret the issue in Romans 13
to be not whether a government is legitimate, but *how* it is to be just and
benevolent.

---

152. John 19 gives a classic example of Jesus' power and Pilate's power. Pilate seems
to think that he has the power to release or to crucify Christ (John 19:10), Jesus on the
other hand replies that his power is "from above," from God, thus he is responsible to
God alone. Indeed, if Pilate finds Jesus to be innocent, a just man (Matt 27:19–24; Mark
15:14; Luke 23:14; John 18:38; 19:4–6), why does he not fulfill his responsibility as a ruler,
why does he not acquit Jesus? Instead, he abuses his power by crucifying Jesus.

Thirdly, the general assumption is that Confucius and Paul have little in common. I once thought Confucius to be anti-religious, a humanist and a political ethicist, preoccupied with retrieving some obscure Golden Age, and that Paul was theological, Christological, and eschatological. But upon closer study I find that their strengths supplement each other's weaknesses. Confucius' suspicion of religion draws attention to Paul's reaction to violence in acts of piety. Confucius' political context also provides a helpful lens for reading political power in Paul's gospel mission. Confucius' ethical insights enable me to better observe the communal problems in Galatia regarding group behavior and identity of such concern to Paul. Paul's Christology clarifies for me the possibility of personal and political salvation for the Chinese. Paul's cross-cultural sensitivity to Jewish and Gentile Christians helps me overcome the danger of ethnocentrism when working with a monocultural text, such as that of the *Analects*.

Lastly, Paul's eschatological definition of the goal (end, *telos*) of history supplements my Confucianist reading of history as a retrieval of a past Golden Age. Eschatology does not negate paleontology, just as the future does not discount history. As a Chinese Christian my worldview has now been stretched to include past, present, and future—the full spectrum of dynamic time. Dynamic time changes and progresses with time-fulfilling and meaningful events, first at the beginning of time when God created, inhabited, and redeemed through his Spirit. Genesis begins with the creative and redemptive process of God in time, and the narrative of time is made possible by the faithfulness of God. Despite the recurring or spiral movement of dynamic time, it has a forward thrust toward Christ, who is the *telos* (goal) of history. The virtue of Christ is faithfulness and love, and hope and the work of Christ is salvation for the sake of humanity and the whole cosmos. Thus, violence and destruction are not the will of God, only wholeness and salvation are. No time or place is outside the reach of God's salvation.[153]

Confucius' moral and political world and Paul's theological world overlap. Confucius articulates how ethics can overcome violence in interpersonal relationships and in government. Paul supplements ethics, or

---

153. Using a musical metaphor to understand eschatology is apt, as Begbie has done: "[B]ecause of its metrical matrix, *music actually depends for its very intelligibility on the enmeshing of nearness and delay,* to a degree unmatched by other art-forms" (*Theology, Music and Time,* 121). Emphasis his.

rather qualifies ethics with and subsumes ethics under, theology, because he believes that Christ has demonstrated to humanity how to be truly human and how to be God's children.

3

Li and Law, *Yue* and Music
in a World of Ritual and Harmony

The function of the *torah* (law) in Judaism and *li* (cultured behavior) in Confucianism was to serve the common good by establishing rules for corporate life. Torah and *li* also had the religious function of leading the community toward holiness. Neither the rules of the *torah* for communal life nor their concept of the people of God as the covenant, however, focused on the individual in isolation. Human beings are communal beings, and both law and *li* were necessary for the well-being of the two communities. Correspondingly, freedom (an issue of major concern in Paul's letter to the Galatians) is defined inter-relationally, rather than as one's personal right independent of others. The task undertaken in Chapters Three and Four is to spell out the ethics of virtue in the two contexts of interest here: Confucius and the Apostle Paul, or let us say Ancient China and Anatolia (called Galatia when Paul wrote his letter to the Christian churches of that region in the first century and today known as central Turkey). While the next chapter focuses on freedom in the context of communal ethics, this chapter looks at law and the community. The understanding of the self and the community in Confucius' and Paul's thought is sketched out first, then we turn to analyze *li* in the *Analects* and law in Galatians. These discussions are followed by an important and interesting insight of Confucius regarding the formation of virtue and community through music as a distinctive form of *yue* ("aesthetic delight" or "harmonious beauty"). Finally, the chapter ends with a consideration of Paul's meta-phorical—I suggest "musical"—theology of communion and "harmony" in the body of Christ.

LAW AND *LI* IN THE CONTEXT OF COMMUNITY

Self and Community

The ideal of harmony as a Confucianist aspiration is often set against the Western concept of the freedom of the individual, called individualism. This strict juxtaposition is not accurate because it is too simplistic. While one can read Paul using the lens of individualism, that lens does not well fit Paul's theology. Paul's theology does have a certain resonance with Confucius' ethics in its understanding of the self and community. Both thinkers understand the self as a social entity, even though Confucius' understanding places a greater emphasis on the social extension of real-ity, from the self to families, to societies, to countries, and eventually to the universe. Paul also assumes in all his letters the priority of the com-munity over the individual. When Paul deals with the issue of Jewish and Gentile relations in Galatians and in Romans, or with the question of communal concord in 1 Corinthians, or with the task of reconciliation in 2 Corinthians, or with the joy that comes with team-work in Philippians, he sees the issue at hand in terms of the body of Christ or in terms of adoption as into the family of God as God's sons (and daughters). In Paul's mind something new is happening, or is supposed to happen, and this new thing is the creation of a new social order in Christ. Paul's theol-ogy is about reconciliation with God and with others through Christ, in the belief that it is God's salvific intent that the community of faith becomes the body of Christ for the ministry of reconciliation.

Confucian ethics does not have a notion of reconciliation between human and God, however, its concern for communal edification as the ultimate goal of being human is similar to Paul's concern for reconcilia-tion between different factions in a community. The Confucian ethic of "illustrious virtue and renewing the people" (*minde qinmin*) is carried out in the context of community (*Great Learning* 1:1).[1] The five cardinal, bilateral relations (*wulun*) in Confucianism describe virtue formation in

---

1. See Legge and Yang, trans., *The Four Books*, 24.

the context of the social self: ruler and subjects (benevolence and reverence); father and son (compassion and filial piety); husband and wife (obedience and righteousness); older and younger brothers (mutual respect); friendship (affection, loyalty and trust).

This is not to say there is no concept of individual rights in either Confucian or Pauline thought. Their understanding of the individual, however, lies within the context of the community, rather than thinking of the community as an aggregate of individuals. The idea of the individual conceived of in terms of the community reflects their understanding of right as *freedom for others* and for the common good. It is in this context of community that we discuss how the law serves to define Jewish Christian identity, and how *li* defines the stylized culture of the Chinese.

Paul's View of the Law in Galatians

✧ Functions of the Law in Salvation History

In Galatians Paul addresses the question of the law mainly within the context of salvation history; that is, in terms of what God once did (defining his people by way of the law) and what God is now doing in the new age (by creating a new people through faith without the law). Gal 3:15–20 contains a discussion of the place of the law in creating an inclusive people of God. Paul appeals to the history of salvation to prove (a) that the relationship between the law and Christ does not annul the universal promise of God (3:15–16); (b) that the validity of the law is temporary, having a beginning and an end (3:17–18); and (c) that the law is subordinate to the history of God's saving promises (3:19–20).

Paul's position is that "no one annuls even a person's covenant,[2] or adds to it, once it has been ratified."[3] Paul appeals to the Abrahamic covenant in Genesis 15, which is *God's* testament to Abraham. It is a covenant

2. The word *diathēkē* (covenant) is a Greek (LXX) translation of Hebrew word *berit* (covenant), meaning a will or testament of a person without necessarily having the mutual consent of another party. See Rom 9:4; 11:27; 1 Cor 11:25; 2 Cor 3:6, 14, where the new covenant and old covenant are mentioned, referring to the old dispensation of the law and the new dispensation in the age of the Messiah. The problem here is whether the word *diathēkē* does not also connote the mutual contract between two parties. Though a human illustration, the analogy has ramifications for our understanding of God's covenant with Abraham, Moses, and humanity.

3. My translation.

based on God's grace. Under the Abrahamic covenant to be set apart as God's people is the result of God's initiative and not of human effort. In the offering of sacrifices as the way of finding out God's promise (Gen 15:7–11), Abraham was obedient, but he fell asleep (Gen 15:12). This meant God alone was the actor throughout the whole ritual process. If the old covenant is one of grace rather than works, then "works of the law" are but markers of grace for those already in the covenant. The old and the new covenants point to the *hesed* (steadfastness) of God and to the faithfulness of Jesus Christ. In Paul's mind both covenants are works of God's grace. The marker of the people of God in the new age is the faithfulness of Jesus Christ because the self-sacrificing love of Jesus includes all to be the people of God. The faithfulness of Jesus Christ is the gracious work of the cross, for the cross is God's way of forgiving the world justly (Gal 1:4) and loving the world despite its rejection of God's love. Jesus is faithful to himself and to his understanding of God, this faithfulness is seen in the way of the Cross. Jesus calls for loving enemies, doing good toward one's persecutors, of not returning evil for evil. Jesus cannot preach what he does not practice. Thus the Cross was inevitably Jesus' fate in this world—that is, so long as Jesus was faithful. Paul interprets Jesus' Cross and faithfulness as the faithfulness of forgiving love, of one who lays down his life for another, even the enemies of God. Jesus' faithfulness is consistent with God's faithfulness for God's nature and will cannot be less than Jesus'. Jesus' faithfulness to himself and to God must be also the manifestation of God's own faithfulness and forgiving love. There can be no other Christ than this Jesus because in human experience there is no greater love than the love that sacrifices itself in love and forgiveness.

Those Judaizers in Galatia who claimed the "works of the law" as the marker of the people of God had misunderstood faithfulness of God and Jesus. "Works of the law" are different from the "faithfulness of Christ" in two striking ways. First, the "works of law" cannot initiate anyone (Jew or Gentile) into a covenant (new or old) without discrimination, whereas the "faithfulness of Christ" both marks and equalizes all in becoming God's people through grace. Secondly, while the law protects the Jews before the coming of the Messiah, its role is to point to Christ and to lead to the eschatological reality of God's Spirit, thus the function of the law is temporary in the history of salvation. Let me elaborate on these two points. "custodian" (amah) nanny

✧ God's Faithfulness as the Basis of Abraham's Descendents

First, "works of the law" cannot initiate one into the covenant—Jew or Gentile. The new symbol Christ marks those who rely on his work of crucifixion (i.e., his life of faithfulness); it also initiates them into the community of sons and daughters of God through baptism (i.e., through the death [crucifixion] of the old self).

God's *hesed* (steadfastness) and Christ's faithfulness create a human family without discrimination, whereas, Paul argues, the law is impotent in overcoming the problem of discrimination. Gal 3:16 states that the promises and blessings were given to Abraham and his Seed, Jesus Christ.[4] Paul explains "not to seeds" (plural) but "and to your seed" (singular), referring to Christ.[5] Concurring with N. T. Wright, Daniel Boyarin explains:

> 'Seed' here does not mean Christ per se but rather 'family,' as its Hebrew original often does as well. . . . Now it does not say 'seeds,' i.e. families but 'seed'—family, so it follows that in order for the covenantal promise to come true, all of humanity must be constituted through Christ into a single seed. The law . . . could not be the means by which this will come about, since it divides humanity into families and does not join them into one seed.[6]

"Moses is not the mediator of the 'one family,'"[7] Abraham is. Here Paul is using the Genesis texts where Abraham's seed is the promised Isaac (Gen 17:21; 22:16–17; 24:7),[8] but Paul links Isaac to Christ. Paul is

---

4. *Epaggeliai* ("promises") the plural form is used here (and 3:21; but the singular in 3:14, 17, 18, 22, 29; 4:28), suggesting multiple blessings (fruitfulness, land, God's presence, as in Gen 17:1–9). If so, Paul uses Genesis 17, the text most likely used by the opponents. But Paul ignores the issue of circumcision, instead he focuses on the blessings to Abraham.

5. Paul's interpretation of scripture is not grammatically precise, it is Christologically sound. Verse 16b states, "It does not say, 'and to the seeds,' as if to many, but as to one, 'and to your seed,' who is Christ." The references to "seed" (*spermati*) in Gen 12:7; 13:1, 15; 17:8, 17; 24:7 are used grammatically in the collective sense, because the numerous descendants of Abraham were promised. Therefore, the collective noun makes *spermasin* ("seeds") unnecessary.

6. Boyarin, "Was Paul an 'Anti-Semite'?" 55. See Wright, *The Climax of the Covenant*, 162–68.

7. Wright, *The Climax of the Covenant*, 170.

8. Matera, *Galatians*, 127.

not forcing his christo-centric reading back into the Genesis text to read Abraham's seed as Christ, as though he were rewriting the story. Rather, he is reading the accounts typologically. Scripture proclaims in advance the gospel of Christ's faithfulness by way of the Abrahamic narrative (Gal 3:8): typologically that gospel is preached in the promise and offering of Isaac because Isaac is the Christ typologically. Those who are people of [Christ's] faithfulness are blessed through the faithful Abraham (Gal 3:9): typologically, Christ, not Isaac, serves as the seed and therefore defines Abraham's true descendant because in Christ "all the nations are blessed" in a way (i.e., by faith) Isaac could not (because of works).

Paul's argument that "Abraham's seed is Christ" confronts the opponents with his conviction that the faith and work of Christ is different from the works of the law. The works of the law do not even define who Gentiles are except by negation (the uncircumcised). But the faith and work of the crucified Christ includes the Gentiles as Abraham's sons and daughters by giving them positive self-definition. Moreover, the curse of the law is lifted from Jewish Christians. The only essential identity symbol for the people of God is Christ, the promised Seed of Abraham!

In Paul's understanding, God does not divide humanity into Jews as his favored ones and Gentiles as the aliens of his love. In the very beginning when God made covenant with humanity in Abraham, Jews and Gentiles were already at the center of his love and election and promise. God intended Jews and Gentiles alike to participate equally through Abraham's and Christ's faithfulness. God is doing a new thing when he defines Gentiles not by way of Jewish religiosity and culture but by means of Christ's works.

✧ The Eschatological Inclusion of Gentiles in Christ's Works

Secondly, the "works of the law" point all people to the eschatological salvation of God in Christ through God's Spirit. While the law had its intended purpose before the coming of the Messiah, its function has now ended. This second point is an elaborate one, and I want to delineate it in the following subsections.

Jews and Gentiles in the History of Salvation ✦ The first subpoint has to do with the order and condition of being the people of God—the old and the new covenants, the old and the new people of God. To put our inquiry into the form of a question, In the history of salvation, why is there a distinction between "the Jew first and then the Gentiles"? T. L. Donaldson provides a convincing argument: In Gal 3:1—4:7 Paul dramatizes the eschatological inclusion of the uncircumcised (the Gentiles) among the people of God by "representation and participation."[9] Donaldson interprets the plural "us" in Gal 3:13 as referring to Jewish Christians exclusive of Gentile Christians, thus seeing the redemption of Israel as a prerequisite for (or a condition of) the blessing of the Gentiles.[10] Gal 3:13 quotes Deut 21:22–23 ("Cursed be every one who hangs on the tree.") to mean that the law views anyone crucified as cursed by God. Such a person must be removed from the cross and buried. Christ, the Son of God, is crucified and buried. But his resurrection shows that the law that curses him is now at an end. Christ is not an exception to the law, Christ is the end of the law—by divine demonstration.

It is an Old Testament covenantal symbol that points to Israel's bearing the curse and how God's blessing could remove the curse.[11] In the new age of Christ, "Christ redeemed us from the curse of the law by becoming a curse for us . . . in order that the blessing of Abraham might be given in Christ to the Gentiles" (3:13).

Because the purpose of the law is to identify transgression, "those who rely on works of law" are transgressors. Israel is under the curse of the law because "they do not abide by all that has been written in the book of the law to do it" (Gal 3:10, cf. Deut 27:26). Other people, identified as Gentiles, are also under the curse because they do not have the law, they could not have abided by the law. They are under the sway of the forces of the cosmos (Gal 4:3, 9), they live in opposition to God and hence

9. Donaldson, "The 'Curse of the Law,'" 105. He writes, "The first century Judaism has a pattern of thinking about the Gentile—the strand of eschatological expectation that anticipated a massive turning of the Gentiles to Yahweh as an consequence of the end-time redemption of Israel" (110–11). For a similar argument, see E. P. Sanders, *Paul, the Law and the Jewish People*, 171–73; Beker, *Paul the Apostle*, 331–37.

10. Donaldson, "The 'Curse of the Law,'" 105; Hays, *Faith of Jesus Christ*, 86–92, 116–21. The emphatic placement of "us" (3:13) and "the nations" (3:14) at the beginning of the clauses suggests Paul's intention of contrasting the two groups of people, but then the context of Gal 3:6–14 suggests that the first group of people, i.e., the law observers, are subject to the curse as expressed by "us . . . all who rely on works of law" (105).

11. On the use of Deut 21:22–23 in Gal 3:13, see Caneday, "'Redeemed from the Curse of the Law."

under sin (3:22). Even Israel's possession of the law does not alter this fact. Israel's plight is but a special form of the universal plight. While Gentiles are under the "elemental spirits," they are not under the law, though they live in bondage. For the Jews, to be "under the law" is simply another way of being "under the cosmic elements" (4:3), because human beings are universally in bondage to cosmic principles.[12] The purpose of the law is to clarify the universal human plight. Israel, the people of the law, serves as *representative* of the whole of humankind.

Galatians 3:22 also sets forth the human condition. "All things" (3:22) are in need of redemption—Jews and Gentiles are equally in need of redemption. The enslavement of all things to sin expresses in its way the idea of the universal human condition. Gal 1:4, 4:3, and 9 speak of the same thing—all things are under sin. Sin is understood as a cosmic principle or force that enslaves creations. Paul affirms the goodness of God's creation, of a humanity created in the image and likeness of God. Human sinfulness is not an evil that resides in the individual. The preposition *hypo* ("under") suggests that sin is a power or certain realm or sphere of influence that binds humanity and keeps it from becoming what it knows it is intended to be. The human predicament is that it is bound, unable to live authentically, unable to live freely in righteousness, unable to live in faith with God, and in the trust of neighbors.

The result (the clause in Gal 2:2 is purposive) of being confined under sin is: "so that the promise from the faithfulness of Jesus Christ might be given to those who believe" (Gal 3:22). If Jews and Gentiles are equal in their human predicament, they are also equal in their reception into the covenant of God because of God's promise. The promise here means the same thing as in Gal 3:1–5 and 14, i.e., the promised Holy Spirit. Jews and Gentiles who believe in the faithfulness of Jesus Christ[13] receive God's Spirit, the eschatological sign of God's redeemed community.

The order and condition of the spiritual blessings of the people of God are seen in the process of eschatological salvation. This salvation is

12. Donaldson, "The 'Curse of the Law,'" 103–104. Cf. Beker, *Paul the Apostle*, 188 for the same idea.

13. This is a clear indication that the subjective genitive (faith[fullness] of Jesus Christ) reads better because the objective genitive will make the phrase "those who believe" redundant. See Chapter Six of this book (pp. 380–89) on Paul's uses of both subjective genitive and objective genitive of this phrase.

The myth of a people defines the people (law of Jews), making them exclusive. Christ universalizes the intent of the law, making the promises of God true to their original intent, inclusive of all peoples.

actualized by representation and participation:[14] (1) Christ's death and resurrection comprise the eschatological event in which the powers of this age are defeated and Christ becomes the representative[15] of the age to come, the firstborn from the dead. (2) Christ as a representative figure fully identifies with the human condition even to the point of death (Gal 4:4), so that all can share in his resurrection, and thus be vindicated, justified and given the life of the age to come (Gal 2:20). Finally, (3) the way to receive these benefits is to be "in Christ" (Gal 2:17, 3:26, 28). To be "in Christ" is to participate by faith in Christ's death and resurrection.

Likewise, the wisdom of Christ & East Asian cultures are part of the wisdom in the human tradition & accessible to all.

In Christ God's promise is now open to Jews *and* Gentiles. The law can no longer serve as a feature distinguishing Jews *from* Gentiles. In his death Christ has effectively abolished the restrictive character of enculturation.[16] This by no means denies Israel that the law has a special place in establishing salvation for all people. Donaldson explains that, "By creating a representative sample in which the human plight is clarified and concentrated, they set the stage for redemption."[17] Yet, Israel's theological culture of the law cannot be used as a condition by which other nations become the people of God. Through Christ God extended the Abrahamic promise to the Gentiles. J. C. Beker points out well that "the church of the Gentiles is an extension of the promises of God to Israel and not Israel's displacement."[18]

According to Paul's reading of history, Christ is the true heir of the promise of the universal inheritance and blessing, and therefore Christ determines those who are to be fellow-heirs.[19] All who are "in Christ Jesus" (3:26, 28), Jews or Gentiles, share their status as seed in a derivative way (3:29). Or as Donaldson expresses it, "'In Christ' existence, rather than circumcision or Torah observance, is the defining characteristic of

14. Donaldson, "The 'Curse of the Law' and the Inclusion of the Gentiles," 105.

15. Note that Christ identifies not only with the human situation in general (Gal 4:4) but also with Israel in particular. As Israel's representative, Christ is the representative of all humankind, all can participate in Christ. Cf. Donaldson, "The 'Curse of the Law,'" 106.

16. Cf. Stendahl, *Paul Among Jews and Gentiles,* 78–96; Davies, *Jewish and Pauline Studies,* 123–52.

17. Donaldson, "The 'Curse of the Law,'" 105.

18. Beker, *Paul the Apostle,* 332.

19. Schniewind and Friedrich, "*Epaggellō*," 583.

Abraham's seed."[20] Therefore, if the law defines the people of God in the period of promise, Christ now defines the people of God in the period of fulfillment. The identity symbol in the age of fulfillment is no longer that which separates Jews and Gentiles (law), but the One in whom two are united (Christ).

The Function of the Law and the Eschatological Giving of God's Spirit
Paul believes that the law "is capable of giving life" (Gal 3:12b), which is to say that in its own self-understanding the law is capable of giving life ("He who does them shall live by them"). In one sense this is to say that the law has the power to produce the ethical life for those who walk according to its guidance. The law says two things: (1) whoever does the works of the law lives. This is what the law thinks about itself. *But* contrarily the law says that (2) the righteous live by faith. Faith is not something one *does*. So doing the law does not lead to salvation. Moreover, the Son of God was cursed by the law, yet his resurrection shows that Christ, not the law, is victorious. The law therefore must be at an end. Gal 2:21 makes a similar point, that is, if the law can set a person right with God, then Christ would have died in vain. From the perspective of salvation history, the law was given not to *grant* righteousness *to* anyone. The law was not intended to create descendants of Abraham; the law cannot make people righteous. It was given to highlight the human condition and to limit the effect of sin (Gal 3:19).

Paul believes that righteousness does not come from the law, but through Christ's faithfulness and God's Spirit. If the law could give righteousness, then Christ would have died in vain. Being set right with God (being made righteous) is accomplished by the death of Christ, which is appropriated by faith. In faith, which is a gift of the Spirit, the believer completes—or better, continues—the act started in Christ's own faithfulness, culminating in the Cross. Righteousness in Paul's thought is something God does in Christ, not the Spirit. For faith not to be a *work* it must be a gift, and indeed this is the case: One can never decide to have faith and thereby produce it; unlike works of the law, which one can decide to do or not do and thereby fulfill them. Faith is rather always *experienced* as something given, separate from the decisional activity of the mind; it happens to the individual, it does not come from the individual.

20. Donaldson, "The 'Curse of the Law,'" 100.

Paul makes a distinction (perhaps not very clearly) between being set right with God by Christ's death on the cross and the righteousness that follows as the fruit of faith. Faith and its fruits *are* the work of the Spirit. The Christian virtues "faith, hope, love" are all experienced as gifts of the Spirit. They are not the consequence of decision (work). *At the same time*, there is the expectation, the requirement even, that those who say they *believe in* Jesus as the Christ will *also do* the things (the deeds) consonant with the example of Christ.

While the text in Galatians 3 is not clear on the role of the Spirit in granting righteousness and life, Galatians 4 describes the new reality believers have in Christ, and Galatians 5–6 clarify how God's Spirit gives life and righteousness to those who walk by it. In other words, the function of the law is not to grant righteousness, at most the law can pronounce innocent or guilty those who observe or violate the law. The eschatological Spirit of God through Christ's faith will break the power of sin, grant the believers righteousness, and enable believers to walk in the religious and ethical demands of the new law, namely, the love of God and neighbor. In Phil 3:6–8 Paul recounts his earlier attainment of righteousness according to the law; he also testifies that having once known the surpassing value of Christ, he counted that attainment as loss. The reason for this change of perspective surely has to do with his experience of the Spirit. Here in Gal 3:21, the conditional sentence concludes that the law that could grant such righteousness has never been given.

The eschatological gift of God's Spirit that comes through faith in Christ breaks the power of sin, grants the believer righteousness before God, and enables the believer to walk according to the Spirit. To walk according to the Spirit is to observe the ethical demands of the law but, for the Gentiles at least, the religious demands of the law (its cultic ordinances) are set aside.

Confucius will find Paul's understanding of virtue as the gift and work of the Spirit an alien concept. For Confucius, virtue is attained through works of *li* (ritual propriety). For Paul, virtue is an imitation of Christ—imitation itself is not the work of believers but of the Spirit in believers.

The Guardian Function of the Law and the Age of the Messiah ◆ The universal human predicament has already been explained in Gal 3:22; here in 3:23–24 the function of the law is to guard and to discipline those who are confined under the law (3:23b). Jews are defined by the sphere of influence in which they live, in this case, the law. That existence is temporary, i.e., "before faith came" (Gal 3:23a).

The law has its temporary role in the history of salvation as a *paidagōgos* (Gal 3:24, 25). *Paidogōgos* is a child's supervisor and caretaker from infancy to puberty, thus as a moral tutor and legal guardian, he ruled over the child. We can use the word "custodian" to translate *paidogōgos* to include the above nuances. A custodian is often needed to escort a minor to school, or to serve as a home tutor. As a guardian, the custodian has the responsibility to protect the child from immoral influence and to teach him how to be mature.[21] The custodian's responsibility for ruling, constraining, protecting, and teaching a child is holistic. His task is to fulfill the parent's desire that their child will in time become mature fully and well. As a custodian, the twofold function of the law is to guard and discipline. Just as the custodian protects the child, leading him safely to school, and safely home again, so the law is to protect Israel from the defiling influence of paganism. The law guards Jews from the curse and contamination of sin, marks them as the chosen people of God.

Just as the custodian's responsibility ends when the minor becomes an adult, the law's function ends when the age of the Messiah arrives— "until faith be revealed" (3:23c) or "when the time had fully come" (Gal 4:4). Christ *has* come, says Paul, thus it is no longer necessary for the law to protect and divide Israel from the nations. The word "faith" in 3:23c ("until faith be revealed") has the definite article (*tēn*), suggesting that the phrase is not talking about faith in general or about the principle of believing. Rather, it is more likely to refer specifically to the faith(fullness) of the Messiah. "Faith" (Gal 3:23c) cannot mean the act of believing as such or the response of trust, because both such acts and response were present when the law was in effect. Therefore, faith here must be qualified as either belief *in Christ* or the *faith(fulness) of Christ*. Paul believes that Jewish existence under the law was a temporary one in terms of marking them as God's people; with the coming of the Messiah, the law had done its job. The baton of creating and preserving God's people has been passed to Christ.

---

21. This is the view propounded by Young, "Paidagogos," 156–58.

Paul details the function of the law in Galatians mainly in terms of salvation history; that is, in terms of what God has done and is now doing in the new age. The former language of law and covenant is replaced by the new covenant in Christ. With this as our background in Paul let us turn our attention to Confucius' understanding of *li* and observe how ritual behavior, ethical rules, and the moral obligation derived from Heaven (*tian*) constitute the lifeblood of a community.

Confucius' Understanding of Li in the Analects

✦ Two Meanings of *Li*

The word *li* (禮, not to be confused with the word *li*, 理, meaning reason or order) is one of the most important concepts (along with *ren* [humaneness] and *yue* [music]) in the *Analects*. It is used in its narrow sense to refer to ritual rules and regulations.[22] It is also used broadly to refer to proper norms of behavior expected in various social contexts.[23] *Li* is a common word used in the time of Confucius, meaning rites or rituals that include rites of sacrifice performed on behalf of one's ancestors, the royalty, or deities. Etymologically, the ideograph *li* symbolizes a sacrificial act, and more specifically to a religious ritual of sacrifice. One of the early dictionary meanings of *li* is "treading" or "following."[24] It points to the act or ritual whereby spiritual beings are properly served in order to give human happiness. *Analects* 2:5 mentions the rites of serving one's parents, the rites of burial and the rites of sacrificing to one's ancestors.[25] Confucius' understanding of *li* reflects his concern for a particular order within the patriarchal structure of society, just as the Jewish law is understood as community rules.

Confucius knows the power of *li*, the rites and rituals of the past. *Analects* 3:11 shows that Confucius knew the ancestral sacrificial rites as well.[26] There is another example of Confucius' thorough knowledge

22. Schwartz, *The World of Thought in Ancient China*, 67–68. See also Yao, ed., *RoutledgeCurzon Encyclopedias of Confucianism*, 1:356–58.

23. Those holding this interpretation are Lao, *Zhongguo zhexue shi*, 1:40; Cai, *Kongzi Sixiang Tixi*, 238. See also Yang, *Lunyu Yizhu*, 18–21.

24. *Kangxi Zidian*, 1920.

25. See Chen, *Lunyu Duxun Jiegu*, 15.

26. The context of *Analects* 3:11 is a discussion of various rituals; in particular the

of past rites: When someone asked Confucius about the Di Sacrifice (perhaps in the presence of the emperor—the text is without context), Confucius said, "I do not know. Anyone who knows will find the affairs of the empire as if displayed clearly here—i.e., like his palm" (*Analects* 3:11). Huang explains that "in saying he did not know, the Master was trying to avoid discussing the subject. For it was prescribed by the rituals that a subject should avoid discussing the sovereign's faults in public [in the presence or absence of the emperor]."[27] Confucius knew rites and rituals well, but it was against propriety (*li*) to shame the sovereign in public.

There is another incident recorded in *Analects* 3:1. In 517 BCE, Confucius witnessed how the Discreet (*Di*) Sacrifice was performed in the temple of Duke Hsiang of Lu with only two of the total eight teams of dancers taking part—thus called "eight-team" dance. The rest of the dancers were performing at the estate of the Ji family. Confucius criticized the Ji family for not respecting ritual propriety; he said, "If this can be tolerated, what else cannot be?" (*Analects* 3:1).[28]

A broader understanding of *li* as ritual propriety is needed. *Analects* 17:11 explains that when Confucius spoke of ritual propriety, he meant more than presenting jade and silk according to the requirements of ritual tradition (*Analects* 17:11).[29] *Analects* 2:23 uses the word *li* referring to the proper and stylized behaviors practiced in the Yin and Zhou dynasties. Despite Confucius' respect for traditional ritual practices, his discussion of *li* in the *Analects* does not encourage association of ritual practices with magic and superstition, which were prominent during the

---

Display Sacrifice (Xia-*li*) and the Yin dynasty (Yin-*li*) in *Analects* 3:9. In *Analects* 3:10, Confucius discusses the Discrete Sacrifice (*Di*; so called "discrete" because the wooden tablets of the royal ancestors had to be arranged very discretely in the temple dedicated to the founding fathers of the Zhou dynasty). Confucius states that once the libation was poured, he had no desire to watch any more. The text does not explain why. A commentator of the *Analects*, Huang, explains that "the right to perform the Di Sacrifice, a prerogative of the emperor, was granted to Lu upon the founding of the state to honor Duke Dan of Zhou, its founding father, . . . However, for Lu to continue observing the ritual was a usurpation; furthermore, the order of the tablets was not properly arranged. Hence the Master's aversion to witness the ceremony" (Huang, *Analects*, 61). Jiang Wenye suspects that the Ji family has violated the propriety of ritual and music when they request the "eight-team" dance, since they can only ask for the "six-team" dance; see Jiang, *Kongzi De Yuelun*, 103; Zhu, *Zhongguo Yinyue Wenxueshi*, 136.

27. Huang, *Analects*, 19. See also Chen, *Lunyu Duxun Jiegu*, 34.

28. My translation. See Chen, *Lunyu Duxun Jiegu*, 26–27.

29. See Chen, *Lunyu Duxun Jiegu*, 332.

Xia, Shang, and Zhou dynasties. Confucius seems not to dwell long, if at all, on the world of gods and ghosts. He was concerned with political ethics, the world of humanity. And to say that Confucius is unconcerned with the world of gods and spirits is not to suggest Confucian ethics is not spiritual. His social ethics seeks to draw humanity out of its mundane contexts in order to become fully human on a higher plane. This they do, says Confucius, when they observe *li* (ritual) and embody *ren* (humaneness). His ethics focuses on the present reality, challenging humanity to realize the best possible. He believes that the time of sacredness, of the sage as the exemplary ruler when humanity had reached a degree of excellence, lay in the past. So in the *Analects* references to the *li* of the Zhou dynasty is grounded on the memory preserved in the tradition.

So far we have translated *li* as ritual or rite. However, these English words may arouse in the modern readers, especially Western Protestants, negative connotations—giving a false impression of its true meaning. The terms "ritual" and "rite" are often used in religious contexts to refer to a set of procedures one has to follow if one intends to maintain membership within a given community of faith. So the connotations often associated with the terms, such as "wooden," "fixed," "uncompromising," "mechanical," "imposing," with the overtones of "lifeless," "formality," or "going through the motions"—are all off the mark when it comes to the meaning of *li*. Connotations of this kind fail to translate the tenor of the Chinese word *li* as encompassing, as is the case, compassion and empathy. For example, in *Analects* 17:21, Confucius says that observing the mandate to mourn for a period of three years is not about keeping rigid rules. When his disciple Zai Wo opines that three years is too long and one year sufficient, Confucius replies, "When the gentleman is in mourning: eating delicacies, he does not relish their good taste; listening to music, he does not feel any happiness; living at home, he does not enjoy its comfort. Therefore, he does not do so. Now, if you feel at ease, do so! [i.e., mourn for one year]" (*Analects* 17:20).[30] As soon as Zai Wo left, Confucius disappointedly says that Zai Wo is without *ren* (he is inhumane, not benevolent). Confucius' rationale for teaching Zai Wo to observe the *li* (rite) of mourning for three years is based on *ren* (humaneness) and *ai* (love): "For three years from birth children do not leave their

---

30. Lau, trans., *Analects,* 171; See Chen, *Lunyu Duxun Jiegu,* 336–37.

parents' arms. Three years of mourning is universal, and does Zai Wo love (*ai*) his parents for three years?" (*Analects* 17:21).[31]

Confucius objects to the understanding of *li* as rigid following of traditions or rules. He is disgusted with

> the emptiness and superficiality of his age personified in the figure of the 'village worthy' (*xiangyuan*), who carefully observes all of the outward practices dictated by convention, and in this way attains a measure of social respect and material comfort, but who lacks the inward commitment to the Way that characterizes the true Confucian gentleman [*junzi*]. Confucius refers to the village worthy as the 'thief of Virtue' (17:13), for from the outside he *seems* to be a gentleman and so lays a false claim to virtue. . . . Just as the debased people of his time use the mixed color of purple in place of pure vermilion and confuse the decadent music of Zheng with true music, they mistake village worthies and the 'clever talkers' for true gentlemen. . . . The most prominent and egregious reflection of the sorry state of his contemporaries is the corruption of ritual practice among the political and social elite. . . . Similarly, the overweening pride of the Three Families who ruled Lu in Confucius' time caused them to usurp the ritual privileges properly accorded only to the Zhou kings—a transgression against the very structure of the cosmos that appalled and saddened Confucius (3:1–2, 3:6).[32]

In another passage, Confucius says that he cannot stand seeing those in high places not lenient, those performing rituals (*li*) not reverent, of those observing mourning not in grief (*Analects* 3:26).[33] Empathy, reverence, and grief are part of the self-cultivation of *li*. Following the rites (*li*) is a way to develop one's humanity. One's life and welfare are dependent on others, and one should be grateful to them and repay their goodwill. The *Record of Rituals* (*Liji*) says that if one fails to return a favor, one is violating the rite.[34]

Rites are not merely formalities (*Analects* 3:12, 17:9) as if those who observe them were hypocrites and the rites themselves contrary to good

31. My translation.

32. Slingerland, trans., *Confucius Analects*, xxiv.

33. My translation. See Chen, *Lunyu Duxun Jiegu*, 45.

34. See Chang, "Confucian Theory of Norms and Human Rights," 129.

grace. Nor are they hollow or meaningless acts. As Ames and Rosemont point out,

> A careful reading of the *Analects*, however, uncovers a way of life carefully choreographed down to appropriate facial expressions and physical gestures, a world in which a life is a performance requiring enormous attention to detail. Importantly, this *li*-constituted performance begins from the insight that personal refinement is only possible through the discipline provided by formalized roles and behaviors. Form without creative personalization is coercive and dehumanizing law; creative personal expression without form is randomness at best, license at worst. It is only with the appropriate combination of form and personalization that community can be self-regulating and refined.[35]

克己
复礼
为仁

Li exhibits a form of *decorum* (propriety), a "customary, uncodified law, internalized by individuals, and governing gentlemen in their personal and social lives, in their behavior toward the spirits as well as the rest of the world. For that reason, *li* has the extended meaning of 'correct behavior.'"[36] Rites also require us to have *proper feeling* toward others: "Lin Fang asked about the basis of the rites. The Master said, 'A noble question indeed! With the rites, it is better to err on the side of frugality than on the side of extravagance, in mourning, it is better to err on the side of grief than on the side of indifference" (*Analects* 3:4).[37] Genuine feelings can be expressed when one is wholeheartedly involved. If one can neither participate emotionally (*ruzai, rushenzai*) nor be personally involved in the ritual (*wubu*), it is better not to make sacrifices at all (*Analects* 3:12). One should sacrifice believing the ancestral gods are present (3:12).[38] Reverence and respect are feelings and virtues that are cultivated in the ritual process. Children, in acts of filial piety, provide parents with shelter and food, but more than that, they also serve the parents with respect and a cheerful heart (*Analects* 2:7, 8). Respect is also required of any government official (*Analects* 1:5, 15:8), including a ruler governing the state (*Analects* 6:2).

While the narrow meaning of *li* refers to ritual and rite, Confucius expands and redefines the term to include cultural patterns or styles

35. Ames and Rosemont, *Analects*, 52.
36. Ching, "Human Rights," 74.
37. Lau, trans., *Analects*, 19.
38. See Chen, *Lunyu Duxun Jiegu*, 35.

that are deemed proper and decent. *Analects* 2:23 use the word *li* in a broader sense, referring to the *cultured patterns* of life. With regard to *li* in its broader sense, Van Norden writes, "*li* also includes everything from matters of etiquette to almost the whole of one's way of life, or ethos."[39] Rosemont similarly argues that though largely based on "archaic supernatural beliefs," "a part of the genius of the Master and his followers lies in their giving those ritual practices an aesthetic, moral, political, and spiritual foundation which was independent of their original inspiration."[40] "Propriety" has been an accepted translation of *li* in the past, and I still think that in the broad sense, the Confucian concept of *li* is about propriety. In *Analects* 12:1 we read: "Do not look at what is contrary to propriety (*li*), do not listen to what is contrary to propriety (*li*), do not say what is contrary to propriety (*li*), and do not do what is contrary to propriety (*li*)."[41] Of course, propriety is culturally defined but his does not preclude different cultures from having similar views. For example, in one culture public kissing or hugging may be acceptable, while in another offensive. In one culture burping after meal is a token of appreciation to the host, in another rudeness. Most, if not all, cultures view wearing a swim suit proper on the beach but not in the office. All cultures see murder as a criminal act. All cultures value respect of elders. Some people show respect by means of kneeling and bowing, avoiding mentioning the first name of elders, and taking care of elderly parents in their own home. Others call their elders by their first names to show intimacy, and place them in homes for professional care.

I find Rosemont's translation of the term *li* as "ritual propriety" apt.[42] He writes that ritual propriety in our modern world should be understood

> not simply as referring to weddings, *bar* and *bat mitzvahs*, funerals, and so on, but equally as referring to the simply customs and courtesies given and received in greetings, sharing food, . . . and much more. To be fully civil, then, a Confucian must at all times be polite and mannerly, following closely the customs and rituals

---

39. Norden, ed., *Confucius and the Analects*, 19.

40. Rosemont, "On Confucian Civility," 192.

41. My translation. See Chen, *Lunyu Duxun Jiegu*, 215.

42. Rosemont, "On Confucian Civility," 192; also Ames and Rosemont, *Analects*, 51.

governing these and numerous other interpersonal activities. To do so was to follow the 'human way' (*rendao*).[43]

人 往   仁

仁

Li pertains to the "norms governing polite behavior."[44] The word *li* is commonly used in the Chinese language to modify other nouns, e.g., proper manner (*limou*), courteously give way (*lizan*), ritual etiquette (*liyi*)—indicating that personal and social behaviors are formative for the individual to become fully human. As Wilson says: "More than shaping our raw impulses by any *li* whatsoever, we become fully human when we participate in particularly those *li* our culture(s) deem to be constitutive of the human."[45] *Li* is decorum in everyday social engagement so that the ritual of social interaction with others forms the *virtue of being human.*

↪ *Li* and Ritualized Style—Etiquette

Since both meanings of *li* are used in the *Analects,* it appears that Confucius intends to link ritual appropriateness with a *stylized* way of life, assuming that virtue cultivation is a life long process. *Li* as ritual refers to "a code of propriety that governs all phases of human life, including self-cultivation, personal conduct, and etiquette governing family and social relations, state affairs, and sacrificial rites."[46] Ritual is not simply outward action or performance without content. Ritual has its own narrative and style. A person involved in a ritual immerses himself or herself in the story constructed through a particular cultural prescription of what is right, proper, and beautiful. Of course, a ritual is never an individual belief; it is a creed or the consensus of a community. Fingarette uses the example of handshake as a ritual of social engagement; Gal 2:9 uses similar ritual—"right hand of fellowship."[47] A handshake is not simply a physical act, but by it

43. Rosemont, "On Confucian Civility," 192.

44. Shun, "*Ren* and *Li* in the *Analects*," 53.

45. Wilson, "Conformity, Individuality, and the Nature of Virtue," 97.

46. Huang, *Analects,* 50.

47. The gesture of handshake instills among people the attitude of goodwill. In the ritual of filial piety, the attitudes of reverence and gratitude were instilled. I borrow the handshake illustration from Fingarette, *Confucius—The Secular as Sacred,* 12–13. Fingarette gives the example of handshake as the ceremony of the ritual of agreement or friendship. The practice of handshake is an ancient custom that can be traced back to biblical times (e.g., 1 Macc 6:58), and most notably is Gal 2:9. Grundmann writes: "This usage derives from the custom of giving the right hand at the conclusion of an agreement

two persons are accepting what the larger culture perceives a handshake to be: a form of greeting, an expression of good wishes, or the passing of a blessing between friends. If two people do shake hands, they are bound by the ritual propriety of the handshake. That includes the appropriate timing of extending and retreating the hand, the duration of the handshake, and the amount of force applied. These ritual proprieties involved in the gesture make it a pleasant experience, enabling friendship and goodwill. A simple ritual like the handshake also cultivates the virtuous person in how to extend goodwill. Much more important are other rituals involving complex behaviors and interpersonal relationships. As Fingarette writes, "the peculiarly moral yet binding power of ceremonial gesture and word cannot be abstracted from or used in isolation from ceremony."[48]

The *style* of a ritualized action is also crucial. Style is not like clothing, which can be put on and taken off. Style reflects attitudes, motives, intentions; in short the person that we are. Manners cannot be faked; insincerity comes through. Pretension ends up making other people uncomfortable. As Kuppermans puts it, "Absolute uniformity might well be excessive, but considerable continuity in things that matter (which include close personal relationships) can be important in allowing for a sense of personal integrity."[49] Thus style forms virtue. There is no absolute sense of what correct style is. With one's peers, one often feels comfortable giving stronger handshakes. With an elderly woman the handshake is gentler and slower.

To fine tune the style further, one needs to know intuitively the speed and pressure most comfortable to the recipient. Most of the time, most people shake hands without consciously knowing what is happening—people are *habituated* to act gracefully! The handshake is a form of *art* that none is born with: so it takes learning and practice till it becomes "second nature"; we do not mentally calculate the timing, the duration or the force of the gesture. The up-bringing of children includes schooling them on how and when to shake hands.

By observing and imitating what others have done provides a wide range of styles for various kinds of contexts. In cross-cultural settings and where cultural settings themselves are changing, style is extremely

Spontaneity

---

or alliance" ("Dexios," *TDNT* 2:38). See also Betz, *Galatians*, 99–100.

48. Fingarette, *Confucius—The Secular as Sacred*, 12.

49. Kupperman, "Naturalness Revisited," 51.

difficult to learn. Different styles are appropriate in different situations. How does one determine, for example, whether a bow, handshake, hug, or kiss is appropriate in a particular setting? How do persons from different cultures greet one another without offense? Translate this example into the situation in Galatia, and a similar question can be asked: How can Jewish Christians, such as Peter, know what the accepted behavior of Gentile Christians should be regarding their identity? To such a question, Paul is silent. But Confucius' concept of "the coherence of style"[50] and the stylized behaviors of ritual propriety provides insight.

Confucius' discussion of ritual behavior indicates that *li* (ritual propriety) is not simply a matter of following rules. It is a matter of learning and expressing through stylized patterns of behavior what and how it is to be human.

✎ *Li* and Political Rulers

As used by Confucius, *li* is related to norms of conduct in a hierarchal society. The order and prosperity of the state depend upon the proper positioning of relationships: rulers and ministers, fathers and sons, older and younger brothers, husbands and wives, and mothers and daughters-in-law, etc. In the public arena of politics *li* becomes the constitutional norm as a way of guarding political rulers. Rulers are not simply to expect commoners to be submissive to them. Political rulers ought "to exercise self-restraint and to fulfill ritual propriety" (*keji fuli*). "To exercise self-restraint and to fulfill ritual propriety" is also the responsibility of commoners. As citizens they practice self-discipline and cultivate virtue, so that their personal virtue might enable them to help cultivate civic virtue within the country. The goal for commoners "to exercise self-restraint and to fulfill ritual propriety" (*keji fuli*) also has the purpose of disciplining the ruler, who will thereby be encouraged to stay on the course of self-restraint and fulfill the requirements of propriety. The ruler is expected to take the lead, because *keji fuli* begins with them.

It is a common misunderstanding to think of classical Confucianism as leading inevitably to political conservatism and totalitarianism. It is true that the Confucian *li* (rites) gives authority to rulers, but it is given that they might demonstrate *li* (propriety) and cultivate virtue thereby

克
己
复
礼

---

50. Kupperman, "Naturalness Revisited," 51.

justifying their authority. The hierarchical structure of Confucian society requires authority to be passed from the top to the bottom. So it is also with the cultivation of virtue. The citizen's role is to provide accountability and to discipline political rulers to assure the government practices benevolence. Ultimately, government exists for the sake of modeling and thereby establishing virtue through the act of self-cultivation, that is, becoming fully human through ritual. As Fingarette writes:

> To act by ceremony [*li*] is to be completely open to the other; for ceremony is public, shared, transparent; to act otherwise is to be secretive, obscure, and devious, or merely tyrannically coercive. It is in this beautiful and dignified, shared and open participation with others who are ultimately like oneself (12:2) that [hu]man realizes [oneself].[51]

Confucius' teaching does not simply endorse patriarchal structure, it departs from feudalistic thinking at a critical point. The discussion of justice in the *Analects* (7:16) is telling: "The Master said, 'In the eating of coarse rice and the drinking of water, the using of one's elbow for a pillow, joy is to be found. Wealth and rank attained through immoral means have as much to do with me as passing clouds."[52] Money or status achieved unjustly means nothing (like the passing clouds), justice is found in a society based on goodness and virtue. The Master is satisfied with coarse rice and plain water by means of self-labor in integrity. He does not want to have anything to do with immoral means of wealth and rank.

✧ *Li* and Filial Piety

Confucian ethics views ritual propriety as the power that cultivates benevolence in human beings. We have already seen how the cultivation of the heart, i.e., the sensitivity and the attitude one has toward others, can become the "second nature" (immediate response) of being human. The cultivation of virtue as the "second nature" is for Confucius the cultivation of *the* nature (ideal) of the human being via *li*—stylized behavior or cultured pattern. Let me explain in terms of filial piety.

Confucian ethics sees *li* as the structure that forms *ren* (humaneness), and filial piety as an aspect of *li* that is essential to cultivate people

---

51. Fingarette, *Confucius—The Secular as Sacred*, 16.

52. Lau, trans., *Analects*, 61. See Chen, *Lunyu Duxun Jiegu*, 117.

to become fully human. The filial relationship begins of course at birth, making filial piety the most basic and of the highest excellence in the Confucian ritual. A family welcomes its offspring into a complex network of relationships, from the immediate family of parents and siblings to their relatives, especially to the older generation. The family is the most basic of structural relationships and forms the first community in which one exists. From conception, one learns to relate to parents, to whom they owe the source of life. Loyalty toward them is to respect and to love them, duty is to be obedient to them and to serve them. When Meng Yizi asked Confucius about filial piety, the Master asked him to be obedient always. Fan Chih asked Confucius what he meant by being "obedient always." Confucius explained, "When your parents are alive, comply with the rites (*li*) in serving them; when they die, comply with the rites (*li*) in burying them and in offering sacrifices to them."[53] Confucius seems to imply that obedience to *li* is the way of honoring parents. These filial obligations do not end in death, for the son is "to refrain from altering the ways of the father for three years" (*Analects* 4:20).[54]

Filial piety is the basic virtue of becoming human and ancestor worship is the basic ritual of becoming human. It is so basic in Confucianism that Zhang Funggan called ancestor worship "the religion of heaven and ancestors."[55] The ritual of ancestor worship requires that children observe three years of mourning after the parents die (*Analects* 17:21). The ritual of mourning expresses the irrepayable debt one has toward his parents. Confucius is not concerned about providing shelter and food for one's parents, since these are the basic duties everyone ought to fulfill. The responsibility of filial piety requires *reverence* (*jing*), for even where dogs and horses are sheltered and fed it is the exercise of mere responsibility (*Analects* 2:7). Confucius is concerned about one's "face" (*se*) in fulfilling the responsibility of taking care of parents—the attitude, gestures, and feeling of the sons and daughters (*Analects* 2:8).[56] To show reverence (*jing*) to parents is not merely completing one's duty, but fulfilling one's responsibility with *inner* joy, admiration, and appreciation that *surface* in one's appearance and gesture.

filiality as "caring"?

53. Ibid., 11.

54. My translation.

55. Zhang, "Tianzu Jiao," 1–9.

56. See Chen, *Lunyu Duxun Jiegu,* 16.

In ancient Chinese society, the ritual of filial piety did not need rational justification. It was "the way it is"—how life begins and how life continues and how it ends and how it begins again. While the Confucian understanding of *tian* (Heaven) may have a vague notion of "creator of all things," the most tangible and visible source of life is one's parents. Yearley captures well the *gift* character of life and the feelings of *gratitude* it works toward those from whom it originates:

> People respond strongly to such an origin because they recognize that with it unpayable debts have been incurred. In most relationships, that is, people receive and give in a fashion that allows for repayment; equity can be restored. In these relationships, however, people receive so much that there is no way for them to repay what has been given. When debts exist that cannot be repaid, the only appropriate response is gratitude, reverence, and a set of related reactions.[57]

Filial piety, then, is more than just the ethical obligation to make sacrificial offerings to one's ancestors; it is a way of life based on the awareness of life's origins. It forms human beings of benevolence. Once the ritual of filial piety is learned, one will extend *li* (ritual propriety) toward one's elders into the wider circle of a society.

Northrop points out the difference between Confucianist and Christian epistemologies with regard to the issue of ancestor worship:

> The worship of ancestors is so important in the Chinese religion and culture. Only by putting up tablets which preserve the memory of their differentiated, unique, local, private personalities and by carrying on ceremonies associated with these tablets which keep the memory of their presence and one's sense of indebtedness to them continuously in mind, can a continuity of their full personality beyond the time of death be preserved. Conversely, in the Christianity of the West, in which immortality of the individual personality in its unique differentiations is guaranteed by doctrine, the use of symbols to preserve their memory and of religious ceremonies associated with these symbols is not encouraged, since according to the Western doctrine it is provided for by God Himself.[58]

---

57. Yearley, "An Existentialist Reading of Book 4 of the *Analects*," 262.
58. Northrop, *The Meeting of East and West*, 337–38.

What does Paul think of filial piety? The practice of filial piety, as Confucius advocates it, does not appear in the teaching of Paul. If one is to find its parallel, the slight resemblance will be 1 Tim 5:4, a text probably written by a later disciple of Paul, that advocates showing piety toward one's own family and to repay their parents. 1 Tim 5:4 adds that such doing "is acceptable in the sight of God." Paul's letter to the Ephesians does admonish "honoring of one's parents" (6:2), in accordance to the Mosaic commandment as recorded in Exod 20:12. The Jewish law does not spell out the ethical rationale of honoring one's parents. In contrast, the Confucian ethics gives an elaborate, persuasive argument. Both Confucian ethics and Pauline admonition regarding respect of parents and elders are set in the context of *li* (ritualized requirement) and law respectively. However, Paul's view of interpersonal relationship is different from Confucius' because of Paul's understanding that all relationships are seen in the new light of the new creation, which each person is to become in Christ through baptism. The new creation in Christ is based on love and forgiveness and manifested in the fruits of the Spirit, and that the imminent return of Christ subordinated all relationships to the believers relationship to God, i.e., to love father, mother, sister, etc. not as bilateral relationships, but to love each and all as persons-in-God.

A CHINESE CHRISTIAN THEOLOGY OF *LI* AND LAW

While one may properly argue that Paul's law cannot be equated with Confucius' *li,* we can nevertheless see how both Jewish law and Confucian *li* define the best cultural forms in each ethnicity, so much so that we can call both the Torah and *li* holy. Paul's discussion of the law in Galatians concerns (a) the definition of being Jewish and Gentile within the scheme of God's people, and (b) the function of the law in guiding and preserving God's people, thus redeeming them from the bondage of sin and an evil *aeon.* Paul's concern for the coexistence of Jews and Gentiles in an inclusive people of God finds its parallel in Confucius. Confucius is fully cognizant that as ritual propriety *li* is not simply a matter of social conditioning as though we can choose to abide by it or not. Human beings participate in ritual (*li*) because they want to be formed and shaped by their sacred traditions, and because they believe that ritualized behavior constitutes the way to being more completely human and holy. Fingarette gives an interesting reading of Confucius' understanding of *li* (ritual propriety) that corresponds to how the Galatian Judaizers understood doing the works of the law as members of the covenant ("covenantal nomism"). Fingarette believes that Confucius assumed

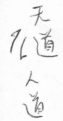

> there is one *li* and that it is in harmony with a greater, cosmic
> *Dao*. . . . He assumes that this *li*, and the cosmic *Dao* in which it
> is rooted, are internally coherent and totally adequate, and that,
> finally, the only moral and social necessity is, therefore, to shape
> oneself and one's conduct in *li*.[59]

Because of that assumption, Fingarette argues that Confucius made the political move of trying to elevate the Zhou-*li* of his home state above the ritual practices of all other states, believing that he could save the world from the deterioration of *li* (and music): "It was a natural tactic for a man of Lu to turn attention not to military conquest but to cultural conquest as the primary basis for order and unity."[60] Is not this conviction similar to that of the Judaizers, who think that law is the only identity symbol worthy of respect? This issue hinges on ritual as forming one's identity in a cross-cultural context, to which we now turn.

Ritual and Identity in Cross-Cultural Context

The initiation rites and rituals by which the Jews preserved their identity as the people of God included circumcision, the observance of days, dietary and sabbath laws. Through them the covenant was maintained and together they constituted the religio-cultural ideals of Judaism. From the Jewish perspective, to become fully human *as a Jew* required this "Torah observance." How to *translate* this Jewish ideal and propriety so that it would have the same meaning for Gentile Christians was another issue altogether.[61]

---

59. Fingarette, *Confucius—The Secular as Sacred*, 57.

60. Fingarette, *Confucius—The Secular as Sacred*, 61. See Wilson's critique of Fingarette's reading, Wilson, "Conformity, Individuality, and the Nature of Virtue," 98–99.

61. I am here thinking of what Tanner has written about the "hybrid, relational affair" of cultural identity: "The distinctiveness of cultural identity is therefore not a product of isolation; it not a matter of 'us' vs. 'them.' Cultural identity becomes, instead, a hybrid, relational affair, something that lives between as much as within cultures" (*Theories of Culture*, 57–58).

Before the incident in Antioch (recorded in Acts 15 and Galatians 2) the Gentile Christians had been fully accepted into the circle of those Jews who believed Jesus was God's Anointed. The pillars of Jerusalem (Peter, James, and John) had agreed that Gentiles need not be circumcised to be considered fellow believers and numbered among the people of God (Gal 2:1–10). Table fellowship in which both Jews and Gentiles took part was a sign of that inclusiveness.

It takes much learning and practice to feel comfortable doing a ritual even in one's own culture. Doing the same gesture in a cross-cultural setting is even more challenging. Fingarette points out two failures of ritual performance entailed in the "lack of learning and skill" and the "lack of serious purpose and commitment." He notes that "beautiful and effective ceremony requires the personal 'presence' to be fused with learned ceremonial skill" and the commitment to convey sincere purpose in one's action.[62] In cross-cultural interaction, these two points are even more significant. Hugging a person or kissing them on the cheek when meeting for the first time may be unpleasant to those coming from a culture that does not observe such customs.

A classic example of controversy on cross-cultural propriety in relation to identity happened in Chinese church history regarding offering food and incense on ancestral altars. To be true to the ethics of filial piety, Chinese have been practicing ancestral veneration (*ji* meaning reverence, implying "worship") as the spiritual and ethical expression of their identity. They use rituals that express not only respect and service to ancestors while they are alive, but also they continue to serve and venerate them as "living dead" after they die, for they are thought still to exist, but in another world (*ying*). As Christians who came from another culture and who believed food-offering and bowing were religious rituals, most missionaries in the nineteenth century prohibited Chinese Christians to practice what they termed "ancestral worship," considering its rituals forms of paganism.[63] The issue of ancestral veneration is complex,

---

62. Fingarette, *Confucius—The Secular as Sacred*, 8.

63. Most Protestant and Roman Catholic missionaries including Walter Henry Medurst and John L. Nevius prior to 1860, and even present-day mainline protestant churches in Asia, take the prohibition position on Chinese practicing ancestral worship. Missionaries such as William Martin, Young Allen, Timothy Richard, and those of the Jesuits represented by Matteo Ricci, held the compromising position towards ancestor worship at the end of the sixteenth century. But the seventeenth century Dominicans and Franciscans held the opposing position, which eventually led to the prohibition of their

and I have shown elsewhere that Christian missionaries failed to see in this rite the subtleness of cross-cultural propriety in the formation of Chinese identity. By suggesting that Chinese Christians offer flowers in place of food, they had asked the Chinese in effect to become Western Christians.[64]

Cross-cultural *li* (propriety) is difficult to achieve. This accounts for Peter's "fear" at Antioch. Peter had been living the style of a Gentile, i.e., socializing with Gentiles. His withdrawal from the fellowship meal was the result of pressure from the circumcision party. But in Paul's mind the issue is one of hypocrisy—his behavior does not match the *li* (propriety) of his new conviction. The ritual propriety consonant with faith in Christ has not been observed. In Galatians Paul attempts to carry out what we have called a *cross-cultural hermeneutics*, that is, he tries to differentiate the old ways of establishing group/self-identity with the new symbol required by Christ. The new symbol of the people of God requires a change in the self-understanding of both Jews and Gentiles. Each group has to learn how to practice "the *li* (propriety) of membership" in the body of Christ in order to belong to a community *and* at the same time to maintain its own group integrity.

There are two things to be said about "the *li* (propriety) of membership" in Christ. First, in Gal 2:15 Paul differentiates Jewish identity from Gentiles *before* the coming of the Messiah: "we, who are Jews by nature, and not sinners from among the nations (or "as the Gentiles are"). The word "we" here refers to Paul, Peter, Jews, and Jewish Christians (such as his opponents in Galatia). This self-definition[65] distinguishes Jews from Gentiles. "Jewishness is determined by birth"[66] as the Jews understand it. Gentiles are sinners precisely because they have no torah and consequently observe no Torah.[67] Possession of the law defines Jews religiously

---

missionary work (in 1720). For more on the various responses to ancestor worship, see Smith, "A Typology of Christian Responses to Chinese Ancestor Worship," 628–47.

64. I have dealt with the issue of ancestral veneration in a number of works: Yeo, *Rhetorical Interaction in 1 Corinthians 8 and 10*, chap. 11; idem, "The Rhetorical Hermeneutic of 1 Corinthians 8 and Chinese Ancestor Worship"; idem, *Jizu Misi*, passim; idem, "Cross-Tradition and Cross-Gender Hermeneutics"; idem, "Paul's Ethic of Holiness and Chinese Morality of *Renren*."

65. Cf. Betz, *Galatians*, 115; Stauffer, "*Egō*" 361–62; Fung, *Galatians*, 113.

66. Betz, *Galatians*, 115.

67. This does not mean Gentiles are lawless and without any sense of right or wrong. Rom 2:15 points out that Gentiles do have conscience and law written in their hearts.

and ethnically. Jews define themselves and others by means of their self-identification. Jews are born Jews because they are born within the covenant-love of God as set forth in the tradition. They are born God's people, graced with God's law, and are called to observe all those works of law (nomistic services) that mark them as people of God. By that definition, all those born outside that covenant are Gentiles, those who are without God's law, and therefore to be reckoned as sinners[68]—"sinners" not in the sense of having committed wrong but in not having the covenantal relationship with God.

This definition of Gentiles centered around the identity of an outsider inevitably leads to an understanding of Gentiles as "no-body"—they are not chosen, they do not have law, etc.; this *"via negativa"* definition does not set a boundary to mark who they are as Gentiles. "Gentile" as a race does not exist. Thus, this definition of Gentiles is inadequate, if not dangerous, because of its implicit theology. Two points can be made here: (1) The self-definition of Jews as the covenanted people of God has the danger of upholding the makers rather than glorifying the faithfulness of God that initiates and sustains who they are as God's people. (2) The definition of others by way of a *via negativa* is a mono-cultural act that has the tendency (a) to view people in the simple dualism of superiority/inferiority; (b) to set up the potential of conflict and thus divide community; and (c) to impose one's way of life on others who are too weak to resist.

Secondly, Paul explains to Jewish Christians that by their own acknowledgment "a person is not made righteous by works of the law but through faith in Jesus Christ" (Gal 2:15), appealing thereby to their awareness of the concept of "being justified/made righteous"[69] (2:16)—being set right before God. In his article, "The Problem at Galatia," David Gordon shows that "faith" in Galatians refers to faith *in Christ,* so much so that Paul uses the two terms ("faith" and "Christ") interchangeably to mean the same thing.[70] The use of the aorist in Gal 2:16 ("we *believed*") cor-

---

68. Matera, *Galatians,* 99 points out 1 Macc 2:48 "Gentiles" and "sinners" are equated: "They rescued the law out of the hands of the Gentiles and kings, and they never let the sinner gain the upper hand."

69. "Being justified" appears three times in Gal 2:16; the verb "being justified" comes from the same root word as the noun "righteousness," and despite linguistic clumsiness, for consistency's sake, one should translate the verb as "being made righteous" or "being rightwise." See Cosgrove, "Justification in Paul," 653–70.

70. Gordon, "The Problem at Galatia," 42–43.

roborates this point: a new and decisive step is necessary for Jews when they place their trust *in Christ*. Here in his own cross-cultural hermeneutics, Paul has already taken a new step, using the concept (*pistis,* faith) not merely of trust but more specifically of *trust in Christ* as the hermeneutical key to refute the misunderstanding of the Jewish Christians and to propose a more inclusive symbol of communal identity.

Even in the old economy of the Torah (law), Jewish identity rested on the gracious election and faithfulness of God. The act of God's grace came first, and upon it the covenantal law was based. The performance of nomistic services, the "works of the law," are to be seen as the way the covenanted people maintained their end of the covenant. The controversy, then, was not to be seen as a disagreement about the means of entering the covenant (since the means had always been and could only be through God's grace), but only about how the covenant was to be maintained, whether by works of the law or by faith in Christ.

"Works of the law" and "faith in Jesus Christ" contrast law or Christ as the identity marker for God's people. Paul dismisses the idea of being justified "by works of the law" (the phrase appears three times in 2:16; cf. 3:2, 5, 10). Paul is not saying that the Mosaic or Abrahamic covenant that the law represents is a perverted view of the law. Such an interpretation tends to see Judaism as a sort of perverted religion. It also totally ignores the Jewish context and the situational character of the Galatian epistle. It assumes too quickly that the guilty conscience of individuals seeks salvation through a legalistic life. The Galatian debate is concerned not with individuals but with the people of God; more precisely, it is concerned not with the legalistic life of the individual but with the identity symbol of the people of God: "justification by faith in Christ" or by "works of law."

Given the audience of Jewish and Gentile Christians (not Jews and Gentiles in general), and of a debate concerning what symbolized one's identity as the covenanted people of God, the phrase "justified" (*dikaioun*; see 2:21; 3:6, 21; 5:5 for *dikaiosynē,* and 2:16 [3x], 17; 3:8, 11, 24; 5:4 for *dikaioō*) cannot refer to entering the covenant of grace, or to the beginning of salvation, or to receiving the imputed righteousness of God. It refers to none to these things and so, I avoid using the word "justified." Instead I use the term "set right" to note that a person or a people maintain(s) the covenant as the way to define his or their relationship with God. The word *dikaioun* can mean "to show justice," "to vindicate someone as just," or "to acquit someone." The emphasis is not about the *sinlessness* of the just; it is about the one (in this case, God) who graciously vindicates or acquits sinners. The emphasis is not about acquittal from guilt and sin in the sense of wrong-doing, it is about having been set right by God from shame and curse so that now propriety, honor, and freedom characterize the new and rightful relationship one has with God.

The subtle distinction I make between "justified" and "set right," between "sinlessness" and "accepted by God" is important. The emphasis on a relationship set right by God based on his gracious acceptance of all defines the *li* (propriety) of membership in the household of God through the work of Christ, and not through cultural distinctions. The emphasis also highlights the fact that maintaining covenantal works as rituals (either "works of the law" or works of mercy and charity in Christian service) is grounded on God's grace, which precedes and sustains the covenant God's has with humanity.

↔ Christian Rituals (Rites) of Baptism and *Agape* Meal

The law and its works (rituals) define the Jews as the people of God within the old covenant: What rituals define the new people of God inclusive of Jews and Gentiles within the new covenant? The *li* (propriety) of membership in the body of Christ has its rituals that enable members to maintain the covenant. Baptism and the love feast (the Lord's Supper celebrated within the context of a fellowship meal) are distinct, but not exclusive, Christian rituals, or in Confucian language, the Christian *li* (ritual propriety). Before explaining how Confucius' understanding of *li* helps me to view Christian rituals, I want to point out the basic difference between them.

The incommensurability between Confucius and Paul is their different understanding of ceremony, rites, or rituals. Whereas ritual (*li*) in Confucius' ethics has its end in forming virtue, Christian rites, such as baptism and the Lord's Supper, do not have as their primary purpose the cultivation of Christian virtue. Christian rites are not ceremonies that promote virtue in the way Confucius thinks of *li* (ritual) as moral. In the Confucian understanding of the moral life as the ideal, *li* (ritual propriety) grounded in *ren* (humaneness/benevolence) is believed to enhance the virtuous life. In Paul, however, the moral life is conceived of as arising from the Spirit. Paul argues that the church does not need the law as a means of virtue formation. Sufficient alone is all-encompassing love, seen as the creative power of the Holy Spirit.[71]

Because of the basically different assumptions concerning *tian* (Heaven) and *Theos* (as God in Christ), Confucius' ethics, centering on the formation of virtue via *li* (ritual propriety), is incommensurate with Paul's ethics in which only the Spirit forms virtue. Paul sees virtue as a gift or fruit of the Spirit apart from learning the traditions of the law, which is the heart of moral education. Confucius' ethics is incomplete without moral training and *li* (as law), although his view accepts a significant role for love, and he is silent on the Spirit. Thus, despite the differences between Confucius and Paul, it is necessary to look at the two traditions from the standpoint of the other and to find ways to glean wisdom from both traditions.

Confucius' emphasis on learning the moral wisdom of the sages would have found Paul's understanding of the role of the Holy Spirit in the moral life of believers quite an alien but supplementary idea. Though Confucius and Paul have incommensurable thoughts, their thoughts can be supplementary through the intertextual reading of Chinese Christians. The case in point is that Chinese Christians believe that the Holy Spirit forms virtue in them *and that* they themselves are actively working with the Spirit in the life of holiness. By equating virtue with the work of the Spirit, the individual claims no *work* on his own. Paul's sees life within the context of God's activity. Life is not just a human phenomenon. It is the arena of God's activity bringing about the fulfillment of God's purposes. Affirming the work of the Spirit to form virtue does not mean that believers are passive. A number of imperatives were used in Galatians 5 to indicate that one should participate actively with the Spirit in the war with the flesh: be gracious toward others, and maintain moral purity. It is here that I see how helpful Confucius' ethics of virtue can be, though Confucius knows nothing of the power of the Holy Spirit.

In a social or cross-cultural context, Paul is using the rituals of baptism (Gal 3:28) and the *agape* meal (implied in 5:13) as the common identity symbols for Jewish and Gentile Christians. From the Confucian perspective, these are not just rigid rituals, rather they are the *li* (ritual propriety) of the new community in Christ. These *li* (ritual propriety) allow participants to live in the larger reality toward which these symbols

71. See Cosgrove, *The Cross and the Spirit*, 182–83.

point. Through participation in that larger reality believers are cultivated and transformed into a new way of life, as symbolized by baptism into Christ and the Lord's Supper. Chinese Christian churches aptly refer to the Eucharist (Thanksgiving Meal, i.e., the Lord's Supper) and the ritual of baptism as *shengli*—holy rite/ritual.

聖礼

Rather than using "works of the law" as the symbol for identifying Christians, Paul uses baptism. While circumcision was a proud sign for the Jews, it was not a "cultured" or stylized sign for the Celtic people of Galatia, to which many of the Gentile Christians belonged. As a sign baptism is applicable to everyone: Jews, Gentiles, males and females, masters and slaves. Baptism is an egalitarian symbol that includes all and brings all together. Paul explains the oneness of Jews and Gentiles using the *li* (rite) of baptism and the imagery of clothing: "For as many of you were baptized into Christ, have clothed yourself with Christ" (Gal 3:27, RSV). The preposition "for" (*gap*) of 3:27 explains 3:26, that Jewish and Gentile believers are sons of God in Christ because they are baptized into Christ. In the immediate context, the imagery of "putting on" Christ as one puts on clothing conveys the oneness of Jews and Gentiles, as the next verse (Gal 3:28) explains that in Christ "there is neither Jew nor Greek, there is neither slave nor free, there is no 'male and female.' For all of you are one person in Christ Jesus."

Baptism is also a ritualized imitation of dying and being raised, symbolizing that believers die to sin and come alive to new life. Although the rite of baptism happens only once for a believer, the ritualized imitation of dying and being raised continue throughout one's life, as one grows into the "second nature" of being like Christ. Paul uses the imagery of putting on clothing (*enedysasthe*) to exhort the believers to take on the spirit of Christ (Gal 3:27) so that they become new spiritual persons.[72] With what one is to clothe oneself is not explicitly stated, but the intended inference is righteousness and salvation a common admonition in biblical texts.[73]

---

72. Alexander the Great liked to put on the clothes of the various gods, and so became Ammon, Artemis, Hermes, Heracles. The imagery of putting on clothing in Gal 3:27 is parallel to Alexander's way of putting on the dress of god. "*Endyō*," BAGD, 264.

73. E.g., Rom 13:12–14; 1 Cor 15:53–54; 1 Thess 5:8; Eph 4:24; and Col 3:10. The Old Testament speaks of being clothed "in righteousness and salvation," e.g., Isa 61:10 ("He has clothed me with the garments of salvation, he has covered me with the robe of righteousness, as a bridegroom decks himself with a garland, and as a bride adorns herself with jewels") and Job 29:14 ("I put on righteousness, and it clothed me; my justice was like a robe and a turban").

The imagery portrays the new life and identity in Christ, which can be characterized as a life of righteousness. Baptism symbolizes the event of Christ's death and resurrection—Jesus' obedience to God, but also the divine affirmation of Jesus' resurrected life.

The imagery and theological significance of baptism is not developed in Galatians as it is in Romans 5–6. Clearly, in the early church baptism was equivalent to circumcision in that it was the rite of initiation into the community of faith. One dies to the old self, just as Christ was crucified; one is raised to new life free of old encumbrances, just as Christ was raised from the dead. Christ's crucifixion resulted from the curse of the law, for apart from the law he would not have been crucified. This is the curse of death, the power of sin. Yet, says Paul, by accepting the cross, which is cursed by the law, Christ has broken the curse of the law, he has conquered the sting of death, and overcome sin by being victorious over it through the power of forgiving love. Resurrection is the fact and symbol of this triumph, and being brought up from the waters of baptism is the (intended) fact and symbol of the new life free from the curse of sin and death experienced by the believer through the power of the Spirit. While the law may for a time continue to be the identity symbol of the people of God ("to the Jew first," writes Paul in Romans), the reality of being in Christ through baptism is the universal alternative to the non-Jew, encompassing new life, blessings, and righteousness.

The second rite Paul advocates is "the Agape" (Gal 5:13: *tēs agapēs* "through [the] love, be enslaved to one another"). The reference can mean the Eucharist (Love Feast) or God's love as exemplified on the cross. Tom Rands argues that the "definite article . . . suggests that Paul had a special kind of love in mind . . . . A close reading of the context supports an interpretation of 'the Agape' as a short hand term referring to the love feast."[74] It can refer to the love feast but it is not limited to it. The immediate context of Galatians 5 suggests not the problem of the common meal at Antioch (although the Antioch incident is one of the main problems faced in Galatians, especially in Chapter 2). The problem is that of the freedom of the believers. The definite article may also refer to the love explicitly manifested in the Christ event. The phrase *dia tēs agapēs* ("through [the] love") recalls Gal 5:6 where it is said that Christ's faith and the believer's faith are expressed through love. "The love" here refers

74. Rand, "The Rhetoric of Ritual," 160; see also idem, "A Call to Koinonia," 79–92.

to the unconditional love of Jesus on the Cross, and the love feast is the ritual that seeks to concretize in a symbolic yet real way a communal life of self-sacrificing love. This is Paul's vision of creating a new community in Christ where communion (*koinōnia*) and mutual service (*diakonia*) define the daily ritual of its members.

"Love" is intentional action that reaches out and relates to others with the purpose of sharing with and building up of others (cf. 1 Cor 8:1). The sending of God's Son and Spirit unto the world is an act of divine love as God seeks to relate and reach out to humanity, in the most intimate and personal of ways. In Galatians 5, Paul writes that the purpose of the freedom God gives is to reach out to others. In other words, love has its goal in human freedom and human freedom is defined as "love in service to others" (Gal 5:13). Human freedom bounded by self-interest only results in bondage and destruction. This "freedom for others" models the shared life of God in Christ and the Spirit.

Envisioning God's New Creation in Christ

Paul concludes his letter to the Galatians with the summarizing statement that "neither circumcision nor uncircumcision is anything, but a new creation" (Gal 6:15). As external signs, circumcision and uncircumcision are meaningless. All that matters is the "new creation" in Christ through God's Spirit (cf. 2 Cor 5:17), or as Gal 5:6 states, "faith working through love." The new creation includes Jews and Gentiles, a new community without discrimination and conflict, because the Spirit has made them one in Christ made real by their love for one another and symbolized by the agape meal.

Paul ends with a traditional blessing now transformed into an exhortation: "Peace and mercy come upon those who conduct themselves according to this rule" (6:16).[75] If Paul here draws upon the Septuagint (LXX) translations of Pss 124:5 and 127:6 for the language of blessings,[76] then it is significant to note that: (a) Paul has extended the "peace upon

75. My translation.

76. As Matera, *Galatians*, 226 suggests. LXX is the abbreviation for Septuagint, the Old Testament translated into Greek from the Hebrew text. The references of the Psalms in the Hebrew Bible are different from that in the Septuagint. Modern translations such as English and Chinese versions follow the references in the Hebrew Bible. Thus Psalm 124 in the LXX is Psalm 123 in the English Bible.

Israel" to all those now in the new creation of Christ; (b) Paul expands the word "Israel" to "the Israel of God," signifying that his understanding of being "in Christ," which is open to Jews and Gentiles, is in no way anti-semitic, because "Israel" as a nation is now changed to "Israel of God" suggesting a people, not a place; and (c) Paul adds the word "mercy" (*el-eos*) to "peace" (*eirēnē*) (Gal 6:16).

Given what we know of how Paul proves that Jews and Gentiles are included in the body (community) of Christ by faith, it is difficult to see how he would make a distinction between the Christian church and Israel. At the time of Paul's writing, Christianity and Judaism were not two different religions, so interpreting "being in Christ" and Israel as two distinct groups would not be helpful. Neither would it be help-ful to think of Israel as limited to ethnicity and heredity. Paul qualifies "Israel" with "of God," he is thinking of salvation history as put forth in Gal 3:1—4:31. "The Israel of God" is a *theological* term. It refers to how God in the very beginning elected a group of people out of the nations to be his people (Abraham and his descendants), and called them to be agents of his will (through the law). "The Israel of God" is not an ethnic term, because Christians are part of the Israel of God and Christians are never referred to as descendants of Christ. Christians are referred to as *heirs* (Gal 4:7). An heir is simply one who inherits something, not a de-scendant necessarily.

Now, in Christ, the definition of Israel has been radically altered from Jews alone to Gentiles also, and the identity symbol changed from circumcision to baptism into Christ, and the task refocused from observ-ing the law to baptism into Christ, so that the whole world, Jews and Gentiles, might be endowed with God's Spirit and truly become chil-dren of Abraham, the Israel of God. The children of Abraham are not defined in terms of heredity, but in terms of spiritual connectedness with Abraham—faith in the God who grants the promise of blessings. The Gentile believers in Galatia are to understand themselves as children of Abraham. The blessing of peace and mercy fall upon them, but also on all those who, like them, walk by the rule of the new creation in Christ. Those who are in Christ fulfill the law through faith expressed in love. They walk by the rule of the new creation and thereby fulfill the law of the Israel of God.

*The Rule of Law/*Li *and Harmony in Society*

Li (ritual propriety) in Confucianism and law in Judaism are alike in their function of defining ideal humanity as those members of the community who observe its rules and rites. The difference between *li* and law lies in their specific content. Whereas the content of *li* is almost exclusively on moral obligation, the content of the Jewish law includes moral and religious dimensions. But both *li* and law are used by the respective traditions as a means of attaining a sanctified life—either before God and/or the people.

Paul's understanding of the function of law is radically different from that of *li* in Confucius' thought and of the law in Judaism. Whereas Confucian and Jewish ethics are based on rites (*li*) and law (Torah) respectively, Pauline ethics is based on the Spirit. Paul does not believe that Christian sanctification can be attained by means of the law, but only by means of the "law of the Spirit" (Gal 3:3–5, cf. Rom 8:2). For both Jewish and Gentile Christians, the life of sanctification in the age of Christ is realized by following the new way of the Spirit. The law has neither its means to save nor its function to define the people of God.

We have already seen how God's Spirit is central to Paul's theology. This fact enabled me in my early Christian life to overcome the Confucian tendency toward legalism. Paul's attitude toward the law is quite negative in terms of his assessment of its limited function in salvation history. Though Confucius' retrieval of a past Golden Age is incommensurate with Paul's apocalyptic framework for salvation history, Confucius would agree with Paul that *torah* (or *li* [ritual propriety] in Confucius' terminology) has a pedagogical function.

Confucianism sees the pedagogical function of law as good *but insufficient*—law can solve disputes, adjudicate conflicts, but it cannot prevent them. Laws and regulations can only go so far, and they are not the humane way of government. The Master said: "If you govern them with decrees and regulate them with punishments, the people will evade them but will have no sense of shame. If you govern them with virtue and regulate them with the rituals, they will have a sense of shame and flock to you" (*Analects* 2:3).[77] In another passage, when Ji Kang Zi asked

---

77. Huang, *Analects*, 52. See Chen, *Lunyu Duxun Jiegu*, 13; Yang, *Lunyu Yizhu*, 25; Zhu, ed., *Sishu*, 190. Cf. *Analects* 8:9.

Confucius about using capital punishment on those who do not practice *dao* (the Way), Confucius replied that if a ruler rules well, he does not need to kill, and then Confucius admonished Ji to rule with *de* (virtue) without exerting physical force (*Analects* 12:19).[78] In other words, the success of a government lies in how little it uses the law; the order and prosperity of a country is served by *li* (ritual propriety).

That is why Confucius turns to virtue and defines government as a ritual (*li*) of virtues—"You will not have difficulties if you are able to rule the state by ritual (*li*) and deference" (*Analects* 4:13).[79] Confucius expands *li* (ritual propriety or holy ceremony) much more positively to refer to a ritualized and aesthetic culture. According to Confucius, ritual propriety is the structure of *ren* (humaneness), the ritual that makes one human. To live a life of *li* is to be in a cultured yet natural pattern of interpersonal relationships that "work through spontaneous coordination rooted in reverent dignity."[80] In our society today, we could hardly charge a person for not being cheerful or dignified. But to cultivate a civil and aesthetic society, styles or ways of being such as dignity, congeniality, and grace are virtues that build community. Style is a difficult category when judging right from wrong. Style reveals the attitude of a person deeper than that of his behavior. It reveals the intentions of a person deeper than that of his actions.[81]

The importance of these distinctions will become clear when we look at modern societies that use the rule of law to maintain social order. Besides some countries whose legal systems are dysfunctional, there are many societies overwhelmed with litigation, and their legal systems are often abused by the self-interest of individuals, lawyers, and corporations. The rule of law may settle disputes based on shared ideas of justice, but it cannot create harmony. The limitations of the rule of law, and the ameliorative effect Confucian ethics might have when supplementing it, has

---

78. See Chen, *Lunyu Duxun Jiegu*, 225.

79. My translation. See Yang, *Lunyu Yizhu*, 82–83.

80. Fingarette, *Confucius—The Secular as Sacred*, 8. Cf. *Analects* 2:3, 13:3.

81. The raging discussion today in the United States concerns the battle between the First Amendment and vulgarity of pornography. Dignity and grace as virtues are losing out to freedom of speech. According to Confucius, *li* and style do not mean *any ways* people *wish* to do. Rather, they are defined by virtues that build up a person or a community.

been expressed by Tu Weiming.[82] He argues that the ethics of Confucius, which focuses on virtues, could beneficially supplement the human-rights consciousness inherent in the rule of constitutional law. He further argues that interpersonal relationships based on trust last longer than adversarial relationships.

We have looked at the nature, the role, the commonalities, and the differences between ritual propriety (*li*) in Confucian ethics and law (Torah) in Jewish tradition as well as in Pauline theology. We have also drawn out the implications of *li* and law for our modern societies and have suggested harmony ("the common good") as the goal (*telos*) of living by the law and *li*. When the common good is coupled with the rule of law, the way of life live together is transformed into virtue.

Our next task is to define "harmony" in relation to the formation of a community, and how different cultures have different ways of expressing aesthetically the way to attain harmony.

YUE (MUSIC), HARMONY/NATURALNESS, AND BEAUTY[83]

The Understanding of Confucius

Confucius suggests that there are times when rituals are used woodenly and inappropriately; in such cases, disharmony and unnaturalness result. Rituals are not artificial gimmicks, they are not just for show. They are powerful enough to bring together a disintegrated community, and to help a morally deteriorated society return to virtue. Whether in government or in the common affairs of interpersonal relationships, according to Confucius, harmony is the way for overcoming chaos, and naturalness is the key for disarming conflict. In seeking modern equivalents for social harmony and naturalness, democracy and its radical exemplification in Quakerism come to mind. Democracy is an effort toward maximum participation within a representative form of government toward the end of achieving freedom for all; Quakers do not act until there is unanimity or consensus, thus allowing the Spirit to lead. In the latter, "speaking

82. Tu, *Confucian Ethics Today*, 151–52.

83. An early draft of this section was published in the following two articles: Yeo, "Musical Harmony according to Confucius and Paul"; "System of Harmony according to Confucius and Paul: Music, Goodness, Beauty."

one's mind" involves listening what others think and feel. In both cases, the harmony of the community is the intended goal toward which the process leads.

In Confucian thought, to which we now turn, harmony and beauty in community can be formed by way of *yue*—"aesthetic delight" (including instrumental music, songs, dances, and poetry that make up the "aesthetic culture"). Aesthetic delight brings about harmony within a person and especially within the community. The following discussion of *yue* as aesthetic delight focuses on music because of Confucius' emphasis on the role of ritual music and *musical harmony* in the moral life of individuals and community. Confucius believes that, as stylized expressions of beauty, music (*yue* 樂) brings about delight/joy (*le* 樂) and harmony (*he* 和) within a community.[84] The same Chinese word (*yue*) can be read as meaning either "music" or "joy." Yet beyond this verbal similarity there is an aesthetic connection as well. Music engenders joy and delight—as well as harmony—as people gather together to make music or sing songs.

◆ Harmony/Naturalness

Ritual propriety and music are so intertwined that the two words *li yue* (propriety and music) are frequently mentioned together in Confucian texts. In the *Record of Rituals* (*Liji*) one reads, "Music is the harmony of heaven and earth; ritual is the order of heaven and earth. Through harmony all things are made known; through order all things are classified. Music is manufactured from heaven; rituals will shape the earth. Overcontrol will produce chaos, over-expressed will cause violence. Manifest the heaven and the earth, then one can stimulate rituals and music."[85] Confucius knew the *Book of Ritual* well. His emphasis on the essential combination of ritual and music in political and moral life is drawn from the ancient Chinese worldview of *yin-yang* and "five elements" (*wuxing*), viz., metal, wood, water, earth, fire. A Taiwanese musician and mu-

---

84. On music in Confucius' age, see So, ed., *Music in the Age of Confucius*, 7–34; Liang, *Music of the Billion*, 47–75; Kaufmann, *Musical References in the Chinese Classics*, passim; Jiang, *Kongzi De Yuelun*, passim; Zhu, *Zhongguo Yinyue Wenxueshi*, passim; Yang, *Zhongguo Yinyue Shigao*, 2 Vols. passim; Liu, *Zhongguo Gudai Yinyueshi Jianshu*, passim; Chen, "Kongzi shiyue meixue zhong de zhengtixing gainian," 1–10; Yung, "The Nature of Chinese Ritual Sound," 13–31.

85. My translation. *Liji*, 113.

sicologist, Jiang Wenye, explains that music in the verse of the *Book of Ritual* quoted above means the harmonious interaction between heaven and earth, between *yang* and *yin,* and that rituals ensure the order of all movements in heaven and earth.[86] According to the worldview of *yin-yang* and the five elements, the cosmos at its primordial beginning was in its mysterious, formless gas-state of "togetherness" called *Taiji* (Great Ultimate or All Togetherness).[87] The Great Ultimate then split into two substances: one light and clear substance and the other, a heavy and substantive kind. The light material rises above and becomes cloud in the heaven; the heavy matter consolidates and sinks to become the earth. Heaven produces heat, therefore it is *yang;* the earth is colder, its nature is *yin.* But heaven and earth interact, the *yang* gas becomes fire, the *yin* gas becomes water. Fire and water interact and produce thunder and lightning, then rain; and consequently, they produce wood (plant), earth, and metal.[88] Jiang explains that in ancient Chinese worldview, sound and pitch are thought of as a type of light gas, therefore music is considered to be celestial substance; music is *yang* and active. Rituals are substances used for the earth, rituals are *yin,* passive.[89] According to this worldview, Confucius believes that music and rituals can harmonize heaven and earth and bring about the moral order called *dao* (the Way). Thus, the *Book of Ritual* reads, "Those who know music will integrate with rituals. Once one have music and rituals, one has virtue (*de*)."[90]

The relationship between *li* and *yue* is "harmony." The key text on the Confucian idea of harmony is *Analects* 1:12, which reads: *li zhi yong, he wei gui* (禮之用, 和為貴), followed by a sentence that reads: "the Way (*dao*) of past kings is beautiful" (*xianwang zhi dao, si wei mei*). These words are said by Master You, not by Confucius himself; but Master You conveys the central idea of his Master Confucius. Soothill translates the words in the first sentence, "In the usages of *decorum* it is naturalness that

86. Jiang Wenye, *Kongzi De Yuelun,* 5.

87. Ibid., 6.

88. Ibid., 6.

89. Ibid. For an excellent account and analysis of music before the age of Confucius, see ibid., 17–75.

90. My translation. *Liji,* 112. See the work of DeWoskin (*A Song for One or Two,* 30–31) who suggests that music in ancient China was thought of as having the function of linking the rulers with the power of heaven, the people with their ruler, the living members with the spirits of their ancestors.

is of value."[91] Waley translates, "In the usages of ritual it is harmony that is prized."[92] Lau's translation is, "Of things brought about by the rites, harmony is the most valuable."[93] And Huang translates, "In the application of the rituals, harmony is most valuable."[94] Most translators render the word *he* (和) as either harmony or naturalness, pertaining to the aesthetic category used in the context—that of the beautiful practice of rituals in government. Kupperman has worked on this text and has rightly proposed that what is meant by decorum/ritual (*li*) and harmony/naturalness (*he*) has to do with how *li* (rituals, i.e., manners and styles of interaction) promotes *he* (harmony, i.e., naturalness) in interpersonal relationships.[95]

The two English words—harmony and naturalness (translating the Chinese word *he*) try to get at "the coherence of oneself," i.e., when one's behavior and one's desire are not in conflict with each other. Harmony or naturalness (*he*) is the delight, the desire, and the ease that results from behaving in a certain way, which we commonly call a "lifestyle" or "way of life" of *wuwei* (effortlessness or naturalness).[96] But "lifestyle" here does not refer to the outward, jaded, merely superficial ornamentation of one's behavior, such as the "lifestyle of the rich and famous." Rather, "lifestyle" as a "way of life" has the tenor Confucius meant for it to have, that of the exemplary person (*junzi*) whose aim of self-cultivation is to be benevolent (*ren*), i.e., one who has realized his/her full humanity. This "way of life" of *internal coherence* (*he*) prompts one to be at home with virtue; there is no discrepancy between one's intent and one's actions. Whether it is a simple handshake or a more elaborate ritual of caring for a bed-ridden parent, Confucius teaches the significance of naturalness (*he*) as an essential virtue. Whether complex or simple, rituals are performed, not just because they are right or proper, but because they produce ease (*he*) and joy (*le*)—and those are characteristics of aesthetic. "Naturalness" (*he*)—or, as Slingerland points out Confucian ethics of *wuwei* (effortless)—means

91. Soothill's translation (*The Analects of Confucius*, 56), followed by Kupperman, "Naturalness Revisited," 42.

92. Waley, *Analects*, 86.

93. Lau, trans., *Analects*, 7.

94. Huang, *Analects*, 49.

95. Kupperman, "Naturalness Revisited," 43. Kupperman's interpretation is similar to Zhu Xi's understanding of *he* as "not forced," "natural," and "decorum." See Zhu, ed., *Sishu*, 86.

96. Cf. Kupperman, "Naturalness Revisited," 44.

"a perfect harmony between one's inner dispositions and external move-ments, and is perceived by the subject to be 'effortless' and free of strain."[97] Naturalness creates the propensity to promote harmony.[98]

There are contexts where ease and fluency may not be present, "for example, in comforting a grieving friend, or in responding to a sum-mons from the ruler (*Analects* 10:3), entering the Palace gate (10:4), or carrying the ceremonial table of jade (10:5)."[99] The decorum (*li*) required in such contexts does not permit one to be at ease, because one is never joyful in grief, or comfortable receiving an authoritative order from the king, or performing a duty in a solemn place. Nevertheless, whether in comforting or in grieving, Confucian ethics suggests naturalness as the desired end. Naturalness or harmony speaks of how one is in sync with the flow of things, whether in celebration or in bereavement.

↭ Harmony and Music[100]

Naturalness and harmony can be understood musically. This under-standing is shared by many ancient cultures, especially those that have pentatonic music. The pentatonic music of ancient China emulates the order and sound of nature;[101] ancient Chinese "music and instruments were part of the calendrical system and the seasons as well as the welfare of the state."[102] One of the oldest Chinese musical instruments, *qin*—a

97. Slingerland, trans., *Confucius Analects*, xix.

98. So, ed., *Music in the Age of Confucius*, 23 quotes *Liji* regarding the efficacy of both rites and music in the life of people: "The rites regulate people's minds. Music unifies their sounds. . . . It is the business of [music and rites] to attune people's feelings and give elegance to their outward manifestations. . . . Music comes from within; rites act from without. Coming from within, music produces the serenity [of the mind]. Acting from without, rites produce the finished elegance [of manner]. Great music must be easy. Great rites must be simple."

99. See Chen, *Lunyu Duxun Jiegu*, 170–71; Kupperman, "Naturalness Revisited," 44.

100. See Lippman, *Musical Thought in Ancient Greece*, 1–21.

101. See Liang, *Music of the Billion*, 47; Jiang, *Kongzi De Yuelun*, 23, 29, 100–103; Lu, "Zhongguo gudai wusheng yinjie xingchen yu fazhan de tansuo," 16–22. See also Jiang Wenye, *Kongzi De Yuelun*, 22–23 on the myths of how Chinese musical instruments came into being. One myth tells that the first Chinese flute was made to imitate the two tones of the sounds made by the male and female mythological birds called phoenix (*fenghuang*).

102. A quote of Needham and Robinson's work in Yung, "The Nature of Chinese Ritual Sound," note 5.

zither with five or seven strings tuned to the pentatonic scale (*gong, shang, jiao, chen, yu*), is thought to be capable of producing natural pitches; the structure of *qin* is thought to be made according to the cosmic pattern.[103] The ancient *qin* in China was customarily played in the hierarchies of listening with the ears (*erting*, hearing) to listening with the heart (*xinting*, sensing) to ultimately listening with *qi* (*qiting*, be transformed)[104]—*qi* being the ether of the universe that sustains one's life as well. Naturalness is like the "hard-wire," the essence, the basic pattern of nature—the way it is supposed to be. But the way (*dao* and *logos*) is not static, it is relational. The Confucian understanding of *dao* is similar to the Greek understanding of *logos* in that both view the cosmos as an organic ordered whole.

The word "harmony" in Greek means "fitting together," and originally refers to joining pieces of wood. Musical harmony is the agreeable adjustment of opposites (e.g., high and low pitches), of different tones (such as the triad to create the consonance of the octave).[105] By analogy, social harmony is the agreeable adjustment of opposing interests and differences among people. Naturalness is understood as a cosmic *ordering* and *union*, for there is a patterning or structure in relationships that produces harmony and joy in the social world.

Harmony is a musical metaphor the *Analects* uses frequently. Confucius uses music and musical metaphors to illustrate the life of virtue, since music plays a significant role in shaping human nature: "A person without *ren* has nothing to do with music" (*Analects* 3:3).[106] Confucius uses music to express beauty and goodness in the ritualizing

---

103. Jiang Wenye, *Kongzi De Yuelun*, 102 describes the symbolic meanings of *qin*: "Its length is 3 feet [in Chinese unit] 3 inches [Chinese unit] 3 *fen* [Chinese unit], symbolizes a year of 366 days; its width is six inches, symbolizes the six dimensions of the cosmos [east, west, north, south, above, below]; its strings produce five tones, symbolizes the five elements of the universe; its middle section is four inches, symbolizes the four seasons." Liang, "Shi lun guqin jinqing de shenjing xinli gongneng xue yu qigong yangsheng shu," 411–13 explains how these five pitches and their corresponding frequencies can affect and preserve one's health and emotions.

104. See Liang Mingyue, "Shi lun guqin jinqing de shenjing xinli gongneng xue yu qigong yangsheng shu," 409–26. The music instrument *qin* was not played for aesthetic performance, but often used for self-cultivation. Liang explains that the scrolls for *qin* are without tableture, thus requiring player to touch (*fu*) the strings in accordance with the rhythm of one's pulses (414–18, 420).

105. Consequently, in the hierarchy of Greek deities, Harmonia is not only the daughter of Zeus and the Altantide Elektra, she is also the mother of the Muses.

106. My translation. See Chen, *Lunyu Duxun Jiegu*, 140; Yang, *Lunyu Yizhu*, 51.

process of becoming human. Goodness is based on moral propriety; beauty is expressed in the musical style of propriety. Music can perfect a person. As *Analects* 8:8 reads, "Be stimulated by the *Odes* [the *Classic of Poetry*], be established in the rites (*li*), and be perfected in music (*yue*, or aesthetic delight)."[107] Music in Confucius' vision is more than simply bells and drums (*Analects* 17:11),[108] it also expresses ethical cultivation and creates personal and social harmony. As Xu Fuguan writes:

> Music has its source in the heart, . . . it [music] involves mostly in the pathos and desires of the heart. But the pathos and desires are well tempered by the harmony of music, thus the conflict between desires and ethical conscience are resolved. At the same time, . . . music brings ethics and pathos into harmony; consequently, pathos is contained and ethics is sustained; both pathos and ethics become one. . . . Therefore Confucius says 'Be stimulated by the *Odes*, be established in the rites, and be perfected in music.' 'Perfect' means union or harmony. In the harmony of ethics (humaneness, *ren*) and biological desires, benevolence becomes not a standard one pursues, but an enjoyment in one's emotions.[109]

"To be perfected in music" means to become fully human, that is, to be the best moral self as one fulfills the heavenly endowed human nature of moral goodness. Confucianism is sometimes called "the culture of *yue*-consciousness" (*yuegan wenhua*), because it believes that ethical pathos unites one with the aesthetic *tian*. *Analects* 6:23 reads: "The wise take joy in rivers, while the benevolent take joy in mountains. The wise are active, while the benevolent are still. The wise are joyful and the benevolent are long-lived."[110] Like the unceasing flow of river, students of the Way should engage in constant reflection toward the goal of benevolence (cf. *Analects* 9:17).[111] Ethical actualization grants one true joy (*le*)

107. My translation. See also *Liji*, 111: "Ritual, music, law and government, their goals are one" (my translation); see Yang, *Lunyu Yizhu*, 179.

108. Yang, *Lunyu Yizhu*, 396.

109. Xu, *Zhongguo Yishu Jingshen*, 27–28. Referred by Chen, "Kongzi shiyue meixue zhong de zhengtixing gainian" 3.

110. Modified Slingerland's translation (*Confucius Analects*, 60). See also *Analects* 7:19, where Confucius describes himself as one who is so driven to teach and learn that he forgets to eat, and he is so joyful (*yue*) that he does not worry at all."

111. *Analects* 9:17 reads: "Standing on the bank of a river, the Master said, 'Look at how it follows on like this, never stopping day or night.'" (Slingerland, trans., *Confucius Analects*, 92). I follow the early commentarial tradition that interprets this text as positive

and therefore music (*yue*) in the heart that comes from Heaven, who is the creator and the field of creation. We have mentioned *Analects* 7:16 in the context of ritual and justice, it also describes the consciousness of joy: "The Master said, 'In the eating of coarse rice and the drinking of water, the using of one's elbow for a pillow, joy (*yue*) is to be found. Wealth and rank attained through immoral means have as much to do with me as passing clouds.'"[112]

During the Eastern-Zhou period at the time of Confucius, music deteriorated and its resources were not preserved. The *Analects* describes a pathetic picture of the musical morale of the day: "The Grand Musician Zhi fled to the state of Qi; the Music Master Gan who played for the second course, fled to Chu; the Music Master Liao from the third course fled to Cai; the Music Master Que from the fourth course fled to Qin. The drummer Fang Shu went to live on the north bank of the Yellow River; the tambour drummer Wu went to live on the north bank of the Han River; the Music Apprentice Yang and the stone chimes player Xiang went to live at the sea's edge."[113] Confucius travels around many states and determines to restore the place of music in the political and ethical life. In an autobiographical note he tells us that, "It was after my return from Wei to Lu [when he edited the *Odes*, or *the Classic of Poetry*] that music was put right, with the *ya* ("Elegance") and the *sung* ("Recitation") [sections in the *Odes*] being assigned their proper places" (*Analects* 9:15).[114] He edited the *Odes*, or the *Classic of Poetry*, an ancient collection of hymns and songs, containing 305 pieces, mostly folk lyrics of the Western Zhou era to Spring Autumn period. Unfortunately, the musical notations to the *Odes* were lost (*Yuejing, the Classic of Music* is said to be the counterpart of the *Odes*),[115] otherwise, we would know much more about Confucius' musical knowledge.

From other sources we can tell that Confucius knew music and poetry very well, since together with rituals, they are integral to his cur-

---

metaphor on cultivation of virtue, thus Confucius is making a recommendation. Later commentarial tradition sees Confucius' lament.

112. Lau, trans., *Analects*, 61.

113. Ames and Rosemont, *Analects*, 217. Cf. Jiang, *Kongzi De Yuelun*, 134.

114. Lau, trans., *Analects*, 81. On the reconstruction of these musical forms, see Jiang, *Kongzi De Yuelun*, 63–75, 134.

115. Yang, *Lunyu Yizhu*, 401.

riculum. He knew how to play a number of musical instruments.[116] He also knew how to sing, and often sang with other people.[117] He discussed music with the music director of Lu, saying, "This much can be known about music. It begins with playing in unison. When it gets into full swing, it is harmonious, clear and unbroken. In this way it reaches the conclusion" (*Analects* 3:23).[118] He knew how to use music to express his emotions.[119] *Analects* 14:39 records a time when Confucius, playing the stone chimes in Wei, was expressing his frustration, and a passerby was able to interpret Confucius' emotional state from the music of the chimes. On another occasion Confucius was able to use music to communicate his refusal to see Ru Bei (*Analects* 17:20).[120] *Analects* 7:14 relates how during his visit to Qi, he heard the music of Emperor Shun (2257–2205 BCE)—called *shao*, the Succession, and for three months he did not notice the taste of meat because he was so overwhelmed with the joy of the music he had heard.[121]

In *Analects* 3:25 Confucius differentiates between Shun's and Wu's music: "The Master said of the *shao* [Shun's music of Succession] that it was both perfectly beautiful and perfectly good, and of the *wu* ["Military Exploits"] that it was perfectly beautiful but not perfectly good" (*Analects* 3:25).[122] Confucius differentiates the music of Shun from that of King Wu (1073–1068 BCE) to indicate the difference between rule by virtue and rule by force. The legendary ruler Yao was said to model his govern-

116. Confucius' music teacher is Shi Xiangzi, according to *Shiji* 47:17. Jiang Wenye, *Kongzi De Yuelun*, 91, 100–104, 116 describes that Confucius knew how to play a number of instruments (bell, stone, *qin*-zither, and *se*-zither [*zhong, qing, qin, se*), knew how to sing, and he taught music.

117. *Analects* 7:32: "When Confucius is with a person who sings well, he will ask him to repeat before joining in in harmony".

118. Lau, trans., *Analects*, 27.

119. On the relationship between music and formation of one's emotive will and consciousness, see Liang, "Shi lun guqin jinqing de shenjing xinli gongneng xue yu qigong yangsheng shu," 409–16; Zatorre, "Musical Perception and Cerebal Function (A Critical Review)," 199–221.

120. Jiang, *Kongzi De Yuelun*, 78 speculates that *the Classic of Music* may be the "Book of Music" in the *Record of History* (*Shiji*) or *Record of Rituals* (*Liji*).

121. Yang, *Lunyu Yizhu*, 154.

122. Lau, trans., *Analects*, 27. Cf. Jiang, *Kongzi De Yuelun*, 33, 85, 90, 113. Jiang thinks that the *shao* music was composed by the musician Kui to magnify the virtuous reign of Emperor Shun. It was said that even the phoenix would come dancing to the music, signifying the blessed reign of Shun.

ment according to Heaven (*tian*) and live a virtuous life. He abdicated the throne not to his son but to a pious, able, and virtuous person—Shun, who became a sage-ruler as well. The enthronement music of Shun and the abdication music of Yao, called *shao*, were both perfectly good and beautiful because no violence was involved in the change of royal positions. The enthronement music of King Wu (his name literally means "the Warrior King") was perfectly beautiful, but not perfectly good, because King Wu used military force to topple King Zhou of the Shang dynasty (*Analects* 3:25). Even though it was good that King Wu got rid of the tyrant—King Zhou, Confucius regards the use of force as less beautiful than the force of virtue. Good and beautiful music is defined not so much in terms of its style and content, but more in terms of its ritualistic function: *aesthetically modeling virtue (de)* in the process of creating social harmony.

We may use *Analects* 3:3 to explain why Confucius' aesthetic culture is grounded on goodness particularly benevolence. The text reads: Confucius said, "If a person is not benevolent, what has he to do with music?"[123] Confucius adored the music of *shao* (Shun's court music) and appreciated *wu* (King Wu's music) of the Zhou dynasty, but he disliked the music of Cheng and the morality of the Cheng people. Why? He said, "The music of Cheng is vacuous and their men dangerous" (*Analects* 15:11).[124] In addition to his moral criticism, Confucius also disliked Cheng music because he claimed it corrupted the classical music of the Shang and Zhou (*Analects* 17:18).[125]

Confucianists believe that music is not a neutral medium, it can form a person and a nation to perfection. It also has the power to corrupt and destroy a person and a nation. The last king of the Shang dynasty was destroyed because of "indecent, excessive, wild, or lewd sound" (*yinsheng*) that corrupted himself and his people.[126] One of the reasons for King

123. My translation. See Chen, *Lunyu Duxun Jiegu*, 28; Yang, *Lunyu Yizhu*, 51.

124. Yang, *Lunyu Yizhu*, 349, explains that the calendar of the Xia dynasty suits better for agricultural activities than the calendar of Zhou dynasty, and the carts of Shang dynasty are much simpler than that of Zhou, but the clothing of Zhou is proper. The word "wu" in Chinese means dance (舞), but here it is pronounced the same as King Wu's music (武), thus it probably refers to King Wu's music.

125. Slingerland, trans., *Confucius Analects*, 207–8 comments that the music of Zheng is artificial and lewd.

126. An account in *Shiji* narrates a famous musician, Juan composed and directed musical dances that intoxicated and corrupted the last emperor of the Shang dynasty, King Zhou, and his people. See Jiang, *Kongzi De Yuelun*, 46–47.

Wu of the Zhou dynasty declared war on the Shang dynasty was that the Shang dynasty had "rejected their ancestor music, and distorted the proper pitches."[127] The Zhou dynasty paid attention to proper rituals *and* music. For Confucius the rituals and music are the two sides of the same coin[128] as he emulates the benevolent rule of the Duke of Zhou by means of rituals and music.[129] *Analects* 1:12 explains that the way of ancient kings was beautiful because the harmony of their music and the goodness of their rituals brought about that beauty and order, from immaterial matters to the great things. The same verse explains that if one aims at harmony for the sake of harmony, and does not use ritual to regulate it, it will not work. Rituals and music reinforce each other in an ethical realm of virtue and harmony.

✧ Poetry and Harmony

Music and poetry are inseparable in ancient China, especially in the context of ritual. In Confucius' time, the lyrics were the *Odes*, one of the basic texts for Confucius' moral education. Confucius summarized the most basic content of the *Odes* as "the determination not deviated from the path of righteousness but to walk in it" (*Analects* 2:2).[130] Singing poetry was a recommended way for his disciples to live in righteousness and to achieve a balanced emotion.[131] *Analects* 3:20 notes that the first

127. See Jiang, *Kongzi De Yuelun*, 49, suspects that proper musical forms were not used anymore, and half pitches were introduced to distort the simple pentatonic pitches.

128. Rituals and music are so intertwined in defining the spirit of China that Confucianists often refer to China as the "State of Ritual and Music" (*liyue zhi bang*).

129. Jiang, *Kongzi De Yuelun*, 61. *Shiji* describes in the forty-year rule of the Duke of Zhou, the prison was not used, rituals and music were properly used, people lived in peace and order, and they sang joyful songs). This is the Golden Age Confucius wishes to recover.

130. My translation. On the six poetic forms preserved in the Zhou dynasty, see Jiang, *Kongzi De Yuelun*, 62–63.

131. See *Liji*, 114 (My translation: "Music is produced by the modulations of the voice, and its source is the heart as it is moved by things. When the heart is moved to sorrow, the sound is sharp; when the heart is moved to pleasure, the sound is gentle; when the heart is moved to joy, the sound is rising; when it is moved to anger, the sound is coarse; when the heart is moved to reverence, the sound is straightforward with humility; when the heart is moved to love, the sound is harmonious and soft. These six sounds are not of human nature; they are produced by external things. On this account the ancient kings were watchful of how things affect the heart").

ode in the *Odes*, "is pleasing without being excessive, is mournful without being injurious."[132] Musical harmony can not only express euphony, it can also express melancholy. Sad music can be welcome, because it reflects the emotion of those in grief or pain, and it soothes the broken hearted. In fact, melancholy and joy must be balanced in one's spirit for the harmonious heart.

The dramatic rendering of poetry in song evokes love and desire for the ideals. As *Analects* 8:15 writes: "The Master said, 'When Chih, the Master Musician, begins to play and when the *Guanju* comes to its end, how the sound fills the ear!'"[133] The *Guanju* is the title of the first ode in *the Odes* that uses the yearning of the osprey (the love bird) to convey a young couple's love for each other.[134] It is similar to the Song of Songs in the Old Testament, thus metaphorically portraying the quest for ideal love. Among his students Confucius took pride in studying poetry with Zigong (*Analects* 1:15) and Zixia (*Analects* 3:8), since they excelled in it.

Another musical metaphor used in the *Analects* is *xing* ("stimulating," "arousing," "inspiring") connoting joy or happiness. The musical metaphor *xing* indicates how the effect of harmony can be healing and restorative to a society, inspiring the people to live virtuous lives. Examples of the harmonious and moral forces of music as expressed in the metaphor *xing* are found in the *Analects*. In *Analects* 15:2, when the disciples were running out of food in Chen during a siege, "none could rise [*xing*] to their feet." And in *Analects* 20:1, where Yao says King Wu restored (*xing*) the states he had destroyed. *Analects* 8:2 speaks of morality as not taught to a person but was stimulated (*xing*) within him; the same verse also states that when an exemplary person (*junzi*) feels affection for his parents, then people are stimulated (*xing*) to *ren* (benevolence or humaneness). *Analects* 13:3 reads, "When affairs do not culminate successfully, rites and music do not flourish/stimulate/resonate; when rites and music do not flourish/stimulate/resonate, punishments will not correct [the people's] crimes."[135] Confucius believed that the rule of law and

---

132. Ames and Rosemont, *Analects*, 86. Yang, *Lunyu Yizhu*, 65.

133. Lau, trans., *Analects*, 25.

134. Yang, *Lunyu Yizhu*, 65, notes that *Guanju* is found in both *the Classic of Poetry* and *the Classic of Music*. Though a love song that expresses passion between a man and a woman, Confucius praises *Guanju* for not being excessive (*ying*).

135. Lau, trans., *Analects*, 121.

punishment would not transform social ills; only rites and music would stimulate people to live a virtuous life and to achieve social harmony.

✦ Ritual, Music, Poetry, Social Order, and Being Human

Confucius believes that the contribution music makes towards social order has to do with the cultured pattern of society, or the ritualized habituation of being human. When coupled with poetry, music provides the medium or the spirit for a community to sing about their yearning and thoughts for a harmonious society.[136] Melody and lyrics are sung as ways to bond the community together by uniting emotional sensibilities with cognitive ones.[137]

In the *Book of Ritual* one reads, "Music comes from yang, rituals come from yin; when *yin* and *yang* harmonize, myriad things are fulfilled" (*Liji* 11:5).[138] Music and poetry are the two essential components of ritual acts. In ancient liturgies or rituals, music accompanied poems, such as those in the *Odes*. From Confucius' point of view, this book was essential to self-cultivation: "The Master said, 'Why is it none of you, my young friends, study the *Odes*? An apt quotation from the *Odes* may stimulate the imagination, endow one with breeding, enable one to live in a community and give expression to grievances" (*Analects* 17:9).[139]

Examples of these various expressions made through the *Odes* can also be seen in Confucius' own life. In the state of Wei where Confucius was playing stone chimes, a man passed by and interpreted the music to be frustrated and heavy laden. The man asked Confucius to stop pla-

---

136. There is a favorite mythological story of Confucianists to account how the sage-emperor Tang Yao (2356–2257 BCE) who heard an old man singing the following song and was pleased by the song: "I work when the sun rises, I rest when the sun sets. I dig the well to drink, I plough the field to eat. The power of the Emperor has nothing to do with me." The farmer sang a simple song with a pentatonic tune, singing about the peace and prosperity of the reign of Yao—the rule of benevolence without the use of force (*wuwei*). See Jiang, *Kongzi De Yuelun,* 33–34 thinks this might be a true story.

137. Confucius says, "To love about it [learning] is better than simply knowing about it; to be experientially delighted (*yue*) is better than simply loving it."

138. *Liji,* 111.

139. Lau, trans., *Analects,* 175. *Zhounan* and *Shaonan* are the first two sections of love songs or about women in the *Classic of Poetry; Zhounan* has eleven songs and *Shaonan* fourteen. It is interesting that Confucius' moral education does not avoid such topics. For more, see Jiang, *Kongzi De Yuelun,* 143.

ing, since nobody would understand his music. Confucius then quoted a verse from the *Odes*: "When the water is deep, go across by wading; when it is shallow, lift your hem and cross."[140] Confucius then offered his interpretation: "That would be resolute indeed. Against such resoluteness there can be no argument" (*Analects* 14:39). Confucius might be *frustrated* in reforming the world, yet through his music he intends to express his resoluteness to do what might not be received well by all, that is, the promotion of humane government.[141] Poetry and music in Confucian political ethics are not means of social control for the sake of "harmony"—as a form. The musical and "poetic justice" as envisioned in benevolent reign of Heaven and virtuous rule of kings for the people is basic to Confucian aesthetic culture, viz., of ritual and music. The language of aesthetics is not simply descriptive, it is also insinuative, enlightening, subversive, and transformative to hegemonic elements in a society,[142] thus it provides a tool for participants a critique of the existing order. In other words, beauty is a category of virtue or goodness called *ren*, as *Analects* 4:1 reads: "To live in the neighborhood of humaneness (*ren*) is beauty." The benevolent politics of Confucius is in fact a harmonious relationship lived out by the rulers and the people, with the emphasis on "cultivating benevolent virtue of the rulers for the sake of bringing peace to the people" (*Analects* 14:42).[143] Music is not the monopoly of the elites, it is the universal gift for all to enjoy.

Confucius believes that statecraft is not a self-consciously government of others, statecraft is musical in the best sense of the word—effortless action (*wuwei*) in harmony with the Way. This point is illustrated in *Analects* 11:26, commonly praised by Confucianists as Confucius' *wu yu Dian ye*, that is, "I agree with Zeng Xi (Dian)." The context of the text is: Zilu sent Zigao (who was young and still in his studies) to serve as the steward of the Ji family. Confucius thinks Zilu is not doing a service to

140. Lau, trans., *Analects*, 145. *Analects* 14:39; Yang, *Lunyu Yizhu*, 336, interprets "the deep water" as symbolizing the chaotic society and "the shallow water" as problems in society that are correctable.

141. See *Analects* 14:42 in Qian, *Lunyu Xinjie*, 537; also Zhu, ed., *Sishu*, 274.

142. Chen, "Kongzi shi yue meixue zhong de zhengtixing gainian," 7. See her discussion in page 8 regarding aesthetics as a political rather than a purely artful language.

143. In the work of Mencius, one of Confucius' disciples called Zigong, says "By seeing the rites of a ruler, we may know the character of his government. By hearing his music, we may know the character of his virtue" (*Mencius* 2a.27). Quoted in So, ed., *Music in the Age of Confucius*, 23.

Zigao. Then other disciples (Zilu, Ran Qiu, Zihua) were asked what they like to do if someone were to use their talents. They all spoke of their aspirations. Confucius disapproved all of them because of their overly focus on statecraft techniques.[144] When it was Zeng Xi's turn, he

> stopped strumming his zither, and as the last notes faded away he set the instrument aside and rose to his feet. 'I would choose to do something quite different from any of the other three. . . . In the third month of Spring, once the Spring garments have been completed, I should like to assemble a company of five or six young men and six or seven boys to go bathe in the Yi river [near Confucius' home] and enjoy the breeze upon the Rain Dance Altar, and then return singing to the Master's house.'[145]

Confucius agreed with Zeng Xi in the matter of "timeliness" (*shi*), a virtue that is aesthetically cultivated best through music. Citing a number of commentaries on *Analects* 11:26, Slingerland explains that

> Only Zeng Xi has transcendent aspirations, only he is able to stir up the sounds of Virtue and give expression to the Master's style and sensibility. . . . Although the various aspects of statecraft pursued by the first three disciples are important, only Zeng Xi perceives that the time is wrong for their application. Mr. Zhou explains that "Zeng Xi wins approval because he alone understands timeliness," and Huang Kan elaborates: "At that time the Way was in decline and the world was disordered, and everywhere people were striving against one another, which is why the disciples all had their hearts set on entering official service. Only Zeng Xi understood the vicissitudes of the age, which is why the Master approved of him."[146]

In Confucianism aesthetics and political ethics are united. Through the improvisation of music, ethics and politics will not be artificial activities but *artful living* of goodness. Once beauty is predicated upon goodness (virtue) and truth (*dao*), rituals and poetry will not be pursued self-consciously, selfishly, or for certain ulterior motives. Confucius taught that a person ought to be lifted by poetry, formed by rituals (*li*), and perfected by music (*Analects* 8:8). Propriety (*li*) sets the parameters

144. Cf. Slingerland, trans., *Confucius Analects*, 124.

145. Ibid., 123.

146. Ibid., 124.

within which individuals can actualize their humanity in *creative and spontaneous ways* through music. Fingarette explains this well,

> The *li* may be thought of as the musical forms within which the musician works—the instrumental colors available, the general principles of harmony, the melodic and rhythmic forms, and the organizational patterns for individual works (the sonata form, the fugue, the symphony—or, for example in Confucius' world, various 'Dances' such as the Succession Dance or the War Dance). . . . physical sounds which otherwise would be mere noise become music when shaped in accord with these norms. . . . One who does expend the effort to learn the *li* ultimately becomes skilled in imaginatively combining and recombining the forms in ways suited to the circumstances, doing so in a critical rather than a slavish way, with spontaneity and elegance—creatively.[147]

Ritual or rite (*li*) is related to virtue cultivation and music because ritual and music bring about harmony in a community and beauty in life. In *Analects* 1:12, ritual propriety and musical harmony are brought together, making the point that the ethical expression of rites needs the harmonizing effects of music. In the cultivation of virtue, rites will regulate our behavior and attitudes; music will harmonize our feelings.[148] When one participates in the rites/rituals of the culture, one is able to live in harmony with others. Such rites extended in ancient China from the simple ritual of the handshake to the elaborate ritual of participating in offering sacrifices to *tian* (Heaven). Confucian political ethics examines the aesthetic arrangement of all participants. Social order and social harmony are similar to musical patterns in the sense that propriety has set forms.

The Confucius' understanding of music is broad, it includes aesthetic expressions through singing, the use of musical instruments, and its elaboration through poetry that brings about harmony within a community. Now, as we turn to Paul's understanding, it is important that we keep these concepts in the foreground.

147. Fingarette, "The Music of Humanity," 345. See *Analects* 2:4; 7:36, 37; 8:1, 2; 13:26; 15:21 for creativity of *li*.

148. In the text, Confucius' disciple, Yuzi said, "The most valuable function of ritual propriety is to achieve harmony. The way of the ancient kings is beautiful" (*Analects* 1:12). Rituals set the path and the boundary for one to learn, but music will make a person learn naturally (cf. *Analects* 16:9: "Knowledge acquired through a natural way is best; next is knowledge through study; next is knowledge through pressure because of difficulties; the worst one is not learning at all despite difficulties").

Music and Its Lyrical Quality in the New Testament

✧ The Tendency of Scholars in Music Studies

Little is known about how Christians of the first century used music in worship. Among scholars of the last twenty years or so, Wendy J. Porter surveys the state of research on early Christian music in her essay, "Misguided Missals: Is Early Christian Music Jewish or Is it Graeco-Roman?" She points out the pitfalls found in the studies of some researchers, the lack of relevant material, as well as the methodological cautions one needs to attend to before forming a conclusion.[149] There is a tendency in scholarship today on New Testament music to be cautious because of scholarship in the past that read later church history into the early church of the New Testament.[150] Only in later church history does the suspicion arise that music in worship distracts worshippers from the Scripture and the proclamation of the Word. The New Testament does not discuss such a problem.[151] If it were encountered in Pauline Christianity, Paul's text would have mentioned it. Similar to Plato's caution of the effect of music on the *ethos* of a people, the medieval churches responded to the problem of how music can have a bad influence on the ethics of believers through habituation. Had the similar problem the medieval churches encountered surfaced in the Pauline churches, Paul would have responded to that issue as well.[152] It is more likely that music was used

149. Porter, "Misguided Missals," 202–27. Likewise, Cosgrove, "Imagining Earliest Christian Music," 1–2 shows that the "sacred bridge" of Eric Werner's work—worship music of the early church is an adoption of that from the synagogue—has been dismantled. In his article "Music and Singing in the Liturgy," 493–507), J. Gelineau also argues that "a search through the NT to discover musical allusions will prove disappointing" (497). Both Cosgrove's and Gelineau's articles discuss musical metaphors in the New Testament. See also the work of Bradshaw (*The Search for the Origins of Christian Worship*, 30–55) and Wainwright (*Doxology*, 46–70, 156–63) for their balanced discussions on this topic.

150. See Bradshaw, *The Search for the Origins of Christian Worship*, 35–36.

151. Blackwell, *The Sacred in Music*, 128.

152. Plato compares bad music (e.g., Bacchic dancing) with bad company, confusion, lack of definition, wantonness, and argues that "musical excess [is] the ruin of the state; musical degeneracy leads to degeneracy in morals" (Lippman, *Musical Thought in Ancient Greece*, 81). Plato restricts musical content in the *Republic* and accepts Dances of War and Dances of Peace. He accepts melodies and rhythms that expressed courage and temperance in the *Laws*. He disapproves of Bacchic dancing in the *Republic*, because of their orgiastic nature.

generously, rather than in a limited fashion, within the churches Paul helped to establish.

While the cautionary attitude of scholarship today concerning music in the New Testament church is to be applauded, an overly discrete attitude toward distinguishing music from singing, chanting, and reading poetry in New Testament churches can be misleading. J. Gelineau's observation on the interconnections between music and singing is helpful. He writes:

> Hebrew and Greek have no separate word for music. The frontier between singing and speaking was far less precise. As soon as speech turned to poetry, or when public and ceremonial speaking was involved, rhythmic and melodic features were incorporated that today would be classified as musical or at least pre-musical. Music and singing could be present even though none of the vocabulary associated with it might be met with.[153]

Along with the idea that meanings conveyed in music and singing are fluid, we can say the same of the relationship between music and reading. Greek language is tonal, thus reading aloud (the norm of ancient reading practices) in the life of first century churches, reading was itself "musical."

⊸ Lyrical Quality of New Testament Texts

Music *per se* is not our concern here, but our focus rests on the nature and function of the lyrics that go with it. In the case of Confucius, what matters is the relationship of ritual music with the *Odes*; in the case of Paul

---

We can understand Amos' attacks on music in the midst of injustice and Isaiah's critique of music in the midst of covenantal betrayal (5:11–12), for they are criticizing not music per se, but wanton attitudes expressed in music. Paul has not associated music with a distraction to worshippers. Much later in the Christian tradition, the Council of Trent—an ecumenical council of the Church (1545–1563)—prohibited abusive use of musical instruments to accompany church music, complicated polyphony that made words hard to understand, the excessive use of noisy instruments, as well as the bad pronunciation, carelessness and irreverent attitude of the church singers. But this is a sixteenth century polemic against church music. Despite the Trent prohibition, Giovanni da Palestrina (1525–1594) was able to form an orchestra of voices (without musical instruments), and composed 106 masses. His aim was perfection in harmony utilizing the human voice.

153. Gelineau, "Music and Singing in the Liturgy," 498.

what matters are such musical expressions as proclamation, psalmody, hymn singing.[154]

Unlike the modern understanding of music as an independent art, we have seen music in Confucius' days as not independent from its lyrics (the *Odes*). Ritual music is most often sung. Likewise, New Testament music has its "intense lyrical quality," as Gelineau puts it. He writes:

[O]ne can . . . recognize an intense lyrical quality in the life of the apostolic Church, particularly in its liturgical assemblies. The Church was born with the proclamation to all nations of the mighty works of God (Acts 2:11). When the Book of Revelation describes the many groups that sing Amen, Alleluia, Holy, and other hymns to God and to the Lamb, the author is using his own experience as a model for the practice of heaven. Other New Testament texts reflect this lyricism. . . . It is quite by chance that we learn that Paul and Silas, when in prison at Philippi, spent the night hours 'praying and singing hymns to God' (Acts 16:23). There is the advice of the epistle to James: 'Is any one cheerful? Let him sing praise' (Jas 5:13). . . . As well as the oft-cited references in Colossians (3:16) and Ephesians (5:19).[155]

Early Christian music was influenced by Jewish and Graeco-Roman cultures, both of which had rich musical heritages.[156] Temple worship and early Christian worship center on word or text *with melody* rather than on performance of instrumental music alone, although there is no evidence of prohibition to instrumental music. We know from the Psalmists and the Old Testament texts that musical instruments, professional temple musicians (1 Chr 15, 25:7) are used in worship and in the synagogue, and

154. In the case of Paul what matters also is such musical expression as cantillation of the word and instrumental music. Gelineau's classification below indicates "the relative importance given to the verbal and the musical elements varies in inverse proportion" (Gelineau, "Music and Singing in the Liturgy," 504).

WORD <————————————————————————————> MUSIC
(3) Chant ("Verbo-Melodism")
(2) Meditation ("Psalmody")   (4) Hymn ("Lied")
Proclamation ("Cantillation")   Acclamation
(1) Ordinary speech   (5) vocalize, Jubilus, Instruments

The wide range of music in relation to words is found in the New Testament, though many of those Gelineau categorized do not yet exist in their developed forms as found in the later church.

155. Gelineau, "Music and Singing in the Liturgy," 498.

156. See Porter, "Misguided Missals," 203–4.

most likely these practices continued into the first century synagogues and churches.[157] Luke 7:32 (also Matt 11:17) seems to suggest that the use of musical instruments alone is appropriate; the verse actually describes a socially dysfunctional situation when the people do not respond to music: "We played the flute for you, and you did not dance; we wailed, and you did not weep" (NIV).

The early church was a singing church,[158] exemplified by Jesus and his disciples, who sang a hymn before going out from the Last Supper (Matt 26:30; Mark 14:26). The Early Christians used the Old Testament as Scripture, and there is no doubt that they used the Psalms in their study, reading, and chanting. Besides new hymns, psalms, and songs of their own creation,[159] the New Testament church also used the Old Testament psalms as their hymn texts. Of all the genres in the Old Testament, the poetic literature, especially the Psalms, became the main source of inspiration for the New Testament church to interpret the Messiah or the Christ.[160] Despite the fact that the Psalms contain only indirect allusions

157. This musical aspect of the New Testament church was a continuation of the Old Testament practice. Songs were used in community gathering to create certain ethos, such as the song of Deborah (Judg 5), the Blessing of Moses (Deut 33), Song of Moses (Deut 32, Exod 15:1–18), also psalms used in Temple worship, such as Psalms 15 (entrance liturgy), 24 (procession), 81 (feast of Tabernacles).

158. Porter, "Misguided Missals," 204. See also Smith, *Musical Aspects of the New Testament*, 59–64.

159. See Luke 1:46–55, 68–79; 2:29–32; John 1:1–16; Phil 2:6–11; Col 1:15–20; 1 Pet 1:3–5; Rev 5:9–10; 19:1, 19:6–9. The New Testament scholar, Ralph P. Martin (*Carmen Christi*, 19), has given clues of hymns mentioned in 1 Cor 14:26; Col 3:16; Eph 5:19–20, and classified the following fairly developed hymns in the New Testament:

(i)   the Lukan canticles;

(ii)   hymns in the Apocalypse;

(iii) Jewish-Christian fragments and ejaculations ('Amen, Hallelu-jah, Hosana, Marana tha, Abba);

(iv)   distinctively Christian forms:

(a) sacramental (Eph 5:14; Tit 3:4–7); (with hesitation Rom 6:1–11; Eph 2:19–22)

(b) meditative (Eph 1:3–14; Rom 8:31–39; 1 Cor 13);

(c) confessional (1 Tim 6:11–16; 2 Tim 2:11–13);

(d) Christological (Heb 1:3; Col 1:15–20; 1 Tim 3:16; John 1:1–14; 1 Pet 1:18–21, 2:21–5; 3:18–21; Phil 2:6–11).

See also Bradshaw, *The Search for the Origins of Christian Worship*, 42–44.

160. See Wainwright, *Doxology*, 211–12 on the use of Psalms (especially 2:7; 16:10; 22; 68:18; 69:21; 110:1, 4; 118:22) by the early church for its Christological formulations.

or prophecies about the coming Messiah, they were used readily also because of their poetic, musical, and memorable quality. Poetry and music
are more easily "transportable" in the mind and heart of people and they
"live on" longer than prose.[161]

The early church did not make music for its own sake, but for the
sake of expressing "a conscious faith [in Christ] . . . [and in] the word of
God."[162] Singing in the early church was a Christian act of worship that
used music "as a support for the words."[163] Early Christian music gave
expression to the new faith of the early believers, a worshipful response
to God's salvation in Christ, and a liturgical call for the faithful to glorify
God and serve one another.

✦ Lyrical Music and Those "In Christ" within Pauline Churches

The use of music in relation to texts in the New Testament church is similar to the ritual setting of music in relation to poetry (the *Odes*) in the day
of Confucius. We know that there was singing in these churches for the
sake of glorifying God and edifying one another. To the church at Corinth
Paul advocates holistic singing, that is, singing "with the spirit and the
mind" (*psalō tō pneumati . . . kai tō voi*; 1 Cor 14:15). The context here
is the discussion of when to speak in tongues—a spiritual or "angelic"
language that needed interpretation—and when to speak with the mind.
It is a question whether tongues can be equated with music. "Tongues"
may be considered as noise, giving the impression that tongues has no
content. But if tongues has no content, it would not need interpretation
(1 Cor 14:27). Paul's concern here is to make tongues, "speech that is not
intelligible" (1 Cor 14:9) meaningful (14:27-28) so that "all may learn
and be encouraged" (14:29). "Tongues" is akin to music without words;
it is a charismatic gift. While Paul himself practices music both with and
without words, he would "rather speak five words with [his] mind, in
order to instruct others, than ten thousand words in a tongue" (14:19;

Wainwright writes that "not only did the Psalms help the primitive church to interpret
Christ, but also Christ in turn became the key for understanding the Psalms" (212).

161. Wainwright writes that "poetry is able to 'speak' transhistorically, transculturally
and transpersonally" (*Doxology,* 194). He also discusses the "memorability of hymns"
(200).

162. Gelineau, "Music and Singing in the Liturgy," 498.

163. Ibid., 503.

RSV). In the same chapter Paul describes the fact that when believers come together (*sunerchomai*), "each one has a hymn, a lesson, a revelation, a tongue, or an interpretation" (14:26), and Paul admonishes them to do "all things for edification" (*panta pros oikodomēn ginesthō*).

The same commitment to use music not for its own sake but for good of the Christian community and for the praise to God is found in Paul's letter to the Colossians. In Col 3:16, singing has both an instructive function (teaching and admonishing) and also a worship purpose as singing "to God." The discussion of Paul in this passage is similar in many ways to the ethical admonition of Confucius. Despite two very different traditions that have their own subjects of adoration (*tian* and *Theos*) and their own understanding of ethics in terms of propriety (*li* and law) and love (*ren* and *agape*), music for both Confucius and Paul can be an expression of joy and gratitude (*yue/xing* and *eucharistomai*). For both Confucius and Paul, music can build up a community; in this way, music is an instrument of love. Paul writes, "Above all put on love, which binds everything together in perfect harmony" (Col 3:14). In the same passage Paul asks the Colossian believers to put on "compassion, kindness, lowliness, meekness, and patience, forbearing one another and . . . forgiving each other, as the Lord has forgiven you" (3:12–13; RSV).

Paul exhorts Christians to "sing psalms, hymns, and spiritual songs to God" (Col 3:16; Eph 5:18–19), tying love of God to music—the unifying (unison) and harmonizing (harmony) effect on a community. In response to the chaotic practice of charismatic gifts and the problem of divisions in the Corinthian church, Paul lifts up love as "the more excellent way" for them to live harmoniously as "the body of Christ" (1 Cor 12:27—13:1). In explaining love Paul thinks of music, for he argues that, without love a person is a noisy gong or a clanging cymbal (1 Cor 13:2); Paul also mentions *aulos* (not a flute but something more like an oboe), harp (*kithara*), and trumpet (*salpigx*) in 1 Cor 14:7–8 when discussing charismatic gifts. According to our modern musical standards, the bell, the cymbal, and the trumpet may sound simple or may be regarded as apotropaic noise-makers. Yet, to the ancient world, bell and cymbal and trumpet when played well—in the sense that they can be understood—calls people together and gives rhythm to their particular acts in the settings of ritual, sacrifice, procession, or even a call to the battlefield. Paul's point in 1 Corinthians 13 and 14 is that love is like music, in that both can unite and build up community.

↩ Singing with the Spirit, Christological Hymns, and Moral Life

Paul's use of musical metaphors is not without problems. He describes the "noisy gong," "the clanging cymbal" (1 Cor 13:1), "the lifeless instruments such as the *aulos* and the harp" (1 Cor 14:7), and "the indistinct sound of the trumpet" (14:8). It is precisely at this point that we need to look at. Paul's emphasis is that the moral life of the believers should match their spiritual vitality, whether they sing "with the spirit" (lower case) or sing "with the mind" (1 Cor 14:15). For Paul, singing with the spirit or with the mind serves a function similar to what music—even in its narrow definition—is supposed to do: to provide harmony and edification to a community.

Paul is so alarmed with what is happening in Corinth and in Galatia because he observes discontinuity between spirituality and morality. Corinthian Christians with abundant spiritual gifts live in strife and immoral chaos; they sing with spirit and mind, but not in harmony as the body of Christ. In effect they are noisy gongs and clanging cymbals. Galatian believers are baptized in Christ and partake of the Love Feast, yet their "being in Christ" as a way of life does not echo harmoniously with their "being in Christ" as a spiritual state. Having not comprehended the spiritual import of faith in Christ, these Christians did not realize the form of moral life required of them. Not living a moral life was the same as not living "in Christ." For Paul "being in Christ" was essentially the same as living a Christ-like life, which he associated with the fruit of the Spirit, enumerated in Galatians. We shall look at Paul's discussion on the ethics of love, freedom, and the fruit of the Spirit in the next chapter. To continue our theme of early Christian music here, we will look at how Christological hymns play an important role not only in worship but also in the moral life of early Christians.

Geoffrey Wainwright's work on the liturgical elements in the New Testament, especially the hymns and the creeds, is helpful to our understanding of how singing and confessing became formative activities of the early Christian community.[164] I limit the scope of Wainwright's contribution to Pauline writings, and I am assuming that worship practices inside and outside of Galatia would be similar.

---

164. Wainwright, *Doxology*, 156–63, 194–217. See also Hengel, *Studies in Early Christology*, 227–92.

Wainwright notes the appearance of the *acclamatory confession*, "Jesus is Lord" in Rom 10:9 and 1 Cor 12:3: The context in the letter to the Romans suggests a baptismal confession, and in the first letter to the Corinthians the worship assembly.[165] Whereas some scholars prefer the juridical locus to the liturgical, Wainwright argues that they are not mutually exclusive, and he cites as evidence the letter of Pliny the Younger, the governor of Bithynia, to Trajan the Emperor. Though the letter of Pliny (ca. 115 CE) is later than letters of Paul, it is significant in showing the power of confession and singing despite persecution. Wainwright notes that

> Pliny's letter to Trajan shows that the appearance before the imperial authorities could itself take on a 'liturgical' complexion: Pliny's test for alleged Christians upon arrest comprised 'reciting a prayer to the gods', 'making supplications with incense and wine before the emperor's statue' (we know the rival confession 'Caesar is Lord'), and 'cursing Christ' (1 Cor 12:3 mentions '*Anathema Iēsous*').[166]

Pliny's letter describes his interrogation of these Christians,

> who persisted [*perseverantes*][167] . . . [And on] a specified day before sunrise they were accustomed to gather and sing an antiphonal hymn to Christ [Latin *carmen . . . dicere*][168] as their God and to pledge themselves by an oath not to engage in any crime, but to abstain from all thievery, assault, and adultery, not to break their word once they had given it, and not to refuse to pay their legal

---

165. Wainwright, *Doxology*, 157. Wainwright notes that the *acclamatory confession* (introduced by the verb *homologein* [to confess that]) is brief, and its "potentially longer and more 'creedal' form . . . which fills out some of the 'work' of Christ" (introduced by the verb *pisteuein* [to believe that] appears in Rom 1:3–4, 4:25, 10:9, 1 Cor 15:3–5, 1 Tim 3:16 (*Doxology*, 157–58).

166. Wainwright, *Doxology*, 157.

167. The Latin word *perseverantes* is related to the Greek word *hypomonē*—or "endured," the central virtue for Christians in the context of persecution.

168. *Dicere* can mean say, chant, or sing, and *carmen* can mean a hymn, a formula, or a declaration. I follow Martin's argument (*Carmen Christi*, 7–8) that "*carmen . . . dicere*" is singing hymn. In both Greek and Latin antiquity we have poetic hymns, which were sung, and prose hymns, which were not. But this differentiation is unnecessary in our discussion here because we follow the broader understanding of music in the work of Gelineau ("Music and Singing in the Liturgy," 503–7). Cf. Hengel, *Studies in Early Christology*, 264–65.

> debts. They then went their separate ways, and came together later
> to eat a common meal, but it was ordinary, harmless food.[169]

Pliny lists the virtues of the Christians along with their confession in Christ and their singing of hymns to Christ. Pliny's letter is a secular, non-Christian account of what Christians did and believed in terms of the ethical and political consequences of their confession and singing.

The Christological hymns were recited or sung in homes, meetings, at the rituals (rites) of baptism and the Lord's Supper. Wainwright states that because "the hymn may range from the rhythmic prose of the *Sanctus,* the *Gloria in excelsis,* and the Eastern odes, to the regular metre, rhyme and strophe of the characteristic Western type," there can be wide variation between the text and the music in hymn singing.[170]

The reading of psalms and singing of hymns united the first century Christians with each other and with Christ. Paul makes much of this musical aspect of their worship as being "united in Christ." We have seen already how the early Christians created and found "harmony" by *singing and confessing* their faith in Christ (see 1 Cor 14:15, 26; Col 3:16; Eph 5:19). We will look at an example from Paul's letter to the Galatians to see how reading, singing, and confessing can create for the believers "harmony" within their cultural diversity (between Jew-Greek, male-female, master-slave, etc.; 3:28). Most scholars think that Gal 3:27–28 reflects the baptismal ritual, and it most probably uses a liturgical form that antedates Paul's time.[171] Poetry and music, creed and song or hymn, are common liturgical elements used in sacraments[172] of baptism and the Love Feast. Gal 3:27–28 is striking because of its quasi-poetic form: "For as many of you as were baptized into Christ have put on Christ. There is neither Jew nor Greek; there is neither slave nor freeman; there is no male and female. For you are all one in Christ Jesus."[173] Betz observes that the ceremony of baptism (3:27) proves the thesis in 3:7 that "it is Christ as the 'Son of God' who makes adoption as 'sons' available through the gift

---

169. The English text of Pliny's letter is taken from Boring et al., ed., *Hellenistic Commentary,* 558.

170. Wainwright, *Doxology,* 199.

171. Betz, *Galatians,* 184, n. 23, and 186.

172. Sacrament as "an outward and visible sign of an inward and spiritual grace" according to *The Common Book of Prayer.*

173. Betz, *Galatians,* 182–83. Betz's translation, *Galatians,* 181.

of the Spirit. The conditions for this adoption [are]: 'through (the) faith and through incorporation in the body of Christ,' i.e., 'in Christ Jesus.'"[174] At the baptismal ritual, these Gentile Christians in Galatia sang and confessed their new creation in Christ; they sang and confessed of Christ who is, in the words of Betz, "the heavenly garment by which the Christian is enwrapped and transformed into a new being."[175] The acts of disrobing, immersion, and robing in baptismal ritual symbolize the believers' "dying and rising with Christ" (Gal 2:19; 5:24; 6:14), and through that ritual they proclaim peace and harmony brought by Christ. Through baptism that symbolizes the new world-order ushered in by Christ, "religious and social distinctions between Jews and Greeks, slaves and freemen, men and women" are abolished.[176] The role of music in the context of liturgy was significant for the moral expression and theological identities of the Gentile Christians in Galatia.

Our next task is to look intertextually between ritual music of Confucius and the lyrical music of Paul. The purpose is to compare and contrast the two systems of harmony.

TOWARD A CHINESE CHRISTIAN UNDERSTANDING OF HARMONY

The *Analects* does not provide an analysis of what music is or how music works; it only gives anecdotes relating how music contributes to the life of virtue within a community. Paul's writings do not contain abundant information on his appropriation of music *per se*, but the role of music in relation to words is significant in Pauline churches as they express hymnically their faith and unity in Christ and in turn experience the oneness of the body of Christ in a manner that only music has the power to give.

Differences between Confucius and Paul on Music

Not only does the New Testament not discuss lyrical music, but, unlike the *Analects* of Confucius, it does not make use of music really or metaphorically to speak about ethics or the common good. We do see

174. Ibid., 186.
175. Ibid., 187.
176. Ibid., 189–90.

early Christian hymn and songs (as texts, not as music) providing expression—often in creedal forms—of Christian faith and belief and therefore of what Christians should be of their behaviors (Gal 5–6) and of one mind about (Phil 2:5–11). But, we do not see lyrical music used as the means toward harmony/naturalness as in Confucius. While there may be some implied use of music for admonition and instruction in Colossians, this reading elides the distinction the writer makes between teaching and admonishing in wisdom and singing with gratitude, although the writer of Colossians does point to the "aesthetic delight" of wisdom, gratitude, and thanksgiving—comparable in some ways to Paul's description of the gifts of the Spirit in Gal 5:22–23.

Though music and poetry in their various forms play important roles in forming the respective communities of Confucius and Paul, their views on the role of music in the formation of virtues contain subtle differences. Whereas Confucius believes the virtue of the community can be formed by rituals (such as that of filial piety) and music (such as singing of the *Odes*), Paul does not believe that in the Christian rites (such as baptism and the Lord's Supper) in and of themselves are the objective basis for the new life in Christ,[177] Betz points out that "Schlier's sacramentalism . . . is wrong," because for Paul:

> the objective basis upon which the Christian existence rests and of which Paul reminds the Galatians is the official declaration of adoption, a legal act which took place at baptism. But this legal basis is only the conclusion of previous events: the christological-soteriological events named in Gal 1:4; 2:20; 3:13; 4:4–5; the gift of the Spirit (3:2–5; 4:6); and the faith of the Galatians in Christ. . . . In other word, the objective basis of which Paul speaks is faith in Christ, but not the sacrament as a *ritus ex opere operato*.[178]

This is of interest because we note even among biblical scholars disagreement on Paul's understanding of the Christian rite. Schlier, a Roman Catholic, views the baptismal rite in a way similar to Confucius' understanding of rite (*li*) and music (*yue*); Betz, a Protestant scholar, opposes Schlier's interpretation. Depending on one's assumption of the relationship between liturgical rites and morality, one may affirm or reject the

---

177. Taken from ibid., 187.
178. Ibid.

commensurability between Confucius' and Paul's understandings of rites in the formation of virtues.

Schlier's view is not a modern understanding. In the context of gnosticism, mystery religions, and many primitive religions that dwell on the power of magic, the language of "putting on Christ" sounds like divine infusion, possession, and transformation through the acts of ritual. Betz points out that Paul seems to be "aware of the danger of 'cultic formalism' inherent in pre-Pauline baptismal theology, and seems to argue against that background in Romans [6:3–8] . . . and critically in 1 Cor 1:13–17."[179] Paul believes that the baptismal rite is grounded in "faith in Christ" and that in turn is grounded in the work of Christ and the gift of the Spirit. While the baptismal rite and the sacrament of the Love Feast can express the work of Christ and the gift of the Spirit and draw community together, they are not the divine means by which virtue is imparted. Paul has trouble accepting the baptismal ritual as the magical means of imparting the essence of God into believers. In contrast, while Confucius is aware of the danger of formalism in ritual (*li*) and music (*yue*), he does believe in their power as two essential means for forming virtue.

Besides these significant differences, Confucius (explicitly) and Paul (implicitly) share a common view of music as a system of harmony that can bring about reconciliation and fellowship in a community.

Ritual, Music, and Harmony

The Confucian language of poetry, ritual, and music may provide a prism for looking at the theology of Paul as found in his letter to the Galatians. In Confucius' mind, the ideal state could be achieved only if the individual, and most particularly the emperor and his retinue, were "stimulated by poetry, formed by ritual, and perfected by music" (*Analects* 8:8); and, as we shall see, although these terms are absent from Paul's thought, the reality to which they point is present. Paul's alarm is caused not only by the Galatians' deviation from his teaching as such, but also by the consequent disharmony produced in the Christian communities both in Galatia and in Antioch.

Confucius uses "poetry, ritual, and music" as the formal rubrics of activities that create propriety in relationships. Paul, on the other hand,

179. Ibid., 188–89.

does not employ rubrics so much as talk about the acts themselves. His language from time to time is poetic, that is, he has a sense of rhythm and juxtaposition. This is in addition to his use of poetry, which was probably sung, as in the Christological hymns. If, for Confucius, by personal commitment and practice the individual is "lifted by poetry, formed by ritual, and perfected through music," then, in Paul, the Christian, through faith is lifted by the gospel, formed by the communal rituals of baptism and table fellowship (the Eucharist), and is perfected by the "song" of the love of God and neighbor, thereby rediscovering the "naturalness" of being refashioned in the image and likeness of God, that is, in the image of the Son of God, Jesus Christ. *[leitourgia]*

In the social context of the gathered community of faith, ritual provides the formal [in the sense of "form"] framework in which music is performed. Ritual seeks to regulate behaviors, attitudes, and feelings, or at least to inspire them. Music is a ritualized cultural pattern that calls vocal harmony into being, and through its expression brings about social harmony within the community. Music sets a text (e.g., the *Odes*) and unites cognition and emotion, thought and feeling. Song and poetry draw the individual away from rigidity, conflict, and isolation and toward harmony and naturalness. According to Confucian ethics, appropriate ritual action produces harmony within a society, creating an integrated community. Today one might question whether Confucius' ideal would lead to little more than social conformity; but the purpose of ritual, as he understood it, is not primarily to bring about "required propriety"; rather, it is to point ahead of itself to the creation of harmony or naturalness. In Galatians 2 Paul provides a contrast between harmony and disharmony, naturalness and unnaturalness, although of course he does not use these terms. Peter serves as the example of disharmony (Gal 2:11–14): While eating with gentiles in one context, he now, out of fear, refuses to join with them in table fellowship. *[S. Baptist teachers]*

Harmony or naturalness, presented as an aesthetic category within an ethical system, is joined to *the beautiful and the good,* together to be held in unity and directed toward the creation of a virtuous community. Harmony cannot be created by beauty alone, no more than harmony can be created by force. Thus, Peter's "unease" at dining with the gentiles, even though they are "believers," disrupts the beauty (fellowship) and the goodness (virtue) of the church in Antioch.[180] Harmony or naturalness is evidence of a virtuous community; beauty and goodness need and affirm each other.

Confucius' understanding of naturalness and harmony brings to mind Paul's words in Gal 2:20: "It is no longer I who live, but Christ who lives in me." Harmony and naturalness are the "hard-wire"—the basic pattern—of heaven that human society ought to emulate.[181] Harmony or naturalness comes as perfection in those who bear the image and likeness of Christ. Abraham (Gal 3:16–18) believes God, responds in obedience, and is "reckoned as righteous" (Gal 3:6), i.e., as one whose actions are "natural" because they are in harmony with the Divine will.

Christ is the perfect image of God, and the God who is in Christ dwells in the Christian (Gal 2:20). This indwelling of the Divine Spirit within the Christian constitutes the source of Christian perfection, that is, perfect love. For Christians, harmony or naturalness are practices of a life lived out of perfect love—language which is similar to the language of "internal coherence" (he) in Confucian' thought. Paul's primary images of harmony, such as "unity in Christ" (Gal 3:28) and being "joint heirs" in the family of God (Gal 4:5–7), are about believers, in community, forming the body of Christ (1 Cor 12), the dwelling place of God (2 Cor 6:16), built upon the foundation or cornerstone of Christ (Eph 2:20). For Paul the image of the body/family of Christ is both reality and metaphor, as in Confucius music is both reality and metaphor; in both ritual practice leads to the reality of personal and social harmony.

Music as Systems of Harmony and Beauty

Though we do not have Paul's deliberation on music in a manner comparable to what Confucius has done in the *Analects*, it is not *music per se* that is important in our search for intertextual connections between Galatians and the *Analects*. Interest here lies in the analogical relationship between *systems of harmony* in the two texts. Whereas Confucius uses the ethics of *li* (ritual propriety) and *yue* (music), Paul uses singing and confession in the rituals of baptism and the fellowship meal based

180. I thank Ron Anderson for helping me see the connection here between Confucius and Paul.

181. See Chapter Two (pp. 115–31) on the relationship between *tian* and *Theos*.

on a theology of the Cross—the crucified Christ. The Cross is a system of harmony because of the virtue and work of Christ whose sacrificial love rejects fear, transcends enmity, and mends division. The Cross is a system of harmony also because it brings about final resolution between life and death. This idea of resolution is expressed in terms of freedom and deliverance from the "evil aeon" (1:4) and "cosmic elements" (4:3, 9) in Galatians. The Cross and its unconditional love reconcile God and humanity and bring about unity of Jews and Gentiles. The Cross as a system of harmony does not rely on traditions of the law or *li,* but on grace and the work of God. Both systems of harmony (music and the cross) bring about concord in the community—and the Cross also brings about the reconciliation between God and humanity. Both systems of harmony are aesthetic representations of transcendence—unity in diversity. Both systems work in the rhythmic, transformative process of mending differences (presence and absence, movement and rest, Jew and Gentile, male and female) and move toward mutual honoring. Both systems engender the language that allows people to participate in awe (ecstasy), holiness (otherness), and grace (gift). Both systems bring participants into doxology. In a discussion of the beautiful and the holy, Don E. Saliers relates liturgical music to doxology:

> Our means of participation in doxology to God is not by abstract rules but embodied cultural forms that open up levels of reality they do not 'contain' in themselves. The very means of singing, praying, and ritual enactment confer something beyond a sum of the various component parts of liturgy. There are rules as well, but these are part of the discipline enabling the arts to become 'artless' in the Christian assembly. . . . St. Basil, in preaching on the Psalms, refers to them as, 'a bond of unity harmoniously drawing people to the symphony of one choir.'[182]

Confucius' notion of music and Paul's theology of the Cross are powerful in the sense that they strike the resonating cords of the heart, and create a beautiful community of the people of God.

This broad metaphorical understanding of music as a system of harmony and beauty is helpful in seeing the role music plays in Paul's theology and in the building of a community. The experience of joining in a lyrical/musical expression of faith, as in the utterance of a hymn to

---

182. Saliers, *Worship as Theology,* 209.

Christ, is one of *unity*. What is created and experienced is something unavailable to individuals as individuals. Early Christians experienced consciously and subconsciously their unity with and in Christ as they said/sung their hymns to Christ; they experienced the "body" of Christ by and when they became a body in song. To reinforce the "harmony" the Gentile Christians now enjoy with the Jewish believers as "Sons of God" in the new creation through Christ, Paul uses an organic metaphor of the *body* in 1 Corinthians—*body* as a music metaphor of harmony. In Galatians the body metaphor is not explicit, although Troy W. Martin has convincingly shown that the metaphor of "brother body" appears in the language of "brothers" in Gal 4:28 and 5:13.[183] Martin reads "brothers" in the texts as referring to different groups of people: In 5:13 "brothers" describes non-Jewish Christians who are formerly pagans, and in 4:28 describes Jewish Christians that include the troublemakers who desire to live under law.[184] Martin contends that the intention of Paul in using the word "brothers" in both cases as nominative (describing) rather than vocative (calling) is not to "call the Galatians to freedom as a goal or end in itself but to be brothers on a condition of freedom."[185] Martin continues to explain the significance of the "brother body" metaphor in relation to the common blood they share in the body of Christ:

> Paul describes both the Galatians, who are non-Jewish Christians, and the agitators, who are Jewish Christians, as brothers who have an obligation and right to share in the Eucharist. Paul's description of both groups as brothers is appropriate to his description elsewhere of the church as the body of Christ. Plutarch describes brothers as being 'one body according to nature (*adelphoi de tou kata physin sōmatos*)' since their bodies are built from the 'frothed blood' [semen] of their father and/or from the 'congealed blood' [*menses*] of their mother. Thus, Paul's description of Christians as brothers is congruent with his description of the church as a body since all share the same blood in the Eucharist just as brothers share the same blood from father and/or mother. Even though the phrase is not used in Galatians, the church could be described as

183. T. W. Martin, "The Brother Body," 5–18.

184. Ibid., 11.

185. Ibid.

the 'brother body,' a body that is extremely difficult to repair once it has been torn apart.[186]

Despite the fact that we have moved from lyrical music in the liturgical context to a "brother body" of Christian rites in Paul's theology, both are concerned with edification and harmony of a community of faith.

It is significant that Paul uses a broad understanding of music, including the metaphorical, as a system of harmony to create a community of concord. Although the ideas are articulated later in church history, Basil of Caesarea, Boethius, and Calvin all see the harmonious role of music in building the Christian community after the virtue of Christ. Basil writes,

> What did the Holy Spirit do when he saw that the human race was not led easily to virtue, and that due to our penchant for pleasure we gave little heed to an upright life? *He mixed sweetness of melody with doctrine* so that inadvertently we should absorb the benefit of the words through gentleness and ease of hearing, just as clever physicians frequently smear the cup with honey when giving the fastidious some rather bitter medicine to drink. Thus he contrived for us these harmonious psalm tunes, so that those who are children in actual age as well as those who are young in behavior, while appearing only to sing, would in reality be training their souls.[187]

Calvin believed that the use of the "organ for praising God and lifting up our hearts to Him, to console us by meditating upon His virtue, goodness, wisdom, and justice, a thing more necessary than one can say."[188] On the metaphorical understanding of music, Boethius (480–524), a Roman Christian philosopher, writes,

> There are three types of music. The first type is the music of the universe (*musica mundana*), the second, that of the human being (*musica humana*), and the third type is that which is created by certain instruments (*musica instruments constituta*) such as the *kithara*, or *tibia* or other instruments which produce melodies. . . . Thus even the humble *musica instrumentalis constituta* was linked through the music of the human soul ultimately to the

---

186. Ibid., 17–18.

187. "Homilia in psalmum," in McKinnon, *Music in Early Christian Literature*, 65.

188. "Foreword" to *Geneva Psalter*, in Strunk, *Source Readings in Music History*, 347.

"resonate"

music of the spheres, for all three were part of the same divinely controlled system. [Humankind] had therefore to strive to make music which synchronized with this harmoniously vibrating universe and which would therefore form a worthy part of God's great symphony of proportions.[189]

The best "musical instrument" is the human voice (not made by human hands). Voices expressed melodically are not only found in the singing of songs, but also in the speaking or utterance of languages, especially those that are tonal—pitched with accents—such as Greek and Chinese. Whether literal or metaphorical, music in Confucius' thought and harmony in Paul's theology create a united "body of Christ," seeking to redeem a chaotic and fallen world.

Can Beauty Save the World?

Can the beauty of music save a fallen world? Both Confucius and Paul are positive in their view of the role music played to bring their respective communities together.[190] This is seen particularly in Paul's aversion to the discord and unreason of speaking in tongues in the Corinthian churches. Because unintelligible ritual speech does not build up the church; lifeless speech, like wooden ritual does not produce harmony or naturalness. It is as if we were presented with "beauty without goodness"—angelic language that does not edify the congregation. So Paul seems to argue that, the internal harmony of Spirit and mind required for intelligible speech is also required to produce social harmony and support the common good. Confucius emphasizes the beauty *and goodness* of *shao* music for it expresses the benevolent virtue of the king, which in turn brings about social harmony and prosperity. Confucius regards beauty as a virtue. In the Bible beauty is not listed as a virtue. Rather, beauty in the Hebrew Scriptures is a divine attribute: The psalmists often praise the beauty of God along with his glory in the context of the liturgical assembly (Pss 27:4; 96:6; cf. Isa 4:2; 28:5). In the New Testament beauty is not men-

189. Wilson-Dickson, *The Story of Christian Music*, 40.

190. Music can also enslave or distract us. Music can draw us away from God to its own beauty, thus becoming an idol "in human form, with human beauty, to be set up in a shrine" of human heart? (Isa 44:13).

tioned as a divine attribute.[191] Perhaps this is because the crucifixion of Christ is often misunderstood as an evil, as Blackwell writes: "Agape or self-giving love, which Christian tradition identifies with God as revealed in Christ, is not identical with harmony as we usually conceive it. The way of Christ is 'the way of affliction.'"[192] I disagree with Blackwell here, for precisely at this point of Christ's suffering salvation is accomplished, the wall of enmity between Jews and Gentiles is torn down, and reconciliation completed. The self-giving love of Christ is the virtue that engenders faith, hope, and love—the Christian virtues.

Although the Bible does not list beauty as a virtue, the early church expresses the conviction of the power of Christian music to bring about reconciliation in a divisive world. Given what Confucius has to say about music in the context of rites and virtue, we can ask the same question about the positive contribution of music to the Christian life. Confucius emphasizes the harmonizing effect of music on community. Some music can hurt and divide community, but music can also heal and pull community together. Salvation in Galatians is essentially about different ethnic groups becoming the people of God *via* baptism and unconditional love (instituted by the Eucharist meal). Consequently, since music was employed in these liturgical contexts, it would not be out of line to suggest that music was used to harmonize factions within the community.

MODERN IMPLICATIONS

This discussion of music as understood by Confucius and Paul has a modern bearing on Chinese communities in mainland China, Taiwan, and Hong Kong who are divided by the straits, by political ideology, and by economical development. The Confucian vision of building an aesthetic society through stylized ritual and harmonious music speaks to the truth that the ultimate goal of politics is not realization of democracy, freedom, equality but the participation, transformation, and enjoyment in Beauty (aesthetic world).[193] Building an aesthetic society does not advocate the

---

191. The word "beauty" appears in Rom 10:15 which quotes Isa 52:7: "How beautiful are the feet of them that bring good tidings."

192. Blackwell, *The Sacred in Music*, 163.

193. Chen, "Kongzi shi yue meixue zhong de zhengtixing gainian," 1.

rule of law but first and foremost, the rule of Beauty, whose curriculum is a benevolent government, graced by music and ordered by rituals.

What unites the Chinese people across the straits seems to be pop culture, especially popular music. There was a saying in the 1970s and 1980s that Deng Xiao-ping ruled during the day, Deng Lijun (Teresa Teng) ruled at night. The people may have listened to the political speeches of Deng Xiao-ping during the day, but all of them listened to singer Deng Lijun at night. It is a known fact that pop concerts held in these "three regions" (China, Taiwan, and Hong Kong) are able to overcome political divides. Music is a language that transcends boundary and touches human hearts, regardless of age, intellect, gender, or ideology.

If pop culture has so much to offer in the task of national reconciliation and in the building of Chinese communities across the straits, Chinese Christians can contribute even more. Culture without theology is like a corpse, or worse, a narcissistic idol or violent demon. Culture then does not have the spiritual resources to critique and renew itself. Yet theology without culture is like an anemic illness, for theology cannot feed on itself, it has to feed on "the nitty gritty" of life.

Christian traditions have long incorporated music as an artifact of worship. Chinese Christians can learn from pop culture and Christian traditions to express their theology, so that both their rituals and their music can be instruments of God's grace. What can Chinese Christians do to help Chinese across the straits to form a new identity in the new creation of God in Christ? Can the Christian rituals of baptism, and the Eucharist, and Christian hymns and songs, as well as acts of mercy and service shape the new Chinese identity in the years ahead, which politics alone seems helpless to do? God is forming his new creation in China through the body of Christ. God has inspired a young peasant woman called Xiaomin nearly a thousand hymns with tunes. She did not complete her secondary school education and she is illiterate in music, yet the collection of her songs and music entitled Canaan Hymns have brought unity, revival, and hope among Chinese churches that are still being persecuted. The Canaan Hymns use lyrical music to create social harmony, enhance worship life, and proclaim the new world order inaugurated by Christ.[194] Though the post-denominational church movement characterizes the Chinese church,

---

194. See the introduction of Canaan Hymns in http://www.chinasoul.com/cross/script/script4.htm

the different practices of observing Holy Communion (Eucharist) still divide Chinese Christianity. It remains a fact that Chinese Christians disagree among themselves regarding the ritual of baptism. As far as church music and singing are concerned, many Chinese churches are adamant that singing traditional hymns and spiritual songs with Western country music is acceptable, while singing hymns with traditional Chinese music or spiritual songs with popular music is prohibited. Many encourage the use of violin, harp, and organ, but object to the use of indigenous Chinese musical instruments such as the *erhu* (a two-string instrument played with a bow), the *zheng* (a zither with thirteen to seventeen strings tuned to pentatonic scale), and the *sheng* (a mouth organ that has seventeen to nineteen pipes seated on a wind chamber). A sociological explanation of this phenomenon is that the initial phase of the gospel proclamation in a new place requires the people to form a new identity as they seek differentiation from their own culture. Contextualization of the gospel in its mature form will usually come later. A sign of hope is witnessed in Chinese Christianity when many of the scores of the Canaan Hymns are in Chinese style—presented with folk accents and in pentatonic scales. Many pieces were performed for recording purposes using both Western and Chinese musical instruments.

Chinese Christians need to reflect on what Christian theology *and* Chinese wisdom can contribute toward their own political culture and identity. As we have explained earlier, Confucian ethics grants resources to Chinese Christians to emphasize rites and music in their political power of forming virtues and community. Confucius once said, "Practice the calendar of the Xia, ride on the plain chariot of the Yin [Shang Dynasty], and wear the ceremonial cap of the Zhou, but, for music, play the *shao* and the *wu*" (*Analects* 15:11).[195] Pauline theology also grants resources to Chinese Christians. In particular Paul's theology of the Cross, his political eschatology, his understanding of community as arising from being-in-Christ, the new law of the Spirit, and the rituals of baptism and the love feast are resources for Chinese Christians to use in building the body of Christ in their midst. Communal practices of Chinese Christians, although expressive of faith, point ahead, as does music in Confucius, to the creation of harmony and naturalness. The transformed

---

195. *Shao* was the music performed at the ceremony when emperor Yao abdicated and Shun became the next ruler; *wu* was the music performed at the ceremony when King Wu became the ruler. Yang, *Lunyu Yizhu*, 349.

lives of Chinese Christians is not for the sake of faith alone, rather they are in Christ for the sake of the world. It is this parallel between Paul and Confucius that enables the author to use a Chinese cultural framework that, rather than being discarded or set in opposition to Christian faith, facilitate a Chinese appropriation of the gospel. In doing so, it is hoped that the resources of Confucius' ethic and Paul's theology will enable Chinese Christian community to express its faith through forms of word, song, and ritual that is "fully Confucianist and fully Christian."

(Chinese)

4

To Be Human and To Be Holy in the New World—To Be the People of God

While the frames of reference for Confucian and Pauline ethics are not the same—one political, the other theological—as a Chinese Christian I have chosen to conflate the two to construct a *political ethics that is theological*. Confucius and Paul meet at the crossroads of (1) *Tian and Theos*, that is, where ethics is graced by Heaven and by God; and of (2) politics and theology, that is, where ethics responded to tumultuous and violent worlds by applying cultural ideals. In the last chapter we saw how Confucius and Paul reappropriated Zhou-*li* (propriety) and *yue* (music) and the Jewish *torah* respectively. The reinterpretation of sacred traditions in each instance aimed at the creation of an inclusive and virtuous community. In this chapter, we want to advance the intertextual reading further by looking at Confucius' and Paul's understanding of what it means to be human and to be holy, as well as at their teaching of the "best moral self" and "cruciform love."

CONFUCIUS AND PAULINE ETHICS: TO BE HOLY AND TO BE HUMAN

There are subtle differences between the ethics of Confucius and Paul. According to Confucius, to be human *is* to be a holy ("religious" or "pious") person.[1] According to Paul, to be holy *is* to be human. Confucius approaches anthropology from a cosmological and social-political perspective; Paul approaches anthropology from a theological, or rather christological, perspective. Paul's anthropology is christologically defined (in Gal 3:28) and is subsumed under divine grace, whereas Confucius understands being human as the endowment of Heaven (*tian*).

The Different Understandings of "Grace" and "Human Nature"

Confucius' cosmic-ethical conception of selfhood views "grace" as *given to all* in creation. Being human is heavenly endowed. A passage within the Confucian canonical text, the *Doctrine of Mean* 1:1 reads, "What *tian* [heaven] has conferred is called nature [*xing*]."[2] That is, all persons are born with the same nature, or ontological reality, which they receive from *tian*.[3] All are endowed with the equal potential of manifesting the ultimate reality (Heaven) in their moral life, for human beings possess a heavenly imparted nature or disposition called *xing*. The word *xing* in Chinese is made up of a phonetic and a radical, implying that the two meanings of the word are interrelated: (a) the phoneme "life" (*sheng*) denotes the breath of life as the endowment of *tian* (Heaven) on all human beings (and, in fact, all creatures); and, (b) the radical "heart" (*xin*) signifies the unique capacity implanted in human nature to be humane and moral.[4] The human heart is different from an animal's heart. In traditional Chinese thought, the human "heart" is considered to be a metaphor for the core of human nature. Animals do not have the capacity of self-reflective thought and moral cultivation; human beings do. The great Confucian master Mencius differentiates a human from an animal according to the moral heart: "Human beings differ from the birds and

---

1. Qian, *Gongzi Yu Lunyu*, 194–95. Tu Weiming writes, "To be religious, in the Confucian sense, is to be engaged in ultimate self-transformation as a communal act. Salvation means the full realization of the anthropocosmic reality inherent in our human nature," *Confucian Thought*, 133.

2. *Doctrine of Mean* (*Zhongyong*) 1:1. Legge and Yang, trans., *The Four Books*, 24–25.

3. Mou, *Xinti Yu Xingti*, 1:26–27.

4. See Alexander, "The Face of Holiness," 25.

beasts but slightly. The mass of people cast it [human nature; *xing*] away, whereas the exemplary person preserves it" (*Mencius* 4b.19).[5]

The heart is the faculty of morality that includes both the reasoning will (mind) and empathetic feeling. Both reasoning will and empathetic feeling are directed toward moral conduct. Mencius identified a universal feeling of commiseration (heart) by noting what everyone feels when they see a child fall into a well. Every person has that feeling of commiseration because every person has the same human nature, the gift of *tian*—and there is no speculation of "Adam's Fall." The human heart and will are not broken; human nature is potentially born good. Unlike the Christian tradition, which understands human creatures as distinct from the Creator, the Confucian tradition perceives human beings as gifted in the cycle of life and as sharing in the same nature of *tian* (Heaven), viz., the universal principle of creativity, morality, and goodness (*Analects* 5:13).[6] Universal *ren* (humaneness) is the ultimate goodness of the universe that is also found in human nature, the "*benxing*" (original nature). Mencius writes, "The feeling of commiseration is the beginning of *ren* (humaneness)" (*Mencius* 3a.6).[7] To realize the moral ideal is the task of each individual as he participates in the ultimate good, symbolized by *tian* or *dao*. In short, "If a person is to do his best with his heart (*jinxin*) benevolently, he knows his nature (*zhixing*). Knowing his nature means that he knows the mandate of Heaven (*zhitian*). He who keeps his heart (*cunxin*) benevolently cultivates his nature (*yangxing*), and consequently serves Heaven (*shitian*). Whether one's life is long or short, the important thing is to cultivate oneself (*xiushen*) in order to establish the mandate of Heaven (*liming*)."[8]

5. My translation. *Mencius* 4b.19. Legge and Yang, trans., *The Four Books*, 416–17.

6. *Analects* 5:13 "Zigong said, 'We hear and receive much from the Master on his cultural refinement, but we do not hear much from the Master on human nature and the *dao* of Heaven.'" Mou explains that the topic on human nature and *dao* of Heaven belonged to tradition older than that of Confucius. Confucius must have known and understood the topic, that is, the creativity or transcendence nature of Heaven *(tian)* is also the nature of human beings. Yet Confucius seldom articulated the topic because, according to Mou, Confucius' ethics emphasized the concrete expressions of the transcendental nature, i.e., humaneness (*ren*), wisdom (*zhi*), and sage (*sheng*). See Mou, *Zhongguo Zhexue De Tezhi*, 40–43.

7. *Mencius* 3a.6. Legge and Yang, trans., *The Four Books*, 320–21.

8. My translation. *Mencius* 7a.1 provides the best summary of Confucius' teaching on *tian* and the moral self. See Zhu, ed., *Sishu*, 650.

Confucius believed that "Human nature is closely similar, but the habits of people are widely different" (*Analects* 17:2). He believed that all are endowed with the same "seed of humanity," but whether every person cultivates the seed to its full potential is another matter. Mencius also understood human nature as naturally good, just as water naturally flows downward (*Mencius* 6a.2).[9] But human nature is constantly influenced by both the conditioning of the environment and by cultivation through learning. The *Doctrine of Mean* (1:1) urges people to follow the moral tendencies of the human heart, "To follow human nature is called the Way (*Dao*); cultivating the Way is called learning (*jiao*)." Heaven is the source of goodness and morality; Heaven has uniquely imparted the good and moral tendencies of the heart to all human beings. Those who walk in the path of the heart cultivate their moral potentiality, thereby abiding in the Way with Heaven itself.

While Confucian ethics, according to Mencius, is based on the goodness of human nature (*xing*), Paul's ethics is based on the human predicament of sin and how its power is overcome in the Cross of Christ. Whether there is a sharp difference between Pauline and Confucianist anthropology is difficult to tell, because Confucius does not deal with what Christians call the "fall into sin." Of course, Confucius and his followers did not deal with "the Christian assumption" that came five centuries later; but they dealt with its equivalent, human finitude. By "the goodness of human nature," Mencius is not saying that humans never sin. Nor is he suggesting that human nature is entirely good. He means that all human beings have the inherent capacity for, and essential human nature of, goodness. Since normative human nature is good, human beings sin because of circumstances, not because of their created nature—"just as barley will produce a good or bad crop depending on cultivation, soil, and rainfall, despite the fact that the seeds are the same" (*Mencius* 6a.4).[10] To say that human nature is good is to say that human beings are inherently capable of initiating (*tuan*) the acts of *ren* (humaneness), *yi* (righteousness), *li* (propriety) and *zhi* (wisdom): "Since all people have these four seeds in them, let them provide for their full development and completion, and the result will be like fire that begins to burn, or of a spring that bursts forth. Provide them with their complete development,

9. Legge and Yang, trans., *The Four Books*, 470–71.
10. Ibid., 472–73.

in curvatus in se — more than environment ?

and they will suffice to protect all within the four seas. Let them be denied that development, and they will not suffice even to serve their own parents" (*Mencius* 3a.6).[11]

The understanding of the goodness of human nature is not incompatible with the Christian theology of the *imago Dei*. Human beings are created in the image of God. Thus though they are creatures, distinct from their Creator, their nature is essentially good. Confucian anthropology basically accepts this Christian reading of human nature. The difference between Confucius and Paul is not about human nature but about sin. Not the origins of human nature, but instead the issue of sin, divides Confucius and Paul. Confucius' ethics begin with the universal goodness inherent to an uncorrupt human nature. However, Paul's theology assumes that all persons live under the enslaving power of sin and are therefore in need of divine grace as it is found in Christ. Confucius would reject the notion that human nature is corrupt to the point that humans live in estrangement from God as a result of sin.[12] It is significant to point out that there is no Chinese word equivalent to the biblical understanding of sin; the Chinese word used to translate sin is "crime" in the Chinese Bible. Confucius does not bring about a union between divine grace and human will in his writings because he does not presuppose a fallenness of humanity. The "sin" Confucianists speak of is the fallenness of one's cultural tradition in the society. *Analects* 19:19 reads, "For a long time those above [ruling elites] have lost the Way and the common people have therefore become confused."[13] The causes of the ritual corruption and decadent music are: (a) "the panlogy of basic human weaknesses: lust, greed, sloth, etc." and (b) "of relatively more timely concern to Confucius—the quality of the tradition into which one is acculturated."[14] Confucianists believe that the personal "sins" are magnified by the cultural "sin"—corrupted tradition. Once the principles of harmony and goodness are restored in the systems of ritual and music according to the ideal traditions, then the character and human nature of a person will be

11. Ibid., 320–21.

12. Alexander, "The Face of Holiness," 32.

13. Slingerland, trans., *Confucius Analects*, xxiii.

14. Ibid. See also Mou Zongsan's understanding of "sin" in Confucianism as an ethical and subjective matter of the heart. Mou, *Zhongguo Zhexue De Tezhi*, 86.

cultivated in a harmonious state "between himself and society and the social order and the cosmos."[15]

For Paul, however, culture and tradition are not the cause of sin. Sin is the enslaving power in the universe that corrupts the image of God in all human beings, and it breaks their moral will to save themselves from their estrangement from God. He sees the reconciling work of Christ on the Cross has broken the dominating power of sin and death, and believers are now able to live a holy life before God and their neighbor through baptism into Christ. Paul sees living a holy life pleasing to God (sanctification) as the faithful response of one justified by the grace of Jesus Christ.[16] We have shown in Chapter Two how Confucian *tian* (Heaven) is different from the Pauline *Theos* (God)—*Tian* reveals its own moral goodness in the world particularly in human nature, but *tian* reveals neither its personhood (if it has) nor its work *personally* in the world. *Theos* is concerned with the redemption of the world and the self-revelation of *Theos* is found in the person and work of Christ. From these different understandings of God/*tian* (theologies) we see how Confucius' and Paul's ethics have different starting points and different ways of understanding the relations between human ethical responsibilities and God's enabling power. The biggest chasm between Confucius and Paul pertains to their understanding of the relationship of human beings to Heaven and to God. The right relationship to *tian* in Confucius' thought is obtained by moral will and consequent acts. In Paul, a relationship is a gift received by faith. In Confucius, salvation comes by following *li (ritual propriety)* in becoming *ren* (humaneness). In Paul, the believer is perfected in love by acknowledging God's forgiving love in Christ and by the imitation of Christ.

Despite their differences, Paul's quite Jewish assumption that sin arises from an evil impulse (*yeser*) challenges human beings to choose between good and evil.[17] This Jewish assumption resonates with the Confucian emphasis on ethical choice and on the cultivation of virtue according to *li* (propriety). But would Paul agree with Confucius by saying that the Jewish law embodied both the proper ethical means and the holy

15. Slingerland, trans., *Confucius Analects*, xxiii.

16. Paul sees the life of holiness (*hagiasmos*) as the obedience of faith (*hypakoen pisteoōs*, cf. Rom 1:5; 15:15), it is the faithful response to divine grace.

17. See Davies, *Paul and Rabbinic Judaism*, 24–26, 30–31, on the good and evil impulses within a person according to rabbinic tradition.

ceremonies to enable human beings to be good? Perhaps we could say that the Pharisaic Paul thought so. But the Christian Paul clearly denied the usefulness of the law in the life of holiness. Confucius sees the necessity of *li* (rites or holy ceremonies) in the formation of virtue; Paul sees the role of the Spirit of God in producing the fruit of the Spirit (virtue). Paul sees "being in Christ" as the goal of salvation. Confucius is more optimistic than Paul about human moral actualization. But whether through divine grace or by means of virtue cultivation, Confucius believes moral perfection is the goal of being human, Paul believes moral perfection is part of the process of salvation, that is, "being in Christ." Paul is too much an eschatological thinker to believe moral perfection as the goal of being human. For Paul "being in Christ"—which carries the certain risk of sharing in Christ's suffering—is for salvation, being at one with God. Being at one with God can be realized now, in this life (and even in the absence of moral perfection) through faith that in Christ one's moral and spiritual imperfection (sin) has been forgiven.

The Life of Holiness and Justification

Paul believes the power of God's Spirit is essential for believers to live a life of holiness, a life pleasing to God. Compared with Confucian ethics, Paul would appear to put less emphasis on the ethical responsibility of the believer. Yet with a closer reading, one may be surprised to see that Paul does not view the life pleasing to God as simply something poured into human beings from a transcendent source; there are *explicit imperatives* Christians must carry out (Galatians 5–6)—we will discuss this point in Chapter Five. Here I want to focus on the continuity between justification and sanctification.

For Paul, the life of holiness (sanctification), which is sustained by the Eucharist, is based upon justification. Justification is a gift of God received by faith. Since reality is not static, new life in Christ is a process. Justification does not stop at restoring our status as acceptable to God. It calls for a response, for obedient living, and living in a trusting relationship. Justification is not just a restoration, it is also the giving of new life. It calls for constant renewal and transformation.

The new life of sanctification has its ground exclusively in the death and resurrection of Christ. Sanctification is not a succession of human works. Sanctification is a process in which the indicative ("you are a new creation") and imperatives (act like a new creation) are harmoniously embraced. The fact of "being in Christ" moves toward "becoming like Christ." Paul is saying in effect that, if one knows one's sins are forgiven, one will respond as fully as one can with a sinless (obedient) life. If one does not stop doing these things (sins) one did not acknowledge that they were sins in the first place, so their forgiveness means nothing to that person, hence he "continues in sin." Diane B. Obenchain writes,

> Jesus offers the gift of forgiveness of sins. . . . The forgiven person is a new creation, a child of God, a member of God's household, ... As a child of God, one puts off ways of feeling, thinking, and acting that are not of God. . . . [I]n compassion, kindness, humility, gentleness, patience, and forgiveness, wrapped in love and ruled by peace and thankfulness, we can offer back to God the new life we have received and seek to use the provisions that we have received to provide for others.[18]

This understanding of ethics is of course distinctively Christian, or rather Pauline, though to my Chinese ears the language may sound Confucianist with respect to a life of holiness as a *process of obedience*.

In their ethical systems, Confucius and Paul share the following views. First, both systems emphasize the ethical life as relational, a consequence of belonging to God the Holy One or to transcendent *tian* (Heaven). Paul argues that the term "holiness" has the meaning of belonging to the Holy One, the Lord. Because one belongs to the Lord, one is one expected to be ethically just and morally good. Similarly, Confucius argues that it is the transcendent *tian* that gives the mandate for human beings to be morally good so that what is immanent (ethics) reflects what is transcendent (*tian*).

Secondly, both Pauline and Confucian ethics understand that the process of sanctification is aimed toward loving one's neighbor. Christians are not under the demand of the law, but they are under the provision to be what God wants them to be, that is, those who love their neighbors. For Paul growth in the process of sanctification is directed toward the ultimate goal of realizing the image of God in human beings. The process is initiated in the life of faith through grace. It is a life of love toward

18. Obenchain, "The Study of Religion and the Coming Global Generation," 3:98–99.

one's neighbor as an expression of a life of faith and love toward God. For Confucius, ethics is the way to become human, and to be human is to love others. Sanctification is a process of human moral perfection achieved by means of fulfilling *daode* (the way of virtue), *tiandao* (the way of Heaven), *rendao* (the way of humanity), and *tianming* (the mandate of Heaven). Confucius advocates that everyone actualizes the mandate of Heaven by committing himself to *ren* (humaneness), because what makes human beings human is *ren* (humaneness). The will of Heaven for any community is to practice the law of life, that is, the law of love.

Before we look at the role love plays in the life of holiness, it is important to recognize that for Confucius, benevolence (*ren*) is ritualized hierarchically and that in Paul love (*apapē*) is not ritualized at all but made virtuous by overcoming human differences in the power of the Spirit. This basic difference in the structures of society *does not necessarily* lead one system of ethic to bondage and the other to freedom. We have seen in the last two chapters (and will discuss further in Chapters Five and Six) that despite the hierarchical structure of Confucian society, Confucius' radical ethics of *de* (virtue), *li* (propriety), and *zhongshu* (single-heartedness and like-heartedness, or loyalty and empathy) are subversive to the oppressive aspects of hierarchy in Chinese society. Thus, though the purpose of Confucius' ethics is to promote social harmony, it has modes of self-criticism to stop from becoming ritualistic, traditionalistic, and autocratic. One such mode is Confucius' understanding of *ren* (humaneness).

A CHINESE CHRISTIAN ETHICS:
RITUAL (LAW) OF LOVE IN THE LIFE OF HOLINESS

Ren *(Humaneness and Benevolence) and Co-Humanity*

↔ The Semantics of *Ren*

Thus far I have translated the word *ren* as benevolence or love. It is, however, necessary to broaden our understanding of this word beyond its translation since the concept is the cornerstone of Confucius' teaching. In the relatively short book of the *Analects*, *ren* is used no less than eighty times. The word can be used either in the narrow sense of one's desirable virtues (e.g., in *Analects* 9:29; 14:28) or more often in the broad sense of the encompassing ethical ideal (e.g., 14:4).[19] In *Analects* 12:22, *ren* is equated with benevolence (for fellow human beings). Readers need to note that the English transliteration "*ren*" can refer to two different Chinese words, 仁 (*ren*) and 人 (*ren*), meaning "humaneness" and "person" respectively. In this section we are discussing the first word 仁. When the two words appear together, the order is always 仁人 (*renren*), meaning "humane person" or "benevolent person." Since Chinese does not have articles, and the word itself does not indicate singular or plural, *renren* can mean a humane person or humane persons.

The Confucian worldview is one of interrelationships, words such as *ren* or *li* are to be understood primarily as relational concepts and consequently defy fixed definition. Given that the *Analects* is not a philosophical treatise with precise use of terms, it has been difficult for scholars to pinpoint the meaning of *ren*. Benjamin Schwartz interprets *ren* as "an attainment of human excellence which—where it exists—is a whole embracing all the separate virtues."[20] Yearley translates *ren* as "virtue,"[21] which is similar to Legge's "virtuous manners."[22] Waley translates *ren* as "goodness," "humane," "human-at-its-best," and Dawson, "humaneness."[23] D. C. Lau writes that *ren* "is basically a character of agents and its application to acts is only derivative."[24] Lau renders *ren* as "benevolence."[25] Other translations are "human-heartedness" (E. R. Hughes), "humanity," "virtue" (H. G. Creel), "human-relatedness," "charity," "humanity" (W. T. Chan), "morality," "compassion" (Lin Yutang), "human-to-humanness" (F. S. C. Northrop).[26]

Part of the difficulty lies in the fact that Confucius was investing new meanings into the term *ren*. He was frequently asked what the term

19. Shun, "*Ren* and *Li* in the *Analects*," 53. See also Yao, ed., *RoutledgeCurzon Encyclopedias of Confucianism*, 2:498–500.

20. Schwartz, *The World of Thought in Ancient China*, 75.

21. Yearley, "An Existentialist Reading of Book 4 of the *Analects*," 245.

22. Legge and Yang, trans., *The Four Books*, passim.

23. Waley, *Analects*, *passim*; Dawson, trans., *Confucius*, passim. Slingerland, trans., *Confucius Analects*, 238 translates *ren* as goodness.

24. Lau, trans., *Analects*, 27; similarly Yang, *Lunyu Yizhu*, 6.

25. Lau, trans., *Analects*, *passim*.

26. Cf. Fung, *A Short History of Chinese Philosophy*, 69–73; Yang, *Lunyu Yizhu*, 18–21, 221; Chan, "Chinese and Western Interpretations of *Ren* (Humanity)," 108–9; Chiu, *The Tao of Chinese Religion*, 191–92. See David Nivison, *The Ways of Confucianism*, 133–48 (on Mencius's *ren*, 3a.5; 7a.45) and 196–97 (Mohist *ren*).

meant, but it is said his audience could not understand his answer, or they rejected what he was saying. In *Analects* 12:22, when asked by Fan Chih the meaning of *ren*, Confucius replied that *ren*) is to love people (*airen*). Let me quote Lau's translation to set the literary context:

> Fan Chih asked about *ren*. The Master said, "Love [*ai*] your fellow men." He asked about wisdom. The Master said, "Know your fellow men." Fan Chih failed to grasp his meaning. The Master said, "Raise the straight and set them over the crooked. This can make the crooked straight." Fan Chih withdrew and went to see Tzu-hsia, saying, "Just now, I went to see the Master and asked about wisdom. The Master said, 'Raise the straight and set them over the crooked. This can make the crooked straight.' What did he mean?" Tzu-hsia said, "Rich, indeed, is the meaning of these words. When Shun possessed the Empire, he raised Kao Yao from the multitude and by so doing placed those who were not benevolent at a great distance. When Tang possessed the Empire, he raised Yi Yin from the multitude and by so doing placed those who were not benevolent at a great distance" (*Analects* 12:22).[27]

So according to *Analects* 12:22, the translation of *ren* as "benevolence" or "love" is apt. But *ren* is not just loving one's fellow beings (12:22); it is to be empathetic/conscientious (*zhong*) and merciful/reciprocal (*shu*, *Analects* 4:15).[28] *Ren* also carries within it all the moral qualities that govern the relationships between two or more human beings.

Ren as Co-humanity

Confucius regards *ren* as the fountain head of all the virtues. The Chinese character for *ren* is composed of two ideograms: "person" connotes self or a human being, and "two" connotes relation.[29] For our purposes here we shall translate *ren* as human-relatedness, human-relatedness, or specifically as love, which is the cardinal principle of human relationships.[30]

27. Lau, trans., *Analects*, 117, 119. See Qian, *Lunyu Xinjie*, 445–46, and Yang, *Lunyu Yizhu*, 279–80.

28. See Chapter Six (pp. 357–63) on *zhong* and *shu*.

29. Tu Weiming says, "Etymologically *ren* consists of two parts, one a simple ideogram of a human figure, meaning the self, and the other with two horizontal strokes, suggesting human relations" (*Confucian Thought*, 84).

30. Fung, *A Short History of Chinese Philosophy*, 69–73; and Chan, "Chinese and

As vividly expressed by Fang Ying-hsien, "in terms of two semiotic foci: *ren* is (1) the tender aspect of human feelings, namely, love, and (2) an altruistic concern for others . . ."[31] However, Fang's first point on feelings is a modern psychological projection on Confucius' thought world, but his second point is well taken. For Confucius says, "In order to establish oneself, one must establish others" (*Analects* 6:30).[32] To be truly human is to be responsible to and for others, but "the others" are not specified in *Analects* 6:30. They could be family members, friends, superiors, or enemies. But the emphasis on edifying and caring for others is clear.

Co-humanity with Authority and Integrity

Ames and Rosemont, tracing the lexicon of *ren*, argue that for Confucius' *ren* means variously "authoritative conduct," "to act authoritatively," or even an "authoritative person."[33] They write,

> 'Authoritative' entails the 'authority' that a person comes to represent in community by becoming *ren*, embodying in oneself the values and customs of one's tradition through the observance of ritual propriety (*li*). The prominence and visibility of the authoritative person is captured in the metaphor of the mountain (6:23): still, stately, spiritual, enduring, a landmark of the local culture and community.[34]

They continue,

> . . . *ren* is one's entire person: one's cultivated cognitive, aesthetic, moral, and religious sensibilities as they are expressed in one's ritualized roles and relationships. . . . *[R]en* is not only mental, but physical as well: one's posture and comportment, gestures and bodily communication. Hence, translating *ren* as 'benevolence' is to 'psychologize' it in a tradition that does not rely upon the notion of psyche as a way of defining the human experience.[35]

Western Interpretations of *Ren*," 109.

31. Taken from Tu, *Confucian Thought*, 84.

32. My translation. See Qian, *Lunyu Xinjie*, 224; Chen, *Lunyu Duxun Jiegu*, 106; Yang, *Lunyu Yizhu*, 141–42.

33. Ames and Rosemont, *Analects*, 48.

34. Ibid., 50.

35. Ibid., 49.

Here Ames and Rosemont criticize an interpretation of *ren* as possessing psychological aspects as in the translation of *ren* as "benevolence." The translation itself, however, does not necessarily give *ren* a psychological dimension. The English word benevolence need not be given or limited to a psychological dimension. "Bene-volence" means to will what is good. What Ames and Rosemont want is to treat *ren* (benevolence) as a way of relating that is ritually proper, respectful, including the right relationship dictated by the hierarchical character of authority. In their analysis of Confucian era bone inscriptions, Ames and Rosemont write:

> An alternative explanation of the character *ren* we might derive from oracle bone inscriptions is that what appears to be the number 'two' is in fact an early form of 'above, to ascend *shang* 上,' which was also written as 二. Such a reading would highlight the growing distinction one accrues in become *ren*, thereby setting a bearing for one's community and the world to come: 'those authoritative in their conduct enjoy mountains . . . are still . . . [and] are long-enduring (6:23; see also 2:1 and 17:3).[36]

In those political or social contexts where rulers and others lost their authority because they loved in word only, Ames and Rosemont' point is well taken.[37] Common people "love" their rulers and inferiors "love" their superiors—out of fear. Confucius had seen the collapse of moral propriety and the social disharmony it created, so his discussion of *ren* (and *li*) was designed to create a new moral order. Confucius' aesthetic project, pertaining to ritual and musical harmony, is based on his keen perception of human *becoming*. The individual becomes human by relating to others; he becomes an authoritative person by benevolent acts toward others. In the language of Mou Zongsan, human *becoming* of *ren* means that a person has moral consciousness or moral mind (*daode xinlin*) and to imitate Heaven's way of creativity (*tian xing jian*) in being virtuous to others.[38]

The individual self is not an isolated entity, an atomized existence, but a living being embedded in relationships. The first character of the word "self" (*ziji*) pictographically depicts "the transverse and lengthwise threads forming the warp and weft of a loom" and the second charac-

---

36. Ibid., 48–49.

37. Ibid., 49: "The human being is not something we are; it is something that we do, and become. Perhaps 'human becoming' might thus be a more appropriate term to capture the processional and emergent nature of what it means to become human."

38. Mou, *Zhongguo Zhexue De Tezhi*, 43.

ter depicts "the human nose, the central and protruding feature of one's face."[39] Niytray explains that,

> In the Confucian view, the *ji* self, or self-in-relation, is responsible *as a self*; it is capable of creating and altering its relations with other selves through the deliberate cultivation of humaneness (*ren*) and the conscious application of ritual form (*li*) in every social interaction. Humaneness and ritual, *ren* and *li*, elevate a person from social animal to what Confucius called the 'gentleman' (*junzi*), an 'authentic' or 'perfected' person.[40]

Or as Ames and Rosemont write,

> no-thing or no-body has an *essence*, but can be defined only 'correlationally,' at any give time, with differing relations holding at other times; we are both benefactors and beneficiaries of our friends, neighbors, lovers, colleagues, and so forth, dependent on specific circumstances.[41]

The interpersonal relationships one has within a community and the acts one does for others constitute together the essence of humanity. To be *ren* (humaneness), to be benevolent or compassionate, is to be in relationship, to be interdependent. *Ren* is the authentic nature of human beings. *Ren* is the way (*dao*) for one to become truly human as he relates to others. In short, *ren* is the ordering principle of a Confucianist society. Though interpersonal relationships change, Confucius saw the five cardinal relations (*wulun*) as basic to the formation of a mature, authentic, and perfect person.

⤷ Five Confucian Basic Relationships (*wulun*)

The five cardinal, bilateral relations, viz., between ruler and subjects, father and son, husband and wife, older and younger brothers, and among friends, are the training grounds of *ren*. The virtues of compassion, righteousness, mutual respect, loyalty, and trust are found in *ren*.

According to Confucius, our immediate family is a microcosm of the larger society we live in, which is why filial piety is the most basic

39. Nyitray, "The Single Thread of A New Confucianism," 197.
40. Ibid., 198.
41. Ames and Rosemont, *Analects*, 24.

moral obligation and virtue. We have seen in the last chapter how filial piety is a ritual that recognizes human mutual indebtedness (no human being exists in isolation, it takes two persons to be human). This "human indebtedness" is good and healthy, and the ritual of filial piety forms individuals into humane persons (*renren*) who understand the benevolent relationship (*ren*) as predicated upon the condition of human frailty and limitation, and thus the necessity of interdependence. This fundamental dependence on others as prerequisite to becoming human is one of the core assumptions of the Confucian ethic of *ren*.

Family is "the locus of where, how, and why we develop into full human beings."[42] The metaphor of the family has been used in politics and government throughout Chinese history. The state is the largest, extended family; it is in Chinese literally the "country-family"—*guojia*. The ruler of a state is called son of Heaven. His moral obligation is to be benevolent, for he is the parent of the people and expected to treat the people as his own children. Common people are called children-citizens—*zimin*, the children of the state.

The five relationships are not on the same level, and some of them depend on others in terms of process of cultivating virtues. "There is a specific hierarchic order defining the unifying relation which joins these five relations to each other."[43] Without trust among friends, it will be difficult to expect trust in government. Without relating well to one's siblings and parents, one will not know how to relate well to friends. Thus, a proper family relation is basic for one to be a social self in the wider world. Confucian ethics is family oriented because it assumes that the family is the most intimate and enduring place for forming human beings. Learning to be human by being children, we learn to be parents as well. Once we learn how to be fully human—how to trust, to love, to forgive, to obey, to serve—in the family context, then we learn how to extend virtuous relations to others—our relatives, our friends, our officials. Ideally, the family relationship in its many and varied occasions teaches us to relate to people outside our family as to our own.

In relating to our own parents, we learn to relate to other parents. The learning process of relating to one (parent) and to many (parents) takes the form of imitation and immersion. From youth, we learn the

42. Rosemont, "On Confucian Civility," 191.
43. Northrop, *The Meeting of East and West*, 326.

(*also Daniel A. Bell*)

intricacies of relationships by immersing ourselves in the particular yet multiply-fluid context of the family. We learn virtue by imitating what our elders do. Act and being are not be dichotomized. Actions reflect the good intention of being a cultured human being; intention is confirmed and realized in the repetitive, life-long process of ritual propriety. These are called customs and rituals.

The immersion process (similar to Northrop's language of "intuitive, aesthetic, undifferentiated continuum") slowly draws us to participate in a ritualized and stylized cultural pattern that is sacred and meaningful. These things are not done for show, but for the excellence of being fully human. Once propriety becomes our "second nature," we are neither ignorant of nor alienated from the rules governing how to relate to other parents and grandparents. Our children and grandchildren and those around us imitate what we do and who we are—both the good and the bad. The Master said, "Look at the means a man employs, observe the path he takes and examine where he feels at home. In what way is a man's true character hidden from view? In what way is a man's true character hidden from view?" (*Analects* 2:10).[44]

Confucius sees the five basic relationships of interconnectedness as: ruler-subject (duty), parent-child (affection), husband-wife (differentiation), older-younger brothers (order), and friends (trust).[45] The first and the last sets of relationships are outside the family structure, but in terms of their nature, they are perceived as being extensions of familial virtues. The second set of relationships is the most important because it is so basic and primordial. Every human being begins life with this set of relationships, thus the practice of virtue here is conditioned by the unrepayable debt one has toward one's parents. In cases where children are born orphans, Confucianist society advocates the virtue of adoption (mostly by the extended family), so that children can grow within the context of the family, immediate or extended.

Though reluctantly Confucian ethics allows subjects to rebel against unfit rulers, but it carries the stern warning against children rebelling against their parents, even when the parents are wrong. They can remonstrate with their parents, but not more. The second set of relationships is therefore primary; and the virtue of affection that it embodies can be ex-

---

44. Lau, trans., *Analects*, 13. See Chen, *Lunyu Duxun Jiegu*, 18.

45. Nyitray, "The Single Thread of A New Confucianism," 197.

tended to characterize in different ways the other four sets of relationships. Confucius assumes that husbands and wives are different (*bie*). Gender differentiation makes their union with one another possible and creative. Differentiated communion and communication in *ren* (humaneness) between husband and wife inculcate the virtues of righteousness and obedience. Sibling relationships in the orderly social world are characterized by the virtues of brotherhood and sisterhood as they care and protect one another. When the three family relationships (second, third, and fourth sets) are extended to one's peers (fifth set), then trustworthiness becomes the virtue of friendship. Extending family relationships upward to ruler and subjects, the virtues required become duty and respect. The relationship existing between government ministers is equivalent to that of friends. The relationship of the common subject to government officials is equivalent to a combination of the fourth and fifth sets of relationship. More importantly, one becomes fully human only when assuming one's full responsibilities within these multiple relationships.

Confucius believes that human nature is similar, that differences appear later in life as a result of practice and learning (*Analects* 17:2). While the average person will change and grow through the learning process, "the highest of the wise and the lowest of the stupid do not change" (17:3).[46] Based on this theory of human nature, Confucius sees filial piety and brotherly love as the most fundamental. In these relationships one begins a life of virtue and of becoming fully human. These "family" relationships can be appropriated analogically across all human relationships.[47]

Confucian ethics possesses great clarity about the contributions of the family in the task of becoming fully human and in the shaping of a civilization. Unfortunately, Chinese societies throughout the contemporary world are bruised by the collapse of the family structure and the devaluing of virtue formation in familial relationships.

No doubt, the Confucian emphasis on family is not without its blind-spots. One can argue that these blind-spots are distortions of the Confucian ethics. Few Chinese families extend their love analogically to outsiders. The idea of the state as a big family may allow a ruler to have absolute sway, beyond the critique of common citizens. The aspiration within Chinese culture for immortality is expressed through marriage

46. Huang, *Analects*, 165.
47. Chang, "Confucian Theory of Norms and Human Rights," 118.

and the family and the bearing of sons.[48] Sadly, this had led to female infanticide.

Biblical and theological resources outside the letter to the Galatians regarding marriage and the family are helpful. The distortions of Confucian ethics regarding the family can be corrected by the teachings of Jesus and Paul. Both value the role of the family and the importance of marriage, but they redefine their proper places in light of God's kingdom. Jesus defines the family not in terms of the *natural* family, but in terms of the *spiritual* family of God. Jesus' brothers and sisters are those who hear and obey the words of God (see Luke 8:19–21; Mark 3:31–35; Matt 12:46–50). Jesus demands his followers to "hate his own father, and mother, and wife, and children, and brethren, and sister, and his own life" (Luke 14:26). Devotion to the Kingdom of God takes priority over love for one's family. Paul captures the same spirit when he lifts up the celibate life as total devotion to God and explains the married life as a distraction from it (1 Cor 7:33–38). The concept of the family of God and of celibacy is an eschatological critique of any preoccupation with the human family or with marriage that diverts attention away from one's ultimate relationships. Such critique can be transformative, especially to the parochial practices of some Confucianist societies. The power of God matches the love of God in his Kingdom. This suggests that in Confucianist families parents should exercise their power in line with their love. The Kingdom of God is all-inclusive; and it implies that family loyalty is a virtue only if it extends care and love for others outside the family.

Renren: *To Be A Benevolent/Humane Person*

Benevolence or humaneness is universally cherished whether it is expressed culturally as *ren* or *agape*. Confucian *ren* and Pauline *agape* are not the same; one is concerned with the love that is extended from the family to others within a structured society, the other is concerned with the self-sacrificing love for others that extends the family of God. The different ways of extending love in Confucian and Pauline ethics can be traced to their different understandings of Heaven (*tian*) and God (*Theos*).[49]

---

48. Mencius (4a.26) teaches that, those without posterity are impious. Legge and Yang, trans., *The Four Books*, 406–7.

49. See Chapter Two (pp. 115–22) on the discussion of *Tian*.

✧ The Move to Full Humanity

Confucius lacks Paul's understanding of the personhood of God, but he does share Paul's awe and reverence in matters related to life and death. Because of this lack of God awareness, the move forward for Confucius is not toward God but toward full humanity, i.e., to creatively fulfill the mandate of Heaven by being *renren* (a benevolent person). To become a benevolent or humane person, one must follow the established norms, rites (*li*), and way (*dao*), and one must be moral (*de*) and love (*ai*) others. If "one observes the rites and rituals and overcomes oneself, one will be benevolent" (*Analects* 12:1).[50] Conforming to the rites and being guided by virtue, one will not only have a sense of shame when one fails to do so, but also one will be able to reform oneself when that occurs (*Analects* 2:3).[51] Confucius believes that once on the road of desiring and pursuing benevolence as one's humaneness (*ren*), one will have the resources to continue (4:6). In contrast to Confucius' forward move toward full humanity, Paul's cry of helplessness, arising from his moral and spiritual frustration and his sense of wretchedness, voices his captivity to the law of sin. Paul cries for help from "God through Jesus Christ our Lord" (Rom 7:24–25). The moral resources for Confucius are rites (*li*) and virtues (*de*); the spiritual resource for Paul is "the law of the Spirit of life in Christ Jesus" (Rom 8:2). In the Confucian tradition, there is little, if any, of the struggles Paul went through regarding power of sin that holds his will captive. For the Confucian tradition, human nature is not a distinct creation of the *tian* and then fallen into sin because of Adam's exercise of will in distrusting God. Rather, the nature of a human person and that of the universe are similar; they all share the nature of creativity, because "what *Tian* imparts to human is called the nature (*xing*)" (*Doctrine of Mean* 1:1) and Heaven is the universal principle of creativity and goodness.[52] Despite these differences, Confucius' understandings of *renren* and full humanity may be compared with Paul's understanding of Jesus Christ as God's Son who loves sacrificially. Jesus is the one unique child (Son) of God's people (family).

---

50. My translation. See Qian, *Lunyu Xinjie*, 413–17; Yang, *Lunyu Yizhu*, 265.

51. See Chen, *Lunyu Duxun Jiegu*, 13.

52. *Doctrine of Mean* (*Zhong Yong*) 1:1. Legge and Yang, trans., *The Four Books*, 24–25.

The *Analects* employs *renren* and *renzhe* as having the same meaning; the terms refer to those who are committed to love others as the law of life. The law of love as the law of life is expressed in *Analects* 15:9 as those *renren* "not saving their own lives but sacrificing them in order to perfect the virtue of benevolence." Unfortunately, Confucius found few he could praise for being *ren*. We are told that there were four such persons. Guan Zhong was one, the other three persons who warranted being called *ren* in the Yin (Shang) dynasty were the viscount of Wei, the viscount of Ji, and Bi Gan. The viscount of Wei was the half brother of King Zhou (a.k.a. Shou-xin, 1099–1066 BCE) of the Yin dynasty. The viscount of Ji and Bi Gan were uncles of King Zhou. *Analects* 18:1 describes how these three persons served a most brutal despot: the viscount of Wei left the despot, the viscount of Ji became his slave, and Bi Gan was killed for his remonstrations against the king (*Analects* 18:1).[53] In Confucius' mind these three exemplary persons of *ren* in the Yin [Shang] dynasty showed in *different* ways their loyal service to a ruler, even though he was a despot. *Renren* is a person who is determined to follow the way of humaneness, even to the extent of putting oneself in danger. Few would have such resolve, for when asked if his disciple Zilu were another example of *renren*, the Master replied "I cannot say." He gave the same reply when asked if Qiu (a.k.a. Ran Qiu) and Chi (i.e., Gongxi Chi) were *ren* (5:8).

Was Confucius a *renren*? Confucius declined to claim himself as such (*Analects* 7:34), but he continued to advocate that one must desire and pursue benevolence: "Is benevolence really far away? No sooner do I desire it than it is here" (7:30).[54] According to Confucius, a benevolent person (*renren*) desires (*yu*) benevolence and finds it close by. In contrast, Paul confesses that evil lies at hand (Rom 7:21), and that a "carnal person sold under sin" (7:14) cannot do the good he wants to do, instead only the evil he does not want (7:18–20). Confucius would say that "there is benevolence in me," but Paul says that "there is nothing good in me" (7:18). In Gal 5:17 Paul speaks of the "desires of the flesh." These different moral tones and anthropologies between Confucius and Paul can be traced to their different assumptions concerning Heaven (*tian*) and God (*Theos*) and concerning human nature, as we have mentioned earlier.

---

53. See Chen, *Lunyu Duxun Jiegu*, 340. King Zhou was defeated by Ji Chang. Ji Chang later became King Wu of the Zhou Dynasty. In his defeat, King Zhou burned himself to death.

54. Lau, trans., *Analects*, 65.

These different views of God and human nature result in different ethics. Consequently, Confucius uses the word "desire" (*yu*) to mean a resolved preference for the highest principle of life—love, whereas Paul uses the words "covet" (*epithymia*) and "will" (*thelō*) to mean desire captivated by sin.

While Confucius sees the resourcefulness in human beings, Paul sees the depravity. Despite the differences between the ethics of Confucius and that of Paul, they share the common view that the person of love is one who seeks to edify others. This is what Confucius means by *renren* and what Paul means by Christ's sacrificial love on the cross. When Confucius was asked by his disciple Zigong if there were people who gave liberally to the common people and brought relief to many and, if so, were they to be considered *renren* (benevolent /humane persons)? Confucius replied that they were more than benevolent, they were perhaps sages. He mentioned that Yao and Shun the sage-rulers would find it difficult to give sacrificially to all people and to bring help to the multitude. Both Yao and Shun had practiced benevolent government by appointing people who were gifted and trustworthy rather than their unworthy sons (*Analects* 6:30).[55] Confucius explained what *renren* means: A *renren* is one who establishes others in order to establish oneself in ritual, and who helps others to succeed. Ames and Rosemont explain that "correlating one's conduct with those near at hand can be said to be the method of becoming"[56] a *renren*. By this measure one could say Jesus Christ qualifies to be a *renren* and a sage (*shengren*), for his passion shows not his preoccupation with death, but his faithfulness in giving himself completely for the sake of humanity. Christ died on the cross because of his *ren*, that is, his sacrificial love. Jesus exhibits the *spiritual and moral* quality to be, in Confucius language, "fully human" through his complete trust and his love for all despite the reality of human sin. The idea of "fully human" is expressed in Confucius' language of a "holy person" (*shengren*).

The "fully human" language in both Confucian ethics and Pauline theology emphasizes the complete love of others. However, there is a difference between Confucius and Paul: for Confucius, everyone ought to attain the goal of becoming a sage, who is fully human; for Paul, everyone

55. Yao used Shun as regent and Shun used Yu. Yao's son Dan zhu and Shun's son Shang-jun were not given the rulership. See Qian, *Lunyu Xinjie*, 224–25; Yang, *Lunyu Yizhu*, 141–42.

56. Ames and Rosemont, *Analects*, 110.

can become fully human by means of Jesus who is not just fully human (a sage), but also *fully divine*. The goal of "fully human" is attainable in Confucianism, though it recognizes that not many will succeed in reaching this. Confucian thought does not presuppose human sin against *tian*, thus human and *tian* are not in estrangement; his ethical thought is on conciliation, not reconciliation, with *tian*. Confucius thought that "the less than human" (any person) can rise to being "fully human" (a sage) through self-cultivation in *ren* (humaneness). However, the idea of progressive sanctification is absent in the fully-human Christology of Paul, because Paul presupposes that the power of sin causes human to be in broken relationship with God and corrupt them morally and spiritually. Pauline theology articulates that human beings cannot mend that relationship—only Jesus can. Jesus can complete the salvation because he is fully God *and* fully human. Only the fully divine, who is infinitely righteous, can forgive infinite sin that is against God. Through the power of righteousness, only the fully human Jesus can restore and save "the less than human" humanity from the power of sin. Thus the unity of Jesus' divinity and humanity is God's work of reconciliation based on Jesus' faithfulness and love. Paul trusts that the Divine can enter the sphere of humanity and become "fully human," *yet* Jesus is *still fully divine*.[57] We mention the text of Gal 4:4–5 in chapter three of this work; the text states that "God sent his Son, born of woman, born under the law, in order that to redeem those under the law, so that we might receive adoption as children" (RSV). Incarnated Jesus is a fully divine Being becoming a fully human being ("born of woman") in the particularity of a Jew ("born under the law"), yet Jesus' divinity is still intact.[58]

---

57. Mou, *Zhongguo Zhexue De Tezhi*, 41, misunderstands the "two natures" of Christ by saying that "Jesus is *not fully* human but God or God becoming Man, that is, God appears in the form of human being." On a succinct explanation of the two natures of Christ pertaining to salvation of humanity, see St. Anselm, *Cur Deus Homo*, 66–67 that articulates how "only God can and only human should" make the reparation for sins against God.

58. Phil 2:6–8 gives evidence also to the unity of the two natures of Christ, as verse 7 writes: "being in the likeness of humans (*homoiōmati anthrōpōn*), and being found in form as humankind (*hōs anthrōpos*). See Dunn, *The Theology of Paul the Apostle*, 203. Cf. Rom 8:3.

❧ *Ren* and Rulers

Paul's understanding of Christ, in the Confucian language of *renren* (a person who loves sacrificially), is subversive to the politics of power concentrated in emperors. Unfortunately, Paul does not address explicitly how divine love could transform the self-love of Roman rulers. It is precisely at this point that Confucius' political ethics is illuminating.

When asked about *ren* by Zizhang, the Master replied saying that whoever is able to practice five virtues would be benevolent: respectfulness, leniency, trustworthiness, industry, and generosity (*Analects* 17:5).[59] The context of this saying is political. Confucius was thinking about a benevolent ruler whose conduct of respectfulness avoid the humiliation of others, whose leniency would win the approbation of the crowd, whose trustworthiness would gain trust, whose industry would bring success, and whose generosity would make him amenable to the delegation of responsibility (*Analects* 17:5).

In a similar context (*Analects* 14:16), when rulership, *ren*, and love for the people was being discussed, Zilu asked Confucius about the case of Duke Huan, who had assassinated his younger brother, Prince Jiu. Prince Jiu had tried to usurp the power of Duke Huan and accede to the throne. One of the prince's tutors, Shao Hu was also killed; another tutor, Guan Zhong, survived. Zilu also asked how benevolent (*ren*) Guan Zhong was. Confucius praised Guan Zhong for being a person of *ren*, stating that when Duke Huan had assembled various princes without the use of war chariots, thereby saving many lives including that of the king and common people, it had been the work of Guan Zhong (*Analects* 14:16). Zigong, another disciple of Confucius, did not quite understand the Master's saying. He questioned whether Guan Zhong was *ren* because he did not die for the prince but had instead helped the Duke kill the prince. Confucius' reply seemed to be along the line of "maintaining the status quo" and keeping the peace and security of a country. But in fact Confucius was thinking along the line of keeping peace in the empire as a way of loving the common people. He explained that Guan Zhong deserved respect for helping Duke Huan become the leader of all the princes and thus saving the country from collapsing or swirling into a civil war. Confucius explained that if it had not been for Guan Zhong,

59. See Chen, *Lunyu Duxun Jiegu*, 328; Yang, *Lunyu Yizhu*, 392–93.

they might have "to wear their hair down, fold their robes to the left, and live like the barbarians" (*Analects* 14:17).[60] A humane or benevolent person (*renren*) in a world of political violence is one who preserves peace and the lives of both ruler and the common people.

Junzi: *The Exemplary Person or the Best Moral Self*

Confucius envisioned saving a politically violent and morally corrupt society by redefining the ritual of love and infusing it into daily existence as the law of life. This Confucian ideal sought to create within society individuals who know how to relate to one another truly as human beings. *Ren* is that virtue; it is the human quality that will save others and oneself. *Ren* had to begin with governors and political leaders, whose moral persuasion (*de*) through humaneness (*ren*) would blow across the land and bring about social harmony and the moral vitality of the common people. Confucius' revolution of virtue was threatening to political leaders. One can understand why his teaching was not received well by those in power.

⊹ *Junzi* and the Best Moral Self

The genius of Confucius lies not only in the redefinition of *ren* despite the hierarchical structure of his society, it is also found in his democratization of the mandate of Heaven (*tianming*) and in the concept of the "best self" (*junzi*). The mandate of Heaven is the right of emperors to rule—but to rule *benevolently*—and it is also the right of *every person* to be a human being—that is, to love others as the expression of one's moral being. *Junzi* once meant "the son of the lord" or "the son of the noble," the few aristocrats who possessed martial and social virtues. Confucius understood that, but he taught that *everyone* could become *junzi*, moral aristocrat, through learning and self-cultivation. This was a revolutionary concept in a society where class struggle was prevalent. Confucius' usage shifted the meaning from class consciousness to an emphasis upon virtue. He taught that, whether from noble descent or not, a person with virtue could become a "son of the lord."

---

60. My translation.

The word *junzi* appears more than a hundred times in the *Analects.*[61] In most cases the word *junzi* can either be a collective noun or refer to one person, since the Chinese language does not use articles, and singular and plural nouns are written exactly the same. This work treats *junzi* as a collective noun, admitting that the *Analects* can also use the word as referring to a single person.

We shall go through the key texts in which the term is used. In *Analects* 10:6 and 16:6 the word *junzi* is used to denote the noble class; but in the *Analects* generally it is more often used to refer to exemplary or excellent persons, those full of humanity, who practice *ren*, and who know ritual propriety well. The *junzi* are, in short, cultured persons. They know the mandate of Heaven (*Analects* 20:3). They care for fundamental things, because only when the root is established can the *dao* (Way) grow (*Analects* 1:2). They do not forsake *ren* for the sake of food (15:32). "In haste and flurry, the *junzi* always adhere to *ren*; in fall and stumble, they always adhere to it" (*Analects* 4:5).[62] The *junzi* are committed to *ren* and to filial piety (*Analects* 8:2), and to keeping the three years of mourning (*Analects* 17:21).

Zilu asked Confucius about the *junzi*. The Master replied, "They cultivate themselves by being respectful." "Is that all?" asked Zilu. "They cultivate themselves by bringing accord to the people. Even a Yao or a Shun [sage-rulers] would find such a task daunting" (*Analects* 14:42).[63] The aspiration of cultivating virtue for the *junzi* is for the purpose of bringing peace to the world.

Junzi practice *dao* (Way) in three ways: "By maintaining a dignified demeanor, they keep violent and rancorous conduct at a distance; by maintaining a proper countenance, they keep trust and confidence near at hand; by taking care in choice of language and mode of expression, they keep vulgarity and impropriety at a distance" (*Analects* 8:4:).[64] *Junzi* are morally persuasive (*Analects* 12:19). They practice five virtues: They are "beneficent without being wasteful, capable of making the people toil without causing resentment, desirous without being greedy, self-

---

61. Based on my calculation on an electronic text of the *Analects*.

62. Huang, *Analects*, 67.

63. Ames and Rosemont, *Analects*, 182.

64. Ibid., 121.

possessed without being swaggering, and awesome without being fierce" (*Analects* 20:2).[65]

Junzi are not mere utensils (*Analects* 2:12; 15:34) but are involved in wide learning. *Junzi* "do not look for a full stomach, nor in their lodgings for comfort and contentment. They are persons of action yet cautious in what they say. They repair to those who know the way (*dao*), and find improvement in their company. Such persons can indeed be said to have love of learning" (*Analects* 1:14; cf. 2:13, 4:22, 24; 12:3, 14:20, 27).[66] *Junzi* act with gravity and dignity, yet in their studies they are flexible (*Analects* 1:8). They "learn broadly of culture (*wen*), discipline this learning through observing ritual propriety (*li*), and moreover, in so doing, can remain on course without straying from it" (*Analects* 6:27, cf. 12:8).[67] *Junzi* are not competitive except in archery (*Analects* 3:7).

Junzi are not resentful when not acknowledged by others (*Analects* 1:1). *Junzi* are concerned by their lack of ability, not by the non-acknowledgment of others (*Analects* 15:19).[68] *Junzi* "do not promote others because of what they say, nor do they reject what is said because of who says it" (*Analects* 15:23).[69] *Junzi* are refined and simple (*Analects* 6:18, 12:8), concerned about not living up to one's name (*Analects* 15:20). *Junzi* "are self-possessed but not contentious; they gather together with others, but do not form cliques" (*Analects* 15:22).[70] *Junzi* "attract friends through refinement (*wen*) and thereby promote" *ren* (*Analects* 12:24).[71]

Junzi are "free from anxiety and fear . . . not conscience-stricken" (*Analects* 12:4).[72] *Junzi* "conduct [themselves] with reverence and do nothing amiss; if they treat others with respect and courtesy, all within the four seas are their brothers. Why should the *junzi* worry about having no brothers?" (*Analects* 12:5)[73] *Junzi* "are proper, but not fastidious" (*Analects* 15:37).[74]

65. Huang, *Analects*, 186.

66. Ames and Rosemont, *Analects*, 74–75.

67. Ibid., 109.

68. My translation.

69. Ames and Rosemont, *Analects*, 189.

70. Ibid.

71. Ibid., 160.

72. Huang, *Analects*, 126.

73. Ibid.

74. Ames and Rosemont, *Analects*, 192.

Junzi neither favor nor disfavor anyone under heaven; they "keep close to whoever is righteous" (*Analects* 4:10; cf. 7:31, 17:23).[75] *Junzi* side with the needy and poor, and do not make the rich richer (*Analects* 6:4). *Junzi* are trustworthy and calm (*Analects* 8:6), they do not associate with those who behave unkindly (*Analects* 17:7). Ames and Rosemont write,

> [*Junzi*] defer on matters [they] do not understand. When names are not used properly, language will not be used effectively; when language is not used effectively, matters will not be taken care of; when matters are not taken care of, the observance of ritual propriety (*li*) and the playing of music (*yue*) will not flourish; when the observance of ritual propriety and the playing of music do not flourish, the application of laws and punishments will not be on the mark; when the application of laws and punishments is not on the mark, the people will not know what to do with themselves. Thus, when [*junzi*] put a name to something, it can certainly be spoken, and when spoken it can certainly be acted upon. There is nothing careless in the attitude of the [*junzi*] toward what is said (*Analects* 13:3).[76]

What *junzi* "hate most is having to declare in favor of something that [they have] already rejected, and then to have to come up with some excuse for doing so."[77]

Junzi have a sense of righteousness as their disposition. They practice propriety (*li*), express it with modesty, and consummate their acts with their trustworthy words (*Analects* 15:19).[78] *Junzi* "have three kinds of conduct that they guard against: when young and vigorous, they guard against licentiousness; in their prime when their vigor is at its height, they guard against conflict; in their old age when their vigor is declining, they guard against acquisitiveness" (*Analects* 16:7).[79] *Junzi* "hold three things in awe: *tianming* [the mandate of Heaven], persons in high station, and the words of the sages."[80] *Junzi* "always keep nine things in mind:

---

75. Huang, *Analects*, 68.

76. Ames and Rosemont, *Analects*, 162. See Qian, *Lunyu Xinjie*, 454–55; Yang, *Lunyu Yizhu*, 286–87.

77. Ames and Rosemont, *Analects*, 195. Yang, *Lunyu Yizhu*, 372–73.

78. Translation altered Ames and Rosemont, *Analects*, 188. Chen, *Lunyu Duxun Jiegu*, 298 notes that the two words "*junzi*" are not in some ancient texts.

79. Ames and Rosemont, *Analects*, 198.

80. Ibid.

in looking they think about clarity, in hearing they think about acuity, in countenance they think about cordiality, in bearing and attitude they think about deference, in speaking they think about doing their utmost (*zhong*), in conducting affairs they think about due respect, in entertaining doubts they think about the proper questions to ask, in anger they think about regret, in sight of gain they think about [righteousness]" (*Analects* 16:10).[81] *Junzi* "detest those who announce what is detestable in others; they detest those subordinates who would malign their superiors; they detest those who are bold yet do not observe ritual propriety; they detest those who, being determined to get what they want, are unrelenting" (*Analects* 17:24).

◆ *Junzi* and *Xiaoren*

Junzi are not *xiaoren* ("little persons" literally: immature persons), who care not for self-cultivation and not being virtuous toward others. *Junzi* are "all-embracing and not partial," *xiaoren* are "partial and not all-embracing" (*Analects* 2:14).[82] *Junzi* "cherish virtue," *xiaoren* "cherish land"; *junzi* "cherish institutions," *xiaoren* "cherish favors" (*Analects* 4:11).[83] *Junzi* are "conversant with righteousness," *xiaoren* are "conversant with profit" (*Analects* 4:16).[84] *Junzi* are "calm and unperturbed;" *xiaoren* are "always agitated and anxious" (*Analects* 7:37).[85] *Junzi*

> are easy to serve but difficult to please. If one tries to please them with conduct that is not consistent with the way (*dao*), they will not be pleased. . . . [*xiaoren*] are difficult to serve but easy to please. . . . [*Junzi*] are distinguished but not arrogant; [*xiaoren*] are the opposite (*Analects* 13:25–26).[86]

Junzi seek harmony but not sameness, *xiaoren* seek sameness and not harmony (*Analects* 13:23).[87] *Junzi* may occasionally not act with *ren*,

81. Ibid., 199.
82. Huang, *Analects*, 55.
83. Ibid., 68.
84. Ibid., 69.
85. Ames and Rosemont, *Analects*, 119.
86. Ibid., 169.
87. My translation.

but *xiaoren* can never be persons of *ren* (*Analects* 14:6).[88] *Junzi* reach for higher things, *xiaoren* reach for lower things (*Analects* 14:23).[89] *Junzi* and *xiaoren* will encounter adversity, but *junzi* will be steadfast in adversity and *xiaoren* simply engulfed by it (*Analects* 15:2).[90] *Junzi* make demands on themselves, *xiaoren* are demanding of others (*Analects* 15:21). *Junzi* learn *dao* to love others, *xiaoren* learn *dao* to use it for themselves (*Analects* 17:4).

✣ *Junzi* and *Ren*

Examples of *junzi* include Confucius' disciples Zijian (*Analects* 5:2) and Zichan, the prime minister of Zheng. In pursuing the *dao* in four areas: "[Zichan] was deferential in serving his superiors, he was generous in attending to the needs of the common people, and he was [righteous] in employing their services" (*Analects* 5:16).[91] Confucius also names Qu Boyu, minister of Wei, as a *junzi*: "When the way prevailed in the state, he gave of his service, and when it did not, he rolled it up and tucked it away" (*Analects* 15:8).[92] Confucius acknowledges that he himself had accomplished little as a *junzi* (*Analects* 7:33). The Master said, "The path (*dao*) of *junzi* has three conditions that I am unable to find in myself: being a person of *ren* and not anxious; being the wise person and not in a quandary; being the courageous person and not timid" (*Analects* 14:28).[93]

From our survey above we can see that the expectations for *junzi* are high. The Master himself humbly acknowledged his deficiency as a *junzi* (*Analects* 14:28). *Junzi* are exemplars of the "best moral self" or the "best of humanity" who embody the many virtues that are condensed in *the one virtue* of *ren* (benevolence as humaneness). Thus, becoming *junzi* (the exemplary person or the best of humanity) and becoming *renren* (the person who loves sacrificially) overlap with each other in Confucian ethics. Both *junzi* and *renren* focus on the cultivation of virtue beginning

88. My translation.
89. My translation.
90. Translation altered from Ames and Rosemont, *Analects*, 184.
91. Ames and Rosemont, *Analects*, 98–99.
92. Ibid., 186.
93. Translation altered from ibid., 178.

with themselves but with the hope that, together with others, they may relate in love, and humanity at its best be formed.

A CHINESE CHRISTIAN ANTHROPOLOGY: SONS OF GOD, *RENREN*, AND *JUNZI*

Being Heirs of God (Sons of God), Becoming Renren and Junzi

The Confucian ideal of becoming *renren* and *junzi* has its emphasis on the best moral self, especially when applied to political leaders. Paul is more interested in the spiritual results of being the people of God and of living in freedom in a mixed community. The concept of the best moral self in *renren* and *junzi* is alien to Pauline ethics because he believes that moral cultivation is the work of God's Spirit and not the work of human beings. Nevertheless, the Confucian understanding of the "best self" does resonate with Paul's deliberation on the heirs of God in the new community formed by Christ.

The debate between Paul and his Judaizing opponents in the Confucianist language was: What or who can create "best selves" as the people of God? Is it the law? Or is it Christ? Paul sees Christ's new community as those redeemed by the faithfulness of Christ (Gal 3:26—4:7). The old symbol, that is, the law, had its function in guarding humanity from sin and its function ended with the coming of the new symbol—Christ (3:23–24). The new symbol does something the old one could not do: (1) It creates sons of God through the faithfulness of Christ (3:26), not through membership in the covenant of law; (2) it brings about the oneness of Jews and Gentiles in Christ (3:27–28), rather than continuing the exclusivistic identity of the people of God; (3) it creates descendants of Abraham according to promise, not according to circumcision (3:29); (4) it delivers believers from the elements of the cosmos, rather than placing them under a curse (4:1–3); and (5) it grants believers the new status as heirs of God (4:4–7).

The Judaizers, however, maintain that the guarding function of the law is able to help Jews to become their best selves (in Confucian language, the *junzi*). Paul sees this as problematic because the symbol of Jewish ethnic identity is such that it cannot help Gentiles become their best selves. In a mixed community of Jews and Gentiles then, the law

new life in christ makes inclusivity possible

has the tendency to create conflict and domination rather than harmony and love. In contrast to the old sphere and the old identity noted in Gal 3:25a, Gal 3:26 describes the new reality and the new symbol: "[F]or you are all sons of God, through faithfulness of Christ Jesus." Galatians 3:25b already mentions the post-law reality in which the custodianship of the law is no longer effective. In the new reality, Jews and Gentiles are set right with God through the faithfulness of Christ, and both groups (all humanity) can live in a loving relationship with each other while maintaining their cultural identity. The new identity of sonship enables them to be, in the language of Confucius, *renren*, that is, to live in love (rather than in fear) and in freedom (rather than in bondage) as *junzi*—mature people of God. *Renren* or *junzi* are morally independent persons who habitually make apt decisions according to the *dao* (principle or way) of   *both / and* life. The true heirs of God will also do the same.

Galatians 3:26 recapitulates 3:25b and describes more precisely the state of believers after the law—sons of God or *junzi*. Paul has already used the term "Son of God" for Jesus Christ (Gal 1:16; 2:20; 4:4, 6). But for the first time in the letter (Gal 3:26), Paul describes for the readers their new name and identity, "sons of God" (see also 4:5–7; 4:30). "Sons of God" includes both male and female, as Gal 3:28 explains.[94] The word "sons" connotes *heirs* who inherit all the blessings, gifts, and graces of the people of God.

The term "sons of God" is used in the Old Testament to connote Israel's pride and privilege within the covenant of God.[95] But now Paul extends the Israelite boundary to include the Gentile believers. The sonship of the Gentile believers in Galatia is made possible only "through faith in Christ Jesus."[96] "In Christ" refers to the sphere in which believers have their new existence as sons of God. This sphere is characterized by freedom, blessing, life, righteousness, maturity, and being Spirit-led.

---

94. See also Chapter Five (pp. 321–25).

95. For example, Exod 4:22–23 ("Thus says the LORD: Israel is my first-born son."); Deut 14:1–2 ("You are sons of the LORD your God. . . . For you are a people holy to the LORD your God; it is you the Lord has chosen out of all the peoples of the earth to be his people, his treasured possession."

96. The faith[fulness] in/of Jesus Christ repeatedly appears in Galatians 3 as well. The article appears only here (3:14) and refers to [the] faith (that we're talking about, that is, faith in Christ). See Chapter Six (pp. 380–89) for a lengthy discussion on the phrase "faith of/in Jesus Christ."

The reality of being in Christ is that all in him are descendants of Abraham and heirs of the promise. "And if you are Christ's, then you are Abraham's seed, heirs according to the promise" (3:29). The promise of God to Abraham and his descendants is the gift of God's own Spirit to dwell in believers to make them God's own. God's Spirit sanctifies believers by making them the vessels as well as the instruments of God's righteousness. It is the work of God's Spirit and not the works of the law that make believers God's special people. Possession of the Spirit thus becomes the identity marker of Christians among all peoples; it does not oppose cultural uniqueness, rather it transcends cultural barriers and makes all peoples into their "best selves." This is the "newness" (the surprise) of God's work.

In Gal 4:6–7 Paul writes, "Because you are sons, God sent the Spirit of his Son into our hearts, crying, 'Abba! Father!' So through God you are no longer a slave but a son, and if a son then an heir." Paul indicates no precise timing regarding one's sonship or for the reception of God's Spirit. He argues that the experience of the Spirit and of sonship is a new reality in salvation history, the old reality is gone.

The new reality of life in Christ and in the Spirit as the new symbols of that identity is salvific and personal in that Christ's faithfulness to God has the power to inspire our faith in God. Jesus' experience of and relational dependence on God are made true again in the life of the believer—as Paul writes, "I live, yet not I but Christ lives in me" (2:20). The uttering of "Abba" (Gal 4:6, cf. Mark 14:36; Rom 8:15) is Jesus' unique address to his Father, connoting absolute trust and intimacy with God. Only through the divine Spirit, who has been sent to dwell among his new community, can one make "Abba" a simple profession of faith.

In the age of the law, the Spirit was sent to a few chosen ones (kings, prophets, priests) to do God's work; now in the age of Christ, the Spirit is promised and given to all. In the old age, the Spirit touched down on the elect few and departed from them when the mission was accomplished. In the new age, the Spirit dwells within believing community. While the Spirit was only an energizing force in the old age, in the new age God the Spirit is present with believers, drawing them into the divine life of the Trinity in mutual trust and sharing, as well as granting them ethical vitality and conviction of divine truths.

The contrasts between the age of the law and that of the Spirit can be seen through the ethical lens of Confucius, particularly his vision of the "best self" in *renren* and *junzi*. The transition from the age of the law to that of Christ is for the purpose of lifting humanity to its best self, to live in moral and spiritual freedom. In the age of the law, human beings lived more like slaves (4:7) under watch and commissioned to serve, similar to what Confucius would say of *xiaoren*, those immature persons bound by immorality. In the age of Christ, the Spirit adopts believers to be sons of God, as Christ is the only begotten Son of God. "So you are no longer a slave but a son, and if a son then an heir through God" (4:7). The purpose of God's salvation is neither to baby-sit humanity nor to protect it from curse and sin. Rather, God's will is that humanity be mature as sons of God so that they become morally responsible for their decisions of faith and action, just as the Son of God ransomed them by being faithful to the Father. One can phrase Paul's understanding of "sons of God" in Confucian language: God wills human beings to desire the way of love (*ren*) and practice the way (*dao*) of the exemplary persons (*junzi*). According to Paul, if human beings are sons of God, then they are heirs of God. The reality of being in Christ not only transfers their existence from immaturity to maturity, from being a custodian of the law to a life of freedom in the Spirit, it also makes them co-heirs with Christ.

Whereas Confucius sees the best moral self (*junzi*) overcoming chaotic society by means of the cultivation of virtue and the extension of harmony to all, Paul looks upon the sons of God as the creation of new humanity. Through faithful participation in the crucifixion and through the working of God's Spirit, Jews and Gentiles can become sons of God and heirs of God's kingdom. Paul's personal testimony (Gal 2:20) that "it is no longer I who live but Christ who lives in me" reflects the *imitatio Christi* of faith. The reality of being in Christ does not abolish cultural differences. It is about harmony, it is not about sameness (cf. *Analects* 13:23). This in-Christ reality heightens cultural distinctions, so that wherever this reality exists uniqueness can be lifted up and celebrated; and what is dominating, bias, parochial, or destructive can be transformed.

Living in the Spirit and Becoming Junzi and Renren

Another point of interaction between Confucian ethics and Pauline theology is their similar emphasis on *the excellence* of the "best self," though Confucius calls it "virtue" (*de, Analects* 2:1–2, 4:11) and Paul the "fruit" (*karpos*, Gal 5:22) of the Spirit. Confucius contrasts virtues and vices, *junzi* (the best moral self) and *xiaoren* (the immature moral self); Paul contrasts the fruit of the Spirit and the works of the flesh, spiritual believers and carnal Christians. By doing so both admonish people to become their "best selves."

The *Analects* seldom commands readers to be *junzi*, it often describes various modes of becoming *junzi* and the ideal to follow to become *junzi*. It often contrasts the two distinctive ways (*junzi* in contrast to *xiaoren*), and leaves it to the readers to contemplate and act accordingly. The lack of explicit imperative is a pronounced feature of this Confucian classic. Compared to the *Analects*, it is striking that in Gal 5:19–23, Paul gives imperatives, though he also explains the consequence of living in the Spirit in contrast to living in the flesh. The contrasting mode of discourse in Paul's letter sounds much like the rhetoric of the *Analects* as it contrasts *junzi* and *xiaoren*.

The works of the flesh are listed, followed by the fruit of the Spirit. "Now the works of the flesh are plain. These are fornication, immorality, licentiousness, idolatry, sorcery, enmity, strife, jealousy, anger, selfishness, dissension, factions, envy, drunkenness, carousing, and things like these. I warn you about such things, as I warned you before, that those who do such things shall not inherit the Kingdom of God" (Gal 5:19–21). In contrast to the "fruit" of the Spirit, "works" denotes the consequence of living under the power of sin and not in the realm of the Spirit.

Paul lists fifteen vices that are stereotypes of the Gentile world, which may or may not reflect the Galatian community. The first three vices (cf. 2 Cor 12:21) are sexual misconducts that are prohibited by the law. Fornication (*porneia*) usually refers to illicit sexual relations (Lev 18:6–18) characteristic of the Gentile world (1 Cor 5:1; 1 Thess 4:3). Immorality (*akatharsia*) denotes sexual impurity or perversion (cf. 1 Thess 4:7, Rom 1:24). Sensuality or licentiousness (*aselgeia*) means excessive indulgence. If Troy Martin's thesis is correct that the Galatian Gentile Christians were reverting to paganism it would include going back to the days when women were excluded from the traditional pagan meals, whereas female slaves, entertainers, and prostitutes were brought in.[97]

---

97. For more on the role of women in the common meal in the ancient world, see Corley, *Private Women*, 53–57.

Paul's words, "Do not use your freedom as an opportunity for the flesh," may be directed at that problem.

The next two vices on the list are sins against God and also prohibited by the law. Idolatry (*eidōlolatria*) is the worship of false gods, placing one's trust in the power of distortion and falsehood. Sorcery (*pharmakeia*; see Exod 7:11, 22; 8:7, 18 on Pharaoh's magicians) portrays the skills one learns to manipulate the power of darkness and deceit and is thus a rejection and suppression of truth and light.

The spiritual discussion of Paul, such as idolatry, does not have its parallel in the sayings of Confucius, but both Confucius and Paul are concerned with ethical issues (such as fornication). The last ten vices of Paul's discussion (5:19–21) are the kind that Confucius is concerned with; they are communal and social misconducts that are destructive to a community in ways harmful both to others and to oneself. They are therefore communal ills to be avoided at all cost: Enmity (*echthrai*), strife (*eris*), jealousy (*zēloi*), anger (*thymos*), selfishness (*eritheiai*), dissensions (*dichostasiai*), factions (*hairesis*), envy (*phthonos*), drunkenness (*methai*), and carousing (*kōmos*). Finally, the words "and things like these" suggest that this is not an exhaustive list of vices. Paul repeatedly warns the congregations that those who do these things cannot inherit the kingdom of God. The heirs of God need to live an appropriate life of righteousness if they are to inherit God's Kingdom. The major emphasis in the list of *social virtues* falls on that which builds up community, rather than on inward spiritual gifts of the believer. In other words, Paul's emphasis is on the *ethos* of the community, rather than on individual spiritual attributes independent of others. Social virtues are also the great concern of Confucian ethics; we have seen how his understanding of *ren* (humaneness), the preservation of peace in a society, and his idea of the cultivation of virtues are all relational. To put together both Confucius' and Paul's ideas of social virtue, one might say: The fruit of the Spirit is most easily realized in a harmonious community where *renren* (benevolent or humane person) and *junzi* (best moral self) abound.

The virtues Paul catalogues are interpreted to be *the singular fruit* of the Spirit who brings about communal unity, a unity we suggest is similar to the Confucian understanding of harmony. So in contrast to the divisive works of the flesh, the Spirit bears only the *one* fruit of a community in harmony. These virtues are love, joy, patience, kindness, goodness, faithfulness, gentleness, self-control (Gal 5:22–23). In the Galatian passage here, the Spirit does not give different fruit to different members, the fruit is given to the community. The people come together and manifest the virtues that constitute the Spirit's fruit (5:22).

The list in Paul's letter to the Galatians (5:22–23) is grouped in the perfect symmetry of a triad. Do they correspond to the vices of sexual, spiritual, and communal sins stated earlier? Probably not. But this list reads like the sayings in the *Analects*, though there are great differences between the two pieces of writing. The first set of the triad begins with "love" (*agapē*). It is not the love of God but the believers' love for one another that flows out of God's love. It is like the self-sharing *ren* (humaneness) that relates and builds up—it is unlike *ren* in that Confucian *ren* does not do away with hierarchical relations whereas Pauline *agapē* does. "Joy" (*chara*) is thankfulness for God's blessings, confidence in Christ's faithfulness, and hope despite the harsh realities of life. It is, in Confucian language, commitment to the way (*dao*) as the *junzi* pursues it and therefore does not depart from it. "Peace" (*eirēnē*) is the confidence and security derived from being set-right by God and from the knowledge that human beings are God's own. It is like the endowment of human nature (*xing*) from *tian* (Heaven).

The second set of the triad begins with "patience" (*makrothymia*). It means the forbearance, endurance, and stamina that come from faithfulness to God. It is like the moral persistency of the *junzi* (the best moral self) to walk in the way of virtue (*dao de*). "Kindness" (*chrēstotēs*) means empathy and generosity; this is akin to the virtue of *ren* (humaneness) that cares for others enough to put self-interest in second place. "Goodness" (*agathōsynē*) means uprightness, similar to the virtue of the exemplary person (*junzi*) in pursuing what is proper, right, and harmonious.

The third set of the triad begins with "faith" (*pistis*). It denotes trust and complete reliance. It is like the virtue of *zhong* (loyalty) in Confucian ethics, which we will discuss in Chapter Six. "Gentleness" (*prautēs*) means humility and meekness; it is like the virtue of *shu* (forgiving) that we will also look at in Chapter Six. "Self-control" (*egkrateia*) means an appropriate exercise of one's power to preserve the harmony and to advance the goodness of a community. It is like the discipline one takes to *keji fuli*—"overcome one's self and fulfill ritual propriety" for the common good of the community. Both Confucius and Paul value social virtues that promote harmony and unity in a mixed community.

Spirit and Law, Li and Ren

There is a subtle but significant difference between the ethics of Confucius and Paul with regard to love (*ren* or *agapē*) and the law (*li* or torah): Paul understands *agapē* (divine love) as superseding the *torah* in that "love fulfills the requirement of the law," whereas Confucius sees the roles of *ren* (benevolence) and *li* (ritual propriety) as mutually supplementary.

In Gal 5:18 Paul writes that those led by the Spirit are not under the law, they are not against the law, in fact they fulfill the law. The fruit of the Spirit fulfills the law—"against such [the fruit of the Spirit] there is no law" (Gal 5:23). However, the works of the flesh not only oppose the Spirit, but also violate the law (5:17). Similarly, we recall, in Confucius' thought ritual propriety (*li*) is grounded in and fulfills *ren*. *Li* should not go against *ren*. In order to be *ren* (benevolent person), one must be persistent in the daily practice of following *li*, the rites/rituals (*Analects* 12:1). This is true especially for political rulers and those who seek to cultivate virtue in themselves in order to be leaders.

Despite the emphasis on rituals and rules in his ethics, Confucius is aware of the dual dangers of ritualism and legalism—which are not the problems faced by the Christians in Galatia. As we have seen in the last chapter, Paul wrestles with his opponents on how to make the Jewish law meaningful to the identity of the Gentile Christians. Though the problems are not the same, the response of Confucius and of Paul to *li* (ritual propriety) and *torah* (Jewish rules of life and faith) are similar in that, both use love (whether *ren* or *agapē*) to subvert law (whether *li* or *torah*), and consequently fulfill the spirit of the law. We shall see in the next section how "loving one's neighbors" for Paul means fulfilling the law. Here we look at how Confucius speaks of fulfilling *li* (rites) by means of *ren* (benevolence), to note the similarity.

Confucius grounds *li* in *ren*. It is possible for a person to love another merely for the sake of duty (although that would be a religious achievement and a noble task). But Confucius teaches that loving for the sake of filial piety can be superficial. The example is given in the *Analects* (2:7)—which I have referred to a number of times already: "Merely to feed one's parents for the sake of piety without reverence . . . even dogs and horses are fed" (*Analects* 2:7). Merely doing what is expected of *li* (rites) is right and dutiful, what is essential, however, is the higher principle of *ren* (humaneness). Therefore, *li* must be grounded in *ren*.[98] *Li* (ritual) without *ren* can degenerate into formalism or the insensitivity that makes one less and less human. *Analects* 3:3 also says, "If a person is without *ren* (humaneness), what has he/she to do with *li* (ritual or ceremonies)?"

Scholars are divided on the question of interpreting the relationship between *ren* and *li*. *Analects* 12:1 seems to put *li* over *ren*. In the essay "*Ren* and *Li* in the *Analects*," Shun summarizes the debate as follows:

> According to Xu Fuguan, one of the most important innovations of Confucius is the discovery of the ideal inner life, which he characterizes in terms of the *ren* ideal. Confucius gives the traditional *li* rules a justification in terms of the *ren* ideal, thereby giving *ren* evaluative priority over *li*. And, according to Lin Yusheng, *ren* is an ideal inner life that has ultimate value, whereas *li* derives its value from *ren* through the instrumental role it plays in the cultivation and development of *ren*. Accordingly, *ren* has evaluative priority over *li*, and provides a perspective from which one can justify the revision of a *li* rule.
>
> This way of interpreting Confucius contrasts sharply with that proposed by Zhao Jibin. . . . According to Zhao Jibin, Confucius regards the content of *ren* as determined by *li*, and the observance of the *li* practices of his time as providing the sole criterion for distinguishing between the possession and lack of *ren*. In doing so, Confucius has given *li* a priority over *ren*. . . . Observance of *li* is the criterion for the possession of *ren*, and Confucius' conception of the *ren* person is just the conception of someone who follows the existing *li* rules in all areas of life.[99]

This is a significant debate for at least two reasons. The first being that if Xu and Lin's reading is correct, then Confucius' teaching can constantly be *reinterpreted* in new contexts and be made relevant based on the conviction that *ren* (humaneness), being the highest principle of life, can change the cultural norms of every land. Wherever Zhao's reading has been preferred, however, with priority given to *li* over *ren*, Confucianist ethics have tended to be conservative.

Second, the two readings have implications for the cross-cultural hermeneutic advanced here. The former reading (*ren* over *li*) allows the ideals of Confucius' teaching to be more easily applied to other cultures

98. This is what Tu Weiming means by "the primacy of *ren* over *li* and the inseparability of *li* from *ren*." See his "*Li* as Process of Humanization," 188.

99. Shun, "*Ren* and *Li* in the *Analects*," 58.

than would the latter reading (*li* over *ren*). While the latter reading defines more precisely than the former the essence of Confucianist anthropology, it seems rigid and therefore difficult to translate across cultural divides. There is no intention here of resolving the tension between these two readings, since each reading has its textual support (with perhaps greater textual support for the first reading),[100] thus making the two interpretations plausible. But I do want to continue this cross-cultural reading of the texts and state up front that my bias prefers the first reading because of my cross-cultural commitment. This commitment is to find meaningful connections across cultures through the comparative readings of texts. I read the *Analects* in light of Galatians, and in the same manner I read Paul's letter to the Galatians in light of the *Analects'* perspective of virtue. To speak of "Paul's way of *renren*" is an example of viewing Paul's reinterpretation of the law via the Confucius' new understanding of *li* (rites) and *ren* (humaneness).

WITHIN THE CONFUCIAN AND PAULINE ETHICS: LOVE FOR ONE'S NEIGHBORS

Can love become legalistic and rigid? Can *ren* become *li* and law? Can the ritual of love overcome ritualism? These questions with which Confucius was concerned with can be phrased in the language of Paul: Can the "law of Christ"—"to bear one another's burden and to love one's neighbor" (Gal 6:2)—ever become a rule of life that binds both Gentile and Jewish Christians, rather than grant them freedom? Paul thinks that the law of Christ or the law of love can guarantee the greatest good and maximum freedom for the Christians in Galatia.

In Gal 5:13–15 Paul suggests that for Gentile believers a life pleasing to God and a life of freedom ought to include the yoke of the law as stated in Lev 19:18. Paul's emphasis here on the necessity to fulfill the whole law recalls his earlier argument in Gal 3:10, 12, and 5:3. The entirety of the law must be upheld if one wishes to receive the blessings the law provides. For those who can do so the law is a blessing; for those who cannot the law becomes a curse. Here, Paul's hermeneutic of loving one's neighbor as a way of loving God is actually commonly used by New Testament writers to maintain the continuity between the Jewish law and Christ.

100. Ibid., 59–61.

New Testament writers reinterpret the fulfillment of the whole Mosaic law in terms of the one commandment in Lev 19:18 (see Matt 5:43; 19:19; 22:39; Mark 12:31; 12:33; Luke 10:27; Rom 13:9; Jas 2:8).[101] Among New Testament writers, Paul, and possibly James also, best understand the radical gospel of Jesus since both Paul and James highlight "loving your neighbor" as the *summation* of Jewish law.[102]

Fulfillment of the Whole Law via Lev 19:18

In Gal 5:14 the whole law is said to "be fulfilled in one word" (*en eni logo*), i.e., the one commandment, of Lev 19:18. The whole law (*ho pas nomos*) refers to the *unity* of all the requirements of the laws. It is different from *holon ton nomon* ("the entire law") in Gal 5:3, which refers to *all the precepts* of the law. The concern of the whole law in Gal 5:14 is about the summation of the whole law into one, thus in a sense understands that all the precepts of the law can be reduced to one.

Scholars disagree on how the law is fulfilled. Stuhlmacher postulates that the "Zion Torah" is inaugurated by the Messiah in the eschatological age through his obedient death so that the Mosaic law, promised to all nations (Mic 4:1–4; Isa 2:2–4; 25:7–9; Jer 31:31–34; Ezek 20; 36:22–28; 40–48), might be made relevant to the Gentiles.[103] Paul may have been influenced by this interpretation of the Messiah, but more evidence of

---

101. R. Akiba (late 1st century CE) says "Love is the greatest principle in the law." The greatest commandment is no doubt the *Shema*, which pious Jews repeat twice daily (Deut 6:4–5: love God with all that you are). However, according to Mark 12:31, Jesus links these two great commandments together ('Love God maximally' and 'love your neighbor as yourself'), and adds that they "are more important than all burnt offerings and sacrifices" (12:33). Jesus is responding to the hostile questions of scribes and Sadducees (v. 28a) regarding the *prote entole* ("chief commandment"). Jesus does not consider burnt offerings and sacrifices ways of loving God. Jesus criticizes the false piety of the Sadducees who are devoted to their liturgical and cultic practices while failing to love their neighbor. According to Matt 22:38–39, Jesus was speaking to Pharisees, the teachers of the law when they ask which commandment is the greatest. Jesus eliminates any possible tension between loving God and loving one's neighbor, by equating the two: "the second is like (*homoia*) it, and the whole Law and Prophets hang on these two commandments." In Matthew the two commandments are not ranked as first and second but simply listed and equated. This is what Paul does in Romans 13 and Galatians 5 as well.

102. Rom 13:9 is a summation of ten commandments (verse 10 says "love is the fulfillment of the law"; see also Jas 2:8 the "royal law" as loving your neighbor).

103. Stuhlmacher, "The Law as a Topic of Biblical Theology," 126.

such a Messianic movement is needed. Galatians makes no mention of the death of the Messiah as fulfilling the Jewish law. It contends that the Messiah died as a curse to lift the curse of the law (Gal 3:13–14), but the language of fulfillment is absent. Stuhlmacher's interpretation would make sense if one were to link the obedient death of the Messiah to the love commandment of Lev 19:18, but again (Gal 5:14) no link is stated. It makes better sense to say simply that the ceremonial requirements of the laws are not applicable to Gentiles, that only the moral-spiritual commandments are apt—which can be summarized by the one commandment of Lev 19:18.

Paul's Reinterpretation of the Whole Law into "Law of Christ"

"Bear one another's burdens, and so fulfill the law of Christ" (Gal 6:2). "Bearing one another's burden" is to encourage solidarity in the community. The "burdens" (*baros*) are not spelled out—Paul's intent is to be general—but they cover all the human frailties and troubles found in a community.[104]

Though the phrase "fulfill the law of Christ" (Gal 6:2) may recall Gal 5:14 ("the entire law is fulfilled in one commandment" [Lev 19:18]), the phrase occurs only here in the New Testament. The closest to it is 1 Cor 9:21, where one finds the words *ennomos Christou* ("under Christ's law"). Here Paul explains that he identifies with those outside the law for the sake of those outside the law (i.e., the Gentiles), even though he believes himself to be "under the law of Christ."[105] A similar occurrence is in Jas 2:8. Though Jas 2:8 does not use the phrase "the law of Christ," his interpretation of the love commandment in Lev 19:18 as the "royal law" (*nomon basilikon*) seems to link the two thoughts found in Gal 6:2 and Gal 5:14.

104. Rom 15:1; 2 Cor 4:17; and 1 Thess 2:7 suggest this meaning also. The spiritual community has the responsibility to support one another, though Gal 6:5 will also add that each individual "will have to bear his own load (*phortion*)."

105. Other New Testament texts define early Christian communities with the word "*nomos*" (law), connoting a Jewish understanding of their Christian convictions, rather than just meaning "principle" or "norm." E.g., Rom 3:27 refers to the "law of faith" (*nomou pisteōs*); Rom 8:2: "the law of the Spirit of life in Christ Jesus"; Jas 1:25: the "perfect law" (*nomon teleion*) and the "law of freedom"; and Jas 2:8: the "royal law" (*nomon basilikon*). By the use of *nomos*, consciously or otherwise, Paul redefines "law" so as to attach by metaphor what is otherwise narrowly defined (by Judaism).

That Jewish law as a whole needs to be fulfilled even in the messianic age is part of Paul's theological conviction. By subsuming the whole of the law under the law of Christ, Paul constructs a new reality and a new identity for Gentile Christians. Notwithstanding the fact that the Gentile Christian movement owes its roots and identity to its Jewish neighbors, Gentile believers are not required to observe the "works of the law." But that is not to say they are lawless people. They have the "law of Christ" to fulfill.

The Significance of Paul's Reinterpretation of the Law

Paul's reinterpretation of whole law by means of one law (Lev 19:18) fleshed out in "the Law of Christ" is significant in the following aspects.

First, the law, in spite of all its multiple precepts, does have *a unity*; in other words, the whole is greater than the parts. How can the fulfillment of one commandment keep the spirit of the law alive? Paul sees the summary of the law in the love commandment and thus understands the purpose and essence of the law as captured by "loving one's neighbors."

Secondly, the use of Lev 19:18 as the fulfillment of the whole law is to be understood as *love for humanity*. Intrinsic to the teaching of Lev 19:18 is God's will for humanity, that is, to be the people of God characterized by love. Love as the ethical dimension of God's will for humanity occupies the main argument of Paul in the last two chapters of Galatians.

The giving of the law is a sacred event in which God wills his people to be his own among the nations and to be people characterized by love. The purpose of the law is to differentiate and to form the identity of the people of God—not to alienate them from other nations but to convey to other nations the will of God—to love one another. The people of God convey the will of God by their moral and theological identity.

Even though Paul has already shown that the law's function (to identity the people of God) ended when the Messiah came, he does not seek to eliminate the law altogether. Paul knows the strength and the danger of using the law for moral formation. In this respect, Paul's theology is similar to Confucian ethics. Paul redefines the relationship between God and human beings in terms of what God has done in Christ. The people of God are called upon to love others as God has loved them. Thus, Paul interprets the law with an emphasis on *loving others*; this is similar to

Confucius' ethic of *renren*—people who are benevolent or humane toward others.

Thirdly, the commandment of love can be said to be *Jewish in origin but fulfilled by the faithfulness of Christ for the sake of Jews and Gentiles*, and thus to become "the law of Christ." As such, it is appropriate to speak of Christ being the end and the fulfillment of the law. And, it is appropriate to speak of "bearing one another's burden as the law of Christ" (Gal 6:2). The law of Christ is the reinterpretation of the Mosaic law through Christ's "faithfulness unto death." One can even say the whole Christ event is hermeneutically summed up by Lev 19:18—if one were to abstract the principle of love for humanity from the love of God in Christ. The law of Christ does not speak of a new law totally different from Mosaic law. In fact, the law of Christ is Mosaic law but read anew in light of the Christ event. According to Paul, it is this reinterpretation of the Jewish law that results in twofold benefits for the people of God:

(a) For Jewish believers, this reinterpretation gives the Mosaic law new life and meaning since the Mosaic law in its custodian role has ceased and since the Jewish believers must live in the power of the Spirit (no longer living under the Mosaic law that manifests and controls sin) as adult heirs of God, living in freedom and in ownership of God's inheritance.

(b) For the Gentile believers, the reinterpretation of the Mosaic law (via Lev 19:18) now makes the God of the Jews relevant to them. This reinterpretation opens up to the Gentiles a new existence in Christ, and one that produces the fruit of the Spirit. To this end the law of Christ is consistent with the intentions of the Mosaic law to grant life.

The controversy concerning which symbol best represents the people of God is ultimately determined by the freedom each gives. Yet, Paul's answer is not "either/or," but "both/and." So the answer for Paul is "the law of Christ."

Fourthly, H. D. Betz makes the subtle differentiation between "the Jew who is obliged to *do* the Torah (cf. 3:10, 12; 5:3; also 6:13) . . . [and] the Christian [who] *fulfills* the Torah through the act of love, to which he has been freed by Christ (5:1, 13)."[106] Judaizers in Galatia thought that

---

106. Betz, *Galatians*, 275.

doing (the Torah) implied being (the people of God). Paul understands that doing often got in the way of, made impossible, being. By fulfilling the law, one does not have to follow every prescription of the law—though doing all the requirements is a noble task—one has to be committed to the essence of the law. The Great Commandment is to love God with all one's being and to love one's neighbor as one's self. Here the law of love changes from doing to *being*. The paradox of the Great Commandment is that love cannot be commanded, yet *being* loving and forgiving (and etc.) can be demonstrated. Jesus lives out the life of love and thereby becomes a model. Fulfilling the law implies an obligation to be true to the spirit of the law. Paul notes to the fact in Galatia that those who receive circumcision do not themselves keep the law (6:13). Paul objects to external laws and ceremonies; he highlights the essence of the law, that is, love. The situation in Confucius' day was similar. A meticulous observance (doing) of the Zhou-*li* or the *Record of Ritual* (*Liji*) can protect one from errors, but it can also be an unbearable burden. "Fulfilling the law" as a whole through love is to know the fundamental thrust of the law and to be able to live one's life out of the freedom to love. Jesus must "break" the law in order to fulfill the (Great) law—being loving. Jesus trusted that the full (whole) law was fulfilled in forgiving love, which he demonstrates and calls for over and over. Jesus goes to the cross not to end the law, but because he trusts that not running away in fear, not hating or killing his enemies, is what love ought to be demonstrating in such moments. More significantly, fulfilling the law in the eschatological age means God's Spirit is guiding and empowering believers to live a life that bears the fruit of the Spirit, rather than struggling without the Spirit (i.e., living in the flesh).

Law, Freedom, and Law of Love

Paul's reinterpretation of the Jewish law by means of love seeks to create harmony and to grant freedom for all. Dieter Georgi argues that after this reinterpretation Paul has arrived at a new understanding of law. Georgi contends that Paul does not see the law as "a demand, a norm, or an authority. It is, rather, an environment of loyalty and solidarity, of fidelity and confidence, of spirit and community. Thus the law becomes a prophetic entity, an expression of creative power and imagination. It establishes neither the past nor the present, binding and limiting the future.

It opens the future and is a message of freedom."[107] This idea is consistent with Paul's understanding of the *law of love* as the law of freedom, that is, love makes us free, and as human beings we are free to love.[108]

It is clear from the example of the Galatian community that those who do the law without observing Lev 19:18 will still end up with divisiveness and self-destruction: "If you bite and tear each other, watch out that you are not consumed by one another" (5:15). Metaphors of animal violence (serpents' biting [*daknein*, cf. Num 21:6], lions' devouring [*katesthiein*], wild beasts' consuming [*analiskein*]) are used to describe the dangers inherent in community strife. Soon the violent behavior within a community will surface when there is no love. Paul has suggested to the Gentile believers in Galatia that though the law plays no role in their religious identity in the age of Christ, the freedom for which Christ redeemed them necessitates that they reinterpret the whole law in the one commandment of Lev 19:18. It is this commandment that guarantees them freedom.

This is what Paul means when he says love your neighbor to fulfill the law, and when in Rom 13:8, he writes, "Leave no debt outstanding, except the debt to love one another." Paul is saying that we can claim completion and perfection in all other religious duties except in the command to love. Christians are always debtors when it comes to loving one's neighbor. The obligation to love one another arises not from what others have done, but from what God has done for all in Christ Jesus—or as Confucius would say, because Heaven (*tian*) has imparted in human beings the nature of *ren* (benevolence/humane), Heaven has mandated all to love (become *renren*).

---

107. Georgi, "God Turned Upside Down," 155.

108. The difference between the Judaizers' and Paul's understanding of the people of God can be expressed in the language of Paul Tillich as heteronomy and theonomy (*The Courage To Be*, passim]). Heteronomy is being directed by someone else's law (constituting inauthentic being, in Heidegger's terms). The Pharisees and, later, the Judaizers, just as Jesus and Paul, thought that in their actions they were being theonomous, that is, being ruled by God. But here, Paul interprets theonomy in a way unacceptable to the Judaizers, just as Jesus acts and words were unacceptable to the Pharisees and Sadducees. For the Apostle Paul, to be the people of God is to be born by the Spirit and to fulfill the law of Christ through loving God and one's neighbor. For Paul, love had nothing to do with circumcision, observance of days, and food laws. See also on this topic Bonhoeffer, *Act and Being*, 150–61.

The paradox of the love commandment is that love cannot be mandated. The law of loving one's neighbor can, however, be practiced by everyone, it is the law of Life, the mandate of *tian* (Heaven). While Confucius uses the language of the "best moral self" (*junzi*) to describe the virtue of a *renren* (a humane person), Paul uses the language of "serving one another in love" to speak of fulfilling the law.

Paul believes in the fulfillment of the old Mosaic laws via the Spirit and the Law of Christ (Gal 5–6). But the Law of Christ for the people of God is not a law that one does, like washing a dish or abstaining from food offered to idols. The command to love is in fact the command *to be*, the fulfillment of one's essential, inherent *being*. The Great Commandment of Jesus is not a law to do but a command to be. The Great Commandment, of which Paul was fully aware, is not a codifiable law. Love cannot be commanded. It is a response to being loved, which is the core message of the gospel. Love, whether divine or human, has to be freely embodied and demonstrated and Paul believes this has happened in Jesus Christ. *To be* the people of God, therefore, is *to be* of love, in response to the self-emptying and self-giving love of Jesus Christ, Son of God.

In his letter to the Galatians, Paul's rule of thumb is love. Paul emphasizes the expression of love over the practice of religious law. Those who oppose Paul, the Judaizers, find Paul's attitude unacceptable. For Paul, the questions are not:

- Can one heal on the Sabbath?
- Should one eat with sinners and Gentiles?
- Ought one to forgive adultery?
- Must the Gentiles be circumcised to have full membership in the people of God?

Rather, the questions of *being, of loving* as the Great Commandment said, are:

- What is the loving thing to do for those in trouble (on the Sabbath or not)?
- How can one extend friendship and forgiveness to sinners and to Gentiles?
- How are they, as the people of God, to embody his love and his freedom?

As noted, love cannot be legislated. Love, like faith, hope, and joy, are gifts of divine grace; they are the fruit of the Spirit, given to those who in faith respond to the love of God in Christ Jesus.

In many ways, a Confucianism of external acts, or formalism, is a departure from Confucius' ethical teachings, which emphasize being and relationship. The closest I can come to connecting Paul's concept of the Spirit with Confucius' ethic is through what F. S. C. Northrop, in his book *The Meeting of East and West,* calls the "intuitive aesthetic character" of Chinese culture. He argues that there is a fluidity and depth beyond mere form in Chinese culture.[109] The ethical teachings of Confucius do not emphasize form (law) but the "intuitive aesthetic character" (cf. spirit) of being human. However, what Northrop describes applies more to Chinese epistemology than to ethics; thus, his concept of the intuitive aesthetic cannot be equated with Paul's understanding of the Spirit.

We have seen that Confucius' understanding of *ren* (humaneness) to be the cord that binds interpersonal relationships together. Whatever the virtue, whether of benevolence (*ren*), empathy (*zhong*), forgiveness (*shu*), or respect (*jing*), Confucian ethics calls upon people to embody that virtue. Self-cultivation is not about adding another "to do" item on the long list of ethical rules. Northrop writes, "For the Chinese, the ethical is grounded in the aesthetic."[110] He continues,

> The Confucian claim, that only if one recognizes this all-embracing aesthetic manifold to be an ultimate and irreducible part of man's nature, will man have the compassionate feeling in himself for human beings other than himself which is necessary to build correct relations within the family and, through them, a good order in the state.[111]

In Confucian teaching, only the ideal human being (*junzi, renren,* sage) is "in part the non-transitory, indeterminate aesthetic continuum

---

109. Northrop, *The Meeting of East and West,* 312–46, 386–89. For example, a Chinese painting may be a few yards long or wide, but the form of the objects painted is not significant. What is significant is the intuitive aesthetic character of the artist and his viewers, and whether they are able to participate in the vastness and tranquility of the work of art, let's say, the juxtaposition of the mountains and water in the painting. Any painter needs to spend hours in nature before picking up the brush to paint a scenic painting.

110. Ibid., 328.

111. Ibid., 334.

that it has any immortality. . . . There is no immortality of the concrete, local, determinate personality."[112] Thus, the Confucian ethic of *ren* assumes that one's true identity is found in others, who are parts of that "indeterminate aesthetic continuum" and "the cherished aesthetic differentiations within it."[113] This ethic calls for all to participate in that which is larger than themselves, in nature and in others. To be *ren* (benevolent) toward others is to affirm the mutual indebtedness of love among all human beings. Does not "that which is larger than themselves" refer to the Spirit that is moving among all people?

BEYOND CONFUCIAN ETHICS: CRUCIFORM *REN* AND LOVE FOR ONE'S ENEMIES

Despite the Confucius' ideal notion of *renren* and Paul's high command of "loving one's neighbor," these two men would find it difficult to accept Jesus' imperative to "love your enemies" (Matt 5:43–48; Luke 6:27–36). Paul's "love your neighbor" in Galatians is still limited to racial, gender, and social differentiation, with a preference to love to those in the household of faith (Gal 6:10). Confucius' understanding of *ren,* comparable to the Stoic ideal of universal brotherhood, is also limited. The extension of self to others often stops short of concern for persons who are not family members. In Confucianism, familism prohibits strangers from being a part of the family/clan relationship.

Jesus' parable of the "Good Samaritan" (Luke 10) and his command to "love your enemies" are both radical extensions of the love command (Lev 19:18). Jesus (according to Matthew and Luke) suggests that to love one's enemies is a mark of a higher righteousness, because even tax-collectors and Gentile sinners "love their neighbors" (Matt 5:46). Matthew's Jesus characterizes the mark of a higher righteousness as "to be prefect as your heavenly Father is" (Matt 5:48); Luke's Jesus characterizes the mark as "to be merciful as your heavenly Father is" (Luke 6:36). The love command pushes the envelope for those who would be children of God from loving the self to the love of the family, friends and neighbors, and ultimately to one's enemies. To be fully human is to embody the law of Life. Jesus said, "Do this . . . and you will live!" (Luke 10:28).

112. Ibid., 337.
113. Ibid., 339.

A comparison of Paul's and Confucius' understanding of loving others is helpful. However, once we compare their explanations of the source and content of love, their views depart from each other radically. Such a contrast is not fully appropriate because Confucius did not know Christ. Confucius may have believed that *tian* (Heaven) imparted *ren* (humaneness) as part of human nature (*xing*), but he did not know of the cruciform love of God as shown on the cross. Paul knows of love among people, and he traces the source of that love to God. God has demonstrated that love by sacrificing his only begotten Son on the cross for the salvation of all people. Paul's understanding of the passion of Christ as the love of God can be used to supplement Confucius' understanding of *ren* (humane, benevolence). The reflection below seeks to construct for Chinese Christians how cruciform love challenges and fulfills the already highly idealized *ren* (humaneness) as taught by Confucius. Paul's theology of cruciform love and Confucius' ethics of humaneness (*ren*) can become the core of a Chinese Christian theological ethics.

The cruciform love of God in Christ is the center of Paul's theology. It is radical of Paul to use the cross as the identity symbol by which Jews and Gentiles are united. The cross is a scandal and a stigma. In contrast to Paul's opponents who boast of the mark of circumcision, Paul places his confidence on nothing but the cross of Jesus Christ. "But far be it from me to boast except in the cross of our Lord Jesus Christ, through which the world has been crucified to me, and I to the world" (Gal 6:14). Paul only boasts in the Lord Jesus Christ (cf. 1 Cor 1:21; 2 Cor 10:17; Phil 3:3), that is, he boasts in the sign of the cross. In a culture in which the cross was reserved for criminals and rebels, Paul's statement that he boasts in the cross is shocking, if not absurd.

The reason for boasting in the cross is because through the cross "the world has been crucified to me, and I to the world." In contrast to the opponents' fear of persecution, Paul openly proclaims his confidence in the cross. The dominion of the present evil age (Gal 1:4; 4:3, 9) has been broken and rendered ineffective ("the world crucified to me"); Paul dies to the power of evil, sin, and death ("I [am crucified] to the world").

The ethical implications of cruciform love for Chinese Christians are significant. The purpose of our work here is to reinterpret Confucian *ren* to have the content of Pauline cruciform love. As we have seen earlier, Confucian *ren* does contain the notion of self-sacrifice (*Analects* 15:9), and that in that sense Jesus can be said to be a *renren*, one whose love for others makes him sacrifice his own life. Confucian *ren*, however, does not contain the idea of "loving one's enemies." Cruciform love reveals that Christ dies for all, including those who crucified him. This forgiving and self-sacrificing love of God for those who oppose and wound him supplements the Confucian *ren*, which often is not taken to mean extending mercy beyond one's community. Cruciform love is God stooping down to reach and save sinners, even though they do not deserve forgiveness.

Both *ren* (benevolence toward others) and *agapē* (divine love) are reciprocal, but *agapē* is unconditional. Cruciform love does not demand of the other the satisfaction of one's own needs. *Ren*, as love, does acknowledge mutual indebtedness as the basic human condition. Cruciform love, however, does not require reciprocity of reward or repayment. *Cruciform ren*, as a self-sacrificing love toward one's enemies, would not manipulate others in order to achieve one's ends.

To be human is to be bound to God; and to be bound to God is to be bound to loving one's neighbor. The test of faith/piety comes when one's neighbors become one's enemies. Although enemies sometimes turn out to be good neighbors, cruciform love continues even when the neighbor is the enemy. This test is especially important in Confucianist and Christian societies where family, clan, and church interests often marginalize outsiders. To live a life of cruciform love is to hear the cry of the forsaken and the despised whom God has given to one's care.

God in Christ reveals to humanity how completely God identifies with "the forsaken and despised neighbor." In Jesus's cry of God-forsakenness on the cross ("Why have you forsaken me?") echoes the cry of humanity in despair and in yearning for hope. Christ, the beloved Son, became the God-forsaken one *on the cross*. He was treated as the victimized other, the rejected neighbor, the crucified enemy. In this human tragedy of crucifixion divine pain is found. Here lie two paradoxes of faith and life in which Confucian ethics can find its fulfillment: (1) Cruciform love is *the* way of *life* because Jesus' suffering love on the cross is God's suffering love for humanity. God is in Jesus *as* the Christ. Humanity can imitate Jesus who reveals what it means to be fully human—in Confucius' language, to be *renren*, that is, to love sacrificially even the enemy. (2) Divine love risks all in obedience even unto death. To risk such love means to trust fully in God, and thus to live fully in one's "best self" to be *junzi*. Living with one's vulnerability in faith does not end in defeat; Jesus was raised from the dead, proving that God has vindicated and exalted Jesus' vulnerable yet confident trust.

Paul's way of highlighting cruciform love enriches Confucius' understanding of *ren* in that, the reality of God in Christ informs the ethics of the people of God, by showing that divine grace is the spiritual force of ethics. Confucius sees morality (*de*) as the expression of heaven, *ren* the essence of being human. The apostle Paul teaches that divine grace is the foundation of ethics, cruciform love the way God redeems the world. For Chinese Christians, who seek to combine Confucian ethics with Pauline theology, cruciform love is the way to become fully human and holy. The cruciform love of Paul's theology and the Confucius' ethics of *renren* both believe that to be human is to reach out in love. Both believe that no human being is alone. The other's welfare is a part of one's well-being; Christ's passion is the peace of all, and divine love the mandate for all to become fully human.

5

Free to Be Human in a World of Difference

The Confucian narrative of the ideal Chinese society and the Pauline narrative of the Christian assemblies (churches) may be resourceful to the problem of co-existence of people in a world of difference. The context of these narratives contains plots of inter-state and inter-ethnic conflicts, as surfaced in ancient China and Galatia respectively. If human ancestry is one (from Adam and Eve), these conflicts are "sibling rivalry," as portrayed most vividly in the story of Cain and Abel (Genesis 4). The story raises the question whether people throughout the ages are born free to do good. Many people seem to be as helpless as Cain in protecting their own siblings. The narrative of every empire, be it Chinese, Babylonian, Greek, Roman, German, or American, proves that human beings are capable of torturing fellow human beings—as Adolf Hilter, Pol Pot, and Milosevic have done. Is the human saga nothing but the replay of the story of Cain and Abel? The language today is of "human sacrifice," "suicide bombers," "human shields," "targets of opportunity," "terrorists," and "axis of evil." The political rhetoric of our day, such as "crusade," "God bless America," "freedom reigns," "ridding the world of evil," and so forth, is often claimed to have as its inspiration the metaphors of the Bible. When the biblical images of "the chosen ones of God" or "the children of light" and the like are interpreted wrongly, they fuse into one the modern egos of self-righteousness. As a consequence, people of God use his name to kill their neighbors and their enemies.

Another biblical text, which is problematic, is Gal 4:21–31. In this passage Paul's deliberation on freedom and ethnic identity sounds ethnocentric and classicist to our modern ears—moreover, it may even be exegetically indefensible. Finding the loci of freedom, identity, and relevance of biblical exegesis are crucial tasks of a Chinese Christian. The task in this chapter is to look at the interpretive principles Paul employs in Gal 4:21–31. I believe Paul has articulated the hope of moral freedom inherent in every human being. His discourse on freedom, and that of Confucius, help us articulate a civil community formed by virtue.

SPIRIT, FLESH, AND FREEDOM IN GAL 4:21–31

The Debate Between Paul and His Opponents: Two Gentile Missions in Galatia

The preceding context of Gal 4:21–31 is 4:8–20, which speaks of Paul's gospel mission among the Gentile churches in Galatia and the "disastrous developments under the tutelage" of the opponents.[1] Galatians 4:21–31 contains Paul's exegetical response to his opponents' scriptural proof. At the heart of the theology of Paul's opponents in Galatia is their conviction that they are the people of God. They believe that their mission to the churches in Galatia is to make them the true descendants of Abraham through Sarah's son Isaac, and that the law-observant mission is based on divine promise and approved by the "present Jerusalem." They see this lineage privileged through Moses, sealed by divine covenant, and codified by the law. They thought Gentiles, Hagar's descendants, had to be circumcised and observe the law if they were to enter the covenant, maintain law-righteousness, and thus become "legitimate" members of the people of God.

In his argument, however, Paul turns to his opponents' basic rhetorical *topos* (the account of Hagar and Ishmael in Genesis 15–21) to show that his opponents have missed the point of the story. The argument in

---

1. I follow Martyn, *Galatians*, 409–66, on the contextual reading of Gal 4:21–31. That is, the pericope is not about Paul's theology of Judaism and Christianity but about two Gentile missions, viz., the law-observant mission of the opponents to the Gentiles in Galatia and the circumcision-free mission of Paul to the Gentiles.

Gal 4:21–31 makes extensive use of the Hebrew Scripture in which Paul offers an alternate reading of the opponents' proof text. In Gal 4:21–31, Paul references Hebrew Scripture in order to counter his opponents' prooftexting. Paul's interpretation confirms that his Gentile mission free of circumcision originates with and is ordained by God. Isaac, says Paul, is the promised son of Abraham *not* because of biological relation but because he is related to Abraham as a result of *divine promise*, and, equally important, Abraham's faith in that promise. According to Paul's counter-argument, although the Judaizers are physically related to Isaac they are spiritually related (thus metaphorically) to Hagar-Ishmael, for they rely on their relationship to Abraham "according to the flesh" (*kata sarka*) and not according to "the promise" (*epaggelias*). Following the allegorical method of his day (and centuries thereafter) Paul simply declares this to be so.

The Allegorical Interpretation of Paul

✧ Allegory and Analogy

Scholars refer to Gal 4:21–31 as "the allegory of Sarah and Hagar, following Paul's own description of this interpretation as allegorical (*atina estin allēgoroumena*).[2] The allegorical method of interpretation was well known to the rabbinic schools of his day. Being a method accepted by his Jewish opponents, Paul answers with a method of their choosing. Paul does not intend to establish the historical accuracy of this Old Testament narrative. Allegory is an extensive form of metaphor.[3] As a form of interpretation, allegory is "the search for secondary and hidden meaning underlying the primary and obvious meanings of a narrative."[4] Or as Hanson defines it, "an allegory is an explanation of the text that replaces

---

2. The word *allēgoroumena* (present participle, nominative neuter plural used substantively) comes from *allo* meaning "another," and *agorouvein* meaning "to speak." It has two possible meanings: (a) to speak allegorically; (b) to interpret allegorically, that is, to draw out the spiritual meaning to underlie the literal sense of the words. Some scholars suggest the word used here has a broader meaning. Hanson, *Studies in Paul's Technique and Theology*, 91. I have consulted the work of Fung, *Zhenli Yu Ziyou*, 285–90. See his insightful reading on this pericope.

3. Mickelsen, *Interpreting the Bible*, 230.

4. Ibid., 228, quoting K. J. Woolcombe.

the literal sense and has a purely arbitrary connection with it."[5] Soulen and Soulen note that "an allegorical interpretation assumes that the text to be interpreted says or intends to say something more than and other than what its literal wording suggests—that it contains hidden within it a deeper, mystical sense not directly disclosed in the words."[6] According to the above definitions of allegory, Gal 4:21–31 is not an allegory in its technical sense because Paul is not searching for secondary meanings but rather deducing principles that are useful in the narrative. Furthermore, Paul is not ignoring the literal meaning of the Old Testament narrative.

Hanson notes that there are at least five different possible translations of *allēgoroumena* in Gal 4:24, and after a lexical investigation he renders it as "these things are intended to convey a deeper meaning."[7] I prefer to call Gal 4:21–31 an analogy, following Ellison's judgment that the passage is "an extreme case of analogy."[8] Paul sees an underlying principle in the relationship between Hagar-Ishmael and Sarah-Isaac[9] analogous to that two kinds of Gentile mission in Galatia. Paul deduces the principle from Old Testament stories and applies it analogously to the situation in Galatia. Just as the son of a free mother was born through promise (Gal 4:23), so also the Gentile Christians in Galatia ought to be born as "children of promise" (4:28) and heirs to the promise (4:30b). Just as the son of the slave mother was not born through the promise, but only according to the flesh" (4:23), so also the Judaizers' "bear children" not according to the promise but only according to the flesh. Just as the allegorized Hagar was in bondage, so also are those who believe in the circumcision of the flesh. Just as Isaac was the son of the free woman, so also are the Gentile Christians who believe in the gospel of Christ. Just as the slave girl and her son are to be thrown out, so also "the Judaizers

---

5. Hanson, *Studies in Paul's Technique and Theology*, 94. Buschel ("Allēgoreō," *TDNT* 1:263) agrees with Hanson but says Paul comes closer to Palestinian allegorizing than to the Alexandrian one.

6. Soulen and Soulen, *Handbook of Biblical Criticism*, 4.

7. Hanson, *Studies in Paul's Technique and Theology*, 94. NIV puts it as "these things may be taken figuratively" which is a better translation than "this is an allegory" in RSV.

8. Ellison, *The Message of the Old Testament*, 90.

9. Cf. Lightfoot, *Galatians*, 180; Ridderbos, *The Epistle of Paul to the Churches of Galatia*, 175; Hanson, *Studies in Paul's Technique and Theology*, 156.

and their totally loyal colleagues who are to be expelled from the Galatian churches (4:30)."[10]

⇔ Three Facts from the Old Testament Narrative

Paul begins his analogical interpretation by appealing to what the law[11] says (4:21b). As he meets the Judaizers on their own ground of the book of the law, Paul states his argument by recalling three facts from the story of Sarah and Hagar:

(1) "Abraham had two sons" (Gal 4:22a). Abraham had other sons,[12] but only the first two sons had to do with becoming the heirs of Abraham, sharing his inheritance (Gen 21:10) and fulfilling God's promise of the covenant (Gen 16:1—17:22). For Paul the two sons provide two distinct paradigms of gospel mission for those under the law and those who believe in Christ.

(2) The two mothers had a different status: one is a slave woman,[13] Hagar; the other is a free woman, Sarah (Gal 4:22b). The point of Hagar and Sarah in the story is not about class or ethnic differences (both are Semites) but about the status of their firstborn— whether born in slavery or in freedom—as the next fact makes clear.

(3) The two sons were born in different ways (Gal 4:23): the son by the slave-maid was born in the ordinary way "according to the flesh" (*kata sarka*), but the son by the free-woman was born as the result of God's promise (*dia tēs epaggelias*).[14] "According to the flesh" and "according to the promise" are contrasted to one another. Though Isaac was begotten and born "according to the flesh" (*kata sarka*) *without* the promise of God, his birth was also

---

10. Lightfoot, *Galatians*, 252 points out that "law" here refers to the Old Testament Scripture because of the indefinite article.

11. Martyn, *Galatians*, 466.

12. Abraham had six other sons by Keturah (Gen 25:1–2). The birth of Isaac is narrated in Gen 21:1–7, and the birth of Ishmael is narrated in Gen 16:1–7.

13. "*Paideia*," BAGD, 603 indicates *paidiskē* is *pais* diminutive, the female gender of *paidiskos*; it refers to little slave-maid. In the New Testament, the term often refers to a slave (cf. Luke 12:45).

14. Burton, *Galatians*, 252 refers *epaggelia* to Gen 15:4; 17:19; and 18:16.

"according to the promise" (*dia tēs epaggelias*) and was significant because of this. The birth of Ishmael was simply "according to the flesh: (*kata sarka*) *without* the promise of God. F. F. Bruce writes that Isaac's birth "took place by the enabling word of God in direct fulfillment of the promise"[15] (cf. Gen 17:17–19). Isaac's birth and existence is meaningless apart from the divine promise.

⤙ 3. Four Applications of Paul's Analogical Interpretation

There are four ways Paul and his readers in Galatia are to apply his analogical interpretation of this Old Testament story to themselves.[16] The applications concern the identity of Gentile Christians in Galatia. They seek to prove which gospel mission is valid scripturally.

(1) "Now you, brothers, like Isaac, are children of promise" (Gal 4:28). Just as Isaac is born through the promise of God (4:23b), so also are the Gentile Christians in Galatia. The promise found in Gal 4:28 has been spelled out earlier in Galatians 3. God has given the promise to the Gentiles. They have received God's Spirit (3:2) by faith in Christ (3:21–22); they have become Abraham's children (3:16–19), and they have escaped the curse of the law (3:14).

(2) Just as he who was born according to the flesh persecuted him who was born through the promise, so in Paul's day Judaizers are persecuting Gentile believers (Gal 4:29a). The account of Ishmael's persecution of Isaac is not recorded in the Bible. Paul may be reflecting here the rabbinic Haggadah tradition, which says: Ishmael was playing with a bow and arrow and under pretext of making a joke shot an arrow at Isaac.[17] In any case Paul most likely had the Genesis passage in mind, and there Ishmael's presence is not so much a threat to Isaac's life but to his freedom,

---

15. Bruce, *Galatians*, 217. Cf. Gen 17:19, 18:9–15.

16. See Fung, *Zhenli Yu Ziyou*, 285–90.

17. Hanson, *Studies in Paul's Technique and Theology*, 97. See Bruce, *Galatians*, 222–24 who gives various historical arguments. RSV's "playing with" is an inaccurate translation, AV's "mocking at" is closer to the intended meaning. The MT has *mšḥq* ("playing") and the LXX has *paizonta* ("playing" or "sporting") in Gen 21:9. Paul's use of "persecution" is a strong word.

security, and privileges as an heir to the promised inheritance.[18] As the texts indicate (Gen 16:12; 17:17–19; and 21:10) Sarah fears that Ishmael, being fourteen years older than Isaac, will get the inheritance.[19] Similarly, the Judaizers in Galatia pressured Gentile believers to accept circumcision as a sign of Jewish identity so that they themselves could escape persecution (6:12). They did not want to appear complicitous to a lax interpretation of the law.

(3) Just as Isaac "is born by the power of the Spirit," so it is with Gentile Christians (Gal 4:29b). In v. 23 Paul describes Isaac as one "born as a result of a promise," but in verse 29 as one "born by the power of the Spirit." The second phrase is a theological expansion of the first and together they describe Isaac and all who live according to the Spirit. Paul's conviction is that the Spirit is the one who fulfills the promise of God. The Spirit is the down-payment and seal of salvation (Eph 1:13; 4:30). The driving theology of Paul's gospel mission emphasizes that Jewish and Gentile Christians are "born by the power of the Spirit" (Gal 4:29) as a result of the promise of God (Gal 4:23).

(4) Paul quotes Genesis: "Get rid of the slave woman and her son, for the slave woman's son will never share in the inheritance with the free woman's son" (Gal 4:30 and Gen 21:10). Here Paul appeals to Sarah's words, but not as a call for Gentile Christians to rise up and expel Jewish Christians from the church; rather, it is a pronouncement of the consequences of holding to circumcision as the mark of the people of God in accordance to the Judaizer's circumcision gospel. The result is: Since those who rely on the flesh to identify themselves are without the Spirit, they are without the promise and "will never share the inheritance" (Gal 4:30).

After all that has been deliberated in Gal 4:21–30, Paul offers in verse 31 a summary of the two consequences of his and his opponents' Gentile mission in Galatia: "the mark of the Spirit" (faith) or "a physical mark on the body" (circumcision). Though the Gentile Christians are

---

18. Ridderbos, *The Epistle of Paul to the Churches of Galatia*, 181 n. 12. Ridderbos is more precise; though he argues that although Paul's use of Gen 21:10 could well be triggered or influenced by his rabbinic background, it was not dictated by it.

19. According to the Old Testament, Ishmael though born outside the promise, was the firstborn of Abraham and therefore a threat to the primogeniture of Isaac.

not the physical descendants of Abraham, they accept the promise by faith, and consequently "are not the children of the slave woman (Hagar), but of the free woman (Sarah)" (Gal 4:31). By comparing the situation in Galatia with the story in Genesis, Paul parallels the freedom of the Gentile Christians that comes from trusting God's promises with the inheritance (of sons of God) and fruit (of the Spirit) that comes from faith in Christ.

MALE AND FEMALE IN THE THOUGHTS OF PAUL AND CONFUCIUS

Paul: Equality and Differentiation

↬ Feminist Critique of Paul?

A current question raised by feminists is whether Paul's theology is sexist, if not misogynist. The theme of sonship is a significant one in Galatians (see 3:7, 26; 4:4, 6, 7, 22, 30) and it is this to which feminists object. Lone Fotum, a feminist scholar, uses what she calls a contextual approach in reading Gal 3:16–18 and 4:1–7, 21–31, and she raises a critical concern regarding Paul's "genderblind" language. She insists that 3:16–18 and 4:1–7 explicitly refers to the male child and to the male heir, and that 4:19, 22–31 refers to sons and not to "children." She writes,

> It is, indeed, evidence of the fact that androcentric normativity is deeply rooted not only in the theological paradigm of creation, according to Gen 1:27a, but also in the ideal of *imitatio Christi* as the encompassing paradigm of Christian existence after baptism in the Spirit (in Christ), . . . No doubt, this fundamental concept of androcentric normality has its pivot in the Adam-Christ typology which is maintained by Paul as an Anthropos speculation in his use of the son and heir motifs. What I would like to emphasize, however, is the observation that the Anthropos speculation is applied by Paul throughout not as an aspect of the androgyne but, on the contrary, as a pattern of life, invested with an exclusively androcentric quality, personified by the male figure of Christ (cf. Gal 4:4–7).
>   . . . As I see it, a collective or inclusive interpretation of the Anthropos motif could be just another way of avoiding the issue of gender and the sexually specific means of repression or gen-

derblind generalization. . . . only by maintaining the male exclusiveness as an eschatological quality of the Christ motif in [Gal 3:]28d along with the concept of androcentric normality and normativity in v. 28c, in accordance with Gen. 1:27a, is it possible to grasp the negative impact of gender and sexuality in the Pauline context. . . . I believe, the key to Paul's argument in Galatians is the presupposition of Jewish discrimination, and in 3:28c the unclean is concretized as Greek, slave and (female) sexuality.[20]

She concludes, "Galatians nowhere gives reason to believe that Paul is at all concerned with the circumstances of women."[21]

✦ 2. Feminist Concerns and Paul's Exegesis in Galatians 4

While I empathize with many of the modern concerns of the feminists to read the Bible, I do not think their interpretation is fair to Paul and accurate to his exegesis. The modern feminist critique of the patriarchal culture in the Bible is that it was biased and dominating. To expect Paul in the first century to be sensitive to twenty-first century concerns is an irrational expectation. The question is, how does Paul change the standards and norms of the first century? Does his preaching of the gospel of Jesus Christ constitute a reinforcement of patriarchal culture? The feminist presupposition that all human beings, male or female, are born equal is a good lens, but the assumption that the circumstances of women then is the same as it is now, so that the problem of male dominance has remained constant is inaccurate. Granted that the woman's role is inadequately defined when it is understood as merely helping males to produce an heir to perpetuate the patriarchal structure of domination, but to use this lens to read the story of Sarah and Hagar is misleading. Neither the writer of Genesis 15–17 nor Galatians 4 describes the male dominance of Abraham as a means for manipulating Sarah and Hagar into child-bearing. The biblical accounts do not make the feminist point that without giving birth to a male child, a woman was shamed as fruitless and useless.

---

20. Fatum, "Women, Symbolic Universe and Structures of Silence," 67–69. See also Fiorenza, *In Memory of Her*, 210–13; Meeks, "The Image of the Androgyne," 165–205.

21. Fatum, "Women, Symbolic Universe and Structures of Silence," 66.

From the feminist point of view, Isaac is chosen as the rightful heir over Ishmael not because Isaac is the promised one, but because of the patriarchal system and the class struggle between the two women. Because of this, the feminist argument is that the story inevitably ends with Isaac as the rightful heir. Once Ishmael is ruled out as the rightful heir, even though he is the firstborn and born with the blessing of Abraham, he is persecuted, as Genesis 17 describes. This explanation is often used as the theological justification that only Sarah's son can be the rightful heir in the family of God. The long history of enmity between these two Semitic tribes is often explained by the story of the family feud between Sarah and Hagar. But the favoritism of Isaac over Ishmael is not the cause; changing the story out of fear of one's identity is. Worse, the insecurity of finding one's identity not in the grace of God but in the proximity and purity of one's own lineage perpetuates violence in the family of Abraham.

Radically different from a literal reading and a claim of one's identity based on the status of one's biological connection with Abraham is Paul's analogical interpretation. For Paul the physical mark of the flesh (circumcision) belongs to the old age, in this new age what is significant is the spiritual mark of God's promise in Christ and the gift of the Spirit. In Galatia the Jewish opponents of Paul first come up with the argument that Jewish Christians are from Sarah and Gentile Christians are descendants of Hagar (the Egyptians, cf. Gen 21:9). Paul's response is that those who think "works of the law" (such as circumcision) make them true heirs are actually aligning with Hagar, and that Gentile Christians without law observance are in fact descendants from Sarah. Paul's counter-argument will only work when he does not count on biological genealogy but on the consequence of one's faith in Christ. In Paul's response to his opponents, he writes, "The women represent two covenants. One covenant is from Mount Sinai and bears children who are to be slaves: This is Hagar. Now Hagar stands for Mount Sinai in Arabia" (Gal 4:24b). The allegorical meaning in this response overshadows the literal, historical meaning of Hagar. In other words, Paul is concerned with the word "Hagar" and its applicability to the covenant at Mount Sinai rather than with the person Hagar and Judaism. The word "Hagar"[22] is meant because: (a) The neuter article before Hagar in the Greek text refers to the word rather than the woman; (b) Hagar is another designation of Mount Sinai as "the name

22. Hanson, *Studies in Paul's Technique and Theology*, 95.

Hagar resembles the Arabic name Sinai. The Arabians are called son of Hagar";[23] (c) The woman Hagar has *no* correspondence with Sinai because according to the Jewish history, the law is given to heirs of Isaac and not to heirs of Hagar. Thus, Paul is *allegorizing*, and not historicizing the Hagar story.[24]

Hagar is interpreted to be representing the theology of Paul's opponents, i.e., a symbol to their Mosaic covenant at Mount Sinai. (The key word is "covenants" in Gal 4:24b). There are not two covenants (Abrahamic and Mosaic covenants) in history but two distinct affirmations of one and the same covenant of grace (Exod 20:2).[25] The intended purpose of God in giving the law is to preserve the people of God (Exod 19:6). In any case, why is Hagar linked to Sinai? Ellis claims the equation of Hagar and Sinai may be onomatology (the word-play of making a name).[26] He writes:

> In so far as onomatology may enter into the passage, there is nothing particularly Alexandrian or rabbinic in it. The significance of names is a frequent phenomenon in the Old Testament itself, both as mere word-play and as illustrative of significant relationships.[27]

In this verse Paul is anxious to remind the readers and the opponents about the corresponding terms of bondage both in figurative Hagar and in the Judaizers' works of the law (given at Mount Sinai). The giving of the law at Mount Sinai is for the heirs of Isaac, the covenanted people of

23. Wuest, *Galatians in the Greek New Testament for the English Reader*, 133.

24. In Paul's interpretation here, Hagar is still being portrayed negatively, but that is not of Paul's choosing; rather it is the assumption of his opponents which Paul uses to prove their argument wrong. Furthermore, Hagar in Galatians 4 is not the historical figure anymore because of the allegorical interpretation of Paul. Take the Hagar story in the Old Testament, for example: Despite the family feud and sibling rivalry, God heard the voice of Ishmael and sent his angel to protect and bless Hagar and Ishmael (Gen 21:17, 25:12). In the biblical narrative, Ishmael is also born out of promise (Gen 16:10), though that promise is given after Hagar's pregnancy. Paul is familiar with these Genesis accounts. The fact that he does not use them suggests that he is arguing with the version of his opponents. See Martyn's reading of Gal 4 without the tendency of anti-Judaism, "The Covenants of Hagar and Sarah," 160–92.

25. Ridderbos, *The Epistle of Paul to the Churches of Galatia*, 175; Kaiser, *Toward an Old Testament Theology*, 268–69.

26. Ellis, *Paul's Use of the Old Testament*, 52–53.

27. Ibid., 53.

the promise, but it is precisely this point that Paul reverses the opponents' claim. The Judaizers believe that their circumcision gospel in Galatia serves to make the Gentiles, like themselves, into the true descendants of the line of Isaac. However, according to Paul, the Judaizers and their followers in Galatia have instead departed from their spiritual relation to Isaac because they have not trusted in the promise of God through Christ. By contrast Paul's gospel is convinced that the Gentile Christians are now spiritually related to Isaac because of Christ's fulfillment of the law.

Paul's theological reinterpretation of circumcision, of the Abrahamic covenant, as well as the concept of the Messiah, is an attempt to fit a new reality. In doing so Paul addresses by implication the problems we face today. Paul was faithful and effective in reflecting critically and theologically on problems comparable to what we call today "racism" and "sexism." Paul took seriously the predominantly patriarchal culture of his day, yet he was able to work out a transformative interpretation within that culture.

✧ Ethnic Differentiation and Unity: "Jews and Greeks"

Paul argues that faith in the faithfulness of Christ is a type of Abrahamic faith in the faithfulness of God and he argues that God's covenant now includes both Jews and Gentiles. It is, he argues, a misunderstanding of the Abrahamic covenant to reduce God's acts in the history of salvation to works of the law such as circumcision. That misunderstanding is exemplified by Paul's opponents in Galatia. From Paul's point of view the gospel of the Judaizers is a scandal because by requiring Gentiles to be Jews as a condition for becoming full members of the family of God they make God partial. Paul argues that anyone who is baptized into Christ and is clothed with Christ is now initiated into God's community (Gal 3:27–28: "For as many of you as were baptized into Christ have put on Christ. There is neither Jew nor Greek, there is neither slave nor free, there is neither male nor female; for you are all one in Christ Jesus").

The three couplets, viz., Jew/Greek, slave/free, male/female, appear together here only in the New Testament.[28] The phrase "there is neither Jew nor Greek" (Gal 3:28) can mean that ethnic identity is erased for those who are in Christ—ethnicity is no longer the symbol of identity it once was. Or it can mean that cultural discrimination is to cease, though differences and identity are still there. The second understanding makes sense because the result of being in Christ cannot be the minimizing, let alone the deletion, of one's cultural, ethnic uniqueness.[29] Were every ethnic group to do that in synagogue or church, then there might be fewer group conflicts, but the result would be conformity and sameness. The Judaizers, on the other hand, implied in their demanding circumcision of the Gentiles, would make one ethnic group a "law observant" people. Circumcision was the mark of the covenant in Paul's day, and by implication of the works of the law (to give a common identity to the people of God) Gentile Christians who do not observe the law remained outside the covenant, a lawless people. The Judaizers believed that Jesus was the Messiah, the Christ. They believed the work of the Messiah was to include Gentiles into the people of God by means of the covenantal laws. Paul disagrees. Paul believes that the inclusion of Gentiles into the covenant is by means of the work of Messiah without works of the law. In other words, faith in the Messiah is sufficient for Gentiles to be the people of God. The Messiah is to have universal significance because faith in Christ is open to anyone and everyone: Jew, Greek, male, female, bond, or free—and by implication, to all "races" and "cultures," worded in modern terms. The unity of Jews and Gentiles found in Christ does not make them one "race" and one "culture."[30] The problem is to overcome the ethnocentric character of the covenant, which only Christ can do.

---

28. First Corinthians 12:13 has the first two couplets but phrases them "Jews or Greeks, slaves or free" (speaking of baptizing into the one body of Christ through the one Spirit). Colossians 3:11 has the first two couplets, but they are inserted with other couplets (Greek and Jew, circumcised and uncircumcised, barbarian, Scythian, slave and free, but Christ is all in all). See Matera, *Galatians*, 146.

29. I do not agree with Mou Zongsan's interpretation of Christian theology and ethic of universalism without differentiation, which he writes "will result in 'rulerless' and 'fatherless' chaos" (Mou, *Zhongguo Zhexue De Tezhi*, 61). He critiques Christian theology for having a "religious morality" without "ethical morality" (63–64). That reading is another misinterpretation, because Christian theology is to contain ethical morality in religious morality, and morality in theology, see Chapter One in this book (pp. 81–89).

30. See Boyarin, *A Radical Jew*, 22–25 on Paul's "erasure of human difference."

The last clause of Gal 3:28 states the new reality in Christ: "for all of you are one in Christ Jesus." The word "one" does not connote the modern myth of sameness or uniformity, which is popularly termed "political correctness," a conformity to a certain ideological position in which no deviation is allowed—under threat of vilification, ostracism, and censorship. Political correctness is a guise for totalitarianism, masked by the appearance of inclusiveness, justice, and freedom. The word "one" signifies the inclusiveness, the union, and the communion of all in Christ. In other words, Christ brings all who are in him into community. The reality of being "in Christ" forms the basis for bringing Jews and Gentiles together (Gal 3:27–28).

Paul's reasoning is: first, that Jews and Greeks are united in Christ because oneness in Christ is based on differences, not sameness. Through differentiation individual identity is clarified; we know who we are. So in Christ there is still Jew and Greek, without uniqueness of ethnicity, the next move of interpretation cannot be completed. The next move is, secondly, "in Christ there is neither Jew nor Greek," i.e., being in Christ is based on mutuality and reciprocity. When two people of different races and cultures or ethnic groups, not to mention gender or generations, are "in love" their differences and their uniqueness do not disappear. Nor do they when they are "in Christ Jesus." The reality or community created in Christ is one of diversity in unity. Diversity means differences that give forth uniqueness, which in turn forms identity. But this identity is formed in a fiduciary community whereby mutuality warrants and supports differences. It is precisely in diversity that interaction among them is necessary. Unity does not mean uniformity, it means reciprocity. Diversity does not mean alienation or domination or self-annihilation, it means celebrating differences and yet holding each other accountable to the shared truth. The principle of the reality in Christ is to overcome the dualism of seeing life in terms of "black and white."[31] If juxtaposing "black

---

31. Anthropologists Brent Berlin and Paul Kay have studied the evolution of language and have noticed that black and white are the first two color terms to emerge in most languages and that other terms were gradually added as cultures became more elaborate. Berlin and Kay, *Basic Color Terms*. Thus in modern Western classifications white is used to mean purity, cleanliness, virginity, virtue, beauty, godliness; black, by contrast, is used to mean ugliness, filthiness, sin, baseness, and devilishness. This categorization is problematic, and is to be rejected as a reference to ethnic identity. It is interesting to note that while most Westerners use white for weddings and black for mourning, Chinese use red in weddings and white in funerals.

and white" polarizes communities and is destructive, why would Paul use the old language of "Jew and Greek" so frequently (e.g., Rom 1:16; 2:9, 10; 3:9; 10:12; 1 Cor 1:22, 24; 10:32; 12:13)? The answer lies in Paul's habit of speaking the language of the common people and yet aiming to transform it (Gal 5:6; 6:15; 1 Cor 7:19; 12:13). We shall return to this point in the following section when we look at Paul's use of the common language of "slave and master" to transform the reality of domination.

↭ Social Equality and Liberation: "Slave and Free"

Just as the new being in Christ transforms the Jew-Greek relationship into a unity in difference, so also are the social distinctions between slaves and free persons, males and females. One may think that it is revolutionary to interpret the second couplet, "there is neither slave nor free" as the elimination of social classes. Some have accused Paul of being socially passive in advocating the acceptance of slavery as a social status (as is implied in 1 Cor 7:21–24).[32] Still, many think that in Gal 3:28 Paul is referring to an "eschatological reality" that will be realized only in the future. Just as he uses the stereotypical "Jew-Greek" language, so also he uses the language of slave and free and this gives the impression that Paul is conservative with regard to the transformation of society.

Paul is consistent in his interpretation of ethnic concern, just as he is in the area of social concerns. The effectiveness of Paul's interpretation is precisely in his using the seemingly stereotypical language of social distinctions to bring about the transformation he seeks. The question for Paul is: What is the problem in the master-slave relationship that needs transformation? The problem in the master-slave relationship is not social class; the problem is domination. In Philemon and 1 Cor 7:21–24, Paul endeavors in an obviously heartfelt way to use the gospel of love to transform the inherently distorted relationship between masters and slaves so that mutuality and respect would replace domination and condescension.[33] Doing away with the slavery system was not a possibility open to Paul, given how ingrained slavery was in the social, economic,

32. In Eph 6:5–8 and Col 3:22–25 the author seeks to transform the responsibility of both slaves and master, even though that author has not gone as far as we might wish toward an egalitarian society.

33. See Yeo, "Feilimenshu de youshui," 177–88.

and political structures of the society. More to the point, Paul's theology was apocalyptic and all his judgments concerning society and its relationships were governed by his belief that the parousia of Christ was the impetus of transformation. Paul's eschatological expectation of the return of Christ precluded any expectation of social transformation through human effort. Paul was not concerned with the elimination of slavery as an institution. He was concerned about abuse and mistreatment and thus about domination of the slavery institution, just as he was concerned with morality in general.

Paul believed that transformation could take place without necessarily changing the nomenclature of society. If the gospel of Christ can transform the relationship between masters and slaves in the church while the social status outside the church remains the same, then a new world order has already arrived. Paul believes that only the love of Christ can overcome the problem of domination in the slave-master relationship. If slaves and masters are brothers in Christ living in the mutual-indebtedness of love, then the problem of domination should not exist even though the social structure might still be there. Paul's use of the common idioms of "Jews and Greeks" and "slave and free" is subtle yet transformative because he needs these linguistic polarities to assert their inherent contrast to life in Christ. That life is lived out in "the body of Christ"—the new alternative to life "in" works of the law. The interpretive lens of "life in Christ" then overcomes and effaces these distinctions in language, and sometimes subverts the inherent polarities in the stereotypical language. Paul is not concerned so much about the elimination of slavery in society. He certainly is concerned about the elimination of slavery in Christ—the prerequisite for being ready for Christ's return. The intent of Paul's interpretation of the reality in Christ was to bring equality and freedom to Jews and Greeks, slave and free.

Why would Paul not stop using the old nomenclature in his discussion of the new reality in Christ? Because the problems of a slavery-holding society do not go away with the demise of nomenclature, such as "slaves" and "masters." In fact, Paul's persistent use of these idioms suggests that the moment one gets rid of the language of domination, one has disempowered himself of the very tools needed to interpret and deal with the problem. The problems of abuses and domination are omnipresent in all human relationships, most vividly seen in that of master-slave.

Without the language of specificity one cannot begin to name the reality and then critically reflect on the problems underlying the reality.

Here Confucius' insight concerning the nature of *ming* (naming) and *shi* (actuality) may help us read Paul's use of language. Confucius believes that *ming*, as the naming function of a language, can transform *shi*, the actuality or the social reality. The two Chinese words *ming* (name) and *ming* (decree or destiny) are cognates, and are often used together (*ming-ming*: decree-name) to refer to the decreeing function of giving a person a name. For example, my given name in Chinese is Khiok-khng (phonetically rendered into English using my family dialect called Chaozhou); it means "diligent." Inherent in the name is the admonition that my destiny is shaped by my willingness to aspire. In a manner comparable to modern speech-act theory, which believes that certain words have the power to perform and to transform, Confucius thinks that *ming* (naming) not only describes but also prescribes, effects, and changes reality. *Analects* 13:3 records Confucius' view of *ming* and the well-governed society: Zilu asks Confucius what will be his top priority if the Lord of Wey asks him to govern his state? Confucius replies, "Proper naming!" (*zhengming*). Zilu complains that Confucius is being too impractical. Confucius replies, "An exemplary person (*junzi*) defers on matters he does not understand. When names (*ming*) are not used properly, language (*yan*) will not be used effectively; when language is not used effectively, matters (*shi*) will not be taken care of; when matters are not taken care of, the observance of ritual propriety (*li*) and the playing of music (*yue*) will not flourish; when the observance of ritual propriety and the playing of music do not flourish, the application of laws and punishments is not on the mark, the people will not know what to do with themselves."[34] Lu Xing, a scholar on ancient Chinese rhetoric, explains the meaning of this saying, "By developing this transformative nature of *ming*, Confucius articulated an ideal way of using speech and language capable of creating order out of disorder and transforming a morally corrupt society into one of *ren* (humaneness), *li* (rites), and *zhongyong* (the Middle Way)."[35] Language, Confucius is saying, has the power to transform society, to cultivate persons, to bring about peace; language can also destroy when it is abused. Paul, too, is aware of the power of language to convict, to convince, and to

34. Ames and Rosemont, *Analects*, 162. See Qian, *Lunyu Xinjie*, 452–53; Yang, *Lunyu Yizhu*, 285–86.

35. Lu, *Rhetoric in Ancient China*, 162.

transform. "His letters are weighty and strong but his physical presence is weak and his speech is of no account," it is said of him (2 Cor 10:10). In his letter to the Galatians and in other letters as well, Paul consistently uses, what Anthony Thiselton calls, "'participatory' language which speaks of sharing in the having-died and being-been-raised of Christ"[36] (Gal 2:20; 3:28; 2 Cor 4:10; 5:14–15; Rom 6:4, 5, 13). This language transforms the world "in accordance with the word: there is a 'world-to-word' direction of fit."[37] Thiselton gives an example of the performative language of the cross:

> The speaking of the words constitutes an act which shapes a state of affairs. . . . The declaration that a particular state of affairs is true ('Christ was buried, and was raised on the third day,' 1 Cor 15:4) has an assertive force, in which the state of affairs to be reported determines the word that is spoken.[38]

In his letters to the Galatians and Philemon Paul uses traditional language as a shared reality he has with his readers. Then in a subtle move forward into the language of faith he transforms the reality the language describes and prescribes, and in so doing the traditional language itself has new meaning. He does that, as we have seen, when speaking of Jews and Greeks. It is the same when he employs the polarities of the "slave and free" and "male and female."

The second couplet in Gal 3:28 is not about the differentiation between masters and slaves. Paul is talking about the new reality of "slave and free" (3:28) in the body of Christ. Despite the distinction of social class in the society, the differentiation of whether one is a slave or free does not hinder their being one in Christ. In fact, Paul believes that the polarities between slave and free and the social structure of division can only be changed by the body of Christ, who has inaugurated a new social order.

✣ Gender Uniqueness and Mutuality: "Male and Female"

In the same vein, Paul's interpretation of the third couplet in Gal 3:28c ("there is neither 'male and female'") does not mean the abolition of sex-

36. Thiselton, *New Horizons*, 19.
37. Ibid.
38. Ibid., 298.

ual differences or the marriage relationship, nor does it mean the creation of some new androgynous being.[39] The couplet is a little different from the first two. Instead of "neither . . . nor," the third couplet has "no . . . and" ("no 'male and female'"; *ouk eni arsen kai thēly*). Betz's observation that if the couplet were "neither male nor female," it would have abundant parallels in the apocryphal and gnostic gospels, which "claim the metaphysical removal of the biological sex distinctions as a result of the salvation in Christ. We must then speak not merely of social emancipation but of androgyny."[40] Betz goes on to suggest that since the wording "male and female" and its linkage to the phrase "one in Christ" (3:28), the couplet may reflect the formula used in Gen 1:27 (LXX, the Greek Old Testament): "male and female he made them" (*arsen kai thēly epoiesen autous*).[41] Betz thinks that the Greek translation of Gen 1:27 "was ready made for interpreting into it, if indeed it is not already contained in it, the myth of the primordial man (*Urmensch*) who is androgynous."[42] The undifferentiated primordial humanity of "male and female" constituted the ideal, "third sex," as articulated by Plato and popularized by many Hellenistic religions of Paul's day.[43] The question is, does Paul embrace the myth of androgynous humanity? I do not think so because Paul negates the formula "male and female" with "no" (*ouk*).

Paul must have had Gen 1:27 in mind when he uses the phrase "no 'male and female,'" as Betz has suggested above. In the context of Genesis 1, the creation of humanity as "male and female" in the likeness and image of God differentiates humanity from other creatures. Human beings are created with a unique status and responsibility. The formula "male

39. Schüssler Fiorenza speculates that Paul's phrase, "there is neither male and female" alludes to Gen 1:27 (probably correctly) and is about gender relation in marriage (probably incorrectly). She writes, "Gal 3:29c does not assert that there are no longer men and women in Christ, but that patriarchal marriage—and sexual relationships between male and female—is no longer constitutive of the new community in Christ" (*In Memory of Her*, 210). If she means that marriage and sexual relationships are no longer conditions for being in the new community of Christ, she is correct. Marriage and sexual relationships have never been conditions for membership in God's community, unless one speaks of circumcision. But if she is saying that patriarchal marriage and certain kinds of sexual relations are problematic, and thus need to be transformed in Christ, then she has a point.

40. Betz, *Galatians*, 196.

41. Ibid., 198.

42. Ibid.

43. Ibid.

and female" in Gen 1:27 portrays the creation of sexes of humanity. I side with majority of scholars in reading Gen 1:27 to mean the undifferentiated humanity—Adam as "male and female."[44] Thus, when Paul alludes to Gen 1:27 in his couplet in Gal 3:28 with a negation, he in effect is saying, there is sexual differentiation and there is unity in Christ.

Paul's interpretation follows the theology of the Genesis writer. For the undifferentiated Adam (humanity) in Gen 1:17 and 2:18–20 goes through the process of differentiation (2:21–23) when Eve, the woman (*'ishshah*), is made out of Adam, the man (*'ish*). In the same spirit Paul affirms the creation of the differentiated humanity (as male and female), for it is through their differences and uniqueness that the individual finds his and her own creative roles.[45] Through differentiation and the meeting of an equal, the man achieves his own identity, as does the woman. The man and the woman are brought to self-awareness only after they encounter each other. In reaching out to the other, one knows who one is and how one is unique. For Paul the new creation in Christ does not eliminate the work of God in creating differentiated humanity. But the work of Christ does bring about reconciliation, and Betz is correct in saying that, for Paul, oneness in Christ is salvation.[46] Oneness does not mean sameness but equality and communion with each other. Man and woman do not just have response-ability toward God (and therefore communion) through language, they also have mutual response-ability to one another through differentiation.

The work of Christ recreates the likeness and image of God in man and woman that was distorted through sin. Sexual differences and patriarchal structures per se are not the issue; sexual differences and patriarchal structures that produce discrimination against sexual uniqueness are. In Paul's mind the absence of distinction between males and females in Christ prompted him—for an additional reason—to reject circumcision, because it excludes women from bearing the sign of the covenant.[47] Circumcision is instituted as the sign of the Abrahamic covenant; it is

44. Westermann, *Genesis 1–11*, 148–51.

45. See my work on Paul as a pro-woman theologian (re: 1 Corinthians 11 and 14), *What Has Jerusalem to Do with Beijing?* 262–308

46. Betz, *Galatians*, 197.

47. The practice of circumcision seems to be about marking the Jewish man's sexual organ different from others. It is this religious rite that authenticates male identity as Jewish, but it excludes, besides the Gentile world, the other half of Judaism—the female.

narrated in Genesis 17, which Paul never refers to in Galatians.[48] Rather, Paul highlights the faith of Abraham (and thus the faith of believers in Christ), the gift of the Spirit, and the sign of the cross (of dying and rising with Christ) as the impartial means for men and women, Jews and Greeks, slave and free to be heirs of God. "Oneness in Christ" speaks of the equality between males and females. The new reality in Christ does not dissolve ethnic, social, or sexual differences and distinctions. It overcomes the barriers and the domination that exists in such differences and distinctions.

✣ Universal Concerns in Paul's Interpretation

Paul's concept of being "in Christ" is powerful. It is a concept that transcends the biases and limitations of words and cultural perceptions and it runs through the whole of his letter to the Galatians. By using "sons" (3:7, 26; 4:5, 6) to refer to believers Paul wants to stress the associated meanings of adoption (4:5) and heirs (4:7). The term *hyiothesia* (adoption) in the writings of Paul (Rom 8:15, 23; 9:4; Gal 4:5; cf. Eph 1:5) has its social and legal background. Any adoption process involves the legal right of a person (whatever the former status, whether poor, classless or slave) to have the full privileges and status of a son (or daughter). The father must treat the adopted son as his very own. Adopted sons cannot be returned to or claimed back by their natural parents. And most importantly, adopted sons are heirs to the family inheritance.[49] Analogously, those who have been adopted into "the realm of Christ Jesus" are free. Paul says that for such adoption into the family of God "neither circumcision nor uncircumcision is of any worth" (Gal 5:6). The term "sons" speaks of privilege, honor, right, status, and a relationship within the Abrahamic

---

48. While Paul does not deal with Genesis 17 directly in Galatians, he does discuss the circumcision issue in 3:10–11. It is likely that in 3:10–11 Paul is refuting the opponents' claim that works of the law (such as circumcision) constitute the only visible sign of anyone in the Abrahamic covenant. Paul quotes (with little change) LXX Deut 27:26 and shows that his opponents are wrong: "Cursed be everyone who does not abide in everything written in the book of the law, and do them" (3:10; RSV). In the MT, Deut 27:26 reads: "Cursed be the one who does not abide the words of this law by doing them" (RSV).

49. Matera, *Galatians*, 151.

covenant and with God. Regardless of gender, ethnicity, or class, all are "sons" or heirs of God and of the Abrahamic covenant (3:7).

The sign of that covenant is faith, a sign with which anyone and everyone can identify. Paul uses phrases, such as "those who from faith" (*hoi ek pisteōs*, Gal 3:7), or "those through faith in Jesus Christ" (Gal 2:16), to qualify the condition necessary for maintaining one's membership within this covenant of grace. He uses "those" (emphatic *houtoi* in Gal 3:7) to refer to both men and women as genderless "sons" of Abraham. He employs the seemingly exclusive Abrahamic covenant, yet he explains it as including Gentiles through faith in Christ (Gal 3:8). In that verse (3:8) Paul quotes Gen. 12:3 and 18:18 to speak of the blessing of Abraham, yet he changes the LXX quotation from "all tribes" (*phylai*) to "all nations/Gentile" (*ethnē*) to include especially the Gentiles (Gal 3:8). He believes that the concept of "the descendants [seed] of Abraham" is still a valid one in the age of Christ, but he reinterprets the collective "seed" as singular "Seed," to designate Christ, and he argues how all humanity are descendants (seeds) of Abraham through that one Seed (Gal 3:16). When Paul uses "seed" in a collective sense, the anarthrous singular ("seed" in Gal 3:29) is used; when he refers to "seed" in a singular sense, the articular singular ("the seed" in Gal 3:16, 19) is used to point to the person of Jesus the Messiah. "God is one" (3:20) emphasizes the oneness of the created family, made up of Jews and Gentiles. Hence, "Moses is not the mediator of the 'one family.'"[50]

For Paul the marks that identified him as a follower of Christ were the scars he bore of persecution (2 Cor 4; cf. Gal 6:17). But in Galatians, he clearly believed that anyone truly in Christ bore the fruit of the Spirit, since faith itself was a work and a gift and a sign of the Spirit.

Confucius on Women, Bie *and* Zhengming

✧ *Junzi*, Ancestor Worship, and Women

Leaving the world of Paul we turn to that of Confucius. Though the issues in both cultures are different, both Paul and Confucius share similar view on holding to the tension between *differentiation and mutuality*, uniqueness and equality—of course, they use their own words, such as

---

50. Wright, *The Climax of the Covenant*, 170.

the "no 'male and female,'" and "one in Christ" of Paul as we have just seen. Confucius uses the language of *bie* (differentiation) and *zhengming* (proper naming). To show their connection is our task at hand.

It is generally thought that Confucianism was a conservative movement and that it was unlikely Confucius himself had an open attitude toward women. Confucius was not critical of the patriarchal assumptions within ancestor worship, but his understanding of ancestor worship was grounded on his moral philosophy of *xiaoti*.[51] The ritual practiced according to this philosophy is called *jici*, and it includes making a sacrifice to the dead as though they were alive. Confucius says, "Death is unknowable because even life is unknowable," and "We do not yet know how to serve people, how can we serve the spirit" (*Analects* 11:12).[52] For this reason, Confucius advocates the practice of propriety toward the living and the dead. In Confucius' philosophy, the ritual of sacrificing to one's ancestors is an act of gratitude that leads to the formation of *ren*.[53]

Because the Chinese worldview holds that children and women do not possess full personhood as adult males do, dead infants and single women are rarely sacrificed to and seldom remembered in the rite of ancestral worship. This ancient worldview is expressed in the old script for the word "ancestor," made up of two pictograms, one resembles the male sexual organ (且), the other the Earth god (示). These are some of the cultural limitations amid the ideals of Chinese culture.

❧ Confucius and Women

Confucius is often perceived as a misogynist. It is true that the *Analects* never mentions a female disciple, and Confucius's discussion of *junzi* is "sexist" (in the modern sense) at least in its English translation, "gentle-

51. The English term "ancestor worship" is taken from Latin terminology, "Manes worship." In Chinese semantics, however, the word "worship" does not appear. The Chinese word used is *jing* (respect) or *ji* (offer sacrifice). It denotes reverence and respect shown in the offering of sacrifices before the spirits or the gods. See Yeo, "The Rhetorical Hermeneutic of 1 Corinthians 8 and Chinese Ancestor Worship," 298–311; idem, *Jizu Misi*, passim.

52. My translation. See Qian, *Lunyu Xinjie*, 389; Yang, *Lunyu Yizhu*, 247.

53. The rite of death is an expression of the living toward the dead, but in a mutual sense; e.g., the ritual of mourning, not only express one's love for the departed, the ritual itself comforts the mourners as they publicly share their emotions among their loved ones.

man." But in Chinese, although the words *junzi* most commonly refer to son(s) (*zi*) of a noble lord (*jun*), the word *zi* can also be used to refer to women. The masculine *junzi*, as it is commonly understood, may reflect the patriarchy of Chinese society, but Ames and Rosemont contend that "there is at least some evidence that women could be regarded as having some of the same qualities of the *junzi* at the time of, or shortly after, the composition of the *Analects*."[54] Since a Chinese word by itself does not indicate number (singular or plural) or gender (masculine or feminine), to translate *junzi* as "gentleman" is inaccurate. A *junzi* is a cultured person, meaning an exemplary person, male or female, whose virtue serves to transform others.[55] A *junzi* is the most excellent human being, he or she can become a *shengren*, or a sage.

Confucius had a mother, a wife, and a daughter (*Analects* 5:1). He had a critical and detached attitude toward Nanzi, the politically powerful and licentious wife of Duke Ling of Wei. It may be in this context that Confucius said, "Women and *xiaren* [morally immature persons] are difficult to deal with, they become insolent if you stay near them, and they become resentful if you keep a distance" (*Analects* 17: 24).[56] The *Analects* are sayings of Confucius, and the context of each saying is difficult to reconstruct. To interpret 17:24 as a blanket statement of Confucius in condemning all women is erroneous. If the word "woman" in 17:24 is not referring to Nanzi, then it is more likely to have a narrower reference than all women. Huang, a commentator of the *Analects*, suggests that "women" here refers to concubines and maid servants and *xiaoren* refers to men servants or eunuchs: "This was an admonition for those who possessed a state [*sic*: an estate] or a noble house."[57]

Less known is Confucius' repeated praise for the woman of Ji outside the *Analects*, i.e., in *Lienu Zhuan* (*Commentary on Women*), *Guoyu* (*National Language*), *Hanshi Waizhuan* (*Exoteric Commentary on the Han School*), *Zhanguo Ce* (*Annals of the Warring States*), and *Liji* (*Record of Ritual*).[58] Confucius praised her for her understanding of *li* (ritual propriety) and of the distinction between men and women. Jing Jiang

---

54. Ames and Rosemont, *The Analects of Confucius*, 40.

55. Yang, *Lunyu Yizhu*, 4 interprets *junzi* to be persons who have virtues (*de*).

56. Cf. Yang, *Lunyu Yizhu*, 406.

57. Huang, *Analects*, 172.

58. Raphals, "A Woman Who Understood the Rites."

was "the woman of the Ji" in the state of Lu. She was the wife of Gongfu Mubo, the mother of Wenbo, and the paternal grandaughter of Ji Kangzi. Confucius most likely had direct contact with her because of his connection with the Ji family (see *Analects* 3:12, 6, 10–11; 6:8; 10:16; 11:17; 12:17–19; 17:1, 4–5). She was a learned woman, able to offer counsel on matters of the state, sacred ritual, the family, marriage, and the art of weaving. She had the courage and the wisdom to admonish her male colleagues when needed and she did so on several occasions. She arranged the marriage of her son, Wenbo. After her son's death, she managed his household.[59]

In her study of Jing Jiang, Lisa A. Raphals suggests that she was a woman who thought highly of Confucius and sent her son to be Confucius' disciple.[60] The intention here is not to argue that Confucius was a feminist—that would be anachronistic and inaccurate. But Raphals' study does raise the question whether the dominant interpretive tradition of the *Analects* and Confucianism is responsible for defining Confucianism as a conservative movement, and for editing out the "counter-cultural edge" in Confucius' gender ethics. Raphals notes that the *Hanshi Waizhuan* elaborates on the virtue of Jing Jiang, but the elaboration was ignored or distorted by the interpretive tradition. The interpretive tradition assumes that, if Jing Jiang was a virtuous woman, she must have mourned at her son's death. The *Hanshi Waizhuan* records her explanation: "Formerly I had this son of mine serve Zhongni [Confucius]. When Zhongni left Lu, my son did not go beyond the suburbs of the capital in sending him off; in making him presents, he did not give him the family's precious objects."[61] Because her son did not respect Confucius according to the propriety of the day, Jing Jiang did not mourn his death. She did not feel the loss of a virtuous son. Raphals also argues, based on the *Zhanguo Ce* version of the Jing Jiang story, that Confucius praised her for being an excellent teacher of her son Wenbo (despite his ultimate disobedience to study), even though women at that time did not have a formal education concerning the self-cultivation of virtue. Raphals concludes, "The implication is that at least women, presumably mothers, are capable of effective teaching without explicit self-cultivation! An extraordinary

59. Ibid., 275–76.
60. See ibid., passim.
61. Ibid., 283.

gendering of virtue!"[62] Despite her example of virtue, the story of Jing Jiang does not appear in the *Analects*. Raphals concludes that

> She may have been able to achieve far more of the learning and status of a *junzi* than would normally have been permitted to, or recognized in, a woman. In this sense, her preeminence was far too particular to be indicative of early Confucian views of the status or potential of women. It does suggest a degree of flexibility (especially in the treatment of elite women) that was to be lost or de-emphasized in later Classical Confucian and Neo-Confucian views of women.[63]

Raphals lifts up the story of an extraordinary woman in the time of Confucius. While the story cannot be used to portray the social norms of women at the time she lived, at least it suggests that their social world was not limited to doing household chores. As far as the cultivation of virtues is concerned, Confucius has an open attitude toward men and women, even though he sees the difference between them.

↬ *Bie*, Yin-Yang, Patriarchy, and *Zhengming*

Confucius' view of the relationship between men and women is based on the notion of *bie* (別)—the distinction between male and female. Generally speaking, a woman's responsibilities are related to the household and to child-rearing, while a man's responsibilities include political and educational activities. While Confucianism may give the impression that it is family oriented, Confucius' personal life seemed to indicate otherwise. He would not sacrifice his work for the sake of his family. In fact, Confucius was not at home for the greater part of his adult life; and once when ill to the point of death, there is no indication that he wanted to be with his wife or daughter or son, he chose instead to be with his friends (as *Analects* 9:12 implies). Love in ancient China cannot be described as a kind of Hollywood romance.

In a manner similar to Paul's understanding of sexual differentiation (see the previous section "Gender Uniqueness and Mutuality"), Confucius believed that one's uniqueness makes one necessary to others and to the whole of society. Implied in his understanding of uniqueness is what oth-

62. Ibid., 284.
63. Ibid., 295.

ers do not have, thus making one's existence necessary and complementary to others. The dynamic interaction between the differences among individuals underlies the process of forming a wholesome community because interpersonal relationships, like all things, are constantly in flux. This understanding of uniqueness and wholeness is popular in the *yin-yang* worldview of change, *yi* or *bian* of Confucius' time. The *yin-yang* worldview sees reality—including cosmic and anthropological realities—as relatedness in change. According to the *Classic of Changes* (*Yijing*), the word *yi* (a pictogram consisting of "sun" and "moon") means chameleon, and the words *yin* and *yang* mean respectively the shaded and sun-lit slopes of mountains. The metaphysical meaning of *yi* as change is derived from the interaction between the sun and the moon, which produce a myriad of shaded and sun-lit areas. The *Classic of Changes* says, "The yin and yang are correlated with the moon and the sun" and "creative yang and the receptive yin are the gateway to change."[64] The idea of the perdurance of all things is integral to the ancient Chinese worldview Confucius believes in when he writes, "Like the river, everything is flowing on ceaselessly, day and night" (*Analects* 9:16). *Yi* (changes) happen in nature and also in human relationships. The dynamic of *yin* and *yang*, that is, male and female, is understood metaphorically as part of the cosmic process of change whose goal is to produce wholeness (*Taiji*). If there were no *yin* and *yang*, nothing would come into being and there would be no wholeness. *Yin* and *yang* each occupies half of the complete circle; they are different from each other to warrant interaction, and they are interactive enough to produce wholeness.

That which is true of the cosmos is also true of human relationships. *Yin* and *yang* are customarily used to refer to female and male relationships, including sexual intercourse. The differences in *yin* and *yang* become creative; in the intercourse of male and female, new life is produced. Because they are in relationship, *yin* (female) needs *yang* (male) to be *yin* and vice versa, neither can exist without the other. *Yin* has part of *yang*, and *yang* has part of *yin*; or, *yin* is in *yang* and *yang* is in *yin*; *yin* (female) is the opposite but not the antagonist of *yang* (male), since the two halves are mutually complementary. Male and female are in mutuality, interdependence, and reciprocity. *Yin* is not inferior to yang; the two are simply

---

64. Ta chuan, sec. 1, chap. 16. Technically, *yin* means the shaded area, and *yang* means the sunlit slope of a mountain, cf. Yeo, "The 'Yin and Yang' of God (Exod 3:14) and Humanity (Gen 1:27)."

different—a difference that brings about an interaction through which wholeness is achieved.

The relationship between female and male and between parents and children is hierarchical but dynamic and contradistinctive. Modern society seems to adore egalitarianism and hate hierarchy. But in pre-modern societies such as ancient China, hierarchy existed (ideally) neither to dominate nor to abuse. In Confucius' thought, hierarchy was necessary for the purpose of role distinction. By it one knows how to relate to others properly and civilly. In Confucius' thinking, hierarchical relationships are dynamic, and distinctive relationships change depending on context. Parents are benefactors, children are beneficiaries—when parents are young, and the children are young. Henry Rosemont continues the illustration as he writes, "When they [parents] are aged and infirm, I [a child] become their benefactor, and the converse holds for my children. I am a benefactor to my friend when she needs my help, a beneficiary when I need hers."[65] In a person's lifetime, he is going to have the role both of the beneficiary and of the benefactor, the parent and the child, of giving and receiving friendship. These manifold roles required of interpersonal relations, which are both dynamic and changing, define who people are as human beings. The better they are able to relate to others in building others up, the better it will be for themselves in walking the "path of humanity" (*rendao*).

Confucian thought believes that the process of life itself, from infancy to adulthood, is a ritual of self-cultivation, of becoming fully human within the web of complex and changing relationships. Human beings express their personhood (and their humanity) only in a social context and also in a specific role, as a parent, a daughter, a friend, a male, or a female, and so forth. There are many ways of being a friend, but there are ways that fall outside the proper behavior of friends, according to the Confucian understanding of propriety. There are ritualized behaviors that both men and women can practice to create an orderly society. Ritualized behaviors are the training ground to form people to be fully human. These ritualized behaviors are called *zhengming*—befitting to one's name—knowing and behaving as one's name prescribes, viz., as a

---

65. Rosemont, "On Confucian Civility," 190.

ruler, a parent, a friend, etc.[66] There is no discrepancy between description and prescription in a name according to the idea of *zhengming*.

Zhengming, behavior befitting of names, refers to the cultivation of virtues that authenticate our humaneness. *Analects* 12:11 reads, "the prince princes, the minister ministers, the father fathers, the son sons."[67] Fingarette explains,

> inherited status is neither necessary nor sufficient to be a prince. Princes who do not prince, i.e., who do not act in relation to their subjects as princes should, may properly be viewed as not authentic princes at all. And on the other hand persons who can act properly as ruler or minister can on that basis be entitled to the status, even if not born into that status. The chief criterion of status is neither birth nor formal office but conduct.[68]

As *Analects* 13:3 explains, if names are not used properly and taken seriously, language loses its power to communicate and tasks remain undone.[69] A name is not simply a word or a concept, but a realized behavior because of the status of the name. Performance of duty as entailed in the name is what matters (see *Analects* 12:11; 13:10).

Confucius' understanding of *zhengming* (names properly used) in the larger cultural context of female-male (*yin-yang*) relations is based upon the uniqueness of social roles. He believes that these differences among human beings make it necessary for everyone to fulfill their position in a society; all are interrelated and complementary to one another for their common good. Coming from a different culture and theological conviction, Paul shares a similar vision of uniqueness in mutuality for different gender and social roles—male and female, Jews and Greeks, slaves and free are one in Christ.

---

66. *Analects* 6:25; 11:16; 12:11; and 13:3.

67. Fingarette, "The Music of Humanity in the *Conversations (Analects)* of Confucius," 335.

68. Ibid., 338. See *Analects* 6:7; 11:23; 14:12, when the qualifications of political leaders were questioned.

69. Lau, trans., *Analects*, 132. See Chen, *Lunyu Duxun Jiegu*, 231–32; Yang, *Lunyu Yizhu*, 287–88.

TOWARD A CHINESE CHRISTIAN UNDERSTANDING OF HUMAN NATURE AND MORAL FREEDOM

The goal of Confucius and Paul to affirm difference/uniqueness and mutuality/oneness is to envision a society where freedom might be achieved for all. This vision assumes that human beings are created equally and for freedom. However, there is a difference between Confucius' view and Paul's view on moral freedom and human nature.

Human Nature and Moral Weakness

ᴥ Confucius' View

We have already seen in Chapter Four Confucius' understanding of human nature—all human beings are born with a similar nature; "nurture" shapes their potentiality differently (*Analects* 6:19, 17:2). The contrast Confucius makes between *junzi* (best moral self) and *xiaoren* (immature moral self) (4:11, 16, 24; 13:7, 37; 13:23, 25, 26; 14:6; 15:24; 16:8) indicates that, in his mind, whereas all human beings are endowed with the same inclination toward goodness, the environment and habituation may cause some to give in to weakness, while others learn to overcome weakness and to do good. Because *xiaoren* (immature moral selves) fail to habituate themselves in virtue, they are incapable of making moral choices; they live in bondage. *Junzi* (the best of moral selves) persist in virtue cultivation, therefore they have resources to make correct moral decisions and live in freedom.

Confucius believes in education and learning, and he believes that morality can be taught. Confucius sees the equality of human beings as (1) the equality of the possibility for actualizing oneself, and (2) the equality of the value of the human being qua human being.[70] Confucius and his disciple Mencius (371–286 BCE) are not of the opinion that a person begins life with his nature completely formed. They often speak of the "seed" or the "beginning" (*tuan*) of human nature. Because of this assumption, they develop an ethical system that helps people to actualize their full moral potential within the Confucian definition of proper relationships.

70. Hsieh, "The Status of the Individual in Chinese Ethics," 310.

Confucius believes that human nature is not morally weak; he never speaks of human nature as evil. *Analects* 5:10 and 6:12 are good texts to support this view. In *Analects* 5:10 we read,

> Zai Yu slept during the day. The Master said: 'Rotten wood is beyond carving; a dung-and-mud wall is beyond plastering. As for Yu, what is the use of reprimanding him?' The Master said: 'At first, my attitude toward men was to hear their words and believe in their deeds. Now my attitude toward men is to hear their words and observe their deeds. It was due to Yu that I have changed this.'[71]

Even though these two sayings of Confucius are found in one verse, most scholars suspect that they were said in two different settings. In any case, we can see that Confucius' judgment of Zai Yu changed. First he chastises Zai Yu and says that he is beyond teaching and reforming. But in the second saying Confucius declares he is now more careful in passing judgment, waiting until after he has heard a person and seen his works.

In *Analects* 6:12, Ran Qiu responds to Confucius, "It is not your way that does not commend itself to me, but that it demands powers I do not possess." The Master replied, "He whose strength gives out collapses during the course of the journey; but you deliberately draw the line"[72] (6:12). Is virtue for Confucius then: (a) *knowing* what is right and doing it, or (b) a *moral force* that causes one to do the right and good thing? In the former case, Zai Yu claims to know his moral obligations but lacks the moral force to fulfill them. The problem with Zai Yu is that he does nothing (such as to seek instruction) for his moral "weakness." He claims not to possess the proper moral will. Virtue, such as benevolence, is not far away. Confucius says, "If I want benevolence, then benevolence is here!" (*Analects* 7:30).

Many Confucianists believe that human nature is endowed by Heaven (*Doctrine of Mean* 1:1).[73] Following Mencius they argue that human nature is good—at least in orientation or potentiality, if not in actuality. Just as the tendency of water is to flow downward, humanity is born

---

71. Huang, *Analects*, 74.

72. My translation.

73. *Doctrine of Mean* (*Zhongyong*) 1:1. Legge and Yang, trans., *The Four Books*, 24–25.

with a propensity toward goodness (*Mencius* 6a.2).[74] The shoot (*tuan*) of goodness is innate in one's nature, thus institutions and social conditions can only bend one's nature. In contrast to Mencius' idea of human nature as inherently good, Xunzi (298–238 BCE) believes that human nature is evil but that it can be corrected by education.[75] The debate between Xunzi and Mencius may be caused by their different definitions of "nature" (*xing*):

> Mencius said, The fact that human beings learn shows that their nature is good. I say this is not so; this comes of his having neither understood human nature nor perceived the distinction between the nature and conscious activity. The nature is what is given by Heaven: one cannot learn it; one cannot acquire it by effort. Ritual and rightness are created by sages: people learn them and are capable, through effort, of bringing them to completion. What cannot be learned or acquired by effort but is within us is called the nature. What can be learned and, through effort, brought to completion is called conscious activity.[76]

Xunzi argues that human beings are not born with virtues. Therefore he emphasizes ritual rather than *ren* as the way for human beings to cultivate themselves. Whether good or evil, the essence of human nature may not be the relevant question; the Confucianist tradition misses the more pertinent question of power of sin in the world. It does not investigate into the captivating power of sin on the human heart because Confucianists assume that the nature of a self-contained universe and the nature of human beings are similar. Confucius and Mencius think of the nature as goodness, whereas Xunzi thinks of it as evil. But, all three think of good and evil in an *ethical* sense. Even in Xunzi's speculation of "evil

74. Legge and Yang, trans., *The Four Books*, 470–71.

75. Xunzi writes, "The nature of human is evil, what is good in him is artificial" (My translation). "One is born with the desires of the ears and eyes and with a fondness for beautiful sights and sounds, and, by indulging these, one is led to licentiousness and chaos, so that the sense of ritual, rightness, refinement, and principle with which one was born is lost. Hence, following human nature and indulging human emotions will inevitably lead to contention and strife, causing one to rebel against one's proper duty, reduce principle to chaos, and revert to violence. Therefore one must be transformed by the example of a teacher and guided by the way of ritual and rightness before one will attain modesty and yielding, accord with refinement and ritual, and return to order. From this perspective it is apparent that human nature is evil and that its goodness is the result of conscious activity" (Bloom, trans., "Xunzi," 1:180).

76. Bloom, trans., "Xunzi," 1:180.

human nature," one is surprised to find a moral optimism that believes ritual propriety can lead one to goodness.

The debate between goodness and evil of human nature is not as important as the discussion of the power of sin and evil. The Confucianist semantic domain of "sin" and "evil" is an ethical one, education and philosophy are therefore the remedies to the problems of sin and evil. Confucianists assume humans, either lacking innate defects or without power of sin, are malleable and perfectible through external will or social conditioning. Confucian tradition understands human beings to be born equal, with the same potential of becoming a "best moral self." Habituation and social environment make people different. Confucius assumes that *tian* (Heaven) endows all with the resource to become benevolent, the highest virtue that characterizes moral freedom. Even though the path to moral perfection is difficult, education by means of virtue cultivation will overcome moral weakness. However, when we turn to Paul we see that the Apostle is not as hopeful as Confucius regarding human endeavor as the way to achieve moral freedom and perfection.

ᴥ Paul's View

Paul has a different understanding of moral weakness and the "moral self" because his understanding of God differs from Confucius' understanding of *tian* (Heaven). Unlike Confucius' natural anthropology, in which *tian* endows everyone with the potential for moral perfection (best moral self), Paul has a spiritual anthropology. Without God's Spirit, Paul sees human beings incapable of achieving moral freedom, since the binding force of the "evil age" and sin render human beings helpless. Without God's Spirit, people are incapable of being free human beings, of being virtuous, of doing good, of loving God and their neighbor. Murphy-O'Connor makes the connection between "sin" in Rom 7:20 ("Now if I do what I do not want, it is no longer I that do it, but sin which dwells within me") and "dangers" in 2 Cor 11:26 ("During my frequent journeys I have been exposed to dangers from rivers, dangers from brigands, dangers from my own people, dangers from Gentiles, dangers in the town and in the country, dangers at sea, dangers at the hands of false brothers"). He writes, "Manifestly Sin in these texts is a symbol or a myth expressive of a world in which individuals were forced to be other than they desired to be; the authentic self was alienated (Rom 7:20). From his own experience as a traveling missionary, Paul learned that people were not selfish because they chose to be. They were forced to be egocentric in order to survive. Their pattern of behavior was dictated by irresistible societal pressures. They were controlled by a force greater than any individual, namely the value system which had developed within their society."[77]

In Gal 6:7–8 Paul addresses the ethical life and its consequences: "Do not be deceived; God is not mocked, for whatever a person sows, this he will also reap. The one who sows to his own flesh will reap corruption from the flesh, and the one who sows to the Spirit will reap eternal life from the Spirit." The exhortation is directed to the members of the Galatian community, to live authentically with themselves, with God, and with the Spirit.[78] "Sowing in the flesh" means giving into or concentrating on the desires of the flesh, whether food or drink or sex or transient "beauty." To these circumcision could well be added. The natural principle of sowing and harvesting applies to the religious and moral life as well: sowing in the flesh produces corruption, and sowing in the Spirit produces the fruit of the Spirit, which is eternal life. The contrast between the flesh and the Spirit was noted previously to speak of the two powers under which a person lives. The phrase "his own flesh" (Gal 6:8) here is odd. It may refer to circumcision—not the act of being circumcised but to what "circumcision" signifies, that is, membership in the people of God. This makes sense when it is read in the context of the "corruption of the flesh" and "eternal life from the Spirit." In other words, he who depends on circumcision to maintain his status as a member of God's people will end up in death; he who depends on the Spirit to do so will receive eternal life. The sowing and reaping imagery suggests the natural cycle of cause and effect; the focus here is not on human endeavor, rather the emphasis is on that to which one intentionally submits, the realm in which he walks and lives.

The contrast between "corruption" (*phthora*) and "eternal life" (*zōēn aiōnion*) suggests mortality and resurrected life respectively (Gal 6:8).[79] If so, this point advances Paul's argument that the new life in Christ ushers the new age of salvation for both Jews and Gentiles, a sign of which is the

77. Murphy-O'Connor, *Paul, A Critical Life*, 101.

78. It is self-deceiving to think one can outwit God. God cannot be "mocked" (*mykterizein*), i.e., "treated with contempt."

79. See 1 Cor 15:42, 50; Rom 2:7; 5:21; 6:22–23.

endowment of the eschatological Spirit. The Spirit will in turn unite Jews and Gentiles as God's faithful, bear fruit to guide and empower the community, and finally grant them resurrected life. In contrast to "sowing to the Spirit" (*eis to pneuma*), sowing to circumcision ("his own flesh") brings forth corruption (Gal 6:8), partly because the realm of circumcision/the law is a realm without the Spirit ("works of the flesh" in Gal 5:19). Even though the play on the word "flesh" (circumcision and human existence without the Spirit) may be confusing, Paul has already shown through an allegorical interpretation in Gal 4:21–31 that those born "according to flesh" are also those who want to hold to circumcision and the law as carnal signs. It is not circumcision per se that Paul objects to, or its role in Judaism; it is rather circumcision as a requirement for membership in the people of God when Christ has shown that faith together with the Spirit—not the works of the law—bring about that membership. In the age of Christ "works of the flesh," are morally invalid for the people of God, because the Spirit of God is now in the eschatological age the giver of new life to a new and inclusive community.

Paul's understanding of existence in the flesh is that it is life without the Spirit. Betz explains the consequence of the works of the flesh,

> Previously Paul had associated "flesh" with circumcision and "the works of the flesh," but in Gal 6:8 he goes further. "Sowing into the flesh" is done by placing one's hope for salvation upon circumcision and obedience to the Jewish Torah, a move which would result in missing salvation altogether (cf. 5:2–12). But the same harvest can be reaped by letting the "works of the flesh" flourish (cf. 5:19–21). A life thus corrupted by the "flesh" cannot "inherit the Kingdom of God" (5:21). In this sense, "sowing into the flesh" means nothing less than "giving an opportunity to the flesh" (5:13), and the very opposite of "crucifying the flesh" (5:24). In either case, the end will be "eternal annihilation."[80]

The consequence to those under the law, those who hold to circumcision and are born without the promise of the Spirit, is slavery. In terms of the moral life, existence without the Spirit results in "fornication, immorality, licentiousness, idolatry, sorcery, enmity, strife, jealousy, anger, selfishness, dissension, factions, envy, drunkenness, carousing, and things like these"

---

80. Betz, *Galatians*, 308–9.

(Gal 5:19–21).[81] "Works of the flesh" denotes the consequence of living under the power of sin and not in the realm of the Spirit. Paul's idea of freedom in the Spirit is unique, one not shared by Confucius' ethical belief that all can live a life of freedom if they but attend to self-cultivation. It is significant to note that, despite the spiritual anthropology of Paul, he shares similar ethical views of Confucius that imperatives are necessary for Christian training of one's moral and spiritual life. Paul understands the fruit of the Spirit not as "virtue" but as divine gift, yet he gives positive and negative imperatives to the Galatian Christians. Though God's grace empowers human effort, it does not take the place of believers' active obedience.

Moral Freedom

⊷ People of God in the Life of the Spirit:
Positive and Negative Freedom

Freedom in Galatians is about freedom from the constraint (negative freedom) of evil and sin, and freedom of life in the community (positive freedom). Galatians 5:1–6 defines for its Gentile readers the new reality of freedom for which Christ redeemed them. The God who calls them has a goal to which they are called: *ep' eleutheria* ("to freedom"), i.e., freedom from the burden of circumcision, the curse of the law, the bondage of sin, and freedom for life in the Spirit, that is, the blessings and righteousness of being in Christ. God's creation of a new humanity in Christ is the work of the Spirit for the sake of the freedom of all.

The danger facing the Christians in Galatia was that they misunderstood the freedom in Christ for the license to do whatever they pleased. Paul warns the readers what not to do and what to do with their new freedom: "Only do not let your freedom become an opportunity for the flesh, but through love be enslaved to one another" (Gal 5:13).

Negative Freedom and the Negative Imperative ⊷ The purpose of God's giving freedom to believers was not to allow "the flesh" to become a sprouting ground of sin. As used in Gal 5:1–26 the word "flesh" has the negative

81. See the section "Living in the Spirit and Becoming *Junzi* and *Renren*" in Chapter Four (pp. 285–91).

connotation of life without the Spirit and in opposition to the realm of the Spirit. The word "flesh" in the negative imperatives in Gal 5:13 ("opportunity for the flesh") and 5:16 ("do not gratify the desires of the flesh) is not a purely anthropological term in the neutral sense. "Flesh" and the "desires of the flesh" refer to neither the carnal aspect of human existence nor the "irredeemable" portions of a human body. Rather, "flesh" is understood in terms of the negative and enslaving power of sin and evil. The human propensity is to live without dependence on God or other people, thus under the negative power of sin and death. The self-centeredness of human beings can be wrongly perceived as freedom, yet it only results in the intensification of the power of sin. For Paul there is no such state as freedom independent of sin or of God; there is only a realm either under God or under sin. Human existence is dependent on one or the other, and the consequences are righteousness and freedom under the realm of God, sin and bondage under the realm of sin. Those who think they can be free independently are actually allowing sin to control their lives; sin will dominate their creaturely existence.

Positive Freedom and the Positive Imperative ✎ In Paul's thought, freedom by definition cannot be used for its own ends. In contrast to negative freedom, Paul has a distinctly spiritual understanding of freedom.[82] Human existence without the guidance of the Spirit is at best self-gratifying and self-absorbing, at worst self-binding and self-destructive. The role of the Spirit is essential in guiding and energizing those who are in Christ, enabling them to live a life of freedom in service to one another. It is this spiritual freedom that occupies Paul's thought in Gal 5:13–26. Those who walk according to the Spirit comprise the community in Christ. The positive imperative is that the Galatians should "walk by the Spirit" (5:16).[83] Here the "Spirit" refers to God's Spirit, which was promised as the eschatological gift for Jews and Gentiles. The role of the Spirit is to bring forth a new community, characterized by love, the consequence of which is bearing the fruits of the Spirit. The Spirit guides the community of Christ to live in freedom and to love God and one another; the Spirit

82. The theme of the Spirit is introduced in Gal 3:2–5. Paul discusses the role of the Spirit in 3:14; 4:6, 29, as well as 5:16–18, 22, 25; 6:1, 8.

83. Paul's thought here has its parallel in the Jewish understanding that those under the law walk (*halak*) by the law (Lev 26:3; Deut 5:33; 11:22; 26:17; 28:9; Pss 1:1–2; 81:33; 86:11). So walking is a metaphor that points to the practice of life or to one's lifestyle.

not only overcomes the controlling power of the flesh, it also binds the community in freedom.

Moral Choice Between Spirit and Flesh ⮞ The reason for the incompatibility of Spirit and flesh lies in their opposing nature: "For the desires of the flesh are against the Spirit, and the Spirit are against the flesh" (Gal 5:17a). These two powers have directly opposite functions: the Spirit of God liberates, saves, empowers, guides, grants life and righteousness; the desires of the flesh control, deceive, deprive, limit, confuse, and kill. Therefore, these two spheres or powers cannot coexist in any community of faith. Since the Spirit and the flesh represent two different realms, Paul argues that the Galatians cannot assume they can do whatever they want (5:17b). They cannot run back and forth between the realms of the Spirit and the flesh, neither can they live without both. The Galatians must chose the Spirit,[84] for not choosing the Spirit is by default to live in the flesh.

⮞ Following the Spirit toward the Freedom of Community

The communal context of freedom is basic in both Confucius' and Paul's teachings. We have seen that Confucius' teaching of *junzi* (best moral self) and *xiaoren* (immature moral self) has to do with one's virtuous life. It is the virtuous life that builds up the community. For Paul the relational ethics of loving those within the body of Christ and the spiritual ethics of following the Spirit have their consequences in the freedom of a community.

We have seen in the last section that the result of the dominion of the flesh is self-centeredness and therefore divisiveness within the community. However, living in the realm of the Spirit means life and freedom for the community. Those who identify with the crucified Messiah gain freedom from the power of bondage, sin, and evil: "Those who belong to Christ have crucified the flesh with its passions and desires" (Gal 5:24).[85] Paul asked the Galatian readers to follow the Spirit and not to do anything that would divide the community: "If we live by the Spirit let us also

---

84. Similarly Matera, *Galatians*, 200, 207.

85. In Rom 6:6 Paul's language is that the "old self" (*ho palaios hemon anthrōpos*) was crucified with Christ.

follow the Spirit. Let us not be conceited, provoking one another, being envious of one another" (5:25–26).

Living in the realm of the Spirit means that believers have to be obedient to the Spirit's leading, and as believers to walk (*stoichein*) in the Spirit. There is no need to be conceited, to provoke one another, or to be envious of others. The promise of blessings to the heirs of Abraham eliminates any need for jealousy or boasting. The presence of God's Spirit in the life of the faithful eliminates strife and dissension in the community. What is meant by "walking in the Spirit" is seen in the two words *peripateite* and *stoichōmen*, used respectively in Gal 5:16 and 5:25. The former has the sense of letting the Spirit direct or control;[86] the latter conveys Paul's desire that the community of faith keep in step with the leading of the Spirit.[87] Paul is exhorting the believers to constantly make the decision to yield themselves to the Spirit. The preservation of unity within a diverse community—such as one that is made up of Jews and Gentiles—could only be realized when those who believe in God realize the truth of living (*zōmen*) in the power of God's Spirit.

✎ Spirit in Paul's Ethics Insightful to Confucius

This discussion of Paul's ethics enables us to see the one weak point in the ethics of Confucius. Confucius' silence concerning human finitude and the power of sin may be due to naive assumptions about human reality. It may be this ignorance that led his ethics into a form of moralism. Even with a charitable reading of both Confucius' creative *tian* (Heaven) cosmology and his concept of the dynamic of *ren* (humaneness) in renewing old traditions, his ethics do not sufficiently take into account the darkness and evil inherent in principalities and powers in the world. Paul's theological ethics, specifically that of the Spirit and the flesh, provide a corrective to this weakness in Confucian ethics. I simply mention two

86. *Peripateō* in Gal 5:16 is used in a figurative sense to refer to how one lives or conducts one's life. In the instance here, "to live one's life" or "to walk in the Spirit" is to "let your conduct be directed by the Spirit." Since the verb is a present active indicative, it has the meaning of continuously allowing the Spirit to control or to direct (5:18 *agesthe*) the various activities of one's life.

87. The word *stoichōmen* in 5:25 implies the more rigid sense of "moving in a definite line." Ridderbos, *The Epistle of Paul to the Churches of Galatia*, 210 n. 24: "as in military formations or in dancing."

assumptions of Confucian ethics, viz., self-cultivation as remedy to social ills and moral deficiency as "evil."

Firstly, Confucius believes that history (the past dynasties) have already demonstrated that peace and order and prosperity are possible in this world, so the task of self-cultivation is to emulate the sages of the past. He believes that human nature is good, that it has been so endowed by heaven, and that self-cultivation is the means for realizing the divine gift of goodness to its fullness. He believes that ethics is the best solution to all the problems of his day. His ethical system is an attempt to overcome the political chaos and violence of his times. The ethical life is the fulfillment of the mandate of heaven; it is the mandate of heaven that humans be moral beings.

Confucius' views concerning rites (in *li*) and social obligations (in *ren*) were revolutionary to a culture that used rites to reinforce the self-interests of the ruling elites. He democratizes the principle of the divine right of the "son of the elite" (*junzi*) and reinterprets the title *junzi* to be the right of everyone to be his best moral self. Central to Confucius' ethical teachings is "a firm belief in the universal perfectibility of all."[88] Everyone can become a sage—at least in theory.[89] Confucius also taught that rulers should rule by virtue and not by force.[90]

In contrast, Paul acknowledges that there is nothing new about the cultivation of virtue (cf. Romans 1–2). Pagans (the Gentiles) have known for long about the moral life within an ethical system. It is written in their conscience (Rom 2:15). For Paul, however, neither the conscience nor the Torah of Judaism has the power to bring about righteousness. They only have the power to bring about condemnation. The Christian, says Paul, believes that God has called him to live the holy life in imitation of Christ through the power of the Holy Spirit in order to have fellowship with God as Father and with His son Jesus Christ. For Paul, self-cultivation is not a solution to the problem of sin. Self-cultivation *may* have its role in

---

88. Bodde, "Harmony and Conflict in Chinese Philosophy," 44.

89. Ibid., 45: "All men may become a Yao or a Shun (legendary sage-rulers)" (*Mencius* 6b.2).

90. Confucius' teachings are greatly distorted: emperors use Confucianism to subdue their subjects, elite groups dominate lower classes, his teachings are turned into rigid rules. Confucius prized social harmony, and harmony with oneself under the mandate of heaven. But Confucius does not condone an emperor's rule by force. To govern by virtue (*de*) is Confucius's first principle of politics. Confucius condemned war, for it disrupts the harmony of the cosmic pattern, and it causes pain and suffering to people.

the life of a believer *only after* the arrival of faith through repentance of sin, and even then, cultivation is always subsumed under the power of the Spirit. Paul's theology is clear: because human beings are sinful, they require the grace of God for their salvation.

Secondly, Confucianists understand that evil and goodness are not opposing forces. For example, death is not evil because it is an integral part of the cosmic process. Just as *yang* and *yin* interact for the sake of wholeness (*Taiji*), goodness without evil would mean that goodness had no counterpart with which to oscillate, and that harmony could not be actualized. Evil in the moral sense refers to the occasional departure from "the harmonious centrality of all things . . . because of [one's] inadequate understanding of the cosmic pattern."[91] Evil is going against the mandate of heaven—the mandate for all to be virtuous (*ming mingde*).[92]

To the contrary, Paul does not idealize human beings and the conditions they live in. For Paul evil is real, its force enslaves all and makes them impotent to be virtuous. Paul argues, quoting the Psalms, "No one is righteous, no not one!" (Rom 3:9) This is why he rejects the notion that an individual could keep the Law as Judaism (and formerly he himself) required.   Paul believes that salvation and damnation are real, in this world and in the next. In the former, an individual gains everything in Christ, including his freedom; in the latter, he loses everything and ends up in bondage to sin. While salvation enables a life of freedom uner the rightousness of God, damnation involves the destruction of self and of relationships with others because of the broken relationship one has with God. Only the work of Christ can overcome the evil aeon and the binding forces of the cosmic elements; human beings cannot defeat the power of sin and death. The Spirit of God can grant believers to live a life pleasing to God and grants them freedom.

A CHINESE CHRISTIAN THEOLOGY OF FREEDOM

Confucius' advocacy of becoming fully human through discipline is a helpful lens for reading Paul's theology. We will use the Confucian idea of the "fully human" as the "best moral self" (*junzi*) or the "humane person"

---

91. Bodde, "Harmony and Conflict in Chinese Philosophy," 40.
92. *Great Learning* 1:1. Legge and Yang, trans., *The Four Books*, 2–3.

(*renren*) to read Paul's ethics of freedom for others, that is, "through love be enslaved to one another" (5:13).

Freedom is understood both by Paul and by Confucius as directed toward others; once others are free, one will be free as well. This is especially true for Confucian ethics, which believes that the freedom of others and of oneself is freedom of all to be fully human. We will look to Confucius' articulation of this relational ethics and in turn use it to read Paul's understanding of the "freedom to serve."

Freedom, Goodness, and Benevolence

Freedom in Confucian ethics has to do with choosing goodness and benevolence (*ren*), particularly as related to the community. As Hsieh Yu-wei writes, "The freedom advocated in Confucian ethics is the freedom to do good or the freedom to choose what is good. It is ethical freedom of choice."[93] In the *Analects*, Confucius says, "When I walk alone with two others, they may serve me as my teachers. Choose what is good and follow it, but avoid what is evil" (*Analects* 7:21).[94] "If you set your mind on *ren*, you will be free from evil" (*Analects* 4:4).[95] These sayings indicate that all one has to do in freedom is within the limit of goodness. In Confucian thought choosing good means to choose *ren*, because *ren* is the principle of the good. In the *Analects*, "Yan Yuan asked about *ren*. The Master said, "To subdue one's self and return to propriety (*li*) is *ren*. If a person can for one day subdue himself and return to propriety (*li*), all under Heaven will ascribe *ren* to him. Is the practice of *ren* from a person himself, or is it from others?"" (*Analects* 12:1).[96] Cheng Chungying writes,

> once one can do right things without reliance on outside authority, one may be said to achieve moral autonomy and moral maturity. This inner transformation with larger and deeper moral freedom and social responsibility speaks to Confucius's notion of 'self-cultivation' (*xiuji*) of virtues one finds originating from oneself.[97]

93. Hsieh, "The Status of the Individual in Chinese Ethics," 310.

94. My translation.

95. My translation. In the *Doctrine of Mean*, "He who attains to sincerity is he who chooses what is good and firmly holds it fast" (20:18). Legge and Yang, trans., *The Four Books*, 40–41.

96. My translation.

97. Cheng, "Confucian Onto-Hermeneutics: Morality and Ontology," 35.

The freedom of an ideal person lies in his or her realization that he or she is free to be fully human, to be a sage in an open and unhindered way. Moral freedom is about building the common good of the community. The *junzi* (best humanity or best moral self) is an ecumenical person and not a sectarian (*Analects* 2:14). "Fully human" therefore means that a person who has the freedom to actualize his best moral self in loving others. He is a sage and a virtuous person who lives harmoniously with others in mutual edification.

To Be Fully Human via Differentiation and Socialization

In the Confucian worldview, the complex interrelationships of human affairs call for individuals to become fully human through the processes of differentiation and socialization. Individuation and actualization of personhood take place in dyadic social relations, the condition for making all fully human.[98] The Confucian notion of the human being is essentially that of a social person who learns the science and art of adjusting to the world. Confucius sees liberal education not only as book learning but also as ritual practices that reinforce the interaction of the self with the larger community (from self, to family, to society, to the nation, to the world). That constant reinforcement of relationships serves as a process of self-cultivation when it is practiced in the spirit of loyalty, reverence, brotherhood, discipleship, and so forth.

Human beings authenticate one another's existence. Becoming fully human is achieved not by detaching oneself from the world but by making sincere attempts to harmonize one's relationship with others. With regard to the social aspect of self-cultivation in the process of becoming fully human, Confucius says, "Virtue does not exist in isolation; there must be neighbors" (*Analects* 4:25).[99] "In order to establish oneself, one helps others to establish themselves; in order to enlarge oneself, one helps others to enlarge themselves" (*Analects* 6:28).

---

98. Tu Weiming observes this Confucian understanding of selfhood cultivation in the grid of the social dyad. Tu argues that "a social dyad is not a fixed entity, but a dynamic interaction involving a rich and ever-changing texture of human-relatedness woven by the constant participation of other significant dyadic relationships." Tu, *Confucian Thought*, 237.

99. Cf. Fingarette, *Confucius—The Secular as Sacred*, 42. *Analects* 4:25.

Human beings are transformed by participation with others in ceremonies that are communal. That is the mandate of Heaven, that all may live in righteousness and orderliness in relation to others in a society of sacredness. To be a *renren* (a humane person) is to express and to participate in the holy as a dimension of human existence. Fingarette writes, "Human life in its entirety finally appears as one vast, spontaneous and Holy Rite: the community of man [humanity]."[100] To be a *renren* is to be courteous, diligent, loyal, brave, broad, kind (*Analects* 13:19, 14:5, 17:6), as actualized in public.

In this vein a word can be said about the Apostle Paul. In his debate with the Judaizers in Galatia, Paul argues similarly for the significance of community over individualism, specifically in his concern for the inclusion of Gentiles into the household of God's elect. He also argues for the necessity of differentiation between Jews and Gentiles in socialization (or coexistence), for in Christ there is always a place for the uniqueness of different ethnicities, yet joined in unity and equality.

Being Fully Human, Social Selves, and Moral Obligation

✧ Social Self and Moral Obligation

Renren as "social self" means that relationships with others constitute who a person is as a human being. A person cannot be "fully human" by himself. The best moral self (*junzi*) can only be achieved by extending a helping hand to others. To be *renren* or *junzi* is to relate to others virtuously, knowing that who one is depends inextricably upon who others are. Consequently, hurting others also means hurting oneself. In a world of violence and war, no one is the winner. In the family or in gang feuds, every member diminishes his/her "best self," becoming less than human when resorting to violence.

The existence and freedom of the Confucian ideal person lies in his or her moral will to be a "best self," and to help others to be their best selves. The notion of freedom here speaks of the obligation one has toward others. All are bound to one another to be human in the task of becoming fully human: In edifying others, a person edifies himself; in

---

100. Fingarette, *Confucius—The Secular as Sacred*, 17. Cf. *Analects* 3:17, 4:5, 6, 8. For a different interpretation of *ren* and *li* in Confucius' thought, see Fung, *A Short History of Chinese Philosophy*, 72–82, 94; and Tu, *Confucian Thought*, 81–92.

being racist toward others, he diminishes his own dignity as a human being; in not forgiving others, he binds himself in hatred; in granting others peace, he is in fuller communion with them. Fingarette expresses this idea differently but well, "My life is not a means to maintaining the relationship; the relationship is my life, not something external to it that I serve. Each such relationship that I live, if it is indeed an authentically humanizing relationship, constitutes my life as being by that much and in that respect a more fully human life."[101] This is not to say that an ideal person does good to others only for the sake of his or her own benefit. Though such hope is surely there, doing good to others is not for selfish reasons. It is done for the sake of benevolence and fulfilling one's humanity. Since humans are social beings and life is public, the excellent person finds his or her home in being benevolent (*ren*). The Master said: "The benevolent man [*renzhe*] is attracted to benevolence [*ren*] because he feels at home in it" (*Analects* 4:2).[102]

Human beings are irreducibly social. Society begins with one's relationship with one's parents and extends outward to one's relationship with the global village. This is the social context where *li* (propriety) and *ren* (humaneness) manifest themselves in concrete ways. On one occasion, Confucius had a dialogue with his disciples, he asked them what they had set their hearts on (ambition in Chinese). Zilu said that he would like to share his carriage, horses, clothes, and furs with his friends, and even if they were worn and torn when given back, he would have no regrets. Another disciple, Yan Yuan said that he would never boast of his goodness and never parade his achievements. Zilu then asked his Master the same question. Confucius replied, "I wish to comfort the old, be truthful to friends, and cherish the young" (*Analects* 5:26).[103]

⋄ Freedom to Serve

Moral obligation toward others is not of the choosing of an autonomous self. Being human is to live in a social context, constantly aware of the dynamic of one's relationships with oneself, with others, and with things.[104]

---

101. Fingarette, "The Music of Humanity," 339.

102. Lau, trans., *Analects*, 29.

103. Huang, *Analects*, 78. See Qian, *Lunyu Xinjie*, 184; Chen, *Lunyu Duxun Jiegu*, 83.

104. Rosemont, "On Confucian Civility," 189.

During a period of desolation and abandonment, Confucius rhetorically defended his need to associate with people of the world, rather than to run away with the birds and beasts (*Analects* 18:6). Rosemont clarifies for us how the modern understanding of the autonomous self cannot understand the Confucian social self:

> The Confucian self is not a free, autonomous individual, but is to be seen relationally: I am a son, husband, father, teacher, student, friend, colleague, neighbor, and more. I live, rather than 'play' these roles, and when all of them have been specified, and their interrelationships made manifest, then I have been fairly thoroughly individuated, but with very little left over with which to piece together a free, autonomous individual. . . . In order to be a friend, neighbor, or lover, for example, I must have a friend, neighbor, or lover. Other persons are not merely accidental or incidental to my goal of fully developing as a human being; they are essential to it. Indeed, they confer unique personhood on me, for to the extent that I define myself as a teacher, students are necessary to my life, not incidental to it.[105]

Unlike our modern thinking of the autonomous self (independent of others and free of responsibilities), the communitarian teachings of Confucius and Paul do not accept the freedom of individuals to be independent as a good moral choice. Confucius and Paul understand that individuals have limited choice to one's socio-historical contexts. Even one's friends and enemies present themselves at the crossroads of life without the exercise of one's will. In Confucian teaching, however there is a strong sense of moral choice, that is, there is a virtuous way to relate to other people, whether parents or strangers. Likewise, for Paul there is a freedom inherent in being human in the presence of the other. While Confucius sees the rationale for the moral obligation toward others as an ethical one, Paul sees the reason for relating virtuously to others a christological one, that is, it is rooted in an act of God. God, the Wholly Other, has become fully human as the Immanent One in Christ (Phil 2:7–8). "Though he was in the form of God" Jesus Christ "did not regard equality with God as something to be exploited"; instead, he "emptied himself, taking the form of a slave, being born in human likeness" (Phil 2:6–7, NRSV). In so doing Christ became neither less than human nor divine, but as a human being was exalted to the fullness of his glory. It

105. Ibid.

is this freedom of Christ to relate to others in humility that serves as the example for humanity to serve others in freedom.

In his letter to the Galatians Paul points out that the communal life of freedom in the Spirit requires guidance from the law of love. The positive end of Christ's giving freedom to humanity is "through love [becoming] slaves to one another" (Gal 5:13, NRSV). The freedom given to believers is to be used to become "slaves to one another" (5:13c). The word *douleuete* is translated literally as "to slave," not "to serve." The term "slave" has a pejorative connotation, thus a more neutral term, "to serve" is used in some translations. But Paul's point of setting "to slave to one another" in the context of freedom and bondage is noteworthy. The word *douleuete* occurs in 4:8, 9, 25 where it also suggests the meaning of enslavement. Paul is undoubtedly making a play on words such as freedom and enslavement to make the point that there is no existence as such outside either the slavery to sin or to righteousness, either to the law or to Christ. But the realm of righteousness, of being in Christ, and the blessings it gives constitutes maximum freedom anyone can ever live. The paradox of Pauline theology, of freedom and slavery, is that the one who seeks to be served by others in order to justify his freedom will eventually live in bondage, while the one who is free will seek to be "a slave" to others in love, i.e., slave not in bondage but *free will to love*.

Paul frequently uses the term "'slave' of Christ" to designate himself and the believer (1 Cor 7:22; Rom 12:11; 14:4, 18). The metaphor has Old Testament roots in the slaves of Yahweh, referring to leaders of Israel such as Moses, David, and Isaiah, thus connoting a position of prestige, privilege, and honor (see Deut 34:5; Josh 1:1; Judg 2:8; 2 Kgs 18:12; Isa 42:19). This meaning is used by Paul (Rom 1:1; Phil 1:1) in addition to the more obvious references to obedience inherent in the slave-master relationship (1 Cor 3:5; 2 Cor 2:14; 3:6; 4:5). Brian J. Dobb surmises that, "To all but the most upper class readers, [*doulos*/slave] may have been heard as a metaphor of power by affiliation with the most important person in the cosmos, much as a member of the *familia Caesaris* might claim his or her unique social status as Caesar's slave."[106] Since the new existence in Christ and in the Spirit is different from being "in the flesh" or "under the law,"

---

106. Dodd, "Christ's Slave, People Pleasers and Gal 1:10," 97, who also gives the reference: Kyrtatas, "Christianity and the Familia Caesaris," 75–86.

Paul understands "the law of love" (6:2) and the new obedience of the "slaves of Christ" as freedom to love and to serve.

In light of the Christ event, Paul identifies himself as one honored to be a "slave" (*doulos*, cf. Rom 1:1; Phil 1:1), honored to be living in the new realm of the righteousness of God and, in the obedience of faith, to serve the living God. It is in serving Christ as Lord that Paul believes human beings find the freedom that leads to righteousness. The truth of the gospel is best expressed in this paradoxical metaphor of faith as a slavery that brings freedom. It thereby points to the fact that Gentiles can enjoy full membership in the people of God without taking up nomistic services.

Both in Pauline theology and in Confucian ethics the mutual indebtedness of love is the guarantee of communal freedom.[107] Confucius believes that *li* is grounded in *ren* and that together they are the agents of freedom for the community. Paul also points out that the communal life of freedom in the Spirit requires guidance from the law of Christ, which is the law of love (Gal 6:2).

FREEDOM, DEATH, AND THE HUMAN STORY

We began this chapter with such concerns as whether the Adam (human) story repeats in history through the violence of his two sons, Cain and Abel. We paid close attention to the biblical narrative and interpretations regarding the sibling rivalry between Ishmael and Isaac. Scripture itself gives examples of interpretation that are hopeful and redeeming. Cain's story is one of violence, shame, and bondage of the will. The biblical story preserves an alternative vision for humanity—that of Abel, the Son of Adam (Man). The honorable title "Son of Adam" is not given to Cain but to Abel—for obvious reasons. Abel's narrative provides life to those whose "blood cries out to Yahweh from the ground" (Gen 4:10), for "though he dies, he continues to speak" (Heb 11:4). Abel was interpreted by early Jewish-Christians to be the innocent victim, the righteous one who ascends to God, who becomes the eschatological judge of all.[108] Wolfgang Roth believes that the author of the Gospel of John uses the story of Abel to reinterpret Jesus as the "Son of Man [Adam]," who was betrayed but

---

107. See the section "Cruciform *Ren*" in Chapter Four (pp. 300–303).

108. Roth, "Jesus as the Son of Man."

raised to life, who as a good shepherd (Abel) lays down his life (cf. John 10:17–18; 12:33; 17:3; 18:32).[109]

Both Abel and Jesus, *mutatis mutandis*, provide the theological language of the cross that grants salvation to the human story. All are created to become fully human. Jesus has died, no one else should, not even Cain. The biblical narrative makes this point clearly, "And Cain said unto Yahweh, My punishment is greater than I can bear. . . . And Yahweh said unto him, 'Therefore whosoever slays Cain, vengeance shall be taken on him sevenfold.' And Yahweh appointed a sign for Cain, lest any finding him should smite him" (Gen 4:13–15, RSV). Jesus has died, no one else should, except maybe Abel and the like. But this is not a death that destroys one's humanity; rather it is a self-sacrificing love one gives even to one's enemies for the sake of love. Those who serve God, who follow Jesus, are often called to face the Cross, for the Scripture says: "Those who love their life will lose it, and those who hate their life in this world will keep it for eternal life" (Matt 10:39, 16:25; Mark 8:35; Luke 9:24, 17:33). Or as Galatians puts it: "through love become slaves to one another" (5:13c, NRSV).

Our discussion in this chapter began with the search for moral freedom in a world of violence. That quest begins with the realization that mutual indebtedness constitutes the essence of being human. The ethics of both Confucius and Paul affirm that our human story is threaded with love, that we are born to be free, free to be of service to others. While Confucius employs the terms "social self" (*renren*) and "best moral self" (*junzi*), Paul intentionally uses the metaphor of "slave" (*doulos*) in speaking of human freedom.

Paul deliberately uses "slave" as a self-reference in relation to God as "master" (*kyrios*) even though the cultural language of slavery denoted bondage. For Paul the Cross has transformed the negative connotations of servanthood and slavery; the world's wisdom is made foolish. He uses the traditional language of slavery, but it is infused with new meaning. The God-Christ paradigm is laid over the master-slave relationship. What is revealed is a master who has absolute power, yet surrenders it on the cross for the sake of love. The Christ, infused with divinity as Son of God, lays aside every claim to power and assumes the role of a human being, remaining obedient in love of God and neighbor to the point of death,

109. Ibid.

even death on a cross (Phil 2:5–11). In this Christian reinterpretation, the *doulos* of God is not one who lives in bondage but in the freedom of love and in the joy of service. The gospel truth is that those who love God and God's creation, that is, the neighbor (including all that is near, such as the cosmos itself) are free—free from any and every kind of bondage. Love cares, and in this world care takes on the servant's role. Paul's conviction is that the theological language of the cross has transformed the cultural language of the empire.[110] The language of the cross has the power to make all to be fully human, so that the human story does not end in violence and despair. It is transformed into a new creation in Christ.

Confucius and Paul's ideas regarding freedom are similar in at least one respect: they both maintain that freedom is constrained by love of others. Their ideas are significant to modern discourse on the topic of political freedom because such freedom is often misunderstood or abused in the West and the East. In his speculation, H. G. Creel tries to account for how Confucianism might have influenced the modern democratic ideal.[111] It is fair to say, however, that Confucius' communitarian ethic does not provide a clear notion of "individual freedom." There is no understanding of the freedom of the individual before Heaven in Confucius' teaching, no impassioned appeal in the *Analects* comparable to Paul's "For freedom Christ has set us free; stand fast therefore, and do not submit again to a yoke of slavery" (Gal 5:1, RSV). In Confucius' thought, freedom is neither a divine gift nor a personal right.

In its democratic spirit, Western civilization, however much it has departed from ecclesiastical traditions and practices, is a product of Christian, and most particularly Protestant, reflection. With its roots in the prophetic traditions of the Old Testament, the New Testament (with which we are here concerned) stresses the unity and equality of all people in Christ, regardless of class, race, gender, or social status. All human beings are equal in their sinfulness, in their need for salvation through repentance, and in their opportunity to experience the freedom that comes through faith in Jesus Christ, the sign of God's forgiving love.

No doubt, the freedom of the individual is a dangerous concept. Many of the problems modern societies in the West face are related to the abuse of freedom, e.g., licentiousness, selfishness, dissension. Nor

110. See Chapter 2 (pp. 144–50) on the subversive political language of Paul.

111. Creel, *Confucius and the Chinese Way*, 254–78 ("Confucianism and Western Democracy"). See also Novak, *Covenantal Rights*, 122.

are these problems absent in a Confucianist society—it is only a matter of degree in regard to human sin. The very concept of freedom of the individual leaves open the possibility of a narcissistic culture. However, without freedom, people cannot become what God intends. This is true of societies as well as individuals. The Apostle Paul calls for a special kind of freedom. It is freedom in Christ; it is a freedom constrained by the love of God, neighbor, and self.

6

Zhongshu (Loyalty-Empathy), Xin (Trust), and Pistis (Faith) in a World of Fear

CIVIL SOCIETY AND CIVILITY

The building of a civil society has been a common pursuit of the East and the West, whether in ancient or modern times.[1] The first meaning of "civil society" refers to the intermediary groups that arise between the family and the state, e.g., various civic clubs. The term "civil society" is commonly used to refer to a society ruled by laws established by the citizens themselves. Thus, the second meaning of "civil society" is related to the first but pays attention to the *process* and the *purpose* of ensuring civility within society. Citizens establish institutions and use the democratic process of inviting every citizen to *participate* in the civil process so that the citizenry itself will embody and sustain the common good. This chapter uses "civil society" with its second meaning, which is found in both the Confucian vision of the *good and beautiful life* and Paul's vision of the *life of love and freedom* lived within the redeemed community, the church, the Body of Christ.

---

1. See in particular Bockmuehl, *Jewish Law in Gentile Churches*, 177–240, on the public ethics of the New Testament and the early church in the context of the Greco-Roman moralist discourses. On *polis* (city) as the context of both Greek and New Testament ethics in Greco-Roman moral philosophy, see Meeks, *The Moral World of the First Christians*, passim.

"Civility and the civil society" have been the subjects of philosophers in the West as they discuss the *politics* (the conduct of the affairs) of the *polis* (city). The word civility comes from the Latin *civitas* (Greek *polis*), meaning city. Civility originates with the emergence of the civil society. Compared with city life, mobility within an agrarian society is limited. In an agricultural society people are born into communities that are familiar to them and they to the community. There is a consensus of mutual politeness and respect with those one knows arising from long-held customs and traditions. With the creation of the cosmopolitan character of city life, where diverse people dwell—most of whom are strangers to one another—and where no common tradition or custom prevails, the virtue of civility is necessary. Civility is a set of behaviors or manners accepted by city dwellers who agree to show respect and politeness in daily interaction with one another. Without civility, misunderstanding, conflict, and violence occur. The purpose of civility is to create an ethos in which persons with diverse cultural, ethical, and religious practices can coexist and live in peace.

In our ethical discourse here, "civil society" refers to the realm of interpersonal relations without which no society, however constituted or ruled, can exist. Civil society means the well-mannered, polite, courteous, humanitarian, kind and gracious community. The good and beautiful life is one in which the social self has ritualized propriety and where love is the basic attitude and the fulfillment of what it means to be human. Benevolence as humaneness *(ren)* expresses the relational mode of human existence in a world of difference. In this chapter, I want to unpack this idea more fully using Confucius' teaching of *zhong, shu, yi, xin*[2] and Paul's understanding of righteousness, faith, honor/shame, and benefaction/curse.

TOWARD A CHINESE CHRISTIAN THEOLOGY OF COMMUNITY

Christian tradition pays attention to the problems of sin and evil and sees salvation of God in Christ as the story of hope and peace for the world.

2. "The Master taught four disciplines: culture *(wen)*, conduct *(xing)*, loyalty *(zhong)*, trustworthiness *(xin)*" *(Analects* 7:25). My translation. See Qian, *Lunyu Xinjie*, 255–56; Yang, *Lunyu Yizhu*, 161.

In the Confucianist tradition, however, Xu Fuguan, a Neo-Confucianist, argues that the "consciousness of concern about the vicissitudes and turmoil" of the age (*youhuan yishi*) is the etiological spirit of Confucianism and the defining spirit of Chinese culture.[3] The "unwholesomeness" Xu mentioned is not a personal insecurity but that of a people-group called the Zhou people and that of their culture. The sea of change that happened between the Shang and Zhou dynasties caused a minority tribe called the Zhou people to worry about the survival of their country, the prosperity of their culture, and to realize that they failed to actualize consummately their heavenly endowed human nature.[4] Based on such consciousness of concern for an ideal and harmonious society, Confucius and Confucianists offer a pragmatic response to cultural chaos, moral corruption, political hegemony by advocating an "ethical consciousness" of cultivating virtues, and by teaching a creative expression of stylized behavior (*li*) as well as aesthetic ethic of goodness (*yue*).[5] In short, this is a "moral religion" (inward transcendence of the human spirit) that seeks to restore the goodness and full potentiality of the human heart/mind (*xin*).[6]

Zhong *and* Shu

According to Confucian thought, in a civil society people treat each other humanly out of the love expressed in the Golden Rule known as *zhong* and *shu*. The word *zhong* can mean variously "to do one's best,"[7] "to fully realize oneself,"[8] "to follow the rituals in service to others,"[9] "loyalty" (Waley, Dawson, Fletcher, Fingarette),[10] "dutifulness" (Slingerland)[11] or more literally, "single-heartedness." Pictographically, the character of *zhong* (忠)

3. Xu, *Zhongguo Renxinglun Shi*, *passim*.

4. Ibid., chapter 2.

5. Ibid.; the thesis of Xu is followed by Mou, *Zhongguo Zhexue De Tezhi*, 16–27. The term "ethical consciousness" is used by Mou (17).

6. Mou, *Zhongguo Zhexue De Tezhi*, *passim*; idem, *Shengming De Xuewen*, 88–89, 119.

7. Lau, trans., *Analects*, 16.

8. This is the interpretation of Zhu Xi on *Analects* 4:15, see his edited, *Sishu*, 121–22.

9. Ivanhoe, "Reweaving the 'One Thread,'" 25.

10. Fletcher, *Loyalty*, 6.

11. Slingerland, trans., *Confucius Analects*, 238.

is made up of an arrow hitting its target (the symbol *zhong* [center] 中 above) and a heart (the symbol *xin* [heart] 心 below). Since the heart is the core of one's rational and emotional faculties, the virtue *zhong* means "conscientiousness, . . . thus [it] points to the heart-mind as a consciously mediating entity, ever aware of and responsive to what lies beyond its boundaries, creating and sustaining itself through self-centering."[12] What lies beyond its boundaries is the encompassing *dao* (the Way) that one is loyal to. Commitment to *dao* assures the members of a society that the duty to serve others with one's best brings about civility.

Confucius' teaching regarding *zhong* appears in a text difficult to interpret, yet it provides a thread for unifying Confucius' teaching. It is found in *Analects* 4:15: "The Master speaks [to Zhengzi], 'My *dao* [teaching] is threaded with one string.' . . . Others ask: 'What does that mean?' Zhengzi replies, 'The Master's Way consists in wholehearted sincerity and like-hearted considerateness, that is all.'"[13] The text is difficult to understand not because the language is cryptic, but because the Master's teaching was interpreted by his disciple Zhengzi and not by the Master himself. Most translators and commentators cross-reference *Analects* 4:15 with 15:3. *Analects* 15:3 discusses the "one thread" teaching of Confucius. Confucius asked Ci if he considered the Master a learned person who had committed everything to memory. Ci said yes, but Confucius replied, "No, I use one string to thread them all."[14] The text, "one string to thread them all," may refer to the synthesizing mastery of Confucius' learning rather than to the unity of Confucius' teaching.

As for *Analects* 4:15, we can take Zhengzi's interpretation as a guide. Zhengzi seems to imply that the one string of Confucius' teaching is made up of two strains of *zhong* and *shu*.[15] *Zhong* means being both honest with oneself and faithful toward others. The latter is also expressed as singleheartedly doing one's best in serving others (*Analects* 1:4; 13:19; 16:10), being loyal, devoted, and trustworthy (*Analects* 1:8; *Analects* 9:25;

---

12. Nyitray, "The Single Thread," 199.

13. My translation. See Chen, *Lunyu Duxun Jiegu,* 54–55. Qian, *Lunyu Xinjie,* 133 does not explain the meaning of *dao*. Here I follow Yang, *Lunyu Yizhu,* 83–84.

14. My translation. See Yang, *Lunyu Yizhu,* 344–45.

15. On various interpretations of this verse in the commentary tradition, see Van Norden, "Unweaving the 'One Thread,'" 218–24. Fingarette, "Following the 'One Thread,'" thinks that Confucian *shu* cannot be appropriated alone, it needs *zhong*. Thus, *zhongshu* appear together in some instances in the *Analects*.

12:10; 15:6). When Confucius was asked how to make common people loyal (*zhong*) to their lords, he replied that first the lords had to be "filial to elders and merciful to juniors" (*Analects* 2:20). The word *zhong* is often used in the *Analects* in the context of ministers serving their lords with utmost sincerity (*Analects* 3:19; 12:14, 12:23; 14:7). *Analects* 5:19 provides an illustration: Confucius commended Prime Minister Zi Wen for his loyal service, even though the minister neither showed any sign of joy when he was promoted nor any sign of sadness when he was dismissed (*Analects* 5:19); the minister was simply faithful apart from praise or rejection. While *zhong* is used in the *Analects* as "mutual devotion" between peers and colleagues and friends, it is quite often used to describe the responsibility of inferiors towards their lord. The word *shu* seems to overcome that asymmetry.

Shu means having a heart like others. Huang translates it as "like-heartedness,"[16] as the Chinese pictograph also suggests—the character "like" (如, *ju*) on top and the character "heart" (心, *xin*) at the bottom of the word *shu*. *Shu* means comparing like things, so the compound character of *shu* means "comparing one heart-mind to another."[17] The English word "empathy" may provide a good translation. For *shu* entails the empathetic ability to extend one's mind and emotion to others. *Shu* includes sensibility to "what the other person wants or does not want."[18] This process of treating others with respect and civility is central to Confucius' thought (cf. *Analects* 6:30).

According to Confucius *shu* also means "not doing to others what you do not desire yourself" (*Analects* 15:24).[19] The context of this verse is when Zigong asks the Master if there is a word or a sentence upon which one could act for the rest of one's life. Confucius replies, "It is *shu*! Do not do to others that which you do not desire yourself." The only two occurrences of the word *shu* in the *Analects* are 4:15 and 15:24. Norden suggests that the definition of *shu* appears elsewhere even though the word itself does not appear, such as 5:12 and 6:30,[20]—and I would add 12:2.

---

16. Huang, *Analects*, *passim*; similarly, Qian, *Lunyu Xinjie*, 132–33.
17. Nyitray, "The Single Thread," 199.
18. Lau, trans., *Analects*, 16.
19. Yang, *Lunyu Yizhu*, 358.
20. Van Norden, "Unweaving the 'One Thread,'" 224.

If the meaning of *shu* in *Analects* 15:24 is like-heartedness (the extension of one's desires to others), then it is similar to what *Analects* 6:30 says regarding benevolence or humaneness (*ren*), except that in 6:30 the concept is expressed positively: "if you want to establish yourself, establish others as well, if you want to be successful, make others successful."[21] *Analects* 5:12 essentially repeats what Confucius says in 15:24. In 5:12 Zigong says that what he does not desire others to place on him, he will also not place on others. And the Master replies that this is beyond his reach. The implication of the Master's comment is that, to treat others with *shu* in the sense of respecting the feeling of others is a highly challenging, if not impossible, task. *Analects* 12:2 couches the teaching ("do not do to others that which you do not like to have done to you") in the context of assuming one's responsibility in a court or a noble house. To Zigong's question of what constitutes humaneness or benevolence (*ren*), Confucius replies that by practicing the virtue of like-heartedness, one will not incur any resentment in the service to one's state or one's family.[22]

Confucius' understanding of *zhong* and *shu* as virtues practiced by all becomes the thread that binds Chinese society. Without these virtues Chinese society falls into chaos. Turning to the situation at Galatia, we want to use the Confucian teachings to read the community Paul labored to build. By reading Paul's theology with Confucius' ethic of *zhong* and *shu* we are by no means suggesting that Paul believes in cultivating these virtues as the means to build community. In fact Paul does not think so, he believes that the righteousness of the community can only be achieved "through the Spirit, by faith" (Gal 5:5). Nonetheless, we will make use of Confucius' language of ethics because the interrelational aspect of Confucius' thought sheds light on the polemic in Galatia.

Shu *in the Galatian Situation*

↔ Self-Forgetting as *Shu*

If we are to apply Confucius' thought to Paul's situation, we must ask, "How valid would it be to expect that the ethical admonition of *shu*, viz.,

---

21. My translation. Cf. Yang, *Lunyu Yizhu*, 141–42.
22. Chen, *Lunyu Duxun Jiegu*, 216.

acceptance of the mutual responsibility of edification and the alleviation of burdens, would be practiced in the churches in Galatia?" Is it feasible to expect *analogical knowing* (do to others what one desires for oneself), hoping that "likeheartedness" would not work its will "imperialistically" despite good intentions of the Judaizers? How does one know that what is helpful and desirable for oneself is also helpful to others? If *shu* operates on the principle of analogical knowing, cannot the claim of freedom for oneself become bondage to others? This becomes a serious problem when we apply the ethics of *shu* to the situation in Galatia. Jewish Christians, contrary to Paul's teaching, required Gentile Christians to practice "covenantal nomism," believing that true freedom existed only within a strict observance of the laws of the covenant. The Judaizers thought of freedom without the law as license, which is bondage to sin; Paul thought that if the Gentile Christians were to live in the law, they would live in bondage and would be fallen from grace.

Fingarette's interpretation of the Confucian *shu* is helpful in this regard. Fingarette makes the point that *shu* is not simply imagining oneself in the other person's situation (self-extension); it is imagining oneself *as* the other (self-forgetting) and then acting in awareness of the other's need. The other person becomes the frame of reference for determining how one should treat others.[23] The process of analogical knowing does not work when a person sees himself as the point of reference and begins with his own agenda. *Shu* requires that the centering subject intentionally works at self-forgetting. Living in the borderland or in alien places is the training ground of *shu*. Similarly, using a cross-cultural reading causes "culture shock" and brings to an end the naive assumption that one's own norms provide the only legitimate reading of the world.

The teaching of the Judaizers constitutes a mono-cultural extension of themselves, expecting Gentile Christians to become Jewish. This Jewish Christian group proclaimed a gospel that was law-observant and supplementary to the gospel of Christ. They believed that Gentiles could become full members of the people of God and overcome the impulsive desires of the flesh by means of the law. Yet Paul names this group "false," their motive "insincere," and their actions "deceitful." Paul's law of Christ is (in our terms) cross-cultural; it frees Gentile believers from the burden of the law and causes them to serve one another. This Christian life is pat-

---

23. Fingarette, "Following the 'One Thread,'" 383–84.

terned after the Cross, which itself is the paradigm of the self-forgetting and self-giving God who acts on behalf of humanity.

↦ "Become as I am, because I also am as you are" (Gal 4:12)

Seeking to model the self-forgetting way of the life of the Cross, Paul appeals to the audience to imitate him, as he also imitates them: "Become as I am, because I also [have become] as you are, brethren, I ask you" (Gal 4:12).[24] The language of imitation refers to how Paul had lived like a Gentile for the sake of the Gentiles. He had fellowship meals with them and he had participated in the community ritual of the agape meal, which re-presented Christ's sacrificial love.[25] Paul's defense recalls the friendship he had enjoyed with his audience during their first encounter when the gospel was preached. He now wants to remind his readers of the good reception they had first given the gospel of Christ and his apostle (Gal 4:12–14).

Paul declares that the Galatians had not treated him unjustly (*adikein*). They had received him as an angel of God, despite "the weakness of the flesh" (*di' asthenian tēs sarchos*; Gal 4:13). Although *asthenia* can refer to a physical illness it is unlikely to be the reason for Paul's initial visit. The sense of the term may be theological, that is, it may well refer to the human weakness of being under the dominion of sin, of living in the present evil age. This weakness may be Paul's rationale for preaching the gospel, viz., in order to fulfill the needs of humanity.[26] Understood in this way the word *asthenia* refers to weakness in the sense of bondage. The weakness, or need, is qualified with *tēs sarchos* (the flesh) without

---

24. My translation.

25. The imitating language can mean generally that (1) Paul is asking the audience to be like him in his desire to be all things to all people, or specifically that (2) Paul is asking the audience to be true to Christ and the gospel. "Meals symbolize proper behavior among social groups in relation to one another and in relation to God" (Feeley-Harnik, *The Lord's Table*, 2).

26. Many proposals ranging from bodily illnesses (fever, headache, epilepsy, eye disease [Gal 4:15], hemmorhia, the thorn in flesh [2 Cor 12:7]) to bodily ailments have been suggested by scholars, but these interpretations have nothing to do with the gospel Paul preached. It is most unlikely that the Galatians welcomed Paul the preacher as an angel of God just because of his physical illness, even if they knew Paul had started his preaching campaign despite his physical disability. Thus, I offer a contextual reading above.

qualifying whose is it; Paul may well be referring to the general state of what "the flesh" symbolizes. Since the word "flesh" in Gal 6:13 means circumcision, the phrase *asthenia tēs sarchos* would then refer to the inadequacy/weakness of circumcision. Paul's call to be an apostle of Christ comes after his awareness that works of the law such as circumcision, are incapable of bringing the Gentiles into the people of God (Galatians 2–4). A self-forgetting and empathetic understanding of the Gentiles causes Paul to recognize the inadequacy of circumcision as a means for including Gentiles as the people of God—though it is a sign of privilege for the Jews as the people of God.

Initially, the Galatians did not reject Paul's proclamation. They received him as a messenger of God (4:14). That the Galatian Gentiles were able to do that is also an act of *shu* (empathy). Gal 4:15–16 provides a narrative of the mutual *shu* that existed in Paul's earliest relationship with the Gentiles of Galatia. In the immediate context of friendship, the happiness Paul recalls in Gal 4:15 refers to the joy and blessedness of the mutually receptive relationship that existed between the Galatian Christians and himself.

✎ The Pain of Betrayal: Where is Empathy? Where is *Shu*?

The mutual *shu* (empathy) that had existed between Paul and the Christians in Galatia soon turns into betrayal. In Gal 4:17–19 Paul laments that the happiness he once enjoyed with the Gentile Christians is now gone, their friendship broken. Understandably, Paul expresses his disappointment that they now treat him as their enemy, that they have departed from Christ's gospel and have turned to a gospel contrary to the one he had preached. If this alien gospel, preached by Paul's opponents, is accepted by the Galatian Christians, Paul's labor in creating Christians is like a miscarriage. He is no more the esteemed apostle, despite the initial friendship they had previously extended to him. In heartfelt anguish, he cries, "My children, with whom again I am in pain until Christ be formed in you" (4:19).

In Confucianist terms Paul the apostle embodies the principles of *zhong* and *zhu*, viz., single-heartedness and like-heartedness, loyalty and empathy. Even when he is betrayed, he still holds to the gospel *dao* (truth), knowing that faithfulness and mutual trust is the way to form the bond of God's community.

Hierarchy and Zhongshu

Unlike Paul, few people act so civilly and few understand so well the dynamics of power present in human relationships. As an apostle of Christ, Paul advocates for the "underdog," such as slaves, females, the poor, the marginalized, the last, and least of society. He does not lead congregations by exerting his apostolic power, rather he relies upon rhetorical persuasion, theological clarification, and the works of Christ to convince them of the gospel's truth.

To use the Confucian language of *zhong* and *shu* to describe Paul is not to gloss over the hierarchical nature of Chinese culture. We will first look at *zhong* and *shu* when practiced together. We want to note as well the way they are critical of dominating and abusive power wherever it occurs, even when hierarchical power structures are deemed the cultural norm. We will then look at how the subversiveness of *zhong* and *shu* can be helpful in interpreting the theology of Paul.

The practice of *zhong* and *shu* requires social reciprocity in the imaginative analogical extension of oneself to the other, engendering an empathetic replacement of one's own situation and needs with those of the other. Thus in Confucian teaching *zhong* and *shu* are often set within the five specific relationships (ruler and subjects; father and son; husband and wife; older and younger brothers; friends), which establish the hierarchical structure of a society. *Zhong* often refers to inferiors serving their superiors with an attitude of devotion, such as in *Analects* 3:19 where Duke Ding asks Confucius how a minister should serve his lord. Some might argue that the word *zhong* is not used in a *specified* inferior-superior relationship.[27] In *Analects* 1:4, Zhengzi says that his daily meditation involves asking himself whether he was serving others (not necessarily his superiors) with loyalty, whether he was honest in his dealings with his trustworthy friends, and whether he authenticated himself by practicing what he preached. It is correct to say that in the *Analects zhong* is used

---

27. Van Norden, "Unweaving the 'One Thread,'" 224, sees "planning for others" in 1:4 as serving the superior (cf. 8:14).

to refer to the devotion one shows toward one's superiors or equals, but *never* toward one's subordinates.[28]

The question of hierarchical structure in Confucianism is a challenging one to modern sensibilities. How can one advocate the teaching of *zhong* and *shu* and not endorse domination and hegemony? David S. Nivison's study of the Confucian Golden Rule is helpful in this regard. He observes that *zhong* is practiced in relationships with one's social superiors (involving loyalty, commitment, and obedience), while *shu* is practiced in relationships with one's social inferiors (involving forgiveness, compassion, and consideration). In both there is an imaginative reversal of positions that helps to replace oneself or to extend oneself in dealing with others, either with *zhong* or *shu*.[29] *Shu* swings the pendulum of asymmetry to the opposite side of *zhong* for those who are in power: superiors expect inferiors to be loyal. But *shu* expects putting oneself, the superior, in the position of the inferior. The inferior needs to figure out how to relate to his superior as a loyal person. With the reversal of roles, which Ivanhoe speaks of as the "principle of reversibility,"[30] the inferior person must imaginatively assume the position of being the superior who *expects* of the inferior wholehearted (*zhong*) service. This expectation then becomes the guide to the actions of the actual inferior. This loyalty is called *zhong*. In the reversal of roles, how does the superior relate to his inferior? In the *shu* relationship, the superior imagines himself to be the inferior who expects kindness and leniency. It is this expectation of the putative inferior that becomes the guide to the actions of the superior.

The principle of reversibility assumes the hierarchical structure of a society. It requires that the superior be *shu* (kind and lenient) and the inferior be *zhong* (loyal); the Confucian texts are silent in requiring the superior to be *zhong* (loyal) toward the inferior and the inferior be *shu* (forgiving) toward the superior.[31] Were the principle of reversibility in both *shu* and *zhong* relationships taken seriously, it could overcome the abuse of power in a hierarchical society where role distinction is believed to be necessary for social harmony. Nivison explains that "both *zhong* and *shu* are conceived quite concretely in terms of familiar social, famil-

---

28. So Ivanhoe, "Reweaving the 'One Thread,'" 21–25.

29. Nivison, "Golden Rule Arguments," 73.

30. Ivanhoe, "Reweaving the 'One Thread' of the *Analects*," 25.

31. Nivison, "Golden Rule Arguments," 76.

ial, and political relationships, in which distinctions of precedence and authority are taken for granted."[32] Thus, four out of the five sets of relationships are guided by the virtues of *zhong* and *shu*.

What happens to the fifth set of the relationship of equals (friend to friend)? Is either *zhong* or *shu* still needed in such a horizontal relationship? Nivison argues that the canonical texts of Confucius are silent concerning the application of *zhong* and *shu* to friendship.[33] But Nyitray is right in saying that "the traditional understanding of the friendship bond was that it occurs between peers yet implicitly mimics the hierarchical fraternal relationship; unlike the fraternal bond, however, friendship allows circumstances to cause the balance of authority and deference to shift from one person to the other."[34] Ideally friends and colleagues are equal, but it can be argued that the Confucian assumption concerning distinction and differentiation is correct in that even in peer and colleague relationships equality is rarely ever achieved. The reason for this is that human interaction does not happen in a vacuum. Nor can abstract pronouncements of equality create the reality of equality. Human beings relate to one another in the complex and changing concreteness of everyday life, which includes the individual's multiple identities according to gender, class, wealth, knowledge, ethnicity, backgrounds, experience, emotions, etc. Competition and conflict often hurt communities because of the desire to be in control, to be superior, to dominate others. This fear could be resolved with the Confucian ethic of *zhongshu* as "reversed imagination." Both *zhong* and *shu*, and especially *shu*, are thus appropriate to relationships of equals as well—though this relationship is a constant shifting of power and is conditioned by a myriad of factors.

The Unity of Zhongshu

One would think that, since inferiors outnumber superiors in any society, the teaching of *zhong* would occupy a more fundamental place than that of *shu* in Confucius' teaching. But this is not the case. In moral learning the virtue of *shu* will be more difficult to acquire than that of *zhong*; thus Confucian moral education emphasizes the power of *shu*. Ivanhoe's the-

32. Ibid., 65.
33. Ibid., 76.
34. Nyitray, "The Single Thread," 212, n. 21.

sis that *shu* is the governor of *zhong* is worth noting. Based on the Golden Rule found in *Analects* 5:12, Ivanhoe reconstructs the context of the discussion to be Confucius's admonition to Zigong to serve with *zhong*:

> [Zigong] was strict with himself, but he was too strict with others (cf. *Analects* 14:31). He did not know when or how to amend, bend, or suspend the *li* (rituals) when they (the *li*) adversely affected others. . . . One of the most insidious forms of such overzealous righteousness is believing in one's selfless devotion to the moral ideal. . . . [Zigong] claims to be *shu*, which is what he is not.[35]

In other words, Zigong thought that his loyalty in his demonstrated strict submission to ritual propriety (*li*) was what others ought to emulate. In Confucius' judgment, however, Zigong did not have the virtue of *shu* (empathy). Thus Confucius' reminder to Zigong of his lack of *shu* helped him to practice *zhong* (loyalty) in fulfilling *li* (rituals) without holding to ritualism as an absolute, and without dehumanizing others or oneself. As such *shu* (empathy) completes what the *zhong* (loyalty) of Zigong lacks. Ivanhoe explains,

> *Shu* helps one avoid becoming a slave to the *li*. It insures that individuals will have an active sense of their co-humanity with others. It guarantees that people will run the rules and not be run by the rules. One is to see oneself as dedicated to serving others according to the rituals, but one is also to see oneself as responsible for the well-being of others. One is to be strict with oneself, but one is to be kind to others. Both of these imperatives are mediated through the rituals. Without a firm commitment to *li*, the "kindness" of *shu* can collapse into vague, formless sentimentality and the "loyalty" of *zhong* can degenerate into blind, mechanistic obedience. Neither *zhong* nor *shu* can be understood apart from the *li*, and only in support of each other do they constitute *ren*.[36]

According to Ivanhoe's interpretation, although *shu* occupies a more prominent place than *zhong* in Confucian ethics, the common thread of *zhongshu* is still intact. Their unity is an essential part of Confucius' teaching of becoming *renren* (humane persons) according to *li* (ritual propriety).

---

35. Ivanhoe, "Reweaving the 'One Thread,'" 27.
36. Ibid., 27.

Zhu Xi, an authoritative commentator on the Confucian classics, explains the coupling relationship between *zhong* and *shu*: "Fully realizing oneself is called *zhong*, and extending oneself is called *shu*."[37] We have added to that understanding the notion of serving others wholeheartedly (as an aspect of *zhong*) and of being empathetic toward each other (as an aspect of *shu*) by way of the critical act of "reversed imagination." *Zhong* and *shu* are not simply acts of "civility" in the sense of "just being nice." Being nice to a murderer does not promote virtue. *Zhong* and *shu* are moral acts of promoting virtue in others according to a shared commitment to truth that builds the community. Murderers are to be taught that killing is a vice because it destroys community and departs from the truth. *Zhong* and *shu* are thus to be guided by *dao*,[38] the truth that inscribes the narrative of the community.[39] With a conviction of what *dao* is, a community has a measure for judging and authenticating civility.

Dao *and the Truth of the Gospel*

Turning to the community at Galatia, we can use the Confucian *zhongshu* and *dao* to understand the way Paul admonishes the congregations. We have mentioned in the last section that for Confucius, *dao* (the Way or Truth) is the authenticating means of civility in a community. Similarly, without understanding the truth of the gospel, Paul cannot know how either covenantal nomism or paganism could mean spiritual bondage for Gentile Christians. Since the church in Galatia was initially grounded in the truth of the gospel, those congregations had the responsibility of restoring any member who had strayed from the community rule. To the Galatians, Paul writes, "Brethren, if a person is overtaken in any trespass, you (pl.) who are spiritual restore such one in a spirit of gentleness, watching yourself lest you (sing.) even be tempted" (Gal 6:1; modified RSV). "You (pl.) who are spiritual" refers to those who live, follow, and walk by the Spirit (5:25, 26, 28), i.e., all the Galatian Christians, whether Jewish or Gentile. They are addressed by Paul as "brethren," signifying Paul's affection for them in the shared relationship they together have in Christ. The word "detected" (*prolambanein*) suggests that the misstep in

---

37. See Van Norden, "Unweaving the 'One Thread,'" 225.

38. See Ivanhoe, "Reweaving the 'One Thread,'" 26. See *Analects* 6:25.

39. See the discussion of *rendao* and *tiandao* in Chapter Two (pp. 112–26).

question may have been unintentionally. Still, the responsibility of the community is to correct any member who has not walked according to the truth.[40]

For one to correct a member who has strayed from the truth requires self-awareness regarding the virtues of loyalty (*zhong*) and empathy (*shu*), the virtues Confucius taught. Spiritual members are asked to restore the wayward "in a spirit of gentleness" (Gal 6:1).[41] The counterpart to this exhortation to restore (*katartizein*) is *the awareness* that one not be tempted: "watching yourself (sing.) lest even you be tempted" (6:1b). Some have counseled others yet have themselves been tempted to do the same thing. The behavior of Peter and other Jewish Christians at Antioch served to illustrate this possibility. Without an awareness of the need for Gentiles to be free, the Judaizers imposed on the Gentile Christians the Jewish laws.

In the case of correcting strayed members, Paul writes, "If someone thinks that he is somebody, although he is not, he is deceiving himself" (Gal 6:3). This exhortation is in the third person singular to form a hypothetical example. It may suggest the Galatian community was faced with the problem of pride and dissension. The phrase, "thinks . . . he is somebody" (*dokei tis einai*) appears in Gal 2:6 and refers to the Jerusalem apostles who "thought [themselves] to be somebody." Paul clarifies by noting that he himself does not entertain such an idea because God shows no partiality. Pride and self-inflation can result in envy, jealousy and dissension in a community. That problem can be checked by building up the character of humility: "Let each one test his own work, and then his reason to boast will be in himself alone and not in his neighbor" (Gal 6:4, RSV). The result of self-examination should be a realistic estimation and knowledge of who one is, rather than a "boasting" in what, in fact, one is not (6:4).[42] Similarly in Romans 1, Paul speaks of self-deception

40. The word *paraptoma* is not a technical word for sin or transgression, but for a wrong step.

41. The word "spirit" (*pneuma*) may mean God's Spirit or the human spirit; here it refers to attitude. The word "gentleness" (*prautētos*) appears in Gal 5:23 as an aspect of the fruit of the Spirit. If Paul is referring back to 5:23, most likely he would have made a more explicit reference of the Spirit. The restoration of a strayed member does not need the Spirit of gentleness; rather, correcting a strayed member with an attitude or spirit of gentleness makes sense. Therefore, Paul here most probably means attitude by the word *pneuma*.

42. See Barclay, *Obeying the Truth*, 161.

of human beings in "suppressing the truth in unrighteousness" (1:18), in order to satisfy one's own passions (1:24), and often at the expense of others (1:29–31). "As creatures with consciences, however, we need moral cover for the unrighteous lives we live. Idolatry provides us with that moral cover (1:23, 25)."[43]

To summarize, persons who serve others wholeheartedly (*zhong*) or relate to others empathetically (*shu*) are those who are self-assured. They do not feel threatened by the act of self-forgetting or self-giving. Self-deception and self-boasting are twins; they inflate the self because they are the result of insecurity in the presence of others. We will see in the next section how mutual respect and mutual honoring further enhance the civility of a community and thus redeem the human tendency to shame and to destroy itself from within.

A CHINESE CHRISTIAN THEOLOGY OF *JING* (RESPECT) AND MUTUAL HONORING

Shame and Honor Culture and *Jing*

The Chinese culture Confucius had in mind and the community Paul wanted to establish in Galatia may both be seen as dyadic cultures. Dyadic cultures are those cultures in which self-worth is determined by the individual's orientation toward the other. Dyadic cultures are based on the concept of *co-humanity*, that is, each person within a community achieves his/her full humanity only in co-relation with another human being. Such cultures recognize that human beings are fundamentally social selves. According to Confucian thought, *renren* (humane persons) realize the goodness of *tian* (heaven) innate in human nature through the practice of communal rituals. Only in community, in striving to relate well with others, can one become fully human. The Greco-Roman understanding of a person as *prosōpon* or *persona* agrees with the Confucian understanding of *renren*—except that the Greco-Roman understanding does not have the moral connotation. The Greek word, *prosopon*, literally means a face; it refers to the mask used in Greek theater.[44] To be a person is to learn the art of bearing another's character, and to know one's

---

43. Cosgrove, "Paul and American Individualism," 79.

44. Alexander, "The Face of Holiness," 32.

own character well enough to allow the two characters to be mutually engaging. Similarly, the Latin word *persona* as seen in *per sonare*, meaning "to sound through," refers to the mouthpiece of the theatrical mask.[45] Alexander writes that, "To be a person in Roman society (or to possess self-identity) was not found through internal projection; that is, to be the bearer of a certain character, a certain external projection. The ancient understanding of personhood involved social confirmation."[46]

The societies in which Confucius and Paul lived were also rooted in a value system of social confirmation called "honor and shame."[47] Social selves derive their *value* or *worth* not from themselves but from others. The value system of a dyadic culture is determined by the honor or shame members grant to one another within the community. Bestowing honor is a means of approving a certain value and of including a person into the community as its own. Giving and receiving honor constantly reinforces the sense of worth and purpose.

Shame works just as effectively in the opposite way: it disgraces, alienates, and dismantles the value system of the one shamed. The purpose of shame is to debase, to disapprove, to curse, and ultimately to ostracize a person. Once a person is excommunicated, he is no longer a "human" being, for he is not a "social" self. Self-deception is the failure to recognize who one is and where one is within the communal network; thinking too highly or too little inflates or deflates self-worth. Self-worth can be restored when the community recognizes one's unique gifts and graces, and that is what Paul seeks to do for the Christians in Galatia.

Jing, *Mutual Respect, and Mutual Honoring*

Confucian ethics of respect (*jing*) is predicated on reverence to Heaven (*jingtian*) because to be reverent to Heaven is to fulfill its mandate of ensuring moral order in human nature and in human society.[48] Mutual benefaction and mutual respect are required if a civil society is to be formed. Rather than condescension, giving esteem is a way of recogniz-

45. Ibid., 27.

46. Ibid., 28.

47. See an extensive discussion of honor and shame by Malina in his *The New Testament World*, 27–57.

48. Mou, *Zhongguo Zhexue De Tezhi*, 24–25.

ing worth. The ethics of Confucius illumines the point well. According to Confucius, esteem, reverence, honor, and respect (*jing*) are the basis of self-cultivation (*Analects* 14:42; 15:5). One ought to offer reverence (*jing*) when observing proper norms of behavior toward others, even after long acquaintance (*Analects* 5:17). One learns the stylized manner of reverence or respectfulness (*jing*) by observing ritual propriety (*Analects* 3:26). One learns the attitude of respectfulness (*jing*) when performing the rites of sacrifice (*Analects* 19:1), which express reverence for the world of the spirits (*Analects* 6:22). One ought to be reverent (*jing*) in serving one's parents (*Analects* 2:7), even when they do not heed one's suggestions (*Analects* 1:7). One ought to be respectful (*jing*) when carrying out official duty (*Analects* 1:5; 5:16; 13:19; 15:38; 16:10). Rulers should teach their people to be dignified in order to learn respect (*Analects* 2:20). An exemplary person (*junzi*) respects (*jing*) and is courteous toward others, he does not wrong others, and his manners are formed according to the rituals of propriety (*Analects* 12:5).

Mutual respect and benefaction are cornerstones of a Confucianist civil society. A similar emphasis is found in the ancient Greco-Roman culture of which the Galatian society was a part. Frederick W. Danker has shown that the dominant feature of the Greco-Roman culture was its association with the motifs of benefaction and honor, both in the display, claim, and acknowledgment of the benefactor's merit or excellence, and in the beneficiaries' response to that merit.[49] The pervasive nature of this cultural pattern is evident in the variety of the media of benefaction (city council documents, published edicts, civic decrees, biographies or autobiographies, oaths, etc.) of beneficiaries (esteemed members, community and military personnel, emperors, deities, statesmen, physicians, philanthropists, etc.), and the merits of benefaction (exceptional character, foresight, leadership).[50]

The question facing Paul in Galatia, at least in part, is how he would form a new system of honor for the Galatian Christians. Paul uses the

49. Danker, *Benefactor*, is a source book containing fifty-three Graeco-Roman inscriptions related to the theme of benefaction (1–316).

50. Danker suggests that "the language and themes of Graeco-Roman inscriptions that reflect the pervasive interest in the function of a benefactor offer a manageable hermeneutical control base for determining the meaning that an auditor or reader of literary documents is likely to have attached to certain formulations and thematic treatment" (Danker, *Benefactor*, 29).

language of honor and shame by reversing the source of approval. God, he argues, is the ultimate source of honor, not Rome and its glory. Paul exhorts his Galatian friends to "sow in the Spirit," meaning by that they should be benefactors to all: "Let us not grow weary in well-doing, for in due season we shall reap, if we do not lose heart. So then, as we have opportunity, let us do good to all [people], and especially to those who are of the household of faith" (Gal 6:9–10; RSV). Paul expects the Galatians to endure in their benefaction to all—"do not grow weary," he writes, "do not lose heart." In the Roman patronage system, slaves, freed persons, and the lower classes generally work for their masters or for the upper class. Paul views this dependence on others as a crucial means of survival, but he redefines the client-patron relationship by the concept of mutuality. In Paul's mind the work of Christ, and of God in Christ, as exhibited in the cross, illumines Paul's understanding of love as seeking the good of the other. The Master (Lord Jesus) has come to serve (see Phil 2:7–8).

The secular culture of Rome operated from the top down, from the emperor to the ordinary citizens of the empire. Paul's view of the egalitarian character of life in Christ is radically counter-cultural. Believers made righteous by the act of God in Christ, have been given the honor of being sons of God. This stands in stark contrast to the emperor cult that believed, for example, that Augustus, the adopted son of Julius Caesar, had the status of a *divi filius* (son of the deified).[51] Paul replaces the Roman emperor with the crucified Messiah and risen Lord as the Benefactor. The death and resurrection of the benefactor Christ had dethroned all deities; the faithful followers of Christ were called to be agents of God in doing good to all.

The benefactions of believers are derivative and imitative of the works of Christ and the Spirit. The fundamental will of God in salvation calls people to be righteous and to be free from any form of domination. God's Spirit dwells among the promised heirs of God and bears fruit that eliminates domination and builds community. Doing good works is a basic purpose in being the people of God.

---

51. The temple of Caesar was built in the reign of Augustus. Julius was acknowledged as god. Numismatic evidence as early as 29 BCE shows the image of Caesar's head on one side of a coin, designating him to be a god, and the other side as Augustus. This numismatic evidence reveals that the head of Augustus had replaced the head of Zeus, and Octavian/Augustus was seen as "son of god."

Abraham's Descendants as the People of and for Blessing

The Abrahamic family is comprised not of physical descendants but of those who have faith in God. The family of God as his New Creation is defined by Christ's faithfulness and obedience, and not by circumcision, Torah, or Zhou-*li*. Blessing through the "obedience unto death" of the Messiah—rather than Torah faithfulness—is Paul's way of understanding the suffering righteous, and the Crucified Messiah being the "suffering righteous par excellence."[52] According to Paul, the resurrection as God's vindication of Jesus is not a vindication of the Law so that the Law becomes a blessing to Jews and Gentiles. Rather, God's vindication of Jesus is the overcoming of the Law as a curse on Jesus and on Law-keepers (Gal 3:10–14).[53] In Romans 8 and 1 Corinthians 15 Paul speaks of the suffering of the whole creation, because of the domination of the power of death. Though the Law has its positive functions, Paul thinks of the inability of Torah faithfulness to overcome the power of death.[54] Paul argues that the Abrahamic family and faithfulness of Christ constitutes of people of faith whose sharing with the suffering of Christ is the way to blessing in an age where the power of death is broken through the works of Christ.

Suffering and blessing are interconnected concepts in Paul's theology. But Paul never exhorts Christians to practice the cross or suffering. "It might be a mistake to speak of 'the way of the cross' in Paul, as if it were a discipline of suffering. Instead, Paul calls for the practice of love, imitating Jesus' other-centered way, obeying God, doing good to all."[55] The self-giving and self-sharing life always carries the risk of suffering, through which blessings are extended to others. Extending of blessings to others can be understood as a way of sharing the suffering of Christ.

People of faith/trust are people of God, and they find wholeness only in service to others, and their purpose in life is to bless others. In Galatians, Paul demonstrates the truth of mutual blessing by noting that God's actions toward Abraham were for the benefit of the Gentiles: "In you shall all the nations be blessed" (Gal 3:8).[56] Paul's interpretive task is

52. Yeo, "Paul's Theological Ethic and the Chinese Morality of *Ren Ren*," 270.

53. Ibid.

54. Ibid.

55. Ibid.

56. Paul's citation in Gal 3:8 is a conflation of the Old Testament Greek (Septuagint) reading of Gen 12:3c ("be blessed in you", cf. Gen 28:14b) and 22:18a ("all nations"; cf.

to prove that people of faith are sons of Abraham and children of God
(Gal 3:8–14) through faith in Jesus Christ. It is God's doing through Jesus'
faithfulness (obedience) that creates a new family based on promise and
blessing. Because they have received the blessing of the heirs of God, they
are to bless others as fulfillment of the ancient covenant promise.

A CHINESE CHRISTIAN THEOLOGY
OF *XIN* AND MUTUAL TRUST

信念

Paul's understanding of the cross as inverting the honor-shame systems
of the imperial culture and, *mutatis muntandis*, of the Judaizers is perceptive in that it reveals the basic problems of society—suspicion of, and the
alienation of, each other. Confucius speaks of trust or trustworthiness
(*xin*) as the glue that holds a society together, and without it, all live in
fear of betrayal. We will look at Paul regarding his argument that the
Christians' faith in Christ and their trust in the faithfulness of Christ are
windows that bring light to the dark world of fear.

Confucian Xin *and Pauline* Pistis *(faith)*

↦ Trust as a Relational Concept

Confucius' understanding of *xin* (trust) and Paul's understanding of *pistis* (faith) are relational rather than cognitive concepts. For whether it is
between human beings and God or between human beings themselves,
trust defines the proximity of their relationships. Confucius explains that
xin (trust) is what a person cannot do without (*Analects* 2:22): "*Xin* is as

---

Gen 18:18b; 26:4b). The words *"panta ta ethnē"* ("all nations") are substituted for the
LXX's *"pasai hai phylai"* ("every race") in Gen 12:3 so as to bring in the word "nation"
desired by Paul because of its contemporary usage in the sense of "Gentiles", who are "the
other" to the Jews. Already in Gen 12:3 and 18:18 the compound word "be blessed" is designed to stress the fact that the blessing of Abraham embraces all races and peoples. Gen
12:3 reads "all the tribes (*phylai*) of the earth will be blessed in you"; Gen 18:18 reads "and
through him all the nations (*ethnē*) of the earth will be blessed." *Ethnē* is used commonly
to refer to Gentiles, it works for Paul to use *ethnē* in Gen 18:18 in place of *phulai* as in Gen
12:3. Thus the quotation reads "all the nations will be blessed in you." This universalist
promise was, however, scarcely taken up in the Jewish treatment of Abraham, said C. K.
Barrett in *From First Adam to Last*, 34, 40. Perhaps this is Paul's radical interpretation in
light of the Christ event.

necessary as is the bar in the yoke of a carriage or the pin for the crossbar of a cart."[57] Without mutual trust (*xin*), a society will collapse, and human interaction becomes impossible.

Xin (trust) is a virtue and a human disposition in the moral world of Confucius; while in the theological world of Paul *pistis* (faith) is also relational, but it is between God and human beings. Paul does not regard *pistis* a virtue, an excellence, a piety. For Paul *pistis* is obedient trust, not trust in some mundane hope, but trust in God whose eschatological kingdom has begun to reign in the world in the faithful work of Christ and his body—the church. For Paul *pistis* refers not to trust in general, but trust in Christ whose faith(fulness) serves as the solid ground for humanity to believe in God without believing in vain.

The difference in understandings of faith/trust between Confucius and Paul lies in their view of time in relation to the salvation of the world. For Confucius the creation of an ideal society of *datong* (Great Harmony)[58] is achieved by retrieving the golden age of Zhou, thus by recovering its ritual propriety (*li*) and virtue (*de*). In that sense Confucius' understanding of *xin* (trust) is trust in social harmony. Paul does not believe in harmony as such. He is not expecting the creation of a Peaceable Kingdom of God. He believes that God has entered the world in a radically new way and that the world is about to be transformed, not by his own doing but by an event, coming out of the future, that is of God's doing. Christ's death and resurrection is the first act of God in this new age; it is only partly here, but it is coming. For Paul faith "can be said to 'come' and 'to be revealed' (Gal 3:23, 25)."[59] Bultmann writes that faith in Christ is granted as a gift in the "eschatological Now":

---

57. My translation. Cf. Yang, *Lunyu Yizhu*, 42–43.

58. Ching, *Mysticism and Kingship in China*, 211–12: In *Shiji* (*Records of History*), there is an account of Confucius as the ideal ruler who brought about an ideal society: "Three months after Confucius had assumed the government of the state [*Lu*], even cattle dealers no longer cheated others by demanding excessive prices; men and women walked along different sides of the road, and objects lost on the streets were no longer picked up. Strangers came from the four directions of heaven, but when they arrived in the towns, they never found it necessary to turn to the police, for they were treated as if they were in their own country" (*Shiji* 47:667b). Similar description of an utopian state was achieved by the Duke of Zhou (Zhou Gong) in *Shiji*: In the forty-year rule of the Duke of Zhou, the prison was not used, rituals and music were properly used, people lived in peace and order, and they sang joyful songs. This is the Golden Age Confucius wishes to recover.

59. Bultmann, *Theology*, 1:329. For Karl Barth the Christ event is God's act for the world pertaining to everyone irrespective of anyone's belief. For Bultmann, Barth's

> The eschatological nature of faith is testified by the fact that Paul does not describe faith as inspired, attributable to the 'Spirit.' Just the opposite: The Spirit is the gift which faith receives (Gal 3:2, 5, 14) and in which the grace of God appropriated by faith becomes effective in concrete living. Therefore, Paul calls the 'love' (*agapē*) in which 'faith' is operating the 'fruit of the Spirit,' just as he regards the Christian 'virtues' as a whole to be such fruit (Gal 5:22). . . . The existing of a Christian in the faith that operates in love is eschatological occurrence: a being created anew.[60]

The eschatological nature of faith of believers is linked to the Christ event; that itself is the eschatological event of the new age when God acted decisively in Christ in history. Believers are those who are created anew in Christ, and through their faith in Christ bear the fruit of the Spirit.

❧ Trust and Word, *Yan* or Kerygma

In Confucius' thinking, *xin* is a relational term. *Xin* is highly intangible, therefore *xin* can be risky. Trusting a person who is not trustworthy may cause the subject to feel betrayed or fooled. In Confucius' thinking, trust is often discernible by means of one's words (*yan*). Confucius' assumption is that words not only communicate one's "substance" (*zhi*), they also actualize the norms and values of cultured behavior. Thus the two characters *xinyan* (literally "trust-words" or "trustworthy words") are used together in the *Analects* (13:20; "Speech must be trustworthy, action must be the follow through").[61] "Trust-words" are words that are to be trusted. Words are not merely sounds, words are embodied in one's behavior. It is unacceptable and shameful for one's "word to out-strip one's deeds" (*Analects* 2:13).[62] It is an honor to be trusted merely because of what one has said, and an equal honor *to fulfill* what one has promised. *Analects* 5:10 reads, "I used to take on trust a man's deeds after having listened to his words. Now having listened to a man's words I go on to observe his

---

understanding of the Christ event had no existential (eschatological) meaning. Thus the new age "comes" with faith; apart from faith the new age exists in Bultmann's mind, not Barth's, in potential.

60. Bultmann, *Theology*, 1:330.

61. Lau, trans., *Analects*, 123. Cf. Yang, *Lunyu Yizhu*, 298–99.

62. Lau, trans., *Analects*, 64.

deeds" (*Analects* 5:10).[63] Thus, those who *waste* or *fail* one's words (*shi-yan*), that is, are unable to fulfill one's words, are shamed (*Analects* 15:8).

Because Confucius is preoccupied with the moral world, he believes that credible words are essential in communicating one's essence or worth to others; words that are trustworthy establish the peace and prosperity of a society. While Paul does not reject the significance of trustworthy words, his concern with the theological world makes him connect *pistis* (faith) with the *kerygma* (the proclamation of the good news in Christ). Bultmann calls this "the dogmatic character" of faith

> insofar as it is acceptance of a word: 'the word of faith' (Rom 10:8) or 'the heard word' (*akoē*, KJV: 'the hearing') of faith (Gal 3:2, 5). Hence, faith can also be called 'faith of the gospel'—i.e. faith in the gospel (Phil 1:27).
>
> 'Faith,' which arises from 'what is heard' (Rom 10:17), consequently contains a *knowing*. . . . We *believe* that if we have died with him we shall also live with him (Rom 6:8f; cf. 2 Cor 4:13f). But since this knowledge can be appropriated only in obedient, comprehending faith, and hence contains an understanding of one's self, knowledge may also appear as arising out of faith. . . .
>
> 'Faith,' . . . also has, on the other hand, 'undogmatic' character insofar as the word of proclamation is no mere report about historical incidents. . . . For the word is *kerygma*, personal address, demand, and promise; it is the very act of divine grace. Hence its acceptance—faith—is obedience, acknowledgment, confession.[64]

While the content and the contour out of which, the faith that Confucius and Paul speak of are different, they do share a conviction that the *xin* or the *pistis* of a person can be strengthened by means of word. For Confucius the integrity of a person can be seen in his trustworthy words, which in turn build up community. For Paul the character of a person, his self-knowledge and his faith, are not a matter of the cultivation of virtue. Rather, they are informed, formed, and renewed by the word of God, the gospel of Christ, the word proclaimed.

---

63. Ibid., 77.
64. Bultmann, *Theology*, 1:318–19.

✧ The Power of Word, Trust, and Obedience

An intertextual reading of the *Analects* and Galatians allows us to see the agreement between Confucius and Paul that words have the power to change reality—whether the word is that of a virtuous person or of the God who raised Jesus from the dead. It is generally acknowledged that the power of words is greater than swords. Confucius believed that words can persuade even barbarians: "If you are honest and trustworthy with your speech and humble and serious in your action, you will not have obstacles even in the lands of the barbarians" (*Analects* 15:6).[65] One word could ruin a nation or make it prosperous (*Analects* 13:15). "When the politics of a government is honest and upright, the speech will be honest and upright" (*Analects* 14:3).[66]

We have seen in Chapter Two, a discussion in the context of the words *dao* and *logos*, how Confucius and Paul hold similar opinions. Their similarity resides in how one's rhetoric reflects one's trust of others. According to Confucius, *xin* (trust) refers to "the commitments that one purports to mean by one's word or comportment, not to engender deceptive expectations."[67] Confucius said, "An exemplary person has righteousness (*yi*) as one's basic disposition (*zhi*), developing righteousness (*yi*) in ritual propriety (*li*), expressing it modestly, and consummating it with one's trustworthiness" (*Analects* 15:18).[68] Thus in Confucian ethics, trust (*xin*), together with deference (*kung*), tolerance (*kuan*), diligence (*min*), and generosity (*hui*), are five types of conduct that lead to *ren* (humaneness), for "if you are deferential, you will not suffer insult; if tolerant, you will win over the many; if you [are *xin*], others will rely upon you; if diligent, you will get results; if generous, you will have the status to employ others effectively" (*Analects* 17:6, similarly 20:1).[69]

The Confucian emphasis on virtuous lives is not as radical as Paul's emphasis on *pistis* as "acceptance of the message"—expressed in different ways as "the *kerygma*" (Rom 10:14–17, 1 Cor 1:21), "the gospel" (1 Cor

65. Lau, trans., *Analects*,158. See Qian, *Lunyu Xinjie*, 553–54; Yang, *Lunyu Yizhu*, 346.

66. Lau, trans., *Analects*, 143. Cf. Qian, *Lunyu Xinjie*, 490.

67. Fingarette, "Following the 'One Thread,'" 389.

68. Translation altered from Ames and Rosemont, *Analects*, 188.

69. Ibid., 204. On *Analects* 17:6 see Qian, *Lunyu Xinjie*, 621–22. On *Analects* 20:1 see Yang, *Lunyu Yizhu*, 392.

15:2), "the testimony" (2 Thess 1:10), "the word" (Eph 1:13), or "the hearing" (Rom 10:16; Gal 3:2, 5).[70]

Before proceeding further, we need to take note that the English language is inadequate in expressing either the meaning or flexibility of the Greek word *pistis* or the Chinese word *xin*. In Chinese and in Greek, *xin* and *pistis* (and their derivatives) are used to express the idea of trust/faith. English uses "faith" and "trust" and "belief/believe" to translate *pistis*. It is redundant in English to speak of a "believers' belief," thus sometimes "belief" is used to denote a set of doctrines to which a believer subscribes. Or we interpret "believers' belief" or "believers' faith" not as a thing a person can possess, but as a trusting response to God and God's words. It is grammatically incorrect to write, "we faith in God" in English, so we say "we have trust in God"; or better still, "we trust God." In the following, I work with these limitations of the English language, and use the words "faith" and "trust" (which also entails the meaning of "obedience") interchangeably to express the Greek word *pistis* or the Confucian idea of *xin*. Except for the christological aspect of Paul's understanding of trust (*pistis*), both Confucius and Paul have similar views in many respects. Yet it is this christological dimension found in Paul that reveals the difference in their understanding of faith. We want here to suggest that Paul's christological understanding of faith can serve as a supplement to that of Confucius.

The Pistis of Christ as the Divine Paradigm of the Fully Human

It sounds strange in English to speak of "Jesus' faith"—though the Greek phrase *pistis Iēsou Christou* can mean that if taken as a subjective genitive—so we use the "faithfulness of Jesus Christ."[71] I have used the work

---

70. Bultmann, *Theology*, 1:89.

71. The phrase "faith/trust in/of Jesus Christ" (*Pistis Iēsou Christou*) in Greek can pose a conundrum, because it is a genitival construction and has two possible meanings. The first treats the construction as a subjective genitive, that is, Jesus as the subject of the phrase; it is he who possesses trust/faith. The second function is called the objective genitive, that is, Jesus is the object of the phrase: faith or trust is placed in Jesus. The English phrase "love of God" can be a subjective genitive (that is God's love) or an objective genitive ([our] love for God). My position in this work is that, *both* subjective and objective genitives are used by Paul with objective as more prevalent. For if we take the "faith of Jesus Christ" to be objective genitive, still Christ's own faith is implicit in what our trust in him, while if we take it to be subjective genitive ("our faith in Jesus Christ"),

of Richard Hays to understand the phrase *pistis* or *pistis Iēsou Christo* in certain verses in Galatians as referring to the "faith(fulness) of Jesus Christ." Without getting into the exegetical details, I simply take Hay's interpretation and modify it to see the inseparable significance between the believers' faith and the faith(fulness) of Christ. That is, Christ's faithfulness becomes the paradigm for humanity in becoming fully human.

✎ Works of the Law and the Faithfulness of Christ

The faithfulness of Christ includes his works, for his obedient trust leads him to the cross, his faithfulness makes him fulfill the works of the kingdom and to bring Jews and Gentiles into it. Paul writes that, "those who are of the 'works of the law'" (*hosoi ex ergōn nomou* in Gal 2:16 [3x], 3:10) stand in contrast to "those who are of [Christ's] faithfulness" (*hoi ek pisteōs* in Gal 3:7, 9). The reason that no one is set right[72] before God by the works of the law in the age of the Messiah is because "the righteous shall live from faith" (3:11b). This is a quotation from Hab 2:4. "The righteous" means the one who is set right as a member of the Abrahamic covenant;[73] "from faith" means on the basis of God's (according to the LXX)[74] and Christ's faithfulness. Paul's intention is to show, in contrast

---

still we are called to trust in the efficacy of his faith.

On the interpretive position of the subjective genitive, I follow the work of Hays, *The Faith of Jesus Christ*, 139–90. See a good collection of essays on this debate in Johnson and Hay, ed., *Pauline Theology*, Volume IV: *Looking Back, Pressing On*. On my argument, see Yeo, "Salvation by Grace Through Faith," 66–77.

72. "Set-right" or "justify" can mean: (1) accepted as a member of God's people; (2) accepted as a righteous/sinless person (ethically) before God; (3) the relationship of a person to God being set right juridically without altering the righteousness/sinfulness of that person. Based on our discussion in 2:16, Paul here does not introduced a new argument regarding the role of the law or works of the law in making a person sinless and therefore righteous in the eyes of God. To "set right" needs to be understood in terms of covenantal language. That is, a person who is already in the covenant is set right in his/her relationship with God and will maintain that relationship by doing "works of the law."

73. Both Cosgrove (*The Cross and the Spirit*, 56–59) and Hays (*The Faith of Jesus Christ*, 207) mention that the early church used to read the phrase "the righteous one" as Jesus. If so, the phrase "from faith" is difficult to explicate: what is the point of saying Jesus lives from faith or through faith? Is Paul trying to prove the significance of Christ's faith? If so, the previous phrase "is justified" should also mean the justification of Christ, but of course that is absurd. It is more likely that the righteous one means those who are set right by God to be in the covenant.

74. While the Old Testament Hebrew text (MT) qualifies faith with "his", that is, the

to the curse that characterizes that those who are under the works of the law, that those under the obedience-faith of Christ will have life.

Galatians 3:12 makes an even sharper differentiation of the "works of the law" and "Christ's faithfulness": "But the law is not from [Christ's] faithfulness." Paul quotes Lev 18:5 to say that the law does have a valid role: "the one who does them will live by them" (3:12). Paul acknowledges the possibility that the law can be practiced and obeyed by members of the Abrahamic covenant (the Jews), even though previously, in 3:10, he has shown how difficult it is "to do everything written in the Book of the law."[75] The initial argument of Gal 3:8–14 centers on the works of the law and on Christ's faithfulness as the identity markers of those belonging to Abraham. The argument gradually touches on the quality of the life of the participants when Paul begins to speak of "curse/blessing" and of the one "hanged on the tree" [cursed] / "shall live" [blessed].[76] Paul appropriately

---

faith of the one who is righteous, the LXX qualifies faith with "my," that is, the faithfulness of God. Paul's quotation leaves out the possessive pronoun, thus making the word "faith" ambiguous. It could mean Christ's faith, or the faith of a person who is set right by God. If the quotation is used to prove scripturally that no one is set right by God by works of the law, the quotation confirms that the one who is set right by God will live from Christ's faith(fulness) whom the believer trusts.

75. This quotation is taken from the section in Leviticus which deals with laws on sexual prohibitions. The OT context is not crucial to Paul. The important point is the stern exhortation and promise of the Lord to the Israelites through Moses: "You shall do my ordinances and keep my statutes and walk in them. I am the Lord your God" (Lev 18:5).

76. The scriptural support for the Messiah becoming a curse in order to redeem Jews and Gentiles from the curse of the law is Deut 21:23, which Paul quotes: "Cursed be everyone hung on a tree" (3:13b). Deut 21:22–23 speaks of the propitiation of Yahweh's wrath toward the criminal hung upon a tree. "Being hung on the tree" is an OT covenantal symbol that points to Israel's bearing the curse and how God's blessing could remove the curse. Deut 21:23 has "cursed by God is everyone hung on a tree," Paul drops the words "by God" so that the subject who cursed the Messiah is not stated. The subject could not be "God" because Christ died under the curse of the law. Paul also changes "everyone" in Deut 21:23 to "the one," meaning Christ. The Deuteronomy text describes the Jewish practice of hanging deceased criminals on a tree for public disgrace. Jesus Christ died on a Roman cross, a punishment that was reserved for non-Romans and the worst of criminals.

The thought of Gal 3:13a is repeated in Gal 4:5: God sent his Son to redeem those under the law. The purpose of Christ's death and of becoming a curse on our behalf is twofold: "in order that the blessing of Abraham might be extended to the Gentiles in Christ Jesus" (3:14a), and "in order that we might receive the promised Spirit through faith" (3:14b).

On the use of Deut 21:22–23 in Gal 3:13, see Caneday, "Redeemed."

emphasizes the law's inability to set people right in their relationship with God and to maintain their membership in the Abrahamic covenant.

✧ The "Faithfulness of Jesus" and the Boasting of the "Works of the Law"

Faithfulness entails faith; that is true for Jesus Christ, and for humanity as well. We have seen how Confucius talks about the kind of commitment and persistence that comes with trust. Trusting and boasting are not two different modes of living—though we often use the word "trusting" positively and "boasting" negatively. For Paul both words speak of the confidence one has. The question is the object one trusts or boasts in, viz., self or God. Bultmann contrasts the attitude of faith in God with that of boasting in self or other things in Paul's understanding:

> The attitude of sinful self-reliance finds its extreme expression in man's 'boasting' (*kauchasthai*). It is characteristic both of the Jew, who boasts of God and the Torah (Rom 2:17, 23), and of the Greek, who boasts of his wisdom (1 Cor 1:19–31). It is also a natural tendency of man in general to compare himself with others in order to have his 'boast' thereby (Gal 6:4). . . . In 'boasting' is revealed a misconstruing of the human situation, a forgetting of the fact implied by the question, 'What do you have that you have not been given? And if it has been given you, why do you boast as if it had not been given you?' (1 Cor 4:7). . . . There is only one valid boast: 'Let him who boasts, boast of the Lord' (1 Cor 1:31; 2 Cor 10:17). Therefore, the Christian must be warned also against haughtily looking down on others (Gal 6:4; Rom 11:17f). And when Paul does once boast, he does it in the 'fool's' role (2 Cor 11–12) which he has adopted; and yet in so doing he turns his 'boasting after the flesh' into a paradoxical 'boasting,' by boasting of his 'weakness' (2 Cor 11:30, 12:9; cf. Rom 5:2). Thus he confesses, 'Far be it from me to boast except in the cross of our Lord Jesus Christ, by which the world has been crucified to me, and I to the world' (Gal 6:14; cf. Rom 5:11).[77]

Bultmann continues to explain that boasting is a universal exhibition of one's fear. In fear humanity seeks reliance on things other than God:

---

77. Bultmann, *Theology*, 1:242.

The *fear* which the man who is concerned for himself has [is] the fear which arises both from zeal in the works of the law and from zeal in wisdom.... The period before faith ... was under the sway of fear.... [It] holds true not only insofar as both Judaism and paganism are under slavery to the 'elemental spirits of the universe,' which for the Jews are represented by the Torah, for the Gentiles by 'beings that by nature are no gods' (Gal 4:1–10), but it especially holds true insofar as 'life after the flesh' leads into slavery to 'flesh' and 'sin.' Both he who 'desires' and he who is 'anxious with care,' both he who 'boasts' and he who 'relies upon' something, in reality makes himself dependent upon that which he supposes he can control.[78]

The radical giving up of boasting in works of the law is the attitude of faith, one that imitates the faithfulness of Jesus Christ. The "works of the law" (which maintain the covenant with God) be nothing more than exhibiting the human response of fear. Though works of the law can be a faithful response to God, for Paul Christ's trust in God is the absolute paradigm, so that even the law becomes secondary as an expression of human trust. There are many theological reasons why Paul thinks this.

The first reason has to do with the Christological qualification of *pistis* (trust). In the case of the Galatians, given that in Jewish self-understanding "covenantal nomism" (maintaining the covenant by law observance) is not antithetical to faith or trust (*pistis*). The only change or extension that the new movement asks for is that the traditional Jewish faith be more precisely defined as faith (*pistis*) in Jesus the Messiah. Being set right by faith is an old Jewish concept, being set right *in and through the* pistis *(faithfulness) of Christ Jesus* is not. In contrast to righteousness under the law, Paul speaks of the righteousness that comes through Christ's faithfulness, which becomes the pattern of human faith in God. Being set right by means of the "faithfulness of Jesus Christ" is something new to Jews. So the "faith of Jesus Christ" becomes a new identity marker for Jewish and Gentile Christians. Only through Christ are believers set right with God through God's gracious justifying works in Christ's obedience.

The second reason is, in light of the reality of Christ's coming (the new inaugurating age, the eschatological Now), were believers still to follow the ritual of the law, then the efficacy of Christ's crucifixion would be denied. Paul ends this section of Galatians (1:10—2:21) stating his pas-

78. Ibid., 1:243.

sionate conviction that Christ's death is the new identity symbol for the people of God. Were the law to remain a valid symbol, Christ would have died in vain: "I have not voided the grace of God, for if righteousness were through the law, then Christ died in vain." Paul is confident that he has neither voided nor nullified (*athetein*, in 2:21; see also 3:5) the grace of God—to the contrary, the grace of God is manifested in Jesus' life and crucifixion.

It is not that the law was incapable of imputing God's righteousness to believers, and for that reason God's Son had to die. It is, rather, that the law and all the works of the law were never designed to include Gentiles as the people of God (Gal 3:21: "For if a law had been given capable of providing life, righteousness would really have been from the law"), so the law's function and requirements are now fulfilled in Christ's faithfulness. For Christ's faithfulness signified by the Cross is the only and sufficient symbol to grant both Jews and Gentiles peaceful coexistence!

⤳ "Trusting in Christ's Faith(fulness)"

The third theological reason Paul differentiates the old identity symbol from the new is to set trust in God over against trust in culture or the world, even if that culture is sacred and its law and *li* (rituals) are ideal. Paul's concern for the identity symbol of the law/*li* is not about its cultural and religious dimensions. It is not that culture is relative and religion absolute; it is not that works of the law are inferior and Christian faith superior. Paul's concern is about the human propensity to trust in law or *li* rather than in God or *tian*. We have discussed in Chapter One that culture and religion are not two separate entities. It is because culture and theology are inseparable, that Paul's theology of the cross constantly deconstructs distorted responses of faith. Faith or trust is the basic human response to one's perceived sacred culture, holding to it and boasting about it. Human beings create gods out of cultural ideals, ideals they believe they can comfortably count on. So Paul's theological response to his Jewish Christian opponents is to call upon them to "trust in Christ's faith(fulness)." What does "Christ's faith(fulness)" mean in the context of his not trusting in the Jewish "theological culture"?

The historical Jesus was Jewish both culturally *and* theologically (popularly understood as "religiously"). His identity—the oneness of his divinity and humanity, and his trust, love, and obedience to God—made him conscious of his mission as the Messiah. He was faithful to God and loved humanity even though his sacred culture (torah obedience) had other visions and prohibitions (e.g., against healing on the sabbath, associating with sinners, etc.). When his calls to be obedient to God and to do the requirements of the law were in tension, Jesus willed to place his ultimate faith in God. Consequently, he was despised as a "law-breaker," charged as a "blasphemous" teacher, and crucified. In other words, Jesus did not place his absolute trust in sacred Jewish culture and its "nomistic services." Jesus was utterly dependent on God and he found expression of that trust in loving humanity without reservation. Jesus was able to see the blind-spots in his own theological culture because his faith in God made him aware of its inadequacy. This point is most vividly seen in the crucifixion, which is central to Paul's theology. Had he obliged himself to do all the requirements of the law, he would have been a perfect Jewish Messiah—or would he? Would he not have made an idol out of the sacred culture?

The implication of Christ's faith in God rather than in the law is that humanity (Jews and Gentiles) is plagued with insecurity, seeking to secure its interests by way of cultural ideals. Not knowing who it is and not being able to comprehend the purpose of its existence, humanity lives in fear that manifests itself in such paranoid actions as self-glorification, cultural boasting, and discrimination against those who are different. Galatians highlights freedom as the context for defining salvation. Indeed, human beings are saved by faith in Christ's faith(fulness) for his faithfulness has redeemed humanity from bondage to freedom, from being slaves to being sons of God, from fear of scarcity to the celebration of plentitude, from cultural boasting to peaceful coexistence, from self-glorification to union with God.

↤ Christian Faith is Faith in Christ Imitating
the Faithfulness of Christ

Christ's faithfulness does not negate or make irrelevant the individual's faith-response in Christ and God; in fact, it requires that people believe in Christ because of what Christ has done—trusting fully in God and obeying God out of love. Christ's faithfulness is the objective identity symbol of the new people of God, inclusive of Jews and Gentiles; their faith in Christ is grounded in Christ's faithfulness, for without it their faith is null, their hope mundane. Because Christ's faithfulness is proven true in God's raising Jesus from the dead, Christ' self-sacrificing love becomes victory over the powers of evil (hatred, revenge, etc.).

Faith in Christ does not end on the cross; suffering and death are not the end result of giving one's self freely in love. The whole Christ event has immediate implications for the faith of human beings in Christ and in God—Christian faith. Christians believe not in a dead hero but a risen Lord. Christian faith is about believing in the ultimate (God) so that one may live faithfully in a world that is penultimate. For Jesus to be faithful to God, being obedient even unto death on a cross, required faith in God.

If Jesus had had no faith, his fear would have handicapped him. Jesus knew that his words and works in the world had something to do with the power behind the world. Fear blurs one's vision. Fear disables one to recognize the power of life over death. Fear gives up on the resource of faith and retreats into paralysis. Christians are adopted sons of God, thus Christian faith models Christ's faith(fulness). Such faith believes that what happens in the world has ultimacy behind it, for woven into the fabric of human existence is both cross and resurrection. This fabric is God's design for creation. What is true for the fully human one, Jesus Christ, is also true for all human beings. The faith and faithfulness of Christ is the divine paradigm for all who believe in God, who believe that God was in Christ and that Christ trusted God, thus human beings are to live in faith, rather than in fear.

To imitate the faith of Christ and to rely on the faithfulness of Christ (cf. Rom 3:26) is to *be* the people of God demonstrating God's self-giving love. The faithful obedience of Jesus is demonstrated in his living for others, "giving himself for us" (Gal 2:20, cf. Rom 15:3). Sharing the faith of Jesus Christ "includes sharing his other-centered way."[79] Cosgrove explains,

> Paul uses the generous love of God in Christ as an example for Christians to imitate, it follows that the moral structure of this love applies to our love for others. Love is not to be based on merit. As a generous or unconditional act, love creates indebtedness,

---

79. Cosgrove, "Paul and American Individualism," 77.

thus producing forms of dependence. . . . The higher rule is the "law of Christ" (Gal 6:2), and to live by this law means seeing oneself as both needing generous love and obliged to show generous love to others. Love outlasts the present evil age [Gal 1:4], remaining the highest value even in the morally perfect world of the new creation (1 Cor 13:8–13). In Paul's understanding, since love is inherently gracious, then the centrality of love for the new creation means that the grace of love is not only a way of dealing with sin but is intrinsically good, a value in itself. . . . Paul thinks of grace as the basic order of unity in Christ, an order of interdependence in which we know ourselves indebted to others and wholly dependent on God who has graced us with each other. Freedom from sin does not obviate love's grace; it enables us to live fully in the grace of love, as both givers and receivers.[80]

In Paul's Christology, the imitation of Christ is not a matter of doing but of being. We have discussed in Chapter Three that the sacraments or rites, as both Confucius and Paul would understand them, are powerful aids in visualizing and experiencing the transformation from doing to being, from the self to God and to others. The old orientation, the old self, dies; in its place a new creation. Ritual propriety (*li*) and sacraments are a matter of being, forming one to be "fully human"—the full nature of Heaven or the complete image of God.

The question in this chapter, extending that of Chapter Three is, whether one can become "fully human" according to Confucian thought? In Pauline thought: Can one, like Jesus, fulfill the "image and likeness of God" that is in Jesus? The answer is ambiguous—yes and no—for Paul and Confucius. For Confucius, everyone can become a sage, become his best moral self, though few truly attain the goal of one's full humanity and becoming benevolent/humane persons (*renren*). Similarly for Paul, Jesus is the *only* Son of God, but as sons of God people are called to imitate Jesus. Christians are not asked to become Christs. Christian reconciliation and communion with God are works of divine grace, which Christians themselves cannot do. Similarly, Confucianists are admonished to become sages and to be one with *tian*; but the difference between Confucius and Paul is that, for Confucius "one with *tian*" means conciliation, but for Paul "one with God" means reconciliation. Confucian thought believes that human nature is derived from the nature of *tian* and that relation-

80. Ibid.

ship has never broken.[81] They believe that becoming *renren* and sages is a cultivation of the human nature, which itself is a heavenly gift. Though Confucianists are not asked to become *tian*, the goal of "becoming one with *tian*" suggests that some people become parts of *tian*. For Confucius, the answer to the question of becoming a sage is ambiguous because the language of heavenly nature (as human nature) always entails cultivation of virtue. Thus in Confucian ethics, those who "know Heaven (*zhitian*) . . . cultivate their nature (*yangxing*), and consequently serve Heaven (*shitian*)."[82] For Paul, the answer to the question of fulfilling the complete image of God in people is ambiguous because the language of ontology (e.g., being people of God) always entails the process of becoming.[83] Thus in Paul's Christology, though the imitation of Christ is a matter of being (rather than doing), *both* "the faith of Christ" *and* "the faith in Christ" are *needed*.

The "faith of Jesus" is in God and in fulfilling the Great Commandment. The faith of Jesus is about being loving toward God and people. Had Jesus not believed in the Great Commandment, he would not have gone to the cross, he would not have asked his enemies be forgiven, etc. But people are asked to believe in Jesus' faith, to *believe* that God, the Creator of the Universe, is behind both the Commandment *and* the Jesus who fulfilled it. If they *believe* that God's forgiving love has been manifested in Jesus Christ, then they respond in loving thankfulness. Salvation is therefore about *being* in God's love, whether or not Christians are always able (as Christ was able) to respond lovingly and forgivingly to life.

The Judaizers in Galatia might be thinking that doing the law was the way, in Confucian language, to be "fully human." Paul disagreed. Paul sees to be fully human is *to be a new creation in Christ*. Christians are "sons of God" made in God's form and likeness. Faith for the Judaizers means doing the laws still for the purpose of realizing their humanity. Faith for Paul means being in Christ. The imitation of Christ is the fulfill-

---

81. Confucian ethics and Pauline theology differ from each other in their different understandings of human nature in relation to nature of *tian* or God.

82. My translation. See Zhu, ed., *Sishu*, 650.

83. In juridical Christology, salvation is never possible until God pronounces one righteous based on a legal system or court of justice. The Pharisaic Paul seems to have a juridical understanding of salvation. In ontological Christology, salvation is always possible because of Christ, the Son of God, has done—restoring God's image in us. Thus, we can become sons of God through faith.

ing of one's being, of achieving "full humanity"—not apart from suffering, but through suffering in love for the other.

↩ Fear of Lawlessness and Sin: Trusting Christ's Life in Us

The Jewish Christians in Galatia are held captive by *fear* (Gal 2:12). In Gal 2:17 Paul raises a question on behalf of his opponents: If in seeking to be God's people by taking up the new identity symbol of Christ, are not those who believe in Christ like Gentile sinners who are without the law? And would that not make Christ "an agent of sin" (*hamartias diakonos*)? The fear of Jewish Christians is that Christ has made them the same as Gentile sinners. This fear is reflected also in Peter and Barnabas when they withdraw their table fellowship from Gentiles (Gal 2:13–14).

Paul's answer to the question in Gal 2:17 is "Let it not be!" or "Certainly not!" Paul argues: "If I build again those things which I tore down, I show myself to be a transgressor" (2:18). Paul's answer seems to accuse Peter of being a transgressor because, by his actions, he has built up the law as a wall discriminating Jews from Gentiles, a wall he had previously torn down when he ate at the table with the Gentiles. The personal narrative of "I" relates the hypothetical possibility of Paul being a transgressor: "If I were to rebuild those things (the law and its nomistic services that would enslave the Gentiles) which I tore down. . . . " The irony is not lost on Paul. In his mind the relationship between the law and transgression has been *redefined*: the law, which was originally given so that transgression would be avoided, now leads people to transgression. The very law that differentiated the sacred from the profane, and Jews from Gentiles, propagates enmity and hatred between peoples.[84]

Paul's own imitation of Christ serves as the paradigm for others, especially Jewish Christians, to deal with their fear: "For through the law I died to the law, in order that I might live to God. I am crucified with Christ. It is no longer I who live, but Christ lives in me. The life I now live in the flesh, I live by the faith in the Son of God, who loved me and gave himself for me" (Gal 2:19–20). Instead of building up what one has torn down (the law), one should *die (apothneskein) to the law and live to God*. That is, one should imitate Jesus who placed his complete faith/trust

---

84. Martyn, *Galatians*, 256. Martyn argues that the personal narrative in this section is Paul's way of presenting himself as the paradigm of human beings (258).

in God and not in the sacred culture (torah).[85] Paul argues that the new existence that comes from faith in Christ and dying to the law will bring life and not transgression.

What does Paul mean by the words "through the law I died to the law"?[86] Given the context, I take it to mean that Paul understood the new paradigm of his life to be Christ: Christ was born under the law (Gal 4:4) and its curse, and was crucified. But Christ became the curse of the law and died under the law so that he would redeem humankind from the curse of the law (3:13) and from the elements of the cosmos (4:3). Christ accomplished all that by having trust in God rather than the law.

Paul responds to the fear of Jewish Christians about the new and the old identity symbols (law and Christ) by summarizing his "trust in the faithfulness of Christ": "I am crucified with Christ. . . . Christ lives in me . . . I live by faith in the Son of God,[87] who loved me and gave himself for me" (2:20). The "I" can be read as autobiographical, it can also be read as representative of humanity (*anthrōpos*). While the law errs in differentiating human beings into Jews from Gentiles, Christ gives human beings new identities and new life. So Paul's participation in the Christ event becomes the paradigm of trust, based on love, that overcomes fear. Paul knows that God through Christ *loves* him, even dying *for* him (accepting the curse of the law). Paul also knows that there are no cosmic powers that can separate him from God's love. Paul trusts that God is love. With the gift of life interpreted by God's love, those who respond with trust and gratitude can do no less but to love. In doing so, one becomes a child of God.

85. See Rom 7:4 "In the same way, you have died to the law through the body of Christ."

86. "Through the law" can have three meanings: (1) the law that acted as a pedagogue that led Paul to Christ (3:24) has ceased its role, therefore Paul can say he has ceased to live in obedience to it as his guardian; (2) the law that serves as God's commandment for believers (Rom 7:11) is rendered ineffective, therefore Christians have died to the law (Rom 7:4); (3) the law that pronounced Christ to be a law-breaker and that crucified Christ as a curse from God constitutes death and crucifixion (3:13). See Martyn, *Galatians*, 257.

87. Paul is not talking about how he lived by faith in the Son of God, rather he is talking about how he lived by the faithfulness of God's Son. "By" is understood in the sense of "through"—participation in the faith or faithfulness of God's Son.

∾ The Ritual of Crucifying Life

The ultimate problem in forming a community does not reside with law (or *li*) or with Christ, rather, it is with the self that is bound by fear. The Confucian understanding of the social self of *renren* (humane persons) suggests what human beings fear is independent and lonely existence—being an unattached self free from *tian* and *dao* and from others. While the problem in Galatia of Jewish and Gentile coexistence may sound like that of a splintered community, the root problem is the broken identity of its constituents who want to act as independent, autonomous, free selves. In Galatians Paul emphasizes group dependence and moral responsibility for members within a community. Bultmann explains that

> the sinful self-delusion that one lives out of the created world can manifest itself both in unthinking recklessness (this especially among the Gentiles) and in considered busy-ness (this especially among Jews)—both in the ignoring or transgressing of ethical demands and in excessive zeal to fulfill them. For the sphere of 'flesh' is by no means just the life of instinct or sensual passions, but is just as much that of the moral and religious efforts of man.[88]

Paul's theological presupposition regarding anthropology is that the "self" is under the control of cosmic elements (Gal 4:3) and the cursing power of the law (3:10), therefore the flesh and its desires (Gal 5:24) are in bondage to sin expressing their works in divisive and conflicting ways within the community (Galatians 5–6). In turning away from God, the "self" seeks itself. A life "after the flesh" is a self-reliant pursuit of one's interest, "to which Christian freedom is not to give free rein."[89] An autonomous self is a form of deception that assumes an individual can be independent from God and others, and that his freedom is without responsibility. Salvation in Christ is a liberation from the imprisonment of self and from the enslavement of one's passions. It is a salvation to "Christ-realization" (Gal 4:19), not "self-realization."[90]

The "self" finds either the law or the Christ appealing as its identity symbol because of the possible liberating role each might play. With

88. Bultmann, *Theology*, 1:239.

89. Ibid.

90. See also other Pauline writings on his other-oriented teaching rather than that of self-fulfillment: Rom 2:7–8; 1 Cor 10:24; and Phil 2:4.

regard to the law, the nomistic ritual process defines the old people of God, granting human selves freedom within the boundary markers of the law. Yet, human fear uses the law and *li* for its own self-interest. Out of fear Judaizers used their cultural ideals to define the identity of the Gentiles. The law provides a sense of security through the establishment of limits. This sense of security is lost if someone, such as the Christian Paul, comes along and argues for a law-free gospel. The Judaizers fear that Paul's law-free gospel will tear down the establishment of limits. The Judaizers required the law to avoid this perplexity. In contrast, Paul seeks to overcome their fear by recognizing a higher law, which is in fact articulated by the law, which is loving God and one's neighbor. Paul also uses the crucifixion of Christ to expand the definition of the people of God. For Paul, the crucifixion of Christ is the enduring state (he uses the perfect tense *systaurōmai* in Gal 2:19) in which the believer can find identity through other-centeredness. This is done through two steps: first, identification with and participation in others; second; trusting in the wholly Other.

First, fear is overcome through identification with and participation in others, which sets the Jewish and Gentile Christians free from bondage to the law. The identification of the self with Christ is the letting go of oneself so as to allow Christ to come in (Gal 2:20). In Gal 2:20 the Greek text both differentiates and identifies "I" with "Christ" in the following word order: "live and no long *I*, lives but in me *Christ*." Here Paul is describing the imitative and participatory process of identifying himself with the life and the crucifixion of Christ. Christian rituals such as baptism and Eucharist are symbols that point to the freedom of the human self in its ability to identify with and participate in others through identification with and participation in Christ. Rom 6:6 speaks of this fact in reference to believers' baptism: "We know that our old self was crucified with him."

The imitation/participating rituals of the baptism and the Eucharist entail not a passive letting go and allowing Christ to live in the "self"; it is the "self" actively living by the faithfulness of the Son of God (Gal 2:20).[91]

---

91. Since the process of identifying with or imitating Christ assumes already the need for faith on the part of the believer, the phrase "I live by faith in/of the Son of God" is to be interpreted as a subjective genitive meaning—"the faith(fulness) of God's Son." The title Son of God, used frequently by Paul (Rom 1:4; 5:10; 8:3, 29, 32; 1 Cor 1:9; 15:28; Gal 1:16; 2:21; 4:4; 1 Thess 1:10), connotes the absolute obedience and utter trust of Jesus

In other words, despite the constraint and the negative influence of the flesh (*sarx*), the problem of fear and insecurity can be overcome not by returning to the self but by participating in the reality of Christ that is larger than ourselves. For the Judaizers the law provides a sense of security through the establishment of limits. This sense of security is lost, for example, when the boundary of fellowship meal for a mixed community is unclear. Fear arises in the knowledge that their identity and religious tradition were relativized. The Judaizers required the law to avoid this perplexity. For Paul fear is overcome by recognizing that there is a higher law, what is in fact articulated in the law of loving God and neighbor. Fear is overcome by connecting to the Source of love and by being propelled toward the goal of loving others.

Secondly, fear is overcome by trusting in the wholly Other.

Trusting in the Wholly Other   (Barthian ?)

Confucius believed that fear is the dark side of human relationships,[92] that trust (*xin*) is the way out of fear. One is gripped by fear when he perceives himself to be at a disadvantage, or his identity threatened, if he does not dominate others. Abuse and violent acts are human responses for coping with fear and suspicion, since most do not recluse themselves or hide. Despite knowing that manipulation and abuse do not restore security, people in general still act in these ways to avoid against vulnerability. They define others through themselves.

↬ Social Self of God and Humanity

The Confucian understanding of interpersonal relations as *ren* (humaneness), *xin (trust)*, *zhongshu* (loyalty and empathy) emphasizes others as the center of one's self; only through others can one become fully human. Similarly, Paul sees Christ as one who lived out his full humanity through

---

toward the Father. This obedience and trust constitute the faithfulness of Christ, which becomes the paradigm of the believers' faith and obedience.

92. See *Analects* 9:29: "The wise are not confused; the benevolent are not anxious; the courageous are not afraid"; *Analects* 12:4: "Sima Niu asked about the exemplary person (*junzi*). Confucius replied, "The excellent person is not anxious or afraid.""

loving others. Instead of defining others via oneself, one finds his identity in others. Trust is the key for one to live as a social self.

Both Confucius and Paul understand humanity as a social construct in which individual selves need trust to be in relationship with others, but it is Paul's understanding of the "community of God," viz., God the Father, Jesus the Son of God, and the Spirit of God, that has direct implications for the "community of humanity." As a social self who lives in co-relationship with others, the human community is made possible only by bonds of mutual trust. The "community of God" is constituted by the reciprocal relationship of love and trust, self-surrender and self-dedication of God, Christ, and the Spirit. This reciprocal relationship is especially vivid in God who is in Christ. The openness of each person in the "community of God" models for humanity the essential ingredients of love for and trust in others in order to secure absolute freedom. This openness to others allows God the Father, Christ the Son, and the Holy Spirit to be in reciprocal relationship of love and trust, self-surrender and self-dedication.

The incarnation and death of Jesus is God's way of revealing to humanity the way of becoming fully human. The transcendence of God does not prohibit the immanence of God from manifesting itself in Christ and in the Holy Spirit. The incarnation of the Word or the Christ is the most vivid manifestation of God's immanence (present in the other) in Jesus. Christ becomes totally human. In the incarnation the otherness (transcendence) of God remains transcendent, unknown and unknowable. The God-in-Christ relates most personally to the other (humanity). The incarnation of Christ is God's way of becoming fully human while remaining fully divine.

↭ Otherness of Self and the Son of God

Paul describes the incarnation of the Son of God as "born of woman, born under the law" (Gal 4:4). The phrase "born of woman" neither emphasizes nor denies virgin birth. The phrase is not as explicit as "born of Mary." Paul highlights the pride/glory, the shame/curse, of woman under the law. Jesus is the son of a woman who has no legal rights. In his incarnation the Christ has given up all the rights and privileges as Son of God, as son of man he becomes an outcast. The second phrase "born under the law" (Gal 4:4) has a similar tone. "Under the law" carries a negative connotation, meaning born under the bondage and curse of the law (see Gal 3:23 and 4:5). Jesus, a full Jew, is as such expected to practice all the requirements of the law. If the Gospel's writers are correct, this "son of the law" did not *fully* obey the law. The two phrases therefore describe Jesus as one who lived at the margin of society, often identical with sinners and outcasts.

However, it is as one "born of woman" and "born under the law" that we see Jesus in his humanity, trusting in God and obedient to God's will. Jesus does not seek security and comfort in the places of royalty, but lives as one who has no where to lay his head. Jesus does not place trust in sacred culture, rather he seeks first God's righteousness and doing God's perfect will. So it is the trust and faithfulness of Christ that redeems those under the law (Gal 4:5)—the Jews, and that redeems the Gentiles who receive adoption as God's sons and daughters. Gal 4:5 uses the word *exagorase* ("ransomed"), the same word used in 3:13 to explain how Christ ransomed those under the law from its curse. The word has its socio-economic background in slave trading. Slaves are ransomed so that they might gain their freedom from a dominating power. The self-sacrifice of Christ on the cross is understood as purchasing those under the law so that they not live under the custodianship of the law anymore, so that they might live in Christ as heirs and live in the power of God's Spirit.

The second purpose God has in sending his Son is "so that we might receive adoption" (Gal 4:5). This second clause is parallel but not subordinated to the first, that is, Paul does not mean that the adoption of Gentiles as God's people is dependent on the ransom of the Jews from the curse of the law. Paul here is not spelling out "the Jew first and then also the Gentile" in terms of salvation history. Rather, Paul explains that the purpose of the Christ event is to liberate both Jews and Gentiles.

To ransom both Jews and Gentiles from slavery and for freedom, Christ became an outcast. He lived a life of love and trust, thus saving humanity from fear and self-destruction. The cruciform love of Christ now stands in contrast to the insecurity of humanity: Christ's trust, humanity's mistrust. God's righteousness is made available to all according to the principle of faith (trust) rather than through conformity to a cultural or religious system. Paul contends that God's love is so ordered on the cross that it makes room for all to become fully human through loving one's neighbor. Paul understands the cross as the voluntary limitation of the divine in which love is exhibited as complete trust (Gal 1:4 "who gave himself for us"; 2:20 "gave himself for me"; 3:13 "he became a curse for us"). Rather than being self-absorbed in fear, Christ's self-sacrifice is *kenotic*, the self-giving love of God who transcends boundaries and as God becomes fully human. Jesus the cursed (*katara* in Gal 3:13) on the cross (death and resurrection) lifted the curse of the law and fulfilled the law by his self-giving love for all.

✧ Love as Reaching Out (*Zhong*) and Self-Forgetting (*Shu*)

Love is self-revealing, it reaches out to others, it shares with all. Love holds love back. There are no preconditions to acts of love. Love is reaching out (*zhong*) and self-forgetting (*shu*), and may sometimes include self-sacrifice. Because love cannot be coerced, love is persuasive and powerful in its transformation of others. As humanity learns the civility of this divine love and grace, societies will become virtuous and at peace. God's love on the cross is full of grace because it comes from the sovereign Creator. Humanity will do well to be at home with each other, as the incarnation and death of God's Son has shown. Through his self-giving and self-forgetting Jesus shows us his obedience and love as he trusted God. Christ's empathy (*shu*) toward humanity is grounded in his trust in God's faithfulness. Thus the humanity of Christ and the divinity of Christ are at one with each other; they are neither mechanical additions nor syncretistic in nature, but a perfect communion and personal union. Christ is loyal (*zhong*) and empathetic (*shu*) towards humanity and trusted God even unto death. The imitation of Christ remains an act of faith. In such act humanity find its fulfillment in others even by becoming vulnerable and open towards others, trusting that honor and blessing arise from honoring and blessing others.

✧ The "Scandal" of the Cross (Gal 5:11)

Christ's love for humanity and his trust in God are life that reached out to others. It is a life that fulfills the Great Commandment, the Law of love. The life of Christ is one of love. Yet, his devotion to being love costs him his life. It is this irony that Gal 5:11 summarizes the power of the Cross as a "scandal." The scandal of the cross (*to skandalon tou staurou*) may be a Jewish view that a crucified Messiah is incredible—not to be believed. For Greeks it is simply foolishness. From a Christian perspective there is no scandal. For the Christians it is a simply truth that since the crucified Jesus is the Messiah then the curse of the law is no curse at all—that law is void. The curse exists only to those outside the faith. God does not send his Son to die as a curse. Christ whom the law pronounced as cursed has lifted the curse of the law and set Jews and Gentiles right with God through his faithfulness via their faith.

The reality of God-in-Christ is that the most powerful, most wise, most gracious God reveals who he is by being love, rather than to retaliate, on the Cross. God reveals his might by surrendering it on the cross. God reveals his grace by blessing all humanity with the endowment of his own Spirit. These are "scandalizing" thoughts. The cross also reveals the impotence of humanity to absolutize its power by coercing or dominating others, the foolishness of humanity to define others through its own ideals, the bondage of humanity to live in constant fear, defensiveness, and self-boasting.

If the "scandal" of the cross is removed, Paul's gospel loses its persuasiveness and power to save. That the scandal is not removed indicates that the power of God's grace to love humanity is still effective in the Christ event.

TOWARD A CIVIL SOCIETY OF TRUST AND *ZHONGSHU*

The question of co-existence and civility is central to both Confucius' and Paul's thought. People of *xin*/trust are people who love, they are "at home with each other" (see *Analects* 4:2), they are fond of *de* (virtue, 9:18, 15:13), *ren* (humaneness; 4:6), *li* (propriety; 1:15, 13:4; 14:41), *yi* (righteousness; 12:20, 13:4), *xin* (trustworthiness; 13:4), *shan* (goodness, 12:19, 15:10). Despite vulnerability and fear, human beings should enjoy each other in the civility of *zhong, shu, xin*, because they are created to be mutual benefactors. Confucius used *li* and *ren* to answer the problems of a splintered society, moral deterioration, and ethnic conflict. He believed that "the person of *ren* is naturally at ease with humanity" (*Analects* 4:2). Humanity is at home with the freedom virtue creates. To be human is to enjoy harmonious relationships with others. The "Confucian Way" is based on two principles: "Do not do unto others what we would not want others to do unto us . . . [and] In order to establish ourselves, we must help others to establish themselves."[93] Practicing the Confucian Way is done in "a series of concentric circles: self, family, community, society, nation, world, and cosmos."[94]

The Confucian worldview assumes the hierarchical differences inherent in the society. These hierarchical differences are consistent with the *yin-yang* understanding that each is necessary to the other. Though *yang* is often accepted as superior to *yin*, neither can displace the other altogether.

The "cosmic hierarchy of balanced inequality" in morality means that the goal of cultivation is to become a sage (*shengren*), one who is "the highest ideal for all humanity. . . . A sage is a being who, to a supreme degree, synthesizes in himself antitheses [in the universe]. More specifically, he is one in whom there is a merging of 'the sublime and the common, the internal and the external.'"[95] However, while hierarchy of inequality in morality can mean social interaction and self-giving love (similar to Paul's understanding of the Law of Christ), hierarchical difference in China unfortunately has given rise to the distorted idea of the need to maintain the *social order*. In the definition of the ruling class social order is understood as a justification for maintaining the status quo of class structure. Social order becomes "a rationalization of existing human *inequalities.* . . . The welfare of the social organism as a whole depends upon *harmonious* co-operation among all of its units and of the individuals who comprise these units."[96] To the contrary, implicit in Paul's theology is the conviction that all human beings are created equal, and their self-worth is not based on merit but divine grace.

The main limitation of Confucian ethics and its concept of civility is the structural problem inherent in the five bilateral relationships (*wulun*). But by incoporating the cruciform love of Christ and his faith(fulness) the understanding of *shu* (empathy) and *xin* (trust) can be extended to strangers and enemies. In the historical communities of Chinese societies Confucianism often exhibits a conservative familialism. Family metaphors and ties tend to become exclusivistic, and the tendency toward

93. Tu, "Joining East and West," 48.

94. Ibid.

95. Bodde, "Harmony and Conflict in Chinese Philosophy," 46. Emphasis mine.

96. Ibid., 63–64; see also *Mencius* 4a.2; 4b.19.

familial hierarchicialism and totalitarianism abound. Membership in any Chinese community is often rather passive and family/clan oriented. Those in power will "*la guanxi*" (make connections or do networking) so as to form new associations, but outsiders are proselytized into the clan system and abused by group members to enhance their influence and personal gain. The witness of Jesus and Paul's own cruciform love do more than equalize the power differential between superior and inferior into the shared trust (*xin*) relationship of friend with friend; it also turns the Confucian system upside down by modeling for humanity how the cursed and rejected Son of God became the person of faithfulness. Thus, human self-transcendence is found in reaching out and self-sacrifice rather than in self-absorption and fear.

In Confucius' teaching, there is a constant sensitizing of what it means to be human in order to create concern for others as human beings, and not as objects. When Confucius returned from the court to his stable and saw the stable was on fire, he asked if anyone was hurt; he did not ask about the horse (*Analects* 10:11). In Paul's terminology, the answer to the co-existence of Jews and Gentiles as God's people is found in the freedom God's Spirit inspires within the believer and in the fruit of the Spirit it bears. God's Spirit wills the faithful to become fully human bearing the image and likeness of God by entering loving relationships with others, and the firstborn (Christ) makes it possible for humanity to co-exist because of the work of grace and faith (trust). Love and trust replace the spirit of timidity, fear, and hatred. Communion replaces division, empathy replaces enmity. The power of Christ's gospel is that it grants righteousness to all who place their faith (trust) in Christ. That faith and grace is concretely expressed in "faith" and "grace" toward others.

In short, the phenomenon of faith itself, and its existential implications, viz., being in Christ, bearing the fruit of the Spirit, etc., is *the* identity marker for Paul, and it supplants any work of the law. The fruit of the Spirit is a sign of faith, but it is not the faith itself. This "faith" is in God as revealed in his Messiah (Christ), for Paul it is eschatological and pertained to eschatological truths. Faith and grace of God are fully expressed to individuals in community. In contrast, Confucius does not discuss faith (*xin*) in *tian*, but he requires something like faith or belief in the moral order of *tian* for one to become his best moral self. This faith (*xin*) is embodied aesthetically in the power of music, communally in the ritual propriety, and relationally in the cultivation of virtues. Virtues, rites, and music are rooted in *tian,* for the order and goodness of *tian* are implanted in human nature, and the way (*dao*) of being human is to be in the harmonious order of *tian.* For Paul, faith, hope, and love are founded in God and in the Christ of God, for God has entered the world with his New Creation to bring about complete salvation over sin and death. The people of God, as the New Creation, are one of God's means for realizing heaven on earth.

EPILOGUE: Implications for the Moral and Theological Identities of Chinese Christians Today

THE ETHICAL AND THEOLOGICAL TASKS OF CHINESE CHRISTIANS

Christian identity is always culturally embodied in a particular host environment (Judea, Galatia, Europe, America, China, etc.), and hence Christians must reflect on how their baptism, membership in church, and experience of the gospel shapes and transforms their existing cultural milieu. The ethical and theological tasks of Chinese Christians are to envision their own identity in the socio-political context of the days. Our hermeneutical task is to take history imaginatively, the future creatively, and to live in the present faithfully. It has been shown in previous chapters how both Confucius and Paul used their ancestral resources to meet the needs of their societies. The cross-cultural interpretation undertaken in this book has shown the possibility of holding to the tension between Confucius' retrospective Golden Age and Paul's eschatological future. Somewhere in the process of intertextual reading the discerning student will note the continuity between the past and the future, and find meaning for present living. The assurance of the past and hope for the future are necessary guides for a life of love in the present. While the future is open, the past is not closed.

402

There are multiple issues in the classical texts of the *Analects* and Galatians that intersect and can offer guidance to modern readers who face the perennial challenges of life, known just as well by the peoples of antiquity. Confucius and Paul never ceased to have hope that the world could change for the better. As a Chinese Christian interpreter, the work of this author on the theological and cultural identity of being Chinese today aligns with the similar aspirations of both Confucius and Paul in their desire to create a community according to the will of God, the *ming* (mandate) of *tian* (heaven).

THEOLOGICO-CULTURAL IDENTITIES: DYNAMIC CHANGE

The Task of Being Creatively Faithful to Living Texts[1]

The aspiration here is not to recreate the particular cultural or theological identity envisioned by a classical text—be it the Pauline sense of a Gentile Christian as defined in Galatians or a Confucian sense of being the best moral self (*junzi*) as presented in the *Analects*. It might be a good historical exercise to figure out whether such identities did or did not exist or what they might look like in modern guise. A romanticized recreation of the past for modern society is not the task here. The author finds it to be the case that the classical texts constantly provide him with helpful ways for looking at himself and his people, even though he is separated from them by more than two thousand years and lives in a different world. One quickly learns that cultural and theological identities keep changing across space and time.

What does it mean to be a Chinese Christian? What are the distinctive features about Chinese culture? What are the basic characteristics of Christian identity? The attempt here is not to be comprehensive in defining Chinese culture or Christian identity; the attempt is to be suggestive. In fact, by working primarily on the *Analects* and Galatians, the author has limited himself to looking at Chinese Christian identity mainly from

---

1. In Chinese terminology the task of being faithful to classical texts is for the purpose of renewing the tradition and advancing a new path for the future, i.e., *fanben kaixin*. This hermeneutic involves the process of "believing the past, doubting the past, and interpreting the past." My work pays attention to the exegetical and theological interpretations of the classical texts.

the particular traditions of the Confucian and the Pauline texts. In using the *Analects*, he is already being selective and discriminatory. Some might observe that most Chinese people today do not know Confucius or *dao* (the way or the truth), *ren* (humaneness), *li* (rituals), *zhong* (loyalty), and *shu* (empathy). It is nevertheless fair to acknowledge that even in the sea of changing culture, there is still a continuity that one can trace. The dynamic change in Chinese culture in the last two millennia might render any twenty-first century Chinese ignorant of Confucius' political ethics, but a certain refrain in the cultural heritage of family life and ethics (e.g., respecting the elders, caring for the extended family, calling seniors by their positions and last names, and valuing education) is still fundamental in any Chinese culture today. The Confucianist ideals of the social self and of being a *renren* (benevolent or humane person) are so important that not even the communist "Cultural Revolution" in recent Chinese history (1966–1976) could erase it.

Might there be the day when the Chinese have no affinity for, not to mention appreciation of, the Confucianist ideals of virtue? That "fractured continuity" between Confucian tradition and modern life may be possible, but then the "museumization" of Confucian ideals in Chinese civilization would make the culture no longer Chinese.[2] Many Chinese are concerned about the obliteration of the historical memory of any culture. A Chinese proverb, however, offers the wisdom of meeting friends in one's study of history (*qianyou guren*). These "ancient friends (*guren*) are, in Christian terms, "clouds of witnesses" (Heb 12:1) or a "communion of saints" (The Apostles' Creed). Our task is to remember the past and work for the future. This task of memory involves making present the transcendence of the past. It involves reconstructing the value of history, beauty, and meaningfulness from the historical texts. It involves living proleptically[3] in God's consummated salvation as the beloved community of love and justice.

2. Levenson, *Confucian China and its Modern Fate*, x.

3. Proleptically is used to mean "full anticipation as if the future event is realized in the present already."

Beauty in Diversity: Journeying to Others and Self

Both Confucian ethics and Pauline theology affirm beauty in diversity and they reject the myth of sameness of modernity. Tu Weiming's warning of the depletion of the Chinese race and its culture needs to be taken to heart:

> The fear, far from that of a population explosion, was actually the depletion of the Chinese race in the Social Darwinian sense. . . . We need to ask, what form of life should the Chinese pursue that is not only commensurate with human flourishing but also sustainable in ecological and environmental terms?[4]

Identifying with Confucius and Paul in terms of their ethics and theology, our cross-cultural and intertextual interpretation here finds journeying with them on the road of being human a hopeful undertaking. The road of being human is a journey toward others, in this case a journey of rediscovering the story of the Chinese people. In discovering Paul, one discovers more about Confucius, and vice versa. Through this pilgrimage into the two traditions, histories, and texts, we have become more than what we used to be. By going over we come back to a different place.

Both the Confucian and Pauline traditions believe that the wisdom to be human is to love, to risk, to reach out, to trust, and to be open to others. Galatians presents the vision of a community of diversity coexisting in freedom as the people of God. The community of Christ is asked to love its neighbors, even when these neighbors are aliens and enemies— people who are different, and whose differences must be appreciated.

CHINESE IDENTITIES: HYBRIDITY AND DIVERSITY

The first implication of reading Confucius and Paul intertextually focusing on their ethical and theological thought, concerns a construction of hybridized identity for Chinese Christians. We have seen in the Overture chapter the significance of identity in the construction of meaning in one's cultural and theological worlds. The author is suggesting that the poetic authoring of self-identity in both its moral and theological aspects is a dynamic process because of the changing world. In this section our

---

4. Tu, "Cultural China," 33.

focus is on the moral and theological identity of the Chinese in light of their concerns in the modern world, particularly in the areas of the politics, economics, and such issues as human rights, freedom, and power and on how these issues impact their self-identities.

The author's reflections on the moral and theological identity of Chinese have been heavily influenced by the two works under consideration of the *Analects* of Confucius and Paul's letter to the Galatians. As a Chinese Christian he feels at home with the uniquely Confucian character of the Chinese culture, whose dominant ethical tradition revolves around the concept of social harmony—but not the concepts of hierarchical differences and social control. He is at home in a harmonious society, where he feels welcomed and enjoys a sense of belonging. However, the blind spot of hierarchical differences used by governments for social control needs be corrected by Pauline theology. Much of what Confucius idealized can be fulfilled realized by Pauline thought regarding the obedient trust of Christ in God's love to be God's will, God's faithfulness to self-giving love to raise his beloved Son, and the work of the Spirit to create a new people of God.

The combined resources of Confucian ethics and Pauline theology provide the best way to view the hybridized identity of the Chinese Christian today. The Confucian effort toward self-cultivation by way of an ethic of virtue is an attempt to construct a "cultured" or "civilized" (*wen*) people. In Confucian ethics the identity of the Chinese is inscribed by the narrative of Zhou-propriety (*li*) and virtues such *as ren* (benevolence), *zhong* (loyalty), and *shu* (empathy). Paul's defense of Gentile Christian identity in Galatia in terms of the righteousness that comes through faith in Christ adds another dimension to Chinese identity beside Confucius. These two compound lenses will be used to discern the moral and theological identity of Chinese today.

China, Chinese, and Overseas Chinese

The author writes as an overseas Chinese,[5] whose voice is embedded in the political, national, cultural, and economic realities of his life. One

---

5. There are 35.5 million Chinese altogether, 86 % in Asia, 11 % in the Americas, and the rest (3%) scattered over the world. See Hughes, *Taiwan and Chinese Nationalism*, 104.

may define "Chinese" as a cultural term, but one cannot escape the complex political connotations of the term or not be saddened by the way these connotations splinter Chinese identity today.

✧ Cultural and Political Identities

In Chinese political history, the "Central/Middle Kingdom" became decentered each time military forces from the periphery attacked the mainland.[6] Tu writes,

> The military and political domination of the Central Country by the Jurchens, the Khitans, the Mongols, and the Manchus in the last millennium was compensated, in cultural terms, by the Sinicization of the Jin, Liao, Yuan, and Qing into legitimate Chinese dynasties. China survived these 'conquests' as a geopolitical entity and Chinese culture flourished.[7]

The question of a "civilizing project," which is nothing less than the conquest of others in the name of promoting virtue and of making citizens out of barbarians, as implied in the words *hua* and *zhong*, is a difficult one to tackle. *Zhonghua* (Chinese) or *huaren* (Chinese people) can be inclusive terms that refer to a common ancestry, traceable according to legend to the Yellow Emperor. Sometimes the Chinese are called the *Yan-Huang zisun*—descendants of the legendary Emperor Yan (a.k.a. Shen Nong, god of husbandry and first pharmacist) and Emperor Huang (whose burial place is in Huangling). *Hua* means "good manner" or "decorum"; *zhong* means "golden mean" or the "balanced middle."[8] One needs to rec-

---

6. The term *zhongguo ren* is quite politicized and should be used only with qualification. *Zhongguo* refers to China as a political or national entity. A more inclusive and neutral term to use is *huaren*, which includes those throughout the world who are ethnically Chinese. But the question is whether the term *huaren* should refer to Han Chinese only, or also to the national minorities in China. The preferred usage in my opinion is the latter.

7. Tu, "Cultural China," 4.

8. Yet no one knows how a people with a common ancestry in the land of *huaxia* became the diverse peoples of enormous geographical diversity and so many mutually incomprehensible dialects. Determining the progenitor of the Chinese people is an unrealistic project of "splitting the gene cell." The legend of Emperors Yan-Huang can provide only an "imagined" identity for those who wish their genealogy to be traced to the royal gene of the emperors. The children and grandchildren of Huang and Yan are an amalgam of many traditions and sub-cultures.

ognize that not only the dominant Chinese group, called the Han, and their Confucian culture, have ideals and virtues; minority tribal groups (*shaoshu minzu*) have their cultural ideals as well.[9] The Confucian ideal is not the only cultural ideal of the Chinese.

Despite ethnic diversity Chinese identity has a certain cohesion or commonality because of Confucian enculturalization, which has taken place sometimes as a result of imperialism, sometimes as welcomed embrace. There was a general conviction held by the Mengs (the Mongolians in the Yuan dynasty) and the Mans (the Manchurians in the Qing dynasty) that Confucianism possessed superior ethical principles. They adopted the Confucian ways of character building, filial piety, and the transformation of others by means of assimilation.

The Confucian promotion of cultural identity by means of virtue and Paul's theology of the people of God made possible by Christ's death and resurrection caution one when boasting of one's hereditary lineage. The Middle Kingdom's (*Zhongguo*) superiority complex is similar to the distinction between Jews and Gentiles or the Greeks and barbarians. The combined wisdom of Confucius and Paul suggests that the common good of a community is built not by privileging the elite but by empowering the lowly. The "best self," understood whether as *junzi* (the exemplary person), *renren* (the benevolent or humane person), "being in-Christ," or as people of God, is the responsible moral agent in the world, who trusts in God or comply to Heaven (*tian*). "Best selves" are not preoccupied with self-cultivation for the sake of boasting, but for the sake of the good of the neighbor. In China many of "the neighbors" are minorities. Paul's wisdom lies in his observation that an inclusive community bears the fruit of the Spirit and blesses and guides its members. An inclusive community affirms the equal rights of every member.

---

9. The word *minzu* (literally "people-tribe") in the usage of early twentieth century intellectuals had no nationalistic overtones; it is used now to refer to the people of a nation and is translated "national," thus connoting a geo-political entity. Minority groups are called *shaoshu minzu*, national minorities. They were once regarded as "barbarians" because they lived on the periphery of the Chinese empire, the Middle Kingdom (*Zhongguo*). Despite its political connotation, *zhonghua minzu* (Chinese national) is the most inclusive term and includes Han and minorities such as Zang (Tibetans), Man (Manchus), Meng (Mongolians), Hui (Muslims), and fifty other minority groups.

✧ Chinese Identity in Relation to China

Being part of migrated communities, overseas Chinese may trace their place of origin to China.[10] The self-consciousness of the author as an overseas Chinese has taught him to align himself with the cultural ideals of Chinese Confucianism and yet not be bound by identification with the geo-political reality of China. The author learns from Paul that, Paul's diasporic life in a multicultural world taught him to critically honor his own tradition without idealizing Jerusalem as the center of the world. One might argue that Paul's understanding of non-Jewish people as *ethnē* (nations or people group) had as its motivation the building of *ecclesial* space (church) for the Gentiles; building the church was a building up of the body of Christ "in the nations" that is, the world. Of course, Gentiles exist only in context of the Jews, and there is no such people as "Gentiles"—there are Greeks, Ethiopians, Cretans, Macedonians, Galatians, etc., but not Gentiles in an ethnic sense. "People group" or *ethnē* may be the non-existent groups, yet it is used by Paul to speak of diversity, in contradistinction to the usage of "Jew" or "Israel" as the only legitimate "people of God." The point is significant to overseas Chinese, because the implication of Paul's gospel is to create a space for all na-

---

10. The terms "overseas Chinese," "Chinese overseas," "diasporic Chinese," "migrant Chinese," the old term *huaqiao* ("Chinese abroad"), and a new term *haiwai zhongguo ren* ("overseas people of China") all refer to the Chinese sojourners who either emigrate or temporarily reside outside mainland China. As such, Chinese-ness is defined by certain ties with China, most often implying the cultural and geo-political mainland of China.

The term *huaqiao* (Chinese abroad) arose in mainland China, a term used a century ago to refer to those Chinese nationals who resided abroad from 1880–1960 without adopting the local nationality. The term is used loosely by the tourist agencies of China to refer to Chinese overseas. Many in Taiwan, Hong Kong, and Singapore thought of themselves as simply Chinese, viz. fully and authentically Chinese. To them, "overseas" connoted either Chinese of lesser degree in terms of cultural identity or those who were living in a foreign land. Neither, they thought, was accurate.

So in the process of historical development and the search for identity, various terms, besides *huaqiao*, were used to highlight this self-consciousness. The cultural (rather than a political) term used to refer to Taiwan and Hong Kong Chinese as well as overseas mainland Chinese is *tongbao*, meaning "compatriots" in the ethnic and cultural sense. The political term *tongzhi* (comrades) is used by mainland Chinese but not to refer to Chinese outside China. Chinese minority communities in diaspora are called *huaren* (Chinese people), a fairly neutral term. In terms of ethnicity in a multicultural world, the Chinese are called *huayi* (Chinese descent), a naturalized foreign national of Chinese descent—either through immigration and re-immigration. See Wang, *Community and Nation*, 1–10.

tions and peoples in God's love. In Israel, there is one Torah, one Holy City Jerusalem, one people of God. But now "in Christ" there are many peoples, and to truly respect their cultures, Paul has demonstrated how he contextualizes the gospel for the Corinthians, the Thessalonians, the Romans, the Galatians—all of whom are *ethnē* (nations or peoples). These new "peoples" of God are bound by the law of love, their holy cities are wherever God's Spirit dwells.

Toward a Chinese Christian Theology of "Being Human": Human Rights in Chinese Identity

As an overseas Chinese, the author lived and worked on Cheung Chau Island in Hong Kong from 1992–1996. He learned from the people in Hong Kong the challenge of cultural identification, and he saw their re-silience in overcoming challenges. He did an unscientific survey in class in early 1996 and was surprised to discover that 75 percent of Hong Kong students did not want to be called *zhongguo ren* (people of China), that is, Chinese in its national and political sense. They preferred to be identified as Hong-Kongers or Hongkongese.

The Basic Law and the Sino-British Joint Declaration granted Hong Kong to be a Special-Administrative Region under the broad principle of "one country, two systems" (coined by Deng Xiaoping, 1902–1997). This relationship is described by the Chinese saying "same bed but different dreams" (*tongchuang yimeng*). Both China and Hong Kong are pragmatic and seek modernization. Though "one country, two systems" recognizes Hong Kong's self-rule, the political process tends to emphasize either "one country" or "two systems," resulting in two different models—absorption or convergence. It is to the advantage of the people of Hong Kong to follow the convergence model, with slow accommodation on both sides. To be Chinese in Hong Kong is such an ambivalent experience because of one of the main points of contention regarding human rights (and the rule of law in the broader sense)—Beijing and Hong Kong do not have similar views on human rights.

Paul's understanding of right and freedom provides a helpful way to view the human rights issues today. "Human rights" are modern terms; they are used here to mean the basic entitlements of a person by virtue of being a human being. These rights include freedoms to live and freedoms of speech and religion; these entitlements safeguard the integrity one has as a human being. Paul would agree with this understanding of human rights, but perhaps with a qualification on human rights within the larger context of powers. Paul establishes his right to be Christ's ambassador (apostle in Galatians 1) and the right of Gentile Christians to have their own ethno-cultural identity within the larger context of cosmic and spiritual powers. These powers come either from the "evil age" (Gal 1:4) and its institutions or from God. Manifestations of the evil age may be neutral, benign, or deadly; but as an apocalyptic thinker, Paul sees binding and dominating powers as "evil," and saving and liberating powers as "holy" (the work of the Holy Spirit [Galatians 5–6]). Although the power human beings has is endowed by God, Paul does not assume that human beings automatically exercise the gift of power to save and to liberate. Paul takes the myth of the fall and the tyranny of sin as negative influences on human rights. Thus, on one hand, Paul affirms the worth and dignity of all human beings as created by God (Gal 2:6; Rom 2:11); but on the other hand, he would disagree with the concept of the "autonomous self" or "self reliance" of the modern world, in which freedom is independent of God (Rom 1:18–32; 1 Cor 15:20–28; Phil 2:10–11) and of others as well as free from duty.

For Paul the freedom and rights of human beings are grace of God and gifts of the Spirit. In other words, Paul is consistent in subjecting the question of human rights to the work of God's Spirit rather than to any institution, so that the rights of a person is preserved by the renewal and guidance of the Spirit. Any institution, secular or religious, will inevitably be naive toward the corrupting influence of power, and impotent in being self-critical. Institutions exhibit the "works of the flesh" that agitate and destroy communities (Gal 5:19–21). When human rights are grounded in the eschatological salvation of God's Spirit, the exercise of one's right is constantly critiqued by the Spirit of the Risen Christ—the Spirit of dying to oneself and living for others. Cosgrove writes,

> In baptism Christians die to every worldly authority (Rom 7:1–6; Gal 2:19, 6:14); they are given a new identity (Gal 3:26–28) and a call in Christ (1 Cor 1:26; Phil 3:14–15; 2 Thess 1:11), with spiritual gifts (1 Cor 12; Rom 12:3–8); they become slaves of Christ

(Rom 6:22; 1 Cor 3:23, 6:20, 7:23) who now owe nothing to anyone except 'to love' (Rom 13:8).[11]

Human rights, for Paul, then are expressed as the law of Christ—
"love your neighbor" (Gal 6:2). Human rights for Paul are freedom to
be who we are in a community without discriminating against others. In
other words, freedom is being "'obliged' to love one another" (Gal 5:13).[12]
Paul is "free with respect to all," yet he has made himself "a slave to all"
(1 Cor 9:19).

It is important to bear in mind that Paul understands the liberating
power of God's Spirit as creating within diversity a community of concord, "against which there is no law" (Gal 5:23). Freedom is achievable
only through God's Spirit and the controlling power of love. The fruits of
the Spirit cannot be produced by law—even the law of nations. The law
of love guarantees human freedom. This Pauline idea of freedom may
be found vaguely, if at all, in Confucius' thinking. Confucius believed
in *de* (virtue) and *ren* (humaneness) rather than in law and punishment
for building a civil society. But Confucius' *li* (ritual requirement) is often
misunderstood as comprised of rigid rules. That is why some scholars
claim that in ancient and modern China there is no concept of "human
rights."[13] Some would even claim that there is no individual identity in
ancient Chinese tradition.[14] Other scholars argue that the concept of
rights did exist in ancient China, but rights were often subsumed under
moral behavior.[15] Julia Ching claims that the understanding of human
rights is found in ancient writings and is a valid Chinese concept, and
that its western version can be traced to the ancient Greeks:

> I would like to describe human rights as a creature of recent birth
> with a fairly long lineage. Its mother is liberal moral and politi-
> cal philosophy—the French Enlightenment and liberal English
> thinking, among other things; its father is international law,
> while its midwife is revolution: first the Revolution of American
> Independence and then the French Republican Revolution of the
> late eighteenth century. . . . But its ancestry includes further back,

11. Cosgrove, "Paul and American Individualism," 89.

12. My translation.

13. See Rosemont, "Why Take Rights Seriously," 167–82.

14. See Wu, "The Status of the Individual," 340–64.

15. Hall and Ames, *The Democracy of the Dead*, passim.

Stoic concepts of natural law and the traditions of Roman civil law on the continent and of the Anglo-Saxon common law to the extent that these lent protection to the rights of citizens and of individuals.[16]

She continues,

The belief in human perfectibility, a cornerstone of Confucian philosophy, implied a belief in personal freedom. But this was more an interior, spiritual freedom to improve one's own moral character. The concept of freedom as a right, such as the right to freedom of thought and religion, to freedom of speech and assembly, was never clearly articulated until modern times, and then under Western influence.[17]

I find Ching's position fair and accurate. According to the Confucian tradition, *zuoren* (being human) is constituted by human rights (*quan*) and human rites (*li*). In Confucian teaching human rites are human rights. Human rites are more than a human right, human rites also make a person to be human and empower him to live out his right as a human being. Human rights are composed of human rites. The Chinese word *quan* means power, with the implication that power makes right, or that one possesses might.

Human rites shape people not so much as individuals but as a community. The power one has in the humanizing process of human rites is to build up the community. Thus, human rights are rendered as rights of the people or of the citizen (*minquan* or *gongminquan*), not mere individual rights.[18] Paul believes that human beings are created with equal rights in relation to one another. "All people are created equal" means equal creaturely status, and this is implied in Paul's understanding of the "impartiality of God" (Gal 2:6; cf. Rom 2:11) and the "oneness of God" (Gal 3:20; cf. Rom 11:6). The hierarchies within, and the discrimination between, the male-female, master-slave, Jew-Gentile distinctions are eradicated by Christ. The communion one has across gender, racial, and social barriers is the work of the Spirit of God. Paul's theology of the impartiality of God in creation and the equality of salvation in Christ can be a helpful catalyst to the issue of citizen rights, or human rights, within a nation. Paul's theo-

16. Ching, "Human Rights," 68–69.
17. Ibid., 73.
18. Ibid.

logical politics knows nothing of the rights of human beings above or in separation from God's sovereignty. Just as government derives its right to rule from God, human rights or citizen rights are subsumed under God's power. Governments are servants of God to executive judgment and to reinforce goodness (Rom 13:1–7). No human law should interfere with a person's or a community's duty to love and to obey God. Neither the separation of church and state nor the privatization of religion is being argued here.[19] Since every political system and ideology has its *mythos* (the comprehensive narrative of a state) they resemble any religion, Paul is correct in saying government derives its authority from God (Rom 13:1–7). By implication a government is a form of religion; a government attempts to actualize its vision (its gospel) of order (peace) and prosperity (salvation) in a country based on its conviction regarding the use of its power and resources in the historical process (eschatology). The question is not whether church and state should be separated; of course they should. The question is how politics and theology can be separated. They can hardly be separated. Since any government and its ideology is susceptible to the power of "fallenness" (sin), the best one can do is to subsume politics under theology, to allow God's word to be a critical guide to the ideology of government. Separation of church and state without the awareness that politics and theology are inseparable inevitably results in another "religious" conviction that promotes secularism as independence from God. A "secular" society has its own concept of the human self, its own laws, its own gods or "ultimate concerns." By no means are we suggesting a theocracy such as that of the Holy Roman Empire. What is being suggested is that Christian theology and the church can be yeast or salt to the world, that they should be, must be. Yet the world and its governments will remain as they are, unable to transcend the power of sin; and the church will always be a part of the world, never free from it or its sins, because those who make it up are both flesh and spirit. However, both Confucius and Paul believed that one's understanding of Heaven (*tian*) and God (*Theos*) could critically inform one's ways of governing, of moral living, etc. For Confucius virtue (*de*) is not just for personal benefit, it is for the sake of maintaining the peace and prosperity of the

---

19. See Chapter Two of this book (pp. 132–58) on the public nature of religious belief, and the intertwined relationship of culture and theology.

world. For Paul the church's mission is to transform the world through the proclaimed word (*kerygma*) and through good works.

Recent Chinese history has witnessed many instances when the Chinese government has interfered in the basic rights of individuals to obey God. Such persecution may be the result of Confucianism, which assumes the divine right of sovereigns to rule as sons of God, and feudal lords to possess and protect. But Confucian teaching also sees *junzi* (the best moral self) as the model for the political ruler, who is to exercise his rights not through military might but through moral persuasion. Unfortunately, Chinese political history has shown emperors to have been totalitarian, and because Confucianism was the civil religion of most dynasties, the phrase, "inner sage, outer king" was an empty one.

The Confucian teachings of loyalty (*zhong*) and filial piety and the concept of *zhengming* (being true to one's name) often preserved the status of rulers. Confucius would go to great length not to allow civil rebellion to happen for the sake of the common people. Yet, his understanding of *zhengming* was so radical that in effect it declared rulers illegitimate if they did not rule with proper *de* (virtue).[20] Ching cites the example of Mencius, the best-known disciple of the Confucian school, who "even formulated a doctrine justifying tyrannicide, declaring that killing a 'tyrant' is not killing a 'king.' In an age when the altars of sacrificing for the good of the earth and grain signified political glory and religious authority of the political rulers, Mencius's words were: 'The people come first; the altars of the earth and grain come afterwards; the ruler comes last' (*Mencius* 7b.14)."[21]

The reception of "Confucian values" by Chinese communities in postcolonial East Asian countries has been wide-ranging. In their programs of modernization and westernization, they have reacted in different ways to Confucianism: some embrace (e.g., Lee Kuan Yew), some reject (e.g., the Chinese Communist Party has recently "rectified" its prior anti-Confucian stance). Most people see Confucian ethics to be useful to political leaders "to help curb rampant corruption and to counter the widespread social malaise that threatens to undermine"[22] law and order. However, Huntington, Cotton, Price, and Pye argue that Confucianism

20. Hall and Ames, *The Democracy of the Dead*, 158.

21. Ching, "Human Rights," 72.

22. Bell and Chaibong, "Introduction: The Contemporary Relevance of Confucianism," 3.

is an obstacle to democratization, citing the following reasons: its basic values on social harmony and common good of the whole easily lead to suppression of dissidents; rights and power are assumed to be coming from the center and the top, that is, the state; the rule of a personalistic (sage) and paternalistic (son of heaven) model does not welcome codification of law.[23] Other scholars point out certain aspects of Confucianism that are compatible with democracy, viz., moral and political space of individual within a society, benevolent rulers to persuade citizens by means of their own virtues, responsibility of government to care for the people, principles of humaneness (*ren*) and righteousness (*yi*) point beyond rule of personality.

He Baogang differentiates among the three models of democracy. His differentiation is helpful in understanding how and why Confucianism can be an obstacle and a resource to the democratization process in Chinese societies. First, the ideology of the radical model of *populist democracy* is rooted in Marxism. Its ideal is moving swiftly to a direct and mass democracy through revolution, such as the case of the Cultural Revolution. Second, the official model of *paternalistic democracy* assumes rights granted by the party-state, with economic rights protected but political rights prohibited. It draws its insight from Marxism and Chinese tradition of paternalism. Third, the *liberal democracy* is a western model (John Locke, J. S. Mill) of a representative and elitist democracy. It affirms the natural rights of individuals and the centrality of human rights.[24] Wholesale westernization or the wholesale adoption of Asian, especially Confucian, values is not the proper path. Bell and Chaibong's "cross-cultural" position is more viable than a simple either/or of East or West. Bell and Chaibong argue for the relevance of Confucianism in modern Chinese society despite the move toward democracy, capitalism, and the rule of law that seem to go against the grain of Confucian teaching. In an edited collection of essays they seek "to articulate a vision of Confucianism that avoids either of these extremes by highlighting the humanistic and liberal elements in the Confucian world view while recognizing its flaws."[25]

23. See He, *The Democratization of China*, 160–61.

24. Ibid., 217, gives a helpful chart of the three models. He discusses the three models on 15–74.

25. Bell and Chaibong, "Introduction: The Contemporary Relevance of Confucianism," 4.

The idea of equality in modern societies has to do with equal protection under the law and equal accountability before the law. The idea of equality is based on the assumption that all are from birth endowed with human rights. It does not mean that people are the same. Human variation makes us unequal. However, for Confucius and Paul "equality" involves giving the less fortunate and the marginalized a head start with extra benefits. Equality as such is not treating all people the same way as if all were born with equal resources, skills, conditions, etc. The understanding of *shu* (empathy) and *ren* (humaneness), of mercy and self-sacrificing love (*agape*), recognizes the unequal conditions of human existence. The equal endowment of human rights is God's gift to all, and it can be realized by including everyone in the democratic process motivated by the liberal spirit of love, *agape* or *ren*.

Equality is difficult to achieve because of the modern assumption that freedom is the pursuit of one's own interests. Paul's theology and Confucius' ethic can provide a corrective to such individualism. Whether one believes in the Christ of God or in Confucius' *tian* (Heaven), all are created free as moral and spiritual agents. Whether one anticipates a new creation in Christ or a recovery of the cultural ideals of the past, freedom is more than the right not to be interfered with. Freedom is also more than the right to accumulate political and economic power. As both Confucian and Pauline traditions teach mutatis mutandis, whatever else freedom may include it carries with it the obligation to receive and to give the unconditional love of God to others.

Human rights are entailed in our duty to God and others—a duty that one does out of freedom and joy. Love knows no obligation. One gets to love, one rejoices in the opportunity. Yet, one is obliged ("enslaved") to God and others to recognize the human rights of others, to treat everyone as unique and worthy of God's love. In loving others, one becomes human. Not to love others is to become less than human oneself. All rights and freedoms are divine gifts, and we are bound to treat all equally with the indebtedness of love. Indeed, "for freedom Christ has set us free, therefore we should not submit to the yoke of slavery" (Gal 5:1).

Today freedom is often defined as "self-realization" and detachment from all duties. Confucius' *renren* and *junzi* indicate that one's best self is a social being who builds up others. Paul's cruciform life also looks upon freedom as "Christ realization" (Gal 4:19). If salvation involves wholeness and the actualization of one's full humanity, then Paul's concept of salvation is at odds with the concept of freedom as self-realization. Salvation liberates from self-centeredness and the tyranny of self-boasting. Both Confucius and Paul present "the road less traveled"—the road to wholeness, in contrast to the road to self-centeredness that inevitably ends in self-absorption and destruction.[26]

Despite the multiple problems raised, being a Chinese Christian today is tied to the pursuit of equality and freedom and human rights. The most challenging case study is about Chinese identity in Taiwan. Chinese identity in Taiwan is contingent upon discerning a Taiwanese Chinese's ethnic consciousness within a multi-ethnic society, upon Taiwan's relationship with China, upon Taiwan's recognition by the international community.

a facile equating of Confucius ≤ Paul + vice-versa? or Paul's Christ 11-18-08

Chinese Identity in Taiwan
↪ Democratic Process, Freedom, and Chinese Identity

Reunification talks and relations between Beijing and Taipei are tense because of political incongruence. At various times Taipei and Beijing recognized respectively the Kuomintang (KMT) or the Chinese Communist Party (CCP) as the only legitimate Chinese government. Taipei and Beijing recognized respectively the Republic of China (ROC, i.e., Taiwan) or the Peoples Republic of China (PRC, i.e., mainland China) was the only legitimate Chinese nation. Interesting enough, both the ROC and the PRC recognize Dr. Sun Yat-sen (1866–1925) as the Founding Father of Modern China, and his idea of a Chinese republic was shared by the KMT and the CCP. Thus the word "republic" appears in both titles, PRC and ROC. There is no doubt that if Beijing and Taipei could both overcome their autocratic past and work toward building democratic republics, citizens in both sides of the Strait would live without fear.

The teachings of Confucius concerning the rule of virtue (*zhengde*) can still be a guide to politics today. It is true that Confucianism was partly responsible for the autocratic government of the Qing dynasty (1644–1911) in that its conservatism was used by the Qing government to resist change. But it is equally true that Sun Yat-sen's republican revolution in 1911 was influenced by the ideal of Confucianism. Wang

26. See Peck, *The Road Less Traveled*, 1–3.

describes Sun's democratization ideal in relation to the Confucian vision of the state as constituted by people who are morally responsible for their own freedom:

> Our three-*min* principles [nationalism, citizens' rights, welfare of human beings] originate from Mencius and are based on Cheng Yichuan. . . . Mencius is really the ancestor of our democratic ideas. . . . The three-min principles are a completion of the development of those three thousand years of Chinese ideas about how to govern and maintain a peaceful world.[27]

Early on, Confucianists such as Kang Youwei (1858–1927) and Liang Qichao (1873–1929) all played important roles in the early democratic movements of China.[28]

Confucian teaching opposes autocratic government, and it interprets "will of the people" to be "will of Heaven," thus to be realized as will of the government. Confucian teaching warns of the negative effect on common people when, for example, government tries to control the national economy. This does not mean, however, that Confucian teaching endorses the unfettered privatization of property.[29] Freedom and the welfare of the people take priority over competing political goods. New Confucian scholars do affirm democracy as compatible to Confucian teachings of spirit of public-mindedness, which is seen in the Confucian utopian ideal of *tianxia wei gong* (all-under-heaven belongs to the public).

With regard to the rule of law, Confucius praised the mediation of disputes and sought to avoid litigation. *Analects* 12:13 says, "The Master said, 'In hearing cases, I am the same as anyone. What we must strive to do is to rid the courts of cases altogether.'"[30] Litigation is a social ill "because it is a deviation from and a disruption of harmonious social relationships. The construction of a harmonious social order is one of the greatest Confucian ideals. This is the famous vision of *datong* (Grand Unity)."[31]

---

27. Taken from Wang, "Confucian Democrats in Chinese History," 78.

28. Ibid., 75–81.

29. See Daniel Bell's article on constraints on the free market when coupled with the ethical values of Confucianism. Bell, "Confucian Constraints on Property Rights."

30. Ames and Rosemont, *Analects*, 157.

31. Chen, "Mediation, Litigation, and Justice," 260.

✧ Toward a Chinese Christian Theology of Freedom

Democracy and Guardianship ✦ Democracy etymologically means the rule of the people. However, the actual rule of all the people is impossible because of various limitations. Not all people are competent. The direct rule of all the people is impractical. Decisions would have to be made by referendum. For these reasons, democracy often refers to the rule of the people through representatives. Still the question of competence is pertinent, for a majority can make wrong judgments, especially when decisions are based on distorted information. Misled, they are unable to make competent and wise decisions. Democracy does not guarantee optimal results or the realization of the ideal intentions of a people. Education becomes one of the crucial factors in ensuring that the citizenry can make informed decisions.

The political scientist Robert A. Dahl suggests "guardianship" as the answer to the problem of competence in democracy.[32] The assumption is that since direct rule by all the people is impractical, and that a small minority of experts can give the most accurate knowledge of the welfare of a community, it is best for elected representatives to rule, while the people participate in the ruling process by electing representatives to voice their concerns and ideas. This small group of representatives are called "guardians," for they are entrusted by the people to seek the good of all, and to do so in a professional manner.[33] Their responsibility is to guard the common good.

Guardianship leaders work with their cabinet or advisors, and more than that, with counselors or even "disciplinarians" (*jian*). Hahm Chaihark, a professor at Yonsei University, argues that modern states can recover Confucian values, such as appointing Confucian scholars not just as counselors, but as disciplinarians, to political leaders. Hahm mentions the fact that political leaders in the Choson dynasty in Korea (1392–1910) were expected to attend royal lectures (*jingyan*) on Confucianism and the art of governance, and rulers could not hold meetings without the presence of at least two historians to record all verbal conversations and gestures, etc. Political rulers were disciplined and lectured to and kept

32. Dahl, *Democracy and Its Critics*, 52–55.

33. Advocates of the guardianship theory are Plato, Confucius, Mencius, Marx, and Lenin. Still, education is the crucial means for guardian rulers to be competent in their craft, and the sage-ruler is the ideal guardian.

under surveillance for proper conduct.[34] The disciplinarian mechanism was put in place to check indiscretion, corruption, and secrecy—illegality in modern nation states.

Though Paul's interpretation of the law as a guardian is not operative in the age of Christ, the notion that the function of the law is to guard people from moral and spiritual bondage is still valid. For Paul the law of love does not negate the guarding function of the law; but in the age of Christ the law is qualified by love and mutual service so that freedom for all might be achieved. In modern societies, if the law of nations can be redefined as the obligation to serve others in order to bring about freedom for all, then a democratic government must pay attention to holding leaders to account and to furthering participation of the people.

◇ Representation, Equality, and Freedom

Other considerations for a democratic government are fair representation and equality of opportunity before the law. Fair representation means that within the democratic structure and in the decision-making process, representation of the whole community ought to be comprehensive, so diverse opinions are voiced and complex issues faced. Fair representation means that the concerns of gender and ethnic groups are presented, but also that groups of different ages, social classes, educational backgrounds, religious beliefs, political convictions, etc., have their voiced represented.

The tension between fair representation and the maximum freedom of all people is a challenging one. Especially in an individualistic society, where freedom and rights of individuals are honored, fair representation ought to include the direct participation of each individual. This hinges on the relation between democracy and liberalism. Liberalism means that freedom of individuals is respected, so that each citizen is free to speak his minds, to seek office, and to vote. Individual society can learn from the insights of Paul and Confucius for a world in need of virtue.

In Paul's world freedom and rights were conditioned by one's social status and its attendant duties. Thus a slave has rights because of his duty as a slave, and a master has rights because of his duty as a master; their

---

34. Hahm, "Constitutionalism, Confucian Civic Virtue, and Ritual Propriety," esp. 46–51.

rights are not equal because their status and duties are different. Paul did not live in a culture that knows of rights regardless of one's social status. In his theology, however, he affirms the rights of those in Christ regardless of their gender, race, and social status (Gal 3:28). In the Confucian ideal, freedoms and rights are circumvented by virtues. Joseph Chan argues: "Now if, as an empirical claim, it is true that freedom of speech in the long run helps society to correct wrong ethical beliefs and to prevent rulers from indulging in wrongdoing, then a Confucian perspective would endorse freedom of political speech."[35] Free speech is consistent with the Confucian ideal of benevolence (*Analects* 15:24). Thus, both Confucius' and Paul's insights can help us locate the modern pursuit of democracy and human rights within the will of God and the cultivation of virtue. These are insights and issues China and Taiwan should discuss as they work toward a modern democratic state.

Hybrid and Multiple Identities ◆ According to Ernest Gellner's "nationalist principle," the question of identity is whether "political and national identity should be congruent."[36] This is particularly true for Taiwan. Can a nation have multiple political systems (such as North and South Koreas and earlier East and West Germany), even though these are intermediate states and reunification is the goal agreed to by each regime? The issue for China and Taiwan is: In a situation where there are two or more political systems (PRC, ROC, HKSAR), how does the international community accept "one nation, two systems" or "one China, three regions"? Is the proposal of "one country, one culture, two governments" a good step toward peaceful reunification? In the 1950s, despite ideological differences, both Mao Zedong (1893–1976) and Chiang Kai-shek believed that China and Taiwan should be united.

Confucius' political ethic of *tianming* was often misunderstood by rulers to mean their divine right as *tianzi* (son of heaven) to command the respect of others. In the West, the nation-state arose in part to counteract imperialism, especially the Holy Roman Empire, in which the Church became the civil government. Ironically the ideology of the modern nation-state has turned out to be an imperialistic or nationalistic project

35. Chan, "A Confucian Perspective on Human Rights for Contemporary China," 229.

36. Gellner, *Nations and Nationalism*, 1.

that had created its own history at the expense of others. A theologico-cultural transformation of China and Taiwan and the global community will be far more significant and comprehensive than the pursuit of the political identity of Chinese-ness. Political identity should follow upon a theologico-cultural Chinese identity.

TOWARD A "THEOLOGICO-CULTURAL" CHINESENESS

Ethnic Identity and "Living Tree"

Chinese Christian theologians, for the sake of Chinese identity, can contribute toward the creation of a future China, which is not only culturally unified but theologically grounded. Chineseness is not just a racial but more importantly, also a theologico-culturally constructed reality, and the political aspect of that reality is only a part of it—though a significant part because political power defines freedom in its social sense. Nevertheless, I agree with Tu Weiming, who writes in his book, *Living Tree*, that cultural space is the salient feature of the dynamic identity of Chineseness.[37] By culture, I mean the ideal way of envisioning how to be fully human according to a particular tradition or philosophical school, in this case, Confucian ethics.

Tu uses his vision of "Cultural China" to deconstruct geo-political China and he creates a cultural space "that both encompasses and transcends the ethnic, territorial, linguistic, and religious boundaries that normally define Chineseness."[38] As an overseas Chinese whose location seems to be peripheral to the locus of being Chinese, I welcome the idea of affiliating with cultural China even if some Chinese are neither proficient in the Chinese language nor having family ties with ancestors in China.

One can construct a vision of Chineseness that is in tune with Chinese history and culture. The "Cultural China" of Tu's postulation consists of the following three "symbolic universes": (1) mainland China, Taiwan, Hong Kong, and Singapore that are populated by ethnic Chinese; (2) overseas or diasporic Chinese throughout the world; and (3) individual professionals (scholars, journalists, industrialists, traders, etc.) who

37. Tu, *The Living Tree*, vi–vii.
38. Ibid., v.

[handwritten margin note: hybridize identity is Julia Ching's hyphenated identity.]

are not racially Chinese but who study and seek to understand Chinese culture.[39] Chinese identity is not a biological necessity, it is the cross-cultural and poetic aspiration of how to be human. Race and ethnicity are not the same. Race is biological, but ethnicity is a poetic (creative and imaginative) cultural identity.

Cultural identity may be traced to a common ancestry, but it is not necessary. Cultural China is able to break down the current Han-race domination. With the Han *ren* as the dominant ethnic group (91 percent), words such as *hua, xia, zhonghua minzu* were often used to imply "cultural superiority and inclusivist expansionism" of any Chinese dynasty that conquered in the name of promoting virtues among the "barbarians."[40] The Han group, originally from northwest China, spread over the land of *huaxia*; initially they made silk and planted rice, soon they learned other skills to make a livelihood. It is important to note that the Chinese are not defined as Han, because being Chinese implies being part of a mixed race or inclusive of various ethnic and sub-ethnic identities, of which Han is one only. This work has advocated the idea of hybridity in any ethnic identity, because there is no such a thing as an ethnic group or race that has a pure bloodline. Along with recognizing this hybridized identity, it is important to "explore the fluidity of Chineseness as a layered and contested discourse, to open new possibilities and avenues of inquiry, and to challenge the claims of political leadership (in Beijing, Taipei, Hong Kong or Singapore) to be the ultimate authority in a matter as significant as [determining what is and is not] 'Chinese.'"[41]

Tu's metaphor of the "Living Tree" (the title of his book) draws attention to change, to what is new and expanding. Tu acknowledges that the cultural alignment required for a Chinese identity "may prove to be too heavy a psychological burden for minorities, foreign-born, non-Mandarin speakers, or nonconformists."[42] Other than that concern, cultural identity can be rooted in the nurturing of a homeland, and to a humanizing com-

---

39. I have an American friend who is of European stock but he has studied in Taiwan and has appreciated and lived out Chinese cultural ideals. The third construction of a "Cultural China" would include him.

40. Harrell, "Introduction," 6. *Hua* or *Huaxia* connotes "cultured" or "civilized" people, so *zhonghua* is often used to refer to people related to the Middle Kingdom. "Central Country" or "Middle Kingdom" signifies the cultural center of the world.

41. Tu, *The Living Tree*, viii.

42. Ibid.

mon code of ethics. Cultural identity also means being faithful to the spirit of creative transformation of old traditions by means of new ones. In my case, the Christian reading of Confucian texts and the Confucian reappropriation of Christian theologies are my way of being faithful to being Chinese. Those Chinese who do not use a Christian lens to read Chinese culture have offered a harsh critique of the ills of Confucianism, believing that by so doing Confucian ideals might gain new life in new contexts. Lu Xun's (1881–1936) satire of Confucianism, for example, described the ills of that tradition as "cannibalistic ritualism."[43]

Confucianist China and the Inclusion of Minorities

While Chinese culture is not just Confucianist, Confucianism is nonetheless a dominant cultural force. Being Chinese in a Confucianist cultural sense means paying respect to ancestors and elders, observing ethical obligations in complex social relationships, pursuing education in service of one's community and country, and practicing the systems of belief that define the norms and values of Chinese societies. But this definition of Chineseness should not be taken as a subscription to Confucian forms of worship (e.g., offering food to the dead and burning incense to the ancestors) but to the practice of Confucian ideals (e.g., reverence for elders). While form and practice are intertwined, an analytical differentiation will help us in defining Chinese culture as predominately Confucianist while not falling into cultural imperialism. Confucian ethical concepts such as *ren* (humaneness) and *shu* (empathy) necessitate that Confucianists respect others; thus, a "cultural China" (or more narrowly speaking, a "Confucianist China") would not judge others based on whether or not they abandoned their own cultural ideals and be proselytized into Confucianism. Rather, the criterion would be whether they agreed to the universal truth (*dao*) expressed in Confucian ethics that to be human is to be *renren* (humane persons), to be *zhongshu* (loyal and empathic), and to be *xin* (trustworthy). Similarly, I understand Christian identity as not requiring the rejection of Chinese culture. Only those aspects of Chinese culture that reject the cruciform life would need to be deconstructed. In other words, a Confucianist China would allow a plurality of identities to coexist.

43. Tu, "Cultural China," 31.

There is a strong tendency in both the Christian and the Confucian narratives to include others, as we have seen in our discussion of *renren* (humane persons), cruciform love, *zhongshu* (loyalty and empathy), and the reinterpretation of the Jewish law. Unfortunately, the word *ren* as "person" (not the Chinese character *ren* as "benevolence") in imperial Chinese history especially has its marginalizing effect. Minorities and barbarians were not considered as *ren* or persons, they were grouped with beasts.[44] The word *ren* as person was used in pre-Confucian times to refer to aristocrats, in distinction from common people. Only under Confucius' influence was the word *ren* (as persons) gradually used to include all human beings. Today Chinese politicians can walk in Confucius' footsteps.

A cultural China can help political China to concentrate on the quality of life of the people, to be aware of the needs of minorities, and to be less paranoid about its "face" (honor)—deemed "lost" to foreign aggressors in the nation's history in the nineteenth and twentieth centuries. Above all, cultural China needs to help political China to live in trust (*xin*), and to prove to its people and the world that only virtue (*de*) rather than military force can gain the trust of its own people, its neighbors and its enemies.

Theological China—God's Country (Shenzhou)?

A cultural China is a theological China, because the cultural ideals of *xin* (trust), *shu* (empathy), *ren* (humaneness), freedom, and power, are only reliable and intelligible when seen in light of Christian theology. Christian theology is not a possession of the West, its "copyright" does not belong to the theologians of the West. Just as the Confucian ideas of *rendao* ("the way of humanity") and *tiandao* ("the way of Heaven") are true, so also is the Christ of Christian theology. Both sets of ideas, Confucian and Christian, have the power to interpret and inscribe the world with truth, goodness, and beauty. They transcend any single group, and they are universally viable for those whose quest is to become fully human.

As a Chinese Christian, the author intends to use a Christian lens to read and transform the Chinese culture. Almost thirty years ago William

44. Graham, *Disputers of Tao*, 19.

Stringfellow understood a similar intertextual work when he used the book of Revelation to read America. What he said about America is comparable to what the author believes the *Analects* and the epistle to the Galatians have to say to China. Stringfellow writes,

> The task is to treat the nation within the tradition of biblical politics—to understand America *biblically*—not the other way, not to construe the Bible *Americanly*. To interpret the Bible for the convenience of America, as apropos as that may seem to be to any Americans, represents a radical violence to both the character and content of the biblical message. It fosters a fatal vanity that America is a divinely favored nation and makes of it the credo of a civic religion . . . It arrogantly misappropriates political images from the Bible and applies them to America so that America is conceived of as Zion: as the Righteous nation, as a people of superior political morality, . . . In archetypical form in this century, material abundance, redundant productivity, technological facility, and military predominance are publicly cited to verify the alleged divine preference and prove the supposed national virtue.[45]

These words are words of wisdom to superpowers and to nations rising to that status.

There is no naive hope that a "Great Awakening," as happened in eighteenth-century America, will take place in China. None can tell. But that is not the point. The point is that theological lenses can be used critically to construct cultural identity of a people. Behind the search for a Chinese Christian identity is the conviction that "cultural China" needs "theological China." Theological China is defined as a civilization that grounds its identity and its *mythos* not so much on territorial sovereignty and material prosperity, but on fulfilling the mandate of Heaven (*tianming*). Heaven is the Source of all truth, goodness, beauty, harmony, justice, freedom, and humanity; will of Heaven is mandating all to love others, that is, to be *renren*. A cultural China without the constant discipline of Heaven's will will end up with cultural boasting. A cultural China without theological reflection will end up with idolatrous absorption of self, rather than with the restoration of a civil community marked by virtue, ritualized by *ren* (humaneness), harmonized by music, and reciprocated with *zhongshu* (mutual loyalty and empathy).

45. Stringfellow, *An Ethic for Christians and Other Aliens in a Strange Land*, 13–14; emphasis his.

The "meta-sin" of any society of "confining grace to race" and of treating its cultural ideals "as a charter of automatic national privilege," marks others as barbarians.[46] The Lord on the Cross is not the emperor but the "rank and file" of common citizens—the weakest and the outcast in the empire. The Cross dethrones all powers and principalities neither by self-assertion nor by humiliating others. Rather, it rules by humble service, initiated through the baptismal ritual of dying to oneself, and being sustained through the ritual of the Eucharist (the Lord's Supper) for cruciform living. This narrative of the Cross is true because history shows that unbridled power ends in bloodshed, and that mercy extended in service to others brings benefactions for all. Paul's declaration, "It is no longer I who live, but Christ who lives in me" (Gal 2:20) summarizes the freedom and faithfulness of God in the Christian's life.

One needs not fear that being servants to one another and to Christ will strip Chinese Christians of their identity or dignity. Paul is sharp on the point that to be a servant of Christ is to be free. But without God's initiative, we are helpless. Even Jesus died in weakness and without the power of God (cf. 2 Cor 13:4). Though crucified in weakness, God raised him from the dead (Gal 1:1). In death, neither the life of Christ nor all humanity counts for anything; in resurrection, God vindicates and restores the dignity and the power of Christ, and consequently for all who are in Christ. The enlightened mind, renewed by God's Spirit, is able to see the Master's will and is full of passion (love) for the good of all (Gal 6:10). It is benevolence (*ren*) that controls humanity and frees humanity to love. The fellowship of those who are inscribed by the narrative of Christ find an identity that holds them together, and that identity in turn calls them to share the suffering and the glory of Christ in the world (Gal 2:20). This vision is countercultural because the empire narrative honors only the privileged, blesses only the powerful, and subdues all enemies. The Cross exemplifies love for one's enemies; it blesses the Gentiles into fellowship with Jews. The Cross honors those who trust in God's grace, rather than those who self-righteously gain membership in God's people. Confucius' political ethics has long articulated, and been a part of *tian's* new creation of persons who love others (*renren*).

(Is Yeo subsuming Confucius under Christ?)

---

46. Wright, *The Climax of the Covenant*, 240–43, refers to Israel's relationship to the law.

(Theological preoccupation)

Both Confucian ethics and Pauline theology are powerful resources for theological China. China once had a beautiful name, that is, the Divine Land (*Shenzhou*) or God's State. At that time, "God's State" meant that God had given the elite the divine right to rule over the people. Some Chinese Christians today argue that Yahweh God had in antiquity claimed China to be the chosen land, and the Chinese to be the chosen people.[47] This would make a nice reading but there is no evidence to show it to be the case. It is doubtful that there was a proto-Christian religion in China's past, and that somehow it was lost through Chinese disobedience. In any case, I am convinced that Chinese identity will be fulfilled when it engages intertextually with the Christian story—as this book has attempted to do.

Chinese-Christian identity (like Greek-, Syrian-, Roman-, etc. Christians before them), though hybridized, is a wholesome one. In a sense all Christians, apart from the Jewish Christians, are hybridized. They are "Gentile Christians" whose identities Paul defended as complete despite their hybridized identities. To be fully Chinese one needs to be a Chinese Christian. To have one more Christian in China does not mean to have one less Chinese. I would see a theologico-cultural China as a manifestation of the reign of God's love and justice. And because the reign of God is "already and not yet (fully)" realized, Christian faithfulness calls one to live in fidelity to one's theologico-cultural identity, holding two aspects of the hybridized life in dialogue and tension. God's new creation of an inclusive community in Christ is ultimately beyond human grasp, because the new life in Christ lies far beyond earthly life. Just as the Confucian lens has helped me reread Paul's theology, the Christian hope continues to refine my Chinese narrative. Paul's eschatology complements the Confucian Golden Age, for the hope of God's creation is salvation in Christ, and the *telos* (goal) of God's creation is peace (Gal 6:6) or "harmony under heaven" (*tianxia taiping*).

---

47. See Yuan, *Shenzhou Chanhuilu*, iv–v. The Chinese title means *China's Confession*, and the publisher is Shenzhou, literally means God's State.

THE CHALLENGE OF CHINESE CHRISTIANS: TOWARD A FIDUCIARY AND GLOBAL COMMUNITY OF THE SPIRIT

The Contribution of Chinese-Christian Theology to the Universal Church

This discussion of Chinese Christian identity does not simply have its Chinese audience in mind. This work is written for non-Chinese Christians as well, especially those in the West. Though the primary purpose of this work is obviously not to construct an indigenous theology for Christians in the West, it has become clear to me that Chinese Christian theology has much to offer the universal church. In almost every chapter of this book, we have pointed out how the Confucian ethics helps to correct or to supplement Paul's theology. The political context of Confucian ethics drives this interpreter to go beyond understanding Paul's theology simply as spiritual, but also as political—whether that political theology be understood in contrast to Roman ideology or to the power dynamic between Jewish- and Gentile Christians in Galatia. The ethical emphasis of Confucius' teaching, in terms of the formation of virtue in interpersonal relationships, challenges the elitist understanding of virtue in the West as an individual's possession of superior goodness. The Chinese Christian understanding of ethics as mutual edification within a community of grace and love corrects the distorted view that assumes ethical responsibility is that of the lonely soul. The Chinese understanding of *renren* (benevolent persons) views Christ's sacrificial love within the context of loving others in the process of becoming fully human. The communal understanding of freedom in Chinese Christian theology challenges the individualistic understanding of freedom in the West as centering in personal rights and in self-service that easily ends up in self-absorption. The Chinese Christian understanding of freedom as mutual indebtedness provides a correction to the notion of individualism. The Confucian understanding of human problem of fear and therefore the basic need of interpersonal relationship of mutual trust offers an alternate interpretation for Christians in the West to read the biblical language of faith neither as doctrinal consensus nor as intellectual belief. Rather, faith is gracious acceptance of others in loyalty (*zhong*), empathy (*shu*), and respect (*jing*). The aesthetic practice of ethics and stylized way of life in Confucian thought may be able to cultivate a technologically

over-charged society to be more humane. The anthropomorphic and re-lational nature of the world may challenge the hegemonic theology that dominates and subdues Heaven (as both creator and field of creatures).

The contribution of Chinese Christian theology to other Christians calls Chinese Christians to be faithful to their cultural identity as they hold it in critical tension with the biblical commitment to life and free-dom. Paul needs Confucius; Christianity needs China.

Mutuality Between Chinese Church and Global Church

China needs Christianity as well. Chinese Christian theology needs be done in constant dialogue with the universal church. The challenge of Chinese Christians is to aim toward a global interpretation. The ambi-guities and uncertainties of one's culturally conditioned and religiously-relative contexts are partially clarified and expanded through the process of global interpretation. This is especially important because culturally-contingent interpretation often has blind-spots and prejudices that ought to be discovered and overcome. Every effort to read with self-conscious cultural sensitivity should also seek cross-cultural and global sensitiv-ity and accountability. Although we cannot hope to achieve any kind of perfect global interpretation, we might think of this aim toward the cross-cultural and global as the eschatological impulse of hermeneutics in the interest of the good of all human beings who must live together in the global village.[48]

The commitment to move toward a global community of interpret-ers does not mean that all will or should agree. The *Analects* (4:3) speaks of the "fiduciary community" that brings about differentiated diver-sity through dialogue, one in which all agree to learn from one another. Different persons have differing visions of the Way. Nevertheless, it is possible for those who differ to be in genuine community with one an-other and to be shaped by each other. In Paul's understanding, the Spirit urges the faithful to become fully human in loving relationships with each other, not erasing all differences but accommodating difference. A fiduciary community is one in which members keep faith with the values of their own culture that they cherish and believe to be true, while taking seriously and being open to the values and perspectives of other peoples.

48. For more, see Yeo, "Culture and Intersubjectivity as Criteria," 81–100.

This "keeping faith" requires seeking the truth together under the eschatological reservation. Hope of authentic community in interpretation is not possible in the presence of cultural imperialism or ideas of cultural relativism but only through cultural dialogue, transformation and humility. This kind of global interpretation remains the challenge of Chinese Christians.

The Christ of God as found in Paul's letter to the Galatians brings Confucian ethics to its fulfillment while protecting the universal church from the aberrations of Chinese history and while protecting China against the aberrations of Christian history in the West. Chinese Christianity has something to give the universal church that needs to be heard. China can develop its distinctive vision of Christianity for the sake of the church universal. Just as theological China is constantly transforming cultural China, God's work in the whole world also constantly needs revitalization, new injections of charisma, new rethinking of its verities, traditions, and practices. Chinese Christianity will have its global mission if it can find its own authentic Chinese-Christian identity. Insofar as that identity brings the best of the Confucian tradition into the Christian story it will help revivify Christianity and compensate for biases in the western-dominated Christian self-understanding. In short, China needs Christianity, Christianity needs China. *Theos* has born Chinese Christians through his Spirit; *Tian* has graced them with moral goodness. They are called to be resident aliens in Jerusalem *and* Beijing, ever becoming the beautiful people of God *and tian.*

Bibliography

Achtemeier, Paul J. "An Elusive Unity: Paul, Acts, and the Early Church." *CBQ* 48 (1986) 1–26.

Aikman, David. *Jesus in Beijing: How Christianity Is Transforming China and Changing the Global Balance of Power*. Washington, DC: Regnery, 2003.

Akenson, Donald Harman. *Saint Saul: A Skeleton Key to the Historical Jesus*. Oxford: Oxford University Press, 2000.

Alexander, Donald. "The Face of Holiness." 87 pages. Manuscript in progress, used with permission.

Ames, Roger T., and Henry Rosemont, Jr. *The Analects of Confucius: A Philosophical Translation*. New York: Random House, 1998.

Ang, Ien. *On Not Speaking Chinese: Living between Asia and the West*. London: Routledge, 2001.

Anselm. *Cur Deus Homo*. Edinburgh: Grant, 1909.

Aristotle. *Nicomachean Ethics*. A Commentary by H. H. Joachim. Edited by D. A. Rees. Oxford: Clarendon, 1951.

Arnold, Matthew. *Culture and Anarchy*. Cambridge: Cambridge University Press, 1932.

Barclay, John M. G. "Mirror-reading a Polemical Letter: Galatians as a Test Case." *Journal for the Study of the New Testament* 31 (1987) 73–93.

———. *Obeying the Truth: A Study of Paul's Ethics in Galatians*. Minneapolis: Fortress, 1988.

Barclay, William. *Flesh and Spirit: An Examination of Galatians 5.19–23*. Nashville: Abingdon, 1962.

Barrett, C. K. "The Allegory of Abraham, Sarah and Hagar in the Argument of Galatians." In *Rechtfertigung: Festschrift für Ernst Käsemann zum 70 Geburtstag*, edited by Johannes Friedrich et al., 1–16. Göttingen: Vandenhoeck & Ruprecht, 1976.

433

———. *Freedom and Obligation: A Study of the Epistle to the Galatians*. Philadelphia: Westminster, 1985.

———. *From First Adam to Last*. London: A. & C. Black, 1962.

———. "Paul and the 'Pillar' Apostles." In *Studia Paulina in honorem Johannis de Zwaan Septuagenarii*, edited by J. N. Sevenster and W. C. van Unnik, 1–19. Haarlem: Bohn, 1953.

Barthes, Roland. *Image, Music, Text*. Edited and translated by Stephen Heath. New York: Hill & Wang, 1977.

Bauer, Walter. *A Greek-English Lexicon of the New Testament and Other Early Christian Literature*. A translation and adaptation of the fourth revised and augmented edition of Walter Bauer's *Griechisch-Deutsches Wörterbuch zu den Schriften des Neuen Testaments und der übrigen urchristlichen Literatur* by William F. Arndt and F. Wilbur Gingrich, Second edition. Revised and augmented by F. Wilbur Gingrich and Frederick W. Danker. Chicago: University of Chicago Press, 1979.

Bauer, Wolfgang. *China and the Search for Happiness: Recurring Themes in Four Thousand Years of Chinese Cultural History*. Translated by Michael Shaw. New York: Seabury, 1976.

Begbie, Jeremy S. *Theology, Music, and Time*. Cambridge: Cambridge University Press, 2000.

Behm, J. "ἀνάθεμα." In *TDNT* 1 (1964) 353–56.

Beker, J. C. *Paul the Apostle, The Triumph of God in Life and Thought*. Philadelphia: Fortress, 1984.

Bell, Daniel. "Confucian Constraints on Property Rights." In *Confucianism for the Modern World*, edited by Daniel A. Bell and Hahm Chaibong, 218–35. Cambridge: Cambridge University Press, 2003.

———, and Hahm Chaibong. "Introduction. The Contemporary Relevance of Confucianism." In *Confucianism for the Modern World*, edited by Daniel A. Bell and Hahm Chaibong, 1–28. Cambridge: Cambridge University Press, 2003.

Berger, Peter L. *Sacred Canopy: Elements of a Sociological Theory of Religion*. Garden City, NY: Doubleday, 1967.

———, and Thomas Luckmann. *The Social Construction of Reality*. Garden City, NY: Doubleday, 1966.

Berger, Peter L., and Hansfried Kellner. *Sociology Reinterpreted: An Essay on Method and Vocation*. Garden City, NY: Doubleday, 1981.

Berlin, Brent, and Paul Kay. *Basic Color Terms: Their Universality and Evolution*. Berkeley: University of California Press, 1969.

Berthrong, John H. *All under Heaven. Transforming Paradigms in Confucian-Christian Dialogue*. SUNY Series in Chinese Philosophy and Culture. Albany: State University of New York Press, 1994.

———. *Transformations of the Confucian Way*. Explorations. Boulder, CO: Westview, 1998.

Betz, Hans Dieter. *Der Galaterbrief. Ein Kommentar zum Brief des Apostels Paulus an die Gemeinden in Galatien*. München: Kaiser, 1988.

———. *Galatians: A Commentary on Paul's Letter to the Churches in Galatia*. Hermeneia. Philadelphia: Fortress, 1979.

————. "Literary Composition and Function of Paul's Letter to the Galatians." *NTS* 21 (1975) 353–79.

Bhabha, Homi, editor. *The Location of Culture*. London: Routledge, 1994.

————, editor. *Nation and Narration*. London: Routledge, 1990.

Blackwell, Albert L. *The Sacred in Music*. Louisville: Westminster John Knox, 1999.

Bligh, John. *Galatians in Greek: A Structural Analysis of St. Paul's Epistle to the Galatians with Notes on the Greek*. Detroit: University of Detroit Press, 1966.

————. *Galatians: A Discussion of St. Paul's Epistle*. London: St. Paul Publications, 1969.

Bloom, Irene, translator. "Xunzi." In *Sources of Chinese Tradition*, Vol. 1: *From Earliest Time to 1600*, compiled by Wm. Theodore de Bary and Irene Bloom, 1:159–82. New York: Columbia University Press, 1999.

Bradshaw, Paul F. *The Search for the Origins of Christian Worship: Sources and Methods for the Study of Early Liturgy*. New York: Oxford University Press, 1992.

Bockmuehl, Markus. *Jewish Law in Gentile Churches: Halakhah and the Beginning of Christian Public Ethics*. Edinburgh: T. & T. Clark, 2000.

Bodde, Derk. *Essays on Chinese Civilization*. Princeton: Princeton University Press, 1981.

————. "Harmony and Conflict in Chinese Philosophy." In *Studies in Chinese Thought*, edited by Arthur F. Wright, 19–80. Chicago: University of Chicago Press, 1953.

Bonhoeffer, Dietrich. *Act and Being: Transcendental Philosophy and Ontology in Systematic Theology*. Translated by H. Martin Rumscheidt. Dietrich Bonhoeffer Works 2. Minneapolis: Fortress, 1996.

Boring, M. Eugene et al., editors. *Hellenistic Commentary to the New Testament*. Nashville: Abingdon, 1995.

Boyarin, Daniel. *A Radical Jew: Paul and the Politics of Identity*. Berkeley: University of California Press, 1994.

————. "Was Paul an 'Anti-Semite'? A Reading of Galatians 3–4." *Union Seminary Quarterly Review* 47 (1993) 48–80.

Brinsmead, Bernard Hungerford. *Galatians, Dialogical Response to Opponents*. Society of Biblical Literature Dissertation Series 65. Atlanta: Scholars, 1982.

Brooks, E. Bruce, and A. Taeko Brooks. *The Original Analects: Sayings of Confucius and His Successors*. New York: Columbia University Press, 1998.

Brown, Raymond. *An Introduction to New Testament*. Anchor Bible Reference Library. New York: Doubleday, 1997.

Bruce, F. F. *The Epistle to the Galatians: A Commentary on the Greek Text*. New International Greek Testament Commentary. Grand Rapids: Eerdmans, 1982.

Bundrick, David R. "Ta Stoicheia Tou Kosmou (Gal 4:3)." *Journal of the Evangelical Theological Society* 34 (1991) 353–64.

Burton, Ernest De Witt. *A Critical and Exegetical Commentary on the Epistle to the Galatians*. International commentary on the Holy Scriptures of the Old and New Testament. New York: Scribners, 1920.

Buschel, F. "ἀλληγορέω." In *TDNT* 1 (1964) 260–63.

Cai, Shangsi. *Kongzi Sixiang Tixi* [*System of Confucius' Thought*]. Shanghai: Shanghai Renmin, 1982.

Caneday, Ardel. "'Redeemed from the Curse of the Law': The Use of Deut 21:22–23 in Gal 3:13." *Trinity Journal* 10 (1989) 185–209.

"Canaan Hymns." http://www.chinasoul.com/cross/script/script4.htm. (Accessed December 10, 2006.)

Capra, Fritjof. *The Tao of Physics: An Exploration of the Parallels Between Physics and Eastern Mysticism*. Boston: Shambhala, 1991.

Chan, Joseph. "A Confucian Perspective on Human Rights for Contemporary China." In *The East Asian Challenge for Human Rights*, edited by Joanne R. Bauer and Daniel A. Bell, 212–39. Cambridge: Cambridge University Press, 1999.

Chan, Wing-tsit. "Chinese and Western Interpretations of *Ren* (Humanity)." *JCP* 2 (1975) 109–15.

———. "The Evolution of the Confucian Concept of *Jen*." *PEW* 4 (1955) 295–319.

Chang, Wejen. "Confucian Theory of Norms and Human Rights." In *Confucianism and Human Rights*, edited by Wm. Theodore de Bary and Tu Weiming, 117–40. New York: Columbia University Press, 1998.

Chen, Albert H. Y. "Mediation, Litigation, and Justice: Confucian Reflections in a Modern Liberal Society." In *Confucianism for the Modern World*, edited by Daniel A. Bell and Hahm Chaibong, 257–87. Cambridge: Cambridge University Press, 2003.

Chen, Shihchuan. *Lunyu Duxun Jiegu* [*Confucian Analects: A Revised Text and New Commentary*]. Hong Kong: Sanlian, 1972.

Chen, Yong. "On the Rhetoric of Defining Confucianism as a 'Religion': A Hermeneutic Reading of the Controversy on Confucian Religiosity and its Significance to the Understanding of Chinese Tradition and Modernity." PhD diss., Vanderbilt University, 2005.

Chen, Zhaoying. "Kongzi shiyue meixue zhong de zhengtixing gainian" ["The Integrative Concept of Confucius' Poetic and Musical Aesthetics"]. http://www.npobook.org.tw/Special/pdf/0401chen.pdf. (Accessed December 2, 2006.)

Cheng, Chungying. "Confucius, Heidegger, and the Philosophy of the *I Ching*: A Comparative Inquiry into the Truth of Human Being." *PEW* 37 (1987) 51–70.

———. "Confucian Onto-Hermeneutics: Morality and Ontology." *JCP* 27 (2000) 33–68.

Cheng, Shude. *Lunyu Jishi* [*The Collective Commentary of the Analects*], 4 vols. Beijing: Zhonghua Shuju, 2006.

Ching, Julia. "Human Rights: A Valid Chinese Concept." In *Confucianism and Human Rights*, edited by Wm. Theodore de Bary and Tu Weiming, 67–82. New York: Columbia University Press, 1998.

———. *Mysticism and Kingship in China: The Heart of Chinese Wisdom*. Cambridge Studies in Religious Traditions 11. Cambridge: Cambridge University Press, 1997.

Chiu, Milton M. *The Tao of Chinese Religion*. Lanham, MD: University Press of America, 1984.

Chopp, Rebecca. "Theology and the Poetics of Testimony." In *Converging on Culture. Theologians in Dialogue with Cultural Analysis and Criticism*, edited by Delwin Brown et al., 56–70. Oxford: Oxford University Press, 2001.

Cole, R. A. *The Epistle of Paul to the Galatians.* Tyndale New Testament Commentary. London: Tyndale, 1965.

"Confucius2000." "Xueren Wenji" ["Collected Essays of Scholars"]. 5 Vols. http://www .Confucius2000.com. (Accessed November 25, 2006.)

Corley, Kathleen E. *Private Women, Public Meals: Social Conflict and Women in the Synoptic Gospels.* Peabody, MA: Hendrickson, 1993.

Cosgrove, Charles H. *The Cross and the Spirit: A Study in the Argument and Theology of Galatians.* Macon, GA: Mercer University Press, 1988.

―――. "Imagining Earliest Christian Music." A paper presented at Society of Biblical Literature, American Schools of Oriental Research, National Association of Baptist Professors of Religion, and Central States Regional Meeting, April 6–7, 2003. 6 pp. Used with permission.

―――. "Justification in Paul: a Linguistic and Theological Reflection." *JBL* 106 (1987) 653–70.

―――. "Paul and American Individualism." In Charles Cosgrove et al., *Cross-Cultural Paul: Journeys to Others, Journeys to Ourselves,* 68–103. Grand Rapids: Eerdmans, 2005.

―――, Herold Weiss, and K. K. Yeo. *Cross-Cultural Paul: Journeys to Others, Journeys to Ourselves.* Grand Rapids: Eerdmans, 2005.

Creel, Herrlee G. *Chinese Thought: From Confucius to Mao Tse-tung.* Chicago: University of Chicago Press, 1953.

―――. *Confucius: The Man and the Myth.* New York: John Day, 1949.

Culler, Jonathan. *On Deconstruction: Theory and Criticism after Structuralism.* Ithaca, NY: Cornell University Press, 1982.

Dahl, Robert A. *Democracy and Its Critics.* New Haven: Yale University Press, 1989.

Danker, F. W. *Benefactor: Epigraphic Study of a Graeco-Roman and New Testament Semantic Field.* St. Louis: Clayton, 1982.

Das, Andrew. *Paul, the Law, and the Covenant.* Peabody, MA: Hendrickson, 2001.

Davies, W. D. *Jewish and Pauline Studies.* Philadelphia: Fortress, 1984.

―――. *Paul and Rabbinic Judaism: Some Rabbinic Elements in Pauline Theology.* 2nd ed. New York: Harper & Row, 1967.

* Dawson, Raymond, translator. *Confucius: The Analects.* Oxford World's Classic. Oxford: Oxford University Press, 1993.   * no Wm. Theodore de Bary*

Deissmann, Adolf. *Light from the Ancient East.* 1927. Reprinted, Eugene, OR: Wipf & Stock, 2004.

DeWoskin, Kenneth J. *A Song for One or Two: Music and the Concept of Art in Early China.* Michigan Monographs in Chinese Studies. Ann Arbor: University of Michigan Press, 1982.

Dibelius, Martin. *From Tradition to Gospel.* Translated by Bertram Lee Woolf. New York: Scribner, 1935.

Dodd, Brian J. "Christ's Slave, People Pleasers and Gal 1:10." *NTS* 42 (1996) 90–104.

Donaldson, T. L. "The 'Curse of the Law' and the Inclusion of the Gentiles: Galatians 3:13–14." *NTS* 32 (1986) 94–112.

Dreyer, June Teufel. "Assimilation and Accommodation in China." In *Government Policies and Ethnic Relations in Asia and the Pacific,* edited by Michael E. Brown and Sumit Ganguly, 351–92. Cambridge: MIT Press, 1997.

Dunn, J. D. G. "Echoes of Intra-Jewish Polemic in Paul's Letter to the Galatians." *JBL* 112 (1993) 459–77.

———. *Romans 1–8*. Word Biblical Commentary 38A. Dallas: Word, 1988.

———. *The Theology of Paul the Apostle*. Grand Rapids: Eerdmans, 1998.

Elliott, John H. "Jesus the Israelite was Neither a 'Jew' nor a 'Christian': On Correcting Misleading Nomenclature." *Journal for the Study of the Historical Jesus* 5.2 (2007) 119–54.

Elliott, Neil. "The Anti-Imperial Message of the Cross." In *Paul and Empire: Religion and Power in Roman Imperial Society*, edited by Richard A. Horsley, 167–83. Harrisburg, PA: Trinity, 1997.

Elliott, Susan Margaret. "The Rhetorical Strategy of Paul's Letter to the Galatians in its Anatolian Cultic Context: Circumcision and the Castration of the Galli of the Mother of the Gods." PhD diss., Loyola University, 1997. [Published as *Cutting Too Close for Comfort: Paul's Letter to the Galatians in its Anatolian Cultic Context*. London: T. & T. Clark, 2003. Not used.]

Ellis, E. E. *Paul's Use of the Old Testament*. Grand Rapids: Baker, 1957.

Ellison, H. L. *The Message of the Old Testament*. Grand Rapids: Eerdmans, 1969.

Engberg-Pedesen, Troels. *Paul and the Stoics*. Edinburgh: T. & T. Clark, 2000.

Eno, Robert. *The Confucian Creation of Heaven: Philosophy and the Defense of Ritual Mastery*. Albany: State University of New York Press, 1990.

Esler, Philip F. *Conflict and Identity in Romans: The Social Setting of Paul's Letter*. Minneapolis: Fortress, 2003.

———. *Galatians*. London: Routledge, 1998.

———. "Group Boundaries and Intergroup Conflict in Galatians: A New Reading of Galatians 5:13—6:10." In *Ethnicity and the Bible*, edited by Mark G. Brett, 215–40. Biblical Interpretation Series 19. Leiden: Brill, 1996.

Fang, Thomé H. "The World and the Individual in Chinese Metaphysics." In *The Chinese Mind: Essentials of Chinese Philosophy and Culture*, edited by Charles A. Moore, 238–65. Honolulu: University Press of Hawaii, 1967.

Fatum, Lone. "Women, Symbolic Universe and Structures of Silence: Challenges and Possibilities in Androcentric Texts." *Studia Theologica* 43 (1989) 61–80.

Feeley-Harnik, Gillian. *The Lord's Table: The Meaning of Food in Early Judaism and Christianity*. Washington, DC: Smithsonian Institution, 1994.

Felski, Rita. "The Doxa of Difference." *Signs* 23 (1997) 1–22.

Fingarette, Herbert. *Confucius—The Secular as Sacred*. New York: Harper & Row, 1972.

———. "Following the 'One Thread' of the *Analects*." *Journal of the American Academy of Religion*, Thematic Issue S (Sept 1980) 373–405.

———. "The Music of Humanity in the *Conversations* (*Analects*) of Confucius." *JCP* 10 (1983) 331–56.

———. "The Problem of the Self in the *Analects*." *PEW* 29 (1979) 129–40.

Fishbane, Michael. *The Garments of Torah: Essays in Biblical Hermeneutics*. Indiana Studies in Biblical Literature. Bloomington: Indiana University Press, 1989.

Fishman, Ted C. *China Inc.: How the Rise of the Next Superpower Challenges America and the World*. New York: Scribner, 2005.

Fletcher, George P. *Loyalty: An Essay on the Morality of Relationships.* New York: Oxford University Press, 1993.

Foley, Edward. *Foundations of Christian Music: The Music of Pre-Constantinian Christianity.* Joint Liturgical Studies. Bramcote: Grove, 1992.

Foerster, Werner. "κύριος." In *TDNT* 3 (1965) 1039–99.

Fredriksen, Paula. "Judaism, the Circumcision of Gentiles, and Apocalyptic Hope: Another Look at Galatians 1 and 2." In *The Galatians Debate: Contemporary Issues in Rhetorical and Historical Interpretation,* edited by Mark Nanos, 235–60. Peabody, MA: Hendrickson, 2002.

Fung, Yulan. *A Short History of Chinese Philosophy.* Edited and translated by Derk Bodde. New York: Macmillan, 1948.

Fung, Ronald Y. K. *The Epistle to the Galatians.* New International Commentary on the New Testament. Grand Rapids: Eerdmans, 1988.

———. *Zhenli Yu Ziyou: Jialataishu Zhushi* [*Gospel Truth and Christian Liberty: A Commentary on Galatians*]. Hong Kong: Christian Witness, 1982.

Gasque, W. Ward. "Images of Paul in the History of Biblical Interpretation." *Crux* 16 (1980) 8–13.

Gaston, L. *Paul and the Torah.* Vancouver: University of British Columbia Press, 1987.

Gaventa, Beverly Roberts. *From Darkness to Light: Aspects of Conversion in the New Testament.* Philadelphia: Fortress, 1988.

Geertz, Clifford. "Religion as a Cultural System." In *Anthropological Approaches to the Study of Religion,* edited by Michael Banton, 1–46. London: Tavistock, 1966.

———. *Works and Lives: The Anthropologist as Author.* Cambridge: Polity, 1988.

Gelineau, J. "Music and Singing in the Liturgy." In *The Study of Liturgy,* edited by Cheslyn Jones et al., 493–507. Rev. ed. Oxford: Oxford University Press, 1992.

Gellner, Ernest. *Nations and Nationalism.* Oxford: Blackwell, 1990.

Georgi, Dieter. "God Turned Upside Down." In *Paul and Empire: Religion and Power in Roman Imperial Society,* edited by Richard A. Horsley, 148–57. Harrisburg, PA: Trinity, 1997.

———. *Theocracy in Paul's Praxis and Theology.* Translated by David E. Green. Minneapolis: Fortress, 1991.

Gordon, T. David. "The Problem at Galatia." *Interpretation* 41 (1987) 32–43.

Graham, A.C. *Disputers of the Tao: Philosophical Argument in Ancient China.* Peru, IL: Open Court, 1993.

The Grand Scribe's Records. Vol. I: *The Basic Annals of Pre-Han China by Ssu-ma Ch'ien.* Edited by William H. Nienhauser, Jr. Translated by Tsai-fa Cheng et al. Bloomington: Indiana University Press, 1994.

The Grand Scribe's Records. Vol. II: *The Basic Annals of Han China by Ssu-ma Ch'ien.* Edited by William H. Nienhauser, Jr. Translated by Weiguo Cao et al. Bloomington: Indiana University Press, 2002.

The Grand Scribe's Records. Vol. VII: *The Memoirs of Pre-Han China by Ssu-ma Ch'ien.* Edited by William H. Nienhauser, Jr. Translated by Tsai-fa Cheng et al. Bloomington: Indiana University Press, 1994.

Gunn, Janet V. *Autobiography: Towards a Poetics of Experience.* Philadelphia: University of Pennsylvania Press, 1982.

Grundmann, Walter. "δεχιός." In *TDNT* 2 (1964) 37–40.

Gutbrod, Walter. "Ἰουδαῖος." In *TDNT* 3 (1965) 369–91.

Guthrie, Donald. *Galatians*. New Century Bible Commentary. London: Nelson, 1969.

Hahm Chaihark. "Constitutionalism, Confucian Civic Virtue, and Ritual Propriety." In *Confucianism for the Modern World*, edited by Daniel A. Bell and Hahm Chaibong, 31–53. Cambridge: Cambridge University Press, 2003.

Hall, David L. "Confucian Friendship: The Road to Religiousness." In *The Changing Face of Friendship*, edited by Leroy S. Rouner, 77–94. Notre Dame: University Notre Dame Press, 1994.

Hall, David L. and Roger T. Ames. *The Democracy of the Dead. Dewey, Confucius, and the Hope for Democracy in China*. Chicago: Open Court, 1999.

Hall, David L. and Roger T. Ames. *Thinking through Confucius*. SUNY Series in Systematic Philosophy. Albany: SUNY, 1987.

Hansen, Chad. *Daoist Theory of Chinese Thought*. Hong Kong: Oxford University Press, 1992.

Hanson, A. T. *Studies in Paul's Technique and Theology*. London: SPCK, 1974.

Harrell, Stevan. "Introduction." In *Negotiating Ethnicities in China and Taiwan*, edited by Melissa J. Brown, 1–10. Berkeley: Institute of East Asian Studies, 1995.

Hauerwas, Stanley. *A Community of Character: Toward a Constructive Christian Social Ethic*. Notre Dame: University of Notre Dame Press, 1981.

Hays, Richard B. *The Faith of Jesus Christ: An Investigation of the Narrative Substructure of Galatians 3:1—4:11*. Society of Biblical Literature Dissertation Series 56. Missoula, MT: Scholars, 1983.

He, Baogang. *The Democratization of China*. London: Routledge, 1996.

He, Guanghu. "Zhongguo wenhua de gen yu hua" ["The Root and Flower of Chinese Culture"]. In "Confucius2000," "Xueren Wenji," Vol. 2. http://www.confucius2000.com/confucian/rujiao/trxdfbykx.htm. (Accessed November 15, 2006.)

He, Yan and Xing Bing. *Lunyu Zhushu [The Commentary of the Analects]*. Beijing: Peking University Press, 1999.

Henderson, John B. *Scripture, Canon, and Commentary: A Comparison of Confucian and Western Exegesis*. Princeton: Princeton University Press, 1991.

Hengel, Martin. *Studies in Early Christology*. Edinburgh: T. & T. Clark, 1995.

Hii, Kong-hock. "Contesting the Ideology of the Empire: Paul's Theological Politics in Romans, with Preliminary Implications for Chinese Christian Communities in Malaysia." PhD diss., Garrett-Evangelical Theological Seminary, 2007.

Horsley, Richard A. "Introduction." In *Paul and Empire. Religion and Power in Roman Imperial Society*, edited by Richard A. Horsley, 10–24. Harrisburg, PA: Trinity, 1997.

Howard, G. *Paul: Crisis in Galatia*. Society for New Testament Studies Monograph Series. Cambridge: Cambridge University Press, 1979.

Hsieh, Yu-wei. "The Status of the Individual in Chinese Ethics." In *The Chinese Mind: Essentials of Chinese Philosophy and Culture*, edited by Charles A. Moore, 307–22. Honolulu: University Press of Hawaii, 1967.

Huang, Chi-chung. *The Analects of Confucius (Lunyu): A Literal Translation with an Introduction and Notes*. Oxford: Oxford University Press, 1997.

Hübner, Hans. *Law in Paul's Thought*. Studies of the New Testament and Its World. Edinburgh: T. & T. Clark, 1984.

Hughes, Christopher. *Taiwan and Chinese Nationalism: National Identity and Status in International Society*. Politics in Asia Series. New York: Routledge, 1997.

Ivanhoe, Philip J. *Confucian Moral Self Cultivation*. New York: Lang, 1993.

———. "Reweaving the 'One Thread' of the *Analects*." *Philosophy East and West* 40 (1990) 17–33.

———. "Whose Confucius? Which Analects?" In *Confucius and the Analects: New Essays*, edited by Bryan W. Van Norden, 119–33. Oxford: Oxford University Press, 2002.

Jensen, Lionel M. *Manufacturing Confucianism: Chinese Traditions and Universal Civilization*. Durham, NC: Duke University Press, 1997.

Jewett, Robert. "The Agitators and the Galatian Congregation." *NTS* 7 (1971) 198–212.

———. *Paul the Apostle to America: Cultural Trends and Pauline Scholarship*. Louisville: Westminster John Knox, 1994.

Jiang, Wenye [Ko Bunya]. *Kongzi de yuelun* [*Confucius On Music*]. Translated by Yang Rubin. Taipei: Himalaya Foundation, 2003. [Originally in Japanese: *Sho dai Shina seigakuko: Ko shi no ongakuron* (Tokyo: Sanseido, 1945).]

Johnson, E. Elizabeth, and David M. Hay, editors. *Pauline Theology*. Vol. 4: *Looking Back, Pressing On*. Atlanta: Scholars, 1997.

Kaiser, Walter C. Jr. *Toward an Old Testament Theology*. Grand Rapids: Zondervan, 1978.

Kangxi Zidian [*Dictionary of Kangxi*]. Taipei: I-wen, 1957.

Kaplan, Robert D. "How We Would Fight China." *The Atlantic* (June 2005) 49–64.

Kaufmann, Walter. *Musical References in the Chinese Classics*. Detroit: Information Coordinators, 1976.

Kennedy, George. *New Testament Interpretation through Rhetorical Criticism*. Studies in Religion. Chapel Hill: University of North Carolina Press, 1984.

Kim, Sung-hae. "Silent Heaven Giving Birth to the Multitude of People." *ChF* 31 (1988) 195–224.

Kitahara, Michio. *Entangled Civilization: Democracy, Equality, and Freedom at a Loss*. Lanham, MD: University Press of America, 1995.

Kittel, Gerhard, and Gerhard Friedrich, editors. *Theological Dictionary of the New Testament*. 10 vols. Translated by Geoffrey W. Bromiley. Grand Rapids: Eerdmans, 1964–1976.

Kotva, Joseph J., Jr. *The Christian Case for Virtue Ethics*. Moral Traditions. Washington DC: Georgetown University Press, 1996.

Kristeva, Julia. "Word, Dialogue and Novel." In *The Kristeva Reader*, edited by Tori Moi, 34–61. New York: Columbia University Press, 1986.

Kroeber, Alfred L., and Clyde Kluckhohn. *Culture: A Critical Review of Concepts and Definitions*. New York: Vintage, 1963.

Kuan, Hsin-chi. "Is the 'One Country, Two Systems' Formula Working?" In *Hong Kong in China. The Challenges of Transition*, edited by Wang Gungwu and John Wong, 23–44. Singapore: Times Academic, 1999.

Kupperman, Joel J. "Naturalness Revisited: Why Western Philosophers Should Study Confucius." In *Confucius and the Analects: New Essays*, edited by Bryan W. Van Norden, 39–52. Oxford: Oxford University Press, 2002.

Kyrtatas, D. J. "Christianity and the Familia Caesaris." In *The Social Structure of the Early Christian Communities*, 75–86. London: Verso, 1987.

Lao, Siguang. *Zhongguo zhexue shi* [*History of Chinese Philosophy*]. 2 Vols. Hong Kong: Chung Chi College, 1974.

Lau, D. C., translator. *Confucius: The Analects*. Harmondsworth: Penguin, 1979.

Legge, James, translator. *Confucian Analects, the Great Learning, and the Doctrine of the Mean*. In series: *The Chinese Classics*. Vol. 1. Oxford: Clarendon, 1893.

————, translator (Chinese to English). 四書 *The Four Books*. Translated (to modern Chinese) by Yang Bojun. Changsha: Hunan Publisher, 1995.

Levenson, Joseph R. *Confucian China and Its Modern Fate*. Berkeley: University of California Press, 1968.

Levine, Amy-Jill. *The Misunderstood Jew: The Church and the Scandal of the Jewish Jesus*. San Francisco: HarperSanFrancisco, 2006.

Liang, Mingyue. "Implications of the De-sensationalized Mental State in *Qin* Music for Health Preservation through *Qi* Energy Transmission." *Hanxue Yanjiu* 19 (2001) 409–26.

————. *Music of the Billion: An Introduction to Chinese Musical Culture*. New York: Heinrichshofen, 1985.

Lightfoot, J. B. *The Epistle of St. Paul to the Galatians*. Grand Rapids: Zondervan, 1962.

Liji [*Record of Rituals*]. Taipei: Shangwu, 1979.

Lin, Yutang. *The Wisdom of Confucius*. New York: Random House, 1938.

Lippman, Edward A. *Musical Thought in Ancient Greece*. New York: Columbia University Press, 1964.

Liu, Shuhsien. "On Confucius' Attitude Toward Gods, Sacrifice, and Heaven." *ChF* 34 (1991) 16–27.

————. *Rujia Sixiang Yu Xiandaihua* [*Confucian Thought and Modernization*]. Beijing: China Broadcasting Television Publisher, 1992.

Liu, Zaisheng. *Zhongguo Gudai Yinyueshi Jianshu* [*Brief History of Ancient Chinese Music*]. Beijing: Renmin Yinyue, 1991.

Lohse, Eduard. "σύν – μετά." In *TDNT* 7:766–97.

Long, Fei. "Yuedao" (1) and (2) ["The Dao of Music" (1) and (2)]. In "Confucius2000," "Shiji" ["Collected Poems"]. http:// www.confucius2000.com/poetry/ ylxdydgdyyzxlgz1.htm). (Accessed November 25, 2006.)

Louden, Robert B. "'What Does Heaven Say?': Christian Wolff and Western Interpretations of Confucian Ethics." In *Confucius and the Analects: New Essays*, edited by Bryan W. Van Norden, 73–93. Oxford: Oxford University Press, 2002.

Luther, Martin. *A Commentary on St Paul's Epistle to the Galatians*. Translated by Theodore Graebner. 2nd ed. Grand Rapids: Zondervan, 1939.

Lu, Xing. *Rhetoric in Ancient China Fifth to Third Century BCE: A Comparison with Classical Greek Rhetoric*. Columbia: University of South Carolina Press, 1998.

Lu, Zhongren. "Zhongguo gudai wusheng yinjie xingchen yu fazhan de tansuo" ["Exploring the Formation and Development of Pentatonic Scale in Ancient China"]. *Journal of Xinghai Conservatory of Music* (2004) 16–22.

Lull, David John. *The Spirit in Galatia: Paul's Interpretation of PNEUMA as Divine Power*. Society of Biblical Literature Dissertation Series. 1980. Reprinted, Eugene, OR: Wipf & Stock, 2006.

Luo, Mengce. *Kongzi Weiwang Erwang Lun* [*On Confucius the King Before Becoming One*]. Taipei: Xuesheng, 1982.

Macintyre, Alasdair. *After Virtue: A Study in Moral Theory*. 2nd edition. Notre Dame: University of Notre Dame Press, 1984.

Makeham, John. *Transmitters and Creators: Chinese Commentators and Commentaries on the Analects*. Harvard East Asian Monographs. Cambridge: Harvard University Press, 2004.

Malina, Bruce J. *The New Testament World: Insights from Cultural Anthropology*. 3rd ed. Atlanta: Westminster John Knox, 2001.

Marcus, Joel. "The Circumcision and the Uncircumcision in Rome." *NTS* 35 (1989) 67–81.

Martin, Ralph G. *Henry and Clare: An Intimate Portrait of the Luces*. New York: Putnam, 1991.

Martin, Ralph P. *Carmen Christi: Philippians 2:5–11 in Recent Interpretation and in the Setting of Early Christian Worship*. Society for New Testament Studies Monograph Series 4. Cambridge: Cambridge University Press, 1967.

———. *New Testament Foundations*. 2 Vols. Grand Rapids: Eerdmans, 1978.

Martin, Troy W. "Apostasy to Paganism: The Rhetorical Stasis of the Galatian Controversy." *JBL* 114 (1995) 437–61.

———. "The Brother Body: Addressing and Describing the Galatians and the Agitators as *Adelphoi* [Brothers]." *Biblical Research* 67 (2002) 5–18.

———. "Pagan and Judeo-Christian Time-Keeping Schemes in Gal 4:10 and Col 2:16." *NTS* 42 (1996) 105–19.

———. "The Physiological Pertinence of PERITOME [Circumcision] in Paul's Epistles." A Paper Presented at 2003 Midwest Society of Biblical Literature. 8 pp. Used with permission.

Martyn, J. Louis. "The Covenants of Hagar and Sarah." In *Faith and History: Essays in Honor of Paul W. Meyer*, edited by J. T. Carroll et al., 160–90. Atlanta: Scholars, 1990.

———. *Galatians: A New Translation with Introduction and Commentary*. Anchor Bible 33A. New York: Doubleday, 1997.

Mason, Steve. "Jews, Judaeans, Judaizing, Judaism: Problems of Categorization in Ancient History." *Journal for the Study of Judaism* 38 (2007) 452–512.

Matera, Frank J. *Galatians*. Sacra Pagina. Collegeville: Liturgical, 1992.

McKinnon, James. *Music in Early Christian Literature*. Cambridge: Cambridge University Press, 1987.

Meeks, Wayne A. *The First Urban Christians: The Social World of the Apostle Paul*. New Haven: Yale University Press, 1983.

―――. "The Image of the Androgyne: Some Uses of a Symbol in Earliest Christianity." *Harvard Theological Review* 13 (1974) 165–205.

―――. *The Moral World of the First Christians*. Library of Early Christianity 6. Philadelphia: Westminster, 1986.

Mickelsen, A. B. *Interpreting the Bible*. Grand Rapids: Eerdmans, 1963.

Moltmann, Jürgen. *The Way of Jesus Christ: Christology in Messianic Dimensions*. Translated by Margaret Kohl. San Francisco: HarperSanFrancisco, 1990.

Mou, Zongsan. "Confucianism as Religion." In *Chinese Essays on Religion and Faith*, translated by Douglas Lancashire, 22–43. San Francisco: Chinese Materials Center, 1981.

―――. *Shengming De Xuewen* [*The Learning of Life*]. Taipei: Sanming, 2004.

―――. *Xianxiang Yu Wuzishen* [*Phenomena and Noumena*]. Taipei: Xuesheng, 1984.

―――. *Xinti Yu Xingti* [*The Subjectivity of Heart and Nature*]. 2 Vols. Taipei: Zhengzhong, 1999.

―――. *Zhongguo Zhexue De Tezhi* [*The Special Features of Chinese Philosophy*]. Taipei: Xuesheng, 1998.

Murphy-O'Connor, Jerome. "Paul in Arabia." *CBQ* 55 (1993) 732–37.

―――. *Paul, A Critical Life*. Oxford: Clarendon, 1996.

Nanos, Mark D., editor. *The Galatians Debate: Contemporary Issues in Rhetorical and Historical Interpretation*. Peabody: Hendrickson, 2002.

―――. "The Inter- and Intra-Jewish Political Context of Paul's Letter to the Galatians." In *Galatians Debate*, edited by Mark D. Nanos, 396–407. Peabody, MA: Hendrickson, 2002.

―――. "What Was at Stake in Peter's 'Eating with Gentiles' at Antioch?" In *The Galatians Debate*, edited by Mark D. Nanos, 282–318. Peabody, MA: Hendrickson, 2002.

Needham, Joseph. "Human Laws and Laws of Nature in China and the West." *Journal of the History of Ideas* 12 (1951) 3–30. [Author has not consulted this article; cited in Derk Bodde, "Harmony and Conflict in Chinese Philosophy," 20. In *Studies in Chinese Thought*, edited by Arthur F. Wright, 19–80. Chicago: University of Chicago Press, 1953.]

―――. *Science and Civilisation in China*. Cambridge: Cambridge University Press, 1954.

Neils, Patricia. *China Images in the Life and Times of Henry Luce*. Savage, MD: Rowman & Littlefield, 1990.

Newbigin, Lesslie. *The Gospel in a Pluralist Society*. Grand Rapids: Eerdmans, 1989.

Niebuhr, H. Richard. *Christ and Culture*. New York: Harper, 1956.

Nivison, David S. "Golden Rule Arguments in Chinese Philosophy." In *The Ways of Confucianism*, edited by Bryan W. Van Norden, 59–76. Chicago: Open Court, 1996.

―――. *The Ways of Confucianism. Investigations in Chinese Philosophy*. Chicago: Open Court, 1996.

Northrop, Filmer Stuart Cuckow. *The Meeting of East and West: An Inquiry Concerning World Understanding*. New York: Macmillan, 1947.

Novak, David. *Covenantal Rights: A Study in Jewish Political Theory*. Princeton: Princeton University Press, 2000.

Nyitray, Vivian-Lee. "The Single Thread of A New Confucianism: Private Virtue and Public Responsibility." In *Taking Responsibility: Comparative Perspectives*, edited by Winston Davis, 196–212. Charlottesville: University Press of Virginia, 2001.

Obenchain, Diane B. "The Study of Religion and the Coming Global Generation." In *God and Globalization*, Vol. 3: *Christ and the Dominions of Civilization*, edited by Max L. Stackhouse and Diane B. Obenchain, 29–109. Harrisburg, PA: Trinity, 2002.

Oepke, Albrecht. "παρουσία." In *TDNT* 5 (1967) 858–71.

O'Neill, J. C. *The Recovery of Paul's Letter to the Galatians*. London: SPCK, 1972.

Oliver, Robert T. *Communication and Culture in Ancient India and China*. Syracuse: Syracuse University Press, 1971.

Pan, Lynn. *Sons of the Yellow Emperor: A History of the Chinese Diaspora*. New York: Kodansha, 1990.

Peck, M. Scott. *The Road Less Traveled: A New Psychology of Love, Traditional Values, and Spiritual Growth*. New York: Simon & Schuster, 1978.

Peterson, Richard. "Revitalizing the Culture Concept." *Annual Review of Sociology* 5 (1979) 137–66.

Porter, Wendy J. "Misguided Missals: Is Early Christian Music Jewish or Is It Graeco-Roman?" In *Christian-Jewish Reactions through the Centuries*, edited by Stanley E. Porter and Brook W. S. Pearson, 202–27. Journal for the Study of the New Testament Supplement Series 192. Sheffield: Sheffield Academic, 2000.

Radl, Walter. *Ankunft des Herrn: Zur Bedeutung und Funktion der Parusieaussagen bei Paulus*. Beiträge zur biblischen Exegese und Theologie 15. Frankfurt: Lang, 1981.

Rand, Thomas Alden. "A Call to Koinonia: A Rhetorical Analysis of Galatians 5:25—6:10." *Proceedings of the Great Lakes and Midwest Societies of Biblical Literature* 15 (1995) 79–92.

————. "The Rhetoric of Ritual: Galatians as Mystagogy." PhD diss., Garrett-Evangelical Theological Seminary/Northwestern University, 2000.

Rankin, H. D. *Celts and the Classical World*. Portland, OR: Areopagitica, 1987.

Raphals, Lisa A. *Sharing the Light: Representations of Women and Virtue in Early China*. Albany: State University of New York Press, 1998.

————. "A Woman Who Understood the Rites." In *Confucius and the Analects: New Essays*, edited by Bryan W. Van Norden, 275–302. Oxford: Oxford University Press, 2002.

Ridderbos, Herman N. *The Epistle of Paul to the Churches of Galatia*. New International Commentary on the New Testament. Grand Rapids: Eerdmans, 1953.

Rorty, Richard. *Philosophy and the Mirror of Nature*. Princeton: Princeton University Press, 1979.

Rosemont, Henry, Jr. "Kiekegaard and Confucius: On Finding the Way." *PEW* 36 (1986) 201–12.

————. "On Confucian Civility." In *Civility*, edited by Leroy S. Rouner, 187–99. Boston University Studies in Philosophy and Religion 21. Notre Dame: University of Notre Dame Press, 2000.

————. "Why Take Rights Seriously? A Confucian Critique." In *Human Rights and the World's Religions*, edited by Leroy S. Rouner, 167–82. Notre Dame: University of Notre Dame Press, 1988.

Roth, Wolfgang. "Jesus as the Son of Man: The Scriptural Identity of a Johannine Image." In *The Living Text: Essays in Honor of Ernest W. Saunders*, edited by Dennis E. Groh and Robert Jewett, 11–26. Lanham, MD: University Press of America, 1985.

Ruskola, Teemu. "Moral Choice in the *Analects*: A Way Without a Crossroads." *JCP* 19 (1992) 285–96.

Qian, Mu. *Gongzi Yu Lunyu* [*Confucius and the Analects*]. Taipei: Liangjing, 1976.

————. *Lunyu Xinjie* [*The Analects: New Interpretation*]. Taipei, Taiwan: Dongda, 2003.

Saliers, Don E. *Worship as Theology: Foretaste of Glory Divine*. Nashville: Abingdon, 1994.

Sanders, E. P. "The Covenant as a Soteriological Category and the Nature of Salvation in Palestinian and Hellenistic Judaism." In *Jews, Greeks and Christians: Religious Cultures in Late Antiquity. Essays in Honor of William David Davies*, edited by Robert Hamerton-Kelly and Robin Scroggs, 11–44. Studies in Judaism in Late Antiquity 21. Leiden: Brill, 1976.

————. *Paul, the Law and the Jewish People*. Philadelphia: Fortress, 1983.

Schniewind, Julius, and Gerhard Friedrich. "ἐπαγγέλλω." In *TDNT* 2 (1964) 576–86.

Schüssler Fiorenza, Elisabeth. *In Memory of Her: A Feminist Theological Reconstruction of Christian Origins*. New York: Crossroad, 1986.

Schwartz, Benjamin I. *The World of Thought in Ancient China*. Cambridge, MA: Harvard University Press, 1985.

Schweizer, Eduard. "Slaves of the Elements and Worshipers of Angels: Gal 4:3, 9 and Col 2.8, 18, 20." *JBL* 107 (1988) 455–68.

Shiji [*Records of History*]. 9 Vols. Beijing: Xinhua Bookstore, 1972.

Shun, Kwongloi. "The Concepts of *Jen* and *Li* in the *Analects*." *PEW* 43 (1993) 457–79.

————. "*Ren* and *Li* in the Analects." In *Confucius and the Analects: New Essays*, edited by Bryan W. Van Norden, 53–72. Oxford: Oxford University Press, 2002.

Slingerland, Edward, translator. *Confucius Analects With Selections from Traditional Commentaries*. Hackett Classics Series. Indianapolis: Hackett, 2003.

Smith, Henry N. "A Typology of Christian Responses to Chinese Ancestor Worship." *Journal of Ecumenical Studies* 26 (1989) 628–47.

Smith, William Sheppard. *Musical Aspects of the New Testament*. Amsterdam: ten Have, 1962.

So, Jenny F., editor. *Music in the Age of Confucius*. Washington DC: Simithsonian Freer Gallery of Art and Arthur M. Sackler Gallery, 2000.

Sontag, Frederick. "The *Analects* of Confucius: The Universal Man." *JCP* 17 (1990) 427–38.

Soothill, W. E., translator. *The Analects of Confucius*. 2nd ed. New York: Paragon, 1968.

Soulen, Richard N., and R. Kendall Soulen. *Handbook of Biblical Criticism*. 3rd ed. Louisville: Westminster John, 2001.

Stauffer, Ethelbert. "ἐγώ." In *TDNT* 2 (1964) 343–62.

Wilfred Cantwell Smith ? Religion as an adjective both - then < now

Stendahl, Krister. *Paul among Jews and Gentiles, and Other Essays*. Philadelphia: Fortress, 1976.

Straus, Virginia. "Making Peace: International Civility and the Question of Culture." In *Civility*, edited by Leroy S. Rouner, 229–45. Notre Dame: University of Notre Dame Press, 2000.

Stringfellow, William. *An Ethic for Christians and Other Aliens in a Strange Land*. 1973. Reprinted, Eugene, OR: Wipf & Stock, 2004.

Strunk, Oliver. *Source Readings in Music History*. New York: Norton, 1950.

Stuhlmacher, Peter. "The Law as a Topic of Biblical Theology." In idem, *Reconciliation, Law, and Righteousness: Essays in Biblical Theology*, 110–33. Translated by Everett R. Kalin. Philadelphia: Fortress, 1986.

Swanberg, W. A. *Luce and His Empire*. New York: Scribner, 1972.

Tamney, Joseph B., and Linda Hsueh-Ling Chiang. *Modernization, Globalization, and Confucianism in Chinese Societies*. Westport, CN: Praeger, 2002.

Tang, Junyi. "Wo duiyu zhexue yu zongjiao jueze" ["My Option Regarding Philosophy and Religion"]. In *Zhongguo Zhexue Sixiang Lunji* [*Collected Essays on Chinese Philosophical Thought*], edited by Xiang Weixin and Liu Fuzeng, 8:186–205. Taipei: Mudong, 1978.

———. *Zhonghua Renwen Yu Dangjin Shijie* [*Chinese Humanistic Culture and Contemporary World*]. Taipei: Xuesheng Bookstore, 1988.

Tanner, Kathryn. *Theories of Culture: A New Agenda for Theology*. Guides to Theological Inquiry. Minneapolis: Fortress, 1997.

Thiselton, Anthony C. *New Horizons in Hermeneutics*. Grand Rapids: Zondervan, 1992.

Thompson, Laurence G. *The Chinese Way in Religion*. Encino, CA: Dickenson, 1973.

Thorp, Robert L. "Erlitou and the Search for the Xia." *Early China* 16 (1991) 1–38.

Tillich, Paul. *The Courage To Be*. 2nd ed. with an Introduction by Peter J. Gomes. New Haven: Yale University Press, 2000.

Tu, Weiming. *Confucian Ethics Today*. Singapore: Federal Publications, 1984.

———. *Confucian Thought: Selfhood as Creative Transformation*. SUNY Series in Philosophy. Albany: State University of New York Press, 1985.

———. "Cultural China: The Periphery as the Center." In *The Living Tree: The Changing Meaning of Being Chinese Today*, edited by Tu Weiming, 1–34. Stanford: Stanford University Press, 1994.

———. "Joining East and West." *Harvard International Review* 20 (Summer 1998) 44–49.

———. "*Li* as Process of Humanization." *PEW* 22 (1972) 187–201.

———, editor. *The Living Tree: The Changing Meaning of Being Chinese Today*. Stanford: Stanford University Press, 1994.

Twiss, Sumner B. "A Constructive Framework for Discussing Confucianism and Human Rights." In *Confucianism and Human Rights*, edited by Wm. Theodore de Bary and Tu Weiming, 27–65. New York: Columbia University Press, 1998.

Tylor, Edward. *Primitive Culture: Researches into the Development of Mythology, Philosophy, Religion, Art, and Custom*. Vol. 1: *The Origins of Culture*. London: Murray, 1871.

Tyson, J. "Works of Law in Galatians." *JBL* 92 (1973) 423–31.

Van Norden, Bryan W., editor. *Confucius and the Analects: New Essays*. Oxford: Oxford University Press, 2002.

———. "Unweaving the 'One Thread' of *Analects* 4:15." In *Confucius and the Analects: New Essays*, edited by Bryan W. Van Norden, 216–36. Oxford: Oxford University Press, 2002.

Waley, Arthur, translator. *The Analects of Confucius*. New York: Vintage Books, 1989.

———. *The Way and Its Power: A Study of the Tao te-ching and Its Place in Chinese Thought*. London: Allen and Unwin, 1934.

Wainwright, Geoffrey. *Doxology: The Praise of God in Worship, Doctrine and Life*. New York: Oxford University Press, 1980.

Wang, Gungwu. *Community and Nation: China, Southeast Asia and Australia*. Sydney: Allen and Unwin, 1992.

———. *Don't Leave Home: Migration and the Chinese*. Singapore: Times Academic, 2001.

Wang, Gungwu and John Wong. "Introduction." In *Hong Kong in China. The Challenges of Transition*, edited by Wang Gungwu and John Wong, 1–22. Singapore: Times Academic, 1999.

Wang, Juntao. "Confucian Democrats in Chinese History." In *Confucianism for the Modern World*, edited by Daniel A. Bell and Hahm Chaibong, 69–89. Cambridge: Cambridge University Press, 2003.

Wang, Pi. *Commentary on the Lao Tzu*. Translated by Ariane Rump. Monograph of the Society for Asian and Comparative Philosophy. Honolulu: University Press of Hawaii, 1979.

Watson, Burton. *The Tso Chuan*. New York: Columbia University Press, 1989.

Watson, Francis. *Paul, Judaism and the Gentiles: A Sociological Approach*. Society for New Testament Studies Monograph Series. Cambridge: Cambridge University Press, 1989.

Werner, Eric. *The Sacred Bridge: The Interdependence of Liturgy and Music in Synagogue and Church during the First Millennium*. 2 Vols. Vol. 1: New York: Columbia University Press, 1959; Vol. 2: New York: Ktav, 1984.

Westerholm, S. *Israel's Law and the Church's Faith, Paul and His Recent Interpreters*. Grand Rapids: Eerdmans, 1988.

Westermann, Claus. *Genesis 1–11, A Commentary*. Translated by John J. Scullion. Continental Commentaries. Minneapolis: Augsburg, 1984.

Williams, Jay G. "On Reading a Confucian Classic: The Rhetoric of the *Lunyu*." *Journal of Chinese Religions* 19 (Autumn 1991) 105–11.

Wilson, Stephen A. "Conformity, Individuality, and the Nature of Virtue: A Classical Confucian Contribution to Contemporary Ethical Reflection." In *Confucius and the Analects: New Essays*, edited by Bryan W. Van Norden, 94–115. Oxford: Oxford University Press, 2002.

Wilson-Dickson, Andrew. *The Story of Christian Music: From Gregorian Chant to Black Gospel: An Authoritative Illustrated Guide to All the Major Traditions of Music for Worship*. Oxford: Lion, 1992.

Wolff, Christian. *Oratio de Sinarum Philosophia Practica: Rede über die Praktische Philosophie der Chinesen*. Edited by Michael Albrecht. Hamburg: Meiner, 1985.

Wong, Siulun. "Changing Hong Kong Identities." In *Hong Kong in China: The Challenges of Transition*, edited by Wang Gungwu and John Wong, 181–202. Singapore: Times Academic, 1999.

Wright, Arthur, editor. *Studies in Chinese Thought*. Chicago: University of Chicago Press, 1953.

Wright, N. T. *The Climax of the Covenant: Christ and the Law in Pauline Theology*. Minneapolis: Fortress, 1992.

Wu, John C. H. "The Status of the Individual in the Political and Legal Traditions of Old and New China." In *The Chinese Mind*, edited by Charles A. Moore, 340–64. Honolulu: University of Hawaii Press, 1967.

Wuest, K. S. *Galatians in the Greek New Testament for the English Reader*. Grand Rapids: Eerdmans, 1944.

Xu, Fuguan. *Zhongguo Renxinglun Shi* [*The History of Human Nature in China*]. Taipei: Shangwu, 1978.

———. *Zhongguo Yishu Jingshen* [*The Artful Spirit of China*]. Tapei: Xuesheng, 1974.

Yang, Bojun. *Lunyu Yizhu* [*Commentary of the Analects*]. Taipei: Wunan, 1992.

Yang, Yingliu. *Zhongguo Yinyue Shigao* [*History of Ancient Chinese Music*]. 2 Vols. Taipei: Danqing Tushu, 1985.

Yao Xinzhong, editor. *RoutledgeCurzon Encyclopedias of Confucianism*. 2 Vols. (A–N; M–Z). London: Routledge, 2003.

Yearley, Lee H. "An Existentialist Reading of Book 4 of the Analects." In *Confucius and the Analects: New Essays*, edited by Bryan W. Van Norden, 237–74. Oxford: Oxford University Press, 2002.

Yeo, Khiok-khng. *Chairman Mao Meets the Apostle Paul: Christianity, Communism, and the Hope of China*. Grand Rapids: Brazos, 2002.

———. "Cross-Tradition and Cross-Gender Hermeneutics: A Confucian Reading of Romans and A Critical Reading of Confucian Ethics." In *Gender, Tradition, and Romans: Shared Ground, Uncertain Borders*, edited by Cristina Grenholm and Daniel Patte, 63–80. New York: T. & T. Clark, 2005.

———. "Culture and Intersubjectivity as Criteria for Negotiating Meanings in Cross-Cultural Interpretations." In *The Meanings We Choose: Hermeneutical Ethics, Indeterminacy and the Conflict of Interpretations*, edited by Charles Cosgrove, 81–100. Journal for the Study of the Old Testament Supplement Series 411. London: T. & T. Clark, 2004.

———. "Feilimenshu de youshui" ["The Rhetoric of Philemon"]. *Journal of the China Graduate School of Theology* 24 (1998) 177–88.

———. *Jizu Misi* [*Ancestor Worship: Rhetorical and Cross-Cultural Hermeneutical Response*]. Hong Kong: Chinese Christian Literature Council, 1996.

———. "Messianic Predestination in Romans 8 and Classical Confucianism." In *Navigating Romans Through Cultures: Challenging Readings by Charting a New Course*, edited by Khiok-khng Yeo, 259–89. New York: T. & T. Clark International, 2004.

———. "Musical Harmony according to Confucius and Paul." *ChF* 5 (2004) 163–89.

———. "Paul's Theological Ethic and Chinese Morality of *Renren*." In Charles Cosgrove et al., *Cross-Cultural Paul: Journeys to Others, Journeys to Ourselves*, 104–40. Grand Rapids: Eerdmans, 2005.

———. "A Political Reading of Paul's Eschatology in 1 and 2 Thessalonians." *Asia Journal of Theology* 12 (April 1998) 77–88.

———. "The Rhetoric of Election and Calling Language in 1 Thessalonians." In *Rhetorical Criticism and the Bible*, edited by Stanley E. Porter and Dennis L. Stamps, 526–47. London: Sheffield Academic, 2002.

———. "The Rhetorical Hermeneutic of 1 Corinthians 8 and Chinese Ancestor Worship." *Biblical Interpretation* 2 (1994) 298–311.

———. *Rhetorical Interaction in 1 Corinthians 8 and 10: A Formal Analysis with Preliminary* Suggests *for a Chinese, Cross-cultural Hermeneutics.* Biblical Interpretation Series 9. Leiden: Brill, 1995.   *Ph.D. dissertation*

———. "Salvation by Grace Through Faith." In *The Wesleyan Tradition: A Paradigm for Renewal*, edited by Paul W. Chilcote, 66–77. Nashville: Abingdon, 2002.

———. "System of Harmony according to Confucius and Paul: Music, Goodness, Beauty." *ChF* 6 (2005) 37–51.

———. *What Has Jerusalem to Do with Beijing? Biblical Interpretation from a Chinese Perspective.* Harrisburg, PA: Trinity, 1998.

———. "The 'Yin and Yang' of God (Exod 3:14) and Humanity (Gen 1:27)." *Zeitschrift für Religions- und Geistesgeschichte* 46 (1994) 319–32.

Young, N. H. "*Paidagogos*: The Social Setting of a Pauline Metaphor." *Novum Testamentum* 29 (1987) 150–76.

Yuan, Zhiming. *Shenzhou Chanhuilu [China's Confession]*. Petaluma: Shenzhou Publisher [China Soul Inc], 1999.

Yung, Bell. "The Nature of Chinese Ritual Sound." In *Harmony and Counterpoint. Ritual Music in Chinese Context*, edited by Bell Yung et al., 13–31. Stanford: Stanford University Press, 1996.

Zatorre, R. J. "Musical Perception and Cerebal Function (A Critical Review)." *Music Perception* 2 (1984) 199–221.

Zhang, Carson Junmai, et al. "Wei Zhongguo Wenhua Jinggao Shijie Renshi Xuanyan" ["A Manifesto on the Reappraisal of Chinese Culture: Our Joint Understanding of the Sinological Study Relating to World Cultural Outlook"]. No pages. Accessed November 9, 2006. Online: http://www.gongfa.com/mouzszhongguowenhuaxuanyan.htm

Zhang, Funggan. "Tianzu Jiao" ["The Religion of Heaven and Ancestors"]. In "Confucius-2000," "Xueren Wenji," Vol. 1. http://www.confucius2000.com/confucian/rujiao/tzjzgctzjsl.htm (Accessed December 1, 2006.)

Zhang, Longxi. *The Tao and the Logos: Literary Hermeneutics, East and West.* Durham: Duke University Press, 1992.

Zhu, Qianzhi. *Zhongguo Yinyue Wenxueshi [History of Chinese Musical Literature]*. Taipei: Xuesheng, n.d.

Zhu, Xi, editor. *Sishu [Four Books]*. Taipei: Taiwan Guji, 1996.

Zuo Zhuan [The Commentary of Zuo]. http://chinese.pku.edu.cn/david/zuozhuan.html. (Accessed November 27, 2006.)

Index of **SUBJECTS**

lord
  as *di* (ruler), 36, 90, 118–19, 162–67,
    320, 359
  as human master/noble (*jun*),
    20–23, 45, 48, 92, 276, 327,
    359, 364, 415
  as Roman emperor, 92, 101, 146–51,
    238–39
  lordship of Christ. *See* Jesus Christ
  lordship of God, 45, 75, 99, 137,
    146, 154, 172, 283, 382
  overlord/hegemon (*ba*), 142–44
love
  of family, neighbors, others, 51, 274,
    300, 353
  of God. *See* God
  of learning, 278
loyalty, *zhong*, 288, 365–67, 404
  zhongshu (single-heartedness, like-
    heartedness, loyalty-empathy),
    18, 261, 358, 366–68, 384, 394,
    398, 401, 425–27

maleness, female, 71, 80, 139, 209,
  219, 239, 245, 270, 283, 286,
  308, 311–32, 364, 413
Mencius, 17, 19, 21, 24, 56, 59, 117,
  122, 161, 169, 171, 228, 254–57,
  262, 270, 333–35, 343, 399, 415,
  419–20
Middle Kingdom, 407–8, 424; *see also*
  China; God's State
multiple other, x–xviii, xix; *see also*
  hybrid identity
music, *yue*, 15, 22–25, 34, 39–42, 46,
  51, 58, 65, 69, 113, 115, 118,
  124–25, 143, 153, 158–59, 162–
  63, 167, 172–257, 265, 279, 320,
  332, 348, 376, 400–401, 427

Paul
  and Confucius. *See* intertextuality
  and Roman ideology, 144–53
  biography of Paul, 25–33
  cross-cultural apostle, 25–33

death of Paul, 32, 301
missionary work/journeys, x, 27–
  32, 72, 98, 100, 145, 337
peace, x, xv, xviii, 15, 19, 24, 38, 48, 83,
  89–90, 109, 143, 147, 149–54,
  163–64, 169, 211–12, 225,
  227–28, 231, 240, 260, 275–77,
  287–88, 303, 320, 343, 348, 356,
  376, 378, 385–86, 397, 414, 419,
  422, 429; *see also* harmony
people of God, xvii, 27, 29–34, 43,
  70–72, 78–84, 100–2, 109,
  133, 136–37, 145, 172, 177–88,
  201–13, 245, 249, 253–305,
  310, 314–16, 338–39, 351, 361,
  363, 373–74, 385, 387, 389,
  401, 405–32
persecution. *See* church
Protestant West, xx, 191, 241; *see also*
  China

reciprocity, xiii–xviii, 96, 98, 148, 263,
  302, 317, 330, 364, 395
ren (person), 43, 410
  xiaoren (immature person), 280–86,
    327, 333, 341
ren (benevolence)
  and *li*, 289–91
  as benevolence, 51, 113, 174,
    207, 226, 265, 281, 287–91,
    297–302, 404–8, 430
  as compassion, 41, 262, 266, 299,
    365
  as humaneness, 58, 113, 174, 191,
    198, 207, 214, 226, 255–56,
    261, 266, 269, 274, 281,
    287–302, 342, 379, 394, 398,
    404–8, 412, 417, 425–27
  as humanness, x, xii
  as love, humanrelatedness, 63, 191
  renren (benevolent person), xxi, 39,
    43, 127, 204, 262, 267, 270–76,
    281–91, 295, 297–303, 339,
    345, 347, 352, 367, 370, 388–92,
    404, 408, 417, 425–30
resurrection of Christ. *See* Jesus Christ

Index of MODERN AUTHORS

Index of **ANCIENT TEXTS**

APOCRYPHA

PSEUDEPIGRAPHA

GREEK WRITINGS

11·24·08   although book is written primarily but also for scholar members
as well as clo
for seniors

Yeo's Christian faith and theological conviction that open him
to claim his own cultural identity in Confucianism.

theology is prior to phenomenology (Obenchain)

The "merit" of Yeo to be included in "value free
academia.

12-7-08 9 a.m., Metropark, Kowloon

Significance of Hong Kong

1958 - Mou Zongsan lectured at Pui Ching (mystities)
Manifesto of Chinese Culture

1988 - Confucian-Christian Dialogue, CUHK

      Le Bang, J. Berling, Berthrong, Tu, 滔, 范, 成

2008 - Pui To Middle School (temporary campus at
                        Precious Blood, Dec. 6, 2008)

大學之道 - education towards maturity -
(nothing to do in universitas) + theologian
                                + medicine

innate given: Imago Dei

明月   良知
illumine   明德

(primary self-cultivation thru human effort a la
                              (Tu)
Living tree - many artforms
enlightful ways of being Chinese.
外